Distance Learning Technology, Current Instruction, and the Future of Education:
Applications of Today, Practices of Tomorrow

Holim Song
Texas Southern University, USA

INFORMATION SCIENCE REFERENCE

Hershey · New York

Director of Editorial Content:	Kristin Klinger
Senior Managing Editor:	Jamie Snavely
Assistant Managing Editor:	Michael Brehm
Publishing Assistant:	Sean Woznicki
Typesetter:	Mike Killian, Sean Woznicki
Cover Design:	Lisa Tosheff
Printed at:	Yurchak Printing Inc.

Published in the United States of America by
Information Science Reference (an imprint of IGI Global)
701 E. Chocolate Avenue
Hershey PA 17033
Tel: 717-533-8845
Fax: 717-533-8661
E-mail: cust@igi-global.com
Web site: http://www.igi-global.com/reference

Library of Congress Cataloging-in-Publication Data

Distance learning technology, current instruction, and the future of education : applications of today, practices of tomorrow / Holim Song, editor.
    p. cm.

 Includes bibliographical references and index.
 Summary: "The aim of this book is to explore current state and future direction of distance education from different research fields, reports and discussions from students, faculty members, researchers, and practitioners in the field of distance education, training development, and performance improvement"--Provided by publisher.

 ISBN 978-1-61520-672-8 (hardcover) -- ISBN 978-1-61520-673-5 (ebook) 1.
Distance education--Computer-assisted instruction. 2. Educational technology.
I. Song, Holim.
 LC5803.C65D575 2010
 371.35'8--dc22
                        2009043101

British Cataloguing in Publication Data
A Cataloguing in Publication record for this book is available from the British Library.

List of Reviewers

Brian Fox, *Santa Fe College, USA*
Chien Yu, *Mississippi State University, USA*
Chris Douce, *Open University, UK*
David Banks, *University of South Australia, Australia*
Deb Gearhart, *Troy University, USA*
Deepak Subramony, *Grand Valley State University, USA*
Deirdre Lawless, *Dublin Institute of Technology, Ireland*
Doug Holton, *Utah State University, USA*
Feng-Qi Lai, *Indiana State University, USA*
Giuliana Dettori, *National Research Council of Italy, Italy*
Glenda Scales, *Virginia Tech, USA*
Glenn Finger, *Griffith University, Australia*
Holly McCracken, *University of Illinois at Springfield, USA*
Julia Thornton, *RMIT University, Australia*
Kenneth Strang, *Central Queensland University, Australia*
Mark Brown, *Massey University, New Zealand*
Michael Sonntag, *Johannes Kepler University, Austria*
Murelli Elena, *Universita Cattolica del Sacro Cuore, Italy*
Roy Rada, *University of Maryland, USA*
Teresa Chen, *California State University, USA*
Thomas Lancaster, *Birmingham City University, UK*
Tina Stavredes, *Capella University, USA*
Wayne Huang, *Kingston University, UK*
Zane Berge, *University of Maryland, USA*

Table of Contents

Section 1
Foundations of Distance Learning Technology

Chapter 1
Gail S. Peters, Ohio Learning Network, USA
Kate M. Carey, Ohio Board of Regents, USA; Ohio Learning Network, USA

Chapter 2
José Magano, Instituto Superior de Ciências Empresariais e do Turismo, Portugal
Carlos V. Carvalho, GILT / Instituto Superior de Engenharia do Porto, Portugal

Chapter 3
Hyacinth Eze Anomneze, Texas Southern University, USA

Chapter 4
Robert D. Wright, University of North Texas, USA

Chapter 5
Jennifer Ehrhardt, netuniversity.se, Sweden; University of West Florida, USA

Chapter 6
Drew Polly, University of North Carolina at Charlotte, USA

Section 2
Applications and Practices of Distance Learning Technology

Detailed Table of Contents

Section 1
Foundations of Distance Learning Technology

This section presents the concepts and foundations of distance learning technology. In addition, this section discusses fundamental elements in designing distance learning environment and strategies to incorporate distance learning technology.

Chapter 1

Gail S. Peters, Ohio Learning Network, USA
Kate M. Carey, Ohio Board of Regents, USA; Ohio Learning Network, USA

This chapter illustrates the innovative curriculum in a free, online course that shows significant promise as one strategy to raise the educational attainment of adults. By looking at the fundamental instructional and delivery issues in providing distance learning to adults, the authors suggest that successes and weaknesses of the program may help other states address the needs of returning adult learners.

Chapter 2

José Magano, Instituto Superior de Ciências Empresariais e do Turismo, Portugal
Carlos V. Carvalho, GILT / Instituto Superior de Engenharia do Porto, Portugal

In Portugal, like in most Western countries, most Higher Education Institutions are already using e-learning platforms. This chapter presents the e-learning initiative of the Higher Institute of Business Science and Tourism (ISCET). This initiative is relevant, precisely because it represents a holistic and revolutionary approach.

Chapter 3

    Hyacinth Eze Anomneze, Texas Southern University, USA

As the global economy moves into a complete dependence on information and technology, the United States has to revisit how information technology is used in schools. Schools no longer imply the actual building with administrative halls and student centers, but also distance learning possibilities. This chapter discusses distance learning technology and its use in the classroom practice.

Chapter 4

    Robert D. Wright, University of North Texas, USA

Traditional classroom practices must be adapted to accommodate the interactive and distributed nature that defines effective contemporary distance learning. The learning theories, cognitive processes, and educational media that shaped the minds of instructional developers, technologists, and teachers who were born in the Twentieth Century differ from those required for Twenty-first Century learning. This chapter examines the changes that Twentieth Century Minds must undergo if they are to successfully design for today's distance learners.

Chapter 5

    Jennifer Ehrhardt, netuniversity.se, Sweden; University of West Florida, USA

In online practice, social constructivism involves students learning from and with each other in computer-mediated collaborative learning communities. In order for students and faculty to succeed in the online social constructivist environment these efforts demand institutional support. This chapter introduces issues facing students and faculty that relate to the implementation of online social constructivism.

Chapter 6

    Drew Polly, University of North Carolina at Charlotte, USA

Educational theorists and researchers have long been calling for learner-centered instruction that situates learners in activities that allow them to explore concepts and construct understanding. This chapter aims to analyze the underlying theories of authentic learning and propose methods to support classroom teachers with the design, implementation and assessment of authentic activities.

Section 2
Applications and Practices of Distance Learning Technology

This section includes contributions that address innovative distance learning technology to solve educational related problems in curriculum and in instruction. Not only does this section speak toward how to use distance learning technology in the teaching and learning process, it also presents examples and strategies on how to use certain technologies to promote active learning. This collection of articles should be required reading for anyone planning to infuse distance learning technology into their teaching and learning practices.

As technology continues to advance and computers become smaller, faster, and more powerful educational institutions are being confronted with multiple, external factors that are driving them towards change e.g. rapid developments in information and communication technology that are part of everyday life, and changing characteristics of learners. This chapter examines how past generations of learning theories and practices have shaped the genealogy of mobile learning.

This chapter provides faculty members and distance learning administrators with a broad overview of the options available to capture, store, edit, distribute, and re-purpose in-class lectures. This chapter also proposes three dimensions to guide the selection of lecture capture systems, review existing technologies for enterprise and individual lecture capture, and discusses the technical and pedagogical challenges associated with implementing lecture capture solutions.

This chapter provides an analysis of business and industry case-based implementations of instructional opportunities within the Second Life three-dimensional virtual world environment, so as to delineate distance learning instructional achievements within virtual worlds and engage in a discussion related to potential implications for higher education.

Online education is characterized by conflicting variables of time, space and interactivity. In response to the market pressure for time and space flexibility, interactivity between student-student and student-teacher usually suffers. This chapter emphasizes the need to balance time, space and interactivity through appropriate blending of tools of interactivity so as to maximize learning as well as business outcomes.

Chapter 11

Screencasts allow a learner to experience a computer-based demonstration again and again at the learner's pace. This chapter outlines the equipment necessary to create screencasts. A selection of software applications is also discussed, and practical tips are provided to help the reader quickly begin creating screencasts.

Chapter 12

Performance of Web-based collaborations depends not only on pedagogical strategies but also on the effectiveness of e-learning systems. The factors that may help designers in creating collaborative environments acceptable to users are considered. Based on two case studies of students evaluating the same environments, this chapter identifies student usability needs for collaborative learning environment design.

Chapter 13

Technologies such as asynchronous and synchronous delivery still need to incorporate these instructional strategies. These technologies can be utilized in traditional, hybrid, and online delivery modalities. As these technologies are introduced, this chapter discusses some concerning interactive instructional strategies and assignments.

Chapter 14

Meaningful interaction and collaboration in online environments needs the consideration of design elements as well as the understanding of the affordances of interactive learning technologies. This chapter presents a 3-dimensional design activity - *social structures*, *tools*, and *learner diversity* - as the fundamental elements that educators and instructional designers need to consider.

Chapter 15

As students increasingly engage with alternative social networking (or realities) there is scope for educators to explore whether they pose opportunities for rethinking learning and teaching spaces. This chapter draws upon two case studies that have provided two distinctly different learning designs for Logistics students and pre-service teachers.

Section 3
Learning Strategy and Challenges for Distance Learning

This section is dedicated to the exploration and discussion of some challenges of distance learning technology. Chapters in this section speak to instructional challenges in higher education online courses, societal issues, legal standards, and International realities universities face in the distance learning market, successful distance learning strategy and perspective.

Chapter 16

This chapter proposes that instructional alignment with pedagogic beliefs is the best instructional foundation for original course designs in this instructional context, and examine three factors unique to this context. This chapter also presents new instructional design models and a new instructional system of design to address the instructional challenges specific to their learning system context.

In today's global economy, both students and workers need to be lifelong learners. While some universities have been slow to recognize these changing needs, others have quickly moved to serve this new academic market. This chapter discusses societal, international, cultural, and technical issues that universities face in providing distance-learning programs to meet the needs of today and the demands of tomorrow.

Chapter 18

Monique Fuchs, Wentworth Institute of Technology, USA
Stephanie Cheney, Wentworth Institute of Technology, USA

Compared to traditional educational offerings, Distance Education requires a significantly different business model involving factors such as learning culture, target audience, infrastructure, course and content development, support models, and others. This chapter presents recommendations and solutions that center around organizational systemic anchoring and faculty development as a critical success factor.

Chapter 19

Julia Penn Shaw, SUNY-Empire State College, USA
Fabio Chacon, Bowie State University, USA

E-Learning has the potential to transform education, deeply changing it at all levels, bringing both benefits and challenges on an international scale. This chapter provides a view of elearning from the perspective of ecological systems with nested levels of structure, organizing principles, and emergent properties.

Preface

Distance education has become a major force in higher education in the United States. Institutions of higher education have increasingly embraced distance education, and the number of students enrolled in distance education is rapidly rising in colleges and universities throughout the United States. According to the U.S. Department of Education, distance education is a steadily growing phenomenon. About 56 percent of all two-year colleges and universities now offer distance learning courses. 34 percent of these institutions offer students the opportunity to complete their degree program solely through distance education. In response to these changes in enrollment demands, many states, institutions, and organizations have been working on strategic plans to implement distance education. At the same time, there are misconceptions and myths related to the difficulty of distance teaching and learning, technologies available to support distance instruction, and the support and compensation needed for high-quality instructors. This confusion swells as higher education explores dozens of distance learning technologies with new ones seeming to emerge each week. Such technologies confront instructors and administrators at a time of continued budget retrenchments and rethinking. Adding to this dilemma, bored students are dropping out of online classes while pleading for richer and more engaging distance learning experiences. Opinions are mixed about the benefits of distance teaching and learning in higher education. Given the demand for distance learning, the plethora of technologies to incorporate into teaching, the budgetary problems, and the opportunities for innovation, distance learning environments are facing challenges, linking pedagogy, technology, and learner needs. Given its popularity and increased usage, it is imperative that administrators and instructors monitor the current state and future direction relating to distance education in order to meet the needs and challenges of tomorrow.

There is substantial effort and research within various disciplines that tackles current state and future direction in distance education dealing the improvement of computer and technology assisted learning settings and environments. Recently there have been several initiatives within the US that focus on strategies and current research approaches to improve the distance learning process with the introduction of advanced web technologies to help learning and fostering innovative learning paradigms. Because of its popularity and increased usage, there is a need to introduce an interdisciplinary approach into the current state and future direction of innovative distance learning approaches. It is imperative that institutions of higher education provide quality distance programs.

The aim of this book is to explore current state and future direction of distance education from different research fields, reports and discussions from students, faculty members, researchers, and practitioners in the field of distance education, training development, and performance improvement. The chapters collected for this book will have influence on future developments in technology-enhanced distance learning both in education and in industry. The book will stimulate administrators and instructors in higher education to focus on current trends as well as future emerging directions in the field of distance education. In addition, this book will offer a critical discussion about distance education, with a focus on the theoretical and practical challenges of distance education in education and current trends, practices, issues, and future directions on the specific distance education areas.

The projected audience for this book includes faculty, K-12 educators, researchers, designers, practitioners and administrators, those developing distance education and training in higher education from the international communities. The goal of this book is to appeal to individuals with a professional interest in current state and future direction in the area of distance education. This book would serve as a resource to instructors, administrators, and students in higher education such as asynchronous learning, authoring tools, building distance learning architectures, collaborative learning, courseware development, developing an organizational distance learning strategy, developing and integrating distance learning solutions, pedagogical issues, societal issues, and quality management and assessment in distance education. The main stakeholders include instructors, K-12 educators, administrators, students, instructional designers, and those who are concerned with ensuring and improving the distance education. We have seen an explosion of strategic improvements and innovations of distance education technologies used in education, business, and industry for the purpose of teaching and learning, training and performance improvement. Researchers and institutions are beginning to see a powerful impact of these technologies in the area of distance learning and teaching. The value of this text will not only add to the body of knowledge of the field of distance education in higher education institutions, but also link theoretical based practices to business and industry.

After an extensive research of major book warehouses, bookstore, and university presses, there remains no work in the area of current states and future directions in distance education. The last book on current states and future directions in distance education was written in 2003. There are several articles relating to current issues and trends in distance directions, but not in the area of future directions of distance education. The texts that focus on current state and future direction do not incorporate a literature on distance education either from the education point of view or from the business/industry point of view of training and performance improvement. This opens a huge market to college faculty, instructional designers, consultants, students, K-12 educators, trainers, etc to learn of the new directions and strategies to promote quality distance teaching and learning. This text will serve the business community, the university — faculty and students, K-12 educations, designers, technology enthusiasts, administrators, and the general public.

The chapters authored were selected based on their expertise within the field as well as their unique perspective on the subject matter. With the combination of non-profit organizations, primary and secondary schools, higher education institution, and the medical industry, a wide range of perspectives were covered in this handbook. Further, this book highlights distance learning technology as a growing field of study which uses technological innovation as a means to solving educational, learning, and development challenges.

The chapters are divided into three major themes. These themes include foundations of distance learning technology, applications and practices of distance learning technology, and learning strategy and challenges for distance learning. This way, distance learning technology book will present different approaches to promoting quality distance learning and development strategies through distance learning technology. Moreover, this distance learning technology book will provide a sure foundation on different types of distance learning technology, tips and strategies on how to use distance learning technology to facilitate active learning, and a discussion on the aspect of distance learning technology and trends. To add, this book will provide a platform and discussion to help faculty, trainers, instructional designers, and teachers to develop online instructional and teaching materials. This book also shows instructors how to create authentic and active learning environments with distance learning technology complete with an assessment and evaluation guide. Lastly, the book provides a platform to assist college and university faculty, trainers, and research to manage and develop eLearning applications with updated strategies that facilitate distance learning and development.

For all practical purposes, this book discusses various methods and tools for assessment, testing and evaluating of effective distance learning technology and strategies for the educational opportunities and learning development challenges. For the future development of distance learning technology, this book gives a discussion on the trends and issues facing the field as well as progression as to where the field may be headed. In the end, this book contains a wide range of ideas, examples, guidelines, stories, models, and solution for anyone interested in the field distance learning technology.

With a diverse and comprehensive coverage of multiple perspectives presented in this authoritative guide, *Distance Learning Technology, Current Instruction, and the Future of Education: Applications of Today, Practices of Tomorrow,* will contribute to a better understanding all topics, research, and discoveries in this evolving, significant field of study. Further, the contributions included in this book will be instrumental in expanding of the body of knowledge to a wider audience. The coverage will provide a strong reference source for researchers and also decision makers seeking to obtain a greater understanding of the concepts, issues, trends, challenges and opportunities within distance learning technology.

It is my sincere hope that the distance learning technology book will assist colleagues, faculty, students, teachers, and business decision makers in enhancing their understanding of this discipline and to effectively integrate distance learning technology to meet the needs of all learning populations. Perhaps this publication will inspire its readers to contribute to the current body of research in this immense field, tapping into possibilities to create, facilitate, and sustain change in educational institutions by making learning and development opportunities open and engaging to participants.

Holim Song
Editor
Texas Southern University

Acknowledgment

As I endeavored to edit the Distance Learning Technology book, I realized how essential the help, encouragement, and support of those with whom we work together. Indeed, this edition could not have come into existence without their tremendous works. I would like to thank all of authors for their continued work and patience and tolerance during the creation of this book. I am surely blessed to have been accompanied by so many distinguished people like you and I am very much indebted to you.

A sincere expression of gratitude goes to my colleagues at Texas Southern University who offered up suggestions, advice, and support. I offer special thanks to Dr. Jay Cummings, Dean of College of Education, for his continuous encouragement; Dr. James Johnson, Associate Dean, for his insightful advice and assistance; Dr. Cherry Gooden, head of Department of Curriculum, for her tireless and hard work in assisting the department and for her encouragement and support. It has been an honor to work under your supervision and guidance.

Also, special thanks go to Elizabeth Ardner and Tyler Heath who are Editorial Assistants. I thank you for all your time and efforts from the beginning of this book to the end. Surely, I could not have made it through this edition without you.

Holim Song

Section 1
Foundations of Distance Learning Technology

Chapter 1
Innovative Curriculum in Distance Learning:
An Ohio Case Study

Gail S. Peters
Ohio Learning Network, USA

Kate M. Carey
Ohio Board of Regents, USA; Ohio Learning Network, USA

ABSTRACT

Ohio is an undereducated state with 21.1% of its adult population holding a bachelor's degree or higher. This chapter illustrates the innovative curriculum in a free, online course that shows significant promise as one strategy to raise the educational attainment of adults. This case study enables readers to look at fundamental instructional and delivery issues in providing distance learning to adults. Successes and weaknesses of the program may help other states address the needs of returning adult learners.

BACKGROUND AND NEEDS ANALYSIS

E 4 ME was born out of a need to target the non-traditional, adult population in Ohio that needs to return to school in order to upgrade skills and knowledge for the demands of the 21st century economy. Nearly 1.5 million Ohio adults had some college education, but no formal degree (OBR, 2004).

In 2003, Ohio was undereducated compared to the rest of the United States, with 21.1% of its adult population 25 and older having a bachelor's degree or higher, compared to 24.4% for the United States (2000 Census). This gap was critical, because

income levels and standards of living were closely tied to education levels. Nationally, bachelor's degree recipients earned nearly $18,000 more than high school graduates earned in 2001. Furthermore, the unemployment rate for workers holding a bachelor's degree was 3.1%, compared to 5.3% for those with only a high school diploma. It was of vital importance that more Ohioans participate in higher education so that our economy could provide the jobs and income levels required to maintain a high quality of life (OBR, 2004).

Ohioans who earned post-secondary credentials would be better positioned to earn more money, contribute more to their communities, pay more taxes to support vital public services, and depend less on public support. Ohio, as a low graduation

DOI: 10.4018/978-1-61520-672-8.ch001

state, ranks 37th in the nation for undergraduate degree completion. For Ohio's workforce to catch up and keep pace at a national level, higher education in Ohio must graduate more people, keep them in Ohio after graduation, and attract more talent to Ohio so the state becomes a net importer of people with college degrees, rather than a net exporter as it is today (Fingerhut, 2008).

No single solution would provide a panacea to solve the educational attainment problem, but through a collaborative effort, Ohioans could be best served. The Ohio Learning Network joined a cadre of organizations to raise educational attainment by providing services and resources to raise the state's educational attainment.

The Regan and Smith Discrepancy Model provided an effective way to determine needs assessment. Distance education was growing rapidly in Ohio colleges and universities in 2003, yet, many adults were unfamiliar with this delivery method. Across the nation, working adults were finding e-learning more flexible than campus-based learning which made an introductory course a reasonable approach for recruiting adults into college.

Ohio's low educational attainment ranking in the nation combined with the charge from the governor and the Ohio Board of Regents to increase the participation of Ohioans in higher education led to the course creation by the Ohio Learning Network (OLN). OLN is a consortium of 83 community colleges and universities within the University System of Ohio, and the state's independent colleges and universities. An initiative of the Ohio Board of Regents, OLN helps Ohioans gain access to higher education through an online catalog of courses and degrees and provides faculty development programs and student support activities.

Adult learning theory drove the design of the E 4 ME course. The course must assist adults in overcoming barriers of time and location as well as provide a cost effective course without unexpected or additional fees attached. The course must be structured to foster short-term success providing immediate results for adult learners. The course experience must build confidence in adults while adequately presenting the challenges of online learning.

DESIGN RATIONALE

Learning theories have their basis in philosophy and psychology and provide the overall framework for teaching and learning activities (Merriam & Caffarella, 1999). The E 4 ME course was designed using a blend of the constructivist approach to teaching and learning as well as the instructivist approach. The course was created with clear performance objectives and has a systematic approach to the learning content to insure consistency in delivery across class sections and among instructors who teach the class concurrently each month. The course also was designed with the needs of the learner in mind, and encourages the learner's interpretations through self-directed exploration of the content, group and individual class exercises, surveys and self assessment activity.

The Morrison/Ross/Kemp Model describes the process used for creating E 4 ME by using nine basic steps in its systematic design process (Gustafson, K. & Branch, R.M. (1997):

- identify *instructional problems*, and specify goals for designing a program;
- examine *learner characteristics* that should receive attention during planning;
- identify *subject content*, and *analyze task* components related to stated goals and purposes;
- state *instructional* objectives for the learner;
- sequence content within each instructional unit for logical learning;
- design instructional strategies so that each learner can master the objectives;
- plan the instructional message and delivery;

- develop evaluation instruments to assess objectives;
- select *resources* to support instruction and learning activities.

Continual revision and formative evaluation processes occurred during each step of the design process and were implemented and documented in building E 4 ME. A final set of activities that accompanies the MRK model includes planning activities, project management, required summative evaluations, and arrangement for necessary services to support the project and instruction once it is implemented. In E 4 ME, these were done by an internal planning team (three full-time staff and two part-time graduate students). Instructional designers can start at any stage in the design process that makes sense to their project. This can be particularly helpful to designers when the development and delivery technology or instructional strategies have already been predetermined as was the case in E 4 ME.

The primary goal for creating the E 4 ME program was to increase educational attainment in Ohio by increasing the number of adults who enrolled in college. Once the course was launched, continuous improvement goals were created: 1) increase the number of adults who completed E 4 ME and enrolled in college; 2) grow the partnerships and fee waivers and 3) increase the number of students working with E Guides and enrolling in college;

Specific course goals were ambitious for a non–credit offering, including:

- Complete the E 4 ME course and receive a certificate of completion;
- Understand how to be successful in an e-learning course;
- Assess their technical skill level;
- Decide if e-learning is right for them;
- Identify some good study habits for e-learning;
- Navigate through and be familiar with the structure of a typical e-learning course;

- Interact with their instructor and other students via the Internet;
- Take quizzes and tests online.

Post course, learners were encouraged to take advantage of an E Guide for assistance in morale or selecting a college and to enroll using an E Fee (a discount incentive from an institution working with the E 4 ME program).

Frey & Alman (2003) report that "Adult learning theory helps faculty understand their students and design more meaningful learning experiences for them. There is not one adult learning theory that successfully applies to all adult learning environments" (p. 8). There were several learning theories that helped inform our decisions as we developed the E 4 ME course for adult learners.

Experiential learning theory, which suggested "that adult teaching should be grounded in adults' experiences, and that these experiences represent a valuable resource" (Brookfield, 1995, p. 4; Cercone, 2008, p. 148). Self-directed learning theory, according to Lowry, "suggested that the locus of control in learning lies with the adult learner, who may initiate learning with or without assistance from others" (Cercone, 2008, p. 148; Lowry, 1989). Transformative learning theory, according to Palloff and Pratt, reminded us that the goal is "to understand why we see the world in the way that we do," and to rid ourselves of "the constraints and limiting perspectives that we brought with us into the learning environment" (Cercone, 2008, p. 149; Palloff and Pratt, 1999). These theories provided our team with a better understanding of the characteristics of adult learners and how these characteristics could influence the design of the E 4 ME learning environment.

The course was designed around five important assumptions about adult learners based on Malcolm Knowles' *Andragogy in Action* (Cercone, 2008; Merriam & Caffarella, 1999; Knowles, 1989):

1. Adult learners are "autonomous, independent, self-reliant, and are self-directed toward goals" (Cercone, 2008, p. 143).

2. Adult students "can build on previous knowledge and experience by relating new information to past events and experience" (Cercone, 2008, p. 144).

3. Adult students "usually know what they want to learn and they like to see the program organized toward their personal goals" (Cercone, 2008, p. 145).

4. Learners "need to know why they should learn something" (Cercone, 2008, p. 145) and how it will benefit them (Knowles, 1989).

5. Adults are "motivated to learn by internal factors rather than external factors" (Cercone, 2008; Merriam & Caffarella, 1999).

The adult learning theories and assumptions influenced the design of E 4 ME by helping our team understand how important it was to make the course learner-centered and self-paced, with an added goal of helping students become more comfortable with self-directed learning. An instructor was made available inside each course to facilitate the course on a daily basis to help students gain confidence as self-directed learners.

A subject content list was developed that enabled the design team to define the tasks and instructional objectives. Tasks were sequenced and assigned to team members, and the results were sub-divided into three sections. Three full-time staff developed the first draft of the instructional content, and the drafts were combined once again and circulated among the project team for full review, critique, and further modification. The final version of the course content was placed into the Course Management System (CMS) and the review and modification process began again. After the initial pilot of the E 4 ME class, the class was opened up to OLN staff, the OLN Governing Board, administrators, and future E 4 ME instructors for evaluation and review. Additional revisions were made. Finally, the course

was offered to the target audience. Periodic evaluation and modifications became an ongoing part of running the E 4 ME course.

The MRK model made anticipating student problems easier and moved the design staff to add innovations. Tech Check helps students assess readiness to begin an online class, including basic computer skill levels, student competencies, and the proper computer set-up requirements needed to successfully take the E 4 ME class. A technical support person was added to each class to help students when they had questions, had problems connecting or navigating inside the course. Lecture-capture tutorials were added to provide an orientation for students.

Consistent, specialized training for the cadre of online instructors helped facilitate and bridge the gap for students who needed more structure while transitioning to a learner-centered environment. Outcomes of training included knowledge of adult learner's unique expectations and needs -- safety, respect, and engagement. Instructors encouraged student engagement in group discussion via the class discussion boards and encouraged students' timely participation in course exercises. Students' past experiences were valued as evidenced by instructor comments on autobiography postings. Student input was frequently encouraged in both personal and group settings.

Several evaluation measures are built into the design of the E 4 ME course. Students are provided with an online evaluation at the end of the last unit and an opportunity to evaluate the course, the instructor, and the quality of the learning experience. External follow-up email messages are sent to students who complete E 4 ME, and to non-completers to inquire about their continued involvement with online learning, and to determine if they have questions or comments they want to share about their learning experience several weeks after the course has ended.

Additionally, focus group comments after the initial launch of the course found that learners liked the content and found it helpful when considering returning to college. Students appreciated the instructor-student contact. Some students expected more interaction among those in the class while others found the level of interaction satisfactory. Some students felt the volume of work in the class was excessive for a non-credit course.

E 4 ME instructors and advisors are periodically sent online evaluations to solicit their feedback and suggestions for ways to improve the course. Quarterly and semi-annual meetings are also scheduled with instructors and advisors to discuss their solicited feedback as a group, and to discuss important updates to the course.

The evaluative data received from E 4 ME students, instructors, and advisors are stored in the customer relational database as a measure to support instruction and learning activities, and to generate reports that are meaningful and helpful to refining the course and validating the E 4 ME program.

E 4 ME COURSE AND RECRUITING PROGRAM

E 4 ME is a free, online course created by the Ohio Learning Network (OLN) to recruit back to school adults who have some college credits but no degree. The month-long, instructor-led course covers admissions, financial aid, academic course searches and degree searches, career counseling, time management, and successful study skills for online students.

Since 2004, more than 1,000 Ohioans have completed the E 4 ME class and 34% who completed E 4 ME have enrolled in college. Significant partnerships have been formed across Ohio as a result of teaching E 4 ME. Residents find the course through local college access programs and community computing centers. Continuing advice and email support is offered to course completers through E Guides, an adult mentor or buddy. An unanticipated benefit of the E 4 ME course is that it is used by some consortium members to help

enrolled students decide if they are good candidates for online learning.

E 4 ME has received four national awards including: Instructional Technology Council (ITC) Awards for Excellence in Distance Learning – Outstanding Online and Blended Courses; Western Cooperative for Educational Telecommunications (WCET) Outstanding Work WOW Award; American Distance Education Consortium (ADEC) Excellence in College and University Distance Education National Awards Program – Honorable Mention Team Award; and National Academic Advising Association (NACADA) which was awarded to George Steele, OLN director of educational access.

E 4 ME is unique in its ability to reach out to all Ohioans at no cost. While many colleges offer an 'intro to e-learning' once enrolled, no other state currently offers a course like E 4 ME. The E 4 ME program targets adults new to distance learning, uncertain about new technology, curious about where or how to begin their transition back to school after a long absence, uneasy with the thought of returning to school as an older or non-traditional student, or faced with barriers that prevent them from attending traditional classes at a college or university. Through E 4 ME, students can make a successful transition into online learning technology and determine the skills that are necessary for a successful return to school. E 4 ME students become self-directed learners with excellent study skills and effective time management. They are comfortable with distance learning technology and enthusiastic about attending college.

The E 4 ME course is divided into six modules, or units, with each unit taking anywhere from 30 minutes up to three hours to complete, depending on the students' abilities. The total time estimated for a student to complete the entire course is between seven and 16 hours. Students are given one month to complete the course at their own pace, but are provided with a course schedule to enable them to pace and plan how they will complete all of the assignments within the month. While self-paced and flexible, in-course assistance is provided from the instructor and from a technical support person.

Each unit in the course can be accessed sequentially or randomly by advancing from one page to the next throughout the course, or by clicking on a table of contents which is located to the left of the course screen. Students are able to stop at any point inside the course and resume where they left off by setting a "bookmark" inside the course to recall where they ended their last session.

Students are invited to tour the course site one day before class begins, and on the first day of class they are greeted by their instructor's welcome message. In addition, instructors post their own autobiographies on the class discussion board in order to get a discussion started the first week of class. Students are encouraged to post their autobiographies within the first week of class and respond to their fellow students' posted autobiographies and messages. This helps build community within each E 4 ME class, and fosters student engagement as early as possible.

Class instructors send periodic messages to students throughout the month to encourage, support, and motivate students, as well as respond to students' inquiries and concerns. Four quiz formats are used inside E 4 ME to introduce students to several testing formats: multiple choice, fill in the blank, essay, and word match. Many quizzes are automatically graded as soon as students complete and submit their responses. Partially graded quizzes are reviewed by class instructors, then graded and sent to students usually within a 24-hour period. Additional feedback is often provided to students with their quiz grades. The course provides opportunities for students to self-assess through interactive class surveys. The surveys enable students to assess their readiness to be a successful online learner, manage their time, and evaluate their readiness to change careers or prepare for a new career.

The course includes several orientation videos to prepare students to use the new online technology, followed by six units of course content. The course content includes: an introduction to the course including instructor expectations, an introduction to e-learning and what it is, an evaluation of whether e-learning is right for the student, help with planning the student's educational path, help with choosing a career or occupation, help with enrolling into a college or university, and steps to take after completing the E 4 ME course.

Students are asked online to evaluate the course, the course content and the instructor after completing E 4 ME. Students who complete all of the class assignments receive a certificate of completion that can be printed out and laminated. Students who complete E 4 ME are also given an opportunity to have extended support after completing the course through a live E Guide who is assigned to answer their questions about preparing to return to school.

THE E 4 ME ENVIRONMENT

The E 4 ME course runs on the WebCT Vista course management platform, and students have a large degree of flexibility inside E 4 ME in terms of what, how, and when they learn. In order to establish a reasonable degree of structure, preliminary course goals are clearly stated at the beginning of the course to enable students to have a productive start and assure them there is a benefit to reviewing the course content inside each unit. Samples of the E 4 ME environment can be seen in Figures 1, 2, 3, 4, 5, and 6.

Each unit has a set of introductory course goals, a pre-test, followed by the course content, and a unit summary. At the end of each unit, there is a brief quiz. The quiz is automatically graded for students, where students receive immediate feedback if the question format is multiple choice, true or false, or word match. Class instructors grade those sections of student quizzes that involve fill in the blank

Figure 1. E 4 ME Homepage – Front Page of E 4 ME Course.

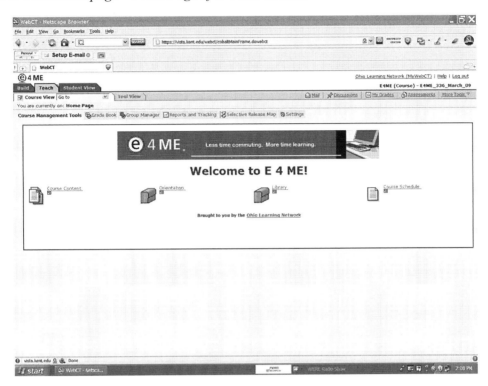

or essay. Turnaround time for instructor-graded quizzes is usually within 24-48 hours.

Students interact with their instructor and fellow students regularly through their mail tool and the class discussion board. Students are sent an external email message prior to the beginning of their class with the Website location, and their password and ID information. All communication thereafter occurs inside the E 4 ME course once students enter the course for the first time.

THE EVOLUTION OF E 4 ME

Issues, Controversies, Problems

E 4 ME was conceptualized in 2003 and first taught in 2004. The staff building the course had never taught online nor created an online course, but had extensive teaching and course development experience. Staff members designing the course were well-versed in student development theory, adult learning theory, curriculum design, non-traditional student advising, and general academic principals and procedures.

The early impetus for E 4 ME came from a statewide group that felt one common orientation course might be useful for members of the consortium. The committee, and a curriculum designer, created an outline for this common course. As often happens with good ideas, time marches on and once the outline was designed, institutions had created orientation courses or had stalled e-learning efforts and the idea of a common orientation fell by the wayside.

Early course development was done by three staff members and two part-time graduate students. One graduate student became the manager of the program, setting up courses, assigning instructors and gathering data. That work moved to a full-time staff member as the course continued to grow in enrollments.

Figure 2. E 4 ME Tutorials – Tutorial Section to Help Students At Start of Course.

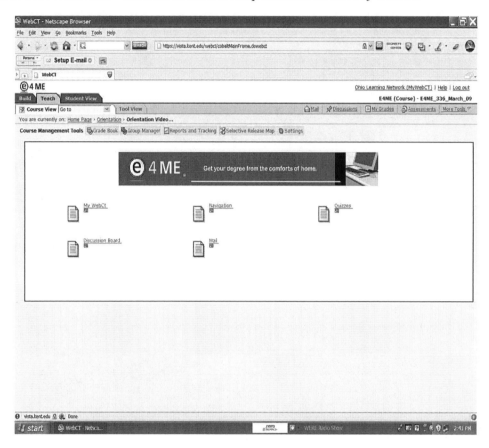

Initially, the course was designed independent of a course management tool because it was felt that a statewide course should be independent from the Course Management System (CMS) wars that were occurring in Ohio and nationwide. Trial and error with software and consulting services for that software led to a course that still needed a student database to capture enrollments, grades, etc. The course quickly moved to a hosted CMS provided by a consortium member because of the accompanying ease of data transfer, course section creation, and the adoption of such tools across the state. It was decided that most students would enter a college using a CMS, so they might as well get familiar with one through the free E 4 ME course.

The course was patterned in part on existing face-to-face orientation and career counseling courses offered by many colleges and universities. Immediately, several issues arose due to the nature of OLN as a consortium. These issues are addressed in a question-and-answer format below. In the true fashion of a skunk works team, the team addressed each question as it arose and designed and documented processes for the course. The team developed levels of expertise and appropriated tasks accordingly across full- and part-time staff and undergraduate student employees.

Should the Course be Offered Centrally or at Each Campus?

The first 'trial' class of students was the OLN Governing Board made up of provosts from member institutions. Some of the board members completed the full course, others jumped into sec-

Figure 3. E 4 ME Course Schedule – Course Syllabus.

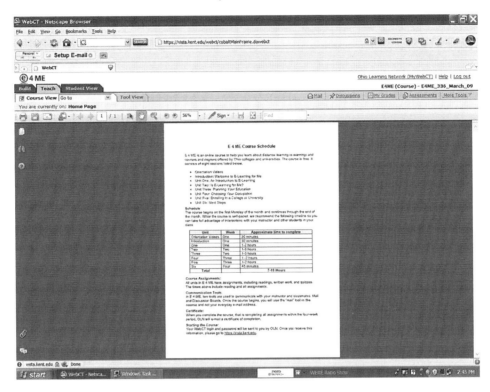

tions to explore key assignments, and all offered input to the course design. Several other 'soft' launches were done in early 2004 with the first general public offering in September, 2004. For course continuity, it was decided to have one course offered at the state level. Many member institutions saw this as yet another benefit provided by OLN and recommended that students take E 4 ME before they enrolled in an online course. Several institutions provided a direct link to the E 4 ME registration page from their distance learning page. In some months, most of the students enrolled were referrals from member institutions.

Should the Course be Taught as Well as Provide a Self-Paced Tutorial?

A self-paced, instructor-led course was designed because most returning adults preferred a hi-tech, hi-touch approach. For adults who preferred a quick tutorial format, the self-paced course al-

lowed them to finish in hours or days, rather than follow the month-long format. Most students finished in the first two weeks.

Should it be Free or Low Cost to Ohioans?

Through the funds provided by the Ohio General Assembly and the Ohio Board of Regents, the course remained free.

What are Finishers Called, Graduates? Completers?

Just as member institutions use the term, "graduates," for those who earn a degree or certificate, "completers," was chosen, as students do not 'graduate' from a single course.

Figure 4. E 4 ME Course Content Page – Course Content of E 4 ME.

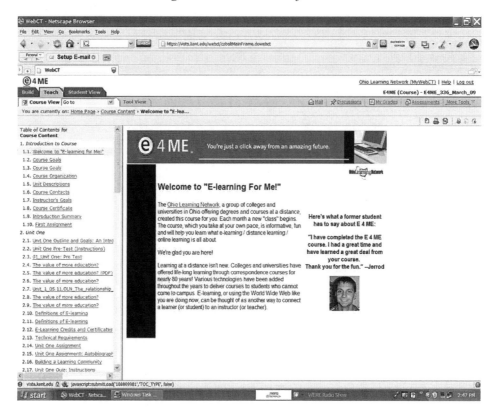

Can Students Receive a Certificate of Completion and can the Certificate be Worth Something at Member Institutions?

Certificates of completion are mailed at the end of the course. Each certificate carries a unique number that allows OLN to track usage of the certificates. Several member institutions offer a discount at the bookstore, a reduced admission fee, or a tuition waiver to E 4 ME completers as an incentive to enroll. This allowed a tracking system to be established if the student took advantage of the fee waiver. Many students enrolled (34%) without notifying OLN or using the fee waiver. A better method to track students without holding social security numbers is under discussion.

Should Non-Ohioans be Able to Enroll in the Course?

Very few non-Ohioans enrolled in E 4 ME. Those who did were often other distance learning professionals who were curious about the course. A small number of 'border state' individuals enrolled in the class and an occasional international student enrolled. More than 95% of the enrolled students have been Ohioans.

If Taught by OLN Staff, how can the Course Scale Beyond a Small Staff (Six) with Teaching Experience?

As the numbers began to grow from less than 75 enrolled a month to close to 200, a way to scale the teaching needed to be addressed. Ohio has two active groups that became partners in the E 4 ME program – college access and community

Figure 5. E 4 ME Mail Tool – Course Communication Tool.

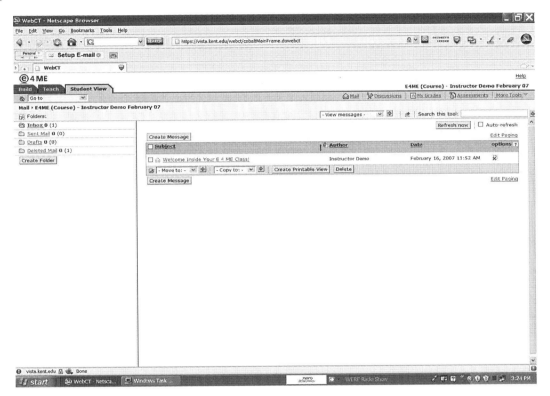

computing. The Ohio College Access Network, also an initiative of the Ohio Board of Regents, has 33 programs in counties across the state. Ohio Community Computing Network (OCCN) is a network of more than 300 small and large organizations that provide free access to computers and the Internet. OLN could never reach adults locally like these two programs, so we created partnerships in which the local organizations promoted, recruited and taught students in E 4 ME classes. OLN paid the organizations per class with a cap of $10,000 annually. To keep consistency in instruction, OLN staff trained the partnership instructors in both teaching the course and using the CMS. The first time instructors taught, they were partnered with an OLN staff member who served as their 'teaching buddy,' offering guidance and help through the first course. OLN purchased statewide, local radio time on adult contemporary stations to promote the E 4 ME course. A tag line identified the local

provider or, where no local provider existed, the URL for registration was provided.

How to Continuously Upgrade the Course Content?

To keep the E 4 ME course fresh and updated, an OLN staff member was assigned to work with all the instructors to gather input for changes and additions to the course. For several years, an annual meeting was held each summer to update instructors on any changes with the course or the course management system and to listen to instructors' suggestions for course improvements. As travel costs increased, distance technologies were employed - both audio and Webinars - to hold meetings.

Figure 6. E 4 ME Discussion Board – Class Discussion Board.

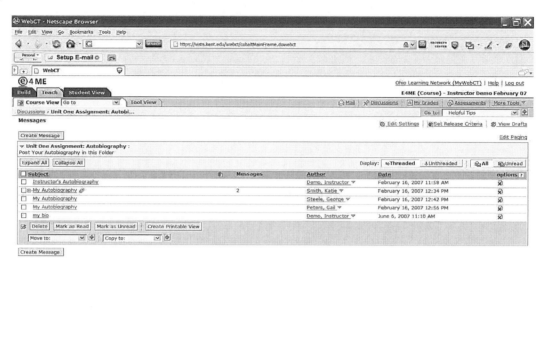

How to Reach Those Completers and Gather Data on Their Next Steps in Lifelong Learning?

Without adequate tracking mechanisms, information on completers remains self-reported data. OLN contracted with external evaluators in 2006 to look at the effectiveness of the course and track activity of the completers. While many did not respond to continued email contacts, those who responded enjoyed the course, and 34% reported enrolling in a college or university.

To aid in tracking students, OLN invested in a Customer Relationship Management (CRM) tool that automates some of the student contact and eases the work of the staff coordinator. The CRM was integrated into the administration of the E 4 ME course in a number of ways. Course registration was the first function modified. The Web form capabilities of the CRM replaced the original Web registration page. This enabled the integrated analytic and marketing capabilities of the CRM. Tracking completers and non-completers allowed the creation of targeted marketing campaigns for specific regions of the state. Specific e-mail campaigns about programs offered by institutions in their region were sent to completers. An e-mail campaign was designed to encourage non-completers to try the course again or contact OLN for assistance. Surveys were targeted to these groups, asking about their reactions to the course and their intended next step plans.

Internal to the course, Web forms were created within the CMS. One Web form collected students' interests in pursuing specific distance learning content after reviewing the course catalog, OhioLearns!. Previously, this data was collected in an aggregate and specific distance learning at the individual level was unknown. The course final evaluation was converted from inside the

Course Management System to inside the Customer Relationship Management tool. The CRM analytical tools gave us a more powerful way to consider students' reactions and make adjustments accordingly.

The critical advantage of the CRM was that any data collected from an individual, whether through an e-mail inquiry incident, a phone conversation, survey results, a Web form, or chat exchange, could be compiled in order to paint a more detailed portrait of that person. Tracking and follow-up with students use timely reminders and messages related to the student's expressed interests.

LESSONS LEARNED AND APPLIED

In every aspect of the program – course design, partnership building, marketing, fee waivers, E Guides – continuous improvements were undertaken to provide the strongest adult recruiting program possible. The course is updated as needed but no less than once per year. The processes are always updated or advanced to serve more students more efficiently. Input from students, instructors, partners and staff keep the course and program always advancing.

Efficiencies have been created in the four years of the full E 4 ME program in updating the course content and managing the classes. Partnership funds were adjusted to reflect actual work rather than perceived work so to best use state resources. Class sizes have been adjusted to reflect the amount of students who sign up but never attend a class. Individual instructors were used heavily in 2006-2007, but that practice has been reduced in 2008 to more effectively use the partnership organizations.

Late in 2007, OLN received a $522,200 grant from the Lumina Foundation for Education for an innovative way to recruit and retain low-skilled adult learners called "QuickStart to College." The E 4 ME course provided some of the essential content for the QuickStart course. The remaining content mimics a first-year experience course. In the QuickStart program, adults often have low math and English skills and additional tutoring is provided prior to placement tests to help reduce remediation of these adults. Without the successes of the original E 4 ME program, the QuickStart project would not have been conceived.

In its inaugural offering, 120 low-skilled adults enrolled in QuickStart. Many were recruited directly from Adult Basic Literacy programs and state jobs programs. Like adults in the E 4 ME class, those in QuickStart have found their technology skills have increased during the course. The content has helped them be more self confident in their abilities.

FUTURE TRENDS

With its four national awards, E 4 ME is a successful recruiting tool for online learners. Its future can take many forms. It can continue as it is with existing partnerships and average monthly enrollment near 200. It can be reconfigured into a high school version. It can be done in partnership with local Adult Basic Literacy programs. In the summer of 2008, the Ohio Board of Regents pulled the Ohio Learning Network into a closer organizational structure. The Ohio Board of Regents will determine the future growth and directions for E 4 ME.

All the evidence across the nation suggests that adults are finding online learning a good way to earn college degrees. In Ohio, approximately 50% of all online learners are over the age of 25. Most colleges and universities see this trend increasing for adults. A course like E 4 ME offers an efficient and effective way to recruit adults for college, to explore online learning with little investment, and to take a small step toward lifelong learning.

Ohio will continue to grow its online offerings in the public colleges and universities. As courses like E 4 ME prepare students to be more successful in online and distance courses, their futures will be positive.

CONCLUSION

E 4 ME is a flexible, low cost, informative first step to returning to college for adults. A self-paced modular format meets their needs. Using a course management tool gives adults the skills they will need should they return to college. A brief biography helps adults reflect and sharpen writing skills. They appreciate the availability of an instructor for information and guidance.

Students who take E 4 ME prior to enrolling in a college or university online class find they are more aware of what is expected in an online course. College and university faculty and distance education personnel believe the E 4 ME experience assists students with decision-making about distance and online courses.

From the success with E 4 ME, the Ohio Learning Network created a new adult program for lower skilled, post-General Education Diploma (GED) adults called QuickStart to College, funded by the Lumina Foundation for Education. The QuickStart course adapts content from E 4 ME and local college First Year Experience courses to create an eight-week modular hybrid course that has successfully recruited 70% of participants into college.

Lumina believes that education is the foundation for individual opportunity, economic vitality and social stability. The Foundation's goal is to raise the proportion of the U.S. adult population who earn college degrees to 60% by the year 2025, an increase of 16 million graduates above current rates. The United States remains an undereducated nation and adults are key to our country's continuing economic future. Courses like E 4 ME are necessary to help adults transition into lifelong learners.

ACKNOWLEDGMENT

The authors thank George Steele, director of educational access at the Ohio Learning Network for his contributions to this chapter.

REFERENCES

Brookfield, S. (1995). Adult learning: An overview. In A. Tuinjman (Ed.), *International Encyclopedia of Education*. Oxford, UK: Pergamon Press. Retrieved November 23, 2008, from http://www.fsu.edu/~elps/ae/download/ade5385/Brookfield.pdf

Cercone, K. (2008). Characteristics of adult learners with implications for online learning design. *AACE Journal, 16*(2), 137–159.

Fingerhut, E. (2008). Raising educational attainment in Ohio. *Strategic Plan for Higher Education 2008-2017*. Retrieved November 21, 2008, from http://uso.edu/strategicplan/downloads/documents/strategicPlan/USOStrategicPlan.pdf

Frey, B. A., & Alman, S. W. (2003). Applying adult learning theory to the online classroom. *New Horizons in Adult Education, 17*(1), 4–12.

Gustafson, K., & Branch, R. M. (1997). *Instructional design models*. Syracuse, NY: ERIC Clearinghouse on Information and Technology.

Knowles, M. (1984). *Andragogy in Action*. San Francisco: Jossey-Bass.

Knowles, M. (1989). *The making of an adult educator: An autobiographical journey*. San Francisco: Jossey-Bass.

Lowry, C. M. (1989). Supporting and facilitating self-directed learning. *ERIC Digest, 93*. Retrieved November 23, 2008, from http://www.ntlf.com/html/lib/bib/89dig.htm

Merriam, S. B., & Caffarella, R. S. (1999). *Learning in adulthood* (2nd ed.). San Francisco: Jossey-Bass.

Ohio Board of Regents. (2004). *The Performance Report for Ohio's Colleges and Universities, 2003.* Retrieved March 19, 2009, from http://regents.ohio.gov/perfrpt/2003

Ohio Board of Regents. (2004). *Adult Educational Attainment by Age Group 1990 and 2000 Census Results. Prepared for the Governor's Commission on Higher Education and the Economy.* Retrieved November 22, 2008, from http://regents.ohio.gov/perfrpt/special_reports/Degree_Attainment_by_Age_Group_90_2000_Census.pdf

Palloff, R. M., & Pratt, K. (1999). *Building learning communities in cyberspace*. San Francisco: Jossey-Bass.

Smith, P. L., & Ragan, T. J. (2005). *Instructional Design* (3rd ed.). Hoboken, NJ: Wiley.

Wedman, J., & Tessmer, M. (1991). Adapting instructional design to project circumstance: The layers of necessity model. *Educational Technology*, *31*(7), 48–52.

KEY TERMS AND DEFINITIONS

Adult Learner: is a term used to describe any person socially accepted as an adult who is in a learning process, whether it is formal education, informal learning, or corporate-sponsored learning. Adult learners are considered distinct from child learners due primarily to the work of Malcolm Knowles, who developed the principle of andragogy. Adult learners fall into the category of non-traditional students, whom the National Center for Education Statistics defines as meeting at least one of the following seven criteria: Delays enrollment (does not enter postsecondary education in the same calendar year that he or she finished high school), Attends part-time for at least part of the academic year, Works full-time (35 hours or more per week) while enrolled, Is considered financially independent for purposes of determining eligibility for financial aid, Has dependents other than a spouse (usually children, but sometimes others), Is a single parent (either not married or married but separated and has dependents), Does not have a high school diploma (completed high school with a GED or other high school completion certificate or did not finish high school).

Andragogy: consists of learning strategies focused on teaching adults. It is often interpreted as the process of engaging adult learners in the structure of the learning experience. The term was developed into a theory of adult education by Malcolm Knowles. Knowles held that andragogy should be distinguished from the more commonly used pedagogy. Knowles' theory is frequently stated as four simple postulates: 1) Adults need to be involved in the planning and evaluation of their instruction, 2) Experience (including mistakes) provides the basis for learning activities, 3) Adults are most interested in learning subjects that have immediate relevance to their job or personal life (readiness to learn), 4) Adult learning is problem-centered rather than content-oriented (orientation to learning).

CRM: Customer Relationship Management tools are software and databases designed to maintain data and provide direct communications to and with customers, or in this case, students.

Educational Attainment: is a term commonly used by statisticians to refer to the highest degree of education an individual has completed. The US Census Bureau Glossary defines educational attainment as "the highest level of education completed in terms of the highest degree or the highest level of schooling completed."

Experiential Learning: focuses on the learning process for the individual (unlike experiential education, which focuses on the process of transacting between teacher and learner). An example of experiential learning is going to the zoo and learning through observation and interaction with the zoo environment, as opposed to reading about animals from a book. Thus, one makes discoveries and experiments with knowledge firsthand, instead of hearing or reading about others' experiences.

Innovative: refers to a new way of doing something. It may refer to incremental, radical, or revolutionary changes in thinking, products, processes, or organizations. In many fields (such as in the arts, economics, business, or government) to be innovative, something must be substantially new or different. In economics, the change must increase value, produce value or add customer value. The goal of innovation is positive change, to make someone or something better. Innovation leading to increased productivity is the fundamental source of increasing wealth in an economy.

Learning Theory: is an attempt to describe how we learn, thereby helping us understand the inherently complex process of learning. Learning theories provide us with vocabulary and a conceptual framework for interpreting the examples of learning that take place, and suggest where to look for solutions to practical problems. There are three main categories or philosophical frameworks under which learning theories fall:

behaviorism, cognitivism, and constructivism. Behaviorism focuses on the objectively observable aspects of learning. Cognitive theories look beyond behavior to explain brain-based learning. And constructivism views learning as a process in which the learner actively constructs or builds new ideas or concepts.

Online Learning: is a type of Technology Supported Learning/education (TSL) where the medium of instruction is computer technology. In some instances, no in-person interaction takes place. E-learning is used interchangeably in a wide variety of contexts. In companies, it refers to the strategies that use the company network to deliver training courses to employees. In the USA, it is defined as a planned teaching/learning experience that uses a wide spectrum of technologies, mainly Internet or computer-based, to reach learners. Lately in most universities, e-learning is used to define a specific attendance mode for a course or programs of study where the students rarely, if ever, attend educational facilities face-to-face, because they study online.

Chapter 2
From Traditional Teaching to Online Learning:
Revolution or Evolution

José Magano
Instituto Superior de Ciências Empresariais e do Turismo, Portugal

Carlos V. Carvalho
GILT / Instituto Superior de Engenharia do Porto, Portugal

ABSTRACT

In Portugal, like in most Western countries, most higher education institutions are already using e-learning platforms. However, this does not mean that these institutions are now offering distance education programmes but rather that they are using these tools as content repositories to support normal f2f academic disciplines. Therefore effective e-learning adoption is still limited to episodic, non systematic, initiatives. This chapter presents the e-learning initiative of the Higher Institute of Business Science and Tourism (ISCET). This initiative is relevant, precisely because it represents a holistic and revolutionary approach. All the students of ISCET were involved and there was a provision of online environments for the entire body of subjects offered in ISCET. The evaluation of the experimental stage setup the path to a systematic approach to distance education in the institute and provided valuable clues for other institutions that want to replicate ISCET's e-learning initiative.

INTRODUCTION

The adaptation of the Institutions of Higher Education (IES) to the knowledge society is having a profound impact in terms of paradigms, organizational structures, educational and social methodologies and practices (UNESCO, 1998; CRE, 1998, Daniel, 1996). This view of the dynamic and rapidly evolving world has been fully substantiated and demonstrated since UNESCO's original statement ten years ago. Now, more than ever, Universities are required to be able to prepare World Citizens, capable of living and working in a globalized society, with improved skills and competences. We've been watching for these past years how uncertain this society is, how difficult it is to achieve balance in such a world and how deep and large are the variations that arise from the global market. Anyone who cannot cope with this will be limited to small, unimportant roles.

DOI: 10.4018/978-1-61520-672-8.ch002

In Europe, the Bologna declaration changed the Higher Education panorama. This declaration, resulting from the common agreement of the Ministers of Education of over 20 European countries, promotes the creation of a two-cycle system with comparable degrees (undergraduate and graduate) and a common credit system with high degree of students and teachers mobility. Above all it promotes recognized quality assurance procedures (ECEM, 2000). The adaptation to the Bologna declaration has also lead to the adoption of new, student-centered, learning/ teaching paradigms.

E-learning has already overcome the initial misgivings arising from a traditionalist vision of Distance Education and it is regarded as a valid means to enhance learning (Moore, 1996). E-learning promotes an increased responsibility by students in their learning. The student controls various aspects of the process, as the choice and access to sources of information, time and location of such access, the processes of interaction with other participants, etc.. Simultaneously, the teacher gets the role of tutoring and guiding the students in their cognitive development. Thus, e-learning converges with the fundamental objectives expressed in the declaration of Bologna. In Portugal, although most of the institutions of higher education have e-learning initiatives, there are actually only a few that promote alternative forms of learning. They rather focus on the use of the e-learning platforms to support static contents of face-to-face (f2f) academic disciplines.

The Higher Institute for Business Science and Tourism (ISCET) is a private establishment of higher education and offers degrees in the areas of Tourism, Management of Human Resources, Social Service, Labor and Social Psychology, International Business Relations and Marketing. ISCET values, in all circumstances, the relation with business in the exploitation of its scientific areas of expertise and in the characterization of their students and teachers. ISCET also encourages and promotes the exchange of teachers and students through protocols with other institutions and regular contact with centers of excellence and seeks to encourage research, as a dimension of the activity of teachers and students (ISCET, 2008).

The e-learning initiative of ISCET presents innovative aspects that promote its scientific interest. The size of the institution allowed for an integral approach, including an holistic assessment of the process. This made possible to examine the change in the organizational culture introduced by the initiative.

This article describes the goals, methodology and evaluation of the initial stages of this initiative and presents the conclusions and recommendations that lead to its systematization.

BACKGROUND

What exactly is e-learning? When does an initiative / methodology / model carries a more generic definition of the use of ICT's for teaching / learning for e-learning itself or one of its variants (like blended-learning)? When a term is as widespread as e-learning is today it ends up failing to reflect what it actually means. People just assume that their interpretation is shared by others and build conversations based on completely different ideas.

The multiplicity of the available definitions does not help to a clear identification. Jay Cross, who in 1998 introduced the term, says that its ambiguity is so great that he prefers not to use it anymore.

A common definition that can be found on the Internet is: "The use of communication technologies to create, promote, distribute and facilitate learning, anywhere anytime." The credit must be assigned to Elliot Masie. It is an elegant but very broad definition. E-learning becomes a large bag of methodologies. However, putting a set of pdf files on the Internet and answering questions from students via e-mail is not e-learning!

The definition of Gomes (2005) clears very well the ground. We can be a little more flexible, indicating that e-learning is any methodology of teaching / learning that integrates activities, supported by Information and Communication Technologies, essential for achieving the objectives of the learning paths.

Studies show that these processes of personalization of learning, that give more responsibility to students, increase the efficiency of learning and create professionals with greater capacity to react to changes in the work environment (Vaz de Carvalho, 2001). The use of technology in the teaching / learning must, however, go through a strategically planned process involving the senior levels of management. But at the same time it is not realistic to attempt to impose models of teaching / learning if the teachers do not feel comfortable with all its components, particularly those concerning technology.

Laurillard (2004) proposes that educators must "…exert some influence over the way in which e-learning is used in universities, and direct its power overtly towards the needs of learners". The perception of teachers regarding the introduction of e-learning focuses on a set of points relating to problems and goals for improvement. This subject was evaluated in previous studies (Cardoso, 2000; Mingle, 1995; Vaz de Carvalho, 2001) which identified the critical factors of success. We can cite, as fundamentals, the need for human resources training (in particular, the teachers), the need to manage expectations and fears and the creation of enlarged communities. Above all, the construction of a shared vision and understanding of the role of technology in higher education institutions is required. This vision must be built together and not imposed by higher structures.

AN HOLISTIC APPROACH TO E-LEARNING IN HIGHER EDUCATION

The e-learning initiative of ISCET derived from the strategic vision of the Institute but also from the necessary conformance to the academic paradigm of the Bologna declaration.

Strategy and Issues

The pre-Bologna reality of ISCET reflected issues and problems that were common to all the Portuguese Higher Education environments:

- High absenteeism from students
- Reduced understanding of the theoretical concepts explained in lectures
- Lack of help and support documentation
- Limited range of exercises
- Lack of self-evaluation activities
- Reduced contact student-teacher
- Reduced level of cooperation

In many situations, these issues reduce the learning process to "study for the exam", normally in the few days preceding the examination, without time for maturation of ideas, understanding of the facts and phenomena and, above all, without an effective knowledge construction. This lack of effectiveness was in fact one of the motivators of the Bologna process.

As mentioned earlier, by its nature and scientific area of action, ISCET is characterized by a close relationship with the labor market. Hence there was the immediate perception that the adoption of e-learning could contribute to greater flexibility of access to a diversity of students. In particular, to mature, professionally experienced students. At the same time, students and teachers demanded access to Information and Communication Tools (ICT) for teaching/learning they already had this technology available elsewhere (home or employment);

ISCET also recognized that the technological environments might increase the effectiveness and efficiency of the learning process and that the adoption of e-learning could contribute to a better positioning of the market.

Therefore, as a result of the previous analysis, ISCET adopted these objectives for its e-learning initiative:

- To extend access to courses easing contact with tutors and institution;
- To promote the autonomy of students so that they take responsibility for their learning process;
- To strengthen active learning through collaboration, team work, and communication;
- To train teachers and administrators so they feel comfortable and motivated in using ICT in education.

Solution and Approach

The generic model adopted departed from the traditional model incorporating new mechanisms for access to information, discussion of concepts and practice following instructional design principles. This is a model successfully used before and which seeks to contribute to the resolution of the issues identified in pre-Bologna model (Vaz de Carvalho, 2001).

The pedagogical model adopted seeks to resolve these problems,

- Allowing the acquisition of knowledge to be made on an individual basis, at the pace of each student, by providing documentation, case studies, exercises and self-evaluation
- Providing discussions for the analysis of theoretical concepts in order to enhance the understanding and cognitive achievement
- Increasing group activities, promoting diffusion of knowledge among students

- Providing exercises so that students can learn by comparing / example and through self-assessment
- Increasing the forms of communication between students and teacher, in person or electronically

In this particular situation, the environment provided to students consisted of the following main tools:

- Syllabus with learning objectives, bibliography, assessment methodology, teacher information. A template based system allowed teachers to easily and quickly produce this kind of information
- Study guides
- Extended documentation, including slides, text, interactive multimedia materials, glossaries, etc..
- Additional reference material as tutorials, exercises and projects
- Assignment delivery
- Discussion through forums and chat rooms
- Self-assessment with automatic correction and direct communication with the teacher, through a messaging system

In order to support students in their academic process and increase social interaction there were areas for:

- Organizational Support
- Registration and management
- Global Forum with free interaction between students and teachers
- Individual user profile

Approach

The implementation process proceeded through the following steps in accordance with well established instructional design models:

1. Analysis of requirements - this step analyzed the organizational strategy, the characteristics of the target audience and the various academic offerings of ISCET.
2. Simultaneously, the technological environment was defined, including the e-learning platform to be used. All disciplines were supported by this platform.
3. Creation of training and helpdesk services - It was necessary to set up a help desk, with technical knowledge. They were trained in management and administration of the learning platform, particularly involving concepts and practice of installation, configuration and updating but also security, user and course management. The helpdesk team was well qualified to act as the first level of support for teachers and students.
4. Hosting platform for the management of learning - at this stage the technical support to the implementation of the e-learning initiative, including the management of storage systems and integrity of data was setup.
5. Training in technical and pedagogical aspects of e-learning for teachers. It included: introduction to the learning platform; management of courses and disciplines; online activities and resources; e-moderating; definition and layout of the learning environment.
6. From this stage it was possible to redesign, with the teachers, the pedagogical methodologies to be adopted in each discipline. The processes of design and educational development, the timing of activities and responsibilities of the various actors were defined.
7. Monitoring and evaluation of the implementation in e-learning - the evaluation methodology was designed, with the selection of tools for data collection. Later on, data collection allowed establishing conclusions and producing recommendations. The results supported the public presentation of the initiative, in conferences and workgroups.

Evaluation Approach and Data Collection

A set of propositions directed the study on the integration of e-learning and how it affected the teaching/learning of ISCET and, in particular, its key stakeholders - students and teachers:

*   e-learning enables students and teachers flexible (time and location) access to content
*   e-learning promotes the autonomy of students in the exploration and exploitation of information sources
*   e-learning enhances the active participation in learning through collaboration and team work
*   e-learning depends on teacher and administrator training so that they feel comfortable with the teaching tools
*   e-learning is reinforced if adequately supported by user helpdesk systems

These propositions guided the process of determining and measuring specific evaluation criteria. The timetable for data collection was in accordance to the teaching process. The unit of analysis encompassed the entire set of students and teachers involved. They were considered as a single group, regardless of their course and year of registration. Thus, it was possible to assemble a broad range of data eliminating variables that were not useful for this assessment.

Selected sources of data were the following:

1. Records: detailed data on access to the e-learning platform that included location and time distribution, access to various resources and tools and user profiling.
2. Questionnaires: distributed to students with open and closed questions to assess...
    *   Degree of qualification and use of ICT tools

○ Availability of access at home, at school and at work

○ Levels of access

○ Degree of use of tools

○ Perception of interest and ease of use of tools

○ Access to documentation, exercises, tests and self-evaluation, communication tools such as forums, chat rooms and other

○ Perception of interest and effectiveness of e-learning

3. Focus Group: an interview, with a semiformal structure, with a small group of teachers. The discussion was moderated in order to lead the group to the objectives of the meeting. The focus-group is a method to group ideas and perceptions concerning a particular subject. The difficulties of this tool are mainly related to disputes of ideas and the inhibition of the individual to expose the group, so the performance of the moderator is crucial (Fern, 1983). The points raised were:

○ Prior training of teachers and students

○ Introduction of new teaching methodologies including the need for conversion of content between models of education

○ Recognition of the educational innovation of teachers

○ Existence of support services to the teacher and student

○ Procedure to monitor students

○ Importance of technology (including multimedia) in the design and development of content

○ Importance of the e-learning platforms and other tools

○ Importance of technological literacy of students and teachers

○ Culture of change of management bodies of Universities, including the

definition of strategies and availability of equipment for virtual campuses

○ Importance of national and regional policies for e-learning and advanced training, including the accreditation of actions

○ Importance of Research and Development

○ Impact of legislation on copyright and accessibility

Analysis of Results

The use of different sources of data enabled a triangular analysis, which resulted in more precise conclusions. The chain of evidence resulted cognitively more coherent and more significant. Thus, the assessment was significant, both by the volume of data obtained and by its diversity. The systematization of procedures for data collection has helped to increase the neutrality of them, particularly with regard to the questionnaires. The set of data is too large to be fully presented here, so we opted to select and show those most directly connected to the study guidelines.

Student Characteristics

A first set of data identified the characteristics of the students in terms of use of the Internet and its tools. The collected data transmitted the evidence of the Internet access by the students. Indeed, its omnipresent use translates into a real possibility of implementing courses and disciplines through e-learning. Therefore, it is a public for whom the Internet is a fundamental tool of work, education and leisure. The use of electronic mail and Web browser is very frequent. The level of use of synchronous communication tools (Messenger or Skype) reflect a chance to explore in terms of learning.

It is clear that this is the ideal audience for the implementation of e-learning: it has a complete mastery of the Internet and its tools; they know and use it for professional and education purposes so they are prepared to make e-learning their predominant method of learning.

Interest and Ease of Use of the Tools of E-Learning

This set of data quantified users' (students and teachers) access and their use of the teaching tools available in the various disciplines. The global figures are very significant: for a total of 330 users, only 3 remained inactive throughout the implementation period.

Most notable is the predominant use on working days. At the same time, the records indicate a predominant use from the school itself. Being a professional public, this seems to outline a clear distinction between their personal and professional life. These results are curious, since one could expect greater access from the outside.

Regarding the use of teaching tools, discipline information (objectives, program, syllabus, assessment, bibliography, etc.) or specific material was available in various formats (slides, books, articles, external references, glossary, etc.) and frequently accessed. Online assignments were also used frequently. Forums were important elements of building learning communities. The use of this tool, in some cases, has been the result of collaborative activities such as case studies and projects. In comparison, synchronous tools as the chat were used in a very limited way. (This evaluation does not include the analysis of the use of electronic mail, because it was not directly connected to the e-learning platform).

Perception of Interest and Effectiveness of E-Learning

The following citations depict the views and perceptions of students and teachers in relation to the e-learning initiative.

One of the most mentioned positive aspects was the strengthening of ties between students and teachers, but also with the very institution.

"I believe that the implementation of this platform, allowed students access to information vital to their subjects and contributed to the rapprochement of teachers to their students. This seems to be the most positive aspect of e-learning."

"Clearly, the proximity and ease of communication between teachers and students."

"An easier way to ask questions and present doubts, access to syllabus of the disciplines and proximity with colleagues and teachers."

"The possibility of a faster and efficient communication, available to everyone at the same time."

The other predominant aspect was the ease of access to resources that avoid commuting to the Institute.

"Not having to go to the Institute for accessing materials."

"Easy access to content."

"The possibility that we could see the marks through the Internet, instead of having to go to the Institute."

Only one teacher mentioned the benefits associated with new educational models.

"From the perspective of teachers, that is my case, greater regularity of supply of materials and content. The possibility, with greater accuracy, to implement, monitor and intensify a process of continuous assessment and an effective process of self-study by students. Diversification of activities

of teaching / learning. There are indeed many advantages that could be mentioned here."

On the negative side, technical aspects related to the use of the platform were the most frequently mentioned issues.

"Other less positive but more technical in nature was the sometimes difficult access to the platform."

"The difficulties in using the application."

"It's a confusing program, not very intuitive, the level of layout is very weak and could be better organized."

"Just to mention some shortcomings of a technical nature and a lack of perception on the part of students of the benefits they have with this platform at various levels. But it also revealed the lack of regularity of their study and in almost all classes it was necessary to call their attention to this. But I think that was also the result of this is being a process still in its early stages."

Issues that Should be Improved in the E-Learning Initiative of ISCET.

"In my opinion, the programmatic content of the subjects should be placed in a mandatory form, available to the student. This would facilitate the students' life, mainly of working students. I also think that there should be more virtual classes."

"Putting more help content in the disciplines."

Another important aspect is the improvement and enhancement of the platform support, in technical terms:

"Improving aspects of a technical nature."

"Changing the layout."

"Simplifying the use because not all people are familiar with new technologies and even those who regularly deal with programs on the Internet, sometimes may have difficulties."

Also mentioned was the need for training and motivation of users.

"Greater awareness of teachers and students to use."

"Need to use the new tools, not only from the technical point of view but also educational."

At the focus-group, teachers pointed out some aspects which indicate that the Institute is on track for the systematic implementation. In particular, indicated that there is already a culture of acceptance of change by ISCET's board and an institutional strategy for the adoption of technology in teaching / learning. Teachers also realized that the existence of national and regional policies for e-learning and advanced training and the existence of national or EU funding can be a contribution but will not be decisive for the success of the initiative.

CONCLUSION AND FUTURE TRENDS

The use of e-learning raised new possibilities and awakened the stakeholders to new forms of communication and access to learning. This study was based on a set of propositions that we can answer now:

- e-learning enables students and teachers access to content on a remote and adapted temporally
- e-learning promotes the autonomy of students in the exploration and exploitation of information sources

These two propositions were clearly demonstrated by the degree of use and perception of effectiveness of the tools associated. There was a clear successful bet in the independent and autonomous work of the students. The investment made at this level has clearly been satisfactory given the reaction of students.

- e-learning depends on teacher and administrator training so that they feel comfortable
- e-learning is reinforced by user support systems

The initiative was already started with a strong conviction of these propositions. That belief was reinforced by the teachers reaction to the training and support system provided.

- e-learning enhances the active participation in processes of learning through collaboration and team work

The success achieved shows that this approach result in learning gains, whether asynchronous (forums and electronic messages) or synchronous (chats and desktop videoconferencing). Especially it enhances the team work skills groups, leadership and collaboration and increases the connection between teachers and students.

The systematization of the initiative is now a reality and it is fully integrated with the process of teaching / learning of ISCET. There has been a fundamental appropriation of students and teachers and, above all, the institution is already preparing new programmes, courses and initiatives taking into account the results obtained in this phase.

REFERENCES

Cardoso, E., & Machado, A. (2000). Tools for Distributed Learning in the University. In *Proceedings of the Simposium Iberoamericano de Informática Educativa.*

CRE. (1998). *Restructuring the University - New Technologies for Teaching and Learning: Guidance to Universities on Strategy.* Geneva, Switzerland: Association of European Universities.

Daniel, J. (1996). *Mega-Universities and Knowledge Media.* London: Kogan Page.

European Council of Education Ministers. (2000). *Bologna Declaration.* Retrieved from http://www. dges.mctes.pt/NR/rdonlyres/2EC14937-0320-4975-A269-B9170A722684/409/Declaraçãode-Bolonha1.pdf

Fern, E. (1983). *The use of focus groups: a review of some contradictory evidence implications, and suggestion for future research methods series.* Advances Consumer Research

Gomes, M. J. (2005). E-learning: reflexões em torno do conceito, In Proceedings of the *Challenges '05: actas do Congresso Internacional sobre Tecnologias da Informação e Comunicação na Educação, 4,* Braga. Braga, Portugal: Centro de Competência da Universidade do Minho. Retrieved from: https://repositorium.sdum.uminho. pt/handle/1822/2896

ISCET. (2008). *Apresentação.* Retrieved from http://www.iscet.pt/index.php?vr1=10

Laurillard, D. (2004). E-learning in Higher Education. In P. Ashwin (Ed.), *From Changing Higher Education.* London: RoutledgeFalmer. Retrieved from http://www3.griffith.edu.au/03/ltn/docs/E-Learning_in_Higher_Education.doc~

Mingle, J. R. (1995). Vision and reality for Technology-based Delivery Systems in Postsecondary Education. In *Proceedings of the Governor's Conference of Higher Education*, St. Louis, MI.

Moore, M. G., & Kearsley, G. (1996). *Distance Education: a Systems View*. Boston: Wadsworth Publishing Company.

Primary Research Group. (2007). *The Survey of Distance Learning Programs in Higher Education, 2007-08 Edition*. Retrieved from http://tinyurl.com/23zep8

UNESCO. (1998). World Declaration on Higher Education for the Twenty-first Century: Vision and Action. In *Proceedings of the World Conference on Higher Education*, Paris. Retrieved from http://www.unesco.org/education/educprog/wche/declaration_eng.htm

Vaz de Carvalho, C. (2001). *Uma Proposta de Ambiente de Ensino Distribuído*. Unpublished doctoral dissertation, University of Minho, Portugal.

Vaz de Carvalho, C., & Cardoso, E. (2003). O E-Learning e o Ensino Superior em Portugal. In *Proceedings of the Revista do SNESUP – Sindicato Nacional do Ensino Superior*. Retrieved from http://www.snesup.pt/htmls/EEZykEyEVurTZ-BpYlM.shtml

Vaz de Carvalho, C., & Machado, A. (2001a). A Virtual Environment for Distributed Learning in Higher Education, In *Proceedings of the 20th ICDE World Conference on Open Learning and Distance Education*, Dusseldorf.

Chapter 3

Technology in Education:
Integrating Contemporary Technology into Classroom Pedagogy as Foundation to a Practical Distance Learning

Hyacinth Eze Anomneze
Texas Southern University, USA

ABSTRACT

As the global economy moves into a complete dependence on information and technology, the United States has to revisit how information technology is used in schools. Schools no longer imply the actual building with administrative halls and student centers, but also distance learning possibilities. Distance learning is still encountering skepticism from some educators, both in the secondary and post secondary stages of learning. This untamed skepticism is the product of the remains from traditional educators who are yet to answer the what, where, when, who, why and how of modern technology in the classroom. Traditional education wants to teach technology as a core curriculum, to be assessed as such. The universal reality, on the other hand, is that technology is a global culture and language. American students, to some extent, determine how this culture and language is used and spoken, but the fear is that they are doing this outside of the classroom. The goal of technology education must be to make technology so comfortable that its transition to distance learning will be smooth. This is done by recognizing and using technology to motivate learners to want to learn and succeed.

INTRODUCTION

Socrates, the Greek philosopher, told his disciples, "By all means marry. If you get a good wife, you'll be happy. If you get a bad one, you'll become a philosopher and that is a good thing for any man." Things have changed since time of this

DOI: 10.4018/978-1-61520-672-8.ch003

Greek thinker, but the Socratic idea of marriage is metaphorically similar to the use of technology in education: it is a win-win situation. By all means use technology in education. If you are successful, you will be happy (and students will be happier). If you are not successful, you will become a smart thinker and that is a good thing for any teacher and student. Whitney (2007) reflects that while many people use technology from dust till dawn to make

Copyright © 2010, IGI Global. Copying or distributing in print or electronic forms without written permission of IGI Global is prohibited.

decision, communicate, evaluate and distribute information, the same level of technology use cannot be found in schools; "schools which are meant to prepare students for their future careers in the 'real' world."

BACKGROUND: THE WHY OF TECHNOLOGY IN EDUCATION

Technology in educational is no longer an option; the No Child Left Behind Act of 2001 makes technology in education an objective. The law (NCLB Act) states that, "every student should be technologically literate by the eighth grade, regardless of student background or family socioeconomic status." McAnear (2006) describes technology in education as "magic." She concludes that it is magic because it makes complex things simple or makes the impossible possible. A sound technology in pedagogy should motivate students, close their learning gap, and help them master complex concepts.

As education moves away from the melting pot theory, that is characterized by one approach to teaching should fit all learners, to a better appreciation of every learner as unique in both learning style and socio-cultural identity, education becomes a highly engaging environment. Considering more diverse approaches to teaching, Law (2006) suggests that educational research into teaching methods should, "target those students who learn through other modalities than the customary linear-sequential approaches of schools." Law also observes that more research in technology in education will find that learning with technology will "benefit" all students, and will lead to a "significant improvement and engagement in learning from students classified as 'at risk.'" Put simply educational technology must be a tool that increases every student's learning opportunities (Dreier, 2006). A United States Department of Education report agrees that, "students using technology have a distinct advantage over similar students who are not using technology" (Murray, 2001). Technology in education is not an optional tool in learning, but a fundamental necessity that every student must have and use in order to be more competitive.

Technology in Schools

Not all technology use within an educational system qualifies as technology in education. The use of $180,000 for Radio Frequency Identification (RFID) in Spring, Texas (Jones, 2006) on school busses to fight kidnapping in a town that has "never" had a kidnapping is a good preemptive undertaking, but does not classify as technology in education. Encouraging students, Wilder (2001) notes, to play games on computer during free time, withholding computer use from some students as a punishment, and giving access to others as a reward are not technology use for education. For technology in education to be adequate it should pass the social test. If the human is a social being and learning is a social activity, it is only logical to expect technology in education to make the social growth of students easier. One way to accomplish this is to motivate the student in such a way that they would want to study the content. In order to meet the mandate of the NCLB Act (provide a reasonable opportunity for every student to learn with technology) it is imperative that technology be truly "easy and transparent" "cheap or free" (McAnear, 2006).

An important component of technology in education is availability and access (Gahala, 2006). A National Center for Educational Statistics (cited by Valdez, 2007) reports that there are virtually "no differences in Internet access between poor schools and wealthier schools any more." While this does not suggest that there is equity in technology availability between the rich and poor, it give the impression that when it comes to the most important technology tool, there is a level playing field. Student today are more likely to write a paper and make a presentation that draw from up-to-date sources and state-of-art knowledge. Gahala (2006) finds that school may have computers and technology available, but the one factor that determines their use is where they are located. If computers and technology are not in convenient locations, Gahala sees limited use of them by students and teachers. Computers on Wheel (COW) or mobile computer labs are alternatives that schools can explore.

Technology in Education

Technology is used for a variety of teaching techniques including distance learning; distance learning is an idea that has been in practice for over 150 years (Ndahi, 2006) and is growing. Although some critics argue that distance learning cannot replace the quality of a classroom experience, Ndahi finds that distance learning students "performed equally well and in some courses outperformed their classroom counterparts." Distance learning in colleges is now accepted as an equal alternative to classroom learning and experience. When high schools will fully embrace distance learning is anybody's guess, but it is worthy of more consideration as an alternative teaching method. This consideration is predicated on two facts: as more baby boomer retire schools will need to hire more teacher, and some students do better as distance learners. Getting student to be more comfortable and assertive with the use of technology in their learning is a worthy venture.

Technology in education can also perform some assistive roles and provide new resources that make learning richer. These resources can include virtual field trips, online simulations, and connections to professional experts. For most students, Limited English Proficiency (LEP) students in particular, Rauch (2002) suggests that technology could allow for the option to do public speaking via multimedia presentations. Another assistive role that technology can play in education is improving student to teacher communications. Dreier (2006) sees technology encouraging contacts between students and teacher, "especially those students who were unwilling to speak out in a face-to-face classroom setting." Technology can also be used to respect different talents and learning styles, make students more active and social learners, and to give immediate feedback. In short, technology can be used as a tool to provide unlimited resources to students and teacher and to provide a means for engagement in higher-order thinking skills.

Technology as a Source of Motivation

Jones (2003) describes a motivated learner as one who has a sincere pursuit of competence and investigates the interaction among technology in education, motivation and learning. Jones concludes that allowing the use of technology will increase motivation. The study uses two groups for the study; one group was instructed with web-based technology that requires students to organize information into web pages that are linked together. The second group was instructed in the traditional classroom model. Jones finds that while achievement gains were similar between the two groups, the students instructed with the web-based technology showed higher motivation.

The most important aspect of learning is motivation; according to Wentzel (cited in Zappe, 2002) some of the facts that impact motivation are the nature of the learning task, the evaluation of the task, the reward and feedback system, and the learner's experienced responsibility. This responsibility results when learners are motivated enough to participate in their own learning process. Zappe also reflects that grades are feedback especially when considered as information, which can lead to improvement. The frequency and timely nature of the feedback are directly linked to increased motivation.

Using technology in education does not just serve as motivation for the main-stream students, it also benefits at-risk students. Wilder and Black (2000) studies conclude that technology can serve as a motivation to learn, keep the engagement in learning, and increase the academic success of students with emotional and behavioral disorder. When technology is configured into the educational process, the learner learns and everybody wins.

Expectations of Technology in Education

Catton (2006) observes that since we can only "blindly" predict the jobs and professions that will be available to our learners "12 years from now," our educational objective must focus on producing "fearless students who are able to quickly learn the skills necessary for what ever task is presented to them." Knezek (2006) agrees that education today should train students to be "successful employees and successful learners. Martin (2006) reminds readers that the over-used slogan "lifelong learners" is necessary and wants us to prepare students who must be "learning-efficient" and grow up to be "successful professionally, socially, and personally."

In 1996 the American Society for Training and Development (ASTD) found that 73% of training professionals agree that computer skills are essential for employment and predicted that by the turn of the 21st century 60% of U.S. jobs will "require the use of computer." In education we still find that the primary tool, information technology, that students will use in work force are not integrated into their education. Another handicap to technology in education is that when it used in education, the assessment of students are done through the traditional format.

Imagine this analogy, a coach instructs his or her learners on how to play basketball by occasionally bringing them out to the basketball court, and giving them multiple choice questions on basketball concepts like tackles, blocks, assists, free-throws, and three pointers to test their mastery of the game. Mastery of the game should be based on how well the learners tackles, blocks,

assists, does free-throws, and gets three pointers in an actual games. In the 'real' life that the coach is getting his or her learners ready for success is judged by how well a player tackles, blocks, assists, free-throws, and gets three pointers. In education, we have not aligned what we actually do in the classroom with what professionals do in the real world; the sad part is that we are not running into more time, but less time.

It is not surprising, Norstrom (2006) notes, that the United States is the only industrialized nation that is "completely" dependent on immigration to fill jobs in science and technology. He argues that the reason for this situation is the United States educational philosophy that concentrates on students "merely meeting minimum graduation requirements rather than providing the SciTech skills needed to succeed in today's global economy."

Today's students have multitasking minds, and they are constantly overloaded with information. A study by the North Central Regional Educational Laboratory (Valdez, 2007), an educational think-tanks, wonders why students are expected – and are learning – the high-level skills that includes how to "access, evaluate, analyze, and synthesize" vast quantities of data and yet these students and their teachers are evaluated on the students' ability to pass tests that often do not give any value to the abilities that the students are learning. On paper the state curricula read well, teachers are expected to consider the students' prior knowledge and to use materials that each student can connect in teaching student how to solve complex problems that require knowledge across many layer of subject area. If technology in education is to have a strong footing, we have to rethink how we assess students' learning.

Sonak (2002) reminds us that learning is part of a loop system, consisting of the learner, the instructor (content deliverer) and assessment (test), and for the purpose of education, the learner is the central aspect in this loop." The learner is the ultimate stakeholder. The drill here is that in shaping instruction, delivering content, and designing the rubrics used in learning, the educator must include every possible mean to motivate the learner to want to learn. This is not the educator subjectively considering things that may motivate the learners, but seriously looking at the learners' motivation and interest. The educator must then use these considerations in designing a curriculum.

Studies (Wilder, 2002 and Whitney, 2007) identify technology as a source of motivation for today's students, and using technology in education sustains that motivation and leads to academic achievement. Understanding how learners use technology in their social living becomes a primary factor to consider in determining what to incorporate into lesson design and how to assess the learning progress.

WHAT DO YOUNG PEOPLE USE TECHNOLOGY FOR TODAY?

Teens use technology, especially internet and handheld device, as major tools to maintain and enhance their social and entertainment lives and to communicate with family and friends, locally and internationally. When it comes to the use of technology in school work, most students find it uninspiring; they want to be assigned more and more "engaging" internet and technology activities that are more challenging and relevant to their lives (NCREL 2007, in Reid 1995). There is a gap in the way students perceive information today and the way the previous generations saw information. Students see information as disposable and not static, Hall (2006) writes that students use technology to access, manipulate, and communicate information, and when they are done, they dispose of the information. He concludes that this "is how they create meaning from an increasing complex and diverse world."

Hall attributes some of the difficulty teachers have on their perception of information; teachers that grew up when information was "static" still see knowledge as something to be "absorbed" which "translates to mastery." Today's students do not keep information static, yet they are expected to reproduce static information in most of their high school tests.

Using the downgrading of Pluto from a planet to a sub-planet, Hall (2006) observes how in an age of non-static use of information – all of a sudden – thousands of textbooks, wall charts, 3D models and encyclopedias will become obsolete. Students did not feel any shake up; they accessed the debate in real time, understood it, disposed of the information and moved on. By the next day, they have updated the acronym for remembering the solar system.

There is no doubt that students are using technology to reach the higher order of thinking; advocates for comprehensive technology program in education warm that the emphasis on passing the "state test" may means that the higher order of thinking expectation may be "occurring online; at home, in students' bedrooms instead of in the classroom" (Hall 2006). Moffitt (1996) suggests that effective use of technology in education requires shifting the educational focus from teaching to active learning, and this must include bringing technology that students use outside of the classroom into the classroom. Weber and Custer (2005) suggest that curriculum include not only the student's prior knowledge, but experiences and technology uses. Instead of using the traditional tools and example to demonstrate technological ideas, educators should use materials and examples that students can identify.

The challenge facing today's educators is to use technology in classrooms in such a way that the classes will have students who are eager to learn (Law 2006); in order to reach this goal, Law wants educators to encourage the "evolution" and inclusion of new tools and technologies that allow students to easily "create their own content." Law emphasizes content package "tied" to curriculum with quality and current teaching materials.

Technology in School Curriculum

There are two huddles to information technology in education, technical support and the question of how to integrate the technology into the curriculum. On technical support, Gahala (2006) notes that in technology and education timing is everything; some studies (Gahala, 2006 and Reid, 1995) observe that the best way to win widespread use of technology is to provide just-in-time support assistance. When technical assistance is needed, it must come not tomorrow or next week, but now! On the integration of technology study into the curriculum, Erekson and Shumway (2006) observe that no "consistent plan has emerged for organizing and teaching technology education across states and school districts." Their suggestion is to forget the idea of technology in education as an academic discipline. They advocate the notion that:

"There is a dimension of technology, like literacy, that is culturally universal… the ubiquitous occurrence of technology (like language) in human cultures. Technology cannot be studied in isolation; it is a social process that occurs within a social, environmental, economic, and political milieu" (p. 28).

Erekson and Shumway propose five models for curriculum integration in our schools (p.29):

1. The simultaneous model – students taking courses in different disciplines with the teachers "deliberately" making "ties between the content of the courses."
2. The braided model – content from various disciplines viewed as strands to be visited on some type of "cyclical pattern to develop a spirally organized curriculum."
3. The topical model – a curriculum that focuses on a topic, or theme, throughout the year, or a major portion thereof, across multiple subjects.
4. The unified model – teachers from two or more disciplines working together to "identify a set of unifying ideas," often implemented with team-teaching techniques.
5. The full interdisciplinary model – the merging of the content from two or more disciplines.

A problem that traditional and reluctant teachers may have about integrating information technology into their teaching is the question of where or how to start. The models could give these teachers a front seat, help them understand technology and mentor them through how to incorporate technology into their curriculum. Institutions that prepare teachers can also help by demystifying technology and making it an integral part of the teachers' preparation.

The purpose of the Technology for All Americans Project (Erekson and Shumway, 2006) was to establish technology education as a core subject in the curriculum. Erekson and Shumway call for a rejection of this mandate and the use technology teachers as resources staff (identical to the use of special education teachers). Technology teachers will now be in a position to have a major impact "by helping regular teachers integrate technology into the context of the disciplines." (p. 33). The technology teacher would not be responsible for teaching separate technology education classes. With this time constraints gone, technology teachers would be "totally dedicated to curriculum integration." (p. 33).

As the need for educators increase, teachers must come up with new pedagogical tools to ensure that learners are learning. Ireh (2002) estimates that two million new teachers would be needed in the next decade and these teachers must have "command" of an array of teaching and motivation tools that would guarantee that all students are learning. This means the teacher must be able to use technology to support multiple approaches to teaching complex ideas to different students with diverse learning styles. This is not unreachable, because the self discovery that comes with learning new and advanced way to teach and learn will motivate both the teachers and the learners.

Domine (2006) suggests a 4-step beginner guide to integrating technology into curriculum. **First**, take an inventory of technologies in the school; this list should include TVs, VCRs, projectors, PCs, Electronic white boards etc. **Second**, establish a curriculum goal, like caring communities. Whatever curriculum goal is chosen, it is imperative to define it through district and state curriculum standards. **Third**, identify teaching strategies; this is best done by creating a list of teaching strategies that is very broad and including the elements of reading, writing, listening, speaking, visualization, and cooperative learning. As the teacher makes this list, he or she should move from "teacher-centered to those those are primarily student-centered" (Domine, 2006). **Fourth**, solve the equations; choose from your technology inventory those that will support each teaching strategy or set of goals.

Lesson Plans with Easily Available Technology

Below are summaries of lesson plans that integrate information and multimedia technologies into English Language Arts curricula. Because of some policy issues, it is important to discuss your intentions with the local school administrators before using some of the suggestions; especially the use of cell phones. Despite the controversy about using cell phones in school, it could be a learning tool.

(A) **Multimedia Encyclopedia.** Adapted from Wahl and Duffield (2006). Building a library of images using digital cameras, cell phones with camera, or any other electronic device that takes still photos. The steps listed below could be a start:

    1) **School Rule.** Make sure the school rule will allow the use of these tools, especially the cell phones.

    2) **Curriculum**. Check to make sure that this assignment aligns with your state and district curricula.

    3) **Project Rules.** Go over the project rules – privacy, copy write, school rules, etc.

    4) **Choose a Theme** and group the students into area of study (example is the theme is sports, a group could be assigned to cover basketball and another football etc.)

    5) **Send the Students** on mission; let them capture as many images as they can as possible on their theme. Note that they do not have to go to a professional game to take these photos; a school game will do the job.

    6) **Organize the Photos.** When the photos are taken and uploaded to a computer, the students would use services like Picasa or Flickr (free software) to organize the photos. Picasa, now owned by Google is good, but my favorite is Flickr. Flickr has a group and privacy control and a title column that makes search very easy. You should require the students to include the definition or history of an image in the description section. Flickr also has a theme or sub-grouping ability in its feature.

    7) **Package.** Now collected and edited, students can package their project to be shared online, link it to the school website or format it as an electronic album on a CD rom. Flickr or Photo Story 3.0 will do.

(B) **The World Today.** One of the features included in most cell phone plans is unlimited text messaging. Students love it; teachers hate it. It could be used as a technology tool in education. Let's find out what is happening in our country and world today. Create and post a map of the U.S. and countries of the world and have your students bring out their cell phones and follow the steps below. Follow steps 1 to 3 above. Then:

4) Have students send text messages to people they know around the country and the world and find out celebrations and holidays, what is making the local news, what the hottest music is in their pals' locality or country? Etc.

5) Have the students write their responses on the map. You might give an extra credit to students that get responses from outside the country.

6) Have each student present the locality that he or she contacted people in; it is okay to have multiple responses.

(C) **Audio Bloggin'.** Kolb (2006) has a detailed Language Arts project plan that lets students use their cell phones as a recording device to conduct interviews. The recording is then uploaded to Gabcast.com, a free audio blog and storage site. Gabcast.com also has a toll-free call-in number, so students can use their home phone. You should follow steps 1 to 3 of the Multimedia Encyclopedia project.

(D) **A Multimedia Autobiography.** The steps below could be a start.

1) Have the student create a family tree as a homework assignment. You could give them a template (easily found online) or you can have them create their own; they can stop at grand parents.

2) Have the students interview their parents and the oldest family members. Encourage them to be on the look out for interesting family stories (happy, sad, and funny). They can use any video and audio recoding device (including cell phones) to conduct the interviews.

3) Have the students collect old pictures and videos and scan or rip them into digital formats.

4) Have the students take new pictures and videos. The cell phones that students carry make it easy to interview, snap photos, and take some videos with a simple device. These data can be uploaded to blogger sites like Gabcast.com or blooger.com reducing the risk of loosing them.

5) Package the product. Some students may elect to package their project in a book format that can be printed (with inserted photos and scan family document) and bonded at the local Kinkos. Other students may want to package their projects into a multimedia formats. PowerPoint is very good it allows students to insert videos and commentaries. Other software like Flipalbum and Autoplay Menu Studio could enhance the multimedia presentation and package.

(E) **Letters to the Teacher:** Have your students write a brief email to you every day/week about a book they are reading, respond to the email, and continue the dialogue until the end of the book or the project's due date.

(F) **Other Multimedia and Technology Assignments:** Attached as appendix are assignments that can be used with other distance learning ideas.

The use of simple technology in education is infinite. Instead of having student cook and bring food from different parts of the world, you include an option for them to video and take photos of the cooking process, and package that into a multimedia presentation or a slide show. What about those assignments on what the students did over the summer, weekend or holiday? They could also create digital scrapbooks of these assignments.

ACADEMIC FEEDBACK AND THE ROLE OF TECHNOLOGY

Success in education is a loop, a loop that starts from the learner wanting to learn and ends with the learner wanting to learn, more. A necessary component of this loop is feedback; the learner must know how he or she is doing and progressing to stay motivated. A feedback that does not come is useless and does not help the learner self-regulate, and a late feedback would not be an effective motivator. Timely and informative feedback plays a significant role in learning. Zappe et al (2002) investigated an information feedback that uses a computerized grade tracking system in a rural Pennsylvania high school. Their investigations conclude that motivated individuals sought feedback and in turn performed better academically.

Mayer and Leone (2001) follow the development of a 9th grade, Jeffery. Jeffery has a history of delayed language development, diagnosed with explosive disorder, bipolar disorder, ADHD, and list goes on; based on his description, his success in academics seem impossible. Using technology and interactive media tools presented Jeffery with three learning options: knowledge presentation, knowledge representation and knowledge construction. The result is that Jeffery took ownership of this learning and constructed a remarkable and "sophisticated" interactive multimedia CD-ROM that "tells the life story of the character of Miss Jane Pittman" (based on the book and film The Autobiography of Miss Jane Pittman) Jeffery used Microsoft PowerPoint, photographs, movie segments, graphic timeline and other sources to create this "multi-level thematic analysis of the Miss Jane Pittman. Jeffery's situation summarizes Ireh's (2002) accretion that student can learn and "must move beyond the drill and practices that often characterize technology uses in classroom.

Assessment of Technology in Education

Law (2006) refers to two on-going research projects to evaluate how well students retain information learned through technology versus traditional classroom settings. One of these researches is going in Denver, Colorado and the other in Oakland, California. Until the finding of the research is conclusive, the biggest question in technology in education is assessment. Is it reasonable (Valdez, 2007) to use paper-and-pencil tests to "assess student learning after the student had been taught content through the use of technology?" The NCREL study also studied:

The effects of test administration mode to see whether tests administered on computer versus paper-and-pencil have an effect on student performance on multiple-choice and written test questions. The study found that significantly higher cognitive-level responses are written on computers than those written by hand (Valdez, 2007).

Valdez concludes that technologies used during learning activities should also be used during testing. Further, he contends that student assessment methods should match the medium in which students typically work. No doubt as more and more students do their work with word processors, spreadsheets, and multimedia software, the traditional paper-and-pencil types of assessment will not measure that they have learned. Other alternative forms of assessments that may reflects the student's performance of authentic tasks (NCREL, 2007) could be building electronic portfolios of their work, sharing their work through performances, presentations at open houses, and science fairs. Assessment in technology is best done when it can be ongoing, performance-based, and generative (Rauch, 2002).

Use of Test Scores

Standardized test scores (Dyer, Reed, and Berry, 2006) can be used to measure students' progress in technology use. Dyer and his team found that fourth grade students who had teachers trained with the integrated curriculum performed better on the New York State's Elementary School Science Program Evaluation Test than students who had teacher not trained. These students also performed well above the State average on the mathematics test (p. 9). In this empirical study Dyer and his associates also find that students from an urban high school in Virginia who have taken illustration and design technology courses performed better on their mathematics Standards of Learning (SOL) test than students who did not take the illustration and design technology courses. Finally they observe that students who had not passed the mathematics test did better on their retake examinations after they took an illustration and design technology course.

FROM TRADITIONAL TO DISTANCE LEARNING

Distance learning is general term that described an educational situation where teachers and learners are physically separated, but are in constant communication through the means of information technologies. Distance learning is easier when learners have internet access and are very comfortable using a personal computer. This comfort has to be created in the pre-collegiate years.

China and India (UNESCO, 2001) use television and radio networks, audio and video cassettes housed at local centers, and print materials through the mail for distance education. China does this through the China Radio and Television University (CCRTVU) and in India by the Indria Gandhi National Open University (IDNOU). As worth as distance teaching is, it is not distance learning. Distance Learning, like its traditional counterpart must include the four questions suggested by Dufour (2009): What do we expect the learners to learn? How will we know when they

have learned it? How will respond when they don't learn? How will we respond and enrich when the student learns or already knows it? The implication here is that a distance learning program should include a formative and summative assessment plan, on demand access to learning materials, access to teaching staff, and a team of collaborating educator Dufour (2009) calls a Professional Learning Community.

Considerations before Distance Learning

Before adapting distance learning, an institution must make a shift in its fundamental purpose from a focus on teaching to a focus on learning. Drucker (cited by Dufour, 2009) puts is well when he says, Organizations that build on learning will dominate the twenty-first century. These organizations will also epitomize effectiveness because they use evidence to shape their exiting assumptions, practices, goals, and culture. Ineffective organizations, on the other hand, use their existing assumptions, practices, and culture to distort evidence.

This is why effective learning organizations are seen as fast, flexible, friendly, focus, and fun; Kanter (2004) suggests that in order to promote these characteristics, a learning institution must be organized into teams, not the old fashioned hierarchies. Each team is the collaboration of education professional working interdependently in order to achieve common goals for which they are mutually accountable. Eaker (2009) explains those common goals as including better results for their learners, their team, and their institution.

Every academic institution exits in a community, and a community is a social phenomenon that is always changing and adapting. Distance learning is a response to adapting education to the information society, and team building justifies that fundamental shift of education from teaching to learning. Information technology and teams transform an educational organization to a distance learning institution, making that institution a professional learning community.

Teams take the focus away from teaching to learning and bring about collaboration for student's success. When teams look for results and constantly quiz themselves if an objective will help the learner, this is learning. The inclusion of information technology into this practice is distance learning.

Conditions for a Success Distance Learning Program

Distance learning will continue to grow and institutions will need guidance in order to take full advantage of distance learning; they will need help because distance learning presents a lot of cultural and pedagogical questions. Below are six cultural and pedagogical questions (or conditions) that every distance learning institution must resolve before accepting learners:

1.   Who are our learners? A distance learning program must have a shared vision, mission, goals, and value with its parent institution; the culture and vision of the parent institution must be aligned with the mission and goals of the distance learning system. A medical institution may not be very successful having a distance learning program in pre-law. This shared mission distinguishes one distance learning institution from others. Furthermore, the answers to this question may spring up other questions like, what types of information technologies are suitable for our learners.

2.   What do we expect the learner to learn? A distance learning system must have both formative and summative skills, knowledge, dispositions that students should learn during and at the end of their learning with us. These skills should be clear, explicit and specific. A course that is titled Introduction to Online Library Resources should empower student to desegregate reliable data from unreliable information using specifically acquired skills.

3.   How will they learn it? Unlike classroom-based learning, distance learning is best when the team puts together a timeline and a general study guide that is easy to read, effortless to follow, and simple to assess. A distance learning experiment in Chile (UNESCO, 2001) illustrates this. The teaching material is developed by a team of teachers, students download this material from the institutions cite, and communicate with web-based software. The final part of this learning process is a collaborative project by students. This project takes six months, and the proposal is reviewed by the teaching team. The mid-term and final reports are independently assessed by one of teaching team and an external assessor.

4.   How will we know they have learned? How success is judged and assessed must be standardized by a team. Dufour *et al* (2008) report that teachers and students benefit if periodically formative and summative assessments are created by a collaborative team of teacher (rather than individual teachers) and given to all students for whom the team is responsible. Assessment is not the ends; timely and frequent feedback must stream to the students because, as Dufour *et al* puts it, feedback of learning is an essential part of effective teaching. Two professors in my graduate school are notorious for not giving feedback, and giving every student in their classes the same letter grade of B, every term and every year. This practice will undermine the essence of learning in a distance learning system because distance learners have no other way to monitor learning except through feedback.

5.   How will we respond when they don't learn? A team of professional educators should

collaborate to identify strategies that will improve their individual and collective abilities to make sure that learners are learning. An effective institution uses data from formative (and summative) assessments to drive decision-making. If this is not done, the organization might be institutionalizing failure. Teams have to accept responsibility; if data show that only 24% of students are passing a test, the team has to say that some of that is their fault. A public document in circulation at the college of education of Texas Southern University shows that every year from 2003 to 2008 not more than 24% of the doctoral students passed the college's comprehensive examinations. Fullen (cited by Dufour, 2009) puts is well when he says, "assessment for learning, when done well, is one of the most powerful, high-leverage strategies for improving student learning that we know of." Some school have become very proficient at this; if a student fails a course, instead of paining the student through the entire course, the team of educators identifies the objectives or domains that the student is having difficulty with and uses other methods to re-teach those objectives or domains. When the student masters those isolated skills, they are moved out of that course. When achievement is not used to improvement student's learning in an institution, that institution is not ready for distance learning (or any learning), but merely reinforcing its identity as a failed institution.

6. How will we respond and enrich when students learn or already know it? This is where a distance learning institution can self-leverage and invited the learners to collaborate in some form of student's created learning.

CONCLUSION AND RECOMMENDATION

A distance learning institution is therefore an academic institution that uses information technology to warehouse information, recruit learners, retain learners, inspire learning, assess learning, offers constructive feedback to learners, react to learning, and enrich learning.

Integrating technology into education and assessment can also start from the requirements of the No Child Left Behind act (NCLB) states that, "every student should be technologically literate by the eighth grade, regardless of student background or family socioeconomic status." Local school districts can carefully develop objectives that describe appropriate technology goal for students at each grade level. This must be done in much a way that it includes the usual and social uses of technology by students of every learning level and age. The NCREL (2007) describes this as the "authentic uses of technology."

The careers, interests, social lives, and technology uses of our students are primarily determined by interests outside of the schools and classrooms. To reverse this trend and make our educational institutions a major player in deciding what technology our children should be using, technology in education has to be completely integrated into every curriculum and the assessment of these courses in every high school. A way to begin this is to put serious money, creativity, and research into answering the question, what are children (at every age level) using technology for and what kind of technology should they be using? This question is not easy when mobile phone companies spent $900 million in 2007 (McClellan, 2007) on advertising and most of that money, according to Bridget Russo, a spokesperson for Virgin Mobile (Spitzer, 2003) targeted kids in the 15-18 age bracket. On the other hand, the US department of education office of elementary and secondary education has a $500 million School Improvement Grants budget for 2008 (ed.gov, 2008). This $500 million includes the development and implementation of technology restructuring plans.

In order to actualize technology in education and increase the motivation of students to learn, Wilder (2001) notes that the technology gap between rich and poor, at risk and main stream students cannot continue unchecked. Wilder's investigation finds that this gap "occurs across school districts, within school districts, and across classrooms within a given school." Comer (1999) considers his family history, his success in academics and his work students and parents in 500 schools across the nation and concludes that, "failure in school implies failure in life." If the American culture accepts this premise and we now know that technology in education leads to success for all students, Welter (cited in Wilder, 2001) suggests that cost and knowledge should not prohibit the use of technology. He concludes that, "if we cannot find a way to provide all students, schools, and teachers with universal access to the same advanced information technologies, we are in effect ensuring a form of state sponsored illiteracy and inequity." Jonathan Kozol (2006) calls this inequity, "the restoration of apartheid schooling in America."

When technology use in education is maximized, when the skepticism of reluctant teachers is minimized, and when the trepidation of traditional instructor is controlled can distance learning with technology be truly successful. Ireh (2002) describes this as moving educator beyond the basement and first floor technologies into the upper level that "incorporates advanced and multifaceted technologies."

REFERENCES

Catton, M. (2006). Create Fearless Learners. *Learning and Leading with Technology, 34*. Retrieved September 18, 2008, from http://www.iste.org/Content/NavigationMenu/Publications/LL/LLIssues/Volume_34_2006_2007_/November_No_3_2/LandL_November_2006.htm

Comer, J. P. (1999). *Waiting for a Miracle: Why Schools Can't Solve Our Problems and How We Can.* Canada: Penguin Group.

Domine, V. (2006). 4 Steps to Standards Integration. *Learning and Leading with Technology, 34*. Retrieved September 18, 2008, from http://www.iste.org/Content/NavigationMenu/Publications/LL/LLIssues/Volume_34_2006_2007_/November_No_3_2/LandL_November_2006.htm

Dreier, E. (2006). *Technology: A Catalyst for Teaching and Learning in the Classroom.* North Central Regional Educational Laboratory (NCREL) online publications. Retrieved September 18, 2008 http://www.ncrel.org/sdrs/areas/issues/methods/technlgy/te600.htm

Dufour, R. (2009). *The Power of Professional learning Communities: Bringing the Big Ideas to Life.* Paper presented at the Professional Learning Communities at Work, San Antonio, TX.

Dufour, R., Dufour, R., & Eaker, R. (2008). *Revisiting Professional Learning Communities at Work: New Insights for improving School.* Bloomington, IN: Solution Tree.

Dyer, R., Reed, A., & Berry, R. (2006). Investigating the Relationship between High School Technology Education and Test Scores for Algebra 1 and Geometry. *Journal of Technology Education, 17*, 7-17. Retrieved June 15, 2008 from http://scholar.lib.vt.edu/ejournals/JTE/v17n2/pdf/index.html

Eaker, R. (2009). *What it Means to be a Professional Learning Community*. Paper presented at the Professional Learning Communities at Work, San Antonio, TX.

Erekson, T., & Shumway, S. (2006). Integrating the Study of Technology into the Curriculum: a Consulting Teacher Model. *Journal of Technology Education, 18*, 27-37. Retrieved October 18, 2008 from http://scholar.lib.vt.edu/ejournals/JTE/v18n1/pdf/index.html

Gahala, Y. (2007). *Critical Issue: Promoting Technology Use in School*. North Central Regional Educational Laboratory (NCREL) online publications. Retrieved September 18, 2008 from http://www.ncrel.org

Hall, D. (2006). Pluto is Gone, Is Mickey Next? *Learning and Leading with Technology, 34*. Retrieved June 7, 2008, from http://www.iste.org/Content/NavigationMenu/Publications/LL/LLIssues/Volume_34_2006_2007_/November_No_3_2/LandL_November_2006.htm

Ireh, M., & Bell, D. (2002). *Implementing Faculty Professional Development: The Product-Based Model*. Paper presented at the Preparing Tomorrow's Teachers To Use Technology (PT3) Grantee Conference. Retrieved May 24, 2009, from http://www.eric.ed.gov/ERICWebPortal/custom/portlets/recordDetails/detailmini.jsp?_nfpb=true&_&ERICExtSearch_SearchValue_0=ED469001&ERICExtSearch_SearchType_0=no&accno=ED469001

Issue, C. Developing a School or District Technology Plan. (2007). *North Central Regional Educational Laboratory (NCREL) online publications*. Retrieved September 9, 2008 from http://www.ncrel.org/sdrs/areas/issues/methods/technlgy/te300.htm

Issue, C. Using Technology to Improve Student Achievement. (2007). *North Central Regional Educational Laboratory (NCREL) online publications*. Retrieved September 9, 2008 from http://www.ncrel.org/sdrs/areas/issues/methods/technlgy/te800.htm

Jones, A. (2006). Should RFID Be Used to Monitor Students? *Learning and Leading with Technology, 34*. Retrieved September 18, 2008, from http://www.iste.org/Content/NavigationMenu/Publications/LL/LLIssues/Volume_34_2006_2007_/November_No_3_2/LandL_November_2006.htm

Jones, B. (2002). Students as Web Site Authors: Effects on Motivation and Achievement. *Journal of Educational Technology Systems, 31*(4), 441–461. doi:10.2190/UX5V-WVKL-3EJN-7L0C

Kanter, R. (2004). *Confidence: How Winning Streaks and Losing Streaks Begin and End*. New York: Three Rivers Press

Knezek, D. (2006). Yes to Both. *Learning and Leading with Technology, 34*. Retrieved June 7, 2008, from http://www.iste.org/Content/NavigationMenu/Publications/LL/LLIssues/Volume_34_2006_2007_/November_No_3_2/LandL_November_2006.htm

Kolb, L. (2006). From Toy to Toll. *Learning and Leading with Technology, 34*. Retrieved June 7, 2008, from http://www.iste.org/Content/NavigationMenu/Publications/LL/LLIssues/Volume_34_2006_2007_/November_No_3_2/LandL_November_2006.htm

Kozol, J. (2006). *The Shame of a Nation: The Restoration of Apartheid Schooling in America*. CA: Three Rivers Press.

Law, l. (2006). Fulldome Video: An Emerging Technology for Education. *Learning and Leading with Technology, 34*. Retrieved June 7, 2008, from http://www.iste.org/Content/NavigationMenu/Publications/LL/LLIssues/Volume_34_2006_2007_/November_No_3_2/LandL_November_2006.htm

Martin, H. (2006). Remember the Mantra. *Learning and Leading with Technology, 34*. Retrieved June 7, 2008, from http://www.iste.org/Content/NavigationMenu/Publications/LL/LLIssues/Volume_34_2006_2007_/November_No_3_2/LandL_November_2006.htm

Mayer, M., & Leone, P. (2001). *Hypermedia and Students With E/BD: Developing untapped Talents and Fostering Success*. Retrieved May 24, 2009 From http://www.eric.ed.gov/ERICWebPortal/custom/portlets/recordDetails/detailmini.jsp?_nfpb=true&_&ERICExtSearch_SearchValue_0=ED458738&ERICExtSearch_SearchType_0=no&accno=ED458738

McAnear, A. (2006). The Magic of Emerging Technology. *Learning and Leading with Technology, 34*. Retrieved June 7, 2008, from http://www.iste.org/Content/NavigationMenu/Publications/LL/LLIssues/Volume_34_2006_2007_/November_No_3_2/LandL_November_2006.htm

McClellan, S. (2008). Will Mobile Ads Take Off In '07, Or Be Put On Hold? *Adweek Magazine*. Retrieved June 27, 2008 from http://www.adweek.com/aw/magazine/article_display.jsp?vnu_content_id=1003526234

Moffitt, M. (1996). *Importance of Teaching and Learning Implications When Making Decisions About Technology Acquisition*. North Central Regional Educational Laboratory (NCREL) online publications. Retrieved September 18, 2008 from http://www.ncrel.org

Murray, F. (2001). *The Use of PowerPoint to Increase Reading and Language Skills: A Research-Based Approach*. Retrieved May 24, 2009, from http://www.eric.ed.gov/ERICWebPortal/custom/portlets/recordDetails/detailmini.jsp?_nfpb=true&_&ERICExtSearch_SearchValue_0=ED458738&ERICExtSearch_SearchType_0=no&accno=ED458738

Ndahi, H. (2006). The Use of Innovative Methods to Deliver Technology Education Laboratory Courses via Distance Learning: A Strategy to Increase Enrollment. *Journal of Technology Education, 17*, 33-42. Retrieved September 18, 2008 from http://scholar.lib.vt.edu/ejournals/JTE/v17n2/pdf/index.html

Norstrom, B. (2006). Produce Employees. *Learning and Leading with Technology, 34*. Retrieved June 7, 2008, from http://www.iste.org/Content/NavigationMenu/Publications/LL/LLIssues/Volume_34_2006_2007_/November_No_3_2/LandL_November_2006.htm

Rauch, L. (2002). *Critical Issue: Using Technology to Support Limited-English-Proficient (LEP) Students' Learning Experiences*. North Central Regional Educational Laboratory (NCREL) online publications. Retrieved September 18, 2008, from http://www.ncrel.org/sdrs/areas/issues/methods/technlgy/te900.htm

Reid, K. (1995). *Purchasing Technology Without Making Plans for Student Learning and Curriculum Application*. North Central Regional Educational Laboratory (NCREL) online publications. Retrieved September 18, 2008, from http://www.ncrel.org

Sonak, B., et al. (2002). *The Effort of a Web-Based Academic Record and Feedback System of Student Achievement at the Junior High School Level*. Paper presented at the Annual Meeting of the American Educational Research Association, New Orleans. Retrieved May 24, 2009, from http://www.eric.ed.gov/ERICWebPortal/custom/portlets/recordDetails/detailmini.jsp?_nfpb=true&_&ERICExtSearch_SearchValue_0=ED465768&ERICExtSearch_SearchType_0=no&accno=ED465768

Spitzer, I. (2003). Students Dial Up Cell Phone Service. *North Gate News Online*. Retrieved June 27, 2008 from http://journalism.berkeley.edu/ngno/stories/001538.html

UNESCO. (2001). *Teaching Education Through Distance Learning*. Retrieved June 16, 2009 from http://unesdoc.unesco.org/images/0012/001242/124208e.pdf

U.S. Government. Education. (2008). *Authentic Uses of Technology*. Retrieved June 6, 2008 from http://www.ed.gov/pubs/EdReformStudies/EdTech/overview.html

U.S. Government. Education. (2008). *Executive Summary of the No Child Left Behind Act of 2001*. Retrieved June 11, 2008 from http://www.ed.gov/print/nclb/overview/intro/execsumm.html

U.S. Government. Budget. (2008, June 27). *FY 2008 Budget Summary: Elementary and Secondary Education*. Retrieved June 27, 2008 from http://www.ed.gov/about/overview/budget/budget08/summary/edlite-section2a.html

Valdez, G. (2007). *Technology: A Catalyst for Teaching and Learning in the Classroom*. North Central Regional Educational Laboratory (NCREL) online publications. Retrieved June 6, 2008 from http://www.ncrel.org/sdrs/areas/issues/methods/technlgy/te600.htm

Wahl, L., & Duffield, J. (2006). Multi-modal Vocabulary Building. *Learning and Leading with Technology, 34*. Retrieved June 7, 2008, from http://www.iste.org/Content/NavigationMenu/Publications/LL/LLIssues/Volume_34_2006_2007_/November_No_3_2/LandL_November_2006.htm

Weber, K., & Custer, R. (2005). Gender-based Preferences towards Technology Education Content, Activities, and Instructional Methods. *Journal of Technology Education, 16*, 55-71. Retrieved September 18, 2008 from: http://scholar.lib.vt.edu/ejournals/JTE/v16n2/pdf/index.html

Whitney, J. (2007). *The Use of Technology in Literacy Instruction: Implications for Teaching Students From Lower Socioeconomic Backgrounds*. Retrieved May 24, 2009, from http://www.eric.ed.gov/ERICWebPortal/custom/portlets/recordDetails/detailmini.jsp?_nfpb=true&_&ERICExtSearch_SearchValue_0=ED498986&ERICExtSearch_SearchType_0=no&accno=ED498986

Wilder, L. (2001). *Integrating technology on program Development for Children/Youth with E/BD*. Retrieved May 24, 2009, from http://www.eric.ed.gov/ERICWebPortal/custom/portlets/recordDetails/detailmini.jsp?_nfpb=true&_&ERICExtSearch_SearchValue_0=ED458738&ERICExtSearch_SearchType_0=no&accno=ED458738

Zappe, S., et al. (2002). *The Effort of a Web-Based Academic Record and Feedback System of Student Achievement at the Junior High School Level*. Paper presented at the Annual Meeting of the American Educational Research Association, New Orleans. Retrieved May 24, 2009, from http://eric.ed.gov/ERICDocs/data/ericdocs2sql/content_storage_01/0000019b/80/1a/6b/19.pdf

APPENDIX

1. TV Advertisement/Commercial

Group Project

1. Start a project log and review a media project checklist.
2. Review the laws and cases on copyright, plagiarism, fair use, patent, harassment, and endangerment.
3. Study samples of TV advertisements. Visit http://www.mediacampaign.org/ and click on TV (under AD GALLERY), or http://video.google.com/ or www.freevibe.com/Share/realteens/ads.asp
4. Brainstorm on a general topic that you may want to work on, example Drugs, Education, Family, Gangs, relationship, peer pressure, etc.
5. Discuss why you chose the general topic. You may want to construct the KWL chart.
6. Narrow down your topic, example: "How drug affects concentration and retention" or "High school dropouts" or "helping drop outs find alternative schools" or "Keeping gangs away from young girls."
7. What do you hope to achieve by working on this topic and project? The reasons might seem obvious, but make a good attempt to discuss it.
8. How are you going to present your ideas? Examples: As a narrative; by way of examples; back-track narrative (start from the end and work your way to the beginning)
9. Write a script.
10. Make a list of items and supplies you need.
11. Give assignments to members of your group.
12. WORK ON THE PROJECT
13. Complete your media project checklist.

2. Music/Soundtrack

Group Project

1. Start a project log and review a media project checklist.
2. Review the laws and cases on copyright, plagiarism, fair use, patent, harassment, and endangerment
3. Brainstorm on a general topic that you may want to work on, example Drugs, Education etc.
4. Discuss why you chose the general topic. You may want to construct the KWL chart. Focus on what you KNOW
5. Narrow down your topic, example: "How easy is it to get drugs?" or "Why are so many kids dropping out"
6. What do you hope to achieve by working on this topic and project? The reasons might seem obvious, but make a good attempt to discuss it.
7. How are you going to present your ideas? Examples: As a narrative; by way of example(s); back-track narrative (start from the end and work your way to the beginning)

8.   Listen to samples of soundtrack at home and school
9.   Write a script or create your lyrics
10.   Make a list of items and supplies you need.
11.   Give assignments to members of your group.
12.   WORK ON THE PROJECT
13.   Complete your media project checklist.

3. Radio Advertisement/Commercial

Group Project

1.   Start a project log and review a media project checklist.
2.   Review the laws and cases on copyright, plagiarism, fair use, patent, harassment, and endangerment
3.   Study samples of radio advertisements. Visit http://www.mediacampaign.org/ and click on RADIO (under AD GALLERY)
4.   Brainstorm on a general topic that you may want to work on, example Drugs, Education etc.
5.   Discuss why you chose the general topic. You may want to construct the KWL chart.
6.   Narrow down your topic, example: "How drug affects concentration and retention" or "High school dropouts"
7.   What do you hope to achieve by working on this topic and project? The reasons might seem obvious, but make a good attempt to discuss it.
8.   How are you going to present your ideas? Examples: As a narrative; by way of examples; back-track narrative (start from the end and work your way to the beginning)
9.   Write a script.
10.   Make a list of items and supplies you need.
11.   Give assignments to members of your group.
12.   WORK ON THE PROJECT
13.   Complete your media project checklist.

4. Television News Story

Group Project

1.   Start a project log and review a media project checklist.
2.   Review the laws and cases on copyright, plagiarism, fair use, patent, harassment, and endangerment
3.   Study samples of TV news stories. http://www.channelone.com/video/
4.   Brainstorm on a general topic that you may want to work on, example Drugs, Education, gangs, drunk driving, prom, high school life, etc.
5.   Discuss why you chose the general topic. You may want to construct the KWL chart.

6. Narrow down your topic, example: "How easy is it to get drugs?" or "Why are so many kids dropping out" or "are high school student eating enough"

7. What do you hope to achieve by working on this topic and project? The reasons might seem obvious, but make a good attempt to discuss it.

8. How are you going to present your ideas? Examples: As a narrative; by way of example(s); backtrack narrative (start from the end and work your way to the beginning); investigative report; live news coverage.

9. Write a news script. See

10. Make a list of items and supplies you need.

11. Give assignments to members of your group.

12. WORK ON THE PROJECT

13. Complete your media project checklist.

5. Movie or Campaign Poster

1. Start a project log and review a media project checklist.

2. Review the laws and cases on copyright, plagiarism, fair use, patent, harassment, and endangerment

3. Study samples of movies posters. Visit http://www.mediacampaign.org/ and click on print or banner (under AD GALLERY), or http://www.allposters.com

4. Brainstorm on a general topic that you may want to work on, example Drugs, Education, Family, etc.

5. Discuss why you chose the general topic. You may want to construct the KWL chart.

6. Narrow down your topic, example: "How drug affects concentration and retention" or "High school dropouts"

7. What do you hope to achieve by working on this topic and project? The reasons might seem obvious, but make a good attempt to discuss it.

8. Come up with a good phrase. Make sure every word says and means something very powerful.

9. Write a script (if you need one).

10. Make a list of items and supplies you need.

11. Give assignments to members of your group.

12. WORK ON THE PROJECT

13. Complete your media project checklist.

6. Media Kit

1. Start a project log and review a media project checklist.

2. Review the laws and cases on copyright, plagiarism, fair use, patent, harassment, and endangerment

3. You work for an organization that helps fight Gangs, Drug use, high school drops, helps teen parents etc. Design a media kit for your organization.

4.   Brainstorm on a general problem that your organization does, example Drugs, Education, Gangs etc.
5.   Discuss why you chose the general problem. You may want to construct the KWL chart.
6.   Narrow down your organization's focus, example: "helping drop outs find alternative schools" or "Keeping gangs away from young girls."
7.   What do you hope to achieve by working on this topic and project? The reasons might seem obvious, but make a good attempt to discuss it.
8.   Come up with a slogan for your organization. Make sure every word says and means something very powerful.
9.   Make a list of items and supplies you need.
10. Give assignments to members of your group.
11. WORK ON THE PROJECT.
12. Complete your media project checklist.

7. Cartoons and Story Board

1.   Start a project log and review a media project checklist.
2.   Review the laws and cases on copyright, plagiarism, fair use, patent, harassment, and endangerment
3.   Study samples of Cartoons and Story Board
4.   Brainstorm on a general topic that you may want to work on, example Drugs, Education, Gangs, etc.
5.   Discuss why you chose the general topic. You may want to construct the KWL chart.
6.   Narrow down your topic, example: "Teen helping teen stay drug free"
7.   What do you hope to achieve by working on this topic and project? The reasons might seem obvious, but make a good attempt to discuss it.
8.   How are you going to present your ideas? Examples: As a narrative; by way of examples; backtrack narrative (start from the end and work your way to the beginning)
9.   Write a script.
10. Make a list of items and supplies you need.
11. Give assignments to members of your group.
12. Makes copies of a storyboard template.
13. WORK ON THE PROJECT
14. Complete your media project checklist.

8. Bumper Sticker

1.   Start a project log and review a media project checklist.
2.   Review the laws and cases on copyright, plagiarism, fair use, patent, harassment, and endangerment
3.   Study samples of bumper stickers done by other students.

4. Think of bumper stickers as a kind of Americanized, Japanese Haiku. A concise, positive melding of image/words not meant to incite road rage.
5. Brainstorm on a general topic that you may want to work on, examples Drugs, Education, Gangs etc.
6. Discuss why you chose the general topic. You may want to construct the KWL chart.
7. Narrow down your topic, example: "How drug affects concentration and retention" or "High school dropouts"
8. What do you hope to achieve by working on this topic and project? The reasons might seem obvious, but make a good attempt to discuss it.
9. Come up with a good phrase. Make sure every word says and means something very powerful.
10. Make a list of items and supplies you need.
11. WORK ON THE PROJECT.
12. Complete your media project checklist.

Project Title

1. Briefly describe the idea for your project.
2. How will you benefit from this project? What value does it have? What will you learn from it?
3. How should this project be evaluated? Design a rubric for it.

Chapter 4
When Twentieth Century Minds Design for Twenty–First Century Distance Learning

Robert D. Wright
University of North Texas, USA

ABSTRACT

This chapter examines the changes that twentieth century minds must undergo if they are to successfully design for today's distance learners. Traditional classroom practices must be adapted to accommodate the interactive and distributed nature that defines effective contemporary distance learning. The learning theories, cognitive processes, and educational media that shaped the minds of instructional developers, technologists, and teachers who were born in the twentieth century differ from those required for twenty-first century learning. Raised and educated before computers were personal, in an era when distance learning consisted of adult education correspondence courses or head-in-a-box instructional television, and when instruction delivery was teacher-centered, educational professionals must now utilize theories, strategies, practices, and resources that are foreign to their learning backgrounds and experiences. Just as important, they must overcome views of interactive media and distance learning that differ greatly from those they seek to educate.

INTRODUCTION

As we move further into the Twenty-first Century, the beliefs, theories, practices, and technologies relating to education and learning evolve. Social Constructivist theory continues to anchor the most commonly-held beliefs. While some may argue with the notion that learning only occurs in collab-orative environments (Chafe, 1998), the cognitive focal point of social development theory positions constructivism to effectively identify the dynamics that exist in the learner-centered combination of collaboration and technology that makes interactive, mediated distance learning the ideal learning tool for Twenty-first Century education (Vygotsky in Kearsley, n.d.). However, before this tool can be put to proper use, Twentieth Century Minds must come to new understandings. This chapter will present

DOI: 10.4018/978-1-61520-672-8.ch004

the cognitive theories that serve to explain how Twenty-first Century Learners process information, the generally-accepted learning theories that help to explain how contemporary students acquire knowledge, and the principles and practices that lead to the development of a technology-integrated pedagogy, and the design of mediated resources, to support the collaborative, interactive, and distributive experiences and activities that comprise Twenty-first Century distance learning.

THE PRODUCTS OF TWO CENTURIES

The education of the instructional developers, technologists, and teachers who were born in the Twentieth Century was vastly different from what is being delivered today. Educational computing did not exist for most; distance learning was print-based for many. Instructional media was crude by today's standards; and it was not an element of mainstream education. To understand how Twentieth Century Minds can design for Twenty-first Century Learners, we must first understand the differences between the two.

Twentieth Century Minds

The development of theories, strategies, and practices to nurture today's students are tasks that fall on the shoulders of a generation of instructional developers, technologists, and educators grounded firmly in the Twentieth Century. Many were raised and educated before computer use—both within and outside of education—was commonplace. Early instructional television enjoyed a widespread presence (Saettler, 2004); but most was locally-produced and often of low quality; educational technology was viewed as a scientific development, not as a resource for general education. As such, it was relegated to enrichment activities and not integrated into the classroom routine (Miller & Cruce, 2002). Kept

out of the mainstream, the innovation of educational television failed to alter classroom instruction. The pedagogy that directed the education of Twentieth Century Minds had remained intact for 200 years (Schank, 2004): teacher-centered, content-driven, and totally removed from any real-world context.

Learning Theories

Older members of this group—many of the earliest users of instructional media--were educated in behaviorist environments: teachers utilized sequenced stimulus-response activities and reinforcement strategies in their efforts to produce observable and measurable learning outcomes (Ertmer & Newby, 1993). Younger members of this group were educated in cognitivist settings, where the emphasis on mental structures and thinking processes took the learning strategies and affective traits of the students into consideration. The objectivist view that knowledge existed outside of the human mind and had to be acquired by the learner (Mergel, 1998) persisted until the youngest of the Twentieth Century Minds—many of whom were raised on Sesame Street and were the first users of PC- and console-based games—studied in the early constructivist classrooms where learning experiences led students to create real world meanings (Jonassen, 1991).

One of the earliest successful educational computer games was *The Oregon Trail* (Rawitsch, Heinemann, & Dillenberger, 1974). This role-playing game allowed students to live in the 1800s as hunters, carpenters, farmers, and other roles while learning about history, geography, and the harsh realities of pioneer life. But, educational computer games did not necessarily employ real situations or activities; they did, however, engage students in activities requiring the use of real world decision-making and problem-solving skills (Jiao, 2007). *The Incredible Machine* (Williams, 1995) explored cause and effect, gravity, and other concepts by requiring learners to use levers, ropes, pulleys, generators, even small animals, to create complex devices that, reminiscent of Rube Goldberg, completed relatively simple tasks. *Math Munchers Deluxe* (The Learning Company, 1995) used an adventure game show approach to help students develop math skills. Learners started the game with three "Munchers"; they responded to questions by directing a Muncher to move across a checkerboard to "eat" the correct answers while avoiding Muncher-eating "Troggles". The ability to customize content and vary the levels of difficulty made the game suitable for Grades 3-7.

Early computer games supported a variety of learning theories and instructional approaches. *Math Munchers* encouraged the construction of cognitivist mental models as students played the games and learned through the use of its interactive multimedia. Objectivists could appreciate the opportunities for the transmission of dependable knowledge that games such as *Oregon Trail* could supply. The control that users held in directing and developing the game play of *The Incredible Machine,* and to some extent almost all games, made it an ideal tool for use in early constructivist environments.

Networked and online delivery supported gaming's ability to serve as a collaborative tool. As early as 1986, commercial games such as *Where in the World is Carmen Sandiego*, *SimCity*—even *Choplifter*—were being adapted for educational use (Kaptelinin & Cole, 1996). As the Worldwide Web became more popular, so did the educational use of popular games such as *Civilization* and *Age of Empires* (Bryant, 2008). Games are now finding their way into distance learning. Multiplayer online games such as *World of Warcraft* are being used in distance learning (New Media Consortium, 2007); NASA is developing two MMOGs for educational purposes (National Aeronautics and Space Administration, 2008). And there is a host of online educational games, such as *Ratio Stadium* (Arcademic Skill Builders, 2008), *Big Kahuna Words* (Energames, 2005) and *DimensionM* (Tabula Digita, 2009) that are available

for use in distance learning. Online environments broaden the range and depth of these experiences (Klopfer, Osterweil, Groff, & Haas, 2009; New Media Consortium, 2007; Delwiche, 2006). As a result, the students' perspectives, as well as their realities, developed in ways that differed from those of earlier learners. Knowledge had become more fluid; resources had become more plentiful and engaging; the process for its acquisition was more flexible in structure and more collaborative in nature.

But, early Constructivist theory did not embrace the collaborative strategy that Social Constructivism does. An interesting parallel is that one study of pre-service teachers shows that a vast majority (77%) favored single-player games; an even greater number (89.8%) did not feel that they were part of a "gaming community". Only 1.1% of the respondents felt that multiplayer online gaming was their favorite genre (Rice, 2006). The early days of constructivist learning, distance education, and popular gaming all appear to have taken place as unique and individual experiences. Thus, even today's younger teachers view collaborative experiences—be they gaming or education—as foreign to them. This places them in a separate camp from the Twenty-first Century Learners.

Twenty-First Century Learners

The successful Twenty-first Century classroom is a learner-centered environment (Khan, 2005; Driscoll, 2002). Though done in slightly different fashions, both distance learning and face-to-face environments support the partnering of students and teachers as they collaborate through the use of technology. Such collaboration creates communities of learning that nurture, encourage, and sustain knowledge acquisition, integration, and application (Klopfer, Osterweil, Groff, & Haas, 2009; Klopfer, Osterweil, & Salen, 2009; Hooper & Rieber, 1995). Bielaczyk (2006) notes that students must assume the role of "collaborative

Table 1. Differences that shaped instruction (derived from Ertmer & Newby, Jonassen, Bielaczyk)

For Twentieth Century Minds	For Twenty-first Century Learners
Classroom Instruction	
Teacher-centered	Student-centered
Content-driven	Process-driven
Context-focused	Cross-domain, real world applications
Learning Environment	
Classrooms and labs	Classroom, labs, networks, virtual
Seatwork	Teamwork
Real-time	Synchronous and asynchronous
Learning Theories and Practices	
Behaviorism	Social Constructivism
Stimulus-response activities	Engaging activities
Reinforcement strategies	Exploratory strategies
Cognitivism	Experiential knowledge
Student learning strategies	
Student affective traits	
Constructivism	
Experiential knowledge	
Individual construction	

co-investigators" with each relying on others to serve as resources so that all can succeed. Pooling individual strengths and talents to direct the learning process, learners create a new identity of "students as instructional designers" (p. 305).

Twenty-first Century learning is more than memorization; knowledge is more than a collection of facts (Schrader, Zheng & Young, 2006). Students want learning experiences to be similar to other life events, in that they will be technologically-based and multi-sensory in delivery. Content acquisition now serves with the tools, resources, practices, and strategies that students employ to develop their existing knowledge and to create new understanding (see Table 1). Students want learning to be challenging, even hard. They will accept almost anything as long as it isn't boring (Papert, 1998).

THINKING AND LEARNING AT A DISTANCE

For distance learning to serve as an effective tool for Twenty-first Century Learners, Twentieth Century Minds will reconsider their beliefs concerning the role of technology in instruction. As was noted above, technology has often been employed in enrichment activities and not in mainstream instructional activities. It was often adopted as an improvement over existing presentation or content delivery apparatus (Cerbin, 2001). Chalkboards replaced the spoken word and provided the means to graphically present information; overhead projectors presented larger images to greater numbers of learners; Power-Point® presentations incorporated sound, motion, rich visual information, and links to web sites to even larger student populations. Yet, the pedagogy remained unchanged (Cerbin, 2001). Christenson and Horn (2008) state that a school would "cram the innovation into its existing operating model to sustain what it already does". The potential of these technologies on learning was never explored. In order to improve instruction, Twentieth Century Minds will utilize distance learning to solve problems that hinder student achievement of learning outcomes (Cerbin, 2001).

To successfully design for the Twenty-first Century Learner, Twentieth Century Minds will think in terms of collaborative strategies, distance technology, and interactive environments. Course designers and instructors will become more aware of how students think and learn, of the capabilities and potential of new technologies, and of how the use of these technologies alters the roles and practices of educators. Such awareness will be critical if educators are to direct the application of technology towards solving specific "learning dilemmas" (Cerbin, 2001). To do so, Twentieth Century Minds must first understand how Twenty-first Century Learners think and what they need in order to learn.

Thinking and Learning

A logical start is with the social, yet distributed nature of distance learning. Twentieth Century Minds must understand that "presence"—as experienced by Twenty-first Century Learners—is not tied to physical proximity; it is more a social atmosphere where each participant establishes, develops, and maintains a communal significance and supportive relevance within an ongoing series of mediated, interpersonal communications (Richardson & Swan, 2003). Within this social environment of virtual presence, today's learners utilize multiple mediated streams as they receive and process new information, and integrate it into their existing knowledge base.

This does not happen automatically. Students can develop a sense of isolation due to the lack of visual and verbal cues in their distance learning experiences (Richardson & Swan, 2003). But studies indicate that the traditional classroom components that are missing in distance learning "are compensated for or even paralleled by paralanguage activities that occur in successful, interactive learning environments" (Richardson & Swan, p.69; see also Picciano, 2002; Polhemus, Shih, Richardson, & Swan, 2000). Specific measures that involve the teachers in the learning process, take advantage of the interactive nature of online instruction, and promote communication provide the foundation for effective distance learning, create a sense of presence, promote socialization, and help students to overcome feelings of isolation (Roblyer & Davis, 2008; Aronson & Timms, 2003; Indiana Higher Education Telecommunications System., 2003; Lehman, 2001). Such activities must be designed into Twenty-first Century distance learning experiences; strategies for their use must be included in the pedagogy.

Short, Williams and Christie (1976) theorize that participants in mediated communication develop an understanding of the extent to which each medium is able to support social presence; they also understand that the level of possible social presence varies from one medium to another. Furthermore, knowledgeable participants avoid engaging in activities that exceed a medium's abilities to sustain the desired level of social presence. Successful educators will employ various media in ways that establish levels of social presence that are appropriate for each activity. Cataloging each medium's potential social presence and matching the appropriate tool to the planned activity will be of some value. But, research indicates that social presence is more than a product of a medium's capabilities; it also stems from the learners' practiced and perceived presence in a progression of mediated communications (Gunawardena & Zittle, 1997). Thus, by properly designing mediated activities to include the interactive use of technology by knowledgeable learners, social presence can "be cultured" in the student user population (Richardson & Swan, 2003, p.70).

Such proper design will also consider how knowledge is to be represented and delivered. Of prime importance is the accurate staging of content so that "conceptual relationships and problem solving strategies become internalized appropriately by students" (Locatis, 2001, p. 12); in simpler terms, knowledge must be clearly understood and integrated so that learners can properly apply it within other contexts. Theoretical models that focus on student exploration and knowledge construction support the use of metaphors to present broader, underlying concepts and analogies to supply more specific examples (Locatis, 2001). Metaphors and analogies provide opportunities for learners to interact with conceptual knowledge and to relate it to pre-existing knowledge and more relevant situations. However, such representations must be applied with a broader understanding of what works.

Mayer and Moreno (1997) detail the theory that learners possess separate systems to manage incoming narrative and graphic information in three fundamental cognitive processes. During the initial process of "Selecting", incoming narrative information generates a text base while graphic information produces an image base of learner knowledge. This is followed by "Organizing", where new knowledge in the text base is processed to create verbal models while recently-acquired image base knowledge is processed to create visual models. Finally, the 'Integrating" process uses information from within both models to create a comprehensive understanding that connects the elements involved in the experience, situation, or event being presented. The workings of these processes are unique to each learner. Internal factors such as pre-existing knowledge and cognitive abilities combine with how information is represented and delivered to affect how thinking and learning take place. Most instructors, however, teach in accordance with their own learning styles and often in the same way that they were taught.

Although learning styles vary greatly within typical Twenty-first Century student groups, most instructors fail to consider the diversity. This lack of accommodation represents one of the greatest weaknesses that occur when Twentieth Century Minds design for Twenty-first Century Learners (Combs, 2004).

Willis (2004) and Combs (2004) detail the types of inclusive strategies that accommodate the needs of a broad field of learners:

- Highly motivated and "active" learners work well with frequent group projects and case-based activities.
- Aural learners perform well using a more technological approach; i.e., the use of videos, narrative-centered learning environments and simulations, Microsoft® PowerPoint® presentations and video- or web-conferencing.
- Students who are given underlying rules, theories, and concepts can employ their critical thinking skills to develop courses of action and relevant applications for their newly-constructed knowledge.
- Some students will respond to case-based and problem-based learning activities that can be used to provide information and observations so that underlying principles can be identified, developed and reported upon.
- In the absence of physical activities, kinesthetic learners have been able to work well with a variety of web pages with different types of resources, short, web-based exercises, and interactive simulations.
- Students who learn through reading and writing activities can be accommodated by presenting them with online readings and assessments, and the assignment of a traditional term paper due at the end of the course.
- Online presentations of information will assist more reflective

Table 2. Mayer and Moreno's principles of multimedia learning

Principle	Concept Involved	Processing Involved
Multiple Representation	Presenting both textual and graphic forms is more effective than merely presenting it as text.	Forms are processed into two mental models; connections between them create more thorough understanding.
Contiguity	Presenting textual and graphic forms simultaneously is more effective than presenting them separately.	It is easier to relate the models to each other when both forms exist in working memory at the same time.
Split Attention	With multimedia, spoken words are more effectively processed than textual presentations.	Words are processed verbally, not visually; images are more readily processed when text does not overload or confuse the creation of the graphic model.
Individual Differences	The outcomes from applying the previous principles are largely dependent upon the qualities within each learner.	Those with less prior knowledge benefit more from multimedia representations; those with significant prior knowledge use verbal and textual information to construct the mental images, lessening the impact of contiguity. Sequential learners do not hold visual images in working memory as well as spatial learners; thus, they do not fare as well when processing multimedia.
Coherence	Using fewer images and words is more effective than using more.	Summarized information simplifies model building.

learners with internalization and knowledge construction.

- Outlined presentations of information within a sequentially-organized, but flexible structure of formative and summative activities allows sequential learners to navigate the course content based upon their own preferences and decisions.
- Visual learners, as could be expected, learn best in environments where graphs, charts, illustrations, diagrams, animated simulations, and other visuals are used to present relevant content and in the demonstration of successful learning.

It should be noted that no hard-and-fast lines can be drawn here. While certain methods may dominate a learner's style, most students employ different strategies, depending upon the content and the circumstances. But as Baker and Gloster (1994) note, technology-mediated instruction does require less time than the traditional text and lecture methodology for students to initially achieve the desired learning outcomes; it also offers improved

long-term retention of the acquired knowledge. To develop interactive multimedia in accordance with practices and strategies of Twenty-first Century learning, Mayer and Moreno (1997) suggest applying the processes discussed above to a set of principles for presenting information through the use of multimedia (see Table 2).

Instructional designers and teachers can use these principles to understand how thinking and learning processes are unique to each learner. They should keep in mind that these learning processes are at work within the members of a group. In mediated learning experiences the collaborative efforts of the learners result in a distributed cognition; the results gained from the processing strengths of the individuals benefit all, while the impact of individual weaknesses are overcome. By applying the principles of balanced graphic and textual representations of knowledge, Twentieth Century Minds improve students' learning by making content the object around which cognitive processes are structured, and by guiding students into more advanced levels of the learning experience. Combining the balanced treatment of new information with engaging interaction and personal activities that feed collaborative exercises creates a dynamic relationship between the student, the content, the instructional environment, and the learning process (Indiana Higher Education Telecommunications System, 2003).

This dynamic relationship is nurtured in a social constructivist environment. While not a new concept, social constructivism encompasses the activities that take place in effective distance learning. Supported by the use of technology, students bring their diverse skills and interests into collaborative learning activities, where they interpret information and negotiate meaning to construct shared understanding (Jackson, Karp, Patrick, and Thrower, 2006). The result of such interaction goes beyond the immediate achievement of desired learning outcomes; it also engages higher-level thinking that is more likely to establish student learning strategies that can be effectively applied to other domains (Miller, 1995).

While this general information is useful, Twentieth Century Minds will need to make more specific application of these concepts when designing and executing the collaborative activities that form an essential part of distance education. Cooperative exercises effectively engage the two phases of peer collaboration: interpersonal problem solving, where students interact to direct and support their common knowledge development; followed by an internal drawing of conclusions based upon what was observed and experienced. Discussion boards and collaborative projects offer opportunities for group exploration and dialogue interwoven with individual reflection and the development of information into personal meaning. Such action requires more than a well-designed process; it must be guided by a teacher who understands and is willing to work with the constructivist cognitive progressions that occur in the minds of Twenty-first Century Learners.

In assessing and gathering the technology-based resources to support effective distance learning, Twentieth Century Minds should abandon longstanding beliefs and move beyond years of observation and experience. Today's interactive multimedia and educational games and simulations have little in common with commercially popular gaming products. They are more complex; use of these games encourages the development of a "media literacy", collaborative problem solving, research, critical analysis, and diplomatic skills that will be critical to academic and personal success in the Twenty-first Century (Jenkins, Purushotma, Clinton, Weigel, & Robison, 2006; Kirriemuir, 2006). They do this by placing learners in scenarios where problems must be solved, often through a collaborative process. Students record, interpret, and apply a wide variety of metrics (points earned, levels attained, tools acquired, lives remaining) while seeking solutions (Bryant, 2008). Games can also combine individual activities with group interaction. The math game *Puzzle Now!* presents weekly problems to students in multiple locations on a statewide network. Students at each site solve the problems on their own; they then meet online to discuss the problem, share their problem-solving methods, and evaluate which approaches worked best, and why (Jiao, 2007). Even *World of Warcraft* is capable of developing higher-order thinking skills (Green & Hannon, 2007); the role of "Guildmaster" requires players to:

- engage potential guild members, analyze their talents and skills, and persuade them to join
- design and implement various group strategies
- develop training, in the form of apprenticeships
- resolve conflicts between guild members
- negotiate agreements with outside players and groups

While not geared towards education, even *World of Warcraft* provides opportunities for students to develop higher order skills. They increase the learner's capacity for "strategic thinking, interpretative analysis, problem solving, plan formulation and execution, and adaptation to rapid change" (Federation of American Scientists, 2006, p.1).

Working with remote groups or with individuals distributed within central locations, Twentieth Century Minds will also facilitate the collaborative use of material objects—"cognitive artifacts"—in the physical environment to promote distributed cognition (Hutchins, 2000). These artifacts are "man-made things that seem to aid or enhance our cognitive abilities... some examples are calendars, to-do lists, computers, or simply tying a string around your finger as a reminder" (Soegaard, 2006, p. 1). Lists and other written artifacts transform the concept or task "by re-representing on paper what was previously in the mind of the task performer" (Soegaard, 2006, p. 2). Computer-generated artifacts not only provide reusable learning objects in printed or other physical form; they can also be shared with fellow students at remote locations (Eberhard, 2005). These artifacts "are involved in a process of organizing functional skills into cognitive functional systems" (Hutchins, 2000, p. 8) that work within and between individuals.

While appearing to be highly structured, such interaction can also be quite flexible: a very cohesive group may develop a collective expertise; technological tools (computer programs, mediated simulations, interactive instructional games) can free individuals from the tasks of information development to allow for greater application of that information. In the absence of strong group interaction, such tools facilitate individual proficiency (Hsiao, n.d.); exercises to promote content recall are replaced by activities to increase conceptual understanding (Burns, Heath, & Dimock, 1998). The use of technology to promote engaging, group participation and feedback is enhanced by its ability to provide real-world interactive simulations (Roschelle, Hoadley, Pea, Gordin, & Means, 2000). Thus, Twentieth Century Minds can lead various assortments of Twenty-first Century Learners who possess different learning styles,

employ unique collections of skills, and may or may not work cohesively.

Altered Roles and Practices

Interaction makes for an engaging classroom experience; yet interaction often fails to manifest. The reformatting of traditional learning drills into a gaming structure—edutainment—failed to produce successful learning, engagement or interaction (Kirriemuir, 2006). Twentieth Century Minds must consider how to create an interactive community that will engage the learner. Designers and educators will use peer learning and interaction (in the form of asynchronous discussions, synchronized chats, and group projects) to create learning communities that support thorough and more complex learning (Bransford, Brown, & Cocking, 2000). Lehman (2001) discusses how different forms of interaction--learner-teacher, learner-learner, and learner-content—can be applied in a "Spectrum of Interaction of Activities" (p.3) ranging from simple presentation activities, such as guest speakers, interviews, and the use of case studies, to increasingly more complex actions that require the sharing of personal information, such as the showing of mediated and physical learning objects, participation through interactive and collaborative experiences, and questioning activities that include debates, Q&A sessions, and formative assessment.

Individual, group, and class-wide participation may be more easily promoted by the collection of asynchronous and real-time activities, the increased opportunities for peer-to-peer and learner-to-teacher dealings, and the host of resources that are not dependent upon physical facilities or centralized locations (Han, 1999). Successful engagement comes from structuring these activities, interactions, and resources to allow students to make use of previous knowledge, to extend that knowledge into the current exercise, and to relate the new information with that which was previously gained. These students are more likely to advance than are those who must drill down through background material and navigate clarifying sidebars. Simpler presentation paths—summaries rather than details, simultaneous presentations of both images and text, and the use of spoken words make for uncluttered presentations that need little clarification. This results in more time on task, which leads to improved achievement of student learning outcomes (Boettcher, 2007).

Instructional Designers

Twentieth Century Minds must account not only for the differences in Twenty-first Century Learners, but the application of Twentieth Century tools to Twenty-first Century distance learning technologies. Drawing upon relevant concepts of behaviorist, objectivist, and constructivist traditions frees instructional designers to apply the most suitable approaches to each situation and set of learners (Nam & Smith-Jackson, 2007; Schwier, 1995). Foundational knowledge may be more easily acquired through the application of behaviorist theory to establish proper learning conditions and to detail how they should lead to a specified slate of desired outcomes (Nam & Smith-Jackson, 2007). For example, designers of an advanced computer graphics course could require that each student have access to a computer with Adobe® PhotoShop® and Illustrator®, and that they demonstrate their mastery of the specific basic functions at the beginning of the course. Cognitivist input would call for the use of advanced organizers and process-driven teaching strategies to provide a framework for the instruction (Driscoll, 2000). The computer graphics course could start a module with visual samples that demonstrated the use of advanced techniques and additional skills, followed by presentations and discussions on the specific processes involved. More advanced understanding of the basic concepts could be achieved through collaborative and reflective constructivist approaches (Nam & Smith-Jackson, 2007). The computer graphics

students could be given collaborative project--a school newsletter or departmental booklet—to produce; alternately, individual students could be given an assignment calling for the creation of a visual piece that represented their design philosophy or understanding of a specific process.

Designers will employ a variety of methods as they develop instruction that focuses on the processes of knowledge acquisition, not on the presentation of content. "Continual interactive engagement of students" (Hake, 2008, p.6) in cognitive, hands-on activities, leading to student-to-student and student-to-instructor discussions, can be more effective in promoting higher-order learning than traditional active teacher/passive student approaches. For this reason, long lists, skill and drill exercises, and other traditional strategies relying on rote memorization and reinforcement will give way to the balanced and complementary representation of information through graphic and textual forms that invite interpretation and interaction. "Collaborative experiences among peers will be designed as key factors in virtual environments, cohort sites, and amongst groups of individual distance learners; this will lead students to query each other, exchange resources and information, examine options, and reach consensus (Han, 1999) as they structure and direct their own learning. Designers will also develop "online learning activities that require… students to become familiar with content prior to coming to a class discussion" (Garnham & Kaleta, 2002, p.1) as a means to facilitate student interaction and to make the best use of the synchronous activity times that instructors share with students.

Instructional designers will accommodate an undercurrent of continuous change. "Tools for distance learning must be flexible and adaptable for a variety of different needs and situations–including their own obsolescence, where possible" (Spodick, 1995, p.4). This characterizes distance learning's continual adoption of available technologies in the past: mail-based correspondence courses gave way to radio transmissions; which were later replaced by television broadcasts. However, these approaches offered no effective means of learner-teacher interaction; most were delivered live, which restricted accessibility (Sherry, 1996). Even as satellite and microwave technology expanded the reach of distance education, instruction remained a teacher-driven, one-way experience. In effect, signals had replaced paper as the delivery medium for the correspondence course, with negative impact and outcomes; without interaction, distance learning replicates the traditional independent study correspondence course where the student could become isolated, de-motivated, and ultimately, non-participatory (Roblyer & Davis, 2008; Sherry, 1996). Teleconferencing provided interaction; but was terribly expensive and cumbersome (Spodick, 1995).

Computer-based instruction made for easier, less expensive delivery, and facilitated the rapid revision of content (Spodick, 1995, p. 1). Email improved interaction (Deloughrey, 1994). Distance learning has taken this to the next level. Outside of infrastructure costs, digital duplication and dissemination of resources is virtually cost-free beyond the time and effort for their original creation. In addition, distance learning provides users with greater latitude in the time and location of their studies, a wider variety of tools and resources, opportunities for immediate updates that reflect new knowledge in the field, and near-spontaneous course revisions in response to expressed learner interests and student-teacher interactions. Discussion boards, chat rooms, and video-/web-conferencing provide for a more robust interactive learning environment in which Twentieth Century Minds can design meaningful instruction, with unique features that overcome time and distance barriers, learner differences, and varying degrees of technological literacy.

Teachers

Online instruction requires that teachers develop and enhance their already-existing teaching skills

and strategies (Willis, 2004; Wilkes & Burnham, 1991). This begins with an honest self-assessment of their mastery and use of current technological resources. Understanding the features and capabilities of the available technology enables teachers to pick the most appropriate tools and adopt the best strategies that will enable them to bring their personal brand of teaching into the distance learning arena (Willis, 2004). "Technology alone is unable to create a meaningful learning environment unless we integrate pedagogy with technology." (Khan, 2005, p. 142; also see Indiana Higher Education Telecommunications System, 2003). In re-creating instruction for distance learning "instructors are not merely involved with designing a course, a program, or a session–rather, they are involved in designing an overall experience for the learners" (Lehman, 2001, p.1).

However, distance education pushes teachers into unfamiliar territory. "Many… initially used familiar teaching skills but quickly discovered that they had to rethink their familiar ways as the landmarks and touchstones of teaching were changed or missing" (Diekelmann, Schuser, & Nosek, 1998, p.6; also see Aronson & Timms, 2003). Distance learning offers few of the controls that have defined the traditional classroom: students at remote classrooms can hold off-microphone discussions; real-time chat room sessions often include multiple, yet still-relevant, threads within the discussion; individual students come and go during synchronous activities; and the asynchronous nature of many distance learning elements makes direct teacher control of students impossible.

Distance learning does open up new instructional possibilities. These sometimes appear as challenges. Teacher autonomy—the ability to alter, add, or remove content, presentations and handout materials—is made more difficult by the network of distance learning technicians and instructional support staff who become involved in making the changes to the posted resources, sites, assignments pages, discussion boards, and the remote locations where groups or cohorts meet. The power structure becomes decentralized; control over instruction no longer rests solely with the teacher; the educational process is no longer anchored in the campus classroom (Hewson & Hughes, 2005; Howell, Williams, & Lindsay, 2003). While content may reside on a central server, the scheduled delivery of content now occurs with less restriction: asynchronous courses move beyond the boundaries of class periods, school hours, vacations, and even semesters; the "class" becomes a multi-point, team-taught experience; teachers adapt to delivering instruction, providing guidance, and performing assessment within environments where they exercise only partial control. Successful teachers are aware of the potential in such situations; they share the power, learn from their students, alter old practices and develop new ones so to produce new pedagogies that reflect and meet the needs of Twenty-first Century Learners (Hewson & Hughes; Howell, Williams, & Lindsay; Diekelmann, Schuser & Nosek, 1998).

And as teachers reflect upon how to resolve new situations and challenges, they often move away from traditional pedagogies. They seek new avenues of interaction, using email, phone calls, even faxes to communicate with students (Lehman, 2001). Teachers lecture less, and for shorter periods of time. They ask more questions—not just concerning content, but also seeking to find out if students are "getting it". And students respond. Both instructors and students provide more feedback. The role of "teacher-as-learner" has become familiar within traditional classrooms; in distance learning, the model of "student-as-teacher" emerges. (Diekelmann, Schuser & Nosek, 1998).

As with face-to-face instruction, teachers will need to establish the breadth and depth to which content will be covered. Doing so requires they realize that the presentation of information in distance learning takes more time. Rather than relying on a traditional lecture form of delivery,

a diverse assembly of offline readings, learner-centered activities, asynchronous peer discussions, and the use of various appropriate media allow for a faster pace of instruction, shorter and more meaningful student-teacher sessions, and greater involvement (Willis, 2004, 1995; Howell, Williams, & Lindsay, 2003; Lehman, 2001). They will also have to assume a new role in the instructional process, in what Chester (2007) refers to as a transformation from teacher to "reacher". Reachers move beyond the traditional didactic practices to embrace strategies that empower students and reinforce their assuming of a more responsible role in their own learning.

Han (1999) notes that teacher support for students will also require a greater awareness of how procedural issues should be dealt with and how students want to be perceived. Students' reading levels and prior experiences with distance education can affect the sequence and format in which structural course materials—syllabi, requirements, reading lists, assignment instructions, and schedules—should be presented to maximize comprehension. Lacking the facial and body language cues that are available in traditional classroom settings, distance learners are better prepared, more highly motivated, and more successful when they deal with instructors who provide clear and complete information, demonstrate a willingness to provide feedback to resolve initial concerns, are well-prepared, technologically competent, and readily available to offer support (Kempfert, 2004; Willis, 2004, 1995; Aronson & Timms,2003; Indiana Higher Education Telecommunications System., 2003; Han; Threlkeld & Brzoska, 1994; Egan, Sebastian, & Welch, 1991).

Finally, teachers need to look beyond the distance that separates them from their students. They must take steps to personalize the learning experience. Lehman (2001) suggests the use of large nametags by students at videoconferencing sites, "bio forms" or "bio booklets" to supply personal information, and discussions to promote rapport, understanding, and expression between peers, with instructors, and with course content. "All serious students want to be noticed" (Han, 1999, p.2). They want to interact and be engaged. But, they also want to be acknowledged; they want their questions to be answered, their contributions to be valued, and their interests to be dealt with. By meeting students' procedural communication and recognition needs, teachers increase students' abilities to develop their new roles in the distance learning environment (Han, 1999).

Students

While instructional designers alter their approaches and teachers implement new strategies, students will also see changes to their roles in the learning environment. First and foremost, they will assume a greater responsibility for their own learning (Willis, 2004; Rumble, 2001; Diekelmann, Schuser, & Nosek, 1998). In fact, they will be mandated to assume greater control. Many students become emboldened when they are not in the same room as the teacher; they participate more, can challenge what is taught, and are less afraid to tell teachers what it is they want to learn. They also turn to each other for assistance and support. In remote group situations, they hold off-microphone discussions, offer and seek information, and "appear... to "get further on" by participating in this kind of spontaneous dialogue" (Diekelmann, Schuser, & Nosek, p. 31). This responsibility will require that they become functionally competent with the relevant technology—able to use it on a routine basis; and possess a certain level of ability to overcome technical problems that arise (Willis, 2004). Familiarity with text messaging, social networking, and other technologies does not automatically extend to distance learning tools. Students will need to become proficient in the use of various communication resources—discussion boards, chat rooms, blogs, wikis, assignment submission

sites, the use of attachments, and videoconferences (Willis, 2004; Lehman, 2001).

INSTRUCTION AND ASSESSMENT

It has been stated that online courses must be designed as well as face-to-face programs (Spodick, 1995; Wilkes & Burnham, 1991). While core content need not be altered, its presentation will require developing new strategies and allocating additional time for planning. Twentieth Century Minds that utilize new strategies and take more time will create curricula that are better-designed than their traditional counterparts (Hake, 2008). The roles of both instruction and assessment are changing; they are moving away from traditional content-centered methodologies to outcome-based practices and measures of competency (Howell, Williams, & Lindsay, 2003). What started out in the workplace is finding its way into education; the value traditionally placed on grades and diplomas is now being assigned to demonstrations of expertise, execution, and ability (Callahan, 2003).

Twentieth Century Minds must begin both the instructional and assessment processes by establishing specific standards, detailed methodologies, and schedules that realistically consider the subject matter; and these must be clearly communicated to the student population (Aronson & Timms, 2003). Dealing with diverse groups of students who possess different learning styles, cognitive skills, and levels of pre-existing knowledge can be difficult in distance learning situations. Part of the solution lies in the promotion of student-teacher interactions. However, while these practices establish familiarity and understanding (Lehman, 2001), they have no direct effect on the delivery of instruction. One possible solution is a form of self-pacing, in which students must finish work within a specific window of time, but are free to move forward once they do (Aronson & Timms, 2003). This provides students with a degree of control over their education and prepares them for the real world, where "Incentives will be given to students and institutions to move students through at a faster rate…" (Dunn, 2000, p. 37). It should be noted that this approach works well with cohorts and groups who meet at remote sites; however, learners who embark on individual self-paced courses of study suffer a high attrition rate (Anderson, 2006). A more proactive approach is to offer learners pacing options in their online courses; students at the Florida Virtual School can choose between "accelerated", "normal", and "extended" schedules and must commit to specific completion dates for each instructional segment (Aronson & Timms). As we move further into the Twenty-first Century, and students advance to become lifelong learners, there will be an increased demand for "… short accelerated programs, well-suited for online delivery…" (Gallagher, 2003).

In addition to the pace of instruction, educators will also rethink the role and application of assessment. While objectivist quizzes and testing may be useful in certain circumstances, the high stakes assessment of rote memorization has no place in Twenty-first Century education. Designers and teachers will employ tools to assess students' mastery of content and ability to apply it. A shift to formative assessment provides opportunities for students to see improvements in their work while providing more interaction with teachers. One successful strategy is to establish a schedule of frequent graded and ungraded assessments (Indiana Higher Education Telecommunications System, 2003); another is to require the submission of drafts to written assignments (Aronson & Timms, 2003); both practices provide learners with specific feedback, result in improved performance on graded coursework, and increase instructor familiarity with individual students. Reflective assignments promote higher level thinking and successfully gauge the extent of students' understanding of the material covered. On a group- or class-wide scale, regular collaborative projects can effectively determine the true extent of learn-

ing by requiring students to discuss concepts and achieve consensus—demonstrating the reasoning behind their results (Aronson & Timms; Indiana Higher Education Telecommunications System). Finally, the use of electronic portfolios (ePortfolios) can provide each student with the opportunity to create, update, and reflect upon "a digital repository of artifacts, which they can use to demonstrate competence and reflect on their learning"(ePortfolio Portal, 2004). Some differentiate between the ePortfolios on local storage media and online webfolios. But both can provide a collection of assessment samples, critical writings, and technical and creative works that demonstrates the students' continuing development and showcases their noteworthy achievements. Frequent assessments and the submission of drafts provide students with feedback as they develop their knowledge; these practices also increase the level of teacher-student interaction. The use of ePortfolios allows the feedback and interaction to continue. More important, their use establishes a trail of demonstrated competency and achievement that can serve as a starting point for reflection and as motivation to continue towards a path of lifelong learning.

CONCLUSION

Twentieth Century Minds *can* design interactive media for Twenty-first Century distance learning. Doing so requires that instructional designers and teachers work with an appreciation of the differences between Twentieth Century education as they experienced it, and Twenty-first Century education as it needs to be. The proper design and presentation of interactive and mediated distance education provides Twenty-first Century Learners with the opportunities to take on more responsibility for their education, to interact with peers, and to use technology in individual and cooperative experiences. Effective tools, supportive resources, meaningful activities, and creative practices allow them to explore concepts, to produce knowledge and to apply it, and to collaborate with classmates to achieve, compete, and learn.

REFERENCES

Anderson, T. (2006, February 25). Affinity groups in self-paced online learning. In *Virtual Canuck: Teaching and Learning in a Net-Centric World.* Retrieved November 12, 2008, from http://terrya.edublogs.org/2006/02/25/affinity-groups-in-self-paced-online-learning/

Arcademic Skill Builders. (2009). *Ratio Stadium.* Retrieved March 7, 2009. from http://arcademicskillbuilders.com/games/ratio-stadium/ratio-stadium.html

Aronson, J., & Timms, M. (2003). *Net choices, net gains: Supplementing the high school curriculum with online courses* (WestEd Knowledge Brief). Retrieved December 21, 2008, from http://www.wested org/online_pubs/KN-03-02.pdf

Baker, W., & Gloster, A. (1994). Moving towards the virtual university: A vision of technology in higher education. *Cause/Effect, 17*(2).

Bielaczyk, K. (2006). Designing social infrastructure: critical issues in creating learning environments with technology. *Journal of the Learning Sciences*, *15*(3), 301–329. doi:10.1207/s15327809jls1503_1

Boettcher, J. (2007). Ten core principles for designing effective learning environments: Insights from brain research and pedagogical theory. *Innovate Journal of Online Education, 3*(3). Retrieved September 20, 2007, from http://innovateonline.info/index.php?view= article&id=54

Bransford, J. D., Brown, A. L., & Cocking, P. R. (Eds.). (2000). *How people learn: Brain, mind, experience, and school.* Washington, DC: National Research Council/National Academy Press.

Bryant, T. (2008). *From Age of Empires to Zork: Using games in the classroom.* Retrieved March 22, 2009, from http://www.academiccommons.org/commons/essay/gamesinclassroom

Burns, M., Heath, M., & Dimock, V. (1998). *TAP into learning: Constructivism and technology: On the road to student-centered learning.* Austin, TX: Technology Assistance Program.

Callahan, P. (2003, March 28-30). *Proceedings of the University Council for Educational Administration 88th Annual Conference,* Chicago, IL. Retrieved November 24, 2008 from http://www.westga.edu/~distance/ojdla/fall63/howell63.html

Cerbin, B. (2001, December 6). Teaching dogs to talk: Bill Cerbin on technology and student learning. *Teaching with Technology Today, 8*(3). Retrieved November 17, 2008, from http://www.uwsa.edu/ttt/articles/cerbin.htm

Chafe, A. (1998). *Computer technology and cooperative learning.* Retrieved September 25, 2007, from http://www.cdli.ca/~achafe/maj_index.html

challenges of participatory culture: Media education for the Twenty-first century [Electronic version]. Retrieved March 19, 2009, from http://www.macfound.org/atf/cf/% 7BB0386CE3-8B29-4162-8098-E466FB856794%7D/DML_ETHNOG_ WHITEPAPER.PDF

Chester, E. (2007). *From teacher to reacher: The common link between uncommon educators.* Retrieved December 12, 2008, from http://www.generationwhy.com/ images/stories/docs/ctr.pdf

Christenson, C., & Horn, M. (2008). *Disrupting class: Student-centric education is the future.* Retrieved March 28, 2009, from http://www.edutopia.org/student-centric-education-technology

Combs, L. (2004). The design, assessment, and implementation of a web-based course. *Association for the Advancement of Computing In Education, 12*(1), 27–37.

DeLoughry, T. (1994). Pushing the envelope. *The Chronicle of Higher Education, 8*(41), A36–A38.

Delwiche, A. (2006). Massively multiplayer online games (MMOs) in the new media classroom. *Educational Technology & Society, 9*(3), 160–172.

Diekelmann, N., Schuster, R., & Nosek, C. (1998). *Creating new pedagogies at the millenium: The uncommon experience of University of Wisconsin-Madison teachers using distance education technologies.* Retrieved November 17, 2008, from http://www.uwsa.edu/ttt/ articles/

Driscoll, M. (2002). *How people learn (and what technology might have to do with it).* Syracuse, NY. ERIC Document Reproduction Service No. ED470032

Dunn, S. (2000, March/April). The virtualizing of education. *The Futurist, 34*(2), 34–38.

Eberhard, S. (2005). *Can dual coding theory be used to develop reusable learning objects in a multilanguage distance education environment?* Retrieved March 19, 2009 from http://74.6.239.67/search/cache?ei=UTF-8&p=cognitive+artifact%2C+distance+learning&fr=moz2&u=www.unm.edu/~eberhard/Portfolio/Lit_review.doc&w=cognitive+artifact+artifacts+distance+learning+learnings&d=XH9S352uSiTJ&icp=1&.intl=us

Egan, M., Sebastian, J., & Welch, M. (1991, March). Effective television teaching: Perceptions of those who count most...distance learners. In *Proceedings of the Rural Education Symposium,* Nashville, TN.

Energames. (2005). *Big Kahuna Words* [Online computer game]. Retrieved March 28, 2009, from http://www.game-remakes.com/game.php?id=81

ePortfolio Portal. (2004). *What is an ePortfolio?* Retrieved March 29, 2009, from http://www.danwilton.com/eportfolios/whatitis.php#references

Ertmer, P., & Newby, T. (1993). Behaviorism, cognitivism, constructivism: Comparing critical features from an instructional design perspective. *Performance Improvement Quarterly, 6*(4), 50–71.

Federation of American Scientists. (2006). *National summit on educational games fact sheet.* Retrieved March 19, 2007, from http://www.fas.org/programs/ltp/policy_and_publications/summit/Fact%20Sheet.pdf

from http://www.usask.ca/education/coursework/802papers/mergel/brenda.htm

Gallagher, R. (2003, March). The next 20 years: How is online distance learning likely to evolve? In *Proceedings of the University Council for Educational Administration 88th Annual Conference,* Chicago, IL.

Garnham, C., & Kaleta, R. (2002, March). Introduction to hybrid courses. *Teaching with Technology Today, 8*(6). Retrieved November 17, 2008, from http://www.uwsa.edu/ttt/articles/garnham.htm

Green, H., & Hannon, C. (2007). *Their Space: Education for a digital generation* [Electronic version]. Retrieved March 24, 2009, from http://www.demos.co.uk/files /Their% 20 space%20 %20web.pdf

Gunawardena, C., & Zittle, F. (1997). Social presence as a predictor of satisfaction within a computer- mediated conferencing environment. *American Journal of Distance Education, 11*(3), 8–26. doi:10.1080/08923649709526970

Hake, R. (2008, January). Can distance and classroom learning be increased? *International Journal for the Scholarship of Teaching and Learning, 2*(1). Retrieved November 7, 2008, from http://www.georgiasouthern.edu/ijsotl

Han, X. (1999, November 15). Exploring an effective and efficient online course management model. *Teaching with Technology Today, 5*(2). Retrieved November 17, 2008, from http://www.uwsa.edu/ttt/articles/han.htm.

Hewson, L., & Hughes, C. (2005). Social processes and pedagogy in online learning. *AACE Journal, 13*(2), 99–125.

Hooper, S., & Rieber, L. (1995). *Teaching with technology*. Retrieved September 24, 2007, from http://www .nowhereroad.com/twt/

Howell, S., Williams, P., & Lindsay, N. (2003). Thirty-two trends affecting distance education; an informed foundation for strategic planning. *Online Journal of Distance Learning Administration, 6*(3). Retrieved November 24, 2008, from http://www.westga.edu/~distance/ojdla/fall63/howell63.html

Hsiao, J. (n.d.). *CSCL theories*. Retrieved January 10, 2008, from http://www.edb.utexas.edu/csclstudent/Dhsiao/theories.html#vygot

Hutchins, E. (2000). *Distributed cognition*. Retrieved January 13, 2008, from http://eclectic.ss.uci.edu/~drwhite/Anthro179a/DistributedCognition.pdf

Indiana Higher Education Telecommunications System. (2003). *Guiding principles for faculty in distance learning*. Retrieved November 27, 2008, from http://www.ihets.org/archive/progserv_arc/education_arc/distance_arc/guiding_principles_arc/index.html

Jackson, R., Karp, J., Patrick, E., & Thrower, A. (2006). *Social constructivism vignette*. Retrieved March 20, 2009, from http://projects.coe.uga.edu/epltt/index.php?title= Social_Constructivism

Jenkins, H., Purushotma, R., Clinton, K., Weigel, M., & Robison, A.J. (2006). *Confronting the*

Jiao, B. (2007). *Social constructivism: games, simulations, cases, and problem solving*. Retrieved March 21, 2009, from http://www.bjiao.com/tel7001/book/Games.htm

Jonassen, D. (1991). Objectivism vs. constructivism: Do we need a new philosophical paradigm? *Educational Technology Research and Development, 39*(3), 5–14. doi:10.1007/BF02296434

Kaptelinin, V., & Cole, M. (1996). *Individual and collective activities in educational computer game playing*. Retrieved March 22, 2009, from http://lchc.ucsd.edu/People/MCole/Activities.html

Kearsley, G. (n.d.). *Social development theory (L. Vygotsky)*. Retrieved September 25, 2008, from http://www.gwu.edu/~tip/vygotsky.html

Kempfert, T. (2004, April). Quality online discussions in Women's Studies classes (or in any class). *Teaching with Technology Today, 10*(5). Retrieved November 17, 2008, from http://www.uwsa.edu/ttt/articles/forums.htm

Khan, B. (2005). Learning features in an open, flexible, and distributed environment. *AACE Journal, 13*(2), 137–153.

Kirriemuir, J. (2006). *Literature review in games and learning*. Retrieved September 8, 2007, from http://www.futurelab.org.uk/resources/publications_reports_articles/literature_reviews/literature_Review378

Klopfer, E., Osterweil, S., Groff, J., & Haas, J. (2009). *Using the technology of today in the classroom today*. Cambridge, MA: The Education Arcade, Massachusetts Institute of Technology.

Klopfer, E., Osterweil, S., & Salen, K. (2009). *Moving learning games forward: Obstacles, opportunities & openness*. Cambridge, MA: The Education Arcade, Massachusetts Institute of Technology.

Learning Company. (1995). *Math Munchers* [Computer Game]. Cambridge, MA: Learning Company.

Lehman, R. (2001, February 15). General principles and good practices for distance education. *Teaching with Technology Today, 7*(6). Retrieved December 13, 2008, from http://www.uwsa.edu/ttt/articles/lehman.htm

Locatis, C. (2001). *Instructional design theory and the development of multimedia programs.* Retrieved January 8, 2008, from http://lhncbc.nlm.nih.gov/lhc/docs/published/2001/ pub2001048.pdf

Mayer, R., & Moreno, R. (1997). *A cognitive theory of multimedia learning: Implications for design principles.* Retrieved January 7, 2008, from http://www.unm.edu/~moreno/PDFS/chi.pdf

Mergel, B. (1998). *Instructional design and learning theory.* Retrieved December 14, 2008,

Miller, M., & Cruce, T. (2002). *A Twentieth Century timeline: Classroom use of instructional film, radio, and television.* Retrieved November 20, 2008, from http://www.arches.uga.edu/~mlmiller/timeline/1960s.htm

Miller, S. (1995). *Vygotsky and education: The sociocultural genesis of dialogic thinking in classroom contexts for open-forum literature discussions.* Retrieved January 11, 2008, from http://psych.hanover.edu/vygotsky/miller.html

Nam, C., & Smith-Jackson, T. (2007). Web-based learning environment: A theory-based design process for development and evaluation. *Journal of Information Technology Education, 6,* 23–43.

National Aeronautics and Space Administration. (2008). *NASA MMO game.* Retrieved March 28, 2009, from http://ipp.gsfc.nasa.gov/mmo/index.html

New Media Consortium. (2007). Massively multiplayer educational gaming. In *The Horizon Report 2007 Edition* (pp. 25-27). Austin, TX: New Media Consortium.

Papert, S. (1998). *Does easy do it? Children, games and learning.* Retrieved September 25, 2007, from http://www.papert.org/articles/Doeseasydoit.html

Picciano, A. (2002). Beyond student perceptions: Issues of interaction, presence, and performance in an online course. *Journal of Asynchronous Learning, 6*(1).

Polhemus, L., Shih, L., Richardson, J., & Swan, K. (2000). *Building an affective learning community: Social presence and learning engagement.* Paper presented at the World Conference on the WWW and the Internet (WebNet), San Antonio, TX.

Rawitsch, D., Heinemann, B., & Dillenberger, P. (1974). *The Oregon Trail* [Computer Game]. Lauderdale, MN: Minnesota Educational Computing Consortium.

Rice, J. (2006). *New media resistance: barriers to implementation of computer video games in the classroom.* Retrieved September 18, 2007, from http://www.eduquery.com/papers/Rice/games/New_Media_Resistance.pdf

Richardson, J., & Swan, K. (2003). Examining social presence in online courses in relation to students' perceived learning and satisfaction [Electronic version]. *Journal of Asynchronous Learning Networks, 7*(1), 68–88.

Roblyer, M., & Davis, L. (2008). Predicting success for virtual school students: Putting research-based models into practice. *Online Journal for Distance Learning Administration, 11*(4). Retrieved December 15, 2008, from http://www.westga.edu/~distance/ojdla/ winter114/roblyer114.pdf

Roschelle, J., Hoadley, C., Pea, R., Gordin, D., & Means, B. (2000, Fall/Winter). Changing how and what children learn in school with collaborative cognitive technologies. *Children and Computer Technology issue of The Future of Children, 10*(2), 76-101. Los Altos, CA: The David and Lucile Packard Foundation.

Rumble, G. (2001). Reinventing distance education, 1971-2001. *International Journal of Lifelong Education, 20*(1/2), 31–43.

Saettler, P. (2004). *The Evolution of American Educational Technology.* Englewood, CO: Libraries Unlimited.

Schank, R. (2004). *Making minds less well educated than our own.* Mahwah, NJ: Erlbaum.

Schrader, P., Zheng, D., & Young, M. (2006). Teachers' perceptions of videogames: MMOGs and the future of teacher education. *Innovate Journal of Online Education, 2*(3). Retrieved September 18, 2008, from http://innovateonline.info/index.php?view= article&id=125&action=article

Schwier, R. A. (1995). Issues in emerging interactive technologies. In G. J. Anglin (Ed.), *Instructional Technology: Past, present, and future* (2nd ed., pp. 119-127). Englewood, CO: Libraries Unlimited.

Sherry, L. (1996). Issues in Distance Learning. [from http://www.cudenver.edu/ ~lsherry/ pubs/issues.html]. *International Journal of Educational Telecommunications, 1*(4), 337–365. Retrieved November 25, 2008.

Short, J., Williams, E., & Christie, B. (1976). *The social psychology of telecommunications.* London: John Wiley and Sons.

Soegaard, M. (2006). *Cognitive artifacts.* Retrieved March 19, 2009, from http://www.interactiondesign.org/encyclopedia/ cognitive_artifacts.html

Spodick, E. (1995). The evolution of distance learning. Retrieved November 24, 2008, from http://sqzm14 .ust.hk/distance/evolution-distance-learning.htm

Tabula Digita. (2009). *DimensionM.* Retrieved March 17, 2009, from http://dimensionm.com

Threlkeld, R., & Brzoska, K. (1994). Research in distance education. In B. Willis (Ed.), *Distance Education: Strategies and Tools.* Englewood Cliffs, NJ: Educational Technology Publications, Inc.

Wilkes, C., & Burnham, B. (1991). Adult learner motivations and electronics distance education. *American Journal of Distance Education, 5*(1), 43–50. doi:10.1080/08923649109526731

Williams, K. (1995). *The Incredible Machine* [Computer game]. Bellevue, WA: Sierra On-Line.

Willis, B. (1995). What's different about distant teaching? In *Strategies for Teaching at a Distance, Distance Education at a Distance, Guide 2.* Retrieved November 9, 2008, from http://www.uiweb.uidaho.edu/eo/guide2.pdf

Willis, B. (2004). Common research questions. In *Distance Education at a Glance, Guide 9: Distance Education: Research.* Retrieved December 9, 2008, from http://www.uiweb.uidaho.edu/eo/dist9.html

Chapter 5
Online Social Constructivism:
Theory Versus Practice

Jennifer Ehrhardt
netuniversity.se, Sweden; University of West Florida, USA

ABSTRACT

Renowned Soviet psychologist and father of social constructivist learning theory Lev Vygotsky (1978) stated: "Every function in the child's cultural development appears twice: first, on the social level, and later, on the individual level" (p. 57). In online practice, social constructivism involves students learning from and with each other in computer-mediated collaborative learning communities. In order for students and faculty to succeed in the online social constructivist environment these efforts demand institutional support. This chapter will introduce issues facing students and faculty that relate to the implementation of online social constructivism. Recommendations focusing on online student support and professional development will be offered as well as a discussion of future trends pointing toward a digital divide between the students of institutions who do support these practices and students of institutions in which faculty have to make do.

INTRODUCTION

Renowned Soviet psychologist and father of social constructivist learning theory Lev Vygotsky (1978) stated: "Every function in the child's cultural development appears twice: first, on the social level, and later, on the individual level" (p. 57). One of the cornerstones of Vygotsky's work is the Zone of Proximal Development (ZPD). Focusing on the potential for learner development in context of social interaction, the ZPD is "the distance between the [learner's] actual developmental level as determined by independent problem solving and the level of [the learner's] potential development as determined through problem solving under adult guidance or in collaboration with more capable peers" (Vygotsky, 1978, p. 86). The socially-based knowledge-building process of ZPD can be initiated, for instance, by group work centered around problems, case studies, simulations or projects as well as discussions

DOI: 10.4018/978-1-61520-672-8.ch005

on personal experiences, readings, resources, and learning products. In short, in online educational practice, social constructivism involves students learning from and with each other throughout the semester in computer-mediated collaborative learning communities. The following unedited quotes come from students who experienced this kind of learning environment in the author's social constructivist online course at an American community college:

- *I was able to learn more . . . in an [environment] that was non judgmental of a person but more of the interaction of thoughts and ideas.*

- *It seemed like each person had a different set of examples for each aspect of [the subject], so each [contribution] I read expanded my horizon.*

- *As I read other students' postings I could see how they were thinking, as we all perceive things differently. In essence, we have been teaching one another.*

- *I learned that giving feedback to fellow classmates is also a learning experience for yourself.*

- *At first, I didn't think I needed all that feedback, now I rely on it!* ☺

According to Storey and Tebes (2008), 3.48 million higher education students were estimated to have taken at least one online course in the fall of 2006. This high number of online course offerings coincides with the movement toward institutions of higher education becoming increasingly learning-centered. This kind of institution "places learning first, putting it at the heart of everything that the college does" (Cross, 1998, p. 5). The core principle of the learning-centered college involves all of the stakeholders asking, "Are our students learning? How do we know?" For online faculty, the question "What is the best thing I can do to help my students learn online?" is added to this collection. The current literature on best practices make

the choice clear—adhere to social constructivist learning theory. The virtues of this theory have proven themselves as per empirical research (see McKeachie, 1999; Johnson, Johnson, & Stanne, 2000) as well as practical online experience (see Harasim et al., 1995; Roberts, 2004).

Lynch (2001) reports a drop-out rate of 35-50% for online students. Commenting on the academic failures of online students, Tinto (Personal Communication, August 19, 2008) said "access without support does not constitute opportunity." This sentiment also rings true for faculty who have access to social constructivist learning theory but not the institutional support needed to implement it successfully. Online social constructivism is different from traditional educational models. Hence, the practical application of the theory needs to be supported by institutional staff and administrators based on its own premises, including technology and pedagogy-specific student and faculty preparation, course development, course support, student assessment, course evaluation, and faculty evaluation.

According to Nixon and Leftwich (2002), "collaboration and communication among faculty, staff, and administration . . . is essential in the process of creating and maintaining successful distance learning environments" (p. 23). Accordingly, the primary objective of this chapter is to begin to bridge the gap between faculty experience and administrator comprehension of online social constructivism. For faculty members who have made the leap, this kind of change is all-encompassing and irreversible. It is the basis for their personal integrity as professional educators. Thus, the secondary objective of this chapter is to offer confirmation of some of the struggles social constructivist online faculty face.

The first part of this chapter introduces the fundamental concepts that relate to online social constructivism. The second section discusses issues that pertain to online social constructivist practices, including problems relating to the student and faculty experience. In the third section, recommendations on providing quality institutional support are offered. This chapter concludes with a discussion of future trends that relate to online social constructivism and institutional support.

FUNDAMENTAL CONCEPTS

This section describes the intertwined elements relating to the application of social constructivist learning theory to the online environment. These elements include the theory of social constructivist learning, the method of computer-supported collaborative learning, and the medium of the asynchronous discussion forums.

Theory: Social Constructivism

According to social constructivist philosophy, "learning is not so much about discovering an objective 'truth' that lies somewhere 'out there' in the reality of the world, as it is about a process of making sense of a vast amount of information that surrounds us" (Cross, 1998, p. 18). In the educational arena, social constructivism "emphasizes the interdependence of the learners and the communal nature of the process of knowledge as negotiated and constructed through dialogue, problem-solving, and authentic experiences" (Comeaux, 2002, p. xxvii). As summarized by Benbunan-Fich, Hiltz, & Harasim (2005), "the learner becomes actively involved in constructing knowledge by applying concepts to problems and/or formulating ideas into words, and these ideas are elaborated on through reactions and responses of others" (p. 22).

Social constructivism can be especially useful in higher education as adult students bring experiences and perspectives shaped by unique life experiences. Each of the students have knowledge and skills that they can share while also being able to benefit from those of their classmates. Both the weaker and the stronger student benefit as a result of mechanisms that are inherit to the social constructivist process, including shared cognitive load, (Self-)explanation, and internalization (Dillenbourg, 1999). In addition, the social aspect of this learning environment facilitates an increase in motivation and the reduction of anxiety and uncertainty as the students figure things out together rather than alone (Benbunan-Fich, Hiltz, & Harasim, 2005).

The potential of social constructivist learning theory is supported in empirical research. For example, according to McKeachie (1999), "there is a wealth of evidence that peer learning and teaching is extremely effective for a wide range of goals, content, and students of different levels and personalities" (p. 159). In a meta-analysis of social constructivist learning methods, Johnson, Johnson, and Stanne (2000) concluded that the cooperative and collaborative teaching methods that had been researched produced significantly higher learning achievement than did competitive or individualistic learning.

Method: Computer-Supported Collaborative Learning

In practice online, social constructivism "urges us to forgo our traditional focus on the delivery of instruction and the design of instructional materials, and to instead approach course development in terms of creating virtual spaces that foster and support active learning" (Swan, 2005, p. 6). Any teaching technique that makes students consider the thoughts of fellow students for potential reconstitution or advancement of their own understanding can be considered social constructivist. Comeaux (2002) explains that according to social constructivism, "knowledge is constructed and negotiated in socio/cultural contexts with others in a collaborative process" (p. xxvii).

These learning activities can involve degrees of collaboration (integration), including cooperative learning (delegation) as well as knowledge building (reciprocal support). True student collaboration

69

involves "joint work on tasks, creation of shared definitions, pooling and sharing of knowledge, and creation of emergent outcomes" (Haythornthwaite, 2006, section III). Cooperative learning may involve these aspects as well, but focus less on integration of ideas and more on delegation of tasks that go toward the final learning product. Knowledge-building activities are grounded in the learning community, facilitating collective as well as individual knowledge. Scardamalia and Bereiter (1992: as summarized by Veldhuis-Diermanse, 2002) offer seven principles for the online knowledge building process: (1) treating knowledge as an object; (2) making progress; (3) encouraging synthesis; (4) consequences that make a difference; (5) contributions that matter; (6) maximizing opportunities for cross-fertilization; and (7) integrating sociality.

Through all of these synergetic activities, the sum of the learning derived from the social interactivity is greater than the total of individual learning gains had the students worked alone. As noted by the author's students, collaborative learning affects efficiency (i.e., "Everyone working together seems to accomplish more"), student interest (i.e., "It makes the work much more fun and interesting"), and the social aspect of the student experience (i.e., "I feel completely connected with everyone" and "This helps people with issues of isolation as well as in some cases selfishness").

Medium: Asynchronous Discussion Forums

When applying social constructivist learning theory to the online environment, the "collaborative strategy provides the process and structure for social interaction and technology provides the channels and modalities for communication" (Conway, 2002, p. xviii). While some faculty members may use synchronous and multimedia communication tools, most social constructivist virtual spaces are likely to be managed via asynchronous discussion forums. Harasim et al. (1995)

explain the virtue of this medium being that "the time, place, and pace of education are expanded and more individualized" (p. 12). A discussion forum is an online application that offers participants a text-based interface for electronic message posting. Discussion forums are a feature of most course management systems and can also be set up by way of blogging software. Each post can be viewed and responded to by the other participants. Depending on the software, the messages may be organized chronologically or thematically with either only the message title and author showing or the entire message showing on the discussion web page. Discussion messages can even be edited after having been posted. The two most important features of online discussion forums in creating a social constructivist learning environment are asynchronicity and text-based interaction.

Asynchronicity

The condition of asynchronicity affords the participants the freedom to participate in class discussions beyond set times. In addition, students can prepare in advance of responding by reading the assigned material and searching out additional sources on the subject at hand (Palloff & Pratt, 2001). In an asynchronous environment, all students are afforded the equal opportunity to communicate freely and continuously with each other during several days, if not weeks. Any student can respond to the communication of any other at the most advantageous time as soon as the initial prompt has been posted. This hyper democratic process can take advantage of a richer diversity of perspectives as "students who are reserved and rarely contribute in class make insightful contributions online (Clouder et al., 2006, p. 477). Students' posts can be of any length the instructor dictates or the student desires and written by way of the writing method most conducive to the individual students. The built-in reflection time engages each participant "at length and in detail in the construction of common understanding" (Benbunan-Fich, Hiltz, & Harasim, 2005, p. 22).

Text-Based Interaction

The characteristic of discussion forums being text-based offers a variety of benefits to social constructivist faculty. As asserted by Harasim et al. (1995), "the written word is uniquely suited to the construction, group revision and sharing of knowledge" (p. 3). Crafting the written message engages the student in critical thinking about the content of the text as well as its purpose and audience. The discussion threads created from participant interactions are saved in the forum beyond the time of the discussion. This archival aspect affords the students the opportunity to reread the threads as needed and reflect on "the structure and flow of the entire dialogue as a single object . . . to see the ideas in a new light" (Enyedy and Hoadley, 2006, p. 436). In line with this benefit, the participants may be able to take advantage of the intertextual phenomenon of linking posts and comments across the discussion forum in constructing their communal understanding of the subject matter. From observing these text-based interactions, the instructor can customize teaching by offering critical information and instruction as needed for individual students, a particular group of students, an entire class, or an even larger learning community.

Social constructivist education "creates changes throughout the educational system . . . altering the very tenets we hold as sacred, such as what it means to be a learner [and] how teachers teach" (Hiltz & Goldman, 2005, p. 14). Thus, switching to online social constructivism involves issues for students and faculty alike.

STUDENT ISSUES OF ONLINE SOCIAL CONSTRUCTIVIST PRACTICE

In order for the social constructivist learning process to fulfill its potential, "it is imperative that [the students] be active knowledge-generators who assume responsibility for constructing and managing their own learning experience" (Conrad & Donaldson, 2004, p. 7). More specifically, Curtis and Lawson (2001) have identified seven student behaviors as being supportive of collaborative learning: (1) giving and receiving help and assistance; (2) exchanging resources and information; (3) explaining or elaborating information; (4) sharing knowledge with others; (5) giving and receiving feedback; (6) challenging the contributions of others; and (7) advocating increased effort and perseverance among peers; and monitoring each others' efforts and contributions. And all of these unfamiliar responsibilities are to be enacted via a computer interface. Student problems relating to the online social constructivist experience involve lack of reality check, pedagogical culture shock, getting lost in cyberspace, issues of interdependence, absenteeism, and attrition.

Lack of Reality Check

Distance learning is often promoted as time-saving and convenient. As a consequence, many students misperceive online classes as being easy correspondence courses. Commenting on student propensity for assuming that online courses are easier than face-to-face courses, Hiltz and Goldman (2005) conclude that "for students who want to do as little work as possible for a course, this mode of learning may be considered a burden rather than an opportunity" (p. 13).

The online student needs to be highly motivated to learn, not just to check off another course towards graduation. On the contrary, many online students seem to be looking for a way to graduate sooner by cramming yet another online course into an already over-flowing schedule. There is also evidence of students perceiving online courses as "click 'n' easy," an opportunity for circumventing the face-to-face learning environment for an easier way out. In the reality of social constructivist online courses, however, students need to spend time in the discussion forum several times a week since "the workload in an online class . .

. is significantly higher" (p. 30) than face-to-face classes. As pointed out by Meinke (1994), student reality checking can be facilitated by institutional marketing of online courses being "realistic, clearly emphasizing the discipline and work that will be demanded" (p. 347).

Unfortunately, even if they know what they are getting in to and are highly motivated to learn, online students cannot be assumed to possess the necessary skills required to be successful in a virtual classroom (Stenerson, 1998). For example, Hiltz and Goldman (2005) share that online courses are "not appropriate for students who are deficient in basic reading, writing, and computational skills" (p. 13). Meinke (1994) acknowledges that reading and writing are skills that are frequently emphasized in online courses while also being skills that many students lack. In fact, students may be taking remedial reading and writing classes at the same time that they are taking online courses. In regard to technology, even students who are computer savvy may face difficulty in online classes because their "click-tainment" habits may compromise academic rigor. The issues associated with underprepared students become exacerbated as learning the necessary skills takes both time and energy.

Pedagogical Culture Shock

Once students are in class, social constructivist learning may cause students to experience culture shock. Students are used to teachers giving them clearly defined information directly via lecture. In contrast, the social constructivist instructor offers ill-defined problems and topics for open-ended discussion via website interfaces. When freed from the highly structured face-to-face lecture environment, students live amidst ambiguity (McManus, 2005). As opposed to learning by way of discrete units of content that start and end in intervals, social constructivist learning happens in an organic whirlwind of stimuli that flow pro-

gressively throughout the semester. As described by Hiltz (1994), "the constantly unfolding online dialogues, feedback from the instructor, and interpersonal dramas are sometimes exhilarating, often disappointing, totally unpredictable, and a constant challenge for both teacher and students" (p. 9). In fact, some students get so disoriented that their fear of not making good grades prevents them from enjoying and taking advantage of the learning process. Instead of neat and tidy accrual of grade points throughout the semester, the true benefit of the course design may not be apparent until the coursework is completed in its entirety. While all students may react strongly to this all-encompassing difference, conscientious students who have done well in the traditional setting seem to have the hardest time with this pedagogical shift.

Lost in Cyberspace

In even the most well-designed online courses, students have to navigate through a large number of web pages, and these maneuvers can be tricky. When it comes to online discussions, every point of discussion demands its own location. As much as the faculty member tries to keep the interface organized, the learning community will inevitably resemble a veritable maze with time.

In addition to being potentially confusing, the asynchronous nature of the social constructivist learning community creates a situation in which class is always in play, never at rest. Some students react to this phenomenon by being online during every possible moment. In some cases, their insistent participation is best described as an addiction. However, students are far more likely to fall behind in the continuous discussions. Trying to catch up in class by reading post after post that may have accumulated over the course of several days is overwhelming. Moreover, not all of the text is relevant. According to Haythornthwaite (2006), "the text-based environment may cause too much sharing that is too wide ranging and too encompassing to benefit the learners" (Section II.C).

Interdependent Individuals

During collaborative learning, the students depend on one another rather than the faculty member (Bruffee, 1993). Specifically, every student "must be a contributor to the evolving knowledge base of the group and not just a . . . consumer of the group's services or knowledge base" (Hunter, 2005, p. 163). In essence, all students need to act according to reciprocal altruism. According to Senge (1990), adopting this concept involves "a shift of mind—from seeing ourselves as separate from the world to connected to the world" (p. 12). This concept can perplex online students deeply as many of them choose to take online classes in the belief that their studies would be conducted in isolation. Traditionally, the only time the members of a class interact is when their grades are compared on the curve. Working together is considered cheating.

Interdependence relies on benevolence. However, as every student has the free choice to "disengage from the group or change the way they contribute" (Clouder et al., 2006, p. 477) this relationship is precarious online. For example, a student who had missed the obligatory peer feedback coursework explained the she had been "under the impression that most of the critiquing of others was optional." Likewise, another student asserted that he could not participate in the activities of the online class project because he was taking the course from overseas.

Just as with face-to-face group work, the online learning community is plagued by slackers who compromise the collaborative process. Reacting to this dilemma being magnified online, Swigonski (1994) exclaimed, "Students cannot comment on papers that have not yet been written, and they similarly cannot incorporate peer comments that do not exist!" (p. 367). As a result of a lack of

nonverbal cues to induce guilt and action such as a steely glance, crossed arms, or a sharp tone, it is harder to get participants to behave online. It is easier to ignore a call for participation when it is hosted in a discussion forum or an e-mail server rather than up close and live. When it comes to peer disapproval, help can be conveniently withheld by simply ignoring the post. Even in the case of well-intentioned participants, it is harder to negotiate collaborative activities when it takes several days to receive responses from the discussion participants.

Absenteeism

In spite of the "anywhere" opportunity afforded by distance learning, distance students have a propensity for failing to participate online a lot more often than face-to-face students fail to show up for physical class. The learning of the online students literally resides in their personal environment while the face-to-face student's learning experience is governed by academic time and space. Further, "the lives of online learners are complicated, with numerous distractions and motivational challenges" (Conrad & Donaldson, 2004, p. 19). Since online learning is a more flexible format, students seem empowered to plan events such as long trips, surgery, moves, change of employment, weddings, and births into the semester. In addition, this population seems more vulnerable to unforeseen events. Unfortunately, the consequences of absenteeism are exacerbated online because there simply is no time to waste in building a sound learning community. Students who do not stay on track gain neither the full effect of the course design nor offer their classmates needed support.

Attrition

Palloff and Pratt (2001) describe online students as older, working adults with family responsibilities. When it comes to online course withdrawal,

Conrad and Donaldson (2004) conclude that "the personal hurdles will far outweigh the technological ones" (p. 19). More specifically, Hiltz (1994) offers that the most prevalent reason for online course withdrawal is family or work emergencies. Basically, "the life situation that drew [the students] to distance learning programs to begin with may also interfere with their ability to complete them" (Palloff & Pratt, 2001, p. 47). Because of these circumstances, Diaz (2002) argues that online course withdrawal can be viewed as a mature, well-informed decision in light of these students' circumstances.

Nevertheless, the effects of student course withdrawal can be crippling to the remaining members of the learning community. The realization of the complete loss of a student may be delayed in the asynchronous environment, causing prolonged frustration on the part of the students who are relying on the missing student's participation. Ultimately, it is quite disconcerting to online students to discover that classmate after classmate has dropped out. Even when it is clear that the withdrawn students never belonged in the course at all, the morale of students as well as the faculty member can be affected.

FACULTY ISSUES OF ONLINE SOCIAL CONSTRUCTIVIST PRACTICE

Laurillard (2002) points out that the online facilitation of students' knowledge construction entails different faculty responsibilities than traditional teaching methods. In social constructivist learning environments, the primary responsibilities of the instructor include creating an online environment that fosters participation, encouraging students to discuss with one another, and enabling students to ask questions, risk judgments and opinions, and help each other (Bates & Poole, 2003). While these responsibilities are extremely different from traditional, face-to-face teaching even at the

surface-level, the real differences do not come into effect until the instructor is immersed in the new practices. Lecture notes are then replaced by almost hourly monitoring of discussion forums, second-guessing directions, pondering of student behavior, and the holding of breath in the hope that the end result is learning. The crux is that collaborative learning methods are not techniques that can be added or taken away at will. Rather, it is the channel through which the entire course flows. Faculty issues related to online social constructivism include the practice of planning the unexpected, faculty being out of control, evolutionary practice, exposure to student wrath, and lack of collegial support.

Planning the Unexpected

In a lecture situation, the instructor can explicitly select what concepts the students will be exposed to and even how those concepts are to be experienced by way of verbal and perhaps audio-visual means. In the social constructivist online course, on the other hand, the instructor is opening up the course for unexpected connections to be made by and among unsuspecting students. The primary features the instructor can rely on are the goal of the discussion forum activity, design of the discussion forum, guidelines for discussion posting behavior, and selection of the content to be discussed at what depth and breadth. Optimally, the learning experience should be organized "so that it encourages critical thinking, problem-solving, and collaborative learning skills" (Bates & Poole, 2003, p. 238). In making and implementing these choices, the instructor needs to be intuitive and creative as setting up and maintaining an online learning community is much like playing a finely-tuned instrument. One false move . . . and discord will erupt.

Out-of-Control Faculty

In the face-to-face lecture environment, it is absolutely certain that the faculty member is in control. The faculty member is the focal point of instruction. In the social constructivist learning environment, on the other hand, "the faculty member is no longer in centralized control of the instructional process" (Stenerson, 1998, para. 3.1). Instead, the spotlight moves away from the faculty member to be shared among all of the participants. The faculty member "acts as a facilitator or mentor, not a 'sage on the stage'" (Milter, 2002, p. 9). Because of purposeful peer interaction, students learn from each other rather than the instructor.

While many online courses are "canned" and ready to be rolled out from beginning to end with the click of the mouse, the social constructivist course is in perpetual and perplexing flux. The instructor always stands "ready to adjust activities as the needs of the community dictate" (Conrad & Donaldson, 2004, p. 19). Conway (2002) points out that in the online environment, the capability to "wing it" when needed to fix something on the spur of the moment is constrained both in timing and modality. What would be little more than a simple statement in a face-to-face class has to be carefully considered in an effort to prevent undue confusion as students may be working on different tasks at different paces and accessing class-related information in different ways and at different times.

Evolutionary Practitioner

Knowledge and skills related to advanced research methods come into play as assessment methods need to change radically to accurately measure and evaluate individual student's learning as well as the collective process of the learning community. Basically, just to figure out what is truly going on in class, the faculty member may need to be trained in both quantitative and qualitative research methods. Although training in these essential skills ought to be provided by the institution, faculty members are likely to have to fend for themselves. This is a daunting task, as every lead toward course improvement seems to unravel yet another thread towards dissertation-level study.

Based on inherent circumstances, online learning communities cannot be expected to work flawlessly from the get go. Instead, Draves (2002) describes the realistic progression as "first offering, awful; second offering, not so awful; third offering, not too bad; fourth offering, pretty good" (p. 148). Still, "learning by doing" social constructivism is hard online. In light of these difficulties, Dziuban, Shea, and Arbaugh (2005) warn that a social constructivist instructor is not born, but evolves over time. Meanwhile, social constructivist online practice is a high-risk activity—"Done badly, students can be confused, disoriented, and feel that they have learned nothing" (Bates & Poole, 2003, p. 163).

Exposure to Student Wrath

The virtues of social constructivist learning have proven themselves over and over in this author's experience. But, just because students get a lot out of the social constructivist learning process does not mean that they like it or respect the integrity of the faculty who uses these methods. Deep, transformative learning can be messy and even painful. If students do not "get" what the faculty member is attempting to do for them, they may view coursework as "busy work." Meinke (1994) offers examples of how students may react:

One young man, a fairly good student, insisted that the course required more time than he could afford and much more than other classes . . . Several others felt that the number of assignments were too demanding. In reality I know that most students spent less time on this course than they did in almost any other class. (p. 343)

Meinke concluded that the either the students had not taken other courses that were very demanding, or they were frustrated because the course demanded an unusual degree of self-discipline on their part.

What is worse, some students may view collaborative learning as unfair and even repulsive (Hiltz, 1994). They may even feel cheated by the process (Palloff & Pratt, 2001). Some of these students may choose to lash out. For example, Palloff and Pratt (2001) describe a situation in which two students "flamed" (made a derogatory comment toward) the instructor in the discussion forum. This controversy caused participation to dwindle, never to reach acceptable levels again. As pointed out by Clouder et al. (2006), "emotion that escalates beyond anxiety can get in the way of learning" (p. 473).

Lack of Collegial Support

Teaching can certainly be a lonely occupation. Online teaching can certainly be an even lonelier occupation, especially as the "by far the most common model of online course development is the Lone Ranger approach" (Bates & Poole, 2003, p. 139). Queering chief academic officers about their perceptions of faculty members' acceptance of the value and legitimacy of online learning, Allen and Seaman (2008) found that "associate's institutions show the highest agreement with this statement (72.8 percent) with those at baccalaureate schools having only 39.5 percent agreement" (p. 16). This situation begs to address the question—How can the online instructor possibly be regarded as a competent educator by colleagues if what they do on a daily basis is neither valued nor considered legitimate? This author has been privy to multiple conversations in the faculty lounge as well as public statements in the school paper indicating the consensus that "learning cannot take place online." The heart-ache of peer dismissal was so paramount to Mitner (2002) that the "Lesson Learned" section of one of his articles focused on

this problem in context of a social constructivist online course: "There will always be closed-minded individuals in the ranks of the academy who feel threatened by educational innovations" (p. 20). Whether due to fear or ignorance, McManus (2005) confirms the potential dangers of making waves among colleagues: "If you have not yet attained tenure, and if the senior faculty in your department are known to oppose innovative teaching . . . be careful. Know the politics of your department" (p. 124).

RECOMMENDATIONS

Online social constructivism holds great hope for the future, but only if well supported at the institutional level. In fact, "without appropriate organizational support for technology-based teaching, the workload of university and college teachers becomes impossible" (Bates & Poole, 2003, p. 103). Basically, a total restructuring of higher education is needed to embrace emerging computer-mediated pedagogical practices. Such an effort ought to include the establishment of an adaptive technological and institutional infrastructure, timely personal mentoring for every faculty member regardless of course format and pedagogical inclination, a 24/7 technological help desk for students and faculty, fair compensation for online course development and facilitation, and fair recognition of online faculty excellence. However, there are two institutional responsibilities in particular that require immediate attention in regard to the practice of online social constructivism: prospective online student support and professional development in online pedagogy.

Prospective Online Student Support

The bottom line is clear, "unless the student has at least the minimal required level of motivation and ability to do the required activities in a course, he or she will fail to reach a satisfactory level of learning" (Benbunan-Fich, Hiltz, & Harasim, 2005, pp. 223-24). At the most basic level, online learning is about student fit. Just because students in open access institutions *can* register to take online courses does not mean that they *should be able to do so* without a meaningful reality check. It is simply awful to observe student after student failing to make academic progress because the institution offered an opportunity they were unprepared to take advantage of and were too desperate to resist. Fact is, online learning simply is not appropriate for all students (Hiltz, 1994; Palloff & Pratt, 2001).

The responsibility to make student access a realistic opportunity rests squarely with the institution, especially with the individuals who hold positions that can affect the circumstances surrounding the online student and faculty. Just as advanced courses have pre-requisites, so should online courses. Hiltz and Shea (2005) point out that "students' prior experiences with distance learning courses increase their familiarity with the technological demands of the virtual classroom and their confidence in their ability to take advantage of online learning opportunities available to them" (p. 152). To capitalize on this phenomenon, institutions should require prospective online students to experience online learning in order to earn eligibility to register for online courses. This venture can be set up as a pre-registration Orientation for Online Students or a for-credit Online Student Success course. For example, North Carolina State University instituted a 1-credit online orientation course for students who were new to online learning (Bozarth, Chapman, & LaMonica, 2004). Similarly, Pennsylvania State University has mandated that students attend Online Learning 101 prior to taking online courses.

Conducting these orientation activities online affords the students the opportunity to figure out the technology and pedagogy in the most authentic setting. Regardless of format, at a minimum, this venture should include assessment of necessary computer skills and equipment, experiences relating to the differences between the online and face-to-face formats, and experience with learning tasks derived from a variety of learning theories conducive to distance learning and practice.

Professional Development in Online Pedagogy

One of the fundamental principles of the learning-centered paradigm is that every single member of the institution is responsible for supporting student learning. To apply this process to online learning, all faculty, staff, and administrators who have anything at all to do with the online student and faculty populations should be required to pursue professional development in online pedagogy. Accordingly, at a minimum, this venture should include awareness of necessary computer skills and equipment, the differences between the online and face-to-face formats, and how different learning theories and technologies affect the learning and teaching experience and need for support.

In regard to faculty, Bates and Poole (2003) assert that all instructors in higher education should receive training in education as a prerequisite for teaching with technology. Palloff and Pratt (2001) add that online faculty should receive instruction in techniques for course development, facilitation, and community building. For best practices see *Learning Networks: A Field Guide to Teaching and Learning Online* by Harasim et al. (1995) and *e-Moderating* by Salomon (2000).

Further, to prevent discrimination, all members of the institution who participate in student assessment, course evaluations, faculty evaluation, and promotion efforts should be required to take advantage of professional development related to what constitutes excellence in student and course outcomes and faculty competence depending on course format and pedagogical design.

The optimal medium for this training program is the institution's online course management system. Since no faculty member should be forced to adhere to a certain learning theory, the training ought to be conducted by way of best practices based on several different theories. This way, the participants can gain first-hand experience in the technology as well as different pedagogical methods.

FUTURE TRENDS

There are reasons to be optimistic for the future when it comes to support for online social constructivist learning practices in the global arena. Researchers are increasingly focusing their attention on the nitty-gritty of the student learning experience and the faculty teaching experience in asynchronous discussion forums. Scholarly developments also include the construction of increasingly precise theories to develop instruments for student assessment, course evaluations, and faculty evaluations. Technology experts around the world are working hard to evolve the current hardware and software as well as creating new tools toward increased support for large, multi-generational learning communities that may grow in an organic fashion.

In contrast, at the level of individual faculty members, there are compelling reasons for protecting the progress that has been made and guarding against compromise of the online social constructivist practices. From this author's perspective, the student population that is entering higher education now expresses an even stronger sense of entitlement to "ATM teaching" than the already self-indulgent past generations; administrative pressures to retain students from "click 'n' easy" online coursework is becoming increasingly persuasive; and the technical support staff is becoming increasingly overtaxed from the institution increasing online sections. These pressures have resulted in colleagues backing away from social constructivist practices even when they make the most pedagogical sense.

In 2001, Palloff and Pratt brought up the concept of "Have" and "Have-Not" institutions representing a rift between those that have the money to enter the distance education market and those that do not. However, "with growth of online course enrollments outpacing enrollments in traditional courses by 500%," (Weisenmayer, Kupczynski, & Ice, 2008, p. 1) the choice to go online seems to be forced upon higher education institutions whether they have the means and wherewithal or not. The tension between the pressures to serve the online student population and the poor preparation of the institution to do so inevitably manifests itself in the position of the online faculty. As a result, a new dimension of the digital divide has developed between the students whose faculty has the support they need to provide the best possible learning environment they can for their students and the students whose faculty had to make do with what their institutions are willing to support. Without vigilance on the part of the online learning and teaching process, "the online class might amount to little more than knowing where to click within a labyrinth of links" (Bender, 2003, p. xv). In short, education is at stake.

CONCLUSION

Students who have participated in a successful online social constructivist experience recognize the depth of the knowledge and skills they acquired through social interactions with their online peers. This is evident in the following unedited comments made by students in this author's social constructivist course:

- *The . . . interaction with other students . . . has drastically influenced my learning in this course.*
- *I have learned so much in this class! I never thought I would.*

- *In most classes, students learn some of the material but it seems to be stored only temporarily. I have confidence that the material I studied in this class will be carried with me.*
- *It's one thing to read the material and absorb it for what it is, but it's a completely different story when you discuss, review, revise and gain feedback from others. . . . We learn, grow.*

The final result of their combined efforts—whether tangible in a final product or knowledge building—is a tremendous source of pride for the students who were engaged. In turn, reading the "We did it!" posts in the discussion forums is a tremendous source of pride to social constructivist instructors. As faculty members in learning-centered institutions, social constructivist online instructors are grounded in solid theory as long as they can offer evidence of their students having learned. And every once in a while, students even express their recognition of hard work well done: "I'm really glad that the teacher cares about our learning experience and wants us to understand every concept . . . clearly."

Nevertheless, applying social constructivist learning theory to the online environment is a difficult task. This chapter was written with the hope that its content can offer insight into the struggles within and surrounding social constructivist online learning communities. Still, even faculty members in "Make Do" institutions can make the best of their situation by sharing their perspectives and dealing proactively with their unique needs for support by working with staff and administration. Luckily, as Conway (2002) reminds us, collaboration "creates a final result that is greater than the sum of its parts" (p. xvii).

REFERENCES

Alavi, M. (1994, June). Computer-mediated collaborative learning: An empirical evaluation. *MIS Quarterly*, *18*(2), 159–174. doi:10.2307/249763

Bates, A. W., & Poole, G. (2003). *Effective teaching with technology in higher education: Foundations for success*. San Francisco: John Wiley & Sons, Inc.

Benbunan-Fich, R., Hiltz, R., & Harasim, L. (2005). The online interaction learning model: An integrated theoretical framework for learning networks. In S. R. Hiltz & R. Goldman (Eds.), *Learning together online: Research on asynchronous learning networks* (pp. 19-37). Mahwah, NJ: Lawrence Erlbaum.

Bender, T. (2003). *Discussion-based online teaching to enhance student learning: Theory, practice, and assessment* (1st ed.). Sterling, VA: Stylus Publishing, LLC.

Bozarth, J., Chapman, D. D., & LaMonica, L. (2004). Preparing for distance learning: Designing an online student orientation course. *Educational Technology & Society*, *7*(1), 87–106.

Bruffee, K. A. (1993). *Collaborative learning: Higher education, interdependence, and the authority of knowledge*. Baltimore, MD: The Johns Hopkins University Press.

Clouder, L., Dalley, J., Hargreaves, J., Parkes, S., Sellars, J., & Toms, J. (2006). Electronic reconstitution of groups: Group dynamics from face-to-face to an online setting. *Computer-Supported Collaborative Learning*, *1*(1), 467–480. doi:10.1007/s11412-006-9002-0

Comeaux, P. (2002). Introduction. In P. Comeaux (Ed.), *Communication and collaboration in the online classroom: Examples and applications* (pp. xxv-xxxiv). Boston, MA: Anker Publishing Company, Inc.

Conrad, R. M., & Donaldson, J. A. (2004). *Engaging the online learner: Activities and resources for creative instruction.* San Francisco: Jossey-Bass.

Conway, K. L. (2002). Foreword. In P. Comeaux (Ed.), *Communication and collaboration in the online classroom: Examples and applications* (pp. xvii-xix). Boston, MA: Anker Publishing Company, Inc.

Cross, K. P. (1998, June). *Opening windows on learning* (The Cross Papers Number 2). Alliance for Community College Innovation. Mission Viejo, CA: League for Innovation in the Community College Educational Testing Service.

Curtis, D. D., & Lawson, M. J. (2001, February). Exploring collaborative online learning. *Journal of Asynchronous Learning Networks, 5*(1), 21–34.

Diaz, D. P. (2002, May/June). Online drop rates revisited. *The Technology Source.* Retrieved March 20, 2009, from http://technologysource.org/article/online_drop_rates_revisited

Dillenbourg, P. (Ed.). (1999). *Collaborative learning: Cognitive and computational approaches.* New York: Pergamon.

Draves, W. A. (2002). *Teaching online* (2nd Ed.). River Falls, WI: LERN.

Dziuban, C., Shea, P., & Arbaugh, J. B. (2005). Faculty roles and satisfaction in asynchronous learning networks. In S. R. Hiltz, & R. Goldman (Eds.), *Learning together online: Research on asynchronous learning networks* (pp. 169-190). Mahwah, NJ: Lawrence Erlbaum.

Enyedy, N., & Hoadley, C. M. (2006). From dialogue to monologue and back: Middle spaces in computer-mediated learning. *Computer-Supported Collaborative Learning, 1*(1), 413–439. doi:10.1007/s11412-006-9000-2

Harasim, L., Hiltz, S. R., Teles, L., & Turoff, M. (1995). *Learning networks: A field guide to teaching and learning online.* Cambridge, MA: The MIT Press.

Haythornthwaite, C. (2006, February). Facilitating collaboration in online learning. *Journal of Asynchronous Learning, 10*(1). Retrieved on December 31, 2008, from http://www.sloan-c.org/publications/jaln/index.asp

Hiltz, S. R. (1994). *The virtual classroom: Learning without limits via computer networks.* Norwood, NJ: Ablex Publishing Corporation.

Hiltz, S. R., & Goldman, R. (2005). Learning together online: Research on asynchronous learning networks. In S. R. Hiltz & R. Goldman (Eds.), *Learning together online: Research on asynchronous learning networks* (pp. 3-18). Mahwah, NJ: Lawrence Erlbaum Associates.

Hiltz, S. R., & Shea, P. (2005). The student in the online classroom. In S. R. Hiltz & R. Goldman (Eds.), *Learning together online: Research on asynchronous learning networks* (pp. 145-168). Mahwah, NJ: Lawrence Erlbaum.

Hunter, B. (2005). Learning, teaching, and building knowledge: A forty-year quest for online learning communities. In G. Kearsley (Ed.), *Online learning: Personal reflections on the transformation of education* (pp.163-193). Englewood Cliffs, NJ: Educational Technology Publications.

Johnson, D. W., Johnson, R. T., & Stanne, M. B. (2000). *Cooperative learning methods: A meta-analysis.* University of Minnesota, Minneapolis, MN: Cooperative Learning Center. Retrieved March 26, 2009, from http://www.cooperation.org/pages/cl-methods.html

Laurillard, D. (2002). *Rethinking university teaching: A conversational framework for the effective use of learning technologies* (2nd ed.). New York: Routledge Falmer.

Lynch, M. M. (November/December, 2001). Effective student preparation for online learning. *The Technology Source*. Retrieved March 31, 2009, from http://technologysource.org/article/effective_student_preparation_for_online_learning/

McKeachie, W. J. (Ed.). (1999). *McKeachie's teaching tips: Strategies, research and theory for college and university teachers* (10th ed.). Boston, MA: Houghton Mifflin.

McManus, D. A. (2005). *Leaving the lectern: Cooperative learning and the critical first days of students working in groups*. Boston, MA: Anker Publishing Company, Inc.

Meinke, R. J. (1994). Appendix III: Introductory Sociology with EIES. In S. R. Hiltz (Ed.), *The virtual classroom: Learning without limits via computer networks* (pp. 334-348). Norwood, NJ: Ablex Publishing Corporation.

Milter, R. G. (2002). Developing an MBA online degree program: Expanding knowledge and skills via technology-mediated learning communities. In P. Comeaux (Ed.), *Communication and collaboration in the online classroom: Examples and application* (pp. 3-22). Boston, MA: Anker Publishing Company, Inc.

Nixon, M. A., & Leftwich, B. R. (2002). Collaborative instructional design for an internet-based graduate degree program. In P. Comeaux (Ed.), *Communication and collaboration in the online classroom: Examples and applications* (pp. 23-38). Boston, MA: Anker Publishing Company, Inc.

Palloff, R. M., & Pratt, K. (2001). *Lessons from the cyberspace classroom: The realities of online teaching*. San Francisco: Jossey-Bass Publishers.

Roberts, T. S. (Ed.). (2004). *Online collaborative learning: Theory and practice*. Hershey, PA: Information Science Publishing.

Senge, P. M. (1990). *The fifth discipline: The art & practice of the learning organization*. New York: Currency Doubleday.

Stenerson, J. (1998). Systems analysis and design for a successful distance education program implementation. *Online Journal of Distance Learning Administration, 1*(2). Retrieved October 15, 2008, from http://www.westga.edu/%7Edistance/ojdla/summer12/stener12.html

Storey, V. A., & Tebes, M. L. (2008, Summer). Instructor's privacy in distance (online) teaching: Where do you draw the line? *Online Journal of Distance Learning Administration, 11*(2). Retrieved December 31, 2008, from http://www.westga.edu/%7Edistance/ojdla/summer112/storey112.html

Swan, K. (2005). A constructivist model for thinking about learning online. In J. Bourne & J. C. Moore (Eds.), *Elements of quality online education: Engaging communities*. Needham, MA: Sloan-C. Retrieved March 31, 2009, from http://www.kent.edu/rcet/Publications/upload/constructivist%20theory.pdf

Swigonski, M. (1994). Appendix III: Peer writing groups in the virtual classroom. In S. R. Hiltz (Ed.), *The virtual classroom: Learning without limits via computer networks* (pp. 363-368). Norwood, NJ: Ablex Publishing Corporation.

Velduis-Diermanse, A. E. (2002). *Csclearing? Participation, learning activities and knowledge construction in computer-supported collaborative learning in higher education*. Unpublished doctoral dissertation, Wageningen University.

Vygotsky, L. S. (1978). Internalization of higher psychological functions. In M. Cole, V, John-Steiner, S. Scribner, & E. Souberman (Eds.), *Mind in society: The Development of higher psychological processes* (pp. 53-57). Cambridge, MA: Harvard University Press.

Weisenmayer, R., Kupczynski, L., & Ice, P. (2008, Winter). The role of technical support and pedagogical guidance provided to faculty in online programs: Considerations for higher education administrators. *Online Journal of Distance Learning Administration, 11*(4). Retrieved December 31, 2008, from http://www.westga.edu/~distance/ojdla/winter114/wiesenmayer114.html

Chapter 6
Employing Technology to Create Authentic Learning Environments

Drew Polly
University of North Carolina at Charlotte, USA

ABSTRACT

The increased access to technologies in schools has opened avenues to explore non-traditional styles of teaching and learning. Educational theorists and researchers have long been calling for learner-centered instruction that situates learners in activities that allow them to explore concepts and construct understanding. However, as constructivist theorists and researchers continue to show the benefits of situating learning in meaningful tasks, many barriers still prevent the use of technology-enhanced authentic activities in classrooms (Ertmer, 2005; Shaw, 2003). This chapter aims to analyze the underlying theories of authentic learning and propose methods to support classroom teachers with the design, implementation and assessment of authentic activities.

TECHNOLOGY IN SCHOOLS

Access to technologies in K-12 schools continues to increase. Each year, more money is spent on hardware, software programs and technology-related infrastructure. These vast amounts of money are being invested on educational technologies with the expectation that both teaching and student learning will change for the better. While research indicates that access to technology helps teachers reconsider how their instruction can be more student-centered (Ringstaff, Yokam, & Marsh, 1995), most technology is integrated in teacher-centered, didactic ways (Ertmer, 2005; Wenglinsky, 1999; Mann, 1999). Becker and Ravitz (2001) surveyed secondary teachers and found that less than 25 percent of them were using computers on a weekly basis to enhance instruction. In most cases the technology is used in drill and practice settings, rather than promoting process or higher-order thinking skills (Becker, 2001; Shaw, 2003).

Simultaneous with the increased access to educational technologies, education reforms have called for a paradigm shift towards more learner-centered,

DOI: 10.4018/978-1-61520-672-8.ch006

constructivist-oriented learning environments (Bransford, Brown, & Cocking, 2000; McCombs & Whisler, 1997; Polly, 2008). According to McCombs & Whisler (1997; McCombs, 2003) in learner-centered environments, students:

- learn concepts by completing relevant tasks
- have some ownership of how they learn or how they demonstrate their understanding
- use appropriate resources, including technology, to support learning
- are facilitated by teachers who model and scaffold students' work
- make connections between concepts and authentic situations

In this chapter I use the idea of anchored instruction (Bransford, Sherwood, Hasselbring, Kinzer, & Williams, 1990) to explicate the idea of using technology to connect concepts to authentic situations. An explanation of anchored instruction and authentic learning environments is followed with examples from K-12 schools. Lastly, implications for anchored instruction are discussed.

Anchored Instruction

The promise of anchored instruction, called for teachers to leverage technologies in ways to anchor learning in authentic environments. Bransford et al. (1990) contended that video discs and other technologies can be employed to anchor instruction in authentic tasks. Hannafin (1992) advocated using electronic tools and resources in open-ended learning environments (*OELEs)* to allow students to investigate real-life problems. Bransford and his colleagues in the Cognition and Technology Group at Vanderbilt (CTGV) (1992, 1997) provided a significant bridge from theory to practice with the *Jasper* series, a set of videodiscs that anchors mathematical problem solving in authentic narratives. Students watched the videodisc, then identified and solve problems that were embedded

in the story. The *Jasper* series was the first of many technology-rich activities that attempt to situate learning in authentic contexts. CTGV's endeavor to promote authenticity via technology has been promoted by other researchers (see Griesser, 2001; Herrington & Oliver, 1999; Shyu, 2000).

Those studies continue to support the effectiveness of student learning in technology-enhanced authentic learning environments (CTGV, 1992; Grieser, 2001; Shyu, 2000). Such an onslaught of research, however, begs the questions: what theories are underpinning the notion of authentic activities, and if authentic learning is such an effective method of instruction, why isn't everyone using it?

THEORIES OF AUTHENTICITY

Anchored instruction builds off of the concept of authentic learning environments. The term authenticity has become commonplace in education, yet its definition remains obscure and undefined (Barab, Squire, & Dueber, 2000). Authentic learning environments, traditionally, describe structured activities that have meaningful context (Radinsky et al., 1998). The term "meaningful context", however, is not the same for all people. For example, while investigating the migrating patterns of buffalo may be authentic for children in the midwest, that activity lacks meaning for students who live in a fishing village on the coast of the Atlantic Ocean. Authenticity lies in the eyes of the beholder, since an experience is authentic if and only if the learner can derive meaning from the experience (Barab & Duffy, 2000).

Authentic learning is akin to Dewey's (1910/1978)'s notion of learning through experience, as well as Vygotsky's theory of social learning (1987). Dewey cited the importance of learning through various experiences in life that the learner can participate in. Vygotsky (1987), meanwhile, contends that schooling should introduce learners into various communities of practitioners. In science education courses, Vygotsky would advocate participation in experiences of scientific investigation and inquiry that resemble the activities that practitioners engage in.

When schooling is based on authentic tasks, students become more responsibility for their learning, and actively participate in the collection and analysis of information, as they seek ways to solve specific problems. Most activities bridge many disciplines, bridging numerous content areas, thus enabling them to master content more effectively (Barab and Linda, 2000; Brown, Collins and Duguid, 1989).

Paradoxically, education primarily remains the home of abstract and decontextualized instruction. Brown et al. (1989) concluded that school activities lack value in the real-world, since formal schooling has very little transfer to real-world practice and they contended (p. 36) that "success within school often has little bearing on performance elsewhere." Recent studies (Becker, 2001; Greisser, 2001; Shaw, 2003; Shyu, 2000) have confirmed that although instruction has become more engaging for learners, classrooms still remain a place where students engage primarily in drill and practice activities, providing minimal transfer to real-world settings. In order to transfer to real-world contexts to occur, instruction should be situated in contexts that are as life-like as possible.

Components of Authentic Learning Environments

The literature cites four primary components about authentic environments. These components were identified from Bransford et al.'s (1990) notion of anchored instruction, as well as other writings about authentic learning and situated learning.

Meaningful Tasks

From a constructivist perspective, learners actively create their own understanding of concepts (Scardamalia & Bereiter, 1996). By participating in meaningful tasks, learners are engaged and interested in the task as well as the relation of the task to the world (Bransford et al., 1990). Situated theorists (Brown et al., 1989; Lave & Wenger, 1991) view learning as part of a cognitive apprenticeship, in which learners form a deeper understanding of the work of practitioners. For K-12 learners, meaningful tasks hold different meanings for different students. An authentic task about the geography of the coastal plain of North Carolina will have different amounts of meaning for students living in that area compared to students living in the mountains of North Carolina. Fundamentally, for K-12 learners, meaningful tasks maintain the interest of students and encourage the transfer of knowledge from the learning environment to other situations.

Open-Ended Learning Environments (OELEs)

Authentic learning environments should be open-ended, allowing learners to use resources and complete tasks in multiple ways (Greeno, 1998; Hannafin, 1992). OELEs support a comprehensive learning process, in which learners to examine a meaningful task, choose how to complete it, use appropriate resources and then make sense of their learning. Tasks in OELEs should emphasize the problem solving process, rather than encouraging the student to simply find the correct answer. In K-12 learning environments, learners should have access to educational technologies and web-based resources that they can use to support task completion.

Scaffolds to Support Students

Adequate support must be provided for learners that are engaging in meaningful tasks that are open-ended. Proponents of anchored instruction charge teachers with the responsibilities for designing and supporting tasks (Bransford et al., 1990). Task support includes a variety of scaffolds, such as modeling, providing resources, asking guiding questions and providing just-in-time help (Oliver & Hannafin, 2001). Vygotsky (1918/1987) posited that all learners have a zone of proximal development, which describes the range of tasks that learners can complete with the support of a more knowledgeable other. This idea has been extended by some that view teaching as "assisted performance" where teachers support learning by designing tasks and providing scaffolds during the learning process.

Opportunities to Reflect

Authentic learning environments must also include opportunities to help students reflect on their learning and their process of completing authentic tasks (Brush, 2003; Herrington & Oliver, 1999). Reflective thinking should encourage learners to think about the problem-solving process and reason through other points of view. Reflection increases the likelihood of knowledge being more connected to other concepts, and of transfer of knowledge to similar situations (Brush, 2003).

Examples of Authentic Learning Environments

While the idea of authentic learning is promising, teachers are unlikely to employ such activities without concrete examples. Below are two examples, one for seventh grade mathematics and one for a high school government class.

Seventh grade mathematics: You receive a credit card in the mail. The credit card has a minimum payment of $25 a month and a 10% annual interest rate. You want to buy a $600 entertainment system. If you earn $50 a month babysitting, examine your options of paying off the bill? Which option is the cheapest? If you only made $30 a month babysitting, how would the price you paid for the entertainment system change?

First, the task has authenticity and relevance, as students must form an understanding of credit,

debt and interest. The activity is open-ended with many ways to solve this problem. Activities such as this lend themselves to employing a spreadsheet to provide a visual representation of the data, as well as explore various variables that affect the problem, such as how much of the debt is paid each month. The teacher can serve as a scaffold, providing support on identifying the problem, choosing an approach to the problem and key questions to focus on throughout the activity. The use of a spreadsheet or table can also scaffold learning, by providing a display of data that the learner can manipulate in order to find a solution. This activity also has the potential to be reflective as well. A spreadsheet or calculator will allow students to collect data for various situations, such as 1) paying off the debt as soon as possible, 2) paying slightly more than the minimum payment or 3) paying only the minimum payment. Comparing the various scenarios enables the learner to choose which option is the best, and allows generalizations to drawn from that information.

While authentic learning activities are pretty realistic in mathematics, other life-like situations can also created for other subjects.

High School government: *You are the campaign manager for Douglas Dooright, a candidate for U.S. President. The Presidential Election will be on November 6th. Douglas will by flying around the country making his final bid for votes from October 29-November 5. If he can only make three speeches a day and has only $12,000 to spend on airfare, what will his itemized travel budget look like? Explain why you chose to travel to each location.*

The task described is life-like and meaningful, as the learner takes on the role of a campaign manager, planning the speech schedule for a presidential candidate. This activity builds on skills such as scheduling, money management, and comparing travel fares, which are all meaningful tasks to high school age students. This activity is extremely open-ended, allowing students to decide when traveling occurs, where they will travel and which airfare to use. Once again, the teacher has the potential to serve as a scaffold, as students interpret the problem, choose their approach, and make decisions during their activity. Technology, mainly the World Wide Web, also scaffolds learning by providing just-in-time information on electoral votes, key locations and travel fares whenever the students need it. While, the immediate access to information helps the student in the activity, it has the potential to be a hindrance. Oliver and Hannafin (1999) cited dilemmas with students with managing information in OELE's as learners became inundated with data. This problem can be lessened if the learner participates in reflection and focuses on the problem solving process. Each student is going to have a different travel schedule, since there are numerous cities and numerous airline flights each day. The learning that occurs is not simply how to design a travel itinerary, but how to engage in data-based decision making and support their choices in a logical manner.

Technology's Role in Authentic Learning Environments

Technology has promise to support the enactment of authentic activities in K-12 schools. While authentic learning environments were and are possible in absence of educational technologies, technology supports authentic learning environments by providing immediate access to information, dynamic tools to support task completion, flexibility for students' work in OELE's, and more options for students to create artifacts of knowledge.

In the first example, the use of a spreadsheet allows students to visual represent their investigation in a chart. By using a spreadsheet, students can set up the chart using formulas and investigate scenarios based on how much they pay each month. A calculator could also be used instead of a spreadsheet. But, while a calculator facilitates the calculation of interest and payment, it does not provide a dynamic representation in the form of a chart like a spreadsheet. Without the use of a spreadsheet the activity could be completed, but becomes more focused on performing calculations, rather than representing a problem and making data-based decisions.

In the second activity, the Internet and airfare websites such as www.orbitz.com students have access to airfares quickly. Further, internet-based mapping programs, such as Google Maps can provide information regarding mileage and distance traveled. Students will also want to examine information regarding the electoral college and determine what states had the most value for them, in terms of campaigning. After the necessary information is gathers, a spreadsheet could then be used to store their records and keep a running tally of their travel budget. The process of completing this activity resembles a traditional Webquest (Dodge, 2003), in which students use the Internet to find information and apply it to solve a problem.

In both activities, access to technology is essential. Students must not only be able to get to the technology, but also must have the requisite knowledge to complete the activities (NRC, 2002). In both activities, the requisite knowledge includes being able to set up and manipulate a spreadsheet. The second activity also requires the student to know how to search the Internet for information.

Technology skills are now a part of curricula nationwide, as students learn word processing skills, how to work with spreadsheets, and how to create products such as presentations and webpages (ISTE, 2008; Sargent, 2003). Employing technology-rich authentic activities supports research (NRC, 2002; Market Data Retrieval, 2002) that students should learn these technologies by using them in life-like contexts.

Table 1. Processes of Enacting Authentic Learning Environments

Barrier	Requisite knowledge	Citations
The Design of Authentic Activities	Educators that are incorporating authentic activities into their instruction must be able to: 1) select realistic situations to serve as the context of learning, 2) establish scaffolds to facilitate learning, and 3) design and develop materials to support learning in an authentic context	Barab et al., 2000; Bruning, 1999; CTGV, 1992; Jonassen & Reeves, 1996; Young, 1993;
The Implementation of Authentic Activities	Educators that are incorporating authentic activities into their instruction must be: 1) a facilitator of knowledge construction rather than a dispenser of information, 2) able to scaffold learning, gradually leading students to successful completion of tasks independently 3) able to provide learners with a model of effective strategies	CTGV, 1992; Dodge, 2003; Lave & Wegner, 1991; Moore et. al, 1994; Young, 1993;
The Evaluation of Learning in Authentic Activities	Educators implementing authentic activities must be able to: 1) assess learning in a context similar to that which learning took place 2) identify the criteria upon which the students will be graded 2) evaluate both the final product and process of each student's learning	CTGV, 1992; Dodge, 2003; Moore et. al, 1994; SCANS, 1991; Scardamalia, M, & Bereiter, 1996;

Processes of Enacting Authentic Learning Activities

Authentic activities provide ample opportunity for learning both content and technological skills. These environments situate learning in real-life contexts, which allows students to draw connections between formal education and the real world. However, it would be naïve to not address the processes and associated obstacles that educators face incorporating authentic learning activities into their classrooms. The processes that educators encounter focus on three major areas of authentic activities: the design, the implementation and the assessment of learning. Table 1 provides an overview of these processes.

These processes are closely related to the knowledge that teachers possess. Recently, much has written about teachers' technological pedagogical and content knowledge (TPCK), various components of teachers' knowledge that are related to the successful integration of technology into their classroom (Mishra & Koehler, 2006; Neiss, 2005; Polly & Mims, 2009).

The TPCK framework posits that teachers possess various components of knowledge related to technology, content and pedagogy, and the intersections of those components (e.g., technology and content). In this section I describe the barriers to authentic learning in the context of the TPACK framework.

Design of Authentic Activities

In order for learning to be situated in authentic contexts, teachers must carefully consider contexts that are both authentic and appropriate for their learners. This process requires knowledge of both content (CK) and pedagogy (PK) and the interplay between effective pedagogies for the content that teachers expect students to learn (PCK). If these authentic activities are technology-rich, teachers also then need knowledge of various technologies (TK) how technologies support the learning of content (TCK), and ways to design activities in which technology supports the learning of content (TPACK). While aspects of the TPACK framework are included in the design of authentic activities, teachers' knowledge of content and technology are emphasized more in this part of implementation.

Traditional teacher education programs train pre-service teachers to employ or slightly modify previously created curricula materials that meet the learning objectives of their students (CEO Forum, 1999). Examples of these include textbooks, practice exercises and computer activities. The promise of authentic learning activities hinges on teachers' knowledge related to designing effective tasks. Learner-centered and constructivist epistemologies influence teacher education programs (Bransford et al., 1999; Mouza, 2002). These programs, however, are relatively ineffective at influencing teacher practice since these programs typically prepare teachers out of the context of their classroom, fail to present concrete examples of authentic, and lack adequate practice and support for teachers as they reenter their classroom and attempt to design such activities (Mouza, 2002, Orrill, 1999).

Teachers that situate learning in authentic contexts must be able to scaffold instruction effectively (CTGV, 1992). In authentic learning activities, although students are completing an authentic task, teachers often over teach and instruction reverts back to traditional instructional methods (Barab et al., 2000; Polly, 2006). On the other hand, teachers can also err by providing no support at all, leaving students floundering and in need of guidance (Bruning, 1999). The teacher's role in the implementation of authentic learning activities will be discussed later.

The final dilemma that educators face in designing authentic learning environments is the amount of planning time that is required for the design and development of materials. Teachers must weigh the options between the use of pre-existing and teacher-created materials (CTGV, 1992; Young, 1993). Ideally, teachers would be able to use their planning time to create authentic learning activities and the materials to support them, but that is currently not the case in education. The constraints on a teacher's time to plan instruction results in the employment of materials that are provided by the school, traditionally based on the pedagogy of direct instruction and practice.

Implementation of Authentic Activities

Situating learning in authentic settings has many implications the role of educators during instruction. Literature concerning open-ended learning environments consistently depicts reluctant teachers, who cling to traditional instructional methods, such as drill and practice, rather than situating their students in learning that is more investigation-based and authentic in context (Becker, 2001; R. Hannafin, Burruss, & Little, 1999). Even when curricula or the design of learning environments is learner-centered, teachers still enact teacher-centered pedagogies (Polly, 2006; Stein, Grover, & Henningsen, 1996).

The enactment of authentic activities hinges primarily on teachers' knowledge related to pedagogy and its intersection with other components of the TPACK framework. Knowledge of pedagogy (PK), when enacted in classrooms, reflects teachers' ability to use effective pedagogies. In classrooms' PK is never isolated, but always is accompanied with content (PCK) and in some cases technology and content (TPCK). Therefore, teachers need opportunities to develop their knowledge of pedagogy with specific content and also related to potentially-effective educational technologies.

The most difficult adjustment for teachers used to traditional teaching is the shift from serving as a dispenser of knowledge to a facilitator of learning (Bruning, 1999). Lave and Wegner (1991) noted that authentic learning in non-traditional settings, such as apprenticeships, place the trainer or supervisor in the role of an expert who models best practices and serves as a resource for the learners. These experts facilitate the apprentice by scaffolding learning, leading the learner from needing complete guidance to a condition of self-sufficiency (CTGV, 1991; Greeno et al., 1998; Vygotsky, 1987). Lave and Wegner (1991) discuss the apprentice in a tailor shop. Learning would begin with the simple, yet authentic task of making straight stitches on fabric. The supervisor would then gradually increase the level of difficulty until the apprentice could successfully complete all types of stitches. Scaffolding students' work in authentic learning activities is consistent with Vygotsky's notion of zone of proximal development, where learning is guided at the beginning of the activity, and results with the learner able to complete a task without scaffolds or others assistance (Griesser, 2001; Vygotsky, 1987).

In our example of the credit card problem, educators could effectively scaffold learning by guiding students through the first steps of creating a spreadsheet that would keep track of their money. By informally evaluating students through this process, the teacher can sense whether or not the students are able to complete the task without help. Students who are able to continue independently can do so, with the teacher serving as a type of just-in-time help. Other forms of just-in-time help would be the help menu on a piece of software, the Internet, textbook or other sources of information that the students have access to.

Another role of educators during the implementation of authentic activities is to provide students with a model of effective strategies and problem solving techniques. With elementary school children, teachers can model key behaviors near the beginning of the activity, such as identifying the problem, generating a plan and checking your work. As content becomes richer in middle grades and secondary classrooms, educators still should provide a model of effective problem solving strategies to the learners. Actual practitioners in the field can also be used to model effective behaviors as well. Many governmental agencies, such as the Environmental Protection Agency (EPA) and the National Air and Space Association (NASA) are willing to collaborate with students and educate them about key issues in their field.

The increased access to the World Wide Web, electronic mail and real-time video conferencing enables practitioners and students to work together regardless of their locations.

Assessment of Authentic Activities

Evaluating student learning in authentic activities is another obstacle for educators. Each state currently assesses its students on mastering a set of curriculum standards. In order to progress to the next grade, or for the school to maintain its accreditation and funding, students must demonstrate competency on these measures. Since state-wide assessments frequently are in multiple-choice form, teachers often make the mistake of limiting their own assessment measures to multiple choice forms (Hanny, 2001). While multiple-choice assessments are appropriate in some areas, it becomes quite problematic when an educator insists on assessing student performance in an open-ended activity via an assessment that lacks alignment with both the activities and the goals of the activity.

Teachers' knowledge of content and pedagogy (CK, PK, and PCK) are all explicitly linked to the assessments that teachers use with authentic learning environments. Teachers must know content, and what aspects of content need to be assessed (CK). Further, assessment processes should be aligned to match pedagogies used to teach the content (PCK). As indicated earlier, if technology is associated with the assessments or activities, the technology-related components of the TPCK framework (TPCK, TCK) are also related.

Assessment must be appropriately aligned with the context in which learning occurs and the learning goals (CTGV, 1992). In the case of our two examples of authentic activities, assessment of learning should be based on students' approach to solving problems, as well as the product that they created. Portfolios of student work have become popular, as a collection of artifacts that reflect a student's progress and level of mastery.

Critics contend that educators that evaluate learning in authentic contexts tend to look solely at the final product, ignoring the process skills and thinking involved in completing the task (Bruning, 1999; Tripp, 1994). Learning that is situated in authentic contexts should be evaluated in the context in which the learning occurs (Herrington & Oliver, 1999).

Overcoming the Obstacles of Authentic Learning Activities

"Any organization that adopts a new technology without significant change is doomed to failure," (Schlechty, cited in Caroll, 2000, p. 130).

The past 20 years of education have seen the adoption of new technologies, as computers and other devices have become commonplace in classrooms. However, the use of them is primarily for drill and practice or word processing, not as tools to help students understand concepts or foster higher-order thinking skills (Doherty & Orlofsky, 2001). The endeavor to change these practices and pedagogical beliefs has blossomed in the past decade, as all states are mandating their public school teachers to participate in professional development to become proficient at using these new technologies. However, the mere learning of these technologies does not carry over to classroom practice, as many teachers drift back to the teaching methods that they remember from their experiences as a student (Mouza, 2002).

The TPCK framework shows promise in supporting the enactment of technology-rich authentic learning activities. Opportunities for teacher learning should be comprehensive enough to develop teachers' knowledge of all components related to the TPCK framework, yet flexible enough so that teachers can hone in on specific components of the greatest need.

Orrill (2001) found that teachers learn very little by participating in workshops where they are simply collecting materials and observing how to integrate them into their classroom. Rather, teachers need to participate in activities as learners. This allows them to better understand the logistics behind the activities and how to alter the activity in order to use it in their own classroom (Mouza, 2002). The effective use of technology depends on teachers knowing classroom applications and adapting learning activities to support learning (CEO Forum, 1999; Gabriel & MacDonald, 1996). Hands-on use of technology in professional development programs increases the likelihood that it will be used in the classroom. In order for teachers to successfully adopt technology, they must be engaged in authentic experiences where they see it modeled, reflect on their own practices, and engage in retooling their existing classroom materials (Garet et al, 2001). "In this way the teacher is first the learner using the technology and therefore will model how she learned her way around, learning what resources are available, learning how to use those resources in conducting your activities productively and enjoyably" (NRC, 2002, p.138).

While proficiency in technology remains a barrier for educators, teachers also lack the necessary skills and beliefs needed to implement technology-enhanced authentic activities in their classroom (Ertmer, 2003; Ertmer, 2005; Loveless & Pellegrino, 2007). In order to support teachers in the creation of authentic learning activities, teachers should be situated in authentic activities that center on the design, implementation and assessment of authentic learning environments. Participants should be given the chance to observe exemplar models, design useable activities and develop strategies for assessing learning (Becker & Ravitz, 2001; Loucks-Horsley, 1998). By situating the educators' training in an authentic context they are more apt to make connections between their professional development experience and their activities in the classroom (CEO Forum, 1999; Loucks-Horsley, 1998). When that connection between learning skills and the successful application of them has been made, we know that learning has occurred.

REFERENCES

Barab, S. A., & Landa, A. (1997). Designing effective interdisciplinary anchors. *Educational Leadership, 54*(6), 52–55.

Barab, S. A., Squire, K. D., & Dueber, W. (2000). A Co-Evolutionary Model for Supporting the Emergence of Authenticity. *Educational Technology Research and Development, 48*(2), 37–62. doi:10.1007/BF02313400

Becker, H. J., & Ravitz, J. L. (2001). *Computer use by teachers: Are Cuban's predictions correct?* Paper presented at the annual meeting of the American Educational Research Association, Seattle, WA.

Bransford, J. D., Brown, A., & Cocking, R. (Eds.). (2000). *How people learn: Mind, brain, experience and school, Expanded Edition*. Washington, DC: National Academy Press.

Bransford, J. D., Sherwood, R. D., Hasselbring, T. S., Kinzer, C. K., & Williams, S. M. (1990). Anchored instruction: Why we need it and how technology can help. In D. Nix & R. Spiro (Eds.), *Cognition, education, and multimedia: Exploring ideas in high technology* (pp. 115-141). Hillsdale, NJ: Lawrence Erlbaum Associates.

Brown, J. S., Collins, A., & Duguid, P. (1989, Jan-Feb). Situated cognition and the culture of learning. *Educational Researcher, 18*(1), 32–42.

Bruning, R. H., Schraw, G. J., & Ronning, R. R. (1999). *Cognitive Psychology and Instruction*. Columbus, OH: Merrill.

Brush, T., Glazewski, K., Rutowski, K., Berg, K., Stromfors, C., & Van-Nest, M. H. (2003). Integrating Technology in a Field-Based Teacher Training Program: The PT3@ASU Project. *Educational Technology Research and Development, 51*(1), 57–72. doi:10.1007/BF02504518

Carroll, T. G. (2000). If we didn't have the schools we have today, would we create the schools we have today? *Contemporary Issues in Technology and Teacher Education, 1*(1). Retrieved March 21, 2009, from http://www.citejournal.org/vol1/iss1/currentissues/general/article1.htm

Cognition and Technology Group at Vanderbilt. (1992). The Jasper series: An Exploration of Issues in Learning and Instructional Design. *Educational Technology Research and Development, 40*(1), 65–80. doi:10.1007/BF02296707

Cohen, D. (1990). A revolution in one classroom: The case of Mrs. Oublier. *Educational Evaluation and Policy Analysis, 12*(3), 327–345.

Dewey, J. (1978). How we think. In J. A. Boydston (Ed.), *How we think and selected essays, 1910-1911* (pp. 177-356). Carbondale, IL: Southern Illinois University Press.

Dodge, B. (2003). *The WebQuest Page* [Online]. Retrieved from http://webquest.sdsu.edu/

Doherty, K. M., & Orlofsky, C. (2001, May 10). The new divides. *Education Week on the Web* [Online serial]. Retrieved from http://www.edweek.org/sreports/tc01

Ertmer, P. (2003). Transforming Teacher Education: Visions and Strategies. *Educational Technology Research and Development, 51*(1), 124–128. doi:10.1007/BF02504522

Ertmer, P. A. (2005). Teacher pedagogical beliefs: The final frontier in our quest for technology integration? *Educational Technology Research and Development, 53*(4), 25–39. doi:10.1007/BF02504683

Forum, C. E. O. (1999). *Professional development: A link to better learning.* Washington, DC: CEO Forum.

Gabriel, M. A., & MacDonald, C. J. (1996). Preservice teacher education students and computers: How does intervention affect attitude? *Journal of Technology and Teacher Education, 4*(2).

Greeno and the Middle School Mathematics Through Applications Project Group. (1998). The situativity of knowing, learning and research. *The American Psychologist, 53*(1), 5–26. doi:10.1037/0003-066X.53.1.5

Griesser, S. A. (2001). A Study of Problem Solving Abilities of Seventh Grade Students Who Receive Anchored Problem Solving Instruction. *Science, Mathematics and Environmnetal Education Clearinghouse.* (ERIC Document Reproduction Service No. ED456040)

Hannafin, R. D. (1999). Can teacher attitudes about learning be changed? *Journal of Computing in Teacher Education, 15*(2), 7–13.

Hanny, R. J. (2001). *Teacher Made Tests and the Virginia SOL.* Retrieved January 5, 2003, from http://www.pen.k12.va.us/VDOE/Instruction/wmstds/solass.shtml

Herrington, J., & Oliver, R. (1999). Using situated learning and multimedia to investigate higher-order thinking. *Journal of Educational Multimedia and Hypermedia, 8*(4), 401–421.

International Society for Technology in Education. (2008). *National Educational Technology Standards for Teachers.* Eugene, OR: International Society for Technology in Education. Retrieved March 29, 2009, from http://iste.org

Jonassen, D. H., & Reeves, T. C. (1996). Learning with technology: Using computers as cognitive tools. In D. H. Jonassen (Ed.), *Handbook of research for educational communications and technology* (pp. 693-719). New York: Macmillan.

Lave, J., & Wenger, E. (1991). *Situated learning: Legitimate peripheral participation.* Cambridge, UK: Cambridge University Press.

Loucks-Horsley, S., Hewson, P. W., Love, N., & Stiles, K. E. (1998). *Designing professional development for teachers of science and mathematics.* Thousand Oaks, CA: Corwin Press.

Market Data Retrieval. (2002). *Technology in education, 2002.* Retrieved March 24, 2009, from http://www.schooldata.com/publications3.html

Mishra, P., & Koehler, M. J. (2006). Technological Pedagogical Content Knowledge: A new framework for teacher knowledge. *Teachers College Record, 108*(6), 1017–1054. doi:10.1111/j.1467-9620.2006.00684.x

Moore, J.L., Lin, X., Schwartz, D.L., Petrosino, A., Hickey, D.T., Campbell, O., & Hmelo, C., & Cognition and Technology Group at Vanderbilt (CTGV). (1994). The relationship between situated cognition and anchored instruction: A response to Tripp. *Educational Technology, 34*(8), 28–32.

Mouza, C. (2002). Learning to teach with new technology: Implications for professional development. *Journal of Research on Technology in Education, 35*(2), 272–289.

National Council of Teachers of Mathematics. (2000). *Curriculum and evaluation standards for school mathematics.* Reston, VA: National Council of Teachers of Mathematics.

National Research Council (NRC). (2002). *How people learn.* Washington, DC: National Academy Press.

Niess, M. L. (2005). Preparing teachers to teach science and mathematics with technology: Developing a technology pedagogical content knowledge. *Teaching and Teacher Education, 21*, 509–523. doi:10.1016/j.tate.2005.03.006

Orrill, C. H. (2001). Building Technology-Based, Learner-Centered Classrooms: The Evolution of a Professional Development Framework. *Educational Technology Research and Development, 49*(1), 15–34. doi:10.1007/BF02504504

Polly, D. (2006). *Examining the influence of learner-centered professional development on elementary mathematics teachers' instructional practices, espoused practices, and evidence of student learning.* Unpublished doctoral dissertation, University of Georgia, Athens, GA.

Polly, D. (2008). Modeling the influence of calculator use and teacher effects on first grade students' mathematics achievement. *Journal of Technology in Mathematics and Science Teaching, 27*(3), 245–263.

Polly, D., & Mims, C. (2009). Designing professional development to support teachers' TPACK and integration of Web 2.0 technologies. In T.T. Kidd & I. Chen (Eds.). *Wired for Learning: Web 2.0 Guide for Educators,* 301-316.

President's Committee of Advisors on Science and Technology. (1997, March). *Report on the use of technology to strengthen K-12 education in the United States.* Retrieved from http://www.whitehouse.gov/ WH/EOP/OSTP/NSTC/PCAST/k-12ed.html

Sargent, M. (2003). Spanish for Beginners. *Technology and Learning, 7*(6), 8–9.

SCANS (Secretary's Commission on Achieving Necessary Skills). (1991). *What work requires of schools: A SCANS report for America 2000: Executive Summary.* Washington, DC: U.S. Dept. of Labor.

Scardamalia, M., & Bereiter, C. (1996) Adaptation and understanding: A case for new cultures of schooling. In S. Vosniadou, E. De Corte, R. Glaser, & H. Mandl (Eds.), *International perspectives on the psychological foundations of technology-based learning environments* (pp. 149-163). Mahwah, NJ: Erlbaum.

Shaw, T. (2003). Finding Time to Teach Tech Skills in Context. *Multimedia Schools, 10*(1), 41–42.

Shyu, H. C. (2000). Using video-based anchored instruction to enhance learning: Taiwan's experience. *British Journal of Educational Technology, 312*(1), 57–69. doi:10.1111/1467-8535.00135

Stein, M. K., Grover, B. W., & Henningsen, M. (1996). Building student capacity for mathematical thinking and reasoning: An analysis of mathematical tasks used in reform classrooms. *American Educational Research Journal, 33,* 455–488.

Vygotsky, L. (1987). *Thinking and speech.* In R.W. Rieber & A.S. Carton (Eds.), *The collected works of L.S. Vygotsky. Volume 1: Problems of general psychology* (pp. 37-285). New York: Plenum.

Young, M. F. (1993). Instructional Design for Situated Learning. *Educational Technology Research and Development, 41*(1), 43–58. doi:10.1007/BF02297091

Section 2
Applications and Practices of Distance Learning Technology

Chapter 7
Making a Difference with Mobile Learning in the Classroom

Anjum Najmi
University of North Texas, USA

Jennifer Lee
University of North Texas, USA

ABSTRACT

As technology continues to advance and computers become smaller, faster, and more powerful educational institutions are being confronted with multiple, external factors that are driving them towards change (e.g., rapid developments in information and communication technology that are part of everyday life, and changing characteristics of learners). We have come a long way from the earlier versions of the desktop computer to mini mobile computing devices of PDAs, iPods and stylish smart phones of today. In this chapter, the authors will examine how past generations of learning theories and practices have shaped the genealogy of mobile learning. Next, they focus on the implications, potentials, current practices, and challenges of mobile learning, with the intent to answer the question of how mobile learning can make a difference in the K-16 classroom.

INTRODUCTION

Although classrooms have traditionally been the epicenters of knowledge acquisition, the age of technology has paved the way for a more dynamic system of learning. For most of us, the walls of our classrooms and the number of books in our campus libraries are no longer physical barriers. Instead we are limited by bandwidths, processor speed, the dearth of innovative ideas, and the size of our imagination. It is time for us to rethink what learning is for the individual, community, and organization (Wenger, 1998). In his book "Community of Practice – Learning, Meaning, and Identity," Wenger observed that our institutions have largely "operated on the assumption that learning is an individual process, that it has a beginning and an end, and that it is best separated from the rest our activities." As a result of de-contextualized learning, it is not surprising that our students perceived education as unchallenging or irrelevant.

DOI: 10.4018/978-1-61520-672-8.ch007

Most of us tend to conjure up "images of classrooms, training sessions, teachers, textbooks, homework, and exercises" when we think of learning (Wenger, 1998). We often forget that it is an activity that happens anywhere, anyplace. Wenger believes that we should view learning as social phenomenon instead of relegating it to the realm of "academic enterprise." We learn as much from our informal learning as we do from our formal learning. We need to make education relevant and challenging again. The lack of synergy among those who are in charge of facilitating knowledge construction and those who are acquiring new knowledge have lead to a dire need for a more responsive, less isolated system of learning.

In the last few years, we have heard educators call for change in the way we educate our students. In this country alone, it is estimated that we have over 80 million Millennials who were born between 1978 and 1995. Their enrollment rates in colleges have surpassed previous generations. In addition to being one of the most diverse groups of Americans, Millennials also hold the distinction as the most technologically savvy-users (Howe & Strauss, 2000; Prensky, 2001). As technology continues to push the boundary of learning, mobile computing has emerged as a viable agent of change. It has created many new possibilities that have not existed before.

The traditional model of teaching has served us well in the last 30 years or so but as technology becomes more and more transparent in our daily lives, we need a new paradigm to meet the needs of our current generation of learners. Why is change critical? Jones-Kavalier and Flannigan (2006) paint a stark picture of what is happening in our classrooms today. We have "digitally literate students being led by linear-thinking, technologically stymied instructors." Nowhere is the gulf between instructors and teens more evident than the ownership of mobile communication. According to Harris Interactive (2008), four out of five teenagers in the United States are owners of wireless devices. Many of these users consider mobile phones a social necessity.

Mobile devices have changed the way we view discourse and knowledge in society (Traxler, 2007). Conventional teaching models tell us that teaching happens in the classroom. Mobile learning, on the other hand, takes the learning process from the inside of the classroom to the outside and vice-versa seamlessly. In this chapter, we will examine how past generations of learning theories and practices have shaped the genealogy of mobile learning. Next, we focus on the implications, potentials, current practices, and challenges of mobile learning, with the intent to answer the question of how mobile learning can make a difference in the K-16 classroom.

THE EVOLUTION OF MOBILE LEARNING

It is essential for us to look into the past in order to understand the rise and decline of technologies that were supposed to revolutionize learning in education. From the early use of instructional television in classrooms (Hagerstown, MD and Samoan Islands, 1950), to the use of motion film for classroom instruction (Rochester, N.Y, 1910), to the radio broadcasts of the Little Red Schoolhouse (Chicago, 1920), all have proved that technology alone cannot solve our learning problems (Cuban, 1986). Some forms of technology have met with greater success in learning than others.

At the heart of technological breakthroughs that have seen the miniaturization of computers (from those that took up a whole room to the ones that fit into a pocket) is, the challenge to make teaching and learning relevant and engaging again. With each generation, we have witnessed the push for making learning more accessible and affordable. We have seen the natural transition from traditional face-to-face learning modes to distance learning, and distance learning to mobile learning. For the purpose of this discussion, we will look at Moore and Kearsley's (2005) five generations of distance learning to trace the movement from limited access to open access in education.

The history of education in America can be viewed through three distinctive periods: restricted or elitist; mass education; universal education (Darrell, 1975). The English colonialists who settled in this country modeled many of the oldest institutions like Harvard and Yale after Britain's illustrious universities, Cambridge and Oxford (Frost, 2000; Cook, 2001). The education system at its infancy was very much paternalistic. Before the Revolutionary War, access to education was limited to the privileged few. Brubacher (1997) noted it was a conscious design on the part of the elites.

After the founding the republic, education did not stray very far from its Puritan roots. Upper class families continued sending their privileged sons to colleges that promoted the "republican ideals" while opening up opportunities for a larger segment of the population (Frost, 2000). It was not until Congress passed the Morrill Act in 1862 that many new colleges sprung up to cater to the educational needs of the citizens. The act paved the way for public institutions that we know today. During this period, the first generation of distance learning began in the 1880s when correspondence education via post allowed students the flexibility to study at home (Moore and Kearsley, 2005).

In World War II, the U.S Army used two-way radios for communication. The post-war period used the technology to develop commercial mobile radio-telephones (Goggin, 2006). It was during this period that the second generation of distance learning, radio and television, gained popularity. Many soldiers took advantage of the G.I Bill and attended college. Evans (1991) called the Servicemen's Readjustment Act 1944 or the "G.I Bill" as one of the most important influence in the history of higher education in America. The move opened up opportunities for many first generation college students to pursue higher education. The

bill was the catalyst that started the third period of American education, the era of universal education (Darrell, 1975).

The next generation of distance learning (1960s and 1970s) saw the adoption of the British model of Open University in the United States. The idea was to give learners open access to learning and greater autonomy. During this period the cellular telephony system underwent several rounds of innovation. In 1972, Alan Kay at Xerox, Palo Alto Research Center envisioned a personal and portable computing device for children. Kay (1972, p.4) believed that children learn best by doing and in order to engage them, we must "provide them with something real and enjoyable to 'do' on their way to perfection of both the art and skill." The Dynabook was considered by many researchers to be the conceptual prototype for modern mobile computing devices.

The 1980s saw the emergence of Teleconferencing (audio/video) which was considered the fourth generation of distance education (Moore & Kearsley, 2005). The traditional view of education was still modeled where learning was seen as an activity that happened in the classroom. It would be another decade before the first portable computer appeared on the market. In 1981, the Osborne 1 was introduced and it was a commercial success. Thus, the 1980s saw the creation of the budget friendly personal computers followed by walkmans, personal digital assistants (PDAs), portable games, and cell phones. It was not until the fifth generation of distance learning in the 1990s that we witnessed the adoption of computer and Internet-based virtual classes, and the introduction of e-learning, which may be in the form of asynchronous learning (Moore & Kearsley, 2005).

Mobile computing has come to represent any device that is small, autonomous, and portable. Despite their shared history, many experts do not consider laptops and tablet personal computers to be fully mobile because of their relative bulk and substantial start-up time (Lavoie, 2007).

Instead, the Personal Digital Assistant (PDA) has the distinction of being considered the first portable device. Trinder (2005) noted that people used PDAs differently than personal computers. Since computers were usually turned on once a day, users accepted a longer boot time. For PDA users, longer boot time was unacceptable. They were frequently used throughout the day to retrieve information and as such, the devices were expected to be ready to respond at all times. One of the disadvantages of a PDA was that users had to carry multiple devices. It was not uncommon for users to be owners of pagers, PDAs and cell phones for work purposes. With each round of innovation, we witnessed the steady advanced from wired to the wireless.

Today, mobile learning is the latest catch-all phrase for all things that support learning anytime, anywhere. According to Kukulska-Hume and Traxler (2005, p.3), learning has become "more personal, yet at the same time more connected to the surroundings and with more potential for connected, collaborative activity." Like its older predecessors, d-learning (distance) and e-learning (web), mobile learning has fast become a distinct sector of modern education. It is now simply known as m-learning. What makes mobile learning different from all the other learning modes?

WHAT IS MOBILE LEARNING?

According to Moore and Kearsley (2005, p.3), the litmus test to "discriminate between distance learning and other forms of education that is to ask, where are the principal education decisions made?" Principal decisions made in the classrooms are as viewed as traditional learning whereas decisions that are made outside the classrooms are as defined as distance learning (Moore & Kearsley). Although, distance learning and its subset e-learning share the same principal educational decision, mobile learning straddles both domains. This is because decisions on the nature of instructions for mobile learning can happen inside and outside the classroom. Nyiri (2002) sees mobile learning as simply learning that is "location-dependent" and "situation-dependent." Situation-dependent learning "arises from practical tasks" and multi-sensory content. Content should be designed with practical problems in mind.

Bachfischer, Dyson, and Litchfield (2008, p.287) see mobile learning as "the facilitation of learning and the delivery of educational materials to students using mobile devices via a wireless medium." Even though technology plays a critical role in the new medium, it is important that mobile learning focuses on the learners instead of technological innovations (Sharples, Taylor & Vavoula, 2005). In this context, mobile learning can be viewed as "the processes of coming to know through conversations across multiple contexts amongst people and personal interactive technologies" (Sharples et. al, 2005).

Mobile learning has four perspectives (Winters, 2007). The first perspective argues that it is techno-centric in nature. M-learning is associated with the devices that support the goal. The second perspective sees mobile learning as an extension of e-learning. It represents a continuum based on the use of more sophisticated technology (Mclean, 2003). The third perspective supports the idea that mobile learning augments formal education, while the last perspective favors the learner-centered model of teaching. The last perspective resonates with us more than the others. M-learning effectively connects learners in an information driven society and offers opportunities for spontaneous, personal, informal and context driven learning (Shih & Mills, 2007).

Some common characteristics that relate to this style of learning are:

• Learning is learner-centered based on the individual learner's environment rather than the classroom.

Table 1.

Life Long Learning Skills	New Technology
Highly portable - Available for use wherever the user desires	Personal
Individualized - Adapts to users abilities	User-centered
Unobtrusive - Blends into environment so it is easy to use to capture information and retrieve knowledge	Mobile
Available anywhere - Allows communication with peers, teachers & others	Networked
Adaptable - To users evolving skills and knowledge	Ubiquitous
Persistent - Durable	Durable
Useful - Will remain available despite changes	
Intuitive - Easy to use with no previous experience needed	

- It is context-driven providing relevant information to the user based on the learning task and is across disciplines.
- Learners make meaningful connections to many different resources and other people (interactive).
- Observations and reflections can be instantly published thus motivating learners to become investigators of their own environment.
- The ability to easily capture and record events assists in recall and collaborative reflection.
- Distributed collaborative opportunities are central to learning and greatly enhanced.
- Provide models of real world settings for learners to construct knowledge through active participation (games and simulations).
- Mobile learning applications are used in conjunction with other learning tools. Learning is a process rather than a single event (Corbeil & Corbeil, 2007).

In the April issue of *Computers and Education*, Sharples (2000) discussed the potential for new designs in personal mobile technologies that could enhance lifelong learning programs and continuing educational opportunities. It was based in part on Vygotsky's socio-cultural theory (1978) where learning is social and includes arguing, reflecting

and articulating to others, and Pask's Conversation Theory (1976), which describes learning in terms of conversations between different systems of knowledge. He envisions the convergence of educational thinking and technological development.

Sharples believes learning happens all the time and is influenced by the environment, and the individual's particular situation. It is embedded in everyday life hence it is supported by mobile learning. Learners have the flexibility for learning anytime, anywhere. They need not be tied to a particular location i.e. home, work, the local library, a shopping centre, college or university (Sharples, 2000, p. 180).

Many of the ideas raised in this early article are still evolving and relate to mobile learning today. They are relevant to mobile learning from a socio-constructivist perspective. Table 1 presents an overview of those overarching ideas.

Although desktop computers fulfill some of the same needs, they have their drawbacks when used at schools. According to Penuel (2006), centrally located computer labs in schools limit student access to technology because the computers are only available at certain scheduled times. In addition, the cost and complexity of maintaining computer labs are exorbitant compared to their alternative counterparts like the mobile phones or personal digital assistants (PDAs).

On the other hand, mobile devices are cheap, portable, have little or no start-up time, require little maintenance and are easy to use. In everyday classroom learning, they offer the user flexibility. Students can exchange data quickly and accurately with peers, move between various collaborators, establish face-to-face interaction, use laboratory equipment distributed over the school, and take measurements in the field. Therefore, it is easy to see why m-learning is an attractive alternative in helping educators, administrators, and researchers achieve the nation's vision for the 21st century model of wired schools.

MOBILE LEARNING IN THE CLASSROOM

How does this translate into learning in the classroom? Soloway, Norris, Blumenfeld, Fishman, Krajcik, and Marx (2001) argue that handheld computers offer a one-to-one student to computer ratio and have the potential to make learning in schools truly personal. The extensive popularity of mobile devices makes them familiar entities: users are more willing to learn with them and find them easier to work with. The learning curve is little or non-existent. This creates a sense of ownership, which is directly transferable to learning. Many innovative school districts and universities are beginning to use mobile learning in the classrooms.

Fifth grade students at Trinity Meadows Intermediate (Keller, Texas), are using Verizon phones to access the Internet, a calculator, take photos and video, sketch drawings, beam information to one another and enter data into Microsoft Excel or Word. They snap photos of their school hallway, to measure the length and width, entering the data into their phones to calculate the area as well as perform research on topics such as the Westward expansion (Unmuth, 2009). The Keller ISD, mobile initiative is part of a larger trend of school districts that seek to equip every child with a computer, known as 1:1 computing in order to provide students with richer and more meaningful learning experiences.

Mobile learning is not just about using portable devices to access information but it is about extending learning across different contexts, offering learners a greater range of activity. It takes learning beyond the constraints of location and time, combining both real and virtual environments. Although desktop computers can fulfill some of the same needs, unlike mobile devices they are limited in their use to within four walls of a classroom.

Using PDAs equipped with Global Positioning Systems (GPS) students in Amsterdam, learn about the history of their city in real time by identifying digital materials with specific physical locations. They take an archeological walk starting at the local museum "Het Valkhof." PDA displayed digital documents of Roman buildings are shown mapped onto present-day corresponding suburban buildings. Pop-up windows on the location-based computers describe what was once where the user stands, hyperlinks to contextual information and discussion supported by animations, present pictures of each site of the time. Additional pictures of the visit are taken with the camera of the device and uploaded to a server for future referencing and research (De Kreek, Krijgsman, Kromwijk, Van Kruining, Liemburg & Wang, 2003).

Likewise, at California State University, Monterey Bay (CSUMB) students use wireless laptops, GPS, digital cameras, Tablet PCs, and PDAs for remote data collection to learn about the early historic communities of the California Central Coast e.g. excavations at the San Juan Bautista and Carmel Spanish Mission sites. Site descriptions, numerical data, qualitative observations, schematic sketches of rocks, faults and folds are collected. Ongoing archaeological field notes are maintained by writing notes and drawings directly on to inherently based digital images rather than on to a sketch. Wireless file transfer provides the venue for a mobile wireless classroom, so the instructor can provide a deeper understanding of geologic phenomenon as the need arises. Information is incorporated into professional technical reports by uploading the data to a central website (California State University, 2005).

Thus, connectivity on location enables emphasis on discovery based, problem solving and collaborative learning supporting participatory, dynamic and immersive forms of learning. Such learning experiences are markedly different from those afforded within the four walls of a classroom typically supported by conventional desktop computers. They are richer, deeper and more meaningful to the learner.

When students can choose their own time to learn, greater learner engagement, higher satisfaction and better learning outcomes are achieved. Gomez (2007) examined the effects of delivering course content and lectures via mobile devices (mobile phones) through podcasts, audio and video files. In general, student enjoyment increased and learning outcomes were rated highly. Despite an initial adjustment period, most students enjoyed the ability to access information on their own time and access information easily. Some students were faced with lack of access to required hardware. For others the small screen for mobile phones worked well for short text messages but was not well suited for sustained reading.

Similarly, research has shown review of course material prior to class promotes greater student participation and improves student achievement. Undergraduate students at the Norwegian University of Science and Technology (NTNU) used mobile phones to prepare course content for a Histology class. Prior class preparation was believed to improve student interest, increase student involvement in class and improve learning outcomes. Visual studies of pictures and specimens were essential in the subject along with factual knowledge and reasoning to determine right from wrong. Short video-recorded highlights (four to six minutes) of upcoming lectures with main themes and key elements were made available usually one day, prior to the lecture (Rismark, Solvberg, Stromme, & Hokstad, 2007).

Results indicated students were better prepared in class they used their mobile phones to get information on upcoming lectures, and to access general updates on the subject matter. They were motivated to look up additional information on the subject, using other sources of information e.g. the textbook, the Internet, dictionaries and other reference works. This was precisely the kind of student activity and learning, professors wished to facilitate (Rismark, et. al., 2007).

Furthermore, mobile learning offers a way to engage and motivate low SES and minority learners. Many who are familiar with popular media and own their own mobile phones. M-learning offers such learners the opportunity to learn independently and privately in their own time and space, building their self-confidence and improving their literacy and numeracy skills (National Literacy Trust, 2008).

Similarly, mobile technologies with their wireless capabilities have the potential to connect with a larger number of people allowing them access to educational content beyond the constraints of time and location. Stanford University's International Outreach program in partnership with three Universities in Uganda, Tanzania and South Africa delivered educational content for a business course. Students received a memory card loaded with lectures and were able to access the course Web site, send text messages, and post media to mobile blogs (Biz Ed, 2007). This made access to technology easier increasing the opportunities for improving literacy beyond time and location (National Literacy Trust, 2008).

Today's learners belong to a diverse group of people who are always on the move. They lead busy lives and many have full time jobs. M-learning offers learners the flexibility of learning just in time, just for me, anytime, anywhere. Using small intervals of time learners are able to interpret an illustration or take a quiz while standing in line at the bank. In this way learners continue with

Table 2. Ways of delivering course content (Lui, 2007, p.111)

Instructional approach	Functions
Displaying	Illustrating digital materials (audio/video)
Broadcasting	Transmitting material to all students
Selective and Spot inspection	Obtaining student responses and assignments, quizzes
Individual Learning	Reading learning materials, taking notes, revising work and referencing
Online Learning	Searching, accessing and saving resources with others
Co-operative Learning	Collaborating with peers, co-editing reports etc. via synchronous and asynchronous messages
Integrated-response display	Two-way communication of sharing information between teacher-student and student-student via SMS text

their day-to-day commitments as well as remain connected as they further their knowledge and skills as lifelong learners.

Delivery of educational content via mobile learning is done in several different ways they are presented in Table 2.

MOBILE LEARNING AND THE EDUCATOR

As mobile technologies continue to rapidly advance with smart phones becoming more and more ingrained into contemporary life and social practices, educators face the challenge of meeting the changing needs of different student groups and utilizing new content delivery channels. Educational institutions are facing increasing pressure to teach masses of diverse students expecting both a quality education combined with highly interactive multimedia, as well as provide adequate training and professional development opportunities to their staff so that they may successfully face these challenges.

Mobile technologies continue to change the rhythm of learning and the use of social space. This "on the go" learning style is a stark contrast to how our previous generations were taught. They learnt what they needed to pass a test and they were limited to using resource materials in the library or textbooks and by what they were

able to memorize (Fisher& Baird, 2006, p.12). Education in the 21st century can no longer be defined by static guidelines but rather by growing, changing, and evolving sets of opportunities, projects, technology, and communities. For the most part, colleges and universities are beginning to realize the potential of mobile technology to improve the quality of student learning.

Today's students are incredibly flexible and fluid when it comes to their social connections and their virtual life culture (Alexander, 2004, p.28). They bring to class an extensive network of information input, peer connections, and potential for a much wider scope of application, unrivalled from what traditional education has promoted up to now. Learning for them is customized: with multi-points of inputs, open-ended outputs and customized spaces of interaction (Reynard, 2008). These spaces of interaction are similar to Vygotsky's (1962) notion of the Zone of Proximal Development (ZPD). They are based on the user's style and the influence of the instructor on the learning process, with interdependencies where social space is part of the learning process. The instructor is the facilitator or coach and is as much as part of the learning process as is the student (Reynard, 2008).

When course content is available anytime, anywhere in multiple formats the potential for maximizing learning needs to be accommodated in the planning and delivery of the course. Educators must know how the information is relevant and how it should be worked and used. The challenge to educators is not only "managing" the multitasking of the students but also addressing their insistence upon continual connectivity. At the same time students should be able to access the content in whatever form they find best - customization. They must have the opportunity to use multiple formats to demonstrate or "produce" their knowledge and learning, as well as maximize their connections with the instructor, other students and the larger community (Reynard, 2008). Thus, mobile learning through its flexible, just in time, learning anytime, anywhere can support and provide a platform for such active learning, collaboration, and innovation.

Similarly, to meet changing student expectations and digital learning styles teacher training and professional development opportunities are important. These can vary from classroom to classroom and between educational institutions. M-learning through its ease of use and many affordances supports both formal and informal professional learning opportunities.

Seppala and Alamaki (2003) in a pilot study examined the training and instruction of Finnish pre-service teachers using mobile technology in the classroom. Given that 98% of Finland's university students owned cell phones instruction via mobile learning seemed to be the next step. Supervising teacher and students discussed teaching issues through Short Messaging Service (SMS) text messaging and various media. Digital pictures of the training sessions, learner actions and teaching strategies were taken and uploaded to a central database. Each user could "withdraw" this material at any time for review and study. Feedback was almost instantaneous while assessment was in the form of student teachers creating a portfolio. Results showed multiple benefits to teaching and learning in this manner e.g. convenient access to information and resources, the ability to take notes at any time and the capacity to work on materials anytime, anywhere.

Likewise, through its communicative and interactive features mobile learning supports real time professional learning. Free online services such as Twitter combine blogging, text-messaging and social networking and provide teachers with a quick, informal way to get feedback from others in the field, who have used many of the strategies and share similar interests (Boss, 2007). Scott Walker a teacher in rural Kentucky found this to be a means of sharing latest news, resources, questions, and (sometimes) trivia about education, technology, and other related topics. All he has to do is post a question online and he can learn from the experiences of others (as cited in Boss, 2007). Thus, the use of academic, peer support groups were seen to be more successful and a better use of resources than general professional development workshops.

Furthermore, mobile learning offers educators a means to organize daily events e.g. calendar, contact list, to-do list, and an efficient way to integrate useful data during the learning process e.g. via spreadsheets and media (digital audio/ video). The mobile device allows information to be entered once and then uploaded to the main computer. Thus, it reduces the time teachers spend on class prep time and helps with making the process of recording student progress more efficient, providing the teacher flexibility to access data anytime, anywhere. This minimizes turnaround time of graded work, decreases much of the burdensome paperwork associated with teaching, and helps teachers have more time to interact with students in order to facilitate learning (McClean, Nikonchuk, Kaplo, & Wall, 2006).

Thus, mobile learning offers educators a means of staying informed and connected as well as the flexibility of having access to a range of online resources such as email, blogs, wikis, RSS feeds, chat, podcasts, and social networks, anytime, anywhere. The three elements of mobility that tend to support teaching and instruction in the classroom are: convenience, expediency and immediacy all valuable attributes that help to strengthen professional development (Seppala & Alamaki, 2003).

MOBILE PHONES AND M-LEARNING

As technology changes and new devices continue to emerge, the distinction between the different kinds of mobile devices becomes ever more blurred. Mobile devices are becoming smaller, faster, more powerful, and much more versatile. MacManus (2002) sees the current trend moving towards a single device being capable of handling multiple functions and media types.

As such, we are seeing the convergence of multiple applications into smart phones with email, texting, Internet, and multimedia capabilities with some having the added benefits of Bluetooth and Wi-Fi. Many websites are catering to the ever-growing base of mobile users. With its ability to effortlessly access, create and share information: anytime, anywhere, mobile phones are becoming an invaluable tool for teaching and learning MacManus (2002).

One of the early pioneers of mobile learning in higher education was the Stanford Learning Lab at Stanford University. Results of their language-learning program through mobile phones for Spanish, showed information when delivered in small chunks was easily learned, review and practice of material was effective and automated voice vocabulary lessons had potential. However the tiny screens of the devices were found to be difficult for learning new content and poor audio quality of live tutoring limited comprehension (Brown, 2001).

Thornton and Houser (2002) conducted a case study on Japanese students learning English through SMS via mobile phone. Content was delivered in small chunks for ease of viewing, presented in frequent, short lessons, used in different contexts e.g. episodic stories and assessed twice a week. They found students using mobile phones were able to retain twice the number of vocabulary words and were able to improve (double) their scores than those students who learned the same words via the Web and paper. Participants of the study viewed learning via mobile phone as an effective teaching method and majority of them saw this as a method they would like to continue with for learning (Thornton & Houser, 2002).

Similarly, Mielo (2005) found learning language via mobile phones was successful when content was used for frequent practice of previous and new vocabulary, paced learning, and mastery of specific words and phrases. Student satisfaction and achievement was seen to improve when content was presented in authentic contexts, made personal and was supported by visual content e.g. posting pictures and text to a web site via moblogging. This created further opportunities for language creation (journaling) and collaboration.

Another study revealed a positive correlation between mobile phone use in the classroom and student achievement. Undergraduate students in an Introduction to Sociology class, at Westchester University of Pennsylvania, were able to access course material e.g. practice vocabulary words, definitions and review exam questions, via their web enabled mobile phones. Scores were based off two mid semester tests and in the form of multiple/choice and true/false. Results revealed students who used their mobile phones to retrieve and review information for the two mid-semester tests had an average score of 89% in comparison to students 84% (t=2.50, p < .01) who prepared using handouts and notes (McConatha, Praul & Lynch, 2008).

Results indicated that practice and review of course material via mobile phones make a positive and significant difference in student outcomes (average test scores). This is not to overlook other factors that influence student achievement e.g. some students possess greater willingness to try unique methods of study (McConatha et. al., 2008).

In Texas, the Abilene Christian University (2008) in an initiative to improve student learning and connectivity, equipped all its incoming freshmen with iPhones and iPods. The idea was to help connect students to the campus through news, calendars, course documents and media along with instructional support in the form of in-class quizzing, trivia programs, surveys, polls, grade and assignment tracking tools.

In a similar initiative, Colorado Technical University's (2008), online campus provided a GPS-based tracking system (Mobile Guardian) for students to activate, allowing University police to monitor their safe arrival at a destination. Students receive real time alerts and information as well as track campus shuttle buses, check assignments, study hall availability, co-ordinate group activities and access other campus related events.

Thus, M-learning provides models of real world settings for learners to construct knowledge through active participation in many different ways. It is easily adaptable across all disciplines (language arts, social studies, science, math and fine arts), grade levels, and content areas.

BENEFITS AND DRAWBACKS OF MOBILE LEARNING

Mobile learning not only connects the learner effectively in an information-driven age, but promotes the opportunity for spontaneous, personal, informal, and situated learning in several different ways:

- It engages and intrinsically motivates the learner
- The all in one mobile device (with Internet access) offers users convenience, flexibility, for learning anytime, anywhere
- It empowers teachable moments, learners access information when they are attentive and willing to learn

- It supports real world application of content (problem-based & experiential)
- It supports independent and collaborative learning
- Allows new skills and knowledge to be immediately applied and practiced (as many times as needed)
- Provides access to experts
- Builds a community of practice and supports lifelong learning
- Helps to integrate technology into learning (Ryan, 2007).

Despite its many affordances m-learning is not for all learners and every situation, certain limitations and challenges remain when using this form of learning such as:

- Small screen size and small keyboard can hinder entry/retrieval of information
- Low resolution and limited processing and storage capacity
- Limited battery life and connectivity issues
- Relative high start up cost
- Challenges to the security of the device and its data
- Possibility for mobile devices to be misplaced or stolen
- Difficulty of use of mobile devices in noisy environments
- Fragmented learning: content delivered in chunks can make it difficult for the learner to see the bigger picture
- Can give tech savvy students an advantage over non-technical learners creating a feeling of isolation and a steeper learning curve
- Mobile software applications need to support course content and curricula (Ryan, 2007).

Research has shown the use of certain guidelines can help reduce many of the issues associated

Table 3. Mobile software applications (Thinking machine, 2008)

Instructional approach	Functions
Lava, MiLK, MOLES, Poodle (mobile version of Moodle)	interfaces that offer teachers and students an easy way to interact on an individual and group basis.
Gabcast	a podcast and audio-blogging platform that offers an easy way to create and distribute audio content to mobile devices
Jott and Braincast	audio to text messages
Mobile Notepad	an instant notepad for users
The Series 60 Weblog	a mobile Wikipedia (over 2000 full length articles including 8500 color images)
Delicious Mona	a news aggregator
Mobile SPS	for surveys and polls
Mobile Study	to create online quizzes
Mobango	a Universal Mobile Community that allows mobile phone users to publish, convert and share all kinds of user generated content via the web
Twitter Mobile	for social networking and mini blogging
MySpace Mobile	social network
Flickr: and Bubbleshare	for creating picture/slide projects
Animoto	to create MTV style videos using images and music

with m-learning and can help to ensure successful learning outcomes. Material should be simple, engaging and have functionality. It should be possible to use without having to read through endless directions e.g. just like playing a short game on the same device. Information should be presented in short modules e.g. chunking. Content can be made more meaningful through trivia programs and short quizzes. Discussion forums and blogs can help with finding answers to common questions in the field. The mobility should have the ability to guide and support students and teachers in new learning situations when and where it is necessary (Trifonova, 2003).

FUTURE TRENDS

As technology moves towards convergence and mobile devices become ever more pervasive in our everyday lives, a range of software applications are emerging that enhance the teaching and learning in the classroom with mobile technology. Many are easily downloadable and can be accessed free

of charge. They are formatted to fit the handsets' screens with expandable options, which improves user readability and allows for faster loading of results. They allow learners to design, create, edit, publish and track content over multiple devices in addition to allowing reflection and assessment functions (Thinking Machine, 2008). They are given below in Table 3.

As the sophistication and availability of software increases the computational power of many of these mobile devices improve giving them mini-computer status e.g. smart phone applications for the Blackberry, Windows-mobile and Symbian powered systems. Smart phones such as the iPhone come equipped with software applications to support learning in the classroom. Such as flash cards for learning anatomy (Netters), graphic calculator (Grafly), a grapher with touch capabilities (Grapher), a trigonometry calculator (Visuala), World Wiki: and an interactive periodic table (AR) plus Thesaurus and Dictionary (Apple, 2008).

Thus users not only have connectivity but they have access to a range of software applications.

So they can gain information, write blog posts, listen to podcasts, develop physics models, or simulate flying over the earth when and wherever they want to (Apple, 2008). Learning supported by technology in this manner meets the learning needs of today's learner "the digital native, that is always on the move, is focused on connectedness, and "is experimental and community oriented" (Prensky, 2001, p. 2).

At the same time emerging trends in industry, software-as-a-service are being added to the set of tools being run from, and stored on remote servers rather than local computers e.g. Google Apps (Miller, 2008). Any device with a high-speed connection can give users access to a range of applications, anytime, anywhere. The Internet is a desktop to create, edit, and share media of all kinds. Transference across different browsers and platforms is made easier and applications can be accessed through multiple devices e.g. desktop or mobile. Students and teachers can choose applications fit to purpose rather than be limited to a small number of propriety software, and be burdened by licensing costs (Miller, 2008).

Such advances support m-learning and classroom instruction, as they significantly reduce the cost of using and maintaining technology. They can help schools overcome some of the connectivity costs and interface issues related to using technology in the classroom. Several educational institutions are recognizing the benefits of increased mobility and creativity, and are signing up for cloud computing services (SAS) providing students access e.g. University of Washington, Stanford, MIT, Carnegie Mellon, University of South Carolina, University of California at Berkeley, Abilene Christian University.

Mobile learning is still an emerging field and therefore has many possibilities for further research some of which are: exploring pedagogical approaches to mobile learning in order to determine the most effective conditions that can help to enhance learning. Improving user interfaces e.g. data entry/retrieval tools and functions of mobile learning management systems (web-based) that can enhance teaching and learning. Strengthening connectivity for the user and improving adaptation to the surrounding context in a mobile learning environment, and improving evaluation and quality assurances for the development and implementation of mobile technologies (Trifonova & Ronchetti, 2003).

CONCLUSION

Implications for mobile learning are far reaching and its effects on education are profound. Mobile information and communication technologies are important enablers of the social structure of the 21st Century. Even though m-learning faces numerous challenges, its benefits for teaching and learning outweigh its drawbacks. To what extent mobile learning is adopted by faculty and students in the classroom, will greatly depend on how efficient, and necessary its services and features are perceived to be. The challenges of creating learning to be delivered via mobile phones are not easily solved by teachers many of who are recent 'migrants' to the digital world (Prensky, 2001).

Nonetheless, non-traditional ways of learning such as mobile learning have much to offer today's learners for whom not knowing is an impetus to find out, and using technology is second nature (Peters, 2007, p. 3835). What is important to remember is change does not happen overnight. What can help educators is to avoid thinking in terms of learning paradigms of the past when considering new paradigms of the future (Trifonova, 2003).

REFERENCES

Abilene Christian University. (2008). *Mobile learning and the connected campus*. Retrieved November 20, 2008, from http://www.acu.edu/technology/mobilelearning/index.html

Alexander, B. (2004). Going nomadic mobile learning in higher education. *Educause Review, 39*(5), 28-35. Retrieved October 8, 2008, from http://connect.educause.edu/Library/EDUCAUSE+Review/GoingNomadicMobile-Learnin/40494

Apple. (2008). *All the tools for mobile learning.* Retrieved October 18, 2008, from http://www.apple.com/education/teachers-professors/mobile-learning.html

Bachfischer, A., Dyson, L., & Litchfield, A. (2008). Mobile Learning and Student Perspectives: An mReality Check! In *Proceedings of the Mobile Business. ICMB '08. Seventh International Conference* (pp. 287-295).

Boss, S. (2007). *Twittering, Not Frittering: Professional Development in 140 Characters.* Retrieved October 22, 2008 from http://www.edutopia.org/twitter-professionaldevelopment-technologymicroblogging

Brown, E. (2001). *Mobile learning explorations at the Stanford Learning Lab. Speaking of Computers, 55.* Stanford, CA: Board of Trustees of the Leland Stanford Junior University. Retrieved October 8, 2008, from http://sll.stanfor.edu/projects/tomprof/newtomprof/postings/289.html

Brubacher, J. S., & Rudy, W. (1997). *Higher education in transition* (4th ed.). New Brunswick, NJ: Transaction.

California State University. Monterey Bay. (2005). *Mobile teaching and learning in action.* Retrieved October 18, 2008, from http://wetec.csumb.edu/site/x17155.xml

Christensen, R., Overall, T., & Knezek, G. (2006). Personal educational tools (PETS) for type II learning. *Computers in the Schools, 23*, 173-189. Retrieved October 15, 2008, from http://www.haworthpress.com/store/ArticleAbstract.asp?sid=P2GNR5WRN57M9HWPW66BWKBCMEC30E6&ID=71006

Colorado Technical University. (2008). *Mobile learning at CTUMobile.com.* Retrieved October 28, 2008, from http://www.ctuonline.edu/ctumobile/ Corbeil, J. R., & Corbeil, M. E. (2007). Are you ready for mobile learning? *Educause Quarterly.* Retrieved October 8, 2008, from http://net.educause.edu/ir/library/pdf/eqm0726.pdf

CTIA - The Wireless Association. (2008). *Teenagers a generation unplugged: A national survey by CTIA.* The Wireless Association and Harris Interactive. Retrieved October 8, 2008, from http://www.ctia.org/advocacy/research/index.cfm/AID/11483

Cuban, L. (1986). *Teachers and machines: The classroom use of technology since 1920.* New York: Teachers College Press.

Darrell, B. (1975)... *Peabody Journal of Education, 53*(1), 45–48. doi:10.1080/01619567509538048

De Kreek, M., Krijgsman, A., Kromwijk, R., Van Kruining, M., Liemburg, M., & Wang, J. (2003). *Archeaological walk guided by a PDA.* Retrieved October 8, 2008, from http://www.geoinformatie.nl/courses/yes60504/posters2003/poster_gr3.pdf

Dede, C. (2005). Planning for neo-millennial learning styles. *Educase Review, 28*(1). [Electronic Version]. Retrieved March 29, 2005, from http://www.educause.edu/ir/library/pdf/EQM0511.pdf

Fisher, M., & Baird, D. E. (2006). Making mlearning work: utilizing mobile technology for active exploration, collaboration, assessment and reflection in higher education. *Journal of Educational Technology Systems, 35*(1), 3–30. doi:10.2190/4T10-RX04-113N-8858

Frost, S. (2000). Historical and Philosophical Foundations for Academic Advising. In V. N. Gordon & W. R. Habley (Eds.), *Academic Advising: A Comprehensive Handbook* (pp. 3-17). San Francisco: Jossey-Bass, Inc.

Godwin-Jones, R. (2007). Emerging technologies e-texts, mobile browsing, and rich Internet applications. *Language Learning and Technology, 11*(3), 8. Retrieved October 18, 2008, from http://llt.msu.edu/vol11num3/pdf/emerging.pdf

Goggin, G. (2006). *Cell Phone Culture: Mobile Technology in Everyday Life*. New York: Routledge.

Gomez, S. (2007). Scroll to 'E' for Education. *The Times Higher Education Supplement, 1780,* 13. Retrieved October 18, 2008, from http://www.timeshighereducation.co.uk/story.asp?storyCode=207730&sectioncode=26

Harris Interactive. (2008). *National Study Reveals How Teens Are Shaping & Reshaping Their Wireless World.* Retrieved October, 8, 2008, from http://www.canvasseopinion.com/news/allnewsbydate.asp?NewsID=1334

Howe, N., & Strauss, W. (2000). *Millennials rising: The next great generation.* New York: Vintage Books.

Jones-Kavalier, B. R., & Flannigan, S. L. (2006). Connecting the Digital Dots: Literacy of the 21st Century. *Educause, 29*(2). Retrieved December 1, 2000, from http://connect.educause.edu/Library/EDUCAUSE+Quarterly/ConnectingtheDigitalDotsL/39969

Kay, A. C. (1972). *A Personal Computer for Children of All Ages*. Paper presented at the ACM Conference, Boston.

Kukulska-Hulme, A., & Traxler, J. (Eds.). (2005). *Mobile learning a handbook for educators and trainers*. London: Routledge.

Lavoie, M.-C. (2007). *Enabling contextual mlearning: Design recommendations for a context appropriate user interface enabling mobile-learning.* A Thesis in the Department of Education. Concordia University, Montreal, Quebec, Canada. Retrieved October, 8, 2008, from http://graduatestudies.concordia.ca/thesis/index.php?convocation_year=207&egree=M.A%20Educational%20Technology&f=list&supervisor=

Liu, C. (2007). Teaching in a wireless learning environment: A case study. *Educational Technology and Society, 10*(1), 107-123. Retrieved October 8, 2008, from http://www.ifets.info/journals/10_1/11.pdf

MacManus, T. (2002). Mobile what? The educational potential of mobile technologies. In *Proceedings of the World Conference on E-Learning in Corporations, Government, Health, and Higher Education* (pp. 1895-1898). Retrieved October 8, 2008, from http://www.editlib.org/INDEX.CFM?fuseaction=Reader.ViewAbstract&paper_id=9424

McConatha, D., Praul, M., & Lynch, M. (2008). Mobile learning in higher education: An empirical assessment of a new educational tool. *The Turkish Online Journal of Educational Technology, 7*(3), 1303-6521. Retrieved October 8, 2008, from http://www.scribd.com/doc/4494956/MOBILE-LEARNING-IN-HIGHER-EDUCATION-AN-EMPIRICAL-ASSESSMENT-OF-A-NEW-EDUCATIONAL-TOOL

Mclean, M., Nikonchuk, A., Kaplo, P., & Wall, M. (2006). In sync with science teaching: Handheld computers support classroom and laboratory activities. *The Science Teacher, 73*(7), 26-29. Retrieved October 8, 2008, from http://eric.ed.gov:80/ERICWebPortal/custom/portlets/recordDetails.detailmini.jsp?_nfpb=true&_&RICExtSearch_SearchValue_0=EJ758661&ERICExtSearch_SearchType_0=no&accno=EJ758661

Mclean, N. (2003). *The m-learning paradigm: an overview. A report for the Royal Academy of Engineering and the Vodafone group foundation.* Retrieved October 8, 2008, from http://64.233.169.132/search?q=cache:1HSfJMPzSgcJ:www.oucs.ox.ac.uk/ltg/reports/mlearning doc+the+m-learning+paradigm+an+overview+by+neil+mclean&hl=en&ct=clnk&cd=1&gl=us

Mielo, G. (2005). The medium is the moblog. [from http://direct.bl.uk/bld/]. *Etc.; a Review of General Semantics, 62*(1), 28–35. Retrieved October 8, 2008.

Miller, M. (2008). *Cloud computing: Web based applications that change the way you work and collaborate online.* Indianapolis, IN: Que Publishing

Moore, M., & Kearsley, G. (2005). *Distance Education: a Systems View* (2nd ed.). Belmont, CA: Wadsworth Publishing Company.

Nyiri, K. (2002) Towards a Philosophy of M-Learning. In *Proceedings of the IEEE International Workshop on Wireless and Mobile Technologies in Education (WMTE, 2002),* Teleborg Campus.

Pask, A. G. S. (1976). *Conversation Theory: Applications in Education and Epistemology.* Amsterdam: Elsevier.

Peneul, W. R. (2006). Implementation and effects of one to one computing initiatives: A research initiative. *Journal of Research on Technology in Education, 28*(3), 329–343.

Peters, K. (2007). M-learning: Positioning educators for a mobile, connected future. *International Review of Research in Open and Distance Learning, 8*(2), 3831–1492.

Peters, K. (2007). M-learning: Positioning educators for a mobile, connected future. *The International Review of Research in Open and Distance Learning, 8*(2), 3831-1492. Retrieved October, 8, 2008, from http://www.irrodl.org/index.php/irrodl/article/view/350/914

Prensky, M. (2001). *Digital Natives. Digital Immigrants.* Retrieved December 2, 2008, from http://www.marcprensky.com/writing/Prensky%20-%20Digital%20Natives,%20Digital%20Immigrants%20-%20Part1.pdf

Quinn, C. (2000). M-learning: Mobile wireless in-your-pocket learning. *LineZine,* 1-5. Retrieved November 6, 2008, from http://www.linezine.com/2.1/features/cqmmwiyp.htm

Reynard, R. (2008). *Mobile learning in higher education: multiple connections in learning spaces. Campus Technology.* Retrieved February 26, 2008, from http://campustechnology.com/articles/2008/04/mobile-learning-in-higher-education.aspx

Rismark, M., Solvberg, M. A., Stromme, A., & Hokstad, L. M. (2007). Using mobile phones to prepare for university lectures: Student's experiences. Norwegian University of Science and Technology. *The Turkish Online Journal of Educational Technology, 6*(4), Article 9. Retrieved October 4, 2008 from http://www.eric.ed.gov/ERICDocs/data/ericdocs2sql/content_storage_01/0000019b/80/3c/19/e9.pdf

Ryan, L. (2007). *Advantages and Disadvantages of mobile learning.* Retrieved October, 8, 2008, from the E-articles database.

Seppala, P., & Alamaki, H. (2003). Mobile Learning in Teacher Training. *Journal of Computer Assisted Learning, 19,* 330-335. Retrieved October 8, 2008, from http://www3.interscience.wiley.com/journal/118838489/abstract?CRETRY=1&SRETRY=0

Sharples, M. (2000). The Design of Personal Mobile Technologies for Lifelong Learning. [from http://www.elsevier.com/locate/compedu]. *Computers & Education, 34,* 177–193. Retrieved October 8, 2008. doi:10.1016/S0360-1315(99)00044-5

Sharples, M. (Ed.). (2006). *Big issues in mobile learning* (Report). Nottingham: Kaleidoscope Research. Retrieved October, 8, 2008, from http://www.lsri.nottingham.ac.uk/Publications_PDFs/BIG_ISSUES_REPORT_PUBLISHED.pdf

Sharples, M., Taylor, J., & Vavoula, G. (2005). Towards a Theory of Mobile Learning. In H. van der Merwe & T. Brown (Eds.), *Proceedings of the Mobile Technology: The Future of Learning in Your Hands, mLearn 2005* (pp. 1-9).

Shepherd, C. (2001). *M is for Maybe Tactix: Training and communication technology in context.* Retrieved September 16, 2008, from http://www.fastrak-consulting.co.uk/tactix/features/mlearning.htm

Shih, Y. E., & Mills, D. (2007). Setting the new standard with mobile computing in online learning. *International Review of Research in Open and Distance Learning, 8*(2), 1492–3831.

Soloway, E., Norris, C., Blumenfeld, P., Fishman, B., Krajick, J., & Marx, R. (2001). Devices are ready at-hand. *ACM Communications.* Retrieved October 10, 2008, from http://www.handheld.hice-dev.org/readyATHand.htm

Thinking Machine. (2008). *Using mobile phones to learn.* Retrieved October 8, 2008, from http://thinkingmachine.pbwiki.com/Think%20Mobile%20Phones%20for%20Learning

Thornton, P., & Houser, C. (2002). M-learning in transit. In P. Lewis (Ed.), *The changing face of CALL* (pp. 229-243). Lisse, The Netherlands: Swets and Zeitlinger. Retrieved October, 8, 2008, from http://studypatch.net/mobile/#General

Traxler, J. (2007). Defining, Discussing, and Evaluating Mobile Learning: The moving finger writes and having writ.... *International Review of Research and Distance Learning, 8*(2).

Trifonova, A. (2003). *Mobile learning: A review of the literature* (Technical Report DIT-03-009). Retrieved October 8, 2008, from http://eprints.biblio.unitn.it/archive/00000359/

Trifonova, A., & Ronchetti, M. (2003). *Where is mobile learning going?* Retrieved October 28th, 2008, from http://www.trifonova.net/docs/Where%20is%20Mobile%20Learning%20Going%20(E-Learn2003).pdf

Trinder, J. (2005). Mobile Technologies and Systems. In A. Kukulska-Hulme & J. Traxler (Eds.), *Mobile Learning a handbook for educators and trainers* (pp. 7-24). London: Routledge.

Vygotsky, L. (1962). *Thought and Language.* Cambridge, MA: MIT Press.

Vygotsky, L. S. (1978). *Mind in Society: the Development of Higher Psychological Processes.* Cambridge, MA: Harvard University Press.

Wenger, E. (1998). *Communities of Practice – Learning, Meaning, & Identity.* New York: Cambridge University Press.

Chapter 8

Lecture Capture:
Technologies and Practices

S. Alan McCord
Lawrence Technological University, USA

William H. Drummond
Lawrence Technological University, USA

ABSTRACT

This chapter provides faculty members and distance learning administrators with a broad overview of the options available to capture, store, edit, distribute, and re-purpose in-class lectures. The authors propose three dimensions to guide the selection of lecture capture systems, review existing technologies for enterprise and individual lecture capture, and discuss the technical and pedagogical challenges associated with implementing lecture capture solutions. They close by considering the emerging trend of community captured audio and video and its impact on how students interact with lecture materials.

INTRODUCTION

This chapter explores the linkage between one of the oldest pedagogical forms with one of the newest: how to incorporate the traditional lecture into today's distance learning environments. While there are pedagogical advantages to the traditional lecture, they are by nature ephemeral and historically have not been effectively and consistently captured and repurposed outside the lecture hall.

Today's technologies provide faculty members, institutions, and students with the ability to capture lecture content, annotate and edit the content, store

DOI: 10.4018/978-1-61520-672-8.ch008

the content in repositories, and repurpose selected lecture components into both online and traditional classroom environments. This chapter provides faculty members and distance learning administrators with a broad overview of the options available to accomplish these tasks.

We begin by reviewing the history of the lecture and the emergence of technical alternatives for capturing, storing, retrieving, and re-using faculty lectures. We then address several important questions that institutions need to ask when they consider capturing and re-purposing classroom lectures outside the spatial and temporal boundaries of the traditional classroom. We propose three dimensions to guide this analysis: interaction with lecture content, the technical components of lecture capture systems, and the resources required to implement and maintain these systems.

We move on to review enterprise and individual lecture capture technologies, technologies for editing, storing, and retrieving lectures, and the use of captured lectures within today's course management systems and digital repositories. We review selected full-feature lecture capture systems, web conferencing systems, screen capture systems, audio/video capture systems, and low-cost solutions.

Next we discuss the technical and pedagogical challenges associated with implementing lecture capture systems including the need to redesign traditional lectures, methods for incorporating student interaction in captured lectures, and alternative support models for capturing lectures by faculty, students, or the institution. We conclude with a consideration of future trends in multimedia technology, where students interact with each other via social networks and media-enabled personal communication technologies. We consider the emerging trend of community captured audio and video, its impact on distance learning, and its impact on how students interact with captured materials and apply that material toward their learning outcomes.

LECTURES AND LECTURE CAPTURE

The lecture has been used for centuries as a primary method of transmitting knowledge from a faculty member to a group of students. Lectures are used to help students acquire information, develop critical thinking, and change attitudes (Bligh, 2000), but most lectures concentrate on the one-way transmission of information. Lectures have a long evolutionary history of technical improvement. Originally, lectures consisted of faculty members reading from original texts without any interaction with students; students focused on capturing as

much of the faculty member's lecture information as possible for later study. Francis Hutcheson of the University of Glasgow is credited as one of the first professors to incorporate teacher-student interaction into lecture sessions in the mid-18th century (Herman, 2001). Other pioneering faculty members included scientific or anatomical procedures in their lectures.

The development of "high tech" lectures during the late 19th century featured the use of screen projection of artwork or photographs of original artifacts. Blackboards – and eventually whiteboards – have been used for faculty members to draw diagrams or list important points. Overhead projectors came on the scene in the late 1940s and faculty members began carrying around sheaves – or even "scrolls" – of transparent note sheets to place on the overhead projector or slide across the screen. The advent of presentation software such as PowerPoint provided faculty members with the opportunity to replace their written notes with presentation files, although many faculty members simply transcribed their notes directly to slides, resulting in "death by PowerPoint." These lectures were first displayed using see-through LCD panels mounted atop traditional overhead projectors. These cumbersome displays were replaced by stand-alone projectors and now by wireless connections to students' laptops.

Today many lecture halls witness a ritual of students trooping to the lectern to place their digital voice recorders in strategic positions to capture the faculty member's lecture. Some faculty members post their notes or presentation slides to course management systems and students may take notes as original documents or as comments attached to the faculty member's posted files. Many campuses have established podcasting services to deliver audio copies of lecture materials to students. The digital nature of today's student note-taking – either audio files or documents – make it much easier for students to exchange their notes with their colleagues. While different audio files may contain different quality levels of the lecture, the lecture itself is preserved intact. The interpretations and annotations of the lecture by students may vary depending on students' differing interpretations, which enable students to learn by sharing their notes with others.

The emergence of virtual campuses around the world has spurred development of lecture capture and distribution systems. Over 4,000,000 students are enrolled in online classes in the United States in 2007 (Allen & Seaman, 2008), and the growth rate for online programs far exceeds that for higher education in general. While it is common for institutions to separate on-ground from online programs from pedagogical and learning resources perspectives, some institutions are exploring the advantages of drawing learning objects from common repositories for use both in the on-ground and online classrooms.

Students' use of technology tools has increased dramatically in the past several years, but not necessarily in the same areas invested in by higher education institutions. Students make extensive use of consumer electronics such as media-enabled cell phones and MP3 players, free social networking sites, and a wide range of personal computing and entertainment software. Institutions are investing in wireless networks (which students use off-campus and expect on-campus), course management systems, digital library resources (which students expect to behave as simply as Internet search engines), and email systems (which most students do not use). Students use a mix of personal and institutional technologies, but often use personal technologies as a preferred alternative to institutional technologies. Students also change their consumer electronic devices frequently, and many of these devices use proprietary networking, graphics, and browser technologies (Salaway & Caruso, 2008).

INSTITUTIONAL CONSIDERATIONS

Institutional decisions to implement classroom lecture capture are driven by historic investments but also by current trends and demands. First, students are requesting to have full access to all instructional material and experiences in the classroom or online, including the more ephemeral and interactive aspects of the class (McInnis & Hartley, 2008). Second, today's online students do not expect to receive instruction using old-fashioned "correspondence school" techniques. Furthermore, institutions realize that lectures delivered in the classroom may retain pedagogical value when re-deployed to an online learning environment or used not only to study what happened in a class, but also to prepare for an upcoming class. Third, more students work while attending school, affecting their availability to study (Anderson, 2005). Finally, some institutions may use investments in lecture capture systems to distinguish themselves when compared with their competitors.

Research into student performance in traditional versus hybrid versus online courses seem to show that all three delivery modes can result in equivalent student learning (Young, 2008b). Even though lecture capture systems may not result in a guaranteed increase in student performance, there is some evidence to suggest that lecture capture systems may result in greater student-faculty interaction and additional faculty time being spent on more important tasks (Harley, Henke, & Maher, 2008). There is also evidence that students prefer to have on-demand lecture materials available to them (Nagel, 2008; Sonic Foundry, 2008).

Some faculty fear that making lectures available will result in fewer students attending class (Young, 2009), although there is little substantiated evidence to support this concern and some evidence that lecture attendance and availability of lecture notes and/or audio lectures can positively affect examination performance (Grabe & Christopherson, 2008). There are many approaches to addressing this concern, including one adopted the University of Maryland Baltimore County which combines use of a course management system, lecture capture system, and in-class student response "clickers" to validate attendance and subsequent access to captured lectures (University of Maryland Baltimore County, 2008).

When institutions discuss whether to implement lecture capture solutions, we suggest spending time considering the linkage between these investments and student learning. This dialog will likely focus on three areas: the interaction of students and faculty with lecture materials, technical issues, and the level of resources and support needed to sustain the lecture capture environment. Let's look at these issues in more detail.

Interaction with Lecture Materials

The central issue for lecture materials – whether delivered in a classroom without visual aids or as a pre-recorded online learning object – is **RESPONSIBILITY**. First, institutions need to discuss who is responsible for operating the lecture environment: will it be faculty members, academic departments, instructional technology service units, the campus IT organization, or students? Institutions may decide that a captured lecture is simply an audio file or a "talking head video" of the lecture, or they may decide that a captured lecture should be annotated with metadata or video bookmarks (Haga, 2004), and if so who will be responsible for adding those annotations (Chandra, 2007). Once an institution decides on how lectures will be captured, processed, stored, and retrieved, they have created a service that faculty and students will expect to operate in a reliable and consistent manner. This means that a campus unit will need to assume responsibility for assuring that lectures are indeed captured, edited, stored, and maintained according to agreed-upon service level standards.

Another key issue is **OWNERSHIP** of the intellectual property of the lecture itself. Traditional principles of academic freedom dictate that faculty members are the exclusive owners of their original course materials and students are the exclusive owners of their course notes and class deliverables. Many faculty labor agreements include specific clauses addressing intellectual property, ownership, and compensation. These traditional approaches are quickly challenged when lectures are posted online or when annotated or adapted for other uses. What is the institution's policy regarding ownership of intellectual property, and how might these policies need to be revised or extended when lectures are captured, posted online, and repurposed into other courses? Most institutions claim partial or full ownership when significant resources are used to capture and produce the artifact. Other institutions provide development grants to faculty in exchange for shared ownership of lecture content. Others have adopted an open courseware approach where faculty work is shared freely with other institutions in exchange for attribution and free distribution of derivative works.

A third institutional consideration is the degree of **EXTENSIBILITY** contemplated for captured lectures. Many authors cite the importance of incorporating ancillary materials into on-demand lectures (Cook & Sosin, 2006; Malone, 2003; Sensiper, 2000). Institutions may provide services to summarize, transcribe (via automated or manual techniques), annotate, and otherwise package captured lectures, store them in institutional repositories, link them to course management systems, or even publish them on publicly available web sites. One example of lecture reusability is Cornell University's eClips initiative, which provides over 10,000 short video and audio clips available for integration within campus courses or reference by other institutions (Cornell University, 2008).

Technical Considerations

The central technical consideration for selection of a lecture capture system is **QUALITY**. The discussion of quality begins with a discussion of audio and video capture and delivery formats, audio and video capture hardware, quality levels of archived lectures, transcoding formats for on-demand lectures, and the ability to post-produce captured lectures by adding metadata, annotations, and ancillary materials. Captured lectures should be of sufficient quality to focus students' attention on important content, effectively manage the focus and timing of lecture components, maintain the interest of students, and – most importantly – accurately reflect the original content presented by the faculty member (Heck, Wallick, & Gleicher, 2007).Quality also depends on the resources brought to bear, as we discuss below.

Another important technical consideration is **SCALABILITY**. Some institutions may choose to capture lectures in a few large lecture halls with high-quality equipment and on-site audio-visual staff, use library and instructional technology staff to produce and catalog high-quality learning objects, publishing the resulting lectures to a public web site. Other institutions may choose to capture lectures in hundreds of learning spaces with modest equipment, "smart" podiums, and minimal post-production and automated technology for associating captured lectures with appropriate sections of course management systems. These requirements may limit institutions to choosing between a small number of lecture capture solutions, or may cause the institution to adopt multiple lecture capture approaches for different learning environments. Other scaling issues are driven by the planned rollout of lecture capture services to classrooms: the number of classrooms, their configuration, the timing of hardware installation, and the expected production schedules for lecture content. Note that hardware, software, and network scaling also affect the level of support needed to operate these systems. These issues are addressed in the next section.

A third important technical consideration is the degree to which lecture capture systems comply with **STANDARDS** or use open source technologies. Adherence to video and audio format standards provides broader access to materials and insures long-term sustainability of collections. Some lecture capture systems use proprietary video encoding and require the use of non-standard players to view captured lectures, often in support of the vendor's product pricing models. Open source technologies may be able to be used for servers and databases, and in some cases for lecture capture software itself. The adoption of open source solutions provides institutions with the opportunity to collaborate with sister institutions to extend the capabilities of these systems. It may also provide students with the ability to successfully transition to mobile learning (M-learning) since open source standards will more likely play on their commercially obtained non-proprietary hand-held devices.

Level of Support

The most important support consideration for campus lecture capture solutions is **COST**. Cost components include hardware, software, maintenance, client and/or usage licensing, hosting, bandwidth, technical support, audiovisual support, and library support. Some campuses do not consider the life cycles of these cost components against expected adoption rates. For example, a server may have an expected useful life of three years, but may need to be upgraded in one year if the rollout plan predicts rapid growth of captured lectures. Some campuses do not adequately compare and contrast the cost of implementing commercial products – either remotely hosted or locally installed – with open source products. Open source products may be "free" but require specialized technical staff to implement and maintain the software and to integrate it with course management systems, scheduling, and library systems. True open source projects also include an expectation that partner institutions will commit technical staff to ongoing collaborative development.

Another support consideration for lecture capture systems is providing **SUPPORT** to faculty members and students who use the system. If the institution agrees to focus on producing and repurposing lecture content, then editing and production staff will need to be assigned to provide that service. If the institution agrees to broadly distribute lecture capture functionality to most campus classrooms, then extensive documentation, training, and help desk services need to be designed. The institution also needs to consider where the overall responsibility for lecture capture will reside: with the campus information technology unit, audiovisual department, library, or a federation of individual colleges? These decisions are important as they help the institution define how operating and expansion budgets are developed, where the primary responsibility lies for maintaining service levels, who will interact with vendors and partners, and many other factors that will determine the overall success of its lecture capture investment.

DIMENSIONS OF LECTURE CAPTURE SOLUTIONS

From a process perspective, lecture capture begins with lecture planning where the faculty member lays out instructional objectives, related content, sequencing, and visual aids for the lecture. At this point – even prior to preparing multimedia content and ancillary materials – much of the associated metadata for the lecture can be documented.

During the technical planning phase, the faculty member plans for the delivery of the lecture in the context of the lecture capture system. The faculty member must receive training in the use of the lecture capture system, a capture-enabled lecture hall and/or equipment must be reserved, audiovisual technicians scheduled in some cases, presentation materials loaded to a lecture podium station in some cases, and presentation materials staged on a personal computer or on the network.

The delivery of the lecture itself is the next step in the process. The lecture is captured via the capture system and stored for later processing. During the lecture, one or more audio and video channels are switched by the faculty member or audiovisual technician to provide the captured stream to the storage location. In some cases, the live lecture is streamed synchronously through a streaming server to remote audiences. In other cases, the live lecture is embargoed for editing and publication.

Next the lecture stream is edited for publication. The lecture can be tagged with appropriate metadata, scenes can be defined and tagged, closed captioning can be added, web site links can be inserted, and ancillary materials can be attached to the lecture package. The lecture stream is then encoded in one or more video formats for streaming to one or more types of display devices. Links to the edited lecture package are then loaded to the appropriate area of the course management system and added to the institutional repository if one is available.

Recorded lectures are generally played back by individual students, but some solutions provide students with the opportunity to view on-demand lectures in small groups and interact with each other during the playback (Phung, Valetto, Kaiser, Liu, & Kender, 2007; Shih, Wang, Liao, & Chuang, 2003). Interaction can also be accomplished by embedding the recorded lecture within a discussion forum within a course management system.

The final phase of the lecture capture process manages the life cycle of the lecture. If the lecture is time-sensitive and will be replaced by a future semester lecture, then the current lecture may be removed from the repository or moved to an archive. We recommend, therefore, that retention information be included as part of lecture metadata.

Another important, but often neglected, life cycle issue to be considered is the file format of both the unedited archive and the final product. This is especially true with proprietary systems

Table 1. Interaction dimension

Complexity of Interaction	Elements	Examples
Least Complex	Pedagogy	Lecture design
		Supporting materials
	Playback	Select from a list
		Integrated into CMS courses
		Search for specific content
	Personalization	Annotate the lecture
		Social bookmarking
	Collaboration	Interact with the lecture
		Interact with the CMS through the lecture
		Interact with other students using social networking
	Re-purposing	Store in an Institutional Repository
		Exporting lectures nd lecture chunks
Most Complex	Derivative Works and Creation	Creating original content from existing materials

where file formats are subject to market forces, but even professionally approved standard file formats, such as those adhering to the latest m-learning technology standards, may have a limited life span.

Storage is another issue to be considered. Uncompressed video in the current standard AVI format occupies as much as one megabyte per second of video. Compression reduces file size but lowers the quality of playback and makes editing more cumbersome. We recommend storing archived uncompressed master files as a standard operating procedure for any lecture capture implementation, and that sufficient storage space is allocated for this purpose.

Throughout the lecture capture process, the dimensions introduced earlier again come into play:

1. **Interaction dimension** – describing how students and faculty members interact with lecture content,
2. **Technical dimension** – describing the hardware, software, and functionality of the lecture capture environment; and

3. **Resource dimension** – describing the resource commitments made by the institution, department, faculty member, and student in using the lecture capture environment.

Let's explore these three dimensions in the context of the lecture capture process. The technical and interaction dimensions are presented as "stacks" which approximate the level of sophistication of each dimension.

Interaction Dimension

Table 1 addresses the interaction dimension: how students and faculty interact with the lecture capture solution. The elements of the interaction dimension are grouped to approximate the complexity of the interaction.

Technical Dimension

Table 2 addresses the technical dimension: how lecture capture systems are architected and the services that they provide to students and faculty. The elements of the technology dimension are

Table 2. Technical dimension

Complexity of Technology	Elements	Examples
Least Complex	Audio	Audio capture
	Video	Capture of presentation slides and audio
		Video capture of faculty member (stationary)
		Video capture of faculty member (movement)
		Video capture of faculty and students (class interaction)
		Multi-channel capture including presentation slides, instructor audio, instructor video, and student video
	Storage	Lecture metadata
		Repository
	Delivery	Podcasting and videocasting
		Integration with CMS and scheduling system
		Indexing and searching
	Extension	Scene designation and metadata by scene
		Speech-to-text and cene detection
		Advanced video production, inluding editing and transitions
Most Complex		Overlay of ancillary notes and material, hotlinks

grouped to approximate the complexity of the interaction.

Resource Dimension

Table 3 addresses the resource dimension: what investments need to be made to implement a lecture capture solution. The elements of the interaction dimension are not listed in a hierarchical sequence as they are common across all solutions.

REPRESENTATIVE TECHNOLOGIES

Most enterprise-level lecture capture systems consist of one or more capture workstations, often integrated into a classroom-based "smart podium," a server to store captured and edited lectures, another server to stream lectures to students, and a Web browser interface to view the lecture materials (Apperley, Rogers, & Masoodian, 2002; Moss, 2008). Many systems provide both "real time" lecture streaming and archived playback of lectures. Other systems are based on web

conferencing technologies and capture lectures as part of a real-time collaborative experience (Erol & Li, 2005).

Full-Featured Lecture Capture Systems

Full-featured lecture capture systems are designed and marketed specifically for lecture capture and typically include the ability to accept signals from one or more video and audio sources, record desktop activity and presentation slides and graphics, and deliver these various components to users via an integrated graphical user interface. Table 4 summarizes the features of several of these systems.

Web Conferencing Systems

Designed primarily for synchronous live conferencing, these systems may also be used for lecture capture. Table 5 summarizes the features of several of these systems.

Table 3. Resource dimension

Elements	Examples
Hardware and Software	Server costs (initial) Software costs (initial) Network costs (initial) Lecture capture station costs (initial) Audiovisual equipment purchase and installation
Maintenance	Software costs (ongoing) Audiovisual equipment maintenance (ongoing) Network bandwidth (ongoing and upgrades) Software upgrades (ongoing and upgrades) Storage (ongoing and upgrades)
Technical Support	Systems administration Audiovisual staff Contract administration
Instructional Support	Library staff Classroom scheduling Training
Life Cycle	Servers Network Software Audiovisual equipment

Screen Capture Systems

Screen capture systems typically record screen activity as a series of graphic images strung together on a storyboard to form a movie. Narrations, links, polling questions with branching interactivity, and additional video and audio may be added to the recording. Table 6 summarizes the features of several of these systems.

Audio/Video Capture Systems

These systems specialize in capturing and displaying a multitude of audio and video formats, but not in a player so that only one format may be viewed in a screen at a time. Some solutions leverage students' personal investments in personal digital players such as Apple's iPod (Eisenberg, 2007). Table 7 summarizes the features of two of these systems.

Unbundled and Low-Cost Solutions

Lower-tech and lower-cost methods for capturing classroom lectures are available to faculty members and students. These methods include audio capture, podcasting, webcams, wireless microphones, PowerPoint narration, and a range of open source software tools. There are many options for conversion of PowerPoint lectures to Java or Flash objects that can be loaded to course management systems or posted to web sites (Moss, 2008; Barnes, Scutter, & Young, 2008). While it is quite easy for individual faculty members to capture audio or even video of classroom lectures for personal use, the time required to edit, annotate, store, and distribute video lectures to groups of students is burdensome on individuals (Chandra, 2007; Gregory, 2008).

Another lower-cost approach to lecture captures is the use of student videographers, who are paid to visit classrooms, capture lectures, perform basic editing, and load the captured lectures to web sites or course management systems. This low-tech approach is difficult to scale to large

Table 4. Full-featured lecture capture systems

Product	Discussion
Accordent	www.accordent.com A suite of products including Accordent Media Management System (AMMS), Accordent Capture Station (ACS), Accordent PresenterPRO (APP), and Accordent Engage (AE). AMMS is a secure content management system including metadata search capabilities. ACS is a hardware appliance available in portable and permanently mounted models. The appliance accepts inputs from video, audio, desktop, smart whiteboard, and other VGA-enabled devices. Post-production editing of PowerPoint presentations and still graphics, indexing, and synchronization are included. APP is a web conferencing application with video, audio, chat, and polling features. Slides and still graphics may be edited during post-production. AE is a web conferencing application without video and two-way audio; audio is captured through a telephone connection.
	Advantages: Complete suite of applications. Separate appliance accepts input from multiple sources. Excellent metadata and search capability. Post-production editing options are extensive.
	Disadvantages: Needs separate hardware appliance. Duplicates some functionality of and does not integrate with course management systems. Expensive.
Camtasia Relay	www.techsmith.com/camtasiarelay.asp Camtasia Relay is a screen-capture application with audio that includes automated publishing tools. Authorized users create profiles detailing recording and playback formats (e.g. Flash, Windows Media, MP4) and delivery options (e.g. upload server, notification settings). Users start the application, choose their profile, and record their screen and audio session. The resulting video is automatically processed as instructed by the profile.
	Advantages: Records in a number of formats with a variety of playback options. Simple to use. Inexpensive
	Disadvantages: Difficult to set up on a server.
Echo360	www.echo360.com Echo360 is the result of Anystream's purchase of Lectopia. Features include a central network server with Flash media, optional classroom hardware appliance, course management system integration, classroom scheduling, classroom or campus-wide scheduling, and uncompressed multiple file archiving (e.g. video, screen capture, audio).
	Advantages: System integration. Archives in uncompressed multiple files for easy high-quality editing. Versatile with optional classroom hardware.
	Disadvantages: With classroom hardware, may be expensive. Flash-only format.
Panopto Course-Cast	www.panopto.com CourseCast is an open source thin-client lecture capture system available in hosted or on-site versions. CourseCast can use a PC as a capture station, and accepts multiple sources including screen presentations, video cameras, and audio. These sources are routed to a server where they are combined and delivered via a web-based interface. CourseCast includes a video editing application, indexing, and note capture. Recordings may be saved as uncompressed AVI, Windows Media, or Microsoft Silverlight files. Blackboard course management system integration is available.
	Advantages: Open source. Easy to use. Easy to edit. May archive either uncompressed or compressed.
	Disadvantages: MS file formats only. May need sophisticated back-end support.
Replay	www.replay.ethz.ch Replay is an open source system by the Swiss Federal Institute of Technology. Replay uses a hardware appliance, PlayMobil, to gather analog input signals (e.g. audio, video, VGA), process them, and distribute them via a server and to users with a proprietary player (Interplay). Indexing is accomplished by object character recognition and speech-to-text. Camera tracking of the lecturer, a key goal of the project, reduces the need for technical assistance and editing.
	Advantages: Open source. Indexing with speech-to-text. Camera tracking.
	Disadvantages: Proprietary player. Needs hardware appliance.
Sonic Foundry Mediasite	www.mediasite.com Mediasite works with either a portable or classroom-based hardware appliance that accept inputs from video, audio, desktop, smart whiteboard, and other VGA devices. A hosted or onsite Mediasite server allows users to schedule, organize, index, customize, secure, and track recorded content. Users display Microsoft Silverlight content using a proprietary player that includes polling, live chat, and navigation.
	Advantages: Portable or classroom based. May be hosted or on site. Internal scheduler. Player has many options.
	Disadvantages: Needs hardware appliance. Proprietary player. MS Silverlight file format only.

Table 4. continued

Product	Discussion
Tandberg Content Server	www.tandberg.com/products/tandberg_content_server.jsp Tandberg specializes in videoconferencing and telepresence, the simulation of face-to-face meetings using large screens, special lighting, and specialized room configurations. The Content Server is an extension of this technology, accepts inputs from standard H.323 or SIP video conferencing endpoints, and delivers Windows Media, Quicktime, RealMedia, or MP4 video. Users access video and presentation material using a content viewer that features a video output pane and a presentation or graphic output pane.
	Advantages: Very high-quality. Many file formats.
	Disadvantages: No Flash. Proprietary player. Separate server hardware.
Tegrity	www.tegrity.com Tegrity captures screen activity, audio, and video from cameras connected to the instructor's computer. Editing options include the ability to splice video, import external video clips into a class recording, and add searchable key words at class and chapter levels. Students can record with Tegrity if the professor allows it within a course. Tegrity may be hosted or deployed on a network.
	Advantages: Hosted or on site. Many editing options. May be student-driven.
	Disadvantages: Relatively expensive.
Video Furnace System 4	www.videofurnace.com System 4 is an IP streaming video management and distribution system with minimal auxiliary capture and editing capabilities. The propriety InStream Viewer is delivered as part of the video stream.
	Advantages: Streaming technology. Viewer delivered as part of the stream.
	Disadvantages: Minimal editing and capture options. Proprietary viewer.

Table 5. Web conferencing systems

Product	Discussion
Adobe Connect Pro	www.adobe.com/products/acrobatconnectpro Connect Pro features whiteboard, text chat, audio, video, application sharing, polling, and presentation/graphics capabilities. ConnectPro has a simple video editing applet and a slide layout configuration manager. Finished recordings may be downloaded as FLV movies.
	Advantages: High-quality delivery and playback. Simple editing possible. Full range of features.
	Disadvantages: Flash only. Only simple editing possible. Polling not live in recording. Expensive.
DimDim	www.DimDim.com An open source web conferencing system, DimDim is available as a free hosted solution (up to 20 simultaneous participants and one room) or a hosted or on-site configuration with a maximum of 1,000 participants in multiple rooms.
	Advantages: Open source.
	Disadvantages: Low quality. Open source version limited to 20 participants. No editing. Polling not live in recording.
Elluminate	www.elluminate.com The Elluminate Suite includes Elluminate Live web conferencing, Elluminate Plan scheduler, and Elluminate Publish editor. Elluminate Live has whiteboard, text chat, audio, video, application sharing, polling, and presentation/graphics capabilities. A group of non-enterprise applications called vSpaces is also available.
	Advantages: Scheduler. Editor. Full-featured.
	Disadvantages: Relatively expensive. Polling not live in recording.
Wimba Live Classroom	www.wimba.com Wimba Live Classroom features whiteboard, text chat, audio, video, application sharing, polling, and presentation/graphics capabilities. Other members of the Wimba suite include the Pronto instant messenger, Wimba Voice podcaster, voice announcements, and the Wimba Create a content authoring tool.
	Advantages: Full-featured with Voice Tools. Polling live in recording.
	Disadvantages: Relatively expensive. Not editable.

Table 6. Screen capture systems

Product	Discussion
Classroom Presenter	classroompresenter.cs.washington.edu Classroom Presenter is a tablet PC-based interaction system that shares digital ink on classroom presentation slides. When used as a presentation tool, Classroom Presenter integrates electronic slides and digital ink to combine the advantages of whiteboard and slide-based presentation.
	Advantages: Share "whiteboard" with students. May write with "digital ink."
	Disadvantages: Only for tablet PCs.
Adobe Captivate	www.adobe.com/products/captivate Captivate is a full-featured screen capture system with native compatibility with other Adobe products.
	Advantages: Very easy to use. Many options for elearning.
	Disadvantages: Flash only. Relatively expensive.
CamStudio	www.camstudio.org CamStudio is an open source screen and audio recorder based on RoboDemo, the precursor of Captivate.
	Advantages: Open source.
	Disadvantages: Relatively primitive.
Camtasia Studio	www.techsmith.com/camtasia.asp Camtasia is a full-featured screen capture system featuring advanced editing options (e.g. H.232, audio and video decoupling) and special effects such as screen tilting.
	Advantages: Full-featured. Many file formats.
	Disadvantages: Relatively long learning curve.
Cintinel Capture-Cam Pro	www.cintinel.com CaptureCam-Pro is desktop recording software that captures full motion video, screen, and sound recordings. CaptureCam-Pro produces FLV video in addition to its two proprietary formats.
	Advantages: Easy to use. Flash plus internal file format.
	Disadvantages: Only Flash and proprietary file format.
Impatica for Microsoft PowerPoint	www.impatica.com/imp4ppt Impatica converts narrated PowerPoint lectures into Java applets that play easily over the Internet using a player delivered with the content.
	Advantages: Great compression rate. Relatively easy to use.
	Disadvantages: Only works with PowerPoint. Relatively expensive.
Scate Ignite4	www.scateignite.com Ignite4's features address business training needs. A special feature of Ignite4 is its ability to simultaneously publish in almost any standard video format.
	Advantages: Many file formats. Relatively easy to use.
	Disadvantages: Designed with training rather than education in mind.

numbers of classrooms, but it places virtually no burden on faculty members and involves relatively small investments in video cameras, editing suites, and student salaries.

Many campuses take the step of posting selected lectures on public or protected web sites for on-demand retrieval, sometimes within a social networking environment such as Facebook, Ning, or YouTube. While these lectures may be used by students, they also provide a public service and promote the institution's sense of openness. Examples of public lecture retrieval sites include:

- MIT Video Lectures (ocw.mit.edu/OcwWeb/web/courses/av)
- Open Yale Video Lectures (oyc.yale.edu)
- UC Berkeley Webcasts (webcast.berkeley.edu/courses.php)

Table 7. Audio/video capture systems

Product	Discussion
Apple Podcast Producer	www.apple.com/server/macosx/features/podcasts.html Podcast Producer is included with the Apple Leopard OS X server software suite. Podcast Producer can capture audio, video, and screen content but can do so only one format at a time.
	Advantages: Built in to the OS. Very easy to use.
	Disadvantages: Apple only recording. Only can record one format at a time.
Kaltura	corp.kaltura.com Kaltura is an open source platform for web-deployed video. It may be used to collect and ingest video clips, edit and publish videos, and manage online video.
	Advantages: Open source. Versatile.
	Disadvantages: Tricky to deploy.

- Duke University Mathematics Department (www.math.duke.edu/computing/broadcast.html)
- Princeton University (www.princeton.edu/WebMedia/lectures)

Aggregator sites such as the World Lecture Project (www.world-lecture-project.org) or VideoLectures.net (www.videolectures.net) are also available and seek contributions from institutions, faculty members, and students.

IMPLEMENTATION ISSUES

Interaction Dimension

Questions of authentication and access control should be addressed early in the implementation process. The institution should decide who may access and display stored lectures, who may contribute new lectures, who may annotate existing lectures, and who may repurpose segments of existing lectures into new learning objects. Should access to lectures be open to the public, protected by ID and password, or should a mixed model be used? If a mixed model is used, who has the authority to make decisions about which lectures to post?

Intellectual property policies associated with captured lectures also need to be documented.

Faculty members need to be aware of their rights to captured lecture content and agree to post their lecture materials for their students and perhaps for the general public. If student interaction is shown in the captured lecture, then confidentiality policies and model agreements need to be established.

From the student perspective, how long will students have access to lecture materials for a particular class? Will students be able to download lecture content to their personal computers and retain the content into the future? What about student-created content?

Technical Dimension

From the technical perspective, the institution must procure the necessary hardware, software, and network resources to support implementation of the lecture capture system. Backup and retention practices need to be established, and end-to-end network testing for high-end classrooms should be conducted to insure adequate bandwidth and quality of service to those locations. As lecture capture systems are a real-time service, the technology infrastructure should be hardened to support a degree of redundancy and fail-over to maximize availability and reliability of the lecture capture solution.

The institution will also need to choose which streaming formats supported by the lecture capture solution (e.g. Flash, Windows Media, Real) will be used, and also choose which playback devices will be supported. Each additional display format and playback device adds complexity to both the technical and support environments.

Institutions choosing to capture motion in lecture video usually use videographers, which add significant cost to lecture capture services (Rui, Gupta, Grudin, & He, 2004). Automated camera tracking is available from many vendors but often yields less satisfactory results than traditional videography. Fixed cameras are the lowest-cost option but faculty members need to be aware of motion limitations during their lectures.

Audio capture remains the "weakest link" for full-featured lecture capture solutions. Individual microphones may work for stand-in-place lectures but sound quality suffers when instructors turn to face the screen, retrieve materials, or address individual students. Multiple microphone arrangements are needed when any significant level of classroom interaction is expected, and especially if student questions are to be captured. Multiple microphone arrangements must be well tuned to avoid feedback, especially in large lecture classrooms with speaker systems. It is usually impractical to equip each classroom with high-end audio capture equipment, so institutions may wish to define two or more levels of audio support for different classroom environments.

Resource Dimension

Establishing a life cycle funding model for the lecture capture system is of primary importance. The first step in this process is determining the life cycle of the lecture capture environment being built. Will the infrastructure serve the institution for three years, five years, or longer? How frequently will hardware, software, and capture equipment be refreshed and upgraded? When will another lecture capture approach render the current system obsolete? Within this initial life cycle window, costs for servers, software, storage, and networking can be projected.

If the lecture capture solution requires individual end-user licensing, then licensing costs need to be budgeted in line with the phased implementation plan and expected adoption rate for faculty members and students. A similar approach can be used to schedule classroom redesign or technical upgrades.

Technical, user, and production services also need to be arranged. Institutions will need to establish support hours and response time expectations for technical and end-user support, and to communicate those hours to faculty and students. Initial training for faculty members needs to be arranged where required, and training material needs to be distributed to faculty and students. Self-serve help documentation should be developed to reduce the need for personalized support. Processes for post-producing captured lectured also need to be established, including turnaround time for annotating and editing lectures, packaging lectures with ancillary materials, posting lectures to course management systems or public web sites, and archiving lectures.

If the lecture capture system is part of a larger institutional initiative to store historic lectures, then a retrospective conversion of old audio and video holdings should be scheduled. Archivists should be consulted to determine how best to position the content managed by the current lecture capture system to be converted to potential future formats and archived to the university collection.

From the faculty perspective, support should be provided to help faculty members redesign lectures to make them more compatible with the particular lecture capture system used, post-production issues, repurposing, and academic issues. Lectures can be segmented, Q&A sessions can be interspersed with content, and lecture segments can be designed to support varying levels of live interaction and post-production. Faculty members may redesign course pedagogy to reduce classroom absences by making lecture more interactive, not capturing information about upcoming examinations, delaying the availability of lectures, varying the nature and frequency of assessments, creating more robust examinations, and changing course grading rubrics (McCord, 2009; Young, 2009; Harpp et al., 2004).

FUTURE OPPORTUNITIES

We expect that technologies will continue to evolve faster than pedagogical techniques, but we also expect that technological developments will impact how lecture materials are used by students more than they impact the nature of lectures themselves. Personal and group productivity tools allow students to use advance and post-hoc organizers, inventory and manage ancillary materials, and package a range of multimedia material into personalized study guides. Social networking tools allow students to share their interpretations of classroom and online content and to enrich captured lectures. Personal technologies make it easy to capture audio and video and share this content with others. Students are already capturing, publishing, and commenting on their own multimedia objects (Chandra, 2007), and we expect this phenomenon to become commonplace in our classrooms even if faculty members and institutions do not provide these services.

Social networking is one of the early Web 2.0 tools to receive broad adoption. A majority of students who use social networking sites upload photos, music, or videos to these sites. Almost half of undergraduate students contribute content to photo or video sharing sites, and about one third of students use audio or video editing software to create their own content (Salaway & Caruso, 2008). Captured lectures present an opportunity for students to create their own active learning experiences from otherwise static lectures. User-generated content may be less useful as a way to distribute content than to facilitate learning by "allowing students to articulate their understanding and share that understanding with an audience they value" (Lee, McLoughlin, & Chan, 2008; Lee et al., 2008). Student collaboration is a "safer" learning environment than presenting student understanding to a faculty member, and allows students to leverage group intellectual capital and the "weak ties" of students who are not close friends but who may share information such as classroom notes and their interpretation of classroom lectures (Salaway & Caruso, 2008).

Many undergraduate students are either early adopters or innovators of new consumer multimedia and communication technologies, so undergraduate students are likely to push the use of these technologies in the classroom at faster rates than older students or faculty members. A new generation of personal communication devices makes it easier than ever to capture photos, audio, and video and to integrate these objects into collections. Many of these devices double as cell phones and personal computers and have Internet capability to facilitate rapid uploading of media files. Responding to these new devices, MIT has launched an open source initiative to display web content on smart phones (Young, 2008a). Small handheld video cameras can capture classroom activities with surprising clarity and sound quality. These new devices and their native Internet connectivity spur the generation of podcasts and videos, soften the boundaries between traditional streaming and downloading (Campbell, 2005), and change the locus of control from institutions to students.

The level of interaction within social networks, especially by today's undergraduate students, has caused many commercial course management system vendors to incorporate social networking features into their products. Once a captured lecture is posted to a social networking site, or to a course management system with social networking features, students may arrange study meetings, discuss homework or class activities, or collaborate on assignments. So in addition to integrating lecture capture directly into course management systems, we expect that next-generation CMS products will integrate social networking with lecture capture to support student-generated metadata and linkage between lectures, ancillary materials, and student contributions. Some "lightweight" lecture capture features are already integrated with some CMS environments, and we expect to see a range of lecture capture options available in the near future, with support for student-captured lecture content in addition to integration with higher-end lecture capture systems.

The number of students posting media to social networking sites is likely to result in multiple versions of classroom lectures and other learning materials posted to the same site, all with different camera angles, video and audio quality, metadata tagging, and associated comments from other students. While students are expected to capture classroom lectures at increasing rates by using their own hardware and investing their own time, enterprise lecture capture systems are likely to scale to campus-wide use at a slower pace. Enterprise solutions may capture lecture at higher audio and video quality levels, but they lack sophisticated semantic capabilities and therefore cannot impart to students the context of the lecture and identify the topics addressed in lectures that are most important to students (T. Liu & Kender, 2004). Where campuses choose to post-produce lectures with audiovisual and library staff, "workload on technical staff can rapidly become unmanageable and engender extra costs" (Burdet, Bontron, & Burgi, 2007). We expect that future lecture capture systems will have more automated or "pushbutton" approaches for controlling audio levels, integrating multiple camera views, and capturing motion in the classroom. Research into automated multi-camera control indicates that participants will view automated camera control as having similar quality to multi-camera video produced by a technician (Q. Liu, Rui, Gupta, & Cadiz, 2001). The ability to automate scene recognition, automatically associate useful metadata, and push content to appropriate web sites is an area for future development.

As online learning expands globally, we expect that more institutions will share learning objects – including captured lectures – with each other and will develop common repositories for learning objects. This will be driven in part by government regulations focused on increasing access to higher education, easing transfer requirements between institutions, and controlling costs. In Europe, the Bologna Declaration directed the higher education community to establish common assessment methods and to promote student mobility between institutions (Burdet et al., 2007). The 2008 Higher Education Opportunity Act has directed U.S. institutions to thoroughly document transfer procedures between institutions, which should provide further incentives for institutions to coordinate academic programs and perhaps share content across institutional boundaries.

As institutions capture more lecture material and post these materials online for student access, the question of sustainability is raised. How will legacy audio and video formats be preserved, which lectures should be preserved for posterity, and how will audio and video formats be converted to future formats? Many institutions face this problem today when considering how to migrate their VHS tape libraries to digital formats. While enterprise lecture capture systems may record audio and video in standard formats, many student-generated lectures may be captured in proprietary formats. Students may be able to access these recordings today using compatible display technologies; the potential for losing access to these materials in the future is significant.

CONCLUSION

Lecture capture systems can benefit students in many ways. They can respond to changing student needs for access to lecture information, facilitate the repurposing of unique intellectual content, provide increased access to rich learning materials, and support the use of student e-portfolios.

Lecture capture systems can also benefit faculty members by supporting faculty portfolios, facilitating collaboration between faculty members, and building rich learning environments for students. Lecture capture systems can also benefit institutions by providing high quality video for library collections, marketing initiatives, and community engagement initiatives.

Lecture capture systems have implications for campus classroom design, course management systems, and campus technology infrastructure. In turn, lecture capture systems themselves are impacted by development of video-capable personal communications technologies, video-enabled social networking sites, and the behavior of both students and faculty.

Opportunities exist for research in several areas including instructional effectiveness, student performance, the impact of lecture capture on student evaluations of teaching effectiveness, the impact of lecture capture on institutional reputation, and the impact of lecture capture on student attendance. Early research indicates that students may not skip attendance at classes where lectures are available online, perhaps because today's students assume that learning environments are technologically enabled (Salaway & Caruso, 2008).

Deploying high quality, user-friendly, and reliable lecture capture solutions may help students to prepare for the future virtual workplace. Campuses should plan carefully for deploying lecture capture environments and should be prepared to respond flexibly to changing technologies and student behaviors. Institutions should carefully consider their instructional needs in light of their mission, and thoroughly evaluate the instructional processes and outcomes surrounding the use of the lecture on campus. Only after understanding the place of the lecture in the life of the campus, and the potential to leverage lecture to improve instruction, can we consider whether lecture capture solutions can be used to improve instruction – and which approach to adopt and implement.

REFERENCES

Allen, I. E., & Seaman, J. (2008). *Staying the course: Online education in the United States, 2008.* Needham, MA: Sloan Consortium. Retrieved from http://www.sloanconsortium.org/publications/survey/pdf/staying_the_course.pdf

Anderson, B. (2005). Dimensions of learning and support in an online community. *Open Learning*, *19*(2), 183–190. doi:10.1080/0268051042000224770

Apperley, M., Rogers, B., & Masoodian, M. (2002). LLC lecture capture and editing tool for online course delivery. In . *Proceedings of World Conference on E-Learning in Corporate, Government, Healthcare, and Higher Education, 2002,* 1866–1869.

Barnes, L., Scutter, S., & Young, J. (2008). Using screen recording and compression software to support online learning. *Innovate, 1*(5).

Bligh, D. A. (2000). *What's the use of lectures?* San Francisco, CA: Jossey-Bass.

Burdet, B., Bontron, C., & Burgi, P. (2007). Lecture capture: What can be automated? *EDUCAUSE Quarterly*, *30*(2), 40–48.

Campbell, G. (2005). There's something in the air: Podcasting in education. *EDUCAUSE Review*, *40*(6), 32–47.

Chandra, S. (2007). Lecture video capture for the masses. In *Proceedings of the 12th Annual SIGCSE Conference on Innovation and Technology in Computer Science Education,* Dundee, Scotland (pp. 276-280).

Cook, T., & Sosin, K. (2006). Simulating a dynamic lecture online: Circular flow as an example. *The Journal of Economic Education*, *37*(1), 121–121. doi:10.3200/JECE.37.1.121-121

Cornell University. (2008). *eClips*. Retrieved December 19, 2008, from http://eclips.cornell.edu/homepage.do;jsessionid=7B78294693CBA0AE28AC3D60B6E47F8B

Eisenberg, A. (2007). What did the professor say? check your iPod. *New York Times*. Retrieved from http://www.nytimes.com/2007/12/09/business/09novel.html

Erol, B., & Li, Y. (2005). An overview of technologies for e-meeting and e-lecture. In *Proceedings of the IEEE International Conference on Multimedia and Expo,* Amsterdam, The Netherlands (pp. 1000-1005).

Grabe, M., & Christopherson, K. (2008). Optional student use of online lecture resources: Resource preferences, performance and lecture attendance. *Journal of Computer Assisted Learning, 24*(1), 1–10.

Gregory, J. R. (2008). *Automated classroom video streaming pilot at the University of Minnesota*. Paper presented at the EDUCAUSE 2008 Annual Conference, Orlando, FL. Retrieved from http://connect.educause.edu/Library/Abstract/AutomatedClassroomVideoSt/38874

Haga, H. (2004). Concept of video bookmark (videomark) and its application to the collaborative indexing of lecture video in video-based distance education. *International Journal on E-Learning, 3*(3), 32–37.

Harley, D., Henke, J., & Maher, M. W. (2008). Rethinking space and time: The role of internet technology in a large lecture course. *Innovate, 1*(1). Retrieved from http://innovateonline.info/index.php?view=article&id=3&action=article

Harpp, D. N., Fenster, A. E., Schwarcz, J. A., Zorychta, E., Goodyer, N., & Hsiao, W. (2004). Lecture retrieval via the web: Better than being there? *Journal of Chemical Education, 81*(5), 688–705.

Heck, R., Wallick, M., & Gleicher, M. (2007). Virtual videography. *ACM Transactions on Multimedia Computing, Communications, and Applications, 3*(1), Article 4.

Herman, A. (2001). *How the Scots Invented the Modern World: The true story of how Western Europe's poorest nation created our world and everything in it* (1st ed.). New York, NY: Crown Publishers.

Lee, M. J. W., McLoughlin, C., & Chan, A. (2008). Talk the talk: Learner-generated podcasts as catalysts for knowledge creation. *British Journal of Educational Technology, 39*(3), 501–521. doi:10.1111/j.1467-8535.2007.00746.x

Liu, Q., Rui, Y., Gupta, A., & Cadiz, J. J. (2001). Automating camera management for lecture room environments. In *Proceedings of the SIGCHI Conference on Human Factors in Computing Systems,* Seattle, WA (pp. 442-449).

Liu, T., & Kender, J. R. (2004). Lecture videos for e-learning: Current research and challenges. In *Proceedings of IEEE Sixth International Symposium on Multimedia Software Engineering,* Miami, FL (pp. 574-578).

Malone, J. D. (2003). Shooting the past: An instructional case for knowledge management. *Journal of Information Systems, 17*(2), 7–14. doi:10.2308/jis.2003.17.2.41

McCord, A. (2009). Detection and deterrence of plagiarism in online learning environments. In P. L. Rogers, G. A. Berg, J. V. Boettecher, C. Howard, L. Justice & K. D. Schenk (Eds.), *Encyclopedia of distance learning* (2nd ed.). Hershey, PA: IGI Global.

McInnis, C., & Hartley, R. (2008). *Managing study and work: The impact of full-time study and paid work on the undergraduate experience in Australian universities.* Retrieved December 13, 2008, from http://www.dest.gov.au/sectors/higher_education/publications_resources/profiles/managing_study_and_work.htm

Moss, N. (2008). Incorporating a rich media presentation format into a lecture-based course structure. *Innovate, 1*(2). Retrieved from http://innovateonline.info/index.php?view=article&id=10&highlight=lecture

Nagel, D. (2008). *Lecture capture: No longer optional?* Retrieved October 23, 2008, from http://campustechnology.com/articles/67990/

Phung, D., Valetto, G., Kaiser, G. E., Liu, T., & Kender, J. R. (2007). Adaptive synchronization of semantically compressed instructional videos for collaborative distance learning. *International Journal of Distance Education Technologies, 5*(2), 56–73.

Rui, Y., Gupta, A., Grudin, J., & He, L. (2004). Automating lecture capture and broadcast: Technology and videography. *Multimedia Systems, 10*(1), 3–15. doi:10.1007/s00530-004-0132-9

Salaway, G., & Caruso, J. B. (2008). *The ECAR study of undergraduate students and information technology, 2008.* Retrieved November 1, 2008, from http://connect.educause.edu/Library/ECAR/TheECARStudyofUndergradua/47485

Sensiper, S. (2000). Making the case online: Harvard business school multimedia. *Information Communication and Society, 3*(4), 616–621. doi:10.1080/13691180010002134

Shih, T. K., Wang, Y., Liao, Y., & Chuang, J. (2003). Video presentation recording and on-line broadcasting. *Journal of Interconnection Networks, 4*(2), 199–209. doi:10.1142/S0219265903000829

Sonic Foundry. (2008). *University of Wisconsin study finds strong undergraduate student preference for classes with lecture capture.* Retrieved October 23, 2008, from http://www.sonicfoundry.com/company/pressroom/press-release/University-of-Wisconsin-Study-Finds-Strong-Undergraduate-Students-Preference-for-Classes-with-Lecture-Capture.aspx

University of Maryland Baltimore County. (2008). *UMBC Blackboard - adaptive release.* Retrieved December 19, 2008, from http://www.umbc.edu/oit/newmedia/blackboard/help/audio/audio_directions.html

Young, J. R. (2008a). MIT creates version of its web site for smartphones (and plans to share code). *Chronicle of Higher Education.* Retrieved from http://chronicle.com/wiredcampus/article/3486/mit-creates-version-of-its-web-site-for-smartphones-and-plans-to-share-code

Young, J. R. (2008b). Study finds hybrid courses just as effective as traditional ones. *Chronicle of Higher Education.* Retrieved from http://chronicle.com/wiredcampus/article/3321/study-finds-hybrid-courses-just-as-effective-as-traditional-model

Young, J. R. (2009). The lectures are recorded, so why go to class? *Chronicle of Higher Education.* Retrieved from http://chronicle.com.ezproxy.ltu.edu:8080/free/v54/i36/36a00103.htm

Chapter 9

Yesterday, Today and Tomorrow's Recognition of Industry Applications within Virtual Worlds:
A Meta-Analysis of Distance Learning Instructional Achievements within Virtual World Architectural Environments, and Potential Implications for Higher Education

Caroline M. Crawford
University of Houston – Clear Lake, USA

Marion S. Smith
Texas Southern University, USA

Virginia Dickenson
eLumenata, USA

ABSTRACT

The primary focus of this chapter is to provide an analysis of business and industry case-based implementations of instructional opportunities within the Second Life three-dimensional virtual world environment, so as to delineate distance learning instructional achievements within virtual worlds and engage in a discussion related to potential implications for higher education. This provides the essential link between distance learning imperatives within the business and industry realm through a meta-analysis of industry's virtual world distance learning case-based projects. This analysis offers a framework through which to emphasize the strengths and weaknesses of distance learning projects from yesterday and today, with implications towards tomorrow's higher education distance education learning environments within virtual worlds. The framework through which this occurs is a focused presentation of the cases under review, followed by discussions related to: major areas of concern, integral distance

DOI: 10.4018/978-1-61520-672-8.ch009

learning considerations, successes of the business and industry world within virtual worlds; and potential implications for higher education distance learning within virtual worlds. As there is significant interest in the implementation of distance learning opportunities within virtual words displayed by the business and industry realm, there are innumerable "lessons learned" that will benefit higher education as institutions further enhance their distance learning opportunities within three-dimensional virtual world gaming environments.

INTRODUCTION

As business and industry embraces the strengths of distance learning within virtual world environments, there are a growing number of case studies available. However, up to this point in time, there has not been a thorough analysis of the available business and industry case studies. As such, it is timely and of utmost importance to analyze the distance learning instructional achievements of business and industry within virtual world environments, so as to delineate distance learning instructional achievements within virtual worlds and engage in a discussion related to potential implications for higher education. Further, it is imperative to focus upon potential implications for the success of higher education institutions within virtual worlds. This meta-analysis results in major areas of concern, integral distance learning considerations, and successes of the business and industry world within virtual worlds. Following this focus, a discussion related to potential implications and tomorrow's innovations will be discussed, that will directly assist and advance the efforts of higher education's distance learning opportunities within three-dimensional virtual worlds. As such this chapter's objective is to offer a meta-analysis of business and industry implementation of instructional opportunities within the Second Life virtual world environment, and provides the essential link between distance learning imperatives within the business and industry distance learning virtual world realm and potential benefits and innovations for higher education institutions' distance learning efforts.

Specifically, the discussion focuses upon the Second Life virtual world but the discussion can be framed within other virtual worlds.

BACKGROUND

The virtual world has always polarized persons within all realms of society, from the persons who eagerly engage in the virtual world environment and clearly articulate its potential, to the other end of the spectrum wherein people are comfortable in their "real" life and don't find the virtual gaming environment to hold the same "pull" for their time and attention. Of course, the reality of the societal world is that all things do change, and it is of utmost importance for different realms within society to try and engage with collegial professionals and customers where the professionals and customers naturally assemble. But what is a virtual world? Melbourne Laneways (n.d.) offers the explanation that, "Virtual worlds are computer-based two or three dimensional simulated environments that enable users to inhabit and interact with others through chat, instant messaging and voice, via 'avatars'" (p. 2). As suggested by Gronstedt (2007), "Never has the adage that 'on the Internet nobody knows you're a dog' been more true" (paragraph 5). Interesting questions are posed by Dignan (2006), which reflects concerns of those in business and industry, who are slow to engage in the virtual world gaming environment:

I just don't get the appeal for companies or gamers. My other nagging question: Are corporate activi-

ties in Second Life–the hotels, the PR firm offices, the news bureaus, meetings and brainstorming sessions–all that cutting edge? Why exactly are all these companies popping up in Second Life? Where's the value added? (paragraph 2)

Along these same lines, Athavaley (2007) states that, "For some people, the process may be too innovative. To use Second Life, for example, you have to have a certain processor speed and graphics card to be able to download the software onto your computer. The software isn't compatible with satellite Internet, dial-up Internet and some wireless Internet services" (paragraph 12). Adding value, and the subsequent return on investment, is concerns that continuously arise within business and industry, as well as training needs such as within the higher education realm. Yet there is another opinion. As quoted from Gronstedt (2007):

Second Life isn't your father's two-dimensional Web, that's for sure. It's Web 3-D. Don't let the video game look deceive you. There's no purpose, no score, no winners, and no levels of difficulty. Second Life appropriates the world-building and open-endedness of massively multiplayer games, but that's where the similarities end. Its more than 8 million registered "residents" chat with friends, attend book readings, role play, take classes, and make love. Much has been made of the sleaze in Second Life, but it also has virtual cathedrals, mosques, and synagogues. (paragraph 4)

With this significant number of users within virtual worlds, such as Second Life (Linden Research, Inc., 2008), how do companies most appropriately meet the needs of their clients (also referred to as customers) within innovative and, as yet unrealized, realms? This is the overarching question that drives this chapter forward. Yet, why do companies delve into the realm of virtual worlds? Why is this an interesting topic? Dignan (2006) addresses this need for understanding, as

relates to the potential value the virtual worlds hold for companies:

At the Terra Nova State of Play conference in New York Friday I found my answer. "Companies flock to Second Life because it's not threatening to businesses," says Edward Castronova, an Indiana University professor who runs the university's Synthetic Worlds Initiative. "It's like a Web 3.0 product. It's a 3D Web page. For visitors, a Second Life visit is the equivalent of saying 'I went to the company's Web page.'"

Castronova argues that there are more interesting possibilities for companies experimenting with the dynamics of multiplayer games such as the World of Warcraft. A few companies are studying virtual world design and how it could impact their structure. The problem with selecting a more advanced role playing game over Second Life: "It's a bigger step for a company to allow employees to be a wizard," says Castronova. (paragraphs 4-5)

This is an understandable stance, as "do no harm" to the corporation is of significant import within this shifting economic and societal realm. As suggested by Gronstedt (2007):

… in the Second Life environment, I'm drawn in. Engaged. Compelled. As the Second Life experience becomes richer and the application diffuses more widely, it's hard to imagine how existing voice- and videoconferencing can survive. This "metaverse" takes interaction and collaboration to unprecedented levels. And it's redefining training, from telling and testing to interacting with engaged minds in an immersive 3-D environment. (paragraphs 2-3)

Therefore, the ability to engage the virtual world user through interactivity and virtual collaborative ventures is strength of the environment. It is also of interest that opportunities related to training are advancing. Yet as Dignan (2006) aptly suggests, "we're still in the training wheels stage" (paragraph 7). We're still trying to figure out what's happening, and how to most appropriately frame not only the virtual world environments but also the potential strengths within virtual worlds. Athavaley (2007) further supports this stance through the learning curve realized by virtual world users:

Mishaps involving avatars are generally viewed as amusing. The blunders can even act as ice-breakers. Mr. Krefft, 30, who attended the event as a brunette female avatar named Dragon Ritt, tried to reach into his virtual inventory and hand an H-P employee his resume. Instead, he accidentally handed her a beer. (paragraph 22)

Although the learning curve appears to be taking its toll on some, the realization that three-dimensional virtual environments are a part of the "here and now" is gingerly becoming the recognized norm. To support this stance, Gronstedt (2007) noted several interesting considerations that were occurring in the second half of 2007:

It's hard to imagine why any company would wait until it hits 100 million residents before it starts learning in "Web 3-D." Consider these facts:

- *Gartner Group estimates that 80 percent of active Internet users will be in non-gaming virtual worlds such as Second Life by the end of 2011.*
- *IBM is investing millions of dollars in 25 SL islands, and a bevy of Fortune 100 companies such as Sun, Dell, Intel, Adidas, Toyota, GM, and more are all there.*
- *Hundreds of universities, including Harvard and INSEAD, teach classes in Second Life for credit.*
- *My native Sweden just opened an embassy in Second Life.*

The ability to visualize objects in 3-D is perhaps the most obvious appeal of Second Life training. Car companies can let dealers kick the tires and drive a new car. Pharmaceutical companies can take doctors on a journey through the veins of the body to explain a new cardiovascular medication. And computer companies can magnify a chip or minimize a city to explain the flow of bites and bytes. Participants and walk or fly around and inside 3-D objects. (paragraphs 7-8)

Yet, what about the potentials related to training within the virtual world? What drives business and industry into the virtual world, and what keeps them there?

Which companies should conduct training in the virtual world? Any company that is serious about attracting and keeping talented new employees from the new generation of digital natives. Virtual worlds and games are as familiar to them as television, film, or books are to the older "digital immigrant" generation. The new breed of game-savvy and socially networked employees was born after the PC revolution and want to be engaged, in control, with little patience for the century-old instructor-centric teaching model. With the world's knowledge right at the tip of their thumbs, they require their learning programs to be more engaging, more fun, more interactive, and more mobile. Smart companies are catering to the new generation workers with a new suite of emerging electronic technologies that include podcasting, wikis, blogs, video-based simulations, widgets, and social network sites, and now virtual worlds, all of which are changing the face of workplace learning. (Gronstedt, 2007, paragraphs 11-12)

The desire for talent, as well as savvy instructional design issues related to meeting the shifting training needs of learners, may be driving aspects of business and industry within the virtual world. As such, a meta-analysis of virtual world case studies is necessary and timely.

METHODOLOGY

This research implemented the meta-analysis methodology and, as such, it is appropriate to delineate the expectations inherent in this type of research study. Shachar (2008) offered a strong methodological discussion related to meta-analysis methodology as the preferred method when assessing online learning opportunities; as such, this manuscript will frame this discussion. Shachar (2008) is quoted as stating, "This meta-analytic approach may be the best method appropriate for our ever-expanding and globalizing educational systems – in general, crossing over geographical boundaries with their multiple languages, and educational systems in particular" (p. 1). Further, "It should be noted, that the meta-analytic approach may be the best (if not the only) method appropriate for our ever-expanding and globalizing educational systems – in general, crossing over geographical boundaries with their multiple languages, and educational systems in particular" (Shachar, 2008, p. 2). Further, the strengths of the meta-analysis methodology offers the opportunity to represent small case study opportunities within a larger framework of understanding. As such,

One of the benefits and advantages of conducting meta-analysis, is that it 'gives a voice' to 'small and distinct' studies, each one in itself not strong enough to qualify as being statistically significant, or robust enough to warrant serious consideration. But 'integrated together,' can contribute their findings to the 'big picture.' (Shachar, 2008, p. 3)

This study frames the meta-analysis process within the Glassian Meta-Analysis framework, which is a classic methodological framework. As described by Shachar (2008):

Glass' early meta-analyses set the pattern for conventional meta-analysis: define questions to be examined, collect studies, code study features and outcomes, and analyze relations between study features and outcomes. Features: (1) 'classic'

meta-analysis applies liberal inclusion criteria; (2) the unit of analysis is the study finding. A single study can report many comparisons between groups and subgroups on different criteria. Effect sizes are calculated for each comparison; (3) meta-analysts using this approach may average effects from different dependent variables, even when these measure different constructs. Glassian meta-analysis has proven quite robust when submitted to critical re-analysis. (p. 4)

As such, this meta-analysis methodology will follow Glass' (Glass, 2000; Glass, McGraw & Smith, 1981) meta-analysis methodological structural framework.

Subject Selection Criteria

The reasoning behind the criteria for the subject selection was obvious at this point in the virtual world case study. The reality is that any virtual world case study available at this point in history is not only rare but lacking in strict research expectations. As noted by Shachar (2008):

Many of the researchers collecting, reviewing, and extracting data from previous research studies have regrettably noted that many of said studies suffer from flaws in their research design and/ or their representation (or lack of) of complete statistical findings. Furthermore, many meta-analyses overlap in the periods they cover and the studies they include/ exclude from their data bases.... (p. 10)

The criteria for case study selection within this study is more open-ended than might normally be considered appropriate, due to the lack of prior research within this area of interest. Therefore, a Google Internet search for published case studies that were available for review on the World Wide Web was the basic framework through which to frame the selection criteria. The search verbiage was designated as "virtual world + case studies", and from the responses received evaluated the responses for specific case representations. The viable reports of "cases" became the case studies which were the focus of this virtual world case study meta-analysis. The reason behind the decision to develop an inclusive meta-analysis is as follows:

As one sparrow, does not denote the coming of spring, so do the individual studies not suffice to form an answer regarding the effectiveness of DE. Thus, meta-analysis provides a comprehensive answer to the DE versus traditional education continuing conundrum, by analyzing and synthesizing a wide body of academic comparative studies. (Shachar, 2008, p. 10)

Therefore, "The need is for research that guides practitioners in refining practice so the most effective methods are used" (Shachar, 2008, p. 10), which is the focus of this virtual world case study meta-analysis. As this type of research has not previously been implemented on this level of focus, it is appropriate and important to refine and emphasize the effective aspects of the different virtual world case studies available at this point in time.

Methodological Underpinnings of the Meta-Analysis

The meta-analysis procedures represented by Glass, McGraw and Smith (1981):

requires a reviewer to complete the following steps: carry out a literature research to collect studies; code characteristics of studies; calculate effect sizes as common measures of study outcomes; and search for relationships between study features and study outcomes. (Shachar, 2008, p. 5)

Therefore, these expectations will be met within this study.

Defining the Research Domain

The research domain within this meta-analysis is the case studies focused upon the virtual world environment. The variables focus on factors related to "learning experiences" within virtual world architectural environments, meaning what has been learned within the virtual world experiences, and what can be taken away from the case studies that may potentially impact distance learning instructional environments and potential implications for higher education.

Inclusion Criteria

The criterion within which this study is framed is all important. As such, this should be appropriately framed. The first criterion focuses upon the time element within which this meta-analysis is framed, which is difficult to determine due to the timely implementation of case study reviews within virtual worlds. This researcher frames the time period to occur between 2000-2008. The next criterion regards whether the studies were published or unpublished. As the case studies were located through a Google Internet search for "virtual world case studies", all case studies were published and available for review on the World Wide Web. Criterion three engages in the quality of the case studies. Unfortunately, the case studies were not research-oriented but more appropriately framed as action research and, as such, there is no methodological framework support delineated within any of the case studies represented within this meta-analysis. Yet each case study offers a representation of instructional, societal, and community impact within virtual worlds that may directly impact future innovations within virtual worlds; as such, it is important that the available virtual world case studies be analyzed. Further, Criterion four is not supported, due to the lack of control groups within each of the case studies delineated. Finally, Criterion five emphasizes the quantitative data representation within each case study; unfortunately, these are qualitative reports of each case and, as such, a quantitative data representation is unavailable.

Effect Size Determination

As this is a qualitative case study representation within this meta-analysis, the representation of experimental and control groups within a quantitative framework is unavailable. This study is a case-based qualitative meta-analysis, which does not support a quantitative representation of the effect size determination. As such, the step referred to by Shachar (2008) as "Determining the Individual and Overall Effect Sizes Across Studies" (p. 6) is not included within this methodological overview and progressive representation, as the case studies represented within this meta-analysis are qualitative in nature and not appropriately represented through quantitative structures.

Case Study Search

As noted previously, the case studies represented within this meta-analysis were obtained through a Google Internet-based search, using the relevant word search chain "virtual world + case study". From the search results obtained, the researcher evaluated each result for its viability as a case study that represented full-text representations of the case study.

Relevant Case Study Selection and Database Representation

As the case studies within this meta-analysis are qualitative in nature, the concept of a database is pertinent. As such, the database structure emphasized the ability to offer a "convenient repetitive sorting and extracting of data .... The final set of studies, will be selected from those studies that meet all the inclusion criteria" (Shachar, 2008, p. 6). As such, the case studies within this research study met the inclusion criteria.

Data Extraction and Coding

The relevant information and noteworthy characteristics regarding each case study has been evaluated by two other debriefers and agreed upon as both relevant and noteworthy components within each case study. As such, the relevant information and noteworthy characteristics of each case study have been included within the case-by-case representation and discussion.

Limitations Perceived by Homogeneity and Bias

As the qualitative case study meta-analysis is an initial review of innovative occurrences within the virtual world, that may affect future instructional considerations within the virtual world realm, the lack of homogeneity and parallel structure throughout the case study meta-analysis does not offer the suggestion of quantitative analyses and "chance variation in their results" (Shachar, 2008, p. 7). As the case studies are represented and framed through qualitative means, there is no concern related to the suggestion that "statistically significant results are more likely to be published and cited, and are preferentially published in English language journals" (Juni, Holenstein, Sterne, Bartlett, & Egger, 2001, as stated by Shachar, 2008, p. 7). Finally, due to the qualitative nature of this case study meta-analysis, concerns related to the following limitation is not a viable consideration for this study:

(3) Fail-Safe-N. Since only published studies are analyzed, there is the "file drawer problem," that is, how many studies that did not find significant effects have not been published? If those studies in the file drawer had been published, then the effect size for those treatments would be smaller. (Shachar, 2008, p. 7)

However, a limitation of this study is that only the Internet-published case studies were viable options and there may be innovative case studies that have not been published for consideration.

Of course, there are limitations related to meta-analysis research. As stated by Shachar (2008):

A meta-analysis is not a panacea and/or a perfect solution to all research studies. There are many within the professional statistical community who question its suitability and validity by using buzz-words like "you are comparing apples to oranges," and that the heterogeneity of studies does not allow for true comparisons. (p. 9)

Yet, "even if we do accept some scientific criticism, on the practical side, there is no other better method available to synthesize numerous studies" (Shachar, 2008, p. 9).

A REVIEW OF CASE STUDIES: DISTANCE LEARNING INSTRUCTIONAL ACHIEVEMENTS WITHIN VIRTUAL WORLD ARCHITECTURAL ENVIRONMENTS

Back in 1994, Ressler (1994) of the National Institute of Standards and Technology set up an Open Virtual Reality Testbed and developed a case study "touchstone" document that notes the leading edge virtual reality implementations within the world of manufacturing. Some of the businesses included in the case study analysis were: Ford (Ford Motor Company, 2008); Boeing (The Boeing Company, 2008); Caterpillar (Caterpillar, 2008); Matsuhita's Virtual Kitchen (Johnstone, 2003); Equipment Maintenance at Columbia University (Feiner, MacIntyre & Seligmann, n.d.; Columbia University, n.d.); and, NASA's Hubble Space Telescope Maintenance (National Aeronautics and Space Administration, n.d.), and the Virtual Wind Tunnel (National Aeronautics and Space Administration, 2008). Ressler (1994) summarized, based on these case studies from the mid-1990s, that:

Virtual environment technology is an evolving collection of technologies. The application of virtual environments to help solve manufacturing problems gives manufacturing engineers new tools to solve complex problems. Virtual environments offer the engineer new ways to not only visualize their problem spaces but to interact with their environment. Many manufacturing problems can be readily visualized by images of parts or manufacturing processes. These visualizations, based on reality, can be used as an effective conceptual mechanism for the more complete visualizations embodied by virtual environments. (p. 10)

The realities of return on investment were a reality in the 1990s, much as they are today and will be tomorrow. Yet the Internet was only just being released to the public at this point, so the idea of an Internet-connected virtual world that frames social interaction and networking was not yet a consideration. Again, as noted by Ressler (1994),

Although these early applications are highly constrained they are still useful first steps. Decisions made in the design process are the costliest to correct. Virtual environment techniques can improve the design process by integrating human judgement at a far earlier stage of product design then previously possible. Inexpensive changes to the design and rapid prototyping using these environments should improve the quality and reduce the development time for new products. (p. 11)

Therefore, it is appropriate and necessary to analyze the more recent virtual world innovations as regards business and industry, especially as regards training opportunities, which may offer implications towards higher education institutions. It is appropriate to offer overviews of specific case studies at this point, with the primary focus being the experiential outcomes.

Melbourne Laneways

Melbourne Laneways (Melbourne Laneways, n.d.) was a pilot project that finalized its mission and in August 2008 was removed from Second Life (Linden Research, Inc., 2008). Melbourne Laneways was described as:

Using Second Life as a case study, the project involved the development of a prototype – Melbourne Laneways - created in partnership with Victorian Government agencies Multimedia Victoria, Tourism Victoria and Invest Victoria. Melbourne Laneways captures the quintessential characteristics of Melbourne, such as cafes in hidden laneways and Federation Square. It is currently located on the Australian Broadcasting Corporation's well-established Second Life presence "ABC Island". (p. 2)

This case study focused upon the development of a prototype, so as to evaluate the experience associated with developing a virtual world representation of Melbourne, State of Victoria, Australia, so as to research who visited the site and why they may have visited the site. As stated by the State of Victoria, Australia (2008):

Anecdotal evidence suggests that people are interested in the Melbourne Laneways concept. The visual design attracted visitors, along with a number of thematic and competitive events such as the Melbourne Cup scavenger hunt. The audience responded positively to the information being provided to them, and indicated they would even visit Melbourne based on their experience in Melbourne Laneways. (paragraph 6)

Concerning the daily management of the Melbourne Laneways, the researchers realized three primary components of importance:

In practise, managing a virtual presence requires steadfast dedication to foster collaboration and interaction. The following requirements were identified:

- immersive events that engage residents
- virtual content that directly relates to business objectives
- a strong community group to support the presence (paragraph 7)

As such, the importance related to creating an engaging community wherein persons behind the avatars feel compelled to return to actively connect with the content and with the interactive events offered. The design of the virtual world's ease of engagement with an emphasis upon community gathering, real-world understanding of learner needs, and the "play" aspects of fun scavenger hunt games that further addresses the metaphoric representation's follow-through within the virtual world environment so that the learners were not only tied to business objectives but also "down time" to lessen cognitive load issues were inherent within the environment.

The Philadelphia Museum of Art: Brancusi's Mademoiselle Pogany

Works of art are presented to the world through museum exhibitions, but with the introduction of the Internet there are new ways through which to share the beauties of art with a larger world that wouldn't have the opportunity to otherwise share in the beauty. The Philadelphia Museum of Art launched Branchusi's Mademoiselle Pogany on June 1, 2008 (McCall, 2002) and is designed as "A navigable on-line exhibition built in VRML for the Philadelphia Museum of Art website to describe and set in context a series of sculptures that the artist Brancusi developed over a nineteen-year period" (McCall, 2002, paragraph 1). An interesting discussion as regards virtual museum design follows:

Many virtual museum authors seem to forget that whilst their building is an important part of their presence in the physical world, the museum actually exists as a concept to collect objects and create interpretive displays around them. Too often virtual museums are architectural rather than interpretive or narrative. Narrative Rooms' Mlle Pogany does not replicate a real room to the point of photographic reality. Instead it concentrates on displaying sculptures and related items in a 'suggested' reality. Only two architectural metaphors (inlaid floor and imposing doorways) are needed to situate the user firmly within a museum environment. Thus situated, the user can concentrate on the exhibits themselves.

What also differentiates the Mlle Pogany exhibition from other digital musuems is its use of content and conventions created exclusively for the Web and not transferred from the real museum directly. Too often digital museums show exhibitions that are taking place in the real museums. Whilst this is useful perhaps for the prospective real visitor, a virtual visitor need not be served up a second-hand version of a real exhibition. Photographs of a real exhibition, when condensed into the scale and medium of the Web, serve to tell the virtual visitor nothing about the objects displayed. For instance a photograph of a real exhibition will not show the information boards in sufficient detail for the virtual visitor to participate in any interpretation of objects. Likewise the objects or paintings themselves are unlikely to have been produced in any detail. The Mlle Pogany exhibition uses that museum metaphor of information boards but with thought for the change in medium and scale, reproducing them on an exaggerated scale. Likewise it is selective in the photographs and supporting information that it reproduces at a sensible scale. Much thought has gone into the narrative experience and the way that the technology can be used to bring this out. (McCall, 2002, paragraphs 6-7)

As such, the environment should be interpretive and supportive, rather than the primary focus of the user's experience. Also of note is the emphasis upon the design and development of the environment, wherein the museum metaphor is rethought towards an embellished virtual scale, to enhance the visitor's experience as related to the content. As such, serious consideration was given to the navigation throughout the web site, to try to ease the user's movement throughout the site:

Narrative Rooms decided that the proprietary VRML CosmoPlayer interface was inappropriate for what they were trying to achieve. They found it complicated, offering the average web user too many options for movement, thus allowing too many opportunities to become lost. They felt that this caused the user to concentrate on navigating rather than the actual content of the VRML world. Acting on this they customised the interface, simplifying the navigation only to that available with the familiar mouse. The price paid for this (loss of ability to look down, look up, slide sideways etc.) was felt to be worth it, as the visitor gained concentration and engagement with the content. (McCall, 2002, paragraph 8)

As further noted by McCall (2002),

Tests were then conducted, both internally and within the museum, to check that the assumptions made about ease of navigation held up and to assess how effectively the exhibition was telling its story. This useful process helped the team to make significant technical and editorial adjustments before uploading the exhibition to the Philadelphia Museum of Art web site.

The use of two very basic architectural metaphors, that of the doorway and the floor, to suggest the space of the exhibition certainly has an aesthetic justification, but it is also a practical response to the necessity of keeping files small. McCall states that his colleague Hank Graber is a 'genius' at compression! The entire exhibition has a file size of only 400 kilobits. (paragraphs 16-17)

The size considerations are of import, due to the speed by which users can download files and manipulate their way through the navigation structure; however, the integration of a metaphor is of import to frame the user's conceptual framework of understanding (Vygotsky, 1935, 1962, 1978, 1981; Wertsch, 1985) as well as concerns related to file size. Also of interest is the use of a museum map structure that allows the user to track where they are in the museum, and which way they are facing so as to move forward appropriately.

Such a juxtaposition of 2-D and 3-D touches on one of the fundamental questions about 3-D navigation on the Web: how successful is it?

One of the claims for 3-D is that it provides a more intuitive interface than 2-D because it is more like the real world. Anyone who has suffered through the experience of navigating the typical VRML world on-line can tell you that it is nothing like the physical world; neither is it "naturally" more intuitive than other media that have had time to develop and whose conventions and vocabulary have become a well understood part of the culture. (McCall, 2002, paragraphs 10-11)

As such, the use of the tracking map, to support the user's understanding of location and forward movement, offers the two-dimensional interface, to allow the users to more appropriately frame and navigate the three-dimensional virtual world. The virtual world considerations emphasized within this case focus upon: ease of navigation such as through the creation of a built-in navigation support for users; creative, stimulating virtual environments instead of "real world" architectural representations; an emphasis upon content and conventions designed for the virtual world instead of physical world; an emphasis upon virtual world design and development to support learner's understanding; and, a streamlined virtual world environment so as to ease download volume issues.

Dynamic Retailing: Virtual Furniture Sold by Ikea in World

The concept of designing one's own space within a virtual world engages in a person's desire for a perfect conception of one's alternative world possibilities. Carter (2008) describes Ikea's venture into the virtual world as:

Players of The Sims 2 will soon be able to add Ikea furniture to their virtual homes as part of a marketing deal between the Swedish company and Electronic Arts, the computer game's producer.

EA has formed an unusual partnership with Ikea to make a selection of the retailer's furniture and home furnishings available to players of The Sims 2, sequel to The Sims - the life simulator that is the best-selling PC game series ever. (Carter, 2008, paragraphs 1-2)

As such, the concept of choosing virtual furniture to develop one's own spatial environment is a basic instinct in a person's conception of their alternative virtual life. Ikea has delved into the concept of virtual retailing, described as:

Creating 3D representations of real world products and using them as the prime focus for a retail transaction or environment is called dynamic merchandising. Both metabrands and real world products can use this technique to sell.

Interestingly, the concept of dynamic merchandising is also the basis for a newly emerging marketing facet in virtual worlds - Product placement. (Kzero, 2007a, paragraphs 1-2)

An interesting concept of dynamic retailing, especially as regards product placement, is the idea of:

... creating objects at sizes far larger than normally expected can bring advantages. These include:

- *Interaction. Particularly applicable when recreated real world products, being able to examine and interact with them on a supersized scale brings consumers closer to the product*
- *Uniqueness. With so much of the virtual landscape in normal size, creating objects on a larger scale means they stand-out.*
- *Experience. There's some great examples in Second Life and There of places containing objects at fantastically large scales. And, these places seem extremely successful at driving traffic and creating communities.*
- *Product placement. For the time-being at least, placing supersized real world objects into virtual worlds acts as a simple yet effective method of product placement.* (Kzero, 2007b, paragraphs 3-4)

As suggested by the Ikea company, "The Ikea UK marketing manager, Anna Crona, added that the Sims tie-up fitted neatly with the brand's current marketing line, that home is the most important place in the world" (Carter, 2008, paragraph 7). To more appropriately delineate the expectations of the Ikea marketing effort, focused upon personalizing the virtual world environment:

The success of The Sims has generated a number of online communities committed to the game and eager to share content they have created inside the game," said Nancy Smith, the EA global president for The Sims label.

As a result, we know not only players' passion for creating their own content but their desire to interact with brands. It's an environment in which players like to blur the line between the digital and real world. (Carter, 2008, paragraphs 5-6)

This add-on software package supports the virtual world user's need to not only personalize their world, but also to develop a level of comfort within the virtual world through the integration of "comfort" brands, such as Ikea. In turn, this virtual venture is a brilliant marketing effort to further engage the intended audience. Concerning the future possibilities related to the integration of product placement marketing efforts within the virtual environment:

With UK games industry turnover now outstripping film box office receipts, brand owners' interest in games as an advertising medium is growing fast, according to Mark Boyd, the head of content at advertising agency BBH, which is exploring in-game advertising for a number of leading brands. ...

The games industry has been built on high street sales rather than advertising revenue so it's not surprising many companies have been slow to evolve in-game advertising. This, however, is now beginning to change, said Boyd. (Carter, 2008, paragraphs 13,16)

This shift towards a virtual world wherein marketing efforts are slowly being realized is a natural progression towards a comparable real world and virtual world experience. As such, this case suggests the following: the ability to engage "real world" representations within the virtual world spatial environment; consideration towards lively, energetic product interest within virtual worlds; and, the importance of interaction, uniqueness, and brand experience can emphasize dynamic marketing within virtual worlds.

Geo-Tagging: Philadelphia, Pennsylvania, USA

Creating virtual world cities, so as to reflect real world cities, is an interesting consideration. The GeoSimPHILLY (GeoSim Systems Ltd., 2008) virtual city representation features the ability for: human interaction, which "allows you to see and to be seen by other online Virtual Philadelphia users, and to communicate with them" (GeoSim

Systems Ltd., 2008, paragraph 1); city planning, which "allows you to have a glimpse on how center Philly will look like 5, 10 and 15 years from now" (GeoSim Systems Ltd., 2008, paragraph 2); electronic shopping (e-shopping) opportunities, which "provides you with the experience of "real shopping" by combining standard e-commerce tools with a true-to-life city model" (GeoSim Systems Ltd., 2008, paragraph 3); the ability for local searching, which "combines free-hand 3D-navigation of center Philly with automated searches of businesses, addresses, buildings and city landmarks and customized itineraries" (GeoSim Systems Ltd., 2008, paragraph 4); and, even virtual tours, which "offer guided tours of center Philly customized for particular interests of major groups of tourists and visitors" (GeoSim Systems Ltd., 2008, paragraph 5). The geo-spatial model that represents the downtown city area of Philadelphia is merely a three-dimensional model representation, but is enhanced through the engagement of the visitors through virtual human interactions, forethought concerning city planning, the need for visitors to experience e-commerce as occurs in the real world, searching capabilities in order to locate places of interest, and even a virtual tour which can also occur in the real world of a tourist. As quoted from the GeoSim Systems (Kzero, 2008b):

Virtual Philadelphia conveys to a captivated audience of local residents, national and international tourists and visitors the true experience of being there, combined with a variety of location-related content and useful applications, such as: Local Search, Virtual Tours, City Planning, E-Shopping and Human Interaction. As a user you have the option to walk, hover, jump to and simply roam through true-to-life Virtual Philadelphia, or to meet other users, to click on any building, bus stop or shop to find out more information about it or even to go inside. (paragraph 3)

So, how might the virtual realization of a real-world city, such as Philadelphia, be of interest as a case study?

Initial thoughts - it looks and feels as though it could be a hybrid product mashed together from Google Earth, Maps and Street View. This is mainly because of the four view options available. You can see a typical 'top down' map with street names, a fly-by mode a-la from a aeroplane window looking down onto the virtual city, a hover mode (similar to flying in SL) and finally a walking mode that puts you on da streets. It's a nice mix and works well together. (Kzero, 2008b, paragraph 5)

This mashup-style virtual world suggests the potential for real-world data in a real-time offering. To define a mashup, "In web development, a mashup is a web application that combines data from more than one source into a single integrated tool. The term Mashup implies easy, fast integration, frequently done by access to open APIs and data sources to produce results data owners had no idea could be produced" (Wikipedia, 2008, paragraph 1). As delineated by Kzero (2008):

What I mean by this is obtaining and then augmenting third-party data sources and overlaying them onto and into the virtual city. And, a lot of this third-party geo-data is already available, albeit in different sources and disparately located. The limit of my brain breaks this data down into key distinct groups - aggregated (macro) and individual (micro).

Micro data, in other words information relating to individuals could take mirror worlds to another level completely. The most obvious source of geo-specific data is the mobile phone. It's already possible to calculate the location of a phone using triangulation and there's several companies in the market offering this service. But embedding this data into a virtual space brings the data much more to life. (paragraphs 8, 12)

Therefore, this dynamic, database-driven mashup of the real world and a virtual world is an interesting consideration towards future implications of virtual worlds. Within this case, there are further areas of interest: the human interactions developed to reflect "real world" interactions; an opportunity to experience "real world" daily endeavors such as shopping and visiting "real world" landmarks; "real world" city planning opportunities that may alleviate future development concerns; engage potential "real world" tourists and visitors prior to travel.

German Deutsche Steinkohle AG (DSK): Mining Industry Virtual Reality

Virtual worlds offer opportunities that also allow businesses and industries to introduce product visualization into the organizational process.

Deutsche Steinkohle AG (DSK), a German mining company, is actively engaged in introducing the latest 3D technologies into the company's working processes most notably in the dynamic visualization of mine configuration where 3D visualization allows for an improved decision making process. The simulation of equipment functionality in a virtual environment also helps to estimate at an early stage any potential logistical problems. 3D technology is also used in the introduction of new equipment in both business presentations and personnel training. (Parallel-Graphics, 2008, paragraph 1)

The ability to present a virtual the functionality of the product and to offer training to the business personnel were concerns, and the most appropriate and innovative way through which to safely test the system functions was through the virtual environment framework, wherein "DSK in cooperation with Voest-Alpine-Bergtechnik has developed a new road-header system, AVSA (Alternative Version Simultaneous Activities), which simultaneously performs activities such as cutting, bolting, loading and roof support" (Paral-

lelGraphics, 2008, paragraph 2). To delineate the strengths of this venture:

Hands-on training in the mining industry is very expensive so the use of virtual environments in the first phases of the training process allows the company to avoid operational mistakes and also increase hands-on training safety. Deutsche Steinkohle recognizes Virtual Reality as one of the most important educational tools of the future. (ParallelGraphics, 2008, paragraph 5)

The amount of money involved in the training, the potential return on investment, and the ability to represent the innovative product to current and potential clients is of utmost importance due to the marketing and training possibilities. Through this case interesting concepts are realized: "real world" product visualization; emphasis upon hands-on training within a virtual environment; and, engaging support for sales persons and product marketing opportunities.

Santa Clara Island: University Case Study

Institutions of higher education have taken an interesting step into the virtual world, and Santa Clara University is an interesting case study regarding

... the Santa Clara University's Information Commons and Library replica in Second Life. "The essential challenge posed by Santa Clara Island was to design and build a faithful replica of the Information Commons and Library of Santa Clara University — then in the early phases of construction, that could be used by students and faculty at Santa Clara University to explore innovative ideas for the interior spaces. (New Media Consortium, 2008, paragraph 1)

Further,

The interior of the Information Commons and Library, however, was designed to allow ex-

perimentation with ideas for a reference desk, classroom and theater spaces, group study and reading areas, a store, a multi-purpose studio space, and a café." (New Media Consortium, 2008, paragraph 5)

The concluding realization by Santa Clara University is that, "Now that the build is complete, the library interiors and other campus spaces provide faculty and students with a variety of settings to support classes and learning experiences in Second Life" (New Media Consortium, 2008, paragraph 7). This case emphasized the ability to test and engage in creative interior spatial endeavors such as the design of environments; and, focus upon "real-world" physical space design without monetary allocation and outlay.

BDO Stoy Hawyard: Britain's Sixth-Largest Accountancy Firm

BDO is Britain's sixth largest accountancy firm, which has recently foraged into the virtual world of Second Life. It is rather interesting that an accounting firm was interested in setting up a site to encourage visitors. As described by Kzero (2008b):

'It's nice to see BDO Stoy Hayward - Britain's sixth-largest accountancy firm - taking the plunge into Second Life, the virtual world where users can soclalise, learn new skills and even start a business. Okay, most other firms set up their virtual shops over a year ago (when Second Life was still exciting) but this is an accountancy practice and we hear they can be a little conversative.

So, what delights does BDO have for you on Second Life? On BDO's "island" you can watch three short films about, er, tex investigations. The firm's Daniel Dover said: "These films bring humour to a serious area, demonstrating different situations where people would have benefitted

from taking professional advice". The idea, you see, is to encourage tax dodgers to call BDO before the Revenue comes a-knockin'. Has there been much interest yet? "No phone calls yet', a spokesperson said, "but we're certainly hopeful." (Kzero, 2008a, paragraphs 1-2)

For BDO, it is a perfect time to engage in the virtual world, due to a recent US court ruling in favor of the IRS; however, it is suggested that there are issues with the lack of virtual world space development as regards appropriate marketing of the business product:

The venue itself is a dedicated island and is looking a little empty. Let's not forget there are other ways of launching into Second Life. It would make a great venue for a beach party though, and yes, I'm being serious.

However, perhaps it's the perfect time for BDO to have a presence in SL. A recent ruling in the US by the IRS has put the cat amonst the pidgeons with respect to company employees and contractors in virtual worlds. (Kzero, 2008a, paragraphs 6-7)

As pertains to the idea of engaging virtual world avatars as part-time or full-time employees, such as to set up events to launch or market products, an interesting recent event is:

It certainly is an interesting precedent. With the U.S. Congress looking at virtual worlds from multiple angles and a report still in the works from the Joint Economic Committee on virtual worlds and taxes, an official rule from the IRS could start to see some larger effects.

It's worth noting that it doesn't seem like this ruling wasn't over the virtual/real nature of the job, but over the contractor/employee discussion. Even so, Sweden has already declared in-world transactions taxable, and it looks like the U.S. is starting to view virtual world jobs as just a little more real as well. (Virtual Worlds News, 2008a, paragraphs 3-4)

There are several interesting considerations as regards this case study, such as the world view taken by the accounting firm and the ability for the business to reach its targeted audience. Further, it is interesting to note that virtual worlds are coming into focus by governmental entities, and the virtual world taxable work transaction potentials; how might part-time and full-time employment be shifting within the virtual worlds, and how might this impact businesses and industries. Therefore, this case study emphasizes the following considerations: virtual learning experiences to support and engage within social responsibility; potential marketing towards future clientele; the ability to quickly address changes in organizationally oriented laws and decrees within a virtual world environment; and, emphasize a shift in tax-base considerations within the virtual world.

Coca Cola: Virtual Thirst Campaign within Virtual Worlds

Coca Cola started a virtual thirst campaign within a virtual world, with the primary focus being the ability towards "Integrating real life brands in Second Life" (Virtual Worlds News, 2007a, paragraph 2). The focus was to find an innovative way through which to distribute the brand within the virtual world, and maintain an interest in putting an end to thirst. The winning product idea is described as:

Michael Donnelly from coke Stage three: This idea that crayon brought to us resonated with me and my amangement. It resonated with what we call the "Coke Style of Life," of creativity and fun. The machine would dispense experiences. And the advisory board has since designated a winner, and we're in the production mode of creating this project now. And then we'll distribute it for free

in the hopes that it will distribute virally around the metaverse. (Virtual Worlds News, 2007a, paragraph 6)

There were other ventures, as well, but Donnelly stated that, "I want to make a strong point. SL is important to us, but it always has to be part of an integrated plan. SL was a perfect platform to launch around the world, but we also had mainstream media" (Virtual Worlds News, 2007a, paragraph 9); further, "Coke didn't sell any more cans of soda. It wasn't about selling more cans. That's the most important thing, we can't deny that. But this was about lifestyle branding" (Virtual Worlds News, 2007a, paragraph 14). The importance of lifestyle branding, especially the reflection of lifestyle branding in virtual worlds that will spill over into the real world, is a natural progression for virtual world avatars that are controlled by real world persons with potentially disposable income.

As regards lessons that have been learned by the Coca Cola marketing troupe, integral aspects regarding the reality of marketing real world products within the virtual world have been offered:

Listen and communicate with the community, not at them. Partner with pros, crayon has been phenomenal. SL is community driven not location driven. This is about community, not prims. Success is organic, and being flexible is good. We embraced our critics and changed midstream. Someone said our prize wasn't that good, so we enhanced it. I'd rather people say harsh things about us than nothing about us. Maximize success by using multiple channels. That's just basic marketing 101. Strike a balance between art and science. That's a Coca Cola mantra. There's a lot of science behind the metrics. It's about experience and selling product. (Virtual Worlds News, 2007a, paragraph 16)

As noted in the quotation, it is interesting that the basic aspects of marketing in the real world are also embraced within the virtual world. Listen to the community, communicate with the community, the ability to revise ideas and shift partway through the development process, and making the experience reflect the mantra of the company. This case also emphasized the following points for consideration: the distribution of brands within the virtual world; viral branding of products within the virtual world; marketing of product within the virtual world; the need to enhance communications with the community to whom the product is marketed; and, flexibility is inherently important within the virtual world.

Pepsi: Virtual Collaboration with MTV

Pepsi developed a real world collaboration with MTV that was meant to market the Pepsi brand to the MTV viewers. MTV offered the following statement:

In March, MTV said that it would be pushing its virtual worlds as a channel for advertisers at the upfronts later this week. The major push, it seems, is coming from a new case study of Pepsi's work in vMTV. An online survey of 600 consumers conducted for MTV Networks in January by Harris Interactive and Mauro New Media looked at 300 viewers of "The Hills" and 300 non-viewers. Fans like the on-air "Hills," but they love Pepsi' virtual presence. Users average 28-minutes/ interaction with Pepsi's presence compared to its 30-second televised. (Virtual Worlds News, 2008a, paragraph 1)

Further, an interesting consideration for marketing opportunities is that the time and effort of current and potential customers may be shifting from television-focused time spent towards online time.

As for the upfronts, MTV's pitch is that as advertising's reach on television lags, connected properties

online are a strong alternative. Part of the benefit the study identifies is that there are groups of fans that build the community with identifiable behaviors--a cross between Richard Bartle's archetypes and Malcom Gladwell's Tipping Point theories. "Seekers," 54% of the participants, look for all the content they can find. "Generators," about 33% of the participants, go farther, creating messages, narratives, and avatars. (Virtual Worlds News, 2008a, paragraph 4)

It's an interesting event that occurred, which is "a story that touches on most of the major television plays in virtual worlds" (Virtual Worlds News, 2007b, paragraph 1) when Pepsi integrated its brand into MTV's virtual worlds:

... in particular, their successful relationship with Pepsi. Pepsi, which is now in talks to renew its contract with MTV, was involved with the television version of Laguna Beach, but then decided to follow the reality show into the virtual world. "The opportunity to take it into the virtual world was attractive to us. It was a natural extension," says John Vail, director of interactive marketing at Pepsi. "Laguna Beach consumers consume the show across many different media platforms, and we want to consistently be a part of that experience." (Virtual Worlds News, 2007b, paragraph 1)

This event seemingly enabled Pepsi to become further engaged with their customers and potential customers, as suggested by the following quotation:

What surprised us is how many people have touched the Pepsi brand," notes Tim Rosta, svp of integrated marketing at MTV. "About 85 percent of users in the [virtual] world have actually interacted with that brand. Is it engaging? Yes. Users are interested in replicating what they do in real life. (paragraph 3)

As such, the suggestion that the brand must be engaging and worthwhile within the virtual world is important to realize. However, it is an interesting realization that the real world marketing events can potentially shift into the virtual world and either extend the brand's appeal more fully or pull in new potential customers into engaging with the product through marketing events. This case study focuses upon the following considerations: virtual worlds as a conduit for product placement and advertisement; enhanced shift of the marketing target from television and print media towards online; and, the integral importance related to engaging with the customer base.

Second Health Project: Medicine within the Virtual World

An interesting shift in health considerations is occurring through a United Kingdom medical event occurring in Second Life, wherein "The Second Health Project was unusual in that it was not explicitly focused on building a presence in the virtual world of Second Life, but rather on using that world to tell a visual story about a unique vision for the near-term future in real life" (NMC Virtual Worlds, n.d., paragraph 1). The focus of the experience were based upon the shift from treating illness towards total wellness concerns, as reflected through the following statement: "The explicit outcomes of the project were three videos, each portraying the way a medical situation would be handled under a wholly new system of healthcare — one based on the central idea of wellness as opposed to illness" (paragraph 2). To engage in real world health events within the virtual world,

Animations were created to simulate heart attacks, limps, and the ways in which care givers would interact with their patients. All the uniforms used by these care givers had to be precise, and instantly recognizable by residents in the UK. Of

particular importance was to represent life in a contemporary city in the UK, and avatars had to be created to represent all manner of people, large and small, fit and not-so-fit, and representing a wide range of ethnic groups and races in both their form and clothing. (NMC Virtual Worlds, n.d., paragraph 7)

Interesting is the continued implementation of the medical environment, where "The hospital continues to be used for medical and other training, and can be viewed on Second Health, one of the *Scilands* (Science and Technology in Second Life) islands" (NMC Virtual Worlds, n.d., paragraph 9). This ability to lay out specific forms of medical and related training within a virtual world ensures the "safe" environment through which to engage the learners without the real world concerns related to life and death situations. Considerations related to this case focus upon: the ability for virtual worlds to reflect the inherent shift in major areas of professional focus; and, the ability to create and engage within important training opportunities within a "safe" framework, such as health-related concerns.

Virtual Campuses: Rollings College and University of Potsdam

The investment in a virtual world campus is just as important as the investment higher education institutions make in their real world "bricks and mortar" campus. Interesting aspects concerning the integration of a virtual world into the student interest world in marketing the university and the offering of a parallel virtual campus environment are:

Integrating SL into Student Life Cycle:

1. You can integrate before students come to campus. Do PR events, give tours, and provide video on YouTube for viral marketing. You have a real attraction between campus

faculty and students with tours. It's another channel to communicate. And it enhances brand awareness.

2. Once you're there you can give a virtual class, offer office space and advising.
3. After the student leaves, you can connect your campus organization. You can organize job fairs. And it hasn't been done yet, but it's a great idea to organize venture competitions. (Virtual Worlds News, 2007a, paragraph 23)

Also of interest are the suggestions regarding how one might structure a virtual world campus environment:

How do you structure the virtual campus?

1. You need a walking campus where you arrive.
2. College space.
3. Student Union
4. Research and Development
5. Faculty connections (Virtual Worlds News, 2007a, paragraph 24)

These issues are useful considerations towards framing the needs of higher education institutions within the virtual world. Other than the time and effort necessary to train the faculty, staff and administration in the virtual world realm, there are potential benefits noted:

What are the benefits?

*   Financially, quantitative analysis is difficult. We want to increase enrollment. One student more is good.
*   You also get PR and buzz
*   Non financial
*   New communication channel
*   Connect to students, the millenials (Virtual Worlds News, 2007a, paragraph 28)

These are useful aspects that must be addressed, as lessons learned by the virtual campuses are use-

ful to not only institutions of higher education, as well as business and industry. This case suggests the following considerations of import: meeting the student-client user's interests and needs within the virtual world; emphasis upon marketing the positive "real world" student service and student life, so as to frame the university as an engagingly supportive environment; and, support the student's procedural understanding of the "real world" physical environmental expectations.

CASE STUDY CONCERNS: ISSUES, CONTROVERSIES AND PROBLEMS

With the presentation of the above case studies, the careful delineation, and highlighting of major areas of issues, controversies, and problems should be more fully described. One issue that was clearly of concern, as has also been a concern in the two-dimensional world of web site navigation, is the confusion associated with "offering the average web user too many options for movement, thus allowing too many opportunities to become lost. They felt that this caused the user to concentrate on navigating rather than the actual content of the VRML world. Acting on this they customised the interface, simplifying the navigation" (McCall, 2002, paragraph 8). This need for simple navigation throughout a virtual world is of utmost importance, not only to ensure the return of users but also for ease of site maintenance.

A second area of interest is the experimentation that is occurring within the virtual world architecture, which can have positive or negative outcomes. For example, within today's society, the world of terrorism is a real concern that is further emphasized as relates to the geo-tagging of specific cityscapes, and related mashups of information within the same context, that may have the opportunity to create a dangerously available framework through which to plan and execute terrorist attacks.

As well, concerns related to fully built out virtual world locations must be addressed, to as to engage more fully in community gathering places. After all, the desire for virtual world users to have places to come together is just as necessary as is realized within the real world.

Finally, a growing area of concern within virtual worlds is the issue that revolves around part-time and full-time workers within the virtual world; more to the point, are these workers compensated and, if so, how will this compensation be appropriately taxed? As quoted by the Virtual Worlds News (2008a), "I actually think that this is an interesting precedent - that part-time workers in a virtual world, and using their own equipment, schedule, and judgment to perform tasks, have been ruled as employees," explained Constable (paragraph 2).

Of course, there are always several factors of substantial impact that may be brought forward as a form of virtual world consideration.

CASE STUDY CONSIDERATIONS

As the concerns related to this case study meta-analysis are of integral import, the case study considerations are also of impact within the discussion. This section is offered on a case-by-case basis, wherein each case's considerations are addressed.

The Melbourne Laneways (Melbourne Laneways, n.d.) case study focused upon community engagement, so as to further engage users within a creative environment. Also of impact were the real-world understandings of the learner needs, as tied to "real world" learning objectives. This is of consideration due to the learner and instructor needs within any type of learning environment, but perhaps more so within a novel learning environment within which the learner has not yet created a conceptual understanding of the framework and that has the inherent opportunity to impact the learner success towards meeting learning objectives. As well, this case study emphasized the need for "play" within a virtual learning environment, to support learner's cognitive load issues (i.e., "down time"). Much as within the K-12 learning environments for younger learners through young adults, there is a desire for and cognitive need for a break from the emphasis upon consistent instructional emphasis, which is supported through "play" opportunities.

The Philadelphia Museum of Art launched Branchusi's Mademoiselle Pogany (McCall, 2002), with the focus upon the creation of a virtual opportunity through which to enjoy the museum's show. The ease of navigation, such as through the creation of a built-in navigation support for users, was a major area of effort, so as to support the user's understanding and experience within the environment. Further, the creative, stimulating virtual environments are suggested as being important to the virtual experience, instead of "real world" architectural representations. The third consideration was the integral emphasis upon content and conventions designed for the virtual world instead of physical world, which is suggested as further enhancing the user's experience when viewing and potentially interacting with the represented artistic endeavors. Finally, an emphasis upon virtual world design and development so as to support the learner's understanding of the presented information was stressed. Supporting the learner's understanding is not merely imparting knowledge, such as spooning the knowledge into a person's brain; instead, it is of vital importance to create an environment that supports and enhances the learner's experience so as to appropriately engage with the knowledge and frame the information for understanding and future use. Finally, a virtual world environment must be streamlined, so as to ease the user's efforts related to bandwidth and accessibility of download volume issues.

Virtual Furniture sold by Ikea in World Carter (2008) offered a case study that emphasized the impact of "real world" and virtual world engagement, as well as the potential for reflective engagement between the two worlds. The ability to engage "real world" representations within the virtual world spatial environment is an interesting concept, wherein the users have the opportunity to create their own virtual worlds (and perhaps real worlds) in a way that is comfortable to them; this strength of real world and virtual world interconnectedness engages the user more fully in the product emphasis. The consideration towards lively, energetic product interest within virtual worlds is useful to understand, as the ability to virally engage with users' creative attention and appeal through the implementation of a collegial community environment further enhances one's understanding of peer pressure and the desire to "fit into" a community. Finally, the importance of interaction, uniqueness, and brand experience can emphasize dynamic marketing within virtual worlds.

Geo-Tagging in The GeoSimPHILLY (GeoSim Systems Ltd., 2008) is a case worthy of consideration, for several reasons. An interesting aspect is the emphasis upon the human interactions developed so as to reflect "real world" interactions, to further engage the user and develop a sense of a more realistic experience as well as more fully engage within the virtual environment. Also, an opportunity to experience "real world" daily endeavors such as shopping and visiting "real world" landmarks supports the user's developing understanding of the "real world" environment even though it is a virtual world environment. Economically speaking, the "real world" city planning opportunities that may alleviate future development concerns offer a return on investment option, as the potential mistakes that may occur within the virtual world have the possibility to be addressed within the virtual world. Finally, this is an interesting marketing opportunity, due to the possibility for the city to engage potential "real world" tourists and visitors prior to travel, wherein the users can develop not only an understanding

of the city environment but also concerns related to ease of travel and city engagement.

German Deutsche Steinkohle AG (DSK) (ParallelGraphics, 2008) offers consideration related to an emphasis upon "real world" product visualization, with the return on investment and viability concerns focused in stark relief, prior to any physical building of the product. Also, an emphasis upon hands-on training within a virtual environment is of significant interest; the ability to offer initial knowledge-based understanding prior to "real world" training may be a significant factor towards addressing safety issues. Finally, the type of virtual world may be an engaging environment through which to support sales persons' understanding of the product, the sales persons' ability to represent and discuss the product with potential clients, and perhaps even include product marketing opportunities within a larger realm.

Santa Clara University Island (New Media Consortium, 2008) offers interesting considerations related to the ability to test and engage in creative interior spatial endeavors, such as the design of environments. The ability to design and test a user-friendly physical environment is imperative towards concerns related to usability. Further, the opportunity to focus upon "real-world" physical space design without monetary allocation and outlay emphasizes the appropriate use of time and effort, as well as the potential for a desirable return on investment.

BDO Stoy Hayward (Kzero, 2008a, 2008b) is very interesting. The virtual learning experiences created so as to support and engage within social responsibility is imperative within societal realms, and may well directly impact the opportunity for users to more appropriately communicate and develop respect for those who are different socially, culturally and psychosomatically physically through mediated means. As well, the potential marketing towards future clientele is a strong aspect of this case, as this is of interest to all organizations. Of immense interest, specifically pertaining to this organization but also more holistically for all organizations who are impacted by laws and regulations, is the ability to quickly address changes in organizationally oriented laws and decrees within a virtual world environment. Finally, and again primarily focused upon this organization but the concept may impact other organizations, this case emphasize a shift in tax-base considerations within the virtual world; meaning, this case focuses upon the desire for governmental agencies to tax people's virtual world work as if it is a real world endeavor, which directly impacts the freedom and potential creativity that has heretofore been the "wild wild west" wherein personal agreements superseded governmental taxation.

Coca Cola (Virtual Worlds News, 2007a) and Pepsi's Virtual Collaboration with MTV ((Virtual Worlds News, 2008a) offer case studies with interesting considerations. For example, the distribution of brands within the virtual world is of great interest, specifically focused upon virtual worlds as a conduit for product placement and advertisement, no matter whether the focus is business and industry, higher education, or other realms of consideration. As well, viral branding of products within the virtual world is an important consideration; again, no matter whether the focus is business and industry, higher education or other areas of focus. The marketing of products within the virtual world can be successful endeavors, clearly articulated by both case studies, and with special attention towards the enhanced shift of the marketing target from television and print media towards online. Further, the realized need to enhance communications with the community to whom the product is marketed is of vital importance; specifically, the integral importance related to engaging with the customer base. Finally, flexibility is inherently important within the virtual world.

Second Health Project (NMC Virtual Worlds, n.d.) offers considerations within the case study. One example is the ability for virtual worlds to

reflect the inherent shift in major areas of professional focus, meaning the ability to greatly enhance the disbursement of knowledge and information throughout the societal community. Further, the case suggests that the ability to create and engage in important training opportunities within a "safe" framework, such as health-related concerns, that offers the attainment of knowledge and understanding within a significantly larger scale.

Rollings College and University of Potsdam (Virtual Worlds News, 2007a) delineates important considerations that directly impact virtual world learning environments. The opportunity for organizations to actively engage in meeting the student-client interests and needs within the virtual world, so as to offer opportunities to fully engage within the community, may support and enhance the student-client's experience with the organization. Further, an emphasis upon student service and student life is appropriate, with the focus upon not only engaging more fully with the student body but also to enhance marketing efforts, so as to frame the university as an engagingly supportive environment. Finally, the desire to support the student's procedural understanding of the "real world" physical environmental expectations may be more fully realized within a virtual environment, as it offers the perception and impression of an "anytime, anywhere" service.

Of course, there are always several innovative ideas and potential solutions that may be brought forward as a form of recommendation.

CASE STUDY SUCCESSES: SOLUTIONS AND RECOMMENDATIONS

It is important to address potential solutions and recommendations related to virtual worlds as based upon the case studies. The case studies presented offered innumerable potential solutions and strong recommendations to bring forward and, as such, these shall be further delineated herein. The first recommendation offered by the State of Victoria, Australia (2008) concerns the need "… to foster collaboration and interaction. …: immersive events that engage residents; virtual content that directly relates to business objectives; a strong community group to support the presence" (paragraph 7). The importance that surrounds the ideas of creating an engaging community so as to allow the users to actively connect with the content and with the interactive community events offered are of integral importance.

A second point of interest concerns the virtual world architecture, wherein the virtual world environment should be "rather than interpretive or narrative" (McCall, 2002, paragraph 6). Along these same lines is the need for the environment to be designed for implementation within the virtual world (McCall, 2002), instead of through a desire to reflect the real world environment that may represent "assumptions made about ease of navigation held up and to assess how effectively the exhibition was telling its story" (McCall, 2002, paragraph 16).

Of closely aligned interest to the second point noted is the third point; namely, the dynamic merchandising aspects within the virtual world environments. "Interestingly, the concept of dynamic merchandising is also the basis for a newly emerging marketing facet in virtual worlds - Product placement" (Kzero, 2007a, paragraph 2). Further is the focus upon a community of avatars with similar interests, so as to market appropriately and successfully: interaction; uniqueness; experience; product placement (Kzero, 2007b, paragraph 4). This has been a testing ground within virtual worlds for a period of time and, "'As a result, we know not only players' passion for creating their own content but their desire to interact with brands. It's an environment in which players like to blur the line between the digital and real world'" (Carter, 2008, paragraphs 6).

A fourth area of recommendation is the interest in dynamic, database-driven product visualization through which organizations can not only present their products as a marketing event, but also the opportunity for hands-on training by its employees. The opportunity to safely engage with simulated products creates an opportunity to delve into a more advanced level of testing and product understanding, without the need for on-site tours nor oversight. As well, the opportunity for virtual hands-on training enhances the knowledge base of the users before going on-site for specific real-world hands-on training. As quoted from Deutsche Steinkohle, "Virtual Reality as one of the most important educational tools of the future" (ParallelGraphics, 2008, paragraph 5). This return on investment for worker "seat time" and the sales person's ability to offer virtual product demonstrations is also a significant opportunity towards realizing a swift realization of time, effort and quality.

POTENTIAL IMPLICATIONS FOR HIGHER EDUCATION DISTANCE LEARNING WITHIN VIRTUAL WORLDS

Through a careful review of the case studies, there are several obvious and several innovative areas of interest that offer potential implications towards future and emerging trends.

Potential Implications

The implications inherent within virtual worlds is the alternative forms related to developing communities, whether it be casual social communities, business-related communities, or learning-oriented communities; in the best possible world, the overarching community would integral all aspects of social, business and learning potentials into one community environment. This type of community environment would not only connect different cultures and generations without landlocked concerns, but the ability to develop communities that embrace differing perspectives

Table 1. Wenger's Communities of Practice Stages of Development.

Stages of Development	Typical Activities
Potential	Figuring out colleagues and the community space
Coalescing	Exploring community while making and understanding social community connections
Active	Creative, engaging, developing relationships, adapting to new situations
Dispersed	Maintaining social relationships beyond the end of the specific, active community event
Memorable	Remembering positive experiences from being actively engaged within the community, sharing stories concerning the experience

(Adapted from Community Intelligence Labs, 2001, paragraph 11)

into new channels of communication is a huge consideration. Although digital communities are a "hot" topic at the moment, the realization that communities may contain (and be enhanced by) social components, business-related and marketing components, as well as the lifelong learning and training desires of the Twenty-First Century may more easily develop within the virtual worlds.

An interesting explanation of the design and development stages related to communities of learners, referred to by Wenger as the Communities of Practice is well represented through a delineated stages of development framework, which offers a graphic explanation of the learning community life cycle Community Intelligence Labs, 2001. Table 1 offers an overview of Wenger's Communities of Practice Stages of Development.

The emphasis placed upon the ability of community members to come together, develop relationships through negotiated connections, and then the natural progression towards disbursement and the idea related to "passing it forward" by integrating the community experiences into their conceptual framework of understanding identification and understanding and by taking the experiences into their future community experiences.

Also of interest is the fifteen-step process that is focused upon progressively building communities (Brown, 2001). As quoted by McElrath and McDowell (2008):

Brown's research uses grounded theory based on interviews and archived class intereactions to develop a general theory of how community is created in online classrooms. Briefly described, Brown's 3-stage process consists of stage one, "making friends online;" stage two, "community conferment" or acceptance which occurred when students participated in "long, thoughtful, threaded discussions on a subject of importance;' and stage three "camaraderie," which is achieved "after long-term or intense association with others involving personal communication" (Brown, 2001) (McElrath & McDowell, 2008, paragraph 4).

Therefore, Brown's fifteen-step process that is focused upon progressively building communities is framed as a progression from step one through step fifteen, with the basic Step One described as "Tools" (McElrath & McDowell, 2008, paragraph 5) and Step Fifteen described as "Camaraderie" (McElrath & McDowell, 2008, paragraph 5), with the full list of steps progressively offered as: tools; comfort level; self-assessment and judgments; similarities; needs met; time allotted; supportive interaction; substantive validation; acquaintances/friends; earning trust, respect; engagement; community conferment; widen circle; long term/personal communication; and, camaraderie (Adapted from McElrath & McDowell, 2008, paragraph 5). The aspects related to developing a community environment is basically built in a step-by-step motion, as noted through Brown's (2001) progressive framework.

Pulling these ideas together is the connectivism theory, growing in interest, which is described as:

Connectivism is the integration of principles explored by chaos, network, and complexity and self-organization theories. Learning is a process that occurs within nebulous environments of shifting core elements – not entirely under the control of the individual. Learning (defined as actionable knowledge) can reside outside of ourselves (within an organization or a database), is focused on connecting specialized information sets, and the connections that enable us to learn more are more important than our current state of knowing.

Connectivism is driven by the understanding that decisions are based on rapidly altering foundations. New information is continually being acquired. The ability to draw distinctions between important and unimportant information is vital. The ability to recognize when new information alters the landscape based on decisions made yesterday is also critical. (Siemens, 2004, paragraphs 21-22)

Of course, the basic principles which define connectivism are:

- Learning and knowledge rests in diversity of opinions.
- Learning is a process of connecting specialized nodes or information sources.
- Learning may reside in non-human appliances.
- Capacity to know more is more critical than what is currently known
- Nurturing and maintaining connections is needed to facilitate continual learning.
- Ability to see connections between fields, ideas, and concepts is a core skill.

- Currency (accurate, up-to-date knowledge) is the intent of all connectivist learning activities.
- Decision-making is itself a learning process. Choosing what to learn and the meaning of incoming information is seen through the lens of a shifting reality. While there is a right answer now, it may be wrong tomorrow due to alterations in the information climate affecting the decision. (Siemens, 2004, paragraphs 23)

As such, the realities of communities which allow for opportunities to connect at a more personal level are inherent within the virtual world. The ability to connect, as delineated by the connectivism learning theory, is inherent within the realm of communities; both communities of learning and community building.

Tomorrow's Innovations: Future and Emerging Trends

There are innumerable burgeoning innovative ideas that have already been at the forefront of consideration, as described through the case study discussions. Yet where might these innovations be moving? One emerging trend is the reflection of real-world experiential animations within the virtual world, so as to engage the community in virtual opportunities that are "safe" for testing and training without the concerns related to negative outcomes within the real world.

Another emerging innovation is the continuing related engagement and alignment between real world environments and virtual worlds, such as dynamic merchandising and product placement. To further formulate this initial leap into the virtual world foray, experiential elements and integration of product placement within the virtual world may most likely be enhanced through the community ventures wherein the community expounds upon their real world interests and preferences so as to reflect their fundamental interests within a virtual world.

The ideas of architectural progression within the virtual world are shifting from the desire for a reflection of the real world within the virtual world towards a more progressive view of virtual worlds towards navigability and ease of use. The primary focus relates to advancing the realization of user-friendliness, accessibility and availability, which is a dichotomy that exists for persons desiring a lessening learning curve so as to appropriately engage and navigate within virtual worlds.

A final emerging trend is the innovative integration of the database driven, database—supported product visualization and development, such as the burgeoning interest in mash-ups. The integration of data, video, collaborative webs, mobile broadband issues, and other forms of collective intelligence delve into a virtual world mashup wherein all forms of emerging technologies and resources are integrated so as to be easily available and useful to virtual world participants (The New Media Consortium & EDUCAUSE, 2008).

Of course, these burgeoning innovations have implications towards distance learning and similar forms of training within higher education institutions, as well as business and industry.

Integral Distance Learning Considerations

Virtual worlds are an amazing venue, wherein the initial design and development forays are merely novice opportunities and experiences that can frame future endeavors. Yet how do these considerations impact potential future distance learning opportunities? There is some interesting research and theories to guide this discussion.

For example, TRCLARK LCC (2008) suggests that there are five opportunities through which to impact a person's learning from the designated momentary opportunities for learning listed as: first necessary flash of opportunity being "Learning how to do something for the first time"; second

necessary flash of opportunity being "Learning more based on prior learning experience"; third necessary flash of opportunity being "Learning at the point of application, independent of any prior learning, when previous learning has been forgotten, and/or when adapting performance to unique situations"; fourth necessary flash of opportunity being "Learning when things change in order to adapt to new ways of doing things"; and, the fifth necessary flash of opportunity being "Learning when things go wrong in order to solve a problem" (Adapted from TRCLARK LCC, 2008, p. 23).

This is even more interesting when framed within a virtual world environment. Further, considerations regarding the learning agility aspects are framed through current trends suggested by TRCLARK LCC, 2008):

1. Organizational learning agility is becoming the defining quality of high performance organizations.
2. Individual learning agility is fast becoming a core leadership competency.
3. The learning function is poised to become more strategic and performance driven.
4. The primary responsibility for learning and performance support will be pushed to and shared by front-line managers.
5. Individual employee learning support will become the single most important employee retention factor.
6. The lines between formal and informal learning will continue to blur and ultimately disappear.
7. The lines between learning and knowledge management will continue to blur and ultimately disappear.
8. Learners will personalize their own learning and performance support experiences according to their dispositions and situational needs.
9. Organizations will increasingly emphasize learning through direct experience.

10. Organizations will move en masse to reusable content and multi-channel publishing.
11. Organizations will increase their efforts to harvest the tacit knowledge of retiring workers with post-full-time employee relationships. (TRCLARK LCC, 2008, p. 25-26)

Finally, the virtual world culture can be supported through the leadership that nurtures and promotes an organization society based upon customs and traditions, much like within virtual worlds, as supported through the following aspects that are supported within the organizational culture:

- Modeled
- Communicated
- Taught
- Measured
- Recognized
- Rewarded (TRCLARK LCC, 2008, p. 32)

As regards higher education institutions, it is important to recognize the surrounding atmosphere that delineates between teaching and learning, and the technological framework that drives the environmental needs. As framed by Davis, O'Brien and McLean (2008):

In the higher education sector, three key trends in the management and use of information and technologies are transforming the academic enterprise –

- the blurring of research, learning, and teaching boundaries;
- the proliferation of technologically fueled new ways of communication; and
- recognition of an important trend toward standardization. (p. 68)

After all, institutions of higher education are going through a transformation, wherein all aspects of the environment are shifting towards the following:

- Instruction is a scalable craft and can be standardized, personalized, or self-guided.
- Colleges and universities are largely self-governing.
- The academy is enmeshed in communities served.
- College or university education is accessible to all capable.
- The college or university service base can be local, regional, national, or global.
- The college or university is situated in a place and virtually enhanced.
- Scholars and academic resources are plentiful and easily accessible.
- Colleges and universities are creators of knowledge.
- Colleges and universities are increasingly global. (Adapted from Katz, 2008, p. 7)

Of course, the ivory tower's transformation from an isolated entity towards a more community-oriented, client-driven entity is a progressive endeavor. However, the ability to add the opportunities inherent within a virtual world to the skills and needs of students, the academic customers of today's world, are driving the innovative shifts of academia towards the integral distance learning considerations that will further enhance the communities of tomorrow.

CONCLUSION

Yesterday, today and tomorrow are realities within distance learning instructional achievements, wherein innovative ideas and lessons learned help support and enhance the future of distance learning. However, with the impetus associated with virtual worlds offer potential implications for business and industry communities and training needs, as well as within the realm of institutions of higher education. Through this case study meta-analysis, the cases offered were presented and analyzed, with further in-depth analysis occurring within the realms of case study concerns, considerations, successes, and potential implications for higher education distance learning within virtual world environments. Overarching aspects that were realized as deep areas of concern and the desire for fulfillment related to strong navigational undergirding of the virtual world environment, the engagement in experimentation that has the opportunity to occur "safely" and with fewer return on investment concerns within a virtual world, the desire to develop a viral engagement within the virtual world, and the opportunity to develop engagingly attractive and useful learning opportunities within the virtual world. The recommendations that developed as overarching areas of success were: "… to foster collaboration and interaction. …: immersive events that engage residents; virtual content that directly relates to business objectives; a strong community group to support the presence" (State of Victoria, Australia, 2008, paragraph 7); the virtual world architecture, wherein the virtual world environment should be "rather than interpretive or narrative" (McCall, 2002, paragraph 6); the dynamic merchandising aspects within the virtual world environments; and, the interest in dynamic, database-driven product visualization through which organizations can not only present their products as a marketing event, but also the opportunity for hands-on training by its employees. The case study meta-analysis offered herein engages with the real needs of the virtual world to frame its future within an understanding of yesterday and today, while an understanding concerning and recognition of instructional achievements within virtual world environments strongly supports the future implications related to higher education.

REFERENCES

Athavaley, A. (2007, June 20). *A Job Interview You Don't Have to Show Up For: Microsoft, Verizon, Others Use Virtual Worlds to Recruit; Dressing Avatars for Success.* Microsoft, Verizon, Others Use Virtual Worlds to Recruit; Dressing Avatars for Success. Retrieved from http://online.wsj.com/article/SB118229876637841321.html?mod=tff_main_tff_top

Brown, R. E. (2001). The process of community-building in distance learning courses. *Journal of Asynchronous Learning Networks, 5*(1). Retrieved from http://www.sloan-cwiki.org/wiki/index.php?title=The_Process_of_Community-building_in_Distance_Learning_Classes%2c_JALN_5(2)

Carter, M. (2008, May 15). Ikea to offer virtual furniture. *Guardian News and Media Limited.* Retrieved from http://www.guardian.co.uk/media/2008/may/15/marketingandpr.digitalmedia?gusrc=rss&feed=technologyfull

Caterpillar. (2008). *Caterpillar: Home.* Retrieved December 26, 2008, from http://www.cat.com/

Columbia University. (n.d.). *Virtual Worlds Research at Columbia University's Computer Graphics and User Interfaces Laboratory.* Retrieved from http://graphics.cs.columbia.edu/projects/virtual-worlds.html

Community Intelligence Labs. (2001). *Communities of Practice Learning as a Social System by Eitenne Wenger.* Retrieved from http://www.co-i-l.com/coil/knowledge-garden/cop/lss.shtml

Dignan, L. (2006, December 1). *Second Life: Virtual world training wheels for corporate America.* ZDNet: CBS Interactive Inc. Retrieved from http://blogs.zdnet.com/BTL/?p=4039

Feiner, S., MacIntyre, B., & Seligmann, D. (n.d.). *KARMA: Knowledge-based Augmented Reality for Maintenance Assistance*. Retrieved from http://graphics.cs.columbia.edu/projects/karma/karma.html

Ford Motor Company. (2008). *Ford Motor Company: Cars, Trucks, SUVs, Hybrids, Parts – Ford*. Retrieved from http://www.ford.com/

GeoSim Systems Ltd. (2008). *GeoSimPHILLY*. Retrieved from http://www.geosimphilly.com/index.aspx

Glass, G. V. (2000). *Meta-analysis at 25*. Retrieved from http://glass.ed.asu.edu/gene/papers/meta25.html

Glass, G. V., McGraw, B., & Smith, M. L. (1981). *Meta-analysis in social research*. Beverly Hills, CA: Sage Publications.

Gronstedt, A. (2007, August 20). *Virtual Worlds Learning*. Sales and Marketing.com: Nielsen Business Media, Inc. Retrieved from http://www.salesandmarketing.com/msg/content_display/training/e3icb706624eaa6b047f367f6c5ec543baa

Johnstone, B. (2003). *Kitchen Magician: The surprising leader in the commercial VR sweepstakes is Matsushita?!* Wired Digital, Inc. Retrieved from http://www.wired.com/wired/archive/2.07/kitchen_pr.html

Juni, P., Holenstein, F., Sterne, J., Bartlett, C., & Egger, M. (2001). Direction and impact of language bias in meta-analyses of controlled trials: Empirical study. *International Journal of Epidemiology, 31*, 115–123. doi:10.1093/ije/31.1.115

Katz, R. N. (2008). The Gathering Cloud: Is this the end of the Middle? The Tower and The Cloud: Higher Education in the Age of Cloud Computing. In R. N. Katz (Ed), *EDUCAUSE* (pp. 2-42). Retrieved from http://www.educause.edu/books/

Kzero. (2007a, November 25). *A buyers guide to Virtual Retailing. Part 3 – Dynamic Merchandising*. Retrieved from http://www.kzero.co.uk/blog/?p=1630

Kzero. (2007b, September 30). *Supersize Me. Design values in virtual worlds*. Retrieved from http://www.kzero.co.uk/blog/?p=1064

Kzero. (2008a, May 13). *Sunday Times covers BDO Second Life launch*. Retrieved from http://www.kzero.co.uk/blog/?p=2180

Kzero. (2008b, April 8). *The virtual Streets of Philadelphia and real-time geo-tagging*. Retrieved from http://www.kzero.co.uk/blog/?p=2066

Laneways, M. (n.d.). *Would Your Business Benefit from a Second Life?* Retrieved from http://www.mmv.vic.gov.au/Assets/174/1/SecondLifeReport.pdf

Linden Research, Inc. (2008). *Second Life Official Site*. Retrieved from http://secondlife.com/

McCall, A. (2002). *Creating and Using Virtual Reality: A Guide for the Arts and Humanities*. Retrieved from http://vads.ahds.ac.uk/guides/vr_guide/vlib1.html

McElrath, E., & McDowell, K. (2008, March). Pedagogical Strategies for Building Community in Graduate Level Distance Education Courses. *MERLOT Journal of Online Learning and Teaching, 4*(1). Retrieved from http://jolt.merlot.org/vol14no1/mcelrath0308.htm

National Aeronautics and Space Administration. (2008). *Beginner's Guide to Wind Tunnels*. Retrieved from http://www.grc.nasa.gov/WWW/K-12/windtunnel.html

National Aeronautics and Space Administration. (n.d.). *Hubble Space Telescope Servicing Mission 3A*. Retrieved from http://www.gsfc.nasa.gov/gsfc/service/gallery/fact_sheets/spacesci/hst3-01/reasons%20for%20hubble%20servicing.htm

New Media Consortium. (2008, January 22). *Virtual Worlds Case Study: Santa Clara Island.* Retrieved from http://secondliferesearch.blogspot.com/2008/01/virtual-worlds-case-study-santa-clara.html and http://virtualworlds.nmc.org/portfolio/santa-clara/

ParallelGraphics. (2008). *Virtual Reality in the Mining Industry.* Retrieved from http://www.parallelgraphics.com/products/sdk/success/dsk/

Ressler, S. (1994). *Virtual Reality for Manufacturing – Case Studies.* Open Virtual Reality Testbed: National Institute of Standards and Technology. Retrieved from http://ovrt.nist.gov/projects/mfg/mfgVRcases.html

Shachar, M. (2008). Meta-analysis: The preferred method of choice for the assessment of distance learning quality factors. *International Review of Research in Open and Distance Learning, 9*(3), 1–15.

Siemens, G. (2004, December 12). *Connectivism: A Learning Theory for the Digital Age.* Retrieved from http://www.elearnspace.org/Articles/connectivism.htm

State of Victoria. Australia. (2008). *Virtual Worlds.* Retrieved from http://www.mmv.vic.gov.au/VirtualWorlds

The Boeing Company. (2008). *The Boeing Company.* Retrieved from http://www.boeing.com/

The New Media Consortium, & EDUCAUSE Learning Initiative. (2008). *The 2008 Horizon Report.* Stanford, CA: The New Media Consortium. from http://www.educause.edu/

TRCLARK LCC. (2008). *In Search of Learning Agility: Assessing Progress from 1957 to 2008.* The eLearning Guild. Retrieved from http://www.elearningguild.com/content.cfm?selection=doc.1054

Virtual Worlds, N. M. C. (n.d.). *Virtual Worlds Case Study: Second Health.* Retrieved from http://virtualworlds.nmc.org/portfolio/second-health/

Virtual Worlds News. (2007a, August 26). *Blogging the SLCC: Case Studies – Selling Real Life Products.* Retrieved from http://www.virtualworldsnews.com/2007/08/blogging-the--8.html

Virtual Worlds News. (2007b, November 12). *Virtual MTV a Hit for Pepsi.* Retrieved from http://www.virtualworldsnews.com/2007/11/virtual-mtv-a-h.html

Virtual Worlds News. (2008a, May 5). *Case Study: vMTV's Virtual Hills Makes Pepsi Cooler than MTV's On-Air "The Hills."* Retrieved from http://www.virtualworldsnews.com/2008/05/case-study-vmtv.html

Virtual Worlds News. (2008b, May 12). *IRS Rules Electric Sheep's Second Life Greeters as Part-Time Employees.* Retrieved from http://www.virtualworldsnews.com/2008/05/irs-rules-elect.html

Vygotsky, L. S. (1935). *Mental development of children during education.* Moscow-Leningrad, Russia: Uchpedzig.

Vygotsky, L. S. (1962). *Thought and Language.* Cambridge, MA: MIT Press.

Vygotsky, L. S. (1978). *Mind in Society.* Cambridge, MA: Harvard University Press.

Vygotsky, L. S. (1981). The genesis of higher mental functions. In J. V. Wertsch (Ed.), *The concept of activity in Soviet Psychology.* Armonk, NY: Sharpe.

Wertsch, J. V. (1985). *Cultural, Communication, and Cognition: Vygotskian Perspectives.* Cambridge, UK: Cambridge University Press.

Wikipedia. (2008). *Mashup (web application hybrid).* Retrieved from http://en.wikipedia.org/wiki/Mashup_(web_application_hybrid)

Chapter 10
Blending Synchronous and Asynchronous Interactivity in Online Education

Kamna Malik
U21Global, India

ABSTRACT

Online education is characterized by conflicting variables of time, space and interactivity. In response to the market pressure for time and space flexibility, interactivity between student-student and student-teacher usually suffers. Literature reports lack of interaction as the prime reason for reduced quality in online and hybrid courses. This chapter emphasizes the need to balance time, space and interactivity through appropriate blending of tools of interactivity so as to maximize learning as well as business outcomes. Experience related to blended use of various synchronous and asynchronous tools of interaction is shared.

INTRODUCTION

Interactivity is crucial to learning. It facilitates cognitive involvement, enabling free flow of ideas and development of behavioral skills which are otherwise difficult to learn and transfer. Need for improved interactivity has been one of the key drivers in pedagogical shifts in teaching and learning methods. Case based teaching, class discussions, team assignments, in-class presentations, game simulations and role plays are some of the widely adopted interactive methods to map to different learning objectives in a face to face setting (Bonner, 1999; Van Auken & Chrysler, 2005).

However, interactivity, the much sought after ingredient to effective teaching and learning is often a topic of debate when it comes to distance education. While the need for time and space flexibility is driving even the established brick and mortar institutions towards distance mode of education, maintaining the desired quality of interaction between distant people has been a challenge. To counter this imbalance between time, space and interactivity, educators in their individual or organizational capacities also adopt hybrid forms of education by blending face to face interactions with one or more

DOI: 10.4018/978-1-61520-672-8.ch010

forms of distance education. E.g. bundling limited face to face contact hours with a conventional correspondence based course or providing an option for some online courses with a conventional face to face degree course. However, studies on student satisfaction and engagement still report lack of interaction as a significant weakness of online or hybrid systems while rigidity of time and space continue to be the major weaknesses of a face to face system (Beard & Harper, 2002; Jackson and Helms, 2008). In view of the rising need for time and space flexibility and various resulting patterns of education, it is imperative for educators and administrators to innovate and use the right mix of interactive tools and technologies so as to deliver quality of education at least no less than that in face to face setting. A well implemented online education system holds the potential to reach even beyond the capabilities of face to face setting (Kim & Bonk, 2006) and may even become the paradigm of the future (Hutchinson, 2007). Realization of this depends on how institutions handle the imbalance between the critical factors of time, space and interactivity.

This chapter explores the need and feasibility of blending synchronous and asynchronous interactivity as a way to balance time and space flexibility with the need for quality of interaction. Towards this objective, the chapter aims to:

- Explore the relevance of various forms of interactivity in online education
- Share current practices and related issues in blending synchronous and asynchronous interactivity in an online graduate business school.
- Bring out the suitability of webinars for synchronous and multi-directional interaction between students and teacher.

The remaining chapter is organized as follows. Next section sets the context for online education and related environment variables viz. time, space and interaction. It then shares the current practice of blending synchronous and asynchronous modes of interaction in a predominantly asynchronous, online management course. Related issues, recommendations and directions for further research are presented in an attempt to step forward towards a seamless education suitable to the needs of individual students.

BACKGROUND

With the advent of information technology, many new forms of distance education have evolved in an attempt to make education much more interactive. Such variety of forms have been given different names such as e-learning, m-learning, web based learning, technology enabled learning, online education and so on. Quite often, these names have been used interchangeably and difference between them is somewhat blur. For the purpose of this chapter, online education is used as a term to refer to all variants of distance education, where Information and Communication Technology (ICT) is used in some proportion as a medium for education delivery. Irrespective of the medium, every variant of education ultimately strives and should strive to achieve higher student satisfaction and improved learning outcomes.

Earlier, the only variants of technology based distance education were radio / television for unidirectional lecturing or telephone for personalized tutoring. Over the past two decades, ICT has emerged as an effective substitute. As a result, interactive CDs and hyper text have come into use for instructional design based on text, audio, video and animation thus making way for self paced learning. These days, podcast offers an alternate to radio / television based lecturing and as a means to decrease the cost of production and distribution for institution and to increase the time and space flexibility for learner. Conference based technologies are being adopted to facilitate any-where-fixed time (virtual) class rooms with synchronous interactivity. To take care of stu-

Table 1. Commonly used Tools for Online Education

Sno	Tool for Online Education	Meaning used in this chapter	Involvement of Learner
1	Audio/video based lecture	It involves delivery of a lecture through any technology that supports audio, video or both. The lecture can be a live / pre-recorded session delivered by a subject matter expert. It may be technology specific e.g. meant only for a radio / television / DVD or may be open i.e. compliant with any device such as a media player, mobile phone or computer. Podcast (a digital audio/video file that is downloadable from web and is automatically recognized by podcatchers such as Apple's iTunes or Winamp) and vodcast (a podcast with video) are also being increasingly adopted for small duration lecture or instruction sessions.	Learner is a passive listener and cannot ask questions.
2	Online content	It involves use of technology enabled interface facilitating detailed content for self paced learning, organized using various learning tools such as text, graphics, audio, animation, exercises and self assessment questions. The content may be made accessible through any electronic form such as CD, electronic readers or web.	Learner can perform pre-designed self practice exercises but cannot ask questions.
3	Audio Conference	It involves use of some heavy weight technology that supports one-way or multiple-way interaction for audio based session. For example, using a satellite based studio for telecast of lecture and also to take up queries. Such heavy weight technologies are often beyond individual reach and thus make it necessary for institutions to set up studios where learners can gather in real time, to attend a planned session.	Based on implementation, a learner can listen to and interact with the speaker or all the participants.
4	Video Conference	It is an extension over audio conferencing and involves video transmission over heavy weight technologies.	In addition to audio, a learner can also see the presenter and other participants.
5	Web Based Discussion Board / Blog	It involves use of web technologies such as hypertext and blogs to carry out threaded discussions. Such discussions may involve theme based or open topics and involve written expression with the help of text and graphics.	Learner is an active participant.
6	Webinar	The term implies web based seminar. It involves use of world wide web as against the heavy weight technologies such as a satellite link for audio/video based multi-directional interactions. It also facilitates interactivity with the help of tools such as whiteboard, application sharing, and online chat.	Learner is an active participant

dents with limited connectivity, many institutions adopting this format set up specialized studios or study centers in strategic locations to enable a learner join a scheduled session in a nearby-fixed location. Gradually, web-based systems are also being adopted to offer – any-time-any-where learning systems.

Thus, it is evident that, there exist plenty of technology tools that can bring difference to the learner as well as the educational institutions. Table 1 summarizes the meaning of the commonly used tools used for online education, as referred in this chapter. Their suitability to teaching and learning to a large extent depends on the way an institution responds to the environmental pressures of time flexibility, space flexibility and interactivity. More discussion on their application will be done in later sections of this chapter.

Time Flexibility

Recently, need for time flexibility has turned into a market pressure, with more and more students wanting to study at their own pace either because of individual characteristics such as competence, study habits etc. or because they need to balance work, family and study together. It is also important in cases, where students from different time zones join the same group of study. Responding to this pressure has given rise to a separate community of students – the working executives who have to manage conflicting situations in work, family and study (Dumont, 1996; Greco, 1999) and might otherwise hesitate undertaking any fixed time course on further education due to their unpredictable business pressures.

Space Flexibility

Along with time flexibility, there has been an upsurge in the need for space flexibility. This pressure is increasingly being faced by educational institutions due to many factors such as:

- Increased drop out rates in regular courses due to inability of students to balance their mobility with rigid norms for physical attendance and class participation.
- Need for subject experts beyond the geographical constraints.
- Increasing global competition amongst institutions resulting in an increase in their effort to attract global students

Responding to these factors has another set of associated issues. Quality of traditional teamwork (good coordination processes, members' mutual support, cohesion, etc.) can be hindered by physical distance between team members unless special care is taken in teaching good virtual communication skills (Hoegl & Proserpio, 2004). They can be virtually connected and create a virtual community that serves a social purpose (Prosperpio & Gioia, 2007). The authors highlight three features associated with effective learning that have implications for teaching the virtual generation: active involvement by students in the learning process, facilitative social settings, and problem solving

focus (Alavi, 1994; Alavi, Wheeler, & Valacich, 1995; Johnson & Johnson, 1975). Fast emergence of conference and web based systems is an attempt to cater to this pressure.

Interactivity in Education

Interactivity is a key factor for quality of learning environment (McKavanagh & Stevenson, 1992; Powers and Rossman, 1985; Shankar & Hu, 2006). Most of the pedagogical evolutions have their roots in a drive to increase interactivity amongst student-student and student-faculty. Teaching methods such as class room discussions, role plays, simulation games and in-class presentations (Bonner, 2006; Van Auken & Chrysler, 2005) provide interactive ways to engage students and make them learn better. Interactivity depends on the characteristics of students, faculty and also the teaching pedagogy.

Interactivity has many elaborations in education literature. Bates (1991) argues that interactivity should be the primary criterion for selecting medium for educational delivery. Liu & Shrum (2002) summarize many definitions of interactivity notably those of Blattberg & Deighton (1991); Deighton (1996) and Steuer (1992) and consolidate them as - the degree to which two or more communication parties can act on each other, on the communication medium, and on the messages and the degree to which such influences are synchronized." Liu & Shrum (2002) define three dimensions of interactivity as Active control, Two way communication and Synchronicity that combined together result in improved learning, self efficacy and student satisfaction. Even though, face to face systems are known to be interactive, attaining its ultimate essence largely depends on the course faculty.

Simply said, interactivity implies the reciprocal activity between two individuals that influences each other. In the context of computer based systems, it includes user, computer and web pages.

Figure 1. Forms of Interactivity based on Time and Space Flexibility with suitable tools

	Same Space I	Different Space II
Same Time	**Synchronous** **7**	**Synchronous** **3, 4, 6**
Different Time	**Asynchronous** **1, 2, 3, 4, 5, 6**	**Asynchronous** **0, 1, 2, 3, 4, 5, 6**
	IV	III

Legend:
0 => Correspondence course;
1 to 6 =>Serial numbers of tools of online education listed in table 1;
7=> Face to face setting

When related to ICT, types of interactivity are often linked to time and are termed as either synchronous (same time) or asynchronous (different time). Figure 1 exhibits mapping of tools of online education (as listed in table 1) to time and space independence. Block I of the figure represents face to face scenario of interaction; remaining blocks, more significantly II and III can be seen to represent online mode. Inclusion of 3, 4 and 6 in both the blocks II and III depicts the implementation dependence of related tools viz. audio & video conference and webinar. While the three forms can be used in a synchronous mode for live delivery and interaction, a recording of a session can enable their use in an asynchronous manner. Block IV includes all the tools as listed in block III. Ideally, being at same place during different timings (block IV) does not contribute to interactivity. The only reason for such a scenario can be when many learners come to the same place to access the infrastructure and the recordings. For example, one may go to a designated study center to access the institute's library, recorded conference sessions or lecture podcasts.

Distribution of control between various interacting participants in a synchronous interaction is governed by participating individuals, primarily the faculty. Though, use of ICT based synchronous or asynchronous interaction continues to grow in traditional face to face education, emphasis has been more on use of ICT in distance education. Distance education is more conducive to asynchronous interactions due to associated time and space flexibility, thus it explains the lack of attention given to use of synchronous mode of interaction (Olaniran et al. 2000). Olaniran et al. (2000) also alluded to the steeper learning curve in synchronous interactions when compared to asynchronous interactions. They advocate higher interactivity and immediate feedback as the key benefits of synchronous communications. There are many personality traits such as speaking and listening skills that are better developed when there is synchronicity of interaction (Anderson, 2004). A recent study reveals that synchronous conferencing is found to increase the communications between instructor and students (Grant & Cheon, 2007; Pattillo, 2007).

Based on the type of participants, usually two forms of interaction have been explored in the conventional education literature, they are – student-student and student- teacher interactions.

In the case of online education, computer system and the web become vital medium for interaction and thus the interaction has been considered at four levels (Anderson & Elloumi, 2004; Hillman, Willis & Gunawardena, 1994; Moore, 1989) viz.

- Student - teacher
- Student - Student
- Student - content
- Student – interface

The last two levels of interaction facilitate self paced learning by providing intermediation between faculty and student. Quality of such interaction to an extent is driven by the sophistication of tools used and the quality of content developer and designer. Effective use of interactive technologies such as hypertext, animation and multimedia can improve the quality of interaction between student and content. Quality of student-interface interaction is driven by the quality of course plan. More often, this interface is pre-planned and thus rigid in structure with limited scope for accommodating change once the course has been started.

Quality of interaction in first two categories is less technology driven and thus to quite an extent is in the hands of people. There is a good scope to increase their effectiveness in online education. Literature suggests that student satisfaction with graduate education is related to teacher-student interactions, intellectual stimulation, and peer interaction (Powers and Rossman, 1985) and interactive teaching style may be the best pedagogical approach to Internet-based courses (Arbaugh, 2000a; Arbaugh, 2000b; Leidner & Jarvenpaa, 1995). Another study reports three variables of interaction that are significantly associated with learning as - instructor emphasis on interaction, ease of interaction and classroom dynamics; and suggests that faculty exercises one's own wisdom to facilitate interactions and dynamics in an online program (Arbaugh, 2000b). Tools, as listed in table 1, can make a significant contribution to improve these interactions and ultimately the quality of

education. We will revisit their application in later part of the chapter.

Quality and Online Education

Quality means different to different stakeholders. So is the case with students, faculty and investors – the key stakeholders in an educational institute. From student's perspective, quality of education has been often measured in terms of student satisfaction which in turn depends on student's individual needs and learning style. From faculty's view, quality in education has been related to various metrics such as richness of content, effectiveness of delivery, student engagement, cognitive development and soft skills development. For investors, it is important to improve business returns while still maintaining the desired level of quality by the other two stakeholders.

Kirkpatrick's four-level model has been widely accepted for training evaluation. The model suggests four criteria for training evaluation as Reactions, Learning, Behaviour and Results (Kirkpatrick, 1959a; Kirkpatrick, 1959b; Kirkpatrick, 1960a; Kirkpatrick, 1960b). The model has also attracted its share of criticism (Alliger & Janak, 1989; Islam, 2004). Islam (2004) suggested including 'Financial Returns' as fifth level of evaluation to evaluate the business (invester's) aspect of quality.

Crawford & Yetton (1985) highlighted the difference between satisfaction and performance of participant. While teaching skills do influence the former, it is program design and quality of content that affects the latter. Learning environment has a crucial role to play when it comes to online education. Garrison, Anderson and Archer (2000) suggested that deep and meaningful learning happens in the presence of three component 'presences' viz. cognitive presence, social presence and teaching presence. Cognitive presence supports the development and growth of critical thinking; social presence provides comfort and a sense of belongingness to the group; and teaching presence includes structure, mentoring and subject expertise to give high order learning to students. Academic curricula have highly recognized cognitive development thru five levels of mental activities-namely memorization, analysis, synthesis, making judgment, and application and the same are prevalent in online learning environment also (Robinson and Hullinger, 2008). However, there is a scope for improvement in the degree of student involvement in synthesis and making judgment.

Scope to Improve Interactivity

By virtue of its base in ICT, online education inherently supports time and space flexibility. Significant increase in courses and students in distance and online education (Kolowich, 2009; Sikora & Carrol, 2002) also implies its increasing acceptance. However, there has been a mixed response on the benefits and quality of online programmes. Interactivity particularly is seen as a grey area.

Various studies have reported higher student satisfaction in class room based education and attributed it to the greater interactivity and dynamism possible in a class room setting (Arbaugh, 2000a; Arbaugh, 2000b; Beard & Harper, 2002; Jackson and Helmes, 2008; Hoegl & Proserpio, 2004; Leidner & Jarvenpaa, 1995; Rodriguez et al., 2008; Shanker & Hu, 2006). In a recent paper, Jackson & Helms (2008) presented advantages and disadvantages as reported by various researchers. They cited less time in the classroom, less money on travel, more course availability, decreased student inhibitions through removal of psychological and social barriers to interaction, and increased flexibility as online advantages (e.g., Beard & Harper, 2002; Carrell & Menzel, 2001; Chamberlin, 2001; Guidera, 2004). The lack of student-to-instructor and student-to student interaction is cited as a disadvantage. In addition, other disadvantages include privacy issues, technological difficulties, and a focus on technology

rather than content (Plotrowski & Vodanovich, 2000). Rodriguez et al (2008) reported that online courses promoted basic academic skills development except speaking skills.

Even though faculty and educational institutes involved in online education have been experimenting with innovative use of various interactive technologies, literature, as enumerated above clearly exhibits a need to improve the quality of online education and the quality of interactivity therein.

Bucy (2003) reacted to the volumes of research being done on comparing traditional and online courses, emphasizing that rather than replicating the face to face environment, it is better to focus on what is done better in online learning. Though such emphasis is a sound precautionary note on the risk of blind migration of physical class room onto virtual space, it is worth exploring the comparative studies with a view to provide the best of all the worlds of education and make the convergence of various views of quality happen. It is also important to ensure that a compromised rigour and quality cropping out of less interactivity in online education is not perceived as an easy way out by weaker students or students aiming at some short term goals. It is imperative to adopt a holistic view of education and learning goals and then blend technologies to fit in while balancing time, place and interactivity; rather than taking a loyalist's position on a specific technology and compromising on the goals of learning.

BALANCING TIME, SPACE AND INTERACTIVITY

It is well established that time, space and interactivity are interdependent and largely conflicting variables when it comes to online education. As illustrated in figure 2, change in one variable affects the other two and often results in an imbalance in quality of education. E.g. offering space flexibility can lead to time zone differences resulting

Figure 2. Conflicting Variables in Online Education

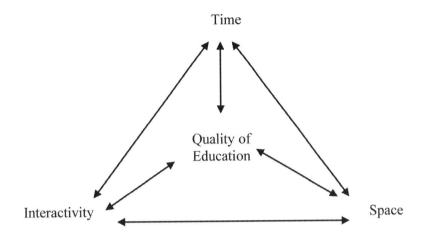

from geographical distances. Offering time and space flexibility may have mixed impact. On one hand, this can enable a pool of students with diverse experience and culture thus broadening the learning horizon which is not easy to get in a fixed time and space setting. On the other hand, time and space flexibility may result in weaker interactivity due to varying characteristics of associated student, faculty and pedagogy. For example, a student who lacks self discipline or is not interactive by instinct may not be able to capitalize on such flexibilities.

While time and space flexibility are the market pressures driving growth of online education business, it is interactivity that can actually enable online education to overcome the oft reported lack of quality and convert it into a complete education system to cater to a definite and distinct target audience.

When it comes to managing interactivity, a significant difficulty lies in balancing synchronous and asynchronous interactions with a view to ensure that right tools are used to allow interaction between any two participants and to achieve improved quality of learning. Based on discussions in the previous sections, figure 3 summarizes that well bended synchronous and asynchronous

tools make the necessary foundation for a holistic learning environment that facilitates student interaction with teachers, peers and various actors who matter to learning; creates a community of learning (Garrison, Anderson & Archer, 2000) and helps to achieve the goals of learning i.e. to acquire mental abilities (Robinson & Hullinger, 2008) and soft skills (Lorenz, 2008) relevant to the course. The blending also needs to take into account individual as well as institutional view of quality of learning.

As depicted earlier in figure 1, asynchronous interactions provide time (and space) flexibility. Synchronous interactions may not be a preferred mode for many who need time flexibility. But literature as elicited above supports some distinct features of synchronous interactivity such as immediate feedback, steeper learning curve, soft skills development (particularly speaking, listening and presentation skills) and ensuring a higher order of learning through application of long term memory for promptness of discussions. A study reports that high order learning happens when the concepts get transferred to long term memory (Ally, 2004). Long term memory is not adequately testable through asynchronous tools as they provide adequate time gap to allow re-

Figure 3. Blending synchronous and asynchronous Interactivity Tools to enable higher interactions and learning outcomes

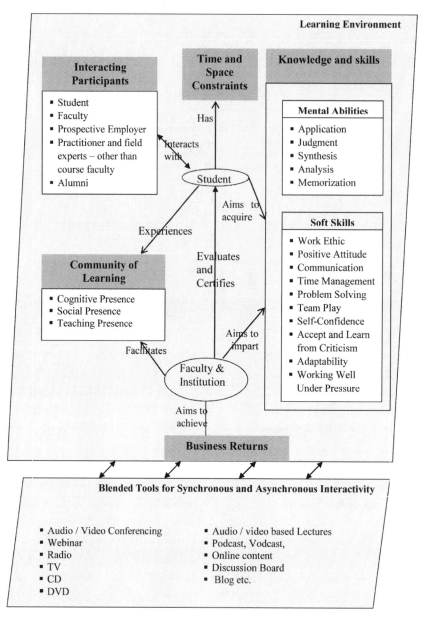

trieval from secondary mediums. An impromptu discussion is the best way to assess and encourage this trait.

Thus, it is suggested to suitably blend the two forms of interaction for optimum outcomes. From the perspectives of ICT tools mapped in figure 1, audio/video conferencing and webinar seem to be

the potential candidates making up for the loss of face to face interactions and still keeping asynchronous option open for the students who cannot join in real time. As audio/video conferencing includes heavy end technologies, webinar appears to be a promising tool for synchronous interactions across the geographies. Of course, this needs a trade off with time flexibility (convenience) and may be seen as a challenge. Technology constraints and weak moderation may also hinder the quality of synchronous interactions.

However, to optimize quality and business, it is important that institutions and faculty continue to experiment with different tools of interactivity to offer better interactivity with reasonable time and space flexibility. Table 1 gave a brief on the relevant tools that can help establish interactions in an online setting. Next section further elaborates the pros and cons of these tools for online education.

Tools of Interactivity

Graphics, animation, voice and hypertext have been widely used tools for student–content and student-interface interactions, making e-learning an acceptable paradigm today. But when it comes to student-student and student-teacher interactions, more sophisticated tools are required for handling complex requirements such as unstructured and voluminous exchange of ideas in limited time and stored in easy to access format for future reference. Figure 1 and table 1 have highlighted the commonly used tools to enable such interactions in online education. These tools have been tried and used in various combinations to generate different flavors of interactivity in online and hybrid education.

Figure 4 exhibits the continuum of interactivity along some of the widely adopted forms of education, with face to face setting and conventional distance (correspondence based) education on the highest and lowest extremes of the continuum respectively. The numbers 0 to 7 marked in the blocks map to the legend in figure 1. All except correspondence course (0) and online/web based content (2) represent tools for person oriented interactions.

A blended system is implementation dependent and thus can lie any where on this continuum depending on the composition of different forms and extent of interactive tools and techniques used. The span of blended systems beyond the lower and upper extremes indicates that wrong strategy for tool adoption can even make or mar the standard level of interactivity.

Some of these tools have very subtle difference, while the others have very thin line difference and can be easily customized by changing the approach to their implementation. Table 2 presents a comparative view of these tools with a view to highlight their common and unique characteristics as well as strengths/weaknesses. As each tool has some inherent strengths and weaknesses, overall degree of effectiveness in a course then depends on the choice and method of mixing different forms. For ease of comparison, table 2 also includes face to face interactions – which may be seen as a benchmark for interactivity. It is possible for institutions to blend multiple such tools to design their own variant of distance education supporting a preferred teaching pedagogy aligned with their business vision as well as the characteristics of courses, faculty and students that they deal with. Appropriate blending also holds the key to personalized education, which is constrained only by the vision of implementers.

It is worth noticing that web-based discussions are largely text based and asynchronous in nature. They offer the best solution in situations where time and space flexibility are crucial. However, they lack in transfer of soft, particularly communication skills. They are also weak in testing the long term memory of students. Webinar is a tool that, if mixed appropriately with web-based education has the potential to bring in the best of face to face interactivity advantages to online education, while adding a lot more flexibility inherent in online medium. What then is needed on part of education providers is a thorough plan on how to trade off between time flexibility and multiple other factors such as teaching pedagogy, subject requirements and learner's style and preferences.

Figure 4. Continuum of Interactivity in Education

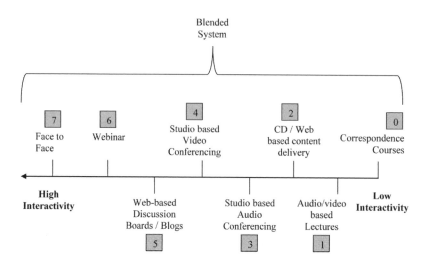

Blending Tools of Interactivity: A Case Study

A study was carried out on the use of tools of interactivity in an online graduate business school that predominantly uses asynchronous mode of interaction. The school uses a web based learning management system (LMS) as the front end for all activities related to teaching and learning. It follows learner centric pedagogy and keeps on innovating and adopting new ways of creating a rich learning experience. There is no lecture based teaching.

Students enrolled in this school are working executives with experience ranging from 6 to 20 years. A student may enroll for one course or a combination of courses leading to a certificate or a degree course. They belong to different nationalities, though majority of them are from Asia. Their job profile needs them to be highly mobile. Many of them work on time bound projects. In brief, they all have high work and family pressures but still have opted for higher studies as a plan to further their career prospects. As per an internal survey carried out by the school in 2008,

65% of students enrolled with the school due to flexibility provided by the online medium. This clearly indicates the importance of time and space flexibility for its students.

To facilitate quality of interaction as well as facilitation, maximum 40 students enrolled for a course are grouped into one section and one subject matter expert is assigned to the section as professor-facilitator (PF).

Tools Used for Interactivity

Interaction between student-student and student-teacher in a section is fairly high and is primarily based on web based discussions or blogs. As 30% of a course assessment is based on participation in theme based discussions, it becomes nearly compulsive for students to exhibit participation which in turn results in high level peer to peer learning - much needed at higher education. This interactivity also draws from quality of facilitation, adequate discussion topics and well defined timelines that makes them interact and exercise critical thinking, thus creating a good cognitive and social presence.

Table 2. A Comparative View of Modes of Interactivity in Education

Mode of Interaction Factors of Interaction and Legend	Face To Face	Audio / Video based Conference	Web based discussion board / Blog	Webinar	Audio/video based Lecture
Type of Interaction	Synch	Synch / Asynch*	Asynch	Synch / Asynch*	Asynch
Time	Fixed	Fixed / Any time*	Any time	Fixed / Any time*	Any Time
Place	Fixed	Fixed	Any Where	Any Where	Any Where
Direction of Interaction	Multi directional	Impl Based	Multi directional	Multi directional	Uni- directional
Communication Skills Transferred	Speaking Listening Writing Body Language	Listening Speaking Body Language (in video based only)	Writing	Speaking Listening Body Language (In video based only)	Listening Body Language (In video based only)
Maximum Participants	As per class room capacity	Limited by studio / server capacity	Limited by server capacity	Limited by Software capacity / license	Meant for stand alone learner
Automatic Log of proceeding	No	Yes	Yes	Yes	No
Flexibility of Entry /Exit for Participants	Low	High Can be User/ Moderator controlled	Very High	High Moderator Controlled	Extremely High
Duration of Interaction	Limited by constraints of logistics	Limited by presenter, studio & support staff availability	Depends on learner's choice, but within bounds of course structure	Defined by Moderator	Limited by Technology

Abbreviations used: Synch - Synchronous; Impl – Implementation

*Applicable for recorded session only]

With a view to enhancing the sense of community, many other tools are also frequently used. Table 3 presents the tools commonly used in this school as against the ones enumerated in table 1. Key resources facilitating the interactivity are also listed. As evident from the table, online content and web based discussion boards are the two major tools used. As the back end support, email is used for student-teacher interaction on adhoc issues and subject related queries. Wiki is used for communication to students for content like student handbook and other policies. Thus, wiki, though indirectly, helps students understand the guiding rules such as performance expectation and assessment guidelines that help them learn and perform better. Face to Face interaction is sometimes used in customized programs, usually on demand of corporate clients.

Though, there is some presence of optional synchronous interactivity in the overall package of student learning, the same has been missing from individual course level deliberations. In its existing format of practice, a webinar brings forth a seminar conducted by a professor for around 45 minutes, followed by question answer session. Such a webinar is open to faculty, staff and students of the school. It is organized during office hours of the university and is optional for students to attend. A downloadable recording of the webinar is made available for future reference.

Table 3. Commonly used Tools in the Online Business School under Study

Sno	Tool of Interactivity	Purpose	Key Resources Involved	Usage Indication
1	Audio/video based lecture	The school does not follow lecture based teaching. However, it frequently uses podcast/ vodcast mainly for giving subject introduction, topic summary, announcements.	PF	17%* of students have ever downloaded a podcast or vodcast.
2	Online content	Prescribed course content is made available to students through the web. The content uses a good mix of multimedia to enable self paced study and practice of an individual student.	Design team and content author(s)	No formal data available but it is expected that every student goes through it.
3	Audio Conference	Not Used		
4	Video Conference	Not Used		
5	Web Based Discussion Board / Blog	This is the prime tool for interaction. 30% of student assessment is based on participation in designated discussions topics.	PF decides on discussion themes; Support staff assists in conversion to LMS format.	Invariably, each student uses discussion forum. Subjective feedbacks indicate high level of benefit that students gain from this.
6	Webinar	Limited use, primarily in first two situations listed below. Situation c is a recent initiative and is elaborated further in this chapter. a. For subject introduction - in the case of corporate students only. b. For generic seminars - where a speaker is invited to talk on a topic related to business and management c. For in-class discussions and assessments	a. PF b. Guest Speaker and Operations Staff	a. Focus is more on orientation to LMS and pedagogy than on actual subject content. b. 27%* students have ever attended or downloaded a recording

* Source: Internal survey of the school, 2008

Scope for Improvement

The school continues to innovate and improve the level of interactivity between student-student and student-teacher to enable a rich learning experience. This drive for continuous improvement has led to many initiatives for better student engagement, richer peer interaction and increased quality of content. While asynchronous interaction based on discussion threads remains the primary mode of interaction and is well aligned to learner-centric pedagogy followed by the school, use of podcast and vodcast is seen as a significant contribution towards creating teaching presence. Despite the very low observed usage of these two forms (17% as per an internal survey, 2008), the school intends to continue with this practice and make it more rigorous and standardized to instill higher value for student.

The internal survey also reported that only 27% of enrolled students had ever attended or downloaded a webinar organized in this format. The prime reasons cited for the same are - mismatch of timing or the topic with that of student's choice. There is no current practice of use of webinar for subject related interactions, soft skill development or student assessments.

As discussed earlier in the background section, synchronous interactivity has its own distinct utility in terms of immediate feedback, soft skills development such as impromptu speaking and presentation skills development and also as a test for application of long term memory thus facilitating high order thinking. With a view to enable students experience a different (and richer) interactivity; a pilot study was carried out with students enrolled for one course.

Methodology and Results

The study involved students enrolled for one course split into two sections. As per the standard assessment scheme of the school, students in this course were expected to carry out a team project towards partial completion of the course and submit their analysis and recommendations to the professor.

Such a submission typically follows a word document or power point presentation file transferred to professor over the LMS. However, in view of the objective of the pilot study undertaken, the students were asked to make their submission more interactive and for this, they could choose the format of the standard power-point (ppt), podcast, vodcast, webinar or any other format that appealed to the team. There was no compulsion on choice of suggested formats and no additional marks were linked to any format of presentation. This was purposefully done to capture the genuine interest and constraints of the students. Vodcast was suggested as an option with a view to increase student collaboration in the absence of professor as well as to exercise speaking and presentation skills of students. Webinar was seen as a clear comprehensive approach towards synchronous interactivity. To enable participation of members having access to limited bandwidth, video was disabled during the webinar and presentation was restricted to audio conferencing only.

As exhibited in table 4, column 2 (labeled First Run), the two sections together had a total of 38 active students at the stage of final project. This number excludes students who had deferred their study for some reason and had thus withdrawn from the course. 50% of the teams chose to submit a vodcast, 30% of them opted to make their presentation through webinar and remaining 20% opted to submit a standard PPT format.

After the student choices were confirmed, time zones of all students who had opted for webinar were gathered to plan for the most convenient time slot for team presentations. In view of students' online session statistics as obtained from LMS (table 5), evening hours were preferred for presentations. Presenting teams were consulted before freezing the final slot for webinar.

A qualitative analysis of team interactions was done based on students' queries to professor, team discussion boards, voluntary informal feedback of students and end term student evaluation of faculty. The team discussion boards were also watched regularly before and after the submissions. Even though only one third of the teams adopted webinar, 80% of the teams willingly adopted a higher level of interaction than a simple PPT. Students who presented their project in the webinar format appreciated the opportunity provided to learn from other teams. Copy of presentations was shared with the section for view by all others who could not attend the webinar.

Driven by the positive feedback of students and in an attempt to gain more confidence on the earlier observations, similar initiative was repeated for another section of the same course – nine months later. This time round, the participation for synchronous interactivity got slightly better reaching close to 43% with 2 teams opting for webinar, while one team opting for a telephone based conferencing system. As business travel and schedule appeared to be a critical issue for students not opting for webinar during the first run, the teams during the second run were given to choose a time slot in the range of 15 days. Table 4, column 3 (labeled 'second run') exhibits the distribution of interactivity choices made by the teams in the second round of study. Figure 5 shows the distribution of time zones for the entire group of students and those participating in webinar during each run. Observations after second run were also in line with the earlier observations.

Table 4. Participants and Choice of Interactivity made by Teams

	First Run		Second Run	
Number of Sections	2		1	
Number of Students	38		28	
Option Suggested	No. of teams that opted	% of Teams that opted	No. of teams that opted	% of Teams that opted
Vodcast	5	50	2	28.57
Webinar	3	30	2	28.57
PPT	2	20	2	28.57
Others (Tele-conferencing)			1	14.29
Total	10	100	7	100

Factors Influencing Choice of Interactivity

Student Characteristics

It was observed that none of the students in the presenting groups had a prior experience with attending webinar or preparing a vodcast. 2% of the students were found hesitant in making even the power-point presentation. Absence of much prior experience led to three visible clusters in the students and they were nearly equally distributed. The three clusters named as per the exhibited behaviour of students are:

- Technology Averse- These were the students with visible technology phobia expressed in many ways with comments such

as – "I have never used such a thing earlier and I am not an IT expert" and "I will have to ask my IT guys in the office to see if they can support me in this". They were hesitant in trying out new technologies and were happy going the straight road. Students belonging to this cluster finally opted for simple power point presentation format for submission.

- Keen Learners – This set of students was enthusiastic about use of webinar, even though some of them did not have prior experience with the tool. Their enthusiasm was judged from their response to faculty's call for applying better tools of interactivity in their own work. All such students approached the faculty within 24 hrs with their queries and confirmation. Most of

Table 5. Summary Statistics of the student group under study – as obtained from LMS

Statistic	Section 1	Section 2
Total user sessions	2803	2649
Average user session length	00:42:14	00:36:37
Average user sessions per day	22	21
Average user sessions per day on weekdays	24	24
Average user sessions per day on weekends	26	28
Most active hour of the day	15:00-16:00	22:00-23:00
Least active hour of the day	6:00-7:00	4:00-5:00

(N=38; Timings in 24 hr format - as per local time of the school)

Figure 5. Distribution of time zones of students

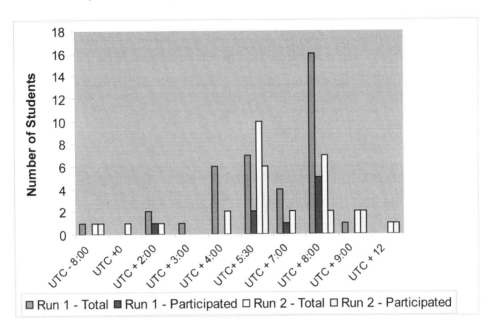

the students in this cluster, participated in the webinar. The ones, who did not, were found to be influenced by team dynamics or business constraints. However, all such students invariably chose to submit a vodcast.

It was observed that students who were highly participative in discussion boards were more responsive to adoption of the new format and were willing to try webinar – this being synchronous and the strongest form of interaction. The students' choice of interactivity was found to be significantly correlated with their assessment scores in discussion based assignments (r=. 0.477, p-value (2-tailed) = 0.045).

• Laggards – This set of students was silent on making any choices and allowed their team mates to lead. There were various factors leading to neutral behavior, lack of participation in the overall course being the primary reason. Some others seemed to be neutral either due to some temporary business or family problems that kept them away from brain storming with team members and hence they chose to remain neutral. They ultimately followed other team members.

During doubt clarifications, it was felt that some students did not want to exert and take the risk of trying out some thing new, if their attempt was not associated with grades.

Student Constraints

Some students had expressed their constraints limiting them from opting for webinar. The constraints reported to professor are broadly classified into three categories.

• Connectivity and accessibility issues - Some students had concerns due to unreliable or slow internet connection in their respective countries. In the absence of a reliable connection, such students were found to be hesitant in committing to a fixed time for participating in the webinar. Some other students were constrained by the infrastructure available at their home and the security/ICT policies based restrictions such as access to audio/video or large file transfer at their work place.

• Business mobility issues- Some students were uncertain of their travel plans and the quality of connectivity they might get in their destination location. Teams where one or more members had to travel finally chose to opt out of webinar.

• Team Dynamics - It was observed that teams that had been working cohesively and were highly interactive within their team discussion board were quicker on making the choice. Most such teams finally exercised an option of webinar or a vodcast. Even if one member in the team had constraints, a cohesive team refrained from choice of webinar. Only teams where all members were equally passive decided on PPT as the format of submission.

As against the initial inhibition of professor, difference in time zones did not emerge as a significant factor (r=0.109; p-value (2-tailed) = 0.521) for student choices. Figure 5 illustrates that most of the students were within the time difference of four hours. There were limited students with wider time difference; however, their participation and choice seemed to derive more from team dynamics than from their location. Active involvement of professor in guiding students, answering their queries and arranging for practice session before final session was instrumental in encouraging students choose better ways of interaction.

Suitability of Webinar

As expressed in table 2, webinar provides synchronous interactivity while still maintaining space flexibility for the participants. The students who participated in the webinar were unanimously posi-

tive about the experience. However, the students who did not participate indicated the constraints associated with application of webinar as a tool for student-teacher-student interactivity. Some clear advantages that have been and can be drawn from the conduct of webinar for student presentations are as follows.

• Mental abilities – Students need to be much more attentive during the real time session as against any asynchronous discussion board. This demands higher use of mental abilities such as synthesis and analysis.

• Soft skills development - As students need to make a formal presentation in front of peers, it promotes speaking and presentation skills. In addition, this generates a sense of competition, self confidence and a spirit to outperform other teams.

• Time management skills development – Students need to adhere to limited time slots, thus exercising very strict control on their content and expression.

• Broad base peer interactions – Webinars, technically can cut across the teams and sections allowing a wider range of students meet and learn from each others' perspective. Such a cross cutting is not possible in section level discussion boards supported by LMS. Listening to or seeing other team mates can also add to the sense of community.

• Immediate feedback and Individual assessment – Faculty may use them as a quick tool to assess the performance of individual team members. Using it in a video format can also help in authentication of students, which is often a concern for students and faculty alike. Students and teachers can also use it for interactive discussion and feedback session on the subject or student performance. Webinar can be particularly helpful in individual project assignments, where a one to one interaction helps a professor gauge the clarity of understanding of the student.

It is worth noting that such advantages have a distinct benefit in an otherwise asynchronous teaching and learning environment. However it is recommended that professor facilitating such interactions should keep following critical factors in view.

- Standardization versus customization – It is easier and cost effective to use a standard pedagogy for all students and 30% may not sound a convincing ratio of students to standardize the use of webinar or vodcast as a medium for interaction amongst peers. Having said so, educational institutes need to accept the fact that every student is different and has different learning style and constraints. Training organizations today need to move towards mass customization (Cohen & Pine II, 2007). Thus, even if there is one segment of the students who can be offered a learning experience of their choice without an overhead to the system, it is worth extending this facility.
- Need for Time Planning – Rigid timing is seen as a major constraint of webinars. As online students are usually working people, it is important that performance expectations and timelines be shared with students much in advance. Despite this, there is a possibility that some students will need last minute adjustments to accommodate their business or family priorities.
- Flexible Facilitation–Students in online education often reside in multiple time zones. Being working executives, they often work during late evenings or week ends. In case, such students work during their office hours, they often are constrained by firewall and other policy restrictions with respect to use of ICT. Faculty needs to be sensitive to such constraints and find flexible ways

to handle unique situations and resulting unique requests. More often than not, synchronous interactions may require faculty to work beyond office hours.

Follow-up of the Pilot Study

The observations and experience of the pilot study have been shared with the faculty of the school. Based on first experience with student presentations, the practice has been repeated for another section of the same course and similar observations have been experienced, as collated in table 4 and figure 5 marked as second run. Though, choice of blending various tools is best left to course faculty, use of webinars has been particularly planned for adoption during evaluation of capstone project where individual student performance is to be assessed. Complexities arising from team dynamics are anticipated to be absent when using webinar for individual participation and assessments.

Pilot study as a research methodology has its own limitations. Further experiments and empirical investigations are required to identify alternate ways of using various tools to improve the learning and business outcomes. Some related research directions have been outlined later in this chapter.

Solutions and Recommendations

Interactivity has a critical role to play towards effective learning. Though technology defines the limits for quality of student-content and student-interface interactions, extent of student-student and student-teacher interactions have a scope for improvement at the level of people and processes. This calls for a mix and match exercise between expected learning outcomes and the abilities of tools of interactivity. While asynchronous interaction provides the much in demand time and space flexibility, synchronous interaction helps nurture many mental abilities and soft skills and is apt for immediate feedback and improvement that is difficult to realize in asynchronous interactions and independent study format.

Online education has a definite and distinct audience and deserves to be treated as a holistic and seamless channel of education. Although, face to face component may not be a feasible solution to offer synchronicity in online courses, web based conference tools (or webinars) have a far greater potential to reach out to individual students across the geographies. As rigid timing is a limitation of synchronous interactions, it is important for educators to use webinars with utmost care and planning for improved learning and assessments rather than as a shear mandate.

Administrators in online education need to be more agile as blending synchronous interactions needs a dynamic planning. Student grouping, course facilitation and tutoring may need to be restructured to enable more convenient way of handling logistics so that students and tutors in neighborhood time zones get into a cluster.

Institutions need to find out the optimum mix of all such forms of interaction so as to maximize on learning as well as business outcomes. While transcending the time and space zones brings in more students; for sustenance, it is imperative that institutions focus on quality of education. This may not necessarily imply a stringent entry and exit criteria for the course or very tight structures, but it certainly calls for a continuously improving teaching and learning process to enable expected learning outcomes and student satisfaction.

It is envisaged that adopters of synchronous interactions will need to resolve the conflict of convenience versus quality. Students who are used to the luxury of time flexibility may resist extra demand on their time and some of them may use it as an excuse too. Resolving this conflict may require assessing the genuineness of student concern. In addition, a prior intimation must be given to students to let them plan their commitments.

Future Trends

Increasing acceptance amongst students and business organizations is a strong indicator that online education is here to stay. In addition to pure online courses, more and more conventional face to face courses are also embracing online format of education. While this growth trend offers unlimited study options for individuals and new markets for educational institutions, key differentiator lies in the way it is implemented by blending various tools and technologies to suit a given context. Further research is suggested to identify such tools, establish agile practices to handle them and explore associated challenges. Empirical investigations are required to study the comparative impact of various tools of interactivity on student engagement, student learning, teacher's life style and academic administration.

Literature describes lack of interactivity as a weakness of online courses and rigid structure as that of face to face courses. Further research should identify the extent to which online students, particularly those working and aiming at live long learning are open to accept rigidity of time, interaction modes and assessments.

As online education has the potential to cater to geographically dispersed students, researchers in online education also need to explore new processes, practices and related tools of interactivity that match the learning styles of individuals. Educators need to analyse the issue of convenience versus quality to identify the balancing factor between the three environmental variables of time, space and interactivity.

Application and empirical study can also be done in face to face systems where synchronous tools like webinar can be used to handle lectures for multiple sections. Blended online interactions can be used for case based analysis or other in-class activities and its impact on teacher, student and institute can be studied.

Online education being a heavy investment proposition, standardization and reuse seem to be a logical way out to meet the economy of scales. However, need for up-to-date knowledge, interactivity and personalized education increase the need for customization and frequent intervention of subject experts. Models and frameworks need to be evolved to help investors identify education delivery models suited to their context.

CONCLUSION

Though, market pressures for time and space flexibility have led to a significant increase in distance education, it is the need for better interaction and overall quality of education that has resulted in the emergence of ICT based variants of distance albeit online education. Literature still shows mixed results on the quality of online and hybrid education.

The chapter analyzed literature from many different dimensions and shared current practices of interactive tools adoption in an online graduate business school that follows a predominantly asynchronous mode of education. Based on a pilot study carried out in the business school, observations and recommendations on use of webinar for student-teacher-student interaction is presented. The pilot study involved use of webinar – a synchronous mode of interaction as applied for multi-directional interactions amongst students and teacher for case based discussion and analysis in an in-class student presentation format. Student response to the use of webinar has been quite positive suggesting the potential for further research and practice to understand and improve upon its utility.

It is recommended that synchronous and asynchronous modes of interaction be blended in the right mix to maximize learning and business outcomes and shape up online education as a seamless mode of education that has the best of all the worlds of education. Technology constraints of today are not long term barriers, thus educators and administrators need to get ready with new skill sets and agile processes. While blending various forms of interactivity and balancing them with time and space convenience, they may need to dynamically handle many trade-offs such as cost versus benefit and convenience versus quality. Better ways of managing these factors need to be explored so as to attain the best of the brick and click.

REFERENCES

139-178. Retrieved April 5, 2009, from http://www.csupomona.edu/~dolce/pdf/guidera.pdf

Alavi, M. (1994). Computer-mediated collaborative learning: an empirical evaluation. *MIS Quarterly*, *18*(2), 159–174. doi:10.2307/249763

Alavi, M., Wheeler, B. C., & Valacich, J. S. (1995). Using IT to reengineer business education: An exploratory investigation of collaborative telelearning. *MIS Quarterly*, *19*(3), 293–312. doi:10.2307/249597

Alliger, G., & Janak, E. (1989). Kirkpatrick's levels of training criteria: thirty years later. *Personnel Psychology*, *42*(2), 331–342. doi:10.1111/j.1744-6570.1989.tb00661.x

Ally, M. (2004). Foundations Of Educational Theory For Online Learning. In T. Anderson & F. Elloumi (Eds.), *Theory and Practice of Online Learning* (pp. 3-31). Athabasca University. Retrieved December 31, 2008, from http://cde.athabascau.ca/online_book/

Anderson, T., & Elloumi, F. (Eds.). (2004). *Theory and Practice of Online Learning.* Athabasca University. Retrieved December 31, 2008, from http://cde.athabascau.ca/online_book/

Arbaugh, J. B. (2000a). Virtual classroom characteristics and student satisfaction in Internet-based MBA courses. *Journal of Management Education*, *24*(1), 32–54. doi:10.1177/105256290002400104

Arbaugh, J. B. (2000b). How Classroom Environment and Student Engagement Affect Leaning in internet-based MBA Courses. *Business Communication Quarterly, 63*(4), 9–26. doi:10.1177/108056990006300402

Bates, A. (1991). Interactivity as a criterion for media selection in distance education. *Never Too Far, 16*, 5–9.

Beard, L. A., & Harper, C. (2002). Student perceptions of online versus on campus instruction. *Education, 122*, 658–663.

Blattberg, R., & Deighton, J. (1991). Interactive Marketing: Exploiting the Age of Addressability. *Sloan Management Review, 33*(1), 5–14.

Bonner, S. E. (1999). Choosing teaching methods based on learning objectives: An integrative framework. *Issues in Accounting Education, 14*(1), 11-39. Retrieved April 5, 2009, from ABI/INFORM Global database. (Document ID: 39568540).

Brower, H. H. (2003). On emulating classroom discussion in a distance-delivered OBHR Course: Creating an on-line learning community. *Academy of Management Learning & Education, 2*(1), 22–36.

Bucy, M. C. (2003). *Online classes: The student experience* (No. AAT 3098412). Corvallis: Oregon State University (Proquest Digital Dissertations).

Carrell, L. J., & Menzel, K. E. (2001). Variations in learning, motivation, and perceived immediacy between live and distance education. *Communication Education, 50*(3), 230–241. doi:10.1080/03634520109379250

Chamberlin, W. S. (2001). Face to face vs. cyberspace: Finding the middle ground. *Campus Technology.* Retrieved April 10, 2009, from http://campustechnology.com/Articles/2001/12/FacetoFace-vs-Cyberspace-Finding-the-Middle-Ground.aspx

Cohen, S. L., & Pine, B. J., II. (2007). Mass Customizing the Training Industry. In *T+D* (pp. 50-54).

Crawford, M. A., & Yetton, P. W. (1985). Do Teaching Skills Matter? An Examination of the Relative Contributions of Teaching Skills and Student Ability in a Postgraduate Executive Development Program. In *Proceedings of the Academy of Management Proceedings* (pp. 124-128). Retrieved from Business Source Premier Database (AN 4978764)

Deighton, J. (1996). The Future of Interactive Marketing. *Harvard Business Review, 74*(6), 151–162.

Dumont, R. A. (1996). Teaching and learning in cyberspace. *IEEE Transactions on Professional Communication, 39*(4), 192–204. doi:10.1109/47.544575

Frydenberg, J. (2007). Persistance in University Continuing Education Online Classes. *International Review of Research in Open and Distance Learning, 8*(3). Retrieved December 31, 2008, from http://www.nosignificantdifference.org/search.asp

Garrison, D. R., Anderson, T., & Archer, W. (2000). Critical thinking in text-based environment: Computer conferencing in higher education. *The Internet and Higher Education, 2*(2), 87–105. doi:10.1016/S1096-7516(00)00016-6

Grant, M. M., & Cheon, J. (2007). The Value of Using Synchronous Conferencing for Instruction and Students. *Journal of Interactive Online Learning, 6*(3), Retrieved December 31, 2008, from http://www.ncolr.org/jiol/issues/PDF/6.3.4.pdf

Greco, J. (1999). Going the distance for MBA candidates. *The Journal of Business Strategy, 20*(3), 30–34. doi:10.1108/eb040004

Guidera, S. G. (2004). Perception of the effectiveness of online instruction in terms of the seven principles of effective undergraduate education. *Journal of Educational Technology, 32*(2/3).

Hillman, D. C. A., Willis, D. J., & Gunawardena, C. N. (1994). Learner interface interaction in distance education: An extension of contemporary models and strategies for practitioners. *American Journal of Distance Education, 8*(2), 30–42. doi:10.1080/08923649409526853

Hoegl, M., & Proserpio, L. (2004). Team member proximity and teamwork in innovative projects. *Research Policy, 33*(8), 1153–1165. doi:10.1016/j.respol.2004.06.005

Hutchinson, D. (2007). Teaching Practices for Effective Cooperative Learning in an Online Learning Environment (OLE). [Retrieved from ABI/INFORM Global Database.]. *Journal of Information Systems Education, 18*(3), 357–367.

Islam, K. (2004). Alternatives for Measuring Learning Success. *Chief Learning Officer, 3*(11), 32-37. Retrieved April 6, 2009, from Business Source Premier (AN 1505760)

Jackson, M.J., & Helms, M.M. (2008). Student Perceptions of Hybrid Courses: Measuring and Interpreting Quality. *Journal of Education for Business, 84*(1), 7-13. Retrieved from Business Source Premier (AN 34772191)

Johnson, D. W., & Johnson, R. T. (1975). *Learning together and alone: Cooperation, competition, and individualization.* Englewood Cliffs, NJ: Prentice Hall.

Kim, K. J., & Bonk, C. J. (2006). The Future of Online Teaching and Learning in Higher Education: The Survey Says… *Educause Quaterly, 29*(4), 22-30. Retrieved March 31, 2009, from http://net.educause.edu/ir/library/pdf/EQM0644.pdf

Kirkpatrick, D. L. (1959a). Techniques for evaluating training programs. *Journal of ASTD, 13*(11), 3–9.

Kirkpatrick, D. L. (1959b). Techniques for evaluating training programs: Part 2—Learning. *Journal of ASTD, 13*(12), 21–26.

Kirkpatrick, D. L. (1960a). Techniques for evaluating training programs: Part 3—Behavior. *Journal of ASTD, 14*(1), 13–18.

Kirkpatrick, D. L. (1960b). Techniques for evaluating training programs: Part 4—Results. *Journal of ASTD, 14*(2), 28–32.

Leidner, D. B., & Jarvenpaa, S. L. (1995). The use of information technology to enhance management school education: A theoretical view. *MIS Quarterly, 19*, 265–291. doi:10.2307/249596

Liu, Y., & Shrum, L. J. (2002). What Is Interactivity and Is It Always Such a Good Thing? Implications of Definition, Person, and Situation for the Influence of Interactivity on Advertising Effectiveness. *Journal of Advertising, 31*(4). Retrieved December 31, 2008, from http://www.accessmylibrary.com/coms2/summary_0286-2773470_ITM

Lorenz, K. (2008). *Top 10 Soft Skills for Job Hunters.* Retrieved December 31, 2008, from http://jobs.aol.com/article/_a/top-10-soft-skills-for-job-hunters/20051107131509990011

McKavanagh, C., & Stevenson, J. (1992, November). *Measurement of Classroom Environment.* Paper presented at the 1992 joint conference of the Australian Association for research in education and the New Zealand Association for research in Education, Deakin University, Geelong.

Moore, M. G. (1989). Three types of interaction. *American Journal of Distance Education, 3*(2), 1–6. doi:10.1080/08923648909526659

Olaniran, B. A. (2006). Applying synchronous computer-mediated communication into course design: Some considerations and practical guides. *Campus-Wide Information Systems*, *23*(3). doi:10.1108/10650740610674210

Pattillo, R. E. (2007). Decreasing transactional distance in a Web-based course. *New Educator*, *32*(3), 109–112.

Plotrowski, C., & Vodanovich, S. J. (2000). Are the reported barriers to Internet-based instruction warranted? A synthesis of recent research. *Education*, *121*, 48–53.

Powers, S., & Rossman, M. (1985). Student satisfaction with graduate education: Dimensionality and assessment in a college education. *Psychology: A Quarterly Journal of Human Behavior*, *22*(2), 46-49. Retrieved April 10, 2009. from Education Resource Information Center, EJ327602.

Proserpio, L., & Gioia, D. A. (2007). Teaching the Virtual Generation. *Academy of Management Learning & Education*, *6*(1), 69–80.

Robinson, C. C., & Hullinger, H. (2008). New Benchmarks in Higher Education: Student Engagement in Online Learning. *Journal of Education for Business*, *84*(2). doi:10.3200/JOEB.84.2.101-109

Rodriguez, M. C., Ooms, A., & Montañez, M. (2008). Students' Perceptions of Online-learning Quality given Comfort, Motivation, Satisfaction, and Experience. *Journal of Interactive Online Learning*, *7*(2), 105–125.

Shanker, M., & Hu, M. Y. (2006). A Framework for Distance Education Effectiveness: An Illustration Using a Business Statistics Course. *International Journal of Web-Based Learning and Teaching Technologies*, *1*(2), 1–17.

Sikora, A., & Carrol, D. (2002). *A profile of participation in distance education: 1999-2000*. National Center for Education Statistics. Retrieved December 31, 2008 from http://nces.ed.gov/pubs2003/ 2003154.pdf

Steuer, J. (1992). Defining Virtual Reality: Dimensions Determining Telepresence. *The Journal of Communication*, *42*(4), 73–93. doi:10.1111/j.1460-2466.1992.tb00812.x

Van Auken, S. V., & Chrysler, E. (2005). The Relative Value of Skills, Knowledge, and Teaching Methods in Explaining Master of Business Administration (MBA) Program Return on Investment. *Journal of Education for Business*, *81*(1), 41–45. doi:10.3200/JOEB.81.1.41-46

Webster, J., & Hackley, P. (1997). Teaching effectiveness in technology-mediated distance learning. *Academy of Management Journal*, *40*, 1282–1309. doi:10.2307/257034

Chapter 11

Screencasts:
Your Technology Professor 24/7

Matthew E. Mooney
Indiana University South Bend, USA

Bruce Alan Spitzer
Indiana University South Bend, USA

ABSTRACT

Screencasts allow a learner to experience a computer-based demonstration again and again at the learner's pace. This means students can review a complicated process or look-up which menu option was selected to get a certain window. Historically, there has been a strong reliance on paper-based support materials. Yet static screen captures don't always tell a learner what steps were taken to get to the window that is shown. Screencasts show exactly what a learner needs to do to complete a given task. Additionally, screencasts are affordable to create and distribute. This chapter will outline the equipment necessary to create screencasts. A selection of software applications will be discussed, and practical tips will be provided to help the reader quickly begin creating screencasts.

INTRODUCTION

Over the years, individuals teaching courses about technology have done their best to provide excellent instructional materials for their students. They've spent countless hours collecting screen captures of menus and windows then developed detailed handouts with step-by-step instructions. They've also devoted considerable class-time to demonstrations. In spite of all of this hard work, students still struggle once they leave the computer classroom. Why does

this happen? Essentially, students learn differently. Some students are so distracted with anxiety while in a computer lab they cannot concentrate. Other students need more individualized, slower-paced instruction. Some students get back to their own computer and find the application looks different on theirs than it did in the classroom. In any case, the goal is good instruction and trying to help students learn a specific application or process.

Wouldn't it be helpful to take classroom demonstrations and package them in a way students could keep? Some sort of package that would allow students to view the same steps over and over

DOI: 10.4018/978-1-61520-672-8.ch011

again would make teachers' lives easier and likely help their students learn the material better. This chapter is about that idea.

BACKGROUND

We've always struggled with printed handouts, or should we say our students have always struggled with printed handouts. We would take a great deal of time to capture the different menu options and windows a student would see when using an application. We would write incredibly detailed descriptions and steps for them, even including call outs and references to the images. Still, many students would experience problems. They would get confused on "where to click" or how we accessed a specific window. We started hearing from them, "I just can't remember what you clicked on," or "I wish you could have shown me that again." Now we can show our students exactly where we clicked, over and over again.

We teach instructional technology in a university school of education. The primary course we teach introduces pre-service teacher education students to using a computer in pedagogically sound ways in classrooms. Our students complete projects using a variety of software applications and online resources. For most of our students, the content in this class is new and goes beyond their usual use of a computer. While they may be comfortable using Microsoft Office applications, checking their email, and surfing the Web, my class introduces them to new applications and resources such as digital photography, podcasting, digital video, and some web development among other things.

We have always encouraged our students to keep their printed materials stored away somewhere for use once they began their teaching career. We never expected them to remember everything covered in class and thought the detailed handouts would be a good resource for them when they wanted to use something we had covered in class

with their students. However, we wanted to give them more. That's where screencasts come in.

Screencasts allow us to capture everything happening on our screens or part of our screens while we narrate what we're doing. Our students see the mouse movements, menu selections, typing, and hear our voice. The use of screencasts allows us to be available to our students any time and anywhere. Additionally, screencasts happen in real-time, so if something takes one minute to complete, our students see it in one minute. Think about the amount of textual descriptions and image captures that are needed to explain something that takes one minute to perform. Screencasts can be used in traditional education classrooms, training environments, distance education situations, and as supplementary materials in textbooks, just to list a few possible uses.

There are a number of great options for capturing a screen and narrating processes. Some of these options are resource intensive and rather expensive. However, there are a lot of wonderful options that are easy to use and quite affordable. The remainder of this chapter will discuss the basic hardware requirements for creating screencasts, introduce some of the software applications that can be used for screencasting, describe different delivery methods of finished screencasts, offer some helpful production tips, and address some potential challenges for those of you that want to begin screencasting. The chapter will conclude with a look to the future.

HARDWARE REQUIREMENTS

Long gone are the days of expensive audio boards. Most modern computers have all the necessary resources for screencasting. The introduction of USB microphones has made recording narration rather simple. As long as the computer used for production has adequate processing power and hard drive space, there should be no problem creating screencasts. Of course, there are always minimum RAM and operating system requirements with any software application. Suffice to say, if the production computer is running at least Windows XP or Mac OS X, software exists to create a screencast. The remainder of this section will offer some ideas on platform decisions, microphones, and room considerations that will help produce quality screencasts.

Platform

You can create screencasts with both Macintosh and Windows platforms; in many cases, it doesn't matter which. For example, if you are preparing a screencast about using a Web-based resource, platform doesn't matter: the Web is basically the same from one platform to the next. Granted, there are sites that are more Windows-centric than others, but overall, platform wouldn't introduce major differences.

Applications offer a lot more variety in their user interface across platforms. If the screencast is to be application-specific, platform will certainly be a concern. In some courses, students learn to use both platforms and learn applications that are only available on one platform. For example, students use Windows when working with Microsoft Access and Macs when using iPhoto. In this situation, screencasts would be created on a platform-specific computer.

If you are in a position where you are getting a new computer to begin creating screencasts, we would recommend purchasing a Mac. While you can create screencasts on either platform, if you need to create screencasts on both platforms, a Mac is a great option that alleviates the need to own two separate machines. It is possible to run both the Mac OS and Windows on the same computer. You can run them simultaneously or independently. We have invested in software for Mac to create screencasts, so we can run Windows XP or Vista using Parallels Desktop. We are able to capture the Windows screen while running my Mac software. What this means is we have one computer to deal with and one application to purchase and learn.

Microphones

A quick Google search for USB microphones will yield hundreds of results ranging from less that $10 to hundreds of dollars. Any of these microphones will work. However, the quality of the microphone will likely have the most influence on the quality of the recording. Even the newest, fastest, and most equipped computer will only record what comes through the microphone. If it's poor quality going in, it will be poor quality coming out. A word of caution however, the most expensive microphone may not provide a quality difference that you can notice. The highest quality microphones provide the best quality when conditions are perfect. Most will not be recording in a professional sound studio, so a $500 microphone is really not necessary.

One of the more popular microphones used by podcasters is the Blue Snowball (http://www.bluemic.com). The Snowball is a rugged and powerful microphone that offers outstanding quality for a modest price.

If you are a person that is often recording screencasts while on the road, you might want to look at the Blue Snowflake. This model is more portable and smaller but offers the same high quality recording capability of the Snowball.

There is one distinct difference between the Snowball and the Snowflake other than size. The Snowflake is a cardioid microphone while the Snowball is both cardioid and omnidirectional. In plain English, the Snowflake is going to record the sound that is directionally in front of the microphone, whereas the Snowball can do that or record sound from all around the microphone. For screencasts, the Snowflake's size, portability and slightly lower prices makes it a perfect choice for someone who needs to have microphone in their bag. If you are going to do most of your recording in your office, you may want to invest in the

Snowball. The added flexibility of the having an omnidirectional microphone is worth the small extra cost. If you ever need a microphone to capture a conversation around a table, the Blue Snowball would be perfect.

Room Considerations

As mentioned above, most will not be recording screencasts in professional recording rooms, and this presents some issues to keep in mind. Most offices have a lot of ambient noise that human brains filter out. Things like fans, furnaces, people walking by, and the campus grounds crews mowing outside are all things that humans block out but a microphone does not. You'll be surprised how much sound a microphone will pick up. Many of these ambient noises are out of your control, so unless you want to record in your office at midnight, you may have to settle for some background noise of people walking by your office. However, most people will respect a "quiet please, recording in session" sign on your door. There are some things you can do to improve your office's recording potential. You can block off a register vent to quiet a furnace or fan, or move your microphone as far away from the source of the noise as possible. Also, if you are using a cardioid microphone, place it so the unwanted sound is at the back of the microphone. This will take advantage of the cardioid design and limit the sound behind the microphone being picked up.

If you notice a lot of echoing in your recordings, you may need to think about something to absorb the sound in your office. Cinderblock walls can give you a lot of sound reflection. Simply hanging some heavy cloth on the wall directly behind your microphone can help absorb the sound of your voice and prevent it from reflecting back at you. You can even purchase acoustic foam to mount to the wall or a board that can be placed behind your microphone. In my experience, simply limiting the distracting noises of furnaces

and fans is often all that is necessary for a good quality recording.

Don't forget to turn your office telephone and cell phone ringer off before you start recording. Inevitably, someone will call just as you are wrapping up a recording.

SOFTWARE

The number of applications available to create screencasts would exceed the page limit of this chapter, possibly even the entire book. There are hundreds of applications available and each one is a viable candidate for screencasts. However, there are a few applications that have been found to be excellent applications for consideration. The following portion of this chapter will describe 3 different applications for both platforms. Additionally, we want to share one open-source application that will work on both platforms. Each application discussed will capture all or part of your screen and allow for audio recording. These are the basic requirements for creating screencasts. Each application will offer additional features or options that may make them more appealing for your specific situation. Additionally, most software developers provide free trials to evaluate the application prior to purchase. We strongly urge you to try any of the applications before purchasing them.

Windows Applications

Adobe Captivate

The most robust and also most expensive application for screencasts is Adobe Captivate (http://www.adobe.com/products/captivate/). Captivate is definitely powerful. For any user who is comfortable with Adobe Flash, the overall interface will be familiar.

Since Captivate is built around the Flash tool sets and interface, you have the ability to add user interaction, decision trees, quizzes, and rich media. While all of these features provide a great deal of flexibility, these features also represent a potential weakness for the applications. There is a much higher learning curve for using Captivate compared to using the other applications that will be discussed in the following sections. Additionally, Captivate outputs Flash movies in the form of .SWF files. While this is an excellent format that nearly any user can view, it does limit your delivery options to some degree.

Additionally, the retail price of Captivate is nearly $700 with an educational price around $250. If you wanted to develop screencasts that include user interaction this is a great tool to use; however, if you simply want to capture and narrate your screen for the development of tutorials and support materials, Captivate may not be the best tool for you.

Camtasia Studio

Camtasia Studio by TechSmith (http://www.tech-smith.com/camtasia) is a very popular screencast application. Camtasia has a familiar "track-based" interface where you have a video track, audio track, and so on. The tracks have a timeline that allows for non-linear editing and moving digital pieces to earlier or later in the presentation. If you have done any audio or video editing, it is likely this interface will feel very comfortable.

Camtasia also offers some nice effects that can add to the production value of your screencast. Things like a built-in zoom and pan allow for the finished screencast to be viewed on virtually any device from a computer screen to a cellular telephone. Camtasia also provides an easy way to add closed captioning, splash screens, and transitions. The ability to add quizzes and surveys is also available in Camtasia. The overall learning curve for Camtasia is easier than Adobe Captivate; however there are still a lot of features to learn if you want to take full advantage of this application.

Camtasia retails for about $300 and is available for around $180 to educational purchasers. It's a feature-rich application that outputs your video in most standard video formats. This allows you a great deal of flexibility for how you will deliver your screencasts to your users.

CamStudio

CamStudio (http://camstudio.org/) is an open source solution that does all the basics, but does for free! CamStudio will record your screen or part of your screen and your narration.

This handy application also does some other things that you would expect to find in other much more costly packages. For example, CamStudio can add captions to your video, or use a web camera to add a picture-in-picture solution.

The native output for CamStudio is a .AVI file, but it also includes .SWF Producer, which allows you to create .SWF files from the .AVI files. Like those produced by Adobe Captivate, .SWF files are very useful; however, there are a few drawbacks to be discussed in a later section.

For creating basic screencasts, CamStudio is a great option. The price is right and the video is very high quality. The application is simple to use and most users figure it out pretty quickly. The only real difficulty found in CamStudio is the download and installation process. For some users, the download might be a little confusing. Since it is an open source application you can download the source code or the application. Some users may select the source code by mistake. Additionally, you need to download and install the codec separately. It seems that enough users have struggled with this and prompted the developer to post a how-to video that walks users through the download and installation process. If you follow the steps outlined in the developer's video, it is quite simple.

Macintosh Applications

iShowU

iShowU by Shiny White Box (http://www.shiny-whitebox.com/) is a nice application for creating screencasts. It actually comes in three different variations: iShowU, iShowU HD, and iShowU Pro. iShowU is for users of OS 10.4. iShowU HD and iShowU Pro are for OS 10.5 users.

All the version of iShowU provide a simple to use interface that output a .MOV QuickTime file. QuickTime files are very nice to work with and provide excellent quality. All versions also have the ability to "follow your mouse" while recording. This means you can have a set recording size that floats around with your mouse as you move around the screen. This is ideal if you have your monitor set to a high resolution. The HD and Pro versions have far more options and the ability to create some custom settings. The HD and Pro versions of iShowU allow you to create presets, in additions to those included with the application. These presets allow you to select and set the audio levels, frame rates, compression settings, codecs and much more. Additionally, the HD and Pro versions allow you to upload your screencasts directly to YouTube. The Pro version allows you to embed watermarks and record keystrokes, and is optimized to use fewer resources.

iShowU offers a wonderful variety of features in an economical packages. The application's retail prices are iShowU for $20, iShowU HD for about $30, and iShowU Pro for about $60. At the time of this writing, there were no educational discounts for these applications.

Snapz Pro X

Snapz Pro X by Ambrosia Software (http://www.ambrosiasw.com/utilities/snapzprox/) has been a long time favorite of developers and tech writers. It started as a screen capture utility and added the ability to perform screencasts a number of years ago.

Snapz Pro X offers a wide variety of options for capturing. Along with changing the selection to be recorded, and the audio options, you can change the color of the video being recorded, set it to follow the mouse, and scale the selection. Snapz Pro X has a very simple interface that allows the use of keystrokes to begin and end a recording. It has proven over the years to be a very powerful tool. Not only can this application be used for screencasting, but also it is equally as valuable as a screen capture tool. Snapz Pro X offers a number of options for capturing still images from your screen. With Snapz Pro X a drop shadow can automatically be applied to a captured still image and it will save the file in nearly any graphics format, along with many other options.

The retail price of Snapz Pro X is about $70. Ambrosia Software offers educational pricing of 20% off the retail price. Ambrosia Software does require that the institution purchases the software, not an individual.

ScreenFlow

ScreenFlow from Vara Software (http://origin.telestream.net/screen-flow/overview.htm) offers one of the most feature rich packages for screencasting. Beyond the ability to capture the video and audio needed for a screencast, ScreenFlow provides a number of very useful post-recording tools. As soon as you finish recording a screen cast, you can begin editing in a timeline and track-based environment.

The editing features of ScreenFlow offer many options. While the application has a simple user interface, it also provides the ability to edit your screencast. ScreenFlow does not allow you to select a specific section of the screen to record. However, you can crop the area once you enter the editing process. There are so many features in ScreenFlow it would be difficult to provide them within the chapter. You can trim and delete sections of your screencast, and you can zoom in and out to highlight specific sections of your screencast. Additionally, you can create callouts that highlight windows or your mouse. When a callout is created, you can change the opacity of the background, blur the background, and even zoom in on just the callout. All of this is done prior to saving your compressed screencast. You also have the ability to save a ScreenFlow file that would allow you to come back and re-edit the file. As for saving your compressed file, ScreenFlow can save your output file in a number of different formats and quality settings.

ScreenFlow is available for a retail price of about $100 and an educational discount of 20% off of the retail price.

Cross-Platform

Jing Project

Jing Project by TechSmith (http://www.jing-project.com/) is an open-source screencasting application that is available for both Mac and Windows. Jing Project provides you with all the basic screencasting features.

The interface is simple to use but is different than most software applications. The interface floats in the corner of your screen until you decide to use it. While the interface is a bit unusual, it is simple to understand and most users quickly become comfortable with it. The quality of the captured video is quite good. The files created by Jing Project are .SWF files. The files can be uploaded directly to a number of online resources or saved locally. Again, the limited variety of output formats could be a concern for some depending on how you want to deliver your screencasts.

Overall, Jing Project is a very viable option for screencasting and should be considered. The fact that it is free and provides software for both Mac and Windows makes it a very useful tool for

individuals looking for a low-cost screencasting application.

DELIVERY OPTIONS

Using screencasts in a classroom or training environment is an excellent way to help learners, students, or employees. However, there are a number of things to consider before you begin recording screencasts. Throughout this chapter, we have mentioned concerns with deliver methods. How you intend to deliver your screencasts has a lot to do with how you will create them and which application(s) will best suit your needs.

A common way of delivering screencasts is through an online venue like Screencast.com, YouTube, and other online video streaming services. However, many people also use syndication through iTunes or course management software at educational institutions.

While all of these methods are very usable, you need to look at your audience to better understand what they need. When we began providing screencasts to our students, we utilized the built-in podcasting features of the university's course management system. This seemed to work well. Students would login and download the files to view. We could have also placed these files on the university's streaming servers. Streaming the screencasts would allow us to provide a bit higher quality video, but we were concerned that students would not have as much access. The geographic location of my campus means that many of our students do not have high-speed Internet available at their homes. Many of our students live in small, rural towns and high-speed access is just not available. In some cases, even the dial-up services are unreliable. So we decided to treat the files like podcasts. This allowed the students to download the files while on campus, burn them to a CD, and take them home.

The following semester, we decided to try something a bit more high-end. We recorded new screencasts in much higher quality and authored a DVD for our students. Each student received a DVD at the start of the semester. They could take it home and watch it on their standard DVD player or on a computer with a DVD drive, or even bring it to class for use with group and individual work sessions. This was a huge hit that cost very little money. The University has a DVD duplicator, and our department supplied the media. Students now have a high quality video of our in-class presentations for all their projects.

Our students are not the only users who benefit from moving screencasts offline. Think about employees who travel. They would not need to have an Internet connection to view the screencasts. Many distance education students could benefit from this as well. They view your screencasts at any time as long as they have access to a DVD player.

We point this out because if you select an application that does not export your screencasts in a format that can be incorporated into a DVD authoring application or at least saved as raw files on a data DVD, you are locking users into having an Internet connection to view your screencasts. The applications that provide more output flexibility allow you to save your screencasts in multiple formats and distribute them through a variety of media.

Helpful Tips

What is "Good Enough?"

Does a higher production value increase learning? In our experience, the answer is no. It's all about the message. If you develop good instruction, a little background noise or some "ums" in your narration aren't going to decrease the learning that might result from someone viewing your screencasts.

While technology has become more affordable and quality continues to increase, do not get caught up in the belief that your screencasts

need to be perfect. Remember that you seldom give a perfect lecture or a perfect training session. When you present information, things happen: you click on the wrong thing, stammer a little, or say the wrong word. You don't need stop and start again every time that happens. In live venues, you simply correct yourself and continue on with the presentation. There is no need to stop and make minor corrections in a screencast either. We admit that we do a retake now and again, but it is typically because we haven't set up the application correctly or have totally lost our train of thought, not because we said "um" or clicked on the wrong button.

Screencasts are intended to make learning better not teaching harder. When you watch a finished screencast, put yourself in the learner's seat. Would you have learned the material? That is the ultimate goal. Should you use a script?

As we mentioned above, there is a point that you just need to "do your thing." Scripts mean you're going to read to your users. Would you use a script in front of a group? You likely would have an outline with the key topics you want to cover. Remember: it's because you are a content expert that you're teaching the class or providing the training.

Before you start screencasting, spend the time preparing the "lecture" or "demonstration" just like you would for a live audience. Make your notes, get all your files together, and prepare. Then start recording your screencasts.

Keep Things Short

Much of this tip depends on your subject matter. When teaching technology courses, our students have told us they prefer short screencasts. So rather than prepare one screencast for the entire project, we might prepare 10 1- to 2-minute screencasts for a project. For example, if our students were learning how to develop a website, we would have a screencast that dealt with the folder structure we wanted. Then we'd have another that introduced them to the application's interface. We might have one on adding a graphic to a page. Each of these screencasts would be very short and focus on a specific task. According to our students, this is much easier that scrubbing through a 5 to 10-minute screencast looking for that topic.

This also makes things easier in the long run. First, it forces us to break the tasks down into smaller pieces. We've found we're much less likely to miss steps when presenting the information in short bursts. Also, if we change something in the project, it's likely going to change a couple of the screencasts, but not all of them. If we had done one screencast for the entire project, we would be recreating the screencast for each small change.

Slow Down

Since you are the content expert, it is very easy to race though these screencasts. You zip your cursor across the screen and open a menu, make a selection, and then shoot back to the other side of the screen, talking all the while. Users new to an application can't move as quickly and easily as you, so you should slow down the process when recording a screencast. Make your mouse movements much slower than normal, take more time to make a menu selection, be deliberate in each and every step of the process. Your students aren't there to ask you to slow down, so we will.

POTENTIAL CHALLENGES

As with any technology, there are always concerns and challenges. Moving to the DVD rather than online delivery is an example of such a challenge. The files students needed to download were very large and it just became cumbersome for them to download the files and me to upload the files.

Also, videos often require specific players for users to view the files. When you author your screencasts, make sure to select a format that is viewable by as many of your users as possible.

While this seems very simple, it often presents a challenge. Version changes and player incompatibility can cause a lot of frustration. Spend a little time thinking this through before you start recording screencasts.

Another challenge we faced was providing content that met accessibility guidelines. Screencasts are very visual and rely on audio cues to help the user. What happens when you have a visually impaired user or a hearing impaired user? We have had students with hearing impairments and began providing closed-captioned screencasts. We did not transcribe our complete narration for the videos. We provided captioned highlights and cues to assist these students. In the case of visually impaired students, we have provided more detailed narration of what we are doing and significantly slowed the pace of our speech.

Regardless of the challenges you face, screencasts provide users with a unique opportunity to learn. From an instructional point of view, we're now able to give our students more realistic support materials that have been developed specifically for their projects.

FUTURE TRENDS

As more and more courses begin to rely on technology, students and instructors are expected to have more and more technology skills. Training materials need to provide a more cohesive and accurate representation of the steps to accomplish a given task. It is far more economical and efficient to have tutorials provided as screencasts than as static paper-based materials.

Companies and organizations that utilize specific software applications can provide screencasts for their employees to view at their desks or at home rather than investing in training centers and travel expenses. One trainer can provide screencasts that can be viewed anywhere and at any time, which results in large financial savings. Additionally, screencasts provide users with the ability to learn at their own pace and review the material as often as they would like. In most cases, this is a preferred solution compared to group training sessions constrained by a specific amount of time with which to cover an amount of material.

Beyond the training needs, screencasts have an excellent application in the world of distance education, regardless of content area. Screencasting applications allow an instructor to record a presentation delivered using presentation software like Microsoft PowerPoint or Apple Keynote. Some of the applications even record the "talking head" of the instructor and integrate that video into the presentation. No longer is it necessary to use expensive hosted solutions to provide narrated lectures. Screencasting can perform these tasks for a fraction of the cost.

Information that is not dependent on classroom interaction can easily be adapted for use in a screencast. Content that does not change regularly is also well suited for screencasts. Education and training have seen an explosion of podcasting; screencasting is the next logical progression.

CONCLUSION

Learning anything that is computer-based presents some challenges. The nature of the computer is that it is fluid and dynamic. When users click on one thing, other things happen. Sometimes one thing will change, sometimes multiple things will change based on that single click of the mouse.

For the learner sitting and watching all of this action projected on a screen, things are happening at a lightening fast pace. It's overwhelming for some and confusing for others. Students hear the presenters' voices and watch cursors fly across the screen. Of course, this is the three-hundredth time the presenter has created a new database, or added an equation into a spreadsheet, or rotated a digital picture. However, presenters sometimes forget that students may be seeing the process for

the first time. Students may not know where to click or which options to select. Good instructors take time with their students and help them as they need. They answer the same questions in each class, sometimes 3 or 4 times in the same class. That is what good teachers do. Why? The answer is simple. Good teachers want their students to learn.

Screencasts can help meet that goal. Teachers can provide students with a way to watch the same event or process over, and over, and over again. Students can hear explanations of processes, watch mouse movements across the screen, and click on something as many times as they need if they have a screencast to which they can refer back.

Every semester we have students who watch a demonstration and complete a project with little or no additional help. However, we also have students who need to see and hear something two and three or sometimes four times before they feel comfortable enough to try it on their own. The use of screencasts lets those students who need to see and hear the demonstration multiple times get that experience while we can work our way around the room to help other students with specific problems. It also lets students experience the demonstration again at a later date. We have students that simply put the DVD we give them in a drawer. Then a couple of years later they need to do something that we covered in class. They pull the DVD out, watch the sections they need, and then get to work. Many of them come back and tell us that they've done just that or something similar every semester.

We have made an investment of time and resources to make our classes more accessible to our students. Screencasts have changed the way our classes run, the way our students learn, and the way we teach. When we purchased our microphones and software, we didn't realize how much those small investments would change our classes. The feedback from our students and their performance in our classes and other classes have shown us it was a great investment.

If you provide in-class demos now, you can easily provide screencasts. Give it a try, your students will thank you for it and your teaching will improve.

Chapter 12
Identifying Student Usability Needs for Collaborative Learning Environment Design

Danuta Zakrzewska
Technical University of Lodz, Poland

Joanna Ochelska-Mierzejewska
Technical University of Lodz, Poland

ABSTRACT

Performance of Web-based collaborations depends not only on pedagogical strategies but also on the effectiveness of e-learning systems. The factors that may help designers in creating collaborative environments acceptable to users are considered. It is shown that usability needs may differ among students attending the same course who have similar technical skills, and it is difficult to determine average user requirements. The research is based on two case studies of students evaluating the same environment. As an experimental result, it is stated that usability requirements may be influenced by learning style preferences, and therefore student groups may be created. Some indications concerning identification of usability needs are presented.

INTRODUCTION

One of the most important factors for measuring the usability of an educational system is learner satisfaction. Identification of portal features, obtaining student approval of the environment in a specified context of use, may be of crucial significance in attaining pedagogical goals as well as building sustainable collaborative communities. Software designers should take into account usability aspects in an educational setting. Development of internet

technologies enables the inclusion of student collaboration as part of e-learning systems, where students may exchange ideas, share knowledge or experience, and discuss problem solutions. Students' attitudes towards participating in collaboration may depend significantly on their acceptance of the collaborative environment and, particularly, on the degree to which it is tailored to meet their needs. Recognition of user requirements at the early stage of development of the portal is the best way to ensure student satisfaction. The learner's role in the process cannot be overestimated. Tailoring the software to user requirements may be difficult in the

DOI: 10.4018/978-1-61520-672-8.ch012

case of different student needs and preferences. Dividing them into groups with similar requirements may help to solve the problem.

In the paper, we consider usability aspects of educational software. The main goal is identification of factors that may help in building collaborative environments which are acceptable to users. The focus is on the student role in creating user-friendly and fully satisfactory portals and, in particular, the significance of the evaluation process. We discuss methods that enable us to discover student requirements. We consider finding groups with similar usability preferences. Our aim is to indicate methods for identifying the factors that are the most important for students and that should be taken into account during the process of creating collaborative learning environments. We propose to use learning styles as the determinant for dividing students into groups. The research is based on two case studies of students' assessment of a system that was used during international collaboration.

BACKGROUND

According to International Organisation for Standardization (1998), software usability may be defined as the extent to which the system can be used by specified users to achieve specified goals with effectiveness, efficiency and satisfaction in a specified context of use. Kukulska-Hulme and Shield (2004) suggest that good usability of computer systems can be only achieved by understanding the psychological, ergonomic, organisational and social factors that determine how people operate. They emphasise the significance of such aspects as satisfaction and enjoyability. Preece, Rogers and Sharp (2002) additionally stress the role of the user's evaluation of prototypes and existing systems. Bell, Zaitseva and Zakrzewska (2007), in turn, present the evaluation of software as crucial in achievement of sustainability of online learning communities.

Squires and Preece (1996) observed that the usability features of educational software have a big impact on achieving educational goals and that researchers do not give enough attention to the fact. Usability of online learning systems has become an object of research in recent years, but there is still no standard methodology for evaluating learning applications (Ardito et al., 2006). According to Nielsen (1993) the usability of software is usually connected with such features as learnability, effectiveness, efficiency, robustness and user satisfaction. Nielsen (1994) formulated software usability heuristics, which Dringus (1995) proposed to use for evaluating interfaces of applications without any modifications. Nielsen's (1994) heuristics, developed to assess user requirements of interactive systems and revised by Schneiderman (1997), were used by Parlangeli, Marchigianni and Bagnara (1999) to evaluate usability of e-learning applications.

Squires and Preece (1999) emphasised the necessity for changes in proposed heuristics to fulfil learners' requirements. They proposed an adaptation of Nielsen's heuristics by using socio-constructivist principles (Philips, 1995; Soloway et al., 1996), such as: matching between designers and learner model, navigational fidelity, appropriate levels of learner control, prevention of peripheral cognitive errors, understandable and meaningful symbolic representations, supporting personal approaches to learning, strategies for cognitive error recognition, diagnosis and recovery, matching with the curriculum.

Quinn, Alem and Eklund (1999) presented a method of evaluating e-learning systems which takes into account design factors and acceptance factors by considering instructional goal and content, learning tasks and aids, and assessment, together with level of motivation to use the system, level of active participation entailed, quality of learning support and level of user satisfaction.

Usability is the feature that decides how the specified goals are achieved. Nogier (2007) defined it as the capacity of an object to be easy to use by a given person to carry out the task for which it has been designed. There are many elements that affect the usability of portals, like front page layout, navigation or supporting tools. Marsico and Levialdi (2004) presented Website design issues with all the factors that influence Website usability. They emphasised the role of the informative content architecture of Websites. They stated that usability may be measured by users' satisfaction with content and amount of information, as well as access policies, type of communication channels, and the cohesiveness of information organisation assigned to participants. Marsico and Levialdi (2004) described user satisfaction as the most significant issue for system usability. That kind of satisfaction may be achieved by user's evaluation of prototypes and existing systems, the role of which was emphasised by Preece, Rogers and Sharp (2002).

Nowadays, educational institutions have to cope with such challenges as teaching to work in teams or enabling students to share distributed knowledge and to diminish individualism, promoting social capital (Lundin & Magnusson, 2003). The value of learning together is emphasised by many authors. Liaw, Chen and Huang (2008) stated that collaboration may enrich students' individual learning experiences by motivating them to seek new insights and perspectives. Schrage (1990) qualified collaboration as necessary for successful problem-solving. Gros (2001), in turn, mentioned collaborative learning as arising from 'information society' needs, which are connected with cooperative relationships, shared decisions, diversity and communication development.

Wang, Tzeng and Chen (2000) proved that Web-based collaborative learning improves achievement of learning outcomes in comparison with Internet-based traditional e-learning. Francescato et al. (2007) showed that students working together online performed better at competence-based tasks than their peers collaborating face-to-face. Comeaux and McKenna-Byington (2003) stated that using Internet technology enhances learner collaboration. Ng and Ma (2002) indicated that Web applications enable learners from different backgrounds and locations to share their personal and team experiences.

Students' attitude towards participating in collaborative activities may depend significantly on their acceptance of the learning environment and interface designers should consider customisation according to students' personal preferences. Preece (2000), considering online communities, claimed that software designers should tailor it to more closely to meet the community's needs. Karger and Quan (2004) stated that personalisation holds great potential to improve people's ability to interact with information.

Soong et al. (2001) presented user adaptation capability as a critical success factor for sustaining a virtual learning community. Teo et al. (2003) emphasised the significance of users' ability to adapt the system to their needs increasing their intention to use it. They proposed the extended Technology Acceptance Model (TAM) of sustainability of virtual learning communities, in which they consider system characteristics of information accessibility and community adaptivity as external variables, which by influencing perceived usefulness and perceived ease of use play a significant role in user acceptance of technology. They also included sense of belonging as a mediating variable between perceived usefulness and intention to use, and between perceived ease of use and intention to use. As regards information accessibility, Teo et al. (2003) defined the type and amount of information, and the cohesiveness of information organisation assigned to participants. By community adaptivity they meant the ability of users and systems to change the rules, structures and content of a virtual community. They showed that both information accessibility and community adaptivity have significant effects on user perceptions and behavioural intention. They indicated that elements such as information content and amount, access policies, the type of communication channels provided and information organisation all have an influence on sustainability of virtual communities.

The relationship between individual learning styles and distance education was examined by a number of researchers. Rovai (2003) showed that teaching methods should vary according to learning styles of learners. Lu, Yu and Liu (2003) and Lee (2001) identified the impact of learning styles on Web-based course performance. Beaudoin (2002) concluded that a necessary element for online course efficacy is the establishment of a collaborative learning environment depending on students' profiling. Alfonseca et al. (2006) stated that collaborative learning may be improved by grouping students according to learning styles. Graf and Kinshuk (2006) confirmed that students with different learning styles have different needs and preferences. Cha et al.(2006) described building a customised interface in an intelligent learning environment related to learners' preferences and connected with their learning styles. The interface guidelines were based on the distinctive characteristics in learning style dimensions suggested by Felder and Silverman (1988), hypothesising learners' behaviour patterns in learning interfaces. Liegle and Janicki (2006) presented an exploratory experiment in which they examined the relationships between learning styles and navigation needs. They concluded that adaptive educational systems may be more effective in achieving educational goals. In the literature there are only a few studies investigating the relationship between learning styles and adaptive hypermedia applications. An overview of the research concerning building adaptive systems, in which dominant learning styles are taken into account, can be found in Stash and Cristea (2004).

USABILITY OF COLLABORATIVE LEARNING ENVIRONMENTS

Issues, Controversies, Problems

Acceptance of Technology

According to the extended Technology Acceptance Model, users should accept technology of collaborative learning environments. Identification of external variables that influence students' perceived ease of use and perceived usefulness may be of crucial significance in interface design. System characteristics as well as characteristics of the usage situation were noted by Wiedenbeck and Davis (1997) as the main elements of external variables. They examined how the interaction style and prior experience with similar software affected users' perceptions of software packages. There were broad investigations of TAM's external variables in the study of Internet-based systems. Lederer et al. (2000) provided instruments for assessing the ease of use and usefulness of Websites. All considered external variables that make the Web useful and easy to use. The tests included ease of understanding, ease of finding and information focus as factors of antecedent ease of use, as well as information necessary to support activities, information quality and information for primary activities. Selim (2003) identified four critical factors for perceived usefulness of course Web sites. He found that course work interactivity, embedding the system with on-line components such as animations and multimedia modules, as well as with tools facilitating the communication and with interactive help explaining Web content, allowed learners to achieve the Web course objectives efficiently. As critical determinants Selim (2003) mentioned consistency, flexibility and efficiency of use and understandability.

Critical Determinants in Educational Environments

In learning environments the critical determinants may differ depending on software functionalities and destination, as well as individual preferences and needs of learners. Designers should take into account such user features as: different technological skills, prior knowledge, interests, motivation, communication skills, creativity and learning styles. Collaborative environments should support learners in finding peers for collaboration, facilitate the communication and exchange of information and the sharing of joint tasks. Special attention should be paid to ease of using communication tools. In the case of international collaboration support for communication in a foreign language may also be of some importance.

The process of designing collaborative software should take into account improvement of the system by addition of adaptation abilities. Embedding environment in special features should be related to the way the collaboration is organised and it should depend on participant characteristics. Designers need to identify factors that are important during different stages of collaborative activities, especially taking into account start of collaboration and its development, as well as critical factors deciding of its sustainability. It is important to determine: what elements influence students' decisions to join the collaboration and what kinds of system features determine whether they are more active than silent? What kinds of factors decide that participants are satisfied? Does the technology have any influence? What does student satisfaction depend on? What is the role of student attitudes towards using the software? What technology features and solutions are essential? What kinds of students' personal characteristics are decisive? What is the role of learning styles? How should designers deal with students' requirements? How can they satisfy them? Answers are usually different for each user. Finding the average student requirements may not be possible. The potential solution may consist in merging users into groups of similar characteristic features. In that case, before starting to allocate environment attributes, crucial for the usability of the software, the designers should identify groups with similar preferences and discover their needs.

Identification of Learner Needs

To adjust the environment to user needs, the process of gathering information about the learners is necessary. There are two approaches to identification of user preferences for tailoring software to student needs: based on data collected explicitly or by implicit methods. Data gathered implicitly are connected with users' behaviours, while in explicit techniques, students complete different kinds of questionnaires, which aim at identification of their preferences or evaluate the software from the perspective of their individual requirements. Both paths for identification of user requirements are presented in Figure 1. The explicit path, in many cases, is connected with creating different versions of the environment, while the implicit one usually allows one to personalise the system. In that case data contained in log files are used to recognise users' patterns from their historical behaviours. Such an approach requires intelligent computational methods and personalization, and is mainly used for recommender systems purposes. For adaptivity goals, the technique of collecting data concerning system evaluation and preferences explicitly seems to be sufficient. Bell, Zaitseva and Zakrzewska (2007) presented usability evaluation as a very important source of information that enables one to adapt the system according to users' expectations and to enhance it with the ability to change rules, structure and contents. This achieves information accessibility and suggests that using the system would be possible without too much effort (perceived ease of use).

For the purpose of Web educational systems, Brusilovsky (2001) defined user individual traits as a group name for user features (like cogni-

Figure 1. Two paths for identification of user requirements

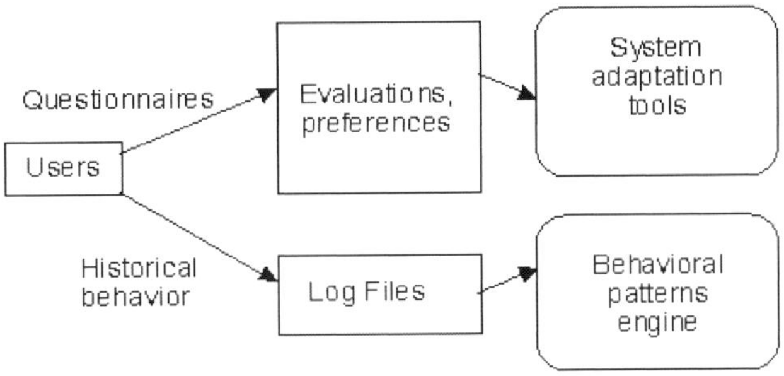

tive factors or simple learning styles), which are stable and usually extracted by specially designed psychological tests. Many researchers agree on the importance of modelling and using individual traits, but there is little agreement on which features can and should be used, or how to use them (Brusilovsky, 2001).

Designing of Collaborative Learning Environments

Identification of student groups participating in the collaborative activities enables the design of the environment according to their needs, taking into account both merits and usability. Participant characteristic features include not only their motivation, preferences and learning styles but also the level of technological skills. The last are especially important in designing such elements as navigation, registration and environmental functionalities. Design of information content should depend on the target user groups and is also of great significance. Information should be presented differently for learners with different characteristics and requirements. Brusilovsky (2001) distinguished two groups of methods: adaptive presentation and adaptive navigation support. The first group was subdivided into text adaptation and multimedia adaptation technologies, and aimed at adapting the content to student goals and other information stored in the student model; the pages are adaptively assembled for

each user (Brusilovsky & Peylo, 2003). Adaptive navigation support is subdivided into link hiding, sorting, annotation, direct guidance, and hypertext map adaptation (Brusilovsky, 2001).

Most developers have a very limited understanding of usability (Andreasen et al., 2006). This is especially easy to notice in the case of Open Source Software, which is very often used as educational environments. What is more, there is lack of both resources and evaluation methods fitting the OSS paradigm (Andreasen et al., 2006). As the most important design categories and the ones that should be evaluated by users, Marsico and Levialdi (2004) cited information representation and appearance; access, navigation, and orientation; and the informative content architecture of Web sites. The first element is connected with the design of homogeneous layout of the whole portal, which will positively influence students' attitudes. Pages together with information content should constitute compact compositions, with both graphics and text content well balanced, which means that users do not pay too much attention to the first component. Information should be complete, compact and presented clearly. The language of all the informative content and help as well as messages, comments and instructions should be understandable for users. There are three main kinds of graphical elements that may be used on Web pages: complementary (to information content), decorative or supporting navigation (links, for example). Portal designers should pay special attention to the layout, as that part is of crucial significance from the perspective of attracting new participants. All the visual elements of the software as well as navigation should support informative content together with required functionalities to fulfil learner needs.

Design of user-centred collaborative environments should consist of defining all the elements according to identification of user requirements. The process should start by recognition of student needs, but even among learners studying the same subject at the same university, it is impossible to define an average student, so multiple versions of the system must be created (Schneiderman, 1997). On the other hand, designing different interfaces for each user can be extremely costly (Gonzales-Rodriguez et al., 2009) and a solution that takes into consideration both aspects should be found.

Solutions and Recommendations

In the present study, we propose to divide students into groups with similar preferences and apply a user-based method to find their usability requirements, which may be taken into account in the process of the development of collaborative environments. Such a solution allows us to tailor the software into needs of group members and does not require too many versions of the system. There are two crucial steps in that approach: identification of groups with similar needs and determination of their profiles. In the first step, it should be decided what kind of criteria should be considered to identify groups of students; in the second one, the focus should be on group characteristics and identification of their needs. The last step may be realised by evaluation of the portal at the early stage of its existence.

In order to demonstrate different kinds of factors that should be taken into account during evaluation of collaborative environments and to show how student preferences differ among learners studying the same course, we now of-

fer two detailed case studies concerning real educational software. The research was done on groups of Polish Computer Science students on the basis of the collaboration established in the CAB (Collaboration Across Borders) Socrates Minerva funded project. During CAB activities, students reviewed their overseas peers' course tasks, by giving feedback from their assessment through their comments and providing advice or suggestions for improvements. They used CAB portal (http://moodle.cabweb.net), which is based on the Open Source educational platform (http://www.moodle.org). The special thing about CAB was the fact that the collaborations were conducted asynchronously and participants very often consisted of volunteers, whose participation was not supervised and depended on students' attitudes towards being active. The idea of the research appeared during observation of collaborative activities, when many complaints concerning usability of the portal interface were made. They were especially numerous at the early stage of the portal existence and students' lack of acceptance of the interface was reflected in their attitudes towards participating in online collaboration with their colleagues from abroad. In both cases students evaluated the interface of CAB portal (the main layout of which is presented in Figure 2), where collaboration activities took place, by answering the same set of questions. In usability evaluation, the focus was on finding portal elements that students find important from the perspective of collaborative activities. To obtain impartial opinions from users, in the first case, the CAB portal was evaluated by external students, who did not participate in any collaborative activity. They did not, however, have chance to discover all the details of portal functionalities, but such choice guaranteed that their opinions did not depend on the quality of assessment of their projects by colleagues from foreign universities. The second case study examined the relationship between dominant learning styles and usability preferences. The main goal of those investigations

Figure 2. Layout of CAB portal

was to check if discovering student groups with similar usability needs is connected with building groups according to learning style profiles.

Questions concerning usability were formulated, taking into account elements that may influence ease of use of CAB environment, that may be considered as external variables of the Technology Acceptance Model and that also belong to design categories mentioned by Marsico and Levialdi (2004). All the questions are presented in Table 1. They may be split into groups of thematic sets associated with such portal features as: general aspects of usability (questions 1 and 2), information content (questions 3-6), layout and graphics (question 7), navigation (question

8), functionalities connected with registration and tools supporting communication in a foreign language (questions 9 and 10).

Case 1. Usability Evaluation

During the tests, 69 Computer Science students, of the same professional skill and who did not take part in any collaboration, evaluated the portal. They answered ten questions (presented in Table 1) concerning usability of CAB collaborative environments. As the aim of the research was not only evaluation of portal usability and finding user requirements but also identification of factors that influence the decision of new

Table 1. Questions concerning usability of cab portal

No	Question
1	What do you think about usability of the portal?
2	What would you change in the portal organisation to make it more usable?
3	Is it easy to find the information on the portal?
4	What kind of information do you consider necessary on the portal?
5	What kind of information do you consider as useless?
6	What kind of information do you think is missing?
7	Do you like the interface? What would you change to make it more usable?
8	Do you like the navigation? What would you change to make it more convenient?
9	What do you think about the registration?
10	What kinds of tools are necessary to support communication in a foreign language?

Table 2. Usability evaluation by external students

Question	Yes	No	Not sure
Do you want to participate in CAB activities?	62.3%	30.4%	7.3%
Is it easy to find the information on the portal?	55.1%	36.2%	8.7%
Do you like the interface?	43.5%	50.7%	5.8%
Do you like the navigation?	30.4%	21.7%	47.8%

learners to join the community and participate in the collaboration, evaluators had to answer two additional questions:

1. Do you want to participate in CAB activities? Why?
2. What should the portal contain that would encourage you to join the community?

The questionnaire responses generated qualitative and quantitative data. The survey results were analysed according to the thematic groups of questions. Quantitative data showed that most of the students would like to join CAB activities, but half of the respondents did not like the portal interface and a considerable percentage of evaluators could not easily find the information that they were looking for. Students focused their evaluation on the interface, not on navigation (almost 50% were not sure whether they liked the navigation or not). All the quantitative data are presented in Table 2. Most students made critical remarks concerning CAB interface and

navigation, which were notified during qualitative data analysis.

Qualitative data were analysed according to thematic groups of questions. While responding, students mentioned two kinds of factors influencing their intention to participate: social (professional) and connected with usability. Table 3 contains both of them. Most students, however, found the idea of joining CAB very interesting, but they emphasised the role of technology in attracting participants and especially that there are many other similar portals on the Web that may catch the attention of students. As the main barriers to membership of CAB activities students specified: lack of time, their own poor English language skills, peers' projects that were not interesting enough to evaluate. They also mentioned the interface as not being user-friendly and the layout of the portal as not attractive enough, but those factors were not mentioned as the most important.

Table 4 contains elements whose presence may influence student decisions about joining the CAB community. Those factors concern these

Table 3. Student opinions concerning intention to participate in cab activities

Factor	Positive	Negative
Social, professional	Evaluation activity seems to be a very interesting experience because it broadens the knowledge and identifies mistakes Critical assessment is motivating. It enables to: get new information, exchange of knowledge, experiences and ideas, improve English language skills Increases personal development	Lack of time There are more attractive events on the Web Evaluation is not professional enough. Poor English language skills Lack of ability to evaluate others Tasks for evaluation are not interesting.
Usability	The idea is very good, but the portal should be more attractive	Interface is not user-friendly Portal layout is not attractive enough

Table 4. What should the portal contain that would encourage you to join the community?

Professional (Social)	Usability
Wide range of tasks for evaluation. Courses and advice Forum topics interesting for students Wide range of information Courses prepared by users Award system Right of each user to present his (her) own task for evaluation	Detailed description of projects to review Easy links to projects Translation tools Editors easy to use Links to references Information in Polish language Possibility of communication in other languages User-friendly interface Easy navigation Search possibilities Easy access to information

aspects: professional (social) and connected with usability. This time, however, while expressing their opinions of intention to participate in CAB community activities, learners paid more attention to ease of use of the technology (compare the right column of Table 4).

Even a quick glance at the list in the second column of Table 4 shows that all the elements mentioned by students which are connected with technology belong to design categories which according to Marsico and Levialdi (2004) are the most important and should be evaluated by users.

Table 5. Some students' remarks concerning cab portal

General	Good idea, interesting goal Possibility of exchanging opinions and meeting interesting people Good place for language skills improvement Interesting proposal for student internationalisation Intuitive functionality Bad first impression, next visit may be problematic Boring when using for a long time Lack of interactivity Not easy to find on Internet
Information content	Interesting discussions and information Small range of information Not easy to find required information Information content limited, too monothematic
Layout and graphics	Poor, uninteresting graphics Monotone, sad colours Archaic and ugly Clear, nice but not attractive Lack of clear menu Clear, changes are not required Easy to read Not being overloaded with graphics is an advantage
Navigation	Not fast Excellent
Functionalities	Registration rules irritating Registration intuitive Easy registration Problems with registration Translation only of titles irritating

Elements presented in the first column of Table 4 are connected with portal functional possibilities, but their presence sends a message to portal designers and facilitators that some additional functionalities may be required.

Table 5 presents more detailed student opinions concerning CAB portal usability elements. In many cases, they are contradictory. It means that, even in such a small group of 69 learners from the same course and of the same level of technological skills, it would be difficult to find average usability standards which may be accepted by all users.

Case 2. Usability and Learning Styles

The aim of the experiment was to examine how students' learning styles influence requirements for interface design. We use Felder learning style index (Felder, 1996; Felder & Silverman, 1988), the same that was used by Cha et al. (2006) in investigations concerning customisation of interface of educational systems. Students with different learning styles evaluated the interface of a CAB portal. Similarly to the survey presented in Case 1, they answered questions concerning graphics, navigation, information content, organisation of layout, supporting tool availability, etc. For that experiment, the 25 most active Computer Science students of the Technical University of Lodz, from among those participating in international collaboration, were chosen to evaluate the environment. The collaboration lasted five weeks and after it was finished, students answered questions (see Table 1), presenting in a descriptive way their opinions connected with usability of the software that they used during their collaborative activities.

As the goal of the research was to investigate how student learning styles influence the evaluation of interface design, at the same time the participants had to fill in an Index of Learning Styles (ILS) questionnaire (Felder & Soloman, 2009). The ILS is a self-scoring questionnaire (see Appendix A) for assessing preferences on

four dimensions of the Felder-Silverman model from eight mutually exclusive pairs: *active* vs. *reflective, sensing* vs. *intuitive, visual* vs. *verbal,* and *sequential* vs. *global.* Learners, as a result of filling in Felder's questionnaire, obtain scores for each of the dimensions. Students may score from one to eleven points for one of the dimensions from the pairs mentioned above. Results indicated students' dominant learning styles, which characterise them as:

- *Active*, who learn by trying things out, working with others or *reflective*, who learn by thinking things through, working alone,
- *Sensing*, who are concrete, practical, oriented toward facts and procedures or *intuitive*, who are conceptual, oriented toward theories and meanings,
- *Visual*, who prefer visual representations of presented material – pictures, diagrams, flow charts or *verbal*, who prefer written or spoken explanations,
- *Sequential*, who are linear, orderly, and learn in small incremental steps or *global*, who are holistic, system thinkers, and learn in large leaps.

Students filled in Felder's questionnaire and answered questions concerning layout, navigation and information content of the CAB portal. The final results of investigations were obtained by analysing both studies for students with at least one preferred learning style (which means they scored more than four for the dimension). In the examined group of students, there were: 8 active, 2 reflective, 11 sensing, 3 intuitive, 13 visual, 1 verbal, 4 sequential and 4 global. After detailed analysis of the survey results we came to the following conclusions:

- *Active* students want efficiency, sites should be loaded quickly, interface should be dynamic, information should be put into order, they need a more colourful interface and they emphasise the importance of re-liability. They find advanced search and move old projects to archive as necessary.

- *Reflective* students like the CAB portal, they emphasise that navigation is intuitive, and find the interface user-friendly as it is not overloaded with graphics.
- *Sensing* students emphasise the neces-sity of menu and that there are too many empty places on the portal, they mentioned the importance of putting more informa-tion content like course plans, they think that the portal should contain more usable information.
- *Intuitive* students find navigation intuitive, they like the CAB interface, but they say it would be good to give more links.
- *Visual* students need more graphics and more colours, they do not find the portal very attractive, but monotone and sad, they would like to have more efficient naviga-tion and a more user-friendly interface, and they mention that advanced and effi-cient search should be improved. Students who are *visual* and *intuitive* at the same time, however, as well as those who are *visual* and *reflective*, like the interface as it is now.
- *Verbal* students are also *reflective* and like the design of the portal.
- *Sequential* students like the graphics but find the interface monotone and com-plain of too much redundant information but on the other hand they want more in-formation concerning the portal and its participants.
- *Global* students have contradictory opin-ions concerning the portal.

Summing up all these results, we concluded that *active sensing visual* students do not like the CAB portal's layout as it is. *Reflective, intuitive, verbal* students find it quite satisfactory.

The research showed the different expectations of students concerning interface design, depend-ing on their dominant learning styles and similar requirements within groups of users with similar learning style preferences. *Active* students should have dynamic content, full of colourful graph-ics, and this last feature is also very important for students whose preferred learning style is *visual*. In both cases, the interface layout cannot be monotone, but the designer should remember, while enhancing the Web sites with graphics not to lose speed and reliability at the same time.

Both considered case studies demonstrate the necessity of taking into account the needs and preferences of different groups of students sepa-rately in the process of developing collaborative environments. The results of the experiments show that evaluation of the software seems to be a good source of information concerning students' opin-ions, and may help in developing the educational system according to learners' requirements. Before designers start to build evaluation tools, however, two actions may be necessary:

- Identification of student groups with dif-ferent needs,
- Identification of factors that characterise each group.

Effects of experiments, described in Case 1, demonstrated that even students attending the same course and with the same technological skills may express contradictory preferences. Before starting the evaluation process, designers should first identify the student features that influence their needs. The example presented in Case 2 indicates the possible solution: using dominant learning styles as criteria for dividing students into groups.

In the next step, designers should build different evaluation tools depending on the target group. In Case 1, responses to the first two questions of the survey showed that students take into account not only usability, but also professional or social aspects of activities on the portal. The last two factors are even more important in the case of participation in collaborative activities (which are rather short-term), while the first one seems to be crucial when joining a portal community. It may mean that usability issues are more important if sustainability of the community is considered. Quantitative data obtained in the experiments of Case 1 showed that some students pay more attention to the interface than to navigation. It suggests that formulation of evaluation tools for each group should be preceded by a general survey, which would aid the choice of detailed aspects of evaluation. Indications concerning building evaluation questionnaires may also be based on dominant learning styles, as they also may determine usability preferences, as shown during investigation of the results from Case 2.

FUTURE TRENDS

Identification of user requirements in collaborative environments, by using evaluation methods is still a matter of interest to researchers and designers. In the near future further improvement of these techniques may be expected, such as personalised, interactive and real-time tools. There will also be further development of methods of analysis of historical learner behaviours, using log files and computational intelligence techniques, in the distance learning area.

The future will, however, belong to technology. When creating environments, educational instructors and designers will include usage of new equipment that enables registration of user preferences, such as tracking eye or gesture-based movements to follow emotional response or capturing touch on multi-touch screens. Student models, similarly to those for business clients, will be created according to the behaviours registered by electronic devices.

One very important research challenge is connected with ubiquitous learning. Students pos-

sessing such devices as personal digital assistants or mobile phones may learn anywhere and any time. In that case their models will depend on the context of use. Ubiquitous systems should be tailored not only to student personal profile but also according to environmental context, such as time zone, location or temperature. Learner requirements should be determined on the basis of the connection of two models: global and context-aware. Investigations in that area will be undertaken together with the development of ubiquitous learning systems by both educational researchers and software designers.

CONCLUSION

This paper considered the identification of student usability requirements in collaborative learning environments. Emphasis was placed on the role of user evaluations as very important tools for achieving usable educational systems acceptable to learners. Investigations were performed on the basis of two case studies. Experiments proved that student needs may differ even for learners attending the same course who have similar technical skills. Examining the relations between learning styles and usability preferences showed that students of the same dominant learning styles may have similar usability requirements.

The case studies demonstrated the necessity of differentiating environments for different groups of students, which may also be connected with building different evaluation tools. Designers, before starting any evaluation process, should identify student groups with different characteristics. This may be done by distinguishing student clusters with similar features such as dominant learning styles, for example. The next step should consist of determination of factors that characterise each group and of building appropriate evaluation tools. Some introductory questions, preceding the evaluation process, as well as group characteristics recognition, may help to indicate crucial issues connected with portal usability and in preparation of the whole survey.

REFERENCES

Alfonseca, E., Carro, R. M., Martin, E., Ortigosa, A., & Paredes, P. (2006). The impact of learning styles on student grouping for collaborative learning: a case study. *User Modeling and User-Adapted Interaction*, *16*(2-3), 377–401. doi:10.1007/s11257-006-9012-7

Andreasen, M. S., Nielsen, H. V., Schrøder, S. O., & Stage, J. (2006). Usability in Open Source Software development: opinions and practice. *Information Technology and Control*, *35*(3A), 303–312.

Ardito, C., Costabile, M., De Marsico, M., Lanzilotti, R., Levialdi, S., Roselli, T., & Rossano, V. (2006). An approach to usability evaluation of e-learning applications. *Universal Access in the Information Society*, *4*(3), 270–283. doi:10.1007/s10209-005-0008-6

Beaudoin, M. F. (2002). Learning or lurking? Tracking the "invisible" online student. *The Internet and Higher Education*, *5*(2), 147–155. doi:10.1016/S1096-7516(02)00086-6

Bell, F., Zaitseva, E., & Zakrzewska, D. (2007). Evaluation: A link in the chain of sustainability. In N. Lambropoulos & P. Zaphiris (Eds.), *User-centered design of online learning communities* (pp. 186-214). Hershey, PA: Information Science Publishing.

Brusilovsky, P. (2001). Adaptive hypermedia. *User Modeling and User-Adapted Interaction*, *11*(1-2), 87–110. doi:10.1023/A:1011143116306

Brusilovsky, P., & Peylo, C. (2003). Adaptive and intelligent web-based educational systems. *International Journal of Artificial Intelligence in Education*, *13*, 156–169.

Cha, H. J., Kim, Y. S., Park, S. H., Yoon, T. B., Jung, Y. M., & Lee, J.-H. (2006). Learning styles diagnosis based on user interface behaviors for customization of learning interfaces in an intelligent tutoring system. In M. Ikeda, K. Ashley, & T.-W. Chan (Eds.), *Proceedings of the Intelligent Tutoring Systems, 8th International Conference* (LNCS 4053, pp. 513-524). Berlin, Germany: Springer-Verlag.

Comeaux, P., & McKenna-Byington, E. (2003). Computer-mediated communication in online and conventional classroom: some implications for instructional design and professional development programmes. *Innovations in Education and Teaching International*, *40*(4), 348–355. doi:10.1080/1470329032000128387

De Marsico, M., & Levialdi, S. (2004). Evaluating web sites: exploiting user's expectations. *International Journal of Human-Computer Studies*, *60*(3), 381–416. doi:10.1016/j.ijhcs.2003.10.008

Dringus, L. (1995). An iterative usability evaluation procedure for interactive online courses. *Journal of Interactive Instruction Development*, *7*(4), 10–14.

Felder, R. M. (1996). Matters of style. *ASEE PRISM*, *6*(4), 18–23.

Felder, R. M., & Silverman, L. K. (1988). Learning and teaching styles in engineering education. *English Education*, *78*(7), 674–681.

Felder, R. M., & Soloman, B. A. (2009). *Index of Learning Styles*. Retrieved March 20, 2009, from http://www.ncsu.edu/felder-public/ILSpage.html

Francescato, D., Mebane, M., Porcelli, R., Attanasio, C., & Pulino, M. (2007). Developing professional skills and social capital through computer supported collaborative learning in university contexts. *International Journal of Human-Computer Studies*, *65*(2), 140–152. doi:10.1016/j.ijhcs.2006.09.002

Gonzalez-Rodriguez, M., Manrubia, J., Vidau, A., & Gonzalez-Gallego, M. (2009). Improving accessibility with user-tailored interfaces. *Applied Intelligence*, *30*(1), 65–71. doi:10.1007/s10489-007-0098-3

Graf, S. & Kinshuk. (2006). Considering learning styles in learning management systems: investigating the behavior of students in an online course. In P. Mylones, M. Wallace, & M. Angelides (Eds.), *Proceedings of the First IEEE International Workshop on Semantic Media Adaptation and Personalization, SMAP 06* (pp. 25-30). Los Alamitos, CA: IEEE Computer Society.

Gros, B. (2001). Instructional design for computer-supported collaborative learning in primary and secondary schools. *Computers in Human Behavior*, *17*(4-5), 439–451. doi:10.1016/S0747-5632(01)00016-4

International Organisation for Standardisation. (1998). *ISO 9241: Software ergonomics requirements for office work with visual display terminal (VDT)*. Geneva, Switzerland.

Karger, D. R., & Quan, D. (2004, January). *Prerequisites for a personalizable user interfa*ce. Paper presented at the Workshop on Bahavior- Based User Interface Customization at the Intelligent User Interface 2004 Conference, Island of Madeira, Portugal.

Kukulska-Hulme, A., & Shield, L. (2004). Usability and pedagogical design: are language learning websites special? In *Proceedings of the World Conference on Educational Multimedia, Hypermedia and Telecommunications 2004* (pp. 4235-4242). AACE Digital Library.

Lederer, A. L., Maupin, D. J., Sena, M. P., & Zhuang, Y. (2000). The technology acceptance model and the World Wide Web. *Decision Support Systems*, *29*(3), 269–282. doi:10.1016/S0167-9236(00)00076-2

Lee, M. (2001). Profiling students adaptation styles in web-based learning. *Computers & Education*, *36*(2), 121–132. doi:10.1016/S0360-1315(00)00046-4

Liaw, Sh.-Sh., Chen, G.-D., & Huang, H.-M. (2008). Users' attitudes toward Web-based collaborative learning systems for knowledge management. *Computers & Education*, *50*(3), 950–961. doi:10.1016/j.compedu.2006.09.007

Liegle, J. O., & Janicki, T. N. (2006). The effect of learning styles on the navigation needs of Web-based learners. *Computers in Human Behavior*, *22*(5), 885–898. doi:10.1016/j.chb.2004.03.024

Lu, J., Yu, C. S., & Liu, C. (2003). Learning style, learning patterns, and learning performance in a WebCT-based MIS course. *Information & Management*, *40*(6), 497–507. doi:10.1016/S0378-7206(02)00064-2

Lundin, J., & Magnusson, M. (2003). Collaborative learning in mobile work. *Journal of Computer Assisted Learning*, *19*(3), 273–283. doi:10.1046/j.0266-4909.2003.00029.x

Ng, E., & Ma, A. (2002). An innovative model to foster Web-based collaborative learning. In *IS2002 Proceedings of the Informing Science+IT Education Conference* (pp. 1165-1171). Informing Science Institute.

Nielsen, J. (1993). *Usability engineering*. Boston, MA: Academic Press.

Nielsen, J. (1994). Heuristic evaluation. In J. Nielsen & R.L. Mack (Eds,), *Usability Inspection Methods* (pp. 25-64). New York: John Wiley.

Nogier, J.-F. (2007). *What is usability?* Retrieved July 27, 2007, from www.usabilis.com/gb/whatis/usability.htm

Parlangeli, O., Marchigianni, E., & Bagnara, S. (1999). Multimedia system in distance education: effects on usability. *Interacting with Computers*, *12*(1), 37–49. doi:10.1016/S0953-5438(98)00054-X

Philips, D. C. (1995). The good, the bad, the ugly: The many faces of constructivism. *Educational Researcher*, *24*(7), 5–12.

Preece, J. (2000). *Online communities: Designing usability, supporting sociability.* New York: John Wiley & Sons.

Preece, J., Rogers, Y., & Sharp, H. (2002). *Interaction design: Beyond human-computer interaction.* New York: John Wiley & Sons.

Quinn, C., Alem, L., & Eklund, J. (1999). A pragmatic evaluation methodology for an assessment of learning effectiveness in instructional systems. In S. Brewster, A. Cawsey, & G. Cockton (Eds.), *Human-Computer Interaction INTERACT99 vol. II* (pp. 55-56). UK: British Computer Society.

Rovai, A. P. (2003). The relationships of communicator style, personality-based learning style, and classroom community among online graduate students. *The Internet and Higher Education*, *6*(4), 347–363. doi:10.1016/j.iheduc.2003.07.004

Schrage, M. (1990). *Shared minds.* New York: Random House.

Selim, H. M. (2003). An empirical investigation of student acceptance of course websites. *Computers & Education*, *40*(4), 343–360. doi:10.1016/S0360-1315(02)00142-2

Shneiderman, B. (1997). *Designing the user interface.* Reading MA: Addison-Wesley.

Soloway, E., Jackson, S. L., Klein, C., Quintana, C., Reed, J., & Spitulnik, J. (1996). Learning theory in practice: case studies in learner-centred design. In [New York: ACM Press.]. *Proceedings of Computer Human Interaction CHI*, *96*, 189–196.

Soong, M. H., Chan, H. Ch., Chua, B. Ch., & Loh, K. F. (2001). Critical success factors for on-line course resources. *Computers & Education*, *36*(2), 101–120. doi:10.1016/S0360-1315(00)00044-0

Squires, D., & Preece, J. (1996). Usability and learning: Evaluating the potential of educational software. *Computers & Education*, *27*(1), 15–22. doi:10.1016/0360-1315(96)00010-3

Squires, D., & Preece, J. (1999). Predicting quality in educational software: evaluating for learning, usability, and the synergy between them. *Interacting with Computers*, *11*(5), 463–466. doi:10.1016/S0953-5438(98)00062-9

Stash, N., Cristea, A., & De Bra, P. (2004). Authoring of learning styles in adaptive hypermedia: Problems and solutions. In *Proceedings of the Thirteenth International World Wide Web Conference* (pp 114-123). New York: ACM Press.

Teo, H.-H., Chan, H.-C., Wei, K.-K., & Zhang, Z. (2003). Evaluating information accessibility and community adaptivity features for sustaining virtual learning communities. *International Journal of Human-Computer Studies*, *59*(5), 671–697. doi:10.1016/S1071-5819(03)00087-9

Wang, W., Tzeng, Y., & Chen, Y. (2000). A comparative study of applying Internet on cooperative traditional learning. In *Proceedings of The 8th International Conference on Computers in Education/ International Conference on Computer-Assisted Instruction 2000* (pp. 207-214). AACE-APC/ National Tsing Hua University, Taiwan.

Wiedenbeck, S., & Davis, S. (1997). The influence of interaction style and experience on user perceptions of software packages. *International Journal of Human-Computer Studies*, *46*(5), 563–588. doi:10.1006/ijhc.1996.0106

APPENDIX

Index of Learning Styles Questionnaire NC State University

For each of the 44 questions below select either "a" or "b" to indicate your answer. Please choose only one answer for each question. If both "a" and "b" seem to apply to you, choose the one that applies more frequently.

1. I understand something better after I
    (a) try it out.
    (b) think it through.
2. I would rather be considered
    (a) realistic.
    (b) innovative.
3. When I think about what I did yesterday, I am most likely to get
    (a) a picture.
    (b) words.
4. I tend to
    (a) understand details of a subject but may be fuzzy about its overall structure.
    (b) understand the overall structure but may be fuzzy about details.
5. When I am learning something new, it helps me to
    (a) talk about it.
    (b) think about it.
6. If I were a teacher, I would rather teach a course
    (a) that deals with facts and real life situations.
    (b) that deals with ideas and theories.
7. I prefer to get new information in
    (a) pictures, diagrams, graphs, or maps.
    (b) written directions or verbal information.
8. Once I understand
    (a) all the parts, I understand the whole thing.
    (b) the whole thing, I see how the parts fit.
9. In a study group working on difficult material, I am more likely to
    (a) jump in and contribute ideas.
    (b) sit back and listen.
10. I find it easier
    (a) to learn facts.
    (b) to learn concepts.
11. In a book with lots of pictures and charts, I am likely to
    (a) look over the pictures and charts carefully.
    (b) focus on the written text.
12. When I solve math problems
    (a) I usually work my way to the solutions one step at a time.
    (b) I often just see the solutions but then have to struggle to figure out the steps to get to them.

13. In classes I have taken
    (a) I have usually gotten to know many of the students.
    (b) I have rarely gotten to know many of the students.
14. In reading nonfiction, I prefer
    (a) something that teaches me new facts or tells me how to do something.
    (b) something that gives me new ideas to think about.
15. I like teachers
    (a) who put a lot of diagrams on the board.
    (b) who spend a lot of time explaining.
16. When I'm analyzing a story or a novel
    (a) I think of the incidents and try to put them together to figure out the themes.
    (b) I just know what the themes are when I finish reading and then I have to go back and find the incidents that demonstrate them.
17. When I start a homework problem, I am more likely to
    (a) start working on the solution immediately.
    (b) try to fully understand the problem first.
18. I prefer the idea of
    (a) certainty.
    (b) theory.
19. I remember best
    (a) what I see.
    (b) what I hear.
20. It is more important to me that an instructor
    (a) lay out the material in clear sequential steps.
    (b) give me an overall picture and relate the material to other subjects.
21. I prefer to study
    (a) in a study group.
    (b) alone.
22. I am more likely to be considered
    (a) careful about the details of my work.
    (b) creative about how to do my work.
23. When I get directions to a new place, I prefer
    (a) a map.
    (b) written instructions.
24. I learn
    (a) at a fairly regular pace. If I study hard, I'll "get it."
    (b) in fits and starts. I'll be totally confused and then suddenly it all "clicks."
25. I would rather first
    (a) try things out.
    (b) think about how I'm going to do it.
26. When I am reading for enjoyment, I like writers to
    (a) clearly say what they mean.
    (b) say things in creative, interesting ways.

27. When I see a diagram or sketch in class, I am most likely to remember
    (a) the picture.
    (b) what the instructor said about it.
28. When considering a body of information, I am more likely to
    (a) focus on details and miss the big picture.
    (b) try to understand the big picture before getting into the details.
29. I more easily remember
    (a) something I have done.
    (b) something I have thought a lot about.
30. When I have to perform a task, I prefer to
    (a) master one way of doing it.
    (b) come up with new ways of doing it.
31. When someone is showing me data, I prefer
    (a) charts or graphs.
    (b) text summarizing the results.
32. When writing a paper, I am more likely to
    (a) work on (think about or write) the beginning of the paper and progress forward.
    (b) work on (think about or write) different parts of the paper and then order them.
33. When I have to work on a group project, I first want to
    (a) have "group brainstorming" where everyone contributes ideas.
    (b) brainstorm individually and then come together as a group to compare ideas.
34. I consider it higher praise to call someone
    (a) sensible.
    (b) imaginative.
35. When I meet people at a party, I am more likely to remember
    (a) what they looked like.
    (b) what they said about themselves.
36. When I am learning a new subject, I prefer to
    (a) stay focused on that subject, learning as much about it as I can.
    (b) try to make connections between that subject and related subjects.
37. I am more likely to be considered
    (a) outgoing.
    (b) reserved.
38. I prefer courses that emphasize
    (a) concrete material (facts, data).
    (b) abstract material (concepts, theories).
39. For entertainment, I would rather
    (a) watch television.
    (b) read a book.
40. Some teachers start their lectures with an outline of what they will cover. Such outlines are
    (a) somewhat helpful to me.
    (b) very helpful to me.
41. The idea of doing homework in groups, with one grade for the entire group,
    (a) appeals to me.
    (b) does not appeal to me.

42. When I am doing long calculations,
    (a)   I tend to repeat all my steps and check my work carefully.
    (b)   I find checking my work tiresome and have to force myself to do it.
43. I tend to picture places I have been
    (a)   easily and fairly accurately.
    (b)   with difficulty and without much detail.
44. When solving problems in a group, I would be more likely to
    (a)   think of the steps in the solution process.
    (b)   think of possible consequences or applications of the solution in a wide range of areas.

Chapter 13
Instructional Strategy Approaches with Technology

Pamela Lowry
Lawrence Technological University, USA

ABSTRACT

Educators need to understand the concepts and strategies pertaining to instructional design. They need to be aware of different models and theories pertaining to learning. Additionally, interactivity and group learning is a very effective approach when designing instruction. It is equally important to incorporate different learning styles of the learner such as auditory, visual, and tactile learners when designing instruction. Technologies such as asynchronous and synchronous delivery still need to incorporate these instructional strategies. These technologies can be utilized in traditional, hybrid, and online delivery modalities. As these technologies are introduced, instructional strategies are discussed concerning interactive instructional assignments.

INTRODUCTION

Concepts such as instructional design, learning theories, instructional strategies, and learning styles are discussed. Different technologies and delivery of instruction illustrate how these concepts can be integrated into learning. To illustrate this, instructional examples are discussed.

CHAPTER OBJECTIVES

At the conclusion of this chapter you should be able to do the following:

- Identify education
- Identify and describe instructional design strategies
- Identify learning theories
- Analyze learning styles
- Compare and contrast different technologies and delivery modalities

DOI: 10.4018/978-1-61520-672-8.ch013

- Discuss future and emerging trends relating to instructional design and technologies

EDUCATION

Education describes all experiences in which people learn. Many of these experiences are unplanned, incidental, and informal (Smith & Ragan, 2005). It is a long-term process of developing individuals. It is derived from the concept life-long learning (Valda, 1998).

The aim of education strives to prepare learners to be analytical thinkers and problem solvers. (Sapieha, 2007). It concerns remembering facts and understanding concepts along with helping the learner to build problem solving skills (Kurtus, 1999). The learners want to expand their knowledge to fulfill an individually identified need. Such learning is active learning (Carney, 2003).

Education is about learning for oneself (Conklin, 2006). It is all about developing a learner's potential, helping them to discover the abilities that they have and giving them the tools to use them.

INSTRUCTIONAL DESIGN

What is instructional design? It refers to the systematic process of translating principles of learning and instruction into plans for instructional materials and activities. It seems that few faculty members have had formal education in instructional design or learning theory. When designing instruction, it is important to think about content, learning activities, and the desired learning outcomes. It requires deliberate instructional design that hinges on linking learning objectives to specific learning activities and measurable outcomes (Oblinger & Lawkins, 2006). Interactivity and group work is a very effective approach when designing instruction. In designing and developing a course it is important to make the content material relevant

(Harvey & Mogey, 1996). By making the course material relevant to the students they are more motivated to learn the material.

Faculty are being challenged to move beyond the notion of a course as covering content to the idea of a course as constructing a series of learning environments and activities (Oblinger & Hawkins, 2006). Faculty are beginning to realize that online instruction is more than a series of readings posted to a course management system such as Blackboard or a website. It requires deliberate instructional design that hinges on linking learning objectives to specific learning activities and measurable outcomes. (Oblinger & Hawkins, 2006).

Models

Different models can be incorporated into the instructional design process. Many of these models are variations of the ADDIE model. ADDIE is short for analyze, design, develop, implement, and evaluate. An instructional designer may utilize an instructional systems design model such as the ADDIE model.

In the analyze phase, the designer develops an understanding of the instructional problem, the goals and objectives are established, and the learning environment and learner characteristics are identified. The design phase is where the instructional strategies are designed and media choices are made. In the develop phase, materials are produced according to decisions made during the design phase. The implement phase includes the testing of prototypes (with targeted audience), putting the product in full production, and training learners and faculty members on how to use the product. The evaluation phase consists of two parts: formative and summative. Formative evaluation is present in each stage. It evaluates the materials to determine the weaknesses in the instruction so revisions can be made to make them more effective. Summative evaluation occurs after the instruction has occurred. It consists of tests for criterion-related referenced items, and provides opportunities for feedback from users.

Two possible models are John Keller's ARCS Model of Motivational Design and the Kemp, Morrison, and Ross Model. John Keller's ARCS Model of Motivational Design involves four steps for promoting and sustaining motivation in the learning process. These steps are Attention, Relevance, Confidence, and Satisfaction. The Kemp, Morrison, and Ross Model involve nine basic steps in the systematic design process (Keller, 2006).

These nine steps are:

- Identify instructional problems, and specify goals for designing an instructional program.
- Examine learner characteristics that should receive attention during planning.
- Identify subject content, and analyze task components related to stated goals and purposes.
- State instructional objectives for the learner.
- Sequence content within each instructional unit for logical learning.
- Design instructional strategies so that each learner can master the objectives.
- Plan the instructional message and delivery.
- Develop evaluation instruments to assess objectives.
- Select resources to support instruction and learning activities

Another model that can apply to education or business utilizing technology is the Human Performance Technology (HPT) model. It can occur at different levels. It stresses a rigorous analysis of present and desired levels of performance, identifies the causes for the performance gap, offers a wide range of interventions with which to improve performance, guides the change management process, and evaluates the results.

The HPT approach includes a variety of instructional and non-instructional interventions to address a performance problem or realize an opportunity. Instructional technology is one of many interventions to improve performance (Klein & Fox, 2004).

Performance Improvement refers to a method for analyzing the way people do their jobs. Are these performance gaps, which is a difference between the present and the desired levels of performance? If performance gaps exit, then explore strategies to improve their performance. Some possible strategies could be workshops, mentoring, courses, professional development conferences, professional development opportunities.

Pedagogical Theories

Instructional design should also incorporate Chickering and Gamson's Seven Principles for Good Practice in Undergraduate Education which leads toward high-quality teaching. The seven principles apply to the hybrid and online instructional environment as well as to a traditional instructional environment. They are clearly applicable to distance learning formats in that they provide instructional strategies focused on the learner, rather than on the medium used to teach the learner (Hutchins, 2003). The seven principles for good practice include (Waterhouse, 2005):

- Encouraging contact between students and faculty
- Developing reciprocity and cooperation among students
- Using active learning techniques
- Giving students prompt feedback
- Emphasizing time on task
- Communicating high expectations
- Respecting diverse talents and ways of learning

Other possible theories are Bloom's Taxonomy of Intellectual Behaviors and Gagne's Nine Events of Instruction. Bloom's Taxonomy students begin working on knowledge behavior and advance to evaluation behavior. Like Chickering and Gamson's Seven Principles, Gagne's Nine Events of Instruction can be used to promote the effective design of elearning resources (Waterhouse, 2005). The nine events are:

- gain attention
- inform students of the objectives
- use recall
- present the material
- provide learning guidance
- elicit performance
- provide feedback
- assess performance
- enhance retention and transfer

Although they have differences, there are several common principles that can be found in all of the above modes or theories on excellence in instructional design. Some include:

- instructional strategies
- interactivity
- prompt feedback
- motivation

LEARNING THEORIES

Instructional designers are very interested in learning theories. These theories attempt to describe, explain, and predict learning. Learning has been defined as "the relatively permanent change in a person's knowledge or behavior due to experience" (Smith & Ragan, 1993). According to Gagne, learning is a change in human capability that persists over a period of time. According to Mayer, learning is the relatively permanent change in a person's knowledge or behavior due to experience. A person could acquire a new skill to enhance their performance. This chapter will address a few of these concepts.

According to this concept map, three particular views of learning include behaviorism, cognitive learning theory, and constructivism (Smith & Ragan, 2005).

Behaviorism

Learning results from behavioral responses to external stimuli. It is really an acquisition of a new behavior. It emphasizes the influence of the environment on learning. Learning occurs when learners evidence the appropriate response to a particular stimulus (Smith & Ragan, 2005). The learner responds to stimuli, reacts to conditional rewards, follows pattern and demonstrates desired behavior. It is the role of the faculty member to determine the desired behavior and to arrange the external environmental conditions that shape a learner's behavior.

Cognitivism

Learning focuses on explaining the development of cognitive structures, processes, and representations that act as a go-between instruction and learning (Smith & Wagner, 2005).

The learner uses old knowledge to create new knowledge. The learner grows in knowledge by modeling expert behavior and by thinking through and figuring things out. Cognitive theorist's view learning as involving the acquisition or reorganization of the cognitive structures through which humans process and store information (Good & Brophy, 1990). It is the role of the faculty member to present new information in a way that helps the learner to encode and retrieve information. Organizing information can help the learner link it to existing information.

Constructivism

Learning is facilitated through construction of mental models. By reflecting on our experiences,

Table 1.

Left-brained learners	Right-brained learners
Adjusts to the environment	Tries to change the environment
Wants to know the rules and stick to it	Often doesn't realize when they do something wrong
Can easily express themselves in words	Often struggles with expressing themselves
Prefers to do one task at a time	More likely able to multitask
Less creative than right-brained learners	More creative than left-brained learners

we construct our own understanding of the world. Learning is simply the process of adjusting our own mental models to accommodate new experiences. (Smith & Ragan, 2005). Constructivism is a paradigm that learning is an active, constructive process. People actively construct or creating their own understanding of the world. It is the role of the faculty member to provide complex questions and to create a collaborative, problem-solving environment to make discoveries.

Brain-Based Learning

Each brain is different so educators should allow learners to customize their own environment. Brain-based learning theory is based on the structure and function of the brain. As long as the brain is not prohibited from fulfilling its normal processes, learning will occur.

The two different sides or hemispheres of the brain are responsible for different manners of thinking. Each of us prefers one mode over the other. The left side of the brain is logical, sequential, rational, analytical, objective, and looks for parts. The right side of the brain is random, intuitive, holistic, synthesizing, subjective, and looks at the whole (Funderstanding, 2001).

According to Hopper 2008, Table 1 summarizes differences between left-brained learners and right-brained learners.

When teaching left and right brained learners be consistent, display rules and expectations, provide a lot of feedback, and give a variety of different assignments to exercise both sides of the brain.

Brain-based research states that learning is best achieved when linked with the learner's previous knowledge, experience, or understanding of a given subject or concept (Thompkins, 2007).

INSTRUCTIONAL STRATEGIES

Interactivity

As assignments are being developed, an important element in instructional design is interactivity. Interactivity involves interacting with fellow students, with the instructor, and the course content. When creating interactive assignments or activities it is a good idea to involve a mixture of individual and group assignments or activities which involve different interactive levels. This allows the students to share ideas or collaborate on an outcome.

Interactivity also increases students' interest; it improves cognitive processes, and it develops group learning skills (Morgan & Kinross, 2002). In designing assignments it is important for students to be a part of a community of students so they do not feel alone. Instructional interactivity actively stimulates the learner's mind to do things that improves ability and readiness to perform effectively (Allen, 2003). It builds an experience that facilitates both deeper understanding and easier recall. It also helps learners retain information, and increase their willingness to spend time with the material. It helps them to stay focused and engaged. This is the process that results in changes in the

Figure 1. Interactivity

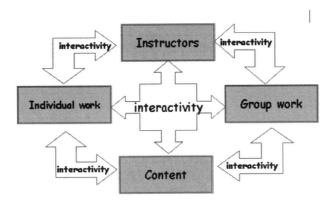

learner's understanding, the learner's perspective, or the cognitive structures of the learner's mind (Kapp, 2006).

Interactivity increases, or elevates learning. Learners learn faster and develop more positive attitudes when learning is interactive. It allows the learner to interact, ponder and consider what they are learning (Kapp, 2006).

The following figure illustrates how interaction is important at each level. Figure 1 was developed by a group of students from Taiwan in the summer of 2008 who were working on their Master of Educational Technology degree from Lawrence Technological University.

Since interactivity is so important, how do you improve it? One can assign a variety of individual and group assignments (Butler, 2003). Some examples could include:

- Essays, reports or short answers tests
- Discussions, debates, collaborative tasks, case studies or role plays
- Multiple choice quizzes, games, self-assessed quizzes, interactive exercises

Group Work or Cooperative Learning

Group learning, also known as cooperative learning, increases opportunities for communications within a group. It can drive collaboration and

group problem solving. Learners are working together to accomplish shared goals. It seems to maximize individual learning and each others' learning within the group.

Group work lends itself to more student participation and involvement. Students working in small groups tend to learn more of what is taught. Students who work in collaborative groups also appear more satisfied with their classes and it makes the assignment relevant to the learners (Davis, 1993).

Cooperative learning is the instructional use of small groups so that students work together to maximize their own and each other's learning. Cooperative learning seems to increase students' achievement, create positive relationships among students, and promote students' healthy psychological adjustment to school (Johnson, D.W., Johnson, R., & Smith, K., 1998). Utilizing cooperative learning seems to provide a structured environment for sharing some of the responsibility for learning.

Cooperative learning promotes the idea that students work to learn and are responsible for one another's learning as well as their own (Slavin, 1991). It can enhance communication and collaborative skills. Students may need help on how to be an effective group member.

Students learn best when they are actively involved in the process. Researchers say that students working in small groups tend to learn more of what is taught and retain it longer than when the same content is presented in other instructional formats (Davis, 1993).

LEARNING STYLES

As a course with interactive assignments is being designed and developed, it is important to keep in mind teaching styles and student's learning styles since not all students learn in exactly the same way. The findings from research on learning styles and how students receive and process information should be included when faculty members design courses. While designing a course, it is important to keep in mind auditory, tactile, and visual learners. The majority of learners appear to be visual learners, followed by auditory learners, then tactile/kinesthetic learners (Waterhouse, 2005). Students will gain more knowledge, retain more information, and perform better when teaching styles match learning styles (Lage, Platt, & Treglia, 2000).

As faculty members design their courses, they cannot develop different ways of teaching for each individual student. Therefore, they should strive to provide a variety of learning experiences such that each learning style is addressed. The use of a variety of styles of activity and interaction can help maintain interest and can also allow a course to cater to different learning styles and especially in an online course (Butler, 2003).

Auditory Learners

An auditory learner is an independent learner. Some important activities for these learners include completing some independent work. Some teaching strategies include lecturing, discussion, verbal questioning and verbal sharing. Because auditory learners like lectures, creating auditory or video recordings of lecture information and posting it to the course website can be effective (Waterhouse, 2005).

Visual Learners

Visual learners tend to be dependent learners that are generally group oriented. Teaching strategies that appeal to visual learners include group learning, demonstrations, and activities that emphasize creativity. Visual aids such as images, diagrams, drawings, charts, and pictures can help them form a visual image.

Tactile/Kinesthetic Learners

Tactile learners tend to learn by doing. They need to be actively engaged in something like open-ended questions. Teaching strategies that appeal to these learners include experiential learning activities and simulations. Tactile/kinesthetic learners have a tendency to be very creative and they like to have learning resources readily at hand (Waterhouse, 2005).

Recommendations to find ways to appeal to the learning preferences of different generations involves maintaining personal contact, getting students active in learning, providing examples that different generations can relate to as a point of reference, being supportive of learning, and encouraging questions of all types, not just content-oriented questions. Maintaining personal contact with students either through email or during synchronous sessions is very important for students. They need to be active in their learning. Faculty members need to be supportive of their learning styles during the course or training through praise, commentary, and constructive criticism. Faculty members should try to make the learners feel comfortable.

TECHNOLOGIES AND DELIVERY OF INSTRUCTION

Technologies can bridge the instructional gap that students face. It is important for faculty members to embrace technology in teaching and some faculty members found that technology has helped them better connect with their students (Carlson, 2004). The concern is not whether technology is used; rather, how does a faculty member ensure quality and achieve learning goals when teaching via a different medium (Hutchins, 2003).

Educators need to be mindful which technologies will be effective and which will not when designing courses. Incorporating new technologies, recognizing differences in learners, and making revisions to curriculum can enhance the learning process. New trend setting technologies are leading to significant changes in teacher-student relationships as well as relationships between students themselves.

If technology is utilized in a course, it is important for the instructor to build confidence in the learner's use of technology. If interactive assignments or activities are used for a course it usually involves an asynchronous environment but these assignments could be utilized in a synchronous environment too. Delivery could be in a traditional, hybrid, or online course environment.

An asynchronous learning environment is one in which students and faculty members are engaged in "anytime-anyplace" learning. Student do not have to be in the same room with other students or their instructor, nor do they all have to be engaged in a learning activity at the same time (Waterhouse, 2005).

A synchronous learning environment is one in which students and faculty members engage each other at the same time, but not necessarily at the same location. Traditional classroom-based learning is a common form of synchronous learning (Waterhouse, 2005).

In a traditional classroom setting, faculty members can use their understanding of their students through observation of body language, verbal response, and eye contact to create an effective learning experience (Bower, 2001). Teaching utilizing synchronous technology, it is more difficult for this to happen. Faculty need to understand student's verbal response and respond to their needs.

Hybrid eLearning delivery mode, which is also referred to as a blended delivery mode, uses the web to enhance face-to-face learning and may decrease the number of face-to-face class sessions needed (Waterhouse, 2005). An online course is delivered entirely using web utilized asynchronous and/or synchronous delivery. The experience of a distance learning student should be as rich, both intellectually and effectively, as the experience of a student in a traditional classroom (Bower, 2001).

It does not matter whether learners are using asynchronous, synchronous, traditional, hybrid, or online it is important to create a comfortable learning environment for learners. Learners should feel that the faculty member is approachable whether they are teaching face-to-face, hybrid, or online.

Instructors/Teachers

According to Watson (2006) research/studies have found that:

- Research clearly indicates training teachers to use technology lowers anxiety and; increase efficacy while improving their skills
- Studies have found that teachers who had training with technology were much more confident about using technology in their classrooms
- Studies found that preservice and inservice teachers taking a college technology integration course had a higher comfort level, confidence, and attitude toward the use of computers, and were more inclined

to integrate new technologies into their classrooms

- Research has proven that professional development workshops for inservice teachers increased the computer self-efficacy levels of the participants

What are some reasons why some instructors/ teachers do not use technology for their traditional, hybrid, or online courses? Some reasons for this include:

- Teachers feel unprepared and anxious when using technology in their lessons
- Lack of pre-service experience and requirements and little emphasis on technology in core education courses (Watson, 2006)
- Educators will not be motivated to use technology unless they see the need and can apply technology immediately to their own teaching situations

What can be done to promote technological use in the classroom? Some examples include:

- Preservice requirements should be increased to demonstrate how to incorporate technology into teaching practices throughout core classes
- In order to prepare teachers, university and collaborative professional development opportunities with technology should be built into teacher education programs
- Use of web 2.0 tools can be a very successful tool to teach teachers for example blogs, social bookmarking, podcasting
- Requiring high school graduation requirements to include a technological component

Teaching Online and Future Trends

Some aspects of eLearning that could influence future trends are students' needs concerning inter-

activity, existing and new technologies, developing quality online courses that are not necessarily conducive to teach online, and motivating more faculty members to teach online.

eLearning is expanding at a very fast rate and will continue to do so. Technologies are constantly changing to incorporate interactivity such as social networking. Social networking will influence the design of existing and future courses using technologies such as Facebook, Twitter, MySpace, and LinkedIn. Social networking focuses on building online communities for students to interact in a variety of ways. It encourages new ways to communicate and share information. These and additional technologies will enable faculty members to effectively design quality online courses even if the courses are not necessarily conducive to teach online.

Even with the growth of online courses many faculty members are still hesitant to teach online. Some feelings they have concerning teaching online are that they feel it is a threat to their job, the quality of instruction is inferior to traditional delivery, and they feel intimidated by the technology.

Teaching online is not for every faculty member but support departments can education/train faculty members to effectively design their courses and overcome their resistance to teach online. As they design their courses it is so important to incorporate what has been discussed in this chapter namely interactivity, group work, and incorporating different learning styles into their assignments/ projects. They need to feel motivated to teach online and feel comfortable with the technology. Hopefully more effective faculty members will find teaching online very gratifying.

EXAMPLE INSTRUCTIONAL ASSIGNMENTS

Designing and organizing materials is very important for learners to know where to find materials so they feel comfortable with class materials. This would apply whether creating a syllabus, assignment, or additional materials. Class materials could be designed and organized into course modules such as material for each week or each unit.

When designing these assignments it is important to make content appropriate, give the students ownership, make it interactive, set targets by utilizing rubrics, enhance students self confidence by providing positive feedback, and making it fun. Developing a process to systematically plan the instruction is very important.

These instructional assignments used both hybrid and online models. The hybrid model used for these instructional activities were half online and half on ground. The online delivery mode was taught entirely on the web which can involve asynchronous and/or synchronous learning environments.

Since online delivery does not meet face-to-face, some students occasionally will have questions pertaining to assignments. To reach out to different learning styles of students, assignments were available in text form, and in an audio version. Some audio versions were in the form of podcasts, archived synchronous sessions, streaming video, and narrated powerpoints. Feedback from students indicated this was very helpful and answered any questions they may have had concerning their assignments.

Evaluating e-Learning Products

This was an individual assignment that required students to select an e-learning product using tools such as podcasting, blogging, webcasting, streaming video, and surveys. It required them to describe the product, evaluate the product, identify strengths and weaknesses of the product, and recommendations. In their evaluation they were required to discuss the instructional design, interactivity, and navigation options of the product. Some examples from this assignment included webcasting, garageband, YouTube, streaming

video, and classroom response systems. The assignment made the students aware of different e-learning products available.

Design and Develop an Online Class Unit

This individual assignment involved having students create a course unit in a course management system such as Blackboard, Moodle, or Sakai. Their course unit needed to include:

- course design
- unit description
- goals
- objectives
- contact information
- instructional materials
- assignments
- external links
- quizzes
- discussion boards
- self evaluation and feedback

Evaluating Online Courses

This was a group interactive assignment that required students to explore online courses available on the web such as MIT and iTunes University. The students had to evaluate whether the course encouraged contact between students and faculty, developed cooperation among students, encouraged active learning, gave prompt feedback, emphasized time on task, communicated high expectations to the students, and respected diverse talents and ways of learning. Their evaluation was based on a rubric which expected overall visual appeal, an introduction, and relevant content.

This assignment allowed students to compare different online courses available on the Internet. By sharing their findings with other students using a synchronous tool, they were able to explain and justify their findings on these courses to the entire class virtually.

Synchronous Group Instructional Research

This was a group interactive assignment that involved researching an assigned topic, creating a PowerPoint presentation, and presenting it in a synchronous tool such as Wimba, Centra, Skype or others. Some topics included learner analysis and motivation, cognitive learning strategies, constructivism approaches to e-learning, and future trends in distance or face-to-face learning. Each group researched the topic utilizing reliable educational technology web sites, articles, and books. Break out rooms were created by each group in their synchronous tool with instructor privileges for these rooms. They were able to upload PowerPoint presentations just as an instructor would. Each group had to present their topic to the rest of the class either synchronously or asynchronously depending on their course delivery. Synchronous delivery students and faculty members engaged at the same time. Asynchronous delivery students invited the rest of the class to their presentation but it was not mandatory for the rest of the class to attend at the time it was presented. Each group archived their presentation so class members could view the session at their convenience.

When a group presented their PowerPoint synchronously, they had to click through their presentation, answer questions, and read chat all at the same time if other students and the instructor attended their session. This taught them that it can be difficult to multitask through different venues and still keep students engaged in their learning. It also provided them with a real life experience to be the instructor during the assignment. The groups needed to interact with each other and change their role from student to instructor. This process emphasized student-to-student interaction through group tasks and cooperative activities which increased as they moved from a teaching to a learning paradigm (Bower, 2001).

The assignment made the students aware of research and opinions of educators pertaining to different topics. The student-to-student interaction through their group work helped them learn from each other.

Discussion Boards

The lack of face-to-face interaction can be substituted by online discussion (Yang & Cornelious, 2005). As a result, this course was designed to have at least one interactive discussion forum for each week of the class whether the course was taught using hybrid or online delivery mode. The discussion forums were based on numerous research papers. Some weeks involved a group of students being responsible for facilitating the forum instead of the professor. In some semesters the instructor would verbally summarize weekly discussion forums for the students using a voice discussion board.

These assignments made the students interact each week with everyone in the class. The majority of weekly discussions were based on outside papers they had to read. Students are expected to answer the specific questions posed, raise questions and add comments to postings by others. They were given points for their weekly discussion forums based on a rubric. This was based on original thoughts not already contained in the threaded discussion, cited examples and ideas, and reasons for agreeing or disagreeing with other postings.

In summary, in a traditional classroom setting, faculty can use their understanding of their students through observation of body language, verbal response, and eye contact to create an effective learning experience (Bower, 2001). The instructor needs to reply more on nonverbal communication cues and employ active listening skills. Faculty members can pose additional questions for clarification and summarize what is said to ensure accurate information exchange (Rybarczyk, 2007). When teaching a class utilizing synchronous technology, the instructor can understand student's verbal response to the content, the assignments, and respond to their needs.

In the past faculty expressed serious concerns and reservations regarding the effectiveness of distance learning (Bower, 2001). In my experience and from discussions with associates from other universities, improved course management systems, such as Blackboard, and improved synchronous technologies such as Wimba have made faculty and students realize how meaningful interaction between faculty and students can take place virtually.

CONCLUSION

As educators develop courses, a number of strategies need to be considered, from what the design should be to what technologies would be effective for the learners. This chapter discussed design models, learning theories, instructional strategies, learning styles, and technologies/delivery of instruction.

Whether you are developing an online course for a university, college, community college, or secondary school as discussed in this chapter, it is important to pay attention to instructional design and learning theories. Student's learning styles are equally important to keep in mind when designing instruction. As asynchronous and synchronous technologies are becoming more user friendly for students, it is also important to remember the Seven Principles for Good Practice in Online Learning. These principles were developed by Arthur Chickering and Zelda Gamson (1987). Even though these principles were for undergraduate education, it is good practice to apply them to all levels of education.

When considering the different strategies discussed in this chapter, educators need to consider asynchronous as well as synchronous technologies. While it may not be possible to utilize everything in this chapter in a single course, it is important to consider everything discussed when designing your instruction.

REFERENCES

Allen, M. (2003). *Michael Allen's Guide to E-Learning: Building interactive, fun, and effective learning programs for any company*. New York: John Wiley & Sons.

Bower, B. L. (2001). Distance Education: Facing the Faculty Challenge. *Online Journal of Distance Learning Administration,* 4(2). Retrieved from http://www.westga.edu/~distance/ojdla/summer42/bower42.html

Butler, K. (2003). *How to Keep Online Students Motivated*. Australian Flexible Learning Community. Retrieved from http://community.flexiblelearning.net.au/TeachingTrainingLearners/content/article_3340.htm

Carlson, S. (2004). The Next-Generation Classroom. *The Chronicle of Higher Education, 50*(25), A26.

Carney, A. L. (2003). *Factors in Instructional Design: Training versus Education.* Paper presented at the Instructional Technology Lab (ITL) Seminar, University of Illinois at Chicago.

Chickering, A. W., & Gamson, Z. F. (1987). Seven principles for good practice in undergraduate education. In *AAHE Bulletin*, March 3-7. Retrieved July 1, 2005 from http://honolulu.hawaii.edu/intranet/committees/FacDevCom/guidebk/teachtip/7princip.htm

Conklin, M. S. (2006). *Difference between education and training*. Megan Squire Conklin blog. Retrieved from http://facstaff.elon.edu/mconklin/2006/10/difference-between-education-and.html

Davis, B. G. (1993) *Tools for Teaching*. San Francisco: Jossey-Bass Publishers.

Funderstanding. (2001). *Right Brain vs. Left Brain.* Retrieved from http://www.funderstanding.com/right_left_brain.cfm

Good, T. L., & Brophy, J. E. (1990). *Educational psychology: A realistic approach (4th ed.).* White Plains, NY: Longman.

Harvey, J., & Mogey, N. (1997). *Implementing Learning Technology.* Learning Technology Dissemination Initiative. Retrieved from http://www.icbl.hw.ac.uk/ltdi/implementing-it/motif.htm

Hopper, C. (2008). *Left vs. Right Which Side Are You On?* Retrieved from http://frank.mtsu.edu/~studskl/hd/learn.html

Hutchins, H. (2003). Instructional Immediacy and the Seven Principles: Strategies for Facilitating Online Courses. *Online Journal of Distance Learning Administration, 6*(3).

Johnson, D. W., Johnson, R., & Smith, K. (1998). *Active Learning: Cooperation in the College Classroom.* Edina, MN: Interaction Book Co.

Kapp, K. (2006). *Design: Advantages of Interactivity.* Karl Kapp Blog. Retrieved from http://karlkapp.blogspot.com/2006/10/design-advantages-of-interactivity.html

Keller, J. M. (2006). *ARCS Design Process.* Retrieved from http://www.arcsmodel.com/Mot%20dsgn%20A%20prcss.htm

Klein, J., & Fox, E. (2004). Performance Improvement Competencies for Instructional Technologists. *TechTrends: Linking Research & Practice to Improve Learning, 48*(2), 22–26.

Kurtus, R. (1999). *Difference Between Education and Training.* Retrieved from http://www.school-for-champions.com/training/difference.htm

Lage, M. J., Platt, G. J., & Treglia, M. (2000). Inverting the Classroom: A Gateway to Creating an Inclusive Learning Environment . *The Journal of Economic Education, 31*(1), 30–43. doi:10.2307/1183338

Learning Theories Knowledgebase. (2008). *ADDIE Model at Learning-Theories.com.* Retrieved from http://www.learning-theories.com/addie-model.html

Morgan, C. K., & Kinross, C. (2002). Facilitating Online Interactivity Among Remotely Located Land Management Students. *Electronic Journal of Instructional Science and Technology.* Retrieved from http://www.usq.edu.au/electpub/e-jist/docs/Vol5_No2/morganrevised.html

Oblinger, D. G., & Hawkins, B. L. (2006). The Myth about Online Course Development. *EDUCAUSE Review, 41*(1), 14–15.

Rybarczyk, B. J. (2007). Tools of Engagement: Using Case Studies In Synchronous Distance-Learning Environments. *Journal of College Science Teaching, 37*(1), 31–33.

Sapieha, S. (2007). *Essay on adult education for use by RM advisory.* Prepared for ARMA Calgary Chapter Board. Retrieved from http://www.arma.calgary.ab.ca/pdfs/Education%20Report2007/Appendix%2024.pdf

Slavin, R. (1991). *Student Team Learning: A Practical Guide to Cooperative Learning (3rd Ed.).* Washington, DC: National Education Association.

Smith, P. L., & Ragan, T. J. (1993). *Instructional Design.* New York: Macmillan Publishing Company.

Smith, P. L., & Ragan, T. J. (2005). *Instructional Design Third Edition.* San Francisco: Jossey-Bass Education.

Sundberg, P. (2003). *Learning and Human Development with Educational Technologies.* EdPsy 317 course offered at University of Illinois, Urbana-Champaign. Retrieved from http://www.ed.uiuc.edu/courses/edpsy317/sp03/learning-maps/sundberg-learning-theories.gif

Thompkins, W. (2007). *Brain-Based Learning Theory: An Online Course Design Model*. Dissertation, Liberty University.

Valda, V. A. (1998). What is technical and vocational education and training? *Quarterly Newsletter of the Technical and Vocational Education and Training (TVET) Council, 1*(1). Retrieved from http://www.tvetcouncil.com.bb/Resource_Centre/TECVOC_Jan_Mar_1998.doc

Waterhouse, S. (2005). *The Power of eLearning*. Upper Saddle River, NJ: Pearson Education, Inc.

Watson, G. (2006). Technology Professional Development: Long Term Effects on Teacher Self Efficacy. *Journal of Technology and Teacher Education, 14*(1), 151–165.

Yang, Y., & Cornelious, L. F. (2005). Preparing Instructors for Quality Online Instruction. *Online Journal of Distance Learning Administration, 8*(1).

KEY TERMS AND DEFINITIONS

ADDIE Model: Instructional design model that stands for analyzing, designing, developing, implementing, and evaluating instructional material

Asynchronous Learning Environment: Students and instructors are engaged in "anytime-anyplace" learning

Education: Describes all experiences in which people learn

Human Performance Technology (HPT): Includes a variety of instructional and non-instructional interventions to address a performance problem

Hybrid eLearning Delivery Mode: Uses the web to enhance face-to-face learning and may decrease the number of face-to-face- class sessions

Instructional Design: Systematic process of translating principles of learning and instruction into plans for instructional materials and activities

Learning: The relatively permanent change in a person's knowledge or behavior due to experience

Online Course: Delivered entirely using web utilizing web utilizing asynchronous and/or synchronous delivery

Social Networking: Focuses on building online communities for students to interact in a variety of ways

Synchronous Learning Environment: Students and instructors engage each other at the same time, but not necessarily at the same location

Chapter 14
Essential Design Features of Online Collaborative Learning

Hyo-Jeong So
Nanyang Technological University, Singapore

Wei-Ying Lim
Nanyang Technological University, Singapore

Jennifer Yeo
Nanyang Technological University, Singapore

ABSTRACT

With the goal of working towards a paradigm shift from delivery-centered to participation-centered pedagogy in mind, this chapter presents a set of essential design features that readers need to consider for designing online collaborative learning environments. Meaningful interaction and collaboration in online environments need the consideration of design elements as well as the understanding of the affordances of interactive learning technologies. This chapter presents a 3-dimensional design activity - social structures, tools, and learner diversity - as the fundamental elements that educators and instructional designers need to consider. It is important to note that the combination of these essential features is not prescriptive, but rather, is situational dependent on the learning context to achieve the "goodness of fit" for the desired learning outcomes. To demonstrate the design and enactment of the 3-D design features, the authors present a case example of a problem-centered learning environment designed for secondary learners' science learning. In conclusion, the authors suggest that while the pedagogical advantages of collaborative learning have been well-supported, more research is needed to better understand the complex nature of designing collaborative learning in online settings, especially through the mediation of emerging technologies such as Web 2.0 technology tools.

INTRODUCTION

One of the prominent trends in K-12 education, higher education and corporate training is the adoption of online learning to complement traditional forms of learning conducted in bounded physical settings. For the past several years, the population of online learners and online courses has been growing substantially (Allen & Seaman, 2007, p. 68; Downes, 2005). It is not uncommon to find

DOI: 10.4018/978-1-61520-672-8.ch014

schools and institutions offering online or blended types of courses to extend learning opportunities beyond classrooms. Further, the recent advances of wireless mobile technologies and social software tools based on Web 2.0 technologies provide new possibilities to design seamless learning spaces cutting across formal and informal settings (Hemmi, Bayne, & Landt, 2009; Sharples, Taylor, & Vavoula, 2007). Now, *learning at anytime and anyplace* seems more possible with such emerging technologies that maximize mobility, connectivity, and versatility.

Despite the increasing adoption of learning technologies, however, pedagogical changes in online learning have been slow, as seen in online courses focusing on content delivery and tutorial based instruction. Simply turning classroom lectures into online learning formats do not necessarily provide learners with the opportunities for rich interactions arising from engagement in activities that make learning experiences meaningful. Instead, it is important to have deep understandings of *how people learn* as well as what new technology can provide for the successful design of technology-integrated learning environments (Bransford, Brown, & Cocking, 2002).

To overcome problems underlying current content-driven practices, a paradigm shift from delivery-centered to participation-centered approach is needed. Beyond downloading learning materials and files, learners should engage in meaningful activities with their peers to develop 21st century learning skills, such as solving ill-structured problems, expressing critical thinking skills, working effectively in teams, adopting diverse perspectives, and creating meaningful content. Towards this paradigm shift, this chapter presents a set of essential design features that readers need to consider for designing collaborative learning activities in online environments.

THEORETICAL BACKGROUND

Situative Perspectives and Collaborative Learning

Drawing on the social-constructivist view of learning which posits that knowledge is constructed as people negotiate meanings with others, situative perspectives of learning expound the social-constructivist construct by emphasizing on the in-situ nature of learning. Learning in this view is performative that is tightly bounded in activity, that is, *practice*. According to Lave and Wenger (1991), *practice* can be thought of as "a way of being that emphasizes on the inherently socially negotiated character of meaning, and the interested, concerned character of thought and action of persons-in-activity" (pp. 50-51). In other words, the knowing, thinking and doing of the persons performing activities in context are based on the situated negotiation and renegotiation of meanings in the particular context. In turn, these meanings are constantly being renegotiated and changed in the course of activity. Thus, practice is social and socially mediated, and the development of human knowing is through participation in a socially constituted world.

Collaborative learning that emphasizes the social construction of knowledge and skills through interaction with others is one approach of translating the social-constructivist theories to instructional situations. Collaboration is conceptualized as a process of shared meaning making that provides opportunities for learners to experience multiple perspectives from others who have different backgrounds, and to develop critical thinking skills through the process of judging, valuing, supporting, or opposing different viewpoints (Fung, 2004; Lipponen, Hakkarainen, & Paavola, 2004). In the continuous process of interaction, prior knowledge is assimilated to bootstrap new understanding. In other words, learners try to make sense of the new knowledge by building on their existing frames of reference in an active constructivist process. Through this experience, learners will come to know or understand the knowledge/concept at hand. Knowledge in this case does not exist as universal information schemas. Rather knowledge is intricately bound to the participation of interaction in activity. Furthermore, learners can develop social and inter-personal skills which are critical to be successful in modern society. In terms of affective advantages, collaborative learning approaches can provide learners with a sense of belonging that promotes participation, community-building, and social presence (Stacey, 2002).

Computer-Supported Collaborative Learning (CSCL)

Various technology tools can play critical roles in supporting collaborative learning in online and offline environments. Computer-supported collaborative learning (CSCL) is a field where the main inquiry of research is about how to utilize the affordances of computers as a mediating tool to support the interaction of participants for shared understanding (Koschmann, Hall, & Miyake, 2002). In knowledge building approaches, for example, a community of learners use a public networked space called Knowledge Forum to share ideas and to work together towards in-depth understanding of certain problems that individual learners may not be able to reach alone (Scardamalia & Bereiter, 2006). Recently, more sophisticated forms of technology, such as 3D simulation, virtual reality, augmented reality, and mobile learning programs (e.g., Pea & Maldonado, 2006; Squire & Klopfer, 2007), have emerged to support collaboration among learners. These emerging technologies can provide a multimedia rich and participatory environment where learners are interacting in situated contexts through multiple forms of representations.

ESSENTIAL DESIGN FEATURES OF ONLINE COLLABORATIVE LEARNING

The goal for CSCL design is to create meaningful interaction and collaborative environments through the mediation of technologies. To achieve this, the consideration of design elements should be coupled with the understanding of the affordances of interactive learning technologies. Drawing on research findings from various studies (discussed below), this section presents the essential design features of online collaborative learning in a 3-dimensional design activity, namely *social structures*, *tools*, and *learner diversity* (see Figure 1) that educators and instructors need to consider. Our rationale for this 3-dimensional design activity is that first, despite the multiple ways online collaborative learning could be design for, it is argued that the three essential dimensions consisting of tools, social structures and learners diversity, are the fundamental considerations that educators and instructors need to consider. Second, it is important to note that the combination of these essential features is not prescriptive, but rather, is situational dependent on the learning context to achieve the "goodness of fit" for the desired learning outcomes (Chee, 2002). By "goodness of fit", we refer to the appropriate use of technology where technology-affordances lend well to the social structures and are apt in terms of learners' ICT literacy. In the following sections, each dimension will be explained in turn.

Social Structures

Assigning learners to groups does not necessarily mean that they would work collaboratively. The ways social structures are setup are important design considerations to facilitate collaboration. Such social structures can be thought of in terms of *participation structures* and *task structures*.

First, it is important to understand the nature of online collaborative learning under different

Figure 1. 3-dimensional design activity

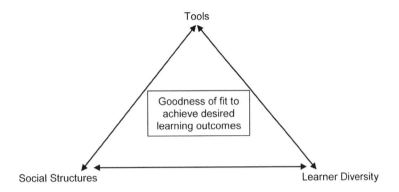

participation structures*, that is, whether participation is mandatory or voluntary. Previous research on the use of online discussion forums, for examples, shows that learners oftentimes post minimum numbers of notes to meet the requirement and to receive grades, and hardly develop a sense of belonging to collaborative knowledge building communities (e.g., Dennen, 2005; Hara, Bonk, & Angeli, 2000; Zhu, 2006). Fung (2003) conducted a research study in a non-mandatory participation structure where learners taking a distance course could voluntarily decide on their participation in online discussion forums. Overall results show that learner participation measured by the number of postings was low, and that the depth of online discussions was rarely observed. Participants reported multiple reasons for this lack of active participation, including the general lack of interest in discussion topics, preference for spending more time on other course-related activities, and low participation from peers.

Whether participation is mandatory or voluntary, cognitive engagement and participation do not happen naturally by simply making collaborative technologies available, but may need instructors' intentional mediating at the initial stage (So, 2009). Then, what scaffolding strategies can instructors employ to facilitate active participation and collaboration among learners? Instructors can provide learners with guidelines for course participations to increase their partici-

pation in online learning activities and essentially promote a sense of learning community. For instance, Rovai (2001) suggested that providing course participation rubric was an effective way of encouraging constructive and active exchange of ideas among learners, and for reducing learner perceptions of psychological distance. Besides the use of static computer-mediated communication tools (e.g., online discussion forums), instructors can consider using social software programs that support content-creation and sharing by learners (e.g., weblogs, wikis, multimedia forums, etc) to encourage participatory learning activities (van 't Hooft, 2008).

More fundamentally, instructors can design learning tasks that provide *authentic meaning-making opportunities for collaboration* to enhance learners' intrinsic motivation for participation. For example, Uribe, Klein, and Sullivan (2003) compared the effect of individual web-based learning versus computer-mediated collaborative learning on solving authentic ill-structured problems in an online course offered to ROTC learners. Realistic military issues that learners might face in the future were used as problem scenarios. Learners in a collaborative learning mode worked together to define problems, gather data, and develop plausible solutions. The researchers found that learners who worked in a collaborative mode performed significantly better than those who worked in an individual mode. Part of this divergence could be explained by learners' satisfaction with the collaborative nature of the problems, the realism of the problems, and the transferability of learned knowledge and skills to real life situations. This case shows that learners' performance and participation can be greatly enhanced when they are engaged in collaborative meaning making processes that are authentic and meaningful to them.

In considering the task structure, it is also important to differentiate collaboration and co-operation. Roschelle and Teasley (1995) defined collaboration as "a coordinated, synchronous activity that is the result of a continued attempt to construct and maintain a shared conception of a problem" (p.70). On the other hand, cooperation emphasizes a task-specialization approach that may give little opportunity for shared meaning making and knowledge co-construction to take place among learners. Researchers such as Paulus (2005) and Lim, Hedberg, Yeo and Hung (2005) suggested that different tasks could lead to different collaboration patterns. In Paulus's study, a group required to synthesize work showed collaborative discourse patterns that was rarely found in other groups that tended to adopt task-specialization approaches. Lim et al's (2005) work found that tasks containing higher degrees of uncertainty and complexity afford greater collaboration and sharing. In sum, these studies suggest that the authentic and complex structure of learning tasks can create the need for learners to work collaboratively.

Tools

According to Sfrad (1998), there are two metaphors of learning: the acquisition metaphor that views learning as a process of acquiring knowledge by individual learners, and the participation metaphor that views learning as a participatory and situated process. Later, Paavola, Lipponen, and Hakkarainen (2004) suggested that knowledge creation by a community of learners is another important metaphor of learning. Such situated practices and knowledge co-construction processes in online environments necessitate the use of tools to support activities. Tools for online collaborative learning can be characterized by the affordances of (a) supporting shared meaning making in a community of learners, (b) enabling seamless collaborative learning not limited by the boundary of physical settings, and (c) enhancing face-to-face and online collaboration.

First, a variety of tools can be used to support shared meaning making and problem-solving processes among learners. Since the use of complex and collaborative tasks often require learners to find additional information to reach solutions, it is useful to provide groups with *shared online spaces* where group members can actively present information, exchange resources, and share ideas (Curtis & Lawson, 2001; McAlpine, 2000). A Computer-Supported Intentional Learning Environment (CSILE), reengineered as a software program called Knowledge Forum, is an excellent example of a technology-mediated environment where learners can share and connect their ideas in a shared space (Scardamalia & Bereiter, 2006). Knowledge Forum has been used in online learning settings to help learners build knowledge with distant peers. For example, van Aalst and Chan (2001) showed the use of Knowledge Forum among learners in two distant countries (Hong Kong and Canada). They found that although learners were located in geographically different areas, participants were able to successfully build knowledge together and be further engaged in the practices of forming an online learning community.

Secondly, tools can be used to enable seamless collaborative learning not limited by the boundary of physical settings. While the main focus of online learning has been to support learning at anytime and at anyplace beyond classroom environments, online learning practices so far have revolved around the use of desktop-computers. Recent advances and adoptions of mobile tools such as Tablet PC, PDA (Personal Digital Assistant),

UMPC (Ultra Mobile PC) and cell phones are interesting since they can enable 1:1 computing, are affordable and promote seamless access to learning materials and collaboration. Now, beyond online learning around the use of desk-top computers, m-learning (i.e., mobile learning) and ubiquitous learning (i.e., U-learning) that utilize the affordances of wireless mobile technology have emerged as a promising trend that can truly support learning at anytime and anywhere.

When discussing educational possibilities of mobile technology, So and Kim (2009) suggested that as the degree of mobility increases, learning patterns can move from centralized to de-centralized systems, from individual learning to collaborative learning, and from one-way communication to many-to-many communication. From collaborative learning perspectives, tools equipped with mobility, portability, and versatility can support collaborative interaction in multiple locations, and filling in white spaces with productive activities. For instance, learners can use the features of multimedia tools and wireless connection to easily create digital artifacts in contexts of their learning and share them with classmates instantly (Pea & Maldonado, 2006; Roschelle, 2003).

Finally, tools can enhance collaboration by providing an appropriate balance between face-to-face interaction and online interaction, and between reality and virtuality. As mentioned earlier, one of the critical problems in current online learning practices is the lack of learners' active participation. For such problems, blended learning that maximizes the best advantages of face-to-face and online interaction has been used to promote more interaction and participation from learners (Graham, 2006). In a blended learning mode, simple tools such as online discussion forums can be used to extend collaborative discussion and problem solving beyond classroom settings. In addition, more sophisticated forms of technology such as virtual reality, online simulations, and 3D virtual worlds (e.g., Second Life) can be used to enhance collaborative learning experiences among multiple users in virtual environments (Squire & Klopfer, 2007).

Learner Diversity

Building on the idea that collaborative learning is about getting learners to experience multiple perspectives from others who have different backgrounds so as to promote the process of judging, valuing, supporting, or opposing different viewpoints, it then warrants a need for the makeup of the group to be diverse. The diversity of the learners' background, knowledge and expertise promulgate rich interactions and exchanges. Take the example of Tapped In (http://tappedin.org/tappedin/), a web-based learning environment created to transform the way teacher professional development is done online, there is a diverse mix of members in the cadre: from the novice to the expert, from apprentice to mentor, from lurker to active participant. By having such diverse makeup of learners, it promotes greater opportunities for sharing of experience, correction of misconception and negotiation of meanings which are characteristics of collaborative learning (Schlager, Fusco, & Schank, 2002).

Of note here is that learner roles (e.g., apprentice) are temporary constructs that evolve throughout the collaboration process. They do not remain static and are reciprocal to the development of interactions. For instance, informal leaders could emerge as interactions develop or that active members who were enthusiastic initially could become less active in the collaboration over time. Educators and instructors should be mindful in their designs to give room for changes to occur. Such dynamism in learners' diversity calls for continuous monitoring by educators and instructors so that learners' interdependency is fostered where one feels responsible for oneself as well as for others. Thus, individual accountability includes two aspects: learners' responsibility for their own learning, and learners' responsibility for helping group members' learning (Abrami, 2001).

Of particular interest in this regard is the conception of *collective cognitive responsibility* where "the condition in which responsibility for the access of a group effort is distributed across all the members rather than being centered in the leaders" (Scardamalia, 2002, p. 68). Learners who take collective cognitive responsibility must recognize that collaborative knowledge building is a continuous process undertaken by a group of learners, and that group effort can create much more synergy than the sum of individual outputs. Learner diversity is also related to idea diversity. When all learners are empowered to engage in the knowledge building process, it creates a rich environment where diverse ideas are valued and advanced to create groups' knowledge innovation. While fostering learners to take collective cognitive responsibility is a complex higher-order activity, prior research shows that well-designed knowledge building environments can enable this to happen even in young learners. For example, Zhang, Scardamalia, Reeve, and Messina (2009) examined how Grade 4 students assumed increasing levels of collective cognitive responsibility to advance their science knowledge through the mediation the Knowledge Forum program. By gradually taking part in online knowledge building processes with flexible participation structures, these younger learners developed high levels of collective cognitive responsibility to advance both individual and groups' knowledge.

A CASE EXAMPLE: ILLUSTRATING 3-D DESIGN FEATURES

The following case example demonstrates the 3-D design features, - social structures, tools, and learner diversity - presented in a problem-centered learning environment, called the THINK cycle. This cycle, modeled after problem-based learning, was designed and developed by a team of secondary science teachers and researchers in Singapore through design research.

First, *social structures* to encourage learners to collaborate are put in place. This is achieved by infusing complexity and uncertainty into the problem, which constitute the two traits that characterize authentic learning. The problem-solving process in the THINK cycle begins with an ill-structured problem modeled after real life problems. For example, in one THINK cycle, learners were tasked to find out the cause of a roller coaster accident. Besides police reports and newspaper reports, no other information was provided to the learners, nor was any relevant content taught in advance as well. Learners had to search for information to close their knowledge gap, deal with many variables involved in this problem such as whether air resistance or friction would affect the stopping distance of a roller coaster cart. There could also be more than one possible cause of the accident. The complexity of problem and uncertainty of situation created the need for learners to work together closely to search for relevant information from different sources, share what they had found, unpack the information in the context of the problem and evaluate the relevance of new information to the problem as they worked towards the common goal of solving the problem. Such questions were unlike end-of-chapter problems, which tended to provide only the necessary information needed to solve the problem in a routine and mechanistic manner.

To ensure active participation among the learners, rules that encourage social and collaborative norms were put in place to shape the behavior of the learners. In the particular THINK cycle described above, rules based on the 12 principles of Knowledge Building (Scardamalia, 2002) were introduced to the learners. These principles include continual improvement of ideas and collective responsibility. The former was introduced to encourage learners to place advancement of the

Figure 2. Screenshot of Knowledge Constructor Environment

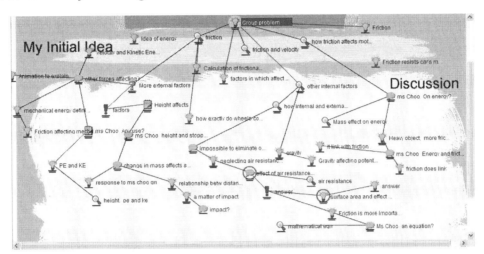

group's and own knowledge as their common goal. The principle of collective responsibility ensured that each learner worked not for himself/herself but saw his/her own contribution as a means to advance the knowledge of the group. These two principles ensured that the learners' end goal was not merely product-driven but process-driven too, as manifested in the learners' engagement in meaningful participation for collaborative knowledge building.

The process of the THINK cycle was mediated by a *CSCL tool* called Knowledge Constructor. Knowledge Constructor is an asynchronous online discussion tool that represents discussion threads in a graphical form. A screen shot of the Knowledge Constructor environment of one of the forum discussions is shown in Figure 2.

Knowledge Constructor provided the tool essential for sharing of ideas with one another in the team and supporting content creation. First, it provided a shared space for easy access to one another's ideas. For example, each little graphical icon in Figure 2 represents a note posted by a particular learner. A note contains written ideas put forth by a learner. These ideas, when posted by individual learners, were recorded permanently on this public space which can be accessed by any registered user. This public display of ideas

facilitated easy retrieval of ideas anytime and anywhere by any one of the members in the group. The permanent record of ideas also allowed for individual and group deliberation over the ideas for a longer period. Notes in such environment tend to show depth via the development of accumulative knowledge that emanates from other members' notes. For example, in Table 1 below, the build-on of note 22 from note 2 showed a long time lag of 2 days between the two notes. However, the quality of note 22 was substantial as learner D expanded on the work-energy equation ($KE_{initial} + PE_{initial} + W_{external} = KE_{final} + PE_{final}$) in note 2 by identifying each of the components in the equation in the context of the problem, thereby unpacking its meaning.

Second, the graphical representation of learners' ideas, with links showing how each idea is built upon, displays the interconnectedness of multiple viewpoints. This feature of Knowledge Constructor supports content creation. Exposing individual responses to ideas allows them to be scrutinized by others and to trigger cognitive activities around the ideas. This feature supporting collaborative learning was evident in Table 2.

Table 2 showed three interconnecting notes (notes 17, 21 and 30) building on the previous one. It showed a negotiation between learner J

Table 1. Unpacking principle of conservation of energy

Note	Author	Date/Time	Content
2	J	2006-08-02 09:28:34	$KE_{initial} + PE_{initial} + W_{external} = KE_{final} + PE_{final}$ The left side of the equation includes the total mechanical energy ($KE_{initial} + PE_{initial}$) for the *initial state* of the object plus the work done on the object by external forces ($W_{external}$) while the right side of the equation includes the total mechanical energy ($KE_{final} + PE_{final}$) for the *final state* of the object.
22	D	2006-08-04 16:37:42	By law of conservation of energy KEinitial + PEinitial + Wexternal = KEfinal + PEfinal KEfinal + PEfinal = 0. Thus, KEinitial + PEinitial must add a negative Wexternal. To calculate Wexternal, we can use the formula: Work = force x displacement x cosine (theta)

and learner M over whether friction should be considered as one of the factors that affect the stopping distance of a roller coaster cart. Learner M's disagreement to neglect both air resistance and friction (see note 21) led Learner J to justify why only air resistance should be neglected and not friction. The public display of each idea allowed learner M and learner J to share ideas they found on the Internet, argue for shared understanding and finally come to resolution to settle their disagreement. These interconnected ideas captured on this CSCL database also allowed these initial decisions to be revisited when the learners were investigating their hypothesis. On reflecting the result of their investigation, the learners realized that "we must account for it (air resistance) in our force diagrams of object moving in the air … (because) Friction often presents itself as drag, when an object is moving through a fluid medium." This realization triggered another cycle of formula construction, hypothesis generation and investigation before a resolution was finally found. This showed how interconnected ideas captured in CSCL system triggered cognitive processes to sustain collaboration learning.

Lastly, to keep online discussion going, new ideas need to be injected. One of the ways to ensure *learner diversity* is to expose different members in the group to different resources bearing different perspectives. In the case example described above, learners were allowed to refer to different resources on the Internet. Their actions on their

Table 2. Does friction affect stopping distance?

Note	Author	Date/Time	Content
1	D	2006-07-26 09:50:39	How does friction affect the point in which the car stops?
17	J	2006-07-26 10:11:51	Once a roller coaster has reached its initial summit and begins its descent, the forces acting upon it are gravity, normal force and dissipative forces such as air resistance. … Finally, air resistance is able to do work upon cars, draining a small amount of energy from the total mechanical energy which the cars possess because it is an external force. Since the effect is small, it is often neglected.By neglecting the influence of air resistance, it can be said that the total mechanical energy of the train of cars is conserved during the ride. …. http://www.glenbrook.k12.il.us/gbssci/phys/mmedia/energy/ce.html
21	M	2006-07-26 10:18:45	if u eliminate other factors like air resistance, friction etc, the roller coaster will never stopp in the first place since energy is neither gain nor lost….
30	J	2006-07-26 10:30:13	friction would affect the roller coaster more than the air resistance and cannot be negligent. friction would cause energy to be converted to heat energy and thus lesser energy would be available for kinetic energy, and distanced object moves is reduced

Table 3. Differing viewpoints

Note	Author	Date/Time	Content
1	D	2006-07-26 09:50:39	How does friction affect the point in which the car stops?
3	K	2006-07-26 09:53:24	Friction plays a major role in actual roller coaster physics, where mechanical energy (the sum of potential and kinetic energy) is not constant. The frictional force itself is in direct opposition to the motion of the coaster. The friction of the wheels on the track, the wheel bearings in oil, and wind drag all contribute to the dissipation of mechanical energy throughout the ride, especially at the end of the ride, when the remaining kinetic energy is transferred out of the system by the application of the brakes.
7	D	2006-07-2609:58:42	in context to my post on "idea of energy", which explains that "In the absence of external forces such as air resistance and friction (two of many), the total amount of an object's energy remains constant.". K's post is stating that "mechanical energy (the sum of potential and kinetic energy) is not constant...

laptop were captured using computer usage observation software, Morae. Observations of the video recordings showed that students shared differing viewpoints offered by different authors of the websites they referred to. Table 3 showed two opposing ideas that the learners obtained from the Internet.

Note 3 showed learner K offering a viewpoint she had gotten from the Internet that "friction plays a major role in actual roller coaster physics". In note 7, learner D offered an opposing viewpoint she found on a different website that external forces such as air resistance and friction were absent. These opposing viewpoints could have formed the basis of argument between learner J and learner M on whether friction and air resistance should be considered in the roller coaster accident. Therefore, learner diversity could be purposefully orchestrated by including expert's voice through Internet search and interpretation by the learners.

FUTURE: 3-DIMENTIONAL DESIGN IN TRANSITION

Looking at the learning of the future, the recent development of Web 2.0 technologies is interesting since it has the potential to support and facilitate participatory communities of practices in online environments. The fast and wide adoption of Web 2.0 tools such as blogs, wikis, and other social networking tools is a socio-technical phenomenon which is indicative of the culture of today's learners, who are the digital natives (Presnsky, 2001). Brown and Adler (2008) argue that Web 2.0 has created a culture of participatory learning called *learning 2.0* wherein the focus is "*learning to be* through enculturation into a practice as well as on collateral learning" (p.30, emphasis added).

As Table 4 summarizes, the growing prevalence of Web 2.0 technologies creates transitional issues in each element of the 3-dimensional design activity. First, the nature of tools in the Web 2.0 era is drastically different from so called Web 1.0 tools that focus on pushing or delivering content. In the Web 1.0 era, users are in a consumer's position to receive ready-made content. On the other hand, Web 2.0 or social networking tools such as Wikipedia, blogs, Flickr, and Facebook are based on pulling and sharing of user-created content, thus giving ample opportunities for leveraging collective intelligence for collaborative knowledge sharing and creation in an open online space. Second, this very nature of open participation in Web 2.0 tools also influences how social structures are set up in online environments. Collaborative learning in the Web 1.0-based environment is often limited to learners who are taking a same class or using the same learning management system.

Table 4. 3-Dimensional design in transition

		Transition	
Tools	Pushed, Content-delivery	→	Pulling, Content-creation
Social structure	Bounded participation	→	Open participation
Learner diversity	Static, Fixed	→	Dynamic Emergent

In the Web 2.0-based environment, however, collaboration becomes fluid as learners can solicit and access participation with peers and partners from anywhere in the virtual world (Lankshear & Knobel, 2006). In turn, the open participation structure naturally influences learner diversity. The composition of learners for collaborative tasks is now dynamic and emergent that groups of learners can be easily formed, modified, or dissolved.

In this transitory period, it becomes clear that one of the challenges in the future learning is how to bring this Web 2.0 phenomenon to create new pedagogical practices to create collaborative learning environments. The digital natives are already using various Web 2.0 tools for personal or social networking purposes. Whether intended or unintended, learners are already exposed to various opportunities for informal learning in this Web 2.0 environment. However, it seems that instructors teaching these digital natives are less aware of such affordances of Web 2.0 and other emerging technologies for pedagogical purposes. Moreover, creating collaborative learning spaces for the new generation of learners requires a cultural shift to embrace openness, participation, and socializing as powerful forces for collaboration across diverse learners.

CONCLUSION

This chapter presented the essential design features of online collaborative learning in a 3-dimensional design activity: social structures, learner diversity, and tools. One case example of secondary learners' science learning was presented to illustrate the enactment of each of the three elements in creating an online learning environment conducive for collaborative knowledge building. Our discussions are based on situative perspectives emphasizing on the in-situ nature of learning and interactive perspectives focusing on meaningful collaboration among learners. From CSCL perspectives, it is clear that online collaborative learning means more than individual learners coming together to complete a task in technology-integrated environments. Instead, learners need to be engaged in meaningful meaning making processes for negotiation, exchange of ideas, and co-construction of knowledge. Technological tools should be designed to support such complex collaborative activities. Online collaborative learning should be designed in social structures in terms of task and participation structures. Further, the diversity of learners' background, knowledge, and expertise should be considered to enrich collaborative learning experiences. Finally, technological tools can be used to support shared meaning making processes and seamless collaboration in face-to-face and online settings. As mentioned earlier, these essential design features should not be taken as prescriptive instructional design strategies, but rather, are situational variables dependent on the learning context to achieve the goodness of fit for the desired learning outcomes. Overall, it is concluded that while the pedagogical advantages of collaborative learning has been discussed and supported in the previous literature, more research is needed to better understand the complex nature of collaborative learning, especially through the mediation of new types of technology such as Web 2.0 technology tools. Further research should examine new emerging technologies and associated teaching and learning practices towards the design of interactive and collaborative learning environments.

REFERENCES

Abrami, P. C. (2001). Understanding and promoting complex learning using technology. *Educational Research and Evaluation, 7*(2-3), 113–136. doi:10.1076/edre.7.2.113.3864

Allen, E., & Seaman, J. (2003). *Sizing the opportunity: The quality and extent of online education in the United States, 2002 and 2003.* Retrieved February 2004, from http://www.sloan-c.org/resources/sizing_opportunity.pdf

Allen, E., & Seaman, J. (2007). *Online nation: Five years of growth in online learning.* The Sloan Consortium.

Bransford, J. D., Brown, A. L., & Cocking, R. R. (2002). *How people learn: Brain, mind, experience, and school.* Washington, DC: National Academy Press.

Brown, J. S., & Adler, R. P. (2008). Minds on fire: Open education, the long tail, and learning 2.0. *EDUCAUSE Review, 43*(1), 16–32.

Chee, Y. S. (2002). Refocusing learning on pedagogy in a connected world. *Horizon, 10*(4), 7–13. doi:10.1108/10748120210452102

Curtis, D. D., & Lawson, M. J. (2001). Exploring collaborative online learning. *Journal of Asynchronous Learning Networks, 5*(1), 21–34.

Dennen, V. P. (2005). From message posting to learning dialogues: Factors affecting learner participation in asynchronous discussion. *Distance Education, 26*(1), 127–148. doi:10.1080/01587910500081376

Downes, S. (2005). E-learning 2.0 [Electronic Version]. *eLearn Magazine.* Retrieved from http://elearnmag.org/subpage.cfm?section=articles&article=29-1

Fung, Y. H. (2004). Collaborative online learning: interaction patterns and limiting factors. *Open Learning, 19*(2), 54–72. doi:10.1080/0268051042000224743

Graham, C. R. (2006). Blended learning systems: Definition, current trends, and future directions. In C. J. Bonk & C. R. Graham (Eds.), *The handbook of blended learning: Global perspectives, local designs* (pp. 3-21). San Francisco: Pfeiffer.

Hara, N., Bonk, C., & Angeli, C. (2000). Content analysis of online discussion in an applied educational psychology. *Instructional Science, 28*(2), 115–152. doi:10.1023/A:1003764722829

Hemmi, A., Bayne, S., & Landt, R. (2009). The appropriation and repurposing of social technologies in higher education. *Journal of Computer Assisted Learning, 25,* 19–30. doi:10.1111/j.1365-2729.2008.00306.x

Koschmann, T., Hall, R., & Miyake, N. (Eds.). (2002). *CSCL 2: Carrying forward the conversation.* Mahwah, NJ: Lawrence Erlbaum Associates.

Lankshear, C., & Knobel, M. (2006). *Blogging as participation: The active sociality of a new literacy.* Paper presented at the American Educational Research Association.

Lave, J., & Wenger, E. (1991). *Situated learning: Legitimate peripheral participation.* Cambridge, MA: Cambridge University Press.

Lim, W. Y., Hedberg, J., Yeo, J., & Hung, D. (2005). *Fostering communities of practice of heads of IT departments using common projects.* Paper presented at the Association for Educational Communications and Technology Leadership and Technology International Convention, Orlando FL.

Lipponen, L., Hakkarainen, K., & Paavola, S. (2004). Practices and orientations of CSCL. In J. W. Strijbos, P. A. Kirschner & R. L. Martens (Eds.), *What we know about CSCL and Implementing it in higher education* (pp. 34-50). Dordrecht, Netherlands: Kluwer Academic Publishers.

McAlpine, I. (2000). Collaborative learning online. *Distance Education, 21*(1), 66–80. doi:10.1080/0158791000210105

Paavola, S., Lipponen, L., & Hakkarainen, K. (2004). Models of innovative knowledge communities and three metaphors of learning. *Review of Educational Research, 74*(4), 557–576. doi:10.3102/00346543074004557

Paulus, T. M. (2005). Collaborative and cooperative approaches to online group work: The impact of task type. *Distance Education, 26*(1), 111–125. doi:10.1080/01587910500081343

Pea, R., & Maldonado, H. (2006). WILD for learning: Interacting through new computing devices, anytime, anywhere. In K. Sawyer (Ed.), *Cambridge Handbook of the Learning Sciences* (pp. 427-442). New York: Cambridge University Press.

Presnsky, M. (2001). Digital natives, digital immigrants [Electronic Version]. *On the Horizon, 9.* Retrieved from http://www.marcprensky.com/writing/Prensky%20-%20Digital%20Natives,%20Digital%20Immigrants%20-%20Part1.pdf

Roschelle, J. (2003). Unlocking the learning value of wireless mobile devices. *Journal of Computer Assisted Learning, 19,* 260–272. doi:10.1046/j.0266-4909.2003.00028.x

Roschelle, J., & Teasley, S. D. (1995). The construction of shared knowledge in collaborative problem solving. In O. M. C. E (Ed.), *Computer-supported Collaborative eLearning* (pp. 69–97). New York, NY: Springer-Verlag.

Rovai, A. P. (2001). Building classroom community at a distance: A case study. *Educational Technology Research and Development, 49*(4), 33–48. doi:10.1007/BF02504946

Scardamalia, M. (2002). Collective cognitive responsibility for the advancement of knowledge. In B. Smith (Ed.), *Liberal education in a knowledge society* (pp. 67-98). Chicago: Open Court.

Scardamalia, M., & Bereiter, C. (2006). Knowledge building: Theory, pedagogy, and technology. In K. Sawyer (Ed.), *Cambridge handbook of the learning sciences* (pp. 97-118). New York: Cambridge University Press.

Schlager, M. S., Fusco, J., & Schank, P. (2002). Evolution of an online education community of practice. In K. A. Renninger & W. Shumar (Eds.), *Building virtual communities: Learning and change in cyberspace* (pp. 129-158). Cambridge, MA: Cambridge University Press.

Sfard, A. (1998). On the two metaphors for learning and the danger of choosing one. *Educational Researcher, 27*(2), 4–13.

Sharples, M., Taylor, J., & Vavoula, G. (2007). A theory of learning for the mobile age. In R. Andrews & C. Haythornthwaite (Eds.), *The Sage Handbook of E-learning Research* (pp. 221-247). London: Sage.

So, H. J. (2009). When groups decide to use asynchronous online discussions: Collaborative learning and social presence under a voluntary participation structure. *Journal of Computer Assisted Learning*, *25*(2), 143–160. doi:10.1111/j.1365-2729.2008.00293.x

So, H. J., & Kim, B. (2009). Teaching and learning with mobile technologies: Educational applications. In M. Pagani (Ed.), *The Encyclopedia of multimedia technology and networking* (2nd ed., pp. 1366-1372). Hershey, PA: Information Science Reference.

Squire, K., & Klopfer, E. (2007). Augmented reality simulations on handheld computers. *Journal of the Learning Sciences*, *16*(3), 371–413.

Stacey, E. (2002). Quality online participation: establishing social presence. In T. Evans (Ed.), *Research in Distance Education 5* (pp. 138-253). Geelong, Australia: Deakin University Press.

Uribe, D., Klein, J. D., & Sullivan, H. (2003). The effect of computer-mediated collaborative learning on solving ill-defined problems. *Educational Technology Research and Development*, *51*(1), 5–19. doi:10.1007/BF02504514

van 't Hooft, M. (2008). Mobile, wireless, connected information clouds and learning [Electronic Version]. *Emerging technologies for learning*, *3*. Retrieved from http://partners.becta.org.uk/upload-dir/downloads/page_documents/research/emerging_technologies08_chapter2.pdf van Aalst, J., & Chan, C. K. K. (2001). *Beyond "sitting next to each other": A design experiment on knowledge building in teacher education*. Paper presented at the first European conference on computer-supported collaborative learning. Maastricht, The Netherlands: University of Maastricht.

Zhang, J. W., Scardamalia, M., Reeve, R., & Messina, R. (2009). Designs for collective cognitive responsibility in knowledge-building communities. *Journal of the Learning Sciences*, *18*(1), 7–44. doi:10.1080/10508400802581676

Zhu, E. (2006). Interaction and cognitive engagement: An analysis of four asynchronous online discussions. *Instructional Science*, *34*, 451–480. doi:10.1007/s11251-006-0004-0

KEY TERMS AND DEFINITIONS

Asynchronous Communication: a form of communication that people send data at different times (e.g. online discussion forum).

Blended Learning: any combinations of learning delivery methods, mostly face-to-face instruction with asynchronous or/and synchronous computer technologies.

Collaborative Learning: an instructional approach in which a small number of learners interact together and share their knowledge and skills in order to reach a specific learning goal.

Collective Cognitive Responsibility: a condition in which responsibility for the access of a group effort is distributed across all the members rather than being centered in the leaders.

Computer-Supported Collaborative Learning (CSCL): a field where the main inquiry of research is about how to utilize the affordances of computers as a mediating tool to support the interaction of participants for shared understanding.

Interaction: a reciprocal communication and learning process between humans or between human and non-human to achieve a certain goal. Four types of interaction include (a) learner - content interaction, (b) learner - instructor interaction, (c) learner- learner interaction, and (d) learner - interface interaction.

Knowledge Building: a community of learners use a public networked space such as Knowledge Forum to continuously share ideas and to work together towards in-depth understanding of certain problems that individual learners may not be able to reach alone.

Knowledge Constructor: an asynchronous online discussion tool that represents discussion threads in a graphical form.

Knowledge Forum: A Computer-Supported Intentional Learning Environment (CSILE), was reengineered as a software program called Knowledge Forum. This is a technology-mediated environment where learners can share and connect their ideas in a shared space.

Learner Diversity: refers to learners' multiple perspectives and different backgrounds to promote the process of judging, valuing, supporting, or opposing different viewpoints.

Mobile Learning (m-Learning): learning that occurs across learning settings or locations through the use of handheld, portable, or wireless devices by learners on the move.

Participatory Learning: situations wherein individuals can contribute to the knowledge building process instead of passively consuming prepackaged knowledge and information; in such cases, anyone with access to the Web has an opportunity to build, tinker with, or share information that might be of value to a growing knowledge base or learning community.

Problem-Based Learning (PBL): a problem-drive learning approach. Learners collectively solve ill-structured problems modeled after real-life situations.

Social Structure: The ways social structures are setup in terms of participation structures and task structures.

Ubiquitous Learning (u-Learning): a type of learning that utilizes the capabilities of mobile and wireless technologies to support seamless and connected learning.

Web 2.0 Technology: Web 2.0: refers to a second generation of Web-based tools, services, and communities, such as blogs, podcasts, RSS feeds, wikis, and social networking software which allow users to interact, collaborate, share, and construct new knowledge collectively. From an educational standpoint, such technologies allow learners to participate in their own learning and contribute to the learning of others, instead of simply passively receiving information and knowledge from experts and course resources. In effect, learning is more personalized, shared, and participatory.

Chapter 15
Alternative Realities:
Immersive Learning for and with Students

Sue Gregory
University of New England, Australia

Torsten Reiners
University of Hamburg, Germany

Belinda Tynan
University of New England, Australia

ABSTRACT

As students increasingly engage with alternative social networking (or realities) there is a scope for educators to explore whether they pose opportunities for rethinking learning and teaching spaces. The authors argue that there is a requirement to shift away from mapping traditional thinking about what constitutes a learning experience when considering virtual worlds. This chapter draws upon two case studies that have provided two distinctly different learning designs for Logistics students and pre-service teachers. These cases, alongside a comprehensive review of the use of virtual worlds in education will draw out issues and factors which need to be considered when pursuing virtual worlds as learning spaces. Specifically, discussion and recommendations will have a focus on pedagogical, organisational, equity and access, cultural, economic and social factors relevant to the use of virtual worlds in distance education.

INTRODUCTION

Over that last years, the Web changed from a *producer-to-consumer* (Web 1.0) to a *consumer-are-producer* (Web 2.0) philosophy where the social networking became the fundamental concept for new services; see Facebook (2009), LinkedIn (2009) or YouTube (2009). Everyone is able to contribute – e.g. writing blogs, twitter or submit

DOI: 10.4018/978-1-61520-672-8.ch015

new Wikipedia entries to a common knowledge base where information is shared rather than collected in decentralized databases for private usage. Collaboration is lived and information becomes a common good being organized by the crowd. One outcome of this era is the virtual worlds which combine most of the features of the Web 2.0 but within a 3-dimensional space, or as it is generally called, world. In this chapter, we take a look at virtual worlds but focus on learning and teaching in this environment as it provides new and challenging opportunities to rethink the classroom and curriculum design, especially in a distance education context.

Despite critics, virtual worlds are emerging as a technology that cannot be ignored for their possibilities for distance education. This chapter has as a focus on two case studies that are drawn from two distinct disciplinary fields and from two distinctly different organisations. The University of New England is a large distance education university located in a regional setting on the Northern Tablelands of New South Wales, Australia. More than 80% of students are learning by distance and are considered to be off campus. The other, the University of Hamburg, is a large urban University located in Germany which has most of its students learning on-campus.

The authors from these varied contexts will illustrate and provide analysis of student experiences (both as on and off-campus students) of two different uses of virtual worlds. This is important for the substantive discussion of factors which may influence the adoption and success, or otherwise, of the use of virtual worlds as a learning and teaching space. Interview extracts with experts, lecturers and students, constitute further data for critical analysis and are included to show that the 'feel' of immersion is not bound to a physical real world but can be simulated and still result in a realistic purposeful learning experience. The interviews reveal learning and teaching requirements and expectations, which are discussed and reviewed alongside the literature and pedagogical models.

The authors are reporting on their experiences in the use of Second Life, a virtual world established by Linden Lab and acknowledges the range and diversity of alternative virtual realities available. They see that there is transferability of ideas and believe the use of one virtual reality over another may not necessarily impact on the ideas. The idea of virtual worlds or 3D-environments is demonstrated and used in many different

forms in the past. For example in movies like the Star Trek Next Generation-series, which used a Holodeck to project different (real) environments into a restricted space, or simulations for training dangerous situations. Nevertheless, the concept, functionality and design of Second Life can be tracked back to the novel "Snow Crash" (Stephenson, 1994), where people escape the real world (as opposed to virtual world) through a technological device into a Metaverse where they are represented by avatars which are virtual representations of themselves. The Second Life world consists of regions, so called islands with 65536 sqm each, which can be designed by their inhabitants without any limitation and used for all purposes like building new homes, businesses (N.N., 2008), educational institutions (SimTeach, 2008), recreation areas, museums (Second Life Wikia, 2008), historical places, governments and embassies like Sweden, Estonia or U.S., or fantasy locations; see also (Second Life Grid, 2008; Second Life Wiki, 2008; Tapley, 2007). The virtual world of Second Life that was used for these projects has been created by the users for the users (Linden Research, 2008b). As at November 2008 there were over 16 million registered users, in a one week period there were over 580,000 members logged in with approximately 60,000 users online at the one time. In relation to educational institutions using Second Life, there are variations with the literature:

- More than 250 universities were using Second Life as an educational tool (Calonge, 2007)
- Over 100 virtual lands currently being used by educational institutions around the world with the majority of University campuses based in the United States (Linden Research, 2007a)
- John Lester, the Academic Program Manger at Linden Lab, states "there are more like 1,000 educational institutions

using Second Life, although it is difficult to actually state accurately" (Conversation with Pathfinder Linden).

Tyke McMillan and Jass Easterman (the author's teacher avatars: Torsten Reiners, Sue Gregory), who facilitate learning experiences within Second Life for students in Information Science (University of Hamburg) and Education (University of New England) for 18 months and 6 months respectively. Tyke and Jass have developed distinct learning strategies for their students that reflect the different disciplinary requirements.

This chapter proceeds to tell the stories of Tyke and Jass, explaining why Second Life was chosen by the two institutions and draws upon relevant literature. The following section presents a brief overview of virtual worlds and provides a basic background for the reader to follow the later scenarios. Section *Virtual worlds and mediating distance learning* introduces the main subject of the chapter by explaining distance learning using examples in Second Life in addition to the given definition in the beginning. The examples are followed by the main contribution, the outline of the two scenarios at the University of New England and University of Hamburg. For both examples, a short background as well as the course experiences are shown, including the current and future intention how to continue from the described outlines. The chapter continues with a discussion on important subjects to consider if being active in virtual worlds: pedagogy of using Second Life, the organisations involved, equity, access, cultural, economic and social issues of students. The paper concludes with an outlook and references.

DEFINING VIRTUAL WORLDS

There are over 70 virtual worlds currently being used by educational institutions around the world. However, the ongoing creation of new worlds for all genres and age groups this number will no doubt increase (Johnson, 2008). Even though some have been available for over ten years, the more popular Second Life has only been available to the public since 2003. Compared to most other worlds, Second Life allows the highest degree of freedom such that members can principally inhabit and build their own 3D world (Linden Research, 2008b) and is therefore the choice of most universities (Jennings & Collins, 2008). Although the story of Second Life includes up and downs, its wide media coverage and discussion in all societies initiated a new era of social environments with a continuously growing number of new virtual worlds opening on a regular basis.

Before we continue, we should have a short discussion about how virtual worlds can be distinguished by their features and the kind of user community; see (Wikipedia, 2009) for a list of classification criteria as well as (Slater, 2004). The largest, and probably most successful kinds in terms of revenue, are the MMORPGs (Massively Multiplayer Online Role Player Game) with Worlds of Warcraft, Everquest, or Star Wars Galaxies. Variations depend on the focus, eg MMOFPS (first person shooter), MMOR (racing), or MMOSG (sports, strategy, social). Linden Lab argues that Second Life is similar to MMO with respect to display and interface and is generally seen as a MMOSG: Creativity, as everything is user generated, ownership, as everything is owned by the creator, fees, not for access but land, and unlimited choices how to behave, what to do and what to become; (Second Life FAQ, 2008). Further classifications are MUVE (*multi-user virtual environment*) and SCMUVE (*social and collaborative*) define the major components of Second Life and similar virtual worlds. Note that despite game-like immersion the term *game* is still not appropriate for SCMUVE due to several criteria like overall goal, bonus like character improvements and classification mechanisms for the main character are missing and there is no real competition in terms of high scores and rules. Virtual worlds might have "game-like immersion and social media functionality", they lack "game-like goals or rules" (Constable, 2007).

It appears that those aged around 20 are engaged with virtual worlds of various types. The classification by (KZERO, 2008) shows that there is a clear focus on age groups below 20 and focus around 20 for socialising and casual gaming. Collins (2008) supports this with statistics from Linden Lab where there is a dramatic increase in users in the 18-20 year age group using Second Life. Even current students in their mid twenties, and therewith in an age group with less interest in virtual worlds according to (KZERO, 2008), join projects in Second Life due to their experiences with social worlds (eg Habbo World, There, Active Worlds and others) or online gaming where they collaborate in teams to compete against other groups (eg, World of Warcraft, Star Wars, Maple Story). Being used to the 3rd dimension and the navigation/interaction through avatars helps them to focus on the exercise while being motivated through the *combination of learning and (private) entertaining* (Remark by Student, 2008). As discussed below, the technology is less a barrier than accelerator for students new to virtual worlds, especially as the projection on the avatar helps on the immersive atmosphere as well faster integration in the virtual team and the media (Lamont, 2007).

With respect to higher education, most of these worlds are of little interest to educators as they provide rather limited opportunities for integration in the curriculum. Nonetheless, the variety and the number of participants with up to 100 million (eg, Habbo World in 2008) requires observation and analysis of developments as the next generations, according to Prensky (2008) and Driver (2008), are engaging with technologies that could impact on how we go about facilitating learning. The next generation, the so-called *digital natives* (Prensky, 2001) are close to the age where they enter university programs. They have a high computer literacy (Myers, 1989) and expect the same from

their teachers. Therefore, it is important to understand the potential of the environments where the next student is self-confident and knows how to navigate and interact. The lecturer needs to take a step towards the students to pick them up for the next learning experience; either in the classroom or the virtual world. It is not important where but how and with what kind of existing knowledge, behaviour, and understanding for inclusion in the next classroom or even curriculum. Therefore, the lecturer has to learn now about virtual worlds.

Virtual Worlds and Mediating Distance Learning

Virtual world's can reduce the isolation that students feel when studying at a distance. It is possible for students in virtual world's to feel as if they are present in a real classroom talking to people as if they were actually standing next to them. In a virtual environment, the only thing students do not get if they were actually with someone are cues relating to body language, but most importantly facial expressions.

Distance learners often express loneliness and mostly choose to study this way due to obligations of work and family lives and would prefer regular face to face instruction (Ostlund, 2008). Students feel they miss collaboration and social activities with others. Distance education can be supported by many technologies, however, according to Belanger & Jordan (2000) some provide almost no interaction of communication between the learner and the instructor, and might even camouflage the size of lectures to the students. Communication technologies make it possible to store, transfer and share information across vast distances and different time zones. Students have the opportunity to engage and immerse in content through the use of a virtual environment (Marshall, 2008). Online communications reduce the distance between people. Online communications through virtual worlds incorporate text, voice and shared experiences making communications much richer (NMC White Paper, 2007). Interactions happen more quickly than they might otherwise.

A rich and dynamic experience asks for a synchronous lecture with all participants being online at the same time period. This might not be given with respect to international classes and, therefore, numerous time zones. Virtual worlds also provide communication channels and documentation possibilities that improve the synchronous and asynchronous collaboration and teaching, whereas the focus in this chapter should be viewed as learning activities with all students being online at the same time and at the same location in the virtual world.

Over the years distance education has moved from print-based correspondence materials towards increased web mediated and frequently blended learning experiences. In addition, teachers have moved from delivering information with limited interaction to more social constructivist online interactive learning experiences. In contrast, virtual spaces offer distance education students alternative opportunities for collaboration with their peers, and immersion in rich, visually interactive and diverse learning experiences (Marshall, 2008), which are controllable, recordable and safe.

The learning experiences of our current generations of distance education students are varied with a range of hybrid and blended models being adopted. The prevalent online options are via use of Learning Management Systems serving up HTML-pages, (enhanced) pod- and vodcasts, wikis, blogs, and various Web 2.0 services (Gregory & Smith, 2008b). These options could be viewed as technology islands, providing multi-media learning cameos rather than complete and controlled and recordable experiences. While the mix of content and media allows students to see and hear their online materials (cognitive domain), it is more difficult for students to 'feel' (affective domain) and thereby achieve a balance of educational objectives. Virtual worlds can provide experi-

ences where students could *feel* like they are in a workshop, tour, or meeting without having to leave their home and thus, for many, mediate distance. There is already evidence to suggest that virtual simulations can create a 'sense' or 'feel' of what it would be like. Students have already indicated "this is great ... love the change almost like face to face with lecturer" (Gregory, 2008). Another student states "I know I keep saying it, but I am absolutely loving this course.:) And not just SL: the entire unit is so well presented - for instance, I have heard your voice! It helps avoid the feeling of isolation so many of us externals feel and the way in which the information is delivered makes it so easy to learn. Thanks!" (Gregory, 2008).

Furthermore, virtual worlds are increasingly being used for simulation (Ramondt, 2008; Addison & O'Hare, 2008; Ryan, 2008; Toro-Troconis et al., 2008), whereas we need to distinguish the one that is generally done in virtual worlds and the one being done with specialized software. The first one is generally running in real time, involves human interaction and does not guarantee 100% accuracy in terms of physical influences. Other simulation might be in real time, but involve large computational power to map all physical properties (wind channel), mechanical devices (flight simulator) and humans participating in the experiment (pilot). Furthermore, pure mathematical or process simulation can run faster to simulate large time frames as well as be repeated for different influence factors. An example where almost all technologies are used is in the area of racing. Racing drivers learn the track by playing console games, while the car is first tested in wind tunnels before driven on test tracks. Note, that especially simulation using realistic models require vast financial resources, whereas virtual worlds compensate this through simplification.

Just imagine an experience were students could feel like they are in a workshop, tour, meeting without having to leave their home. Imagine engaging in an activity where you are talking to someone, collaborating with that person to enhance the learning experience, undertaking an activity that you just couldn't do because of distance, expense, time, danger or difficulty, from your own home. Imagine students becoming so immersed in the learning environment that they always want to attend and loose track of time. Imagine being able to hold a class where you could take into consideration anything that you desired: chemicals, building, tours, excursions, engineering, large construction, land transformation, intricate operations, patients available to demonstrate various medical procedures (Gregory & Smith, 2008a) and all students were totally engaged that they turned up for class, participate and have fun! These are all possible within a (social) virtual environment. According to (Barnes & Tynan, 2007) students would prefer to not attend lectures if there are alternative engaging online sources offered. However, some eLearning platforms are mostly text based, not interactive and made available without sufficient testing, whereas the alternatives are required to be interactive, motivating and pedagogically adequate (Darbyshire, 2005). Note that this observation might contradict with the idea of an ideal student who is attending the classroom session and participates in the activities. Unfortunately, attendance is not always possible due to manifold reasons: eg, illness, family, internship, or time to reach the classroom due to distance or means of transport. Second Life provides a means of education, particularly for those who wish to experience the feelings of 'being there' but aren't able to attend (distance students), and may be more engaging and interactive for the students as an alternative to lectures (internal students). Nevertheless, there are also students who would prefer to stay away from the classroom if there is an adequate choice (covering all learning materials including the parts from the lecture). This can be the comfort of home (learning on the couch while being online in video-conferences or being in a virtual world following the lecture on virtual slides) or, in case of recordings or instalments of learning units, the independence of time and place

of where, when and what to learn. In conclusion, virtual worlds are actually an advantage to reach out for students who would like to stay away from the classroom and still achieve a (virtual) social group or network of all participants. But it is also important that the lecturer is observing the learning progress of all students and intervenes in case of absence or little participation.

Cisco Systems Inc is a large hardware technology manufacture who train remote staff based in Asia pacific region (Collins, 2008) in Second Life. "The sale staff could be working from home but the virtual world enables individuals to see the hardware and the engineer walks them through the 3D hardware at the same time. What happens after the event is important. When finished, participants mingle with others in the audience, which is extremely powerful. Microsoft frequently holds conferences in Second Life, find it very cost effective and there is a lot of interaction after conference presentations". NASA has created an environment for astronauts to practice piloting rockets where atmospheric and other real life situations are incorporated into the training without the expense (Gregory & Smith, 2008b). These examples demonstrate how Second Life can be used as just a meeting place, a place to demonstrate experiments that are not possible, too expensive or dangerous to undertake in real life or to use as a training base, recreating real life and enabling people to come together that could not typically do so due to time, distance and cost constraints.

Charles Nesson from Harvard Law held mock trials in Second Life and found that the sessions ran smoothly through text chat because the participants were more concise with their arguments as opposed to session in a real classroom where the participants tended to speak too long (Constance, 2007). Zagami (2008) also found that the virtual world was an effective environment where students work collaboratively and produced more creative responses when working this way. The Australian newspaper conducted a study from

2002 to 2007 tracking 250 graduate students taking 16 courses, some within the virtual world and some not. It concluded that students using the virtual world developed rapport and stayed interested longer and debated subjects more deeply (MCT, 2008). In Gee (2003), the influence of (serious) games is discussed, especially in identifying with the game character and using the virtual experience to become interested in the subject and doing additional reading in external material. The gaming environment incorporate components with relevance for real-world situation, where the cognitive learning process is embedded in highly motivational settings where the human and the fictional player *melt* as all interactions directly transfer to the game (Clark, 2003).

According to Ondrejka (2007) the features of Second Life enable the emergence of different approaches to education and engage traditional, large-scale educational institutions. He states that residents are approaching learning with a passion and excitement they may not have possessed in school. Bowers (2008) also states his studies supported the notion that educators would use a virtual world again to conduct their classes and its success was due to its immersive environment and the engagement of the users. Lagorio (2007) prefers classes to be discussions and "things pop up in a less linear fashion (in Second Life) than they do in a regular classroom". She finds that students hold after-class discussions about their courses when in Second Life. Ball State University English studies offer students the option of using a virtual world for their learning environment (Robbins, 2007). At their last intake, Spring 2008, there were over 300 student applications and it has been found a very successful and popular environment for learning (Koch, 2007). Koch (2007) quotes Robbins, "in a 20 minute class there is about 20 pages of dialogue … we have great discussions that extend beyond what we'd be able to do in a traditional classroom". However, Brown & Bell (2004) disagree with this notion by stating that

the chat feature of a virtual world can often be out of sequence.

According to Robbins (2007), Second Life is being used in Higher Education in a variety of disciplines, almost any that one can think of. The environment has been established for those who wish to use it. All it requires is a clear understanding, structure and imagination as to how it will be utilised. Kovela (2008) states that the potential uses of a virtual world could include social interaction, collaboration, creative construction, raising awareness, information resource, data visualisation, simple simulation and a teaching and learning environment. When using a virtual world such as Second Life, the educator should have a clear idea of what they wish to achieve for their students, such as the learning outcomes of the course, to make the environment and activities within the environment more meaningful for their students.

To illustrate this independence of place in virtual worlds, we describe use-cases based on classes presented by Tyke and Jass respectively. However, before we describe the course outline in detail, we should have a look at the general classroom design as these demonstrate two variations with their individual pros and cons. Tyke uses the island *University of Hamburg,* which houses the real University with its main building and several areas for projects; see Figure 1 for some impressions of the island. The realistic design for some buildings (1) was chosen as a contrast to the imaginary projects we expected by the students in the surrounding areas, eg the bottle-shaped factory (6) or floating buildings (4) for the role play experiment. Even though the University of Hamburg initially intended not to transfer or project their classes into an exact virtual replica without any further adaptations, we finally agreed on an exact copy of the main building façade including some inner specifics like the most known lecture hall. The latter one was necessary to simplify the announcement of

Figure 1. Impression of the University of Hamburg and its projects: (1) main building and welcome area, (2) aerial view of the island, (3) (4) main classroom and meeting point for classes, (5) sandbox for students, and (6) bottle factory for production process demonstration

classes in the university calendar allowing student to find the real and virtual place (3). As shown in the Scenario 2 below, the classroom is also used to merge the virtual and real world by providing corresponding views allowing the students to choose their preferred environment while not being left out of the (social) integration. The sandbox (5) allows students to experiment with the building process and provide room for the first objects. The factory (6) started in such a box and was later transferred to a reserved area. Other projects and technologies on the University of Hamburg are described below; see also (Burmester et. al,

2008; Reiners and Voß, 2008; Wriedt et. al, 2008, Dreher et al. (2009b).

Meanwhile, Jass created a meeting place, *Education Online Headquarters,* which is used to meet before and after visiting other locations within the virtual world. This ensured that when a lesson was being conducted, the students knew where they have to meet. *Education Online Headquarters* (Figure 2) is a two storey area, traditional indoor area with lounges and coffee tables and a conference style setting in the corner or an outdoor area with picnic benches, log fires, wooden bridge over stream and cushions to sit on. The following

Scenario 1 describes her class and the impressions from the participating students.

SCENARIO 1: JASS EASTERMAN – DISCUSSION GROUPS AND VIRTUAL LECTURES

In comparison to real life, their physical body was allowed to be at any place as long as their avatar appears and is tracked. The first example is a lecture where international experts were invited as guest lecturers who did the teaching without spending any expenses. Beforehand, a designer supported the speaker to setup a look-alike avatar so that students notice and remember the person as well as gadgets to be used for demonstration. Communication was done using a designated chat being monitored by a moderator and either used for immediate questions or later discussions. There was the option of using voice, however it was not necessary and students would require the necessary hardware and know how to use it. It is also higher on bandwidth. However, voice/audio was used on some occasions when required, particularly for demonstrations and performances by the students.

Students enrolled in two technology education units were given the opportunity to participate in virtual world sessions with Jass to assist in the completion of an assessment task. On average there were 6.5 students (out of a possible 12) in attendance on each evening with two guests (this could be educators, student's supervisors and interested people). The evenings were scheduled to be conducted from 7.00 pm to 9.00 pm. Students arrived, on average, 11 minutes prior to the scheduled starting time and left 36 minutes after the scheduled finish time, with sometimes leaving over an hour later. This could be because they were immersed in what was happening or the guest lecturer was still speaking. Jass wasn't able to attend for the full time on two occasions. However, she

placed her avatar inworld to record dialogue. It was found that these non-compulsory sessions drew the students inworld even when there weren't tasks given or lectures to attend. On the first occasion, the dialogue between students began at the normal scheduled start time and concluded 26 minutes after the scheduled finish meeting time. All students within the two units of study received grades of Distinction or High Distinction for their assessment tasks. External markers, not the lecturer, marked these.

All students were informed of and approved the data collection methods prior to commencement. The protocol was also distributed to all participants for later review of the class and preparation for the final assessment task. The protocol was anonymized for all other application, eg, evaluation, reports, or citation in publications. Note, that the usage of avatars even allows hiding any ethical or cultural backgrounds within a class as the true identity must not be revealed to other students. The teacher needs to know more information with respect to authentification and later grading of the course work. Using the chat, even the accent in the voice is masked.

Students in these units attended the meeting place created for these sessions for discussion in the first hour of the scheduled meetings (Education Online Headquarters). The second hour was spent visiting educational institutions in Second Life around the world to hear or see what guest lecturers were doing with their student in the virtual world. This model of workshops was devised after the first session when it became apparent that those participating were studying many different disciplines and therefore it would have been difficult to teach them something specific. These students were studying to become primary, secondary school, or higher education teachers. This meant that their Key Learning Area (KLA) could have been anything from English, Science, Mathematics, Religion, Information Technology, History, Geography, Art, Music, Drama, Economics, etc. And, they were.

Figure 2. (1) Education Online Headquarters; (2) University of Hamburg; (3) St Joseph's College; (4) Griffith University; (5) Disabilities Unit, University of Torino; (6) MacBeth, University of Sydney; (7) Deakin University; (8) Student Performance with voice, dance, lighting – Education Online Headquarters

From week to week, students went to many different universities or schools to listen to the guest educators. They were also given a document with various locations that they could visit according to their particular KLA. These included places such as Vassar which houses a duplicate of the Sistine Chapel, complete with Michael Angelo artwork, the Louvre with its famous glass pyramid roof with artworks such as Leonardo de Vince and Rembrandt or International Space Flight Museum where rockets that have been used in training NASA astronauts are housed, Star Trek Museum to see memorabilia from the television series, or go to a live performance of Shakespeare. They could also visit great icons of the world such as The Great Wall of China, Uluru, Eiffel Tower, London Bridge or the Grand Canyon. Students were able to visit the places of interest on two separate evenings or on other occasions that they were able to do so in their own time. To take students to these locations in reality would be unrealistic, costly and impossible. This was possible in a virtual environment. As one student commented "In a strange way I think exploring a virtual world can actually make that world more real than say looking at pictures or reading texts or even viewing a video" (Gregory, 2008). These students were exploring the possibility of using a virtual world in their future teaching. Learning objectives of their studies were to integrate social computing technologies as tools for learning in an educational setting; strategies for using information from electronic media; and the educational use of software. They were able to achieve these objectives in their Second Life sessions.

Towards the end of the semester, students were to give a short presentation on how they would use Second Life in their future teaching. The group insisted that a stage be created for these presentations. This was an opportunity to teach students some basic building skills so a stage could be created to present their learnings. As talent was found amongst the participants, they also demonstrated these. One student performed by singing, using audio, lighting and dance and was viewed by a very appreciative audience of fellow students and invited guests. Dance is Second Life is scripted and, this particular student, demonstrated skills in enabling her avatar to undertake several dance routines, change the lighting using "particle effects" and sing accompanied by the keyboard through the audio features. Another demonstrated how they had manipulated script to enable a butterfly to move in a pattern around their avatar. Another showed how they could use Dragon Naturally Speaking to speak the text that was written, instead of typing, for others to read. Another discussed how they would use the Shakespeare environment for her students in English. "I will take my... students to the Globe Theatre in-world to experience one of Shakespeare's plays in its correct environment. Along the way I plan on providing my students with several activities that will encourage them to explore and create ideas of their own" (Gregory, 2008).

Some reactions to the workshops from different students (Gregory, 2008):

- "I had my first visit to 2nd life on Wed and it was a blast. I can see the students engaged in this environment and developing understanding in life skills and applying these to real life."
- "Well, had another interesting session in second life last night. It all seems to be coming together as our understanding and control increases. Other students have some useful ideas and have been very creative with their outfits and abilities... I think that this tool has great potential for use in schools once it has been developed to cater for the security issues that will arise. At first I did not see the use for English in particular but have since changed my viewpoint and now feel that it would be a great learning tool for students. It has the capacity to be individualised for every class and teacher and therefore will become essential in the future."
- "I love these discussions Jass! I am going to miss them."
- The weekly sessions … "they are the highlight of my degree"
- "It has been one of the highlights of my entire uni life! (This is my 7th year of uni.... and only performing in operas has been better)"

Below are some images of the excursions that took place in the student workshop – the first image being Education Online Headquarters where students met each week prior to venturing off to their lecture. The following are where students went to attend inworld lectures in Second Life with guest lecturers from around the world.

SCENARIO 2: PRODUCTION AND LOGISTICS IN VIRTUAL WORLDS – CLASS AND PROJECT

The second scenario is placed in the area of production and logistics, and reveals how integrated blended learning can be offered in a real class-

Figure 3. The setting for the blended learning experience

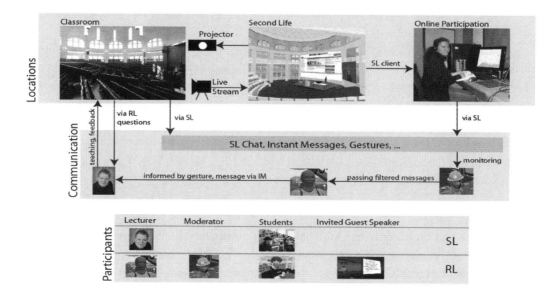

room while students also participate alongside the lecturer in the virtual world. The learning design had a focus on both the real and virtual world. While the virtual world was used to create students' own understandings of logistic operations, the real classroom was used for presenting the traditional learning material like slides and videos covering the basic theory in this field. Nevertheless, all content was also projected into Second Life including a live stream of information from the real world so that students could follow the lecture by attending with their individual avatars. The effect of immersion was enhanced as the live stream provided a window to the physical world. Communication was handled through audio and chats, whereas questions needed to be sent as a chat message to a designated avatar in the role of a moderator, who preselected questions and remarks for the lecturer, who is then being informed by signals, for example, a raised hand of the designated avatar. The setting is outlined in Figure 3.

With respect to the students' experiences with Second Life, the first (optional) session was given in the real-world classroom to introduce the tech-

nology and the procedure for the semester. For the following mandatory sessions, the students could decide if they participate in the classroom or join from any other location via the Second Life client. In addition, Second Life was the main teaching platform as experts and practitioners were invited to demonstrate their logistic operations by meeting at factories, companies or universities within the virtual world. Whereas this causes problems with travelling and financing in the real world, it is more or less *one click* to teleport students to new learning spaces. Here, we experiment with different approaches, whereas Tyke intended to involve the students as much as possible and demonstrated different types of Second Life installations. As mentioned above, Second Life allows a high degree of freedom in design and logic, so that the installations can either be closely related to the real world in terms of processes or design, or use the technology to send out a specific message. In this specific lecture, we visited four locations (Erlenkötter, 2008):

1) **Funny-frisch**: Snack producer who designed the factory and the processes as they are in

reality. This includes planting and harvesting the potatoes on a field, to cleaning, cutting, roasting, flavouring, packing and testing the final product. At each step, the process and product are detailed and explained focusing on the quality aspect and transparency of the product and its ingredients.

2) **Ben and Jerry's:** The ice cream producer targets an audience that is interested in the production process but does not miss on the entertainment part. Before even entering the factory, each visitor can start a game, where cow droppings have to be collected for Linden Dollars and then reused for producing energy and fertilizer. Within the factory, all processes are shown as they occur in the real world, whereas the presentation is exaggerated in terms of having huge comics on the wall and simplified machines that reminds the visitor rather of a walk-in cartoon than a factory.

3) **Fiat:** The car manufacturer concentrates in the demonstration of its Brazilian factory on the environmental aspect. The factory is filled with green areas, trees and clouds. The whole area is covered with trees and other plants. The production process itself is belittled in a way that the focus is set on the process rather than the car. For example, the tires are cut by a huge knife from a sushi-rubber-role, the tires are added in a pit stop style and the final inspection is done under a microscope.

4) **Double Happiness:** The original Double Happiness manufacture is an artist's studio at Eyebeam New York City, where the Second Life factory is fully integrated in the production process of jeans (Hafner, 2008). The main concept behind this setting is about visualizing the concept of sweatshops and its problems for all involved roles – a sweatshop is a working environment with very difficult or dangerous conditions, usually where the workers have few rights or ways to address

their situation. The look is very realistic and includes avatars to actually operate the machines in Second Life for a very small salary an hour of around 90 cents.

The feedback of the students was ambiguous. Besides the fact that it was a new way of learning for them, they liked the freedom to choose from which location they participated without the feeling of being excluded from the class. This was intensified by a *window* to the classroom through the live stream. Nevertheless, the doubts about the usability for the field of production and logistics and if it is a current hype that will disappear over the next years was used to have intensive (mixed world) discussions that are unlikely to happen if the presentation was only done by slides and no further hand-on experiences.

Compared to many other reports where students complain about the technological barrier, we did not have too many complaints. In contrast to the other scenario, most students in Germany have a flat-rate without any quota on the monthly data downloads and a rather large bandwidth up to 16MBit/s. Most of the data transfer resulted from the live stream rather than Second Life and can therefore be compared to video conferencing. Some students did not have an advanced graphic card and had to limit the resolution on their client. Nevertheless, they did not seem to care about this as the content was far more relevant to them than the degree of details like shadows or anti-aliasing. Furthermore, no student was left behind due to their equipment as they could participate in one or the other way: (1) joining the class in a computer lab with well-equipped computers or (2) limiting their experience to the video stream which did cover all content but the participation.

In summary, the students learned about virtual worlds, their usage with focus on production and logistics as well as gained insight of some uses cases. In contrast to a traditional class with frontal presentations, all students participated through an avatar and had the opportunity to visit several location, interview international experts and experience how new installation can be constructed. The general feedback conducted by an anonymous questionnaire showed that more than 80% grade the experience with an A or B and only 12% with a C or D. For the worse grades, the student provided a comment that the grade results from some technical problems at their place with respect to the live stream codec (Second Life was working) and the rather practical than theoretical concept. The later critics are considered for the next class, where Second Life is used as before but the number of visited locations is reduced to have a better coverage about virtual worlds and their advantages/disadvantages in real world scenarios. Other comments in the questionnaire are about the flexibility in how to join the classroom, the invited guest speaker and the *courage* to try new technologies to improve the teaching at the university. Even though most students came to the classroom (overall 65% each session), the experience from home was rated B or better as they had the option to ask question, participate in the excursions and communicate with other students. The communication was very well accepted as they could have private chats not being visible to others. From the perspective of the lecturer, it might be better if students focus 100% on the class; on the other hand, this form of communication is at least not interrupting the class and students pay attention whenever they waited for an answer and came to class despite the option to just meet somewhere else (note that participation was not mandatory to pass). Inviting guest speaker was rated A by all students, besides some comments related to the English language and problems with the accents. In general, we try to have invited guest speakers from other universities or companies in the classroom to provide some insight in real world scenarios, but are limited to local guest due to expenses. With Second Life, it took not more than 30 minutes in communicating the technical details and starting Second Life on the computer of the invited guest speaker. Further-

more, the guests liked this as they did not need to travel but could talk from their office.

The following project is only related to the class as the participating students choose Second Life for their implementation based on their experiences. The project is discussed in more details in Erlenkötter (2008) and described here as it proceeds with the subject from the class. In Hamburg, Information System students have to work on a larger (team) project for 4-6 months, where they have to design and implement a software application while learning about teamwork and collaboration. Instead of providing all details, the assignment was only one sentence (*Use Second Life to demonstrate a production process*) and three milestones: (1) present the project idea and the tasks to achieve these, (2) decide on a possible dissemination channel and (3) implement the production process. The students created a list of ideas, but settled on a production line for soda drinks being bottled and shipped in cases of six bottles each. The decision process was accompanied by contacting several companies to provide input details or even sponsorship, but as expected, without success. Nevertheless, the project was realized within five months and fulfilled the expectations by far. Besides presenting a complete implementation instead of the required prototype, they also paid attention to small details and experimental functionality like small games for an interactive experience. With respect to the dissemination, the students decided on a conference publication (Erlenkötter, 2008) as well as draw the attention of newsagency to the project resulting in full page coverage in a nation-wide newspaper. The outcome of the project is shown in Figure 4.

A later analysis and discussion about the project development showed that the students got most of their motivation from the media itself. Main arguments used by the students are the collaboration as they generally worked from their own computer at home and the immediate visibility of results. In addition, several avatars from all over

Figure 4. Different views of the bottle factory

the world visited their building site and asked questions about the project, which showed the students the relevance of the project. They also admit that it was only possible due to the features in Second Life and that other virtual worlds would probably cause more work in terms of learning the basics and of implementing the production line. None of the students had experience with the script language but managed to get the first implementations after short learning period of just a few days. The project will be continued in two ways: (1) having further student projects that add more features, eg material ordering, sequencing of orders, or integration in a supply chain, and (2) finding sponsors that support the idea and provide the funding to continue the implementation.

PEDAGOGY

The pedagogy around how virtual worlds are used is important. The environment has demonstrated that it can be engaging for students. It appears that where educators choose teaching strategies that can assist students in constructing knowledge that students feel motivated and that their learning is purposeful. The use of a virtual world was

considered in great detail before embarking on its use. Each institution had to decide whether a virtual world could be used as a sound educational tool and be implemented in a pedagogical manner. Virtual worlds support constructivist pedagogy where students use technology to explore and reach an understanding of concepts where they are encouraged to explore and test. Second Life has been created to encourage users to explore and test and educators have the opportunity of using this resource as an enhancement to the pedagogy they already use or as an alternative. When an educator uses Second Life as an educational tool, they are using a "full and diverse range of pedagogic approaches" (Hollins & Robbins, 2008).

The Quality Teaching Framework (NSW Department of Education and Training, 2004), Australia, state that the common traits of good teaching are three-dimensional:

- Teachers construct a learning environment with a high level of intellectual quality
- Teachers make lessons relevant or significant
- Teachers construct a classroom that has a quality learning environment

Intellectual quality builds from a recognition that high quality student outcomes result if learning is focused on intellectual work that is challenging, centred on significant concepts and ideas and requires substantial cognitive and academic engagement with deep knowledge. This is supported by Bloom's Digital Taxonomy (Vieyra, 2006) where the use of a virtual world builds on concepts starting with the lower order thinking skills of remembering, understanding and applying on a continuum to the higher order thinking skills of analyzing, evaluating and creating. When using a virtual world, the users have to firstly learn how to use the environment, as they become more familiar, they are able to undertake other tasks such as learning how to use the environment to support their teaching.

Learning is improved when learning environments provide high level support for learning, such as when educators support their students in a virtual world by teaching them how to operate in the environment and the various protocols for using the environment, creating a quality learning environment. It needs to be a positive, caring, safe and supportive environment, both for the educators and students. Students need to see why, and understand that, their learning matters so that they can see how the virtual world could be significant to their future teaching.

Digital media has had a significant influence on students using a pedagogy that incorporates ambiguity, learning and affect (Carr et al., 2008). Virtual worlds such as Second Life assist their educational needs using methods they can identify with. The pedagogy of educators will vary depending on their level of experience with a virtual world. When viewing any educator that has been using a virtual world for a while, you will be privileged to watch a highly interactive, educational and engaging lesson.

Ryan (2008) describes sixteen pedagogical applications of Second Life. Visualization was used in both scenarios outlined above. In Scenario 1, Jass had students visualizing how they would use the virtual world in their future teaching by offering them a wide range of experiences and in Scenario 2, Tyke required students to visualize how they could set up a bottle factory in Second Life the same as they would in a real situation. Both scenarios used an Interactive Library of virtual resources to create learning environments that balanced technology and good teaching. Students attending sessions in Scenario 1 were both face to face and distance students. The lecturers and students were able to connect but were not in the same physical location. They were situated in various locations around the world. Both scenarios demonstrated the use of sending messages, inventory items or notes via Second Life to students synchronously and asynchronously, so that they would receives these notices when next they logged on. Scenario 2 demonstrated some excellent forms of role-playing, whilst the students in Scenario 1 watched role play being undertaken by others (performances).

An important aspect of Scenario 2 was where students were given the opportunity to test hypotheses through trial and error, although students did this to a certain degree when first learning to use Second Life. Scenario 2 also demonstrated the use of games for learning for students.

Scenario 1 demonstrated Ryan's pedagogical application of soft skill development where the pedagogy is not task-oriented; the virtual world was the "method for practicing the desired skills". This Scenario used a variety of skills such as "critical thinking, problem solving, team building and collaboration" (Ryan, 2008). Jass and Tyke used the virtual world of Second Life for students to research by enabling students to "explore, question and contemplate course material". As Ryan points out, this enabled students to transfer what is learned in the virtual world to a different context.

Again, both scenarios took students on virtual field trips that would not be possible due to a variety of constraints in the real world. Scenario 1 used tours as part of the learning for students so that they could experience a variety of uses of Second

Life in their future teaching. As stated, students stayed over time in the environment because they were engaged, having fun and learning.

As Second Life is a social space, many social activities were undertaken. The format of Scenario 1 was so students could use the environment as a social and learning environment. Scenario 2 found that when some students were in Second Life they were more communicative than when they were in a face to face learning environment.

In Scenario 1, none of the students knew who the other students were in real life. This enabled them to create anonymity if they wished. All students were aware of who all the educators were and Jass knew who all the students were, however the guest lecturers did not know who the students were. This enabled students to be honest and in some cases, take away shy personalities that face to face situations can create for some.

On one virtual lecture in Scenario 1, a guest lecturer discussed how they used machinima with their students, which is the capture of video in Second Life (recording of Second Life role play). Another application of Ryan is recruitment and both institutions had to recruit the support of their institution to embark on this different way of teaching and learning. Ryan also points out that students are under more pressure to increase their expectations when their work is put on display and this is what happened in Scenario 2. These students worked together in given timeframes strove to perform perhaps more than they would have in a face to face situation. Virtual Worlds such as Second Life provide a platform for learning by using building techniques "applying learning by doing". Finally, Ryan's last pedagogical application is virtual action learning, where students learn by "enabling, interaction and collaborative technologies". Both scenarios had students involved in the decision making process. Scenario 2 had students create their bottle factory by utilizing inquiry, action and reflection. Scenario 1 was an open ended learning environment and evolved from student input and academic requirements.

Organisation

Of course, with any venture like this, support and commitment must be sort from the educational institution so that they are able to set up the technical access for educators and students. The University of New England in Armidale, Australia, supported Jass and the University of Hamburg in Germany supported Tyke.

Equity

Students who have the opportunity and availability to use a virtual world are perceived to be 'luckier' than others. Therefore, using a virtual world is not equitable. There are issues involved with access that prohibit some users in being able to participate in a virtual world when they wish to do so. As noted, in some institutions there have been far more applicants than positions available to use Second Life for their studies. The fortunate students that are selected to engage with the environment and educator experience a different learning to the other students. In the scenarios outlined, the use of Second Life was totally voluntary and all students who wished to become involved were able to do so. As the desire to use a virtual world for their studies increases, this may not be the case. Also, as technology improves, all students who would like to use the available technology should be able to do so.

The equity issue is not something that is examined here but the educators are aware of its presence. To date, they have ensured there is not an equity issue with their students, however, this will change as students become more aware of its availability, enjoyment, engagement and different way to learn and wish to become involved in this technique of learning. As improvements in technology, accessibility and broadband increase, we should be able to accommodate this increase in student numbers.

Despite the advantages for the students, there is also another issue about the equity that has to be considered in the future. As shown in the Scenario 2 above, some students said that they would prefer the traditional way of teaching and we have to assume that there is always someone who does not *feel* right to have a virtual avatar instead of participating in person. Therefore, we intend to have further research about the interface between the worlds and how we can merge both worlds in a common learning environment, where the students have a true choice according to their preferences but without missing some experiences. We are aware that some features might not be given in the same way (eg building objects or implementing scripts), so that we focus on the socializing component that includes the classroom, group work and collaboration in a distant education setting.

Access

Access to the hardware and software has been a challenge for some students making it impossible for them to participate. Besides not being able to access Second Life on campus, others have had to upgrade their computers with RAM and video cards. Others found that they didn't have the required bandwidth and withdrew. This barrier to students should be removed as technology is upgraded to be able to deal with these access difficulties. In Australia in July 2008, research from the University of Sydney reported a new ultrafast optical switch on a chip that could speed up the Australian Internet by more than 6000% (Salleh, 2008). In Germany, most students either have a flat rate or access to equipment at the university, therefore, the students did not have the access problems that we expected before the class started. Nevertheless, Second Life is still a platform with limitations. If it comes to media and in-world Internet access, it was rather challenging to setup the live video stream and support students with getting the correct codec installed on their own computers. The feedback, as described above, was very good, even though some students reported

that they could access Second Life only with a low graphics resolution and limited visibility. But as the focus was on interviews and concepts used in the virtual world, the lower resolution had no disadvantages for the students. There can be problems with the voice chat quality and unexpected failures of the Second Life clients and/ or server. We prepared for this by providing the same live stream also on a different server, but never run into troublesome situations. The voice quality, even including guests from the U.S. and Australia, was similar to the one of Skype and only had short periods where noise influenced the quality, but always clear to understand.

Note, that the speed of technology development is increasing and the prototype/beta status of virtual worlds is finally over, we see fewer problems with accessing the virtual worlds. The software is stable and requires fewer resources (graphics and CPU) such that students will not run into the same problems as described above. In March 2009, we used a netbook (Asus Eepc) to run Second Life and actually build something without problems, even though the graphics quality was set to low. Nevertheless, the hardware and software should be tested and the course design adapted to the resources. With respect to experiences in virtual worlds, we can conclude that the time to learn the interface, to navigate and to start being productive is very low compared to many other software applications. Most of the time, participants felt comfortable with the environment as it is in 3D and therefore comparable to the real world, i.e. as the current students are used to this kind of interface due to media like videos and gaming. Administration is only a small task and requires little work as Second Life is a Web-application and not installed at the institution itself. The major administrative part is the assignment/invitation of avatars to groups and recording of the instant messaging for the protocol.

Cultural

By using a virtual world, cultural barriers are lowered as the avatars are, by default, not indicating a relation to the real user. Most students start to individualize the generic avatar and might integrate indications to their culture or social background. But it is not completely visible to others unless being announce by the user itself. For the described scenarios, we chose to have a relative neutral setting and allowed the students to define their identity themselves. Obviously, we had to decide on the language as a commonality to understand each other, but even here, we could hide some of the origin by using instant messaging in some lectures. Typed test is harder to project on a certain culture than spoken words.

In the two scenarios, it is a requirement of students to be able to speak their native tongue (i.e. German or English) to enrol in their studies. Therefore, all barriers are removed as all students perceive others in the virtual environment to be the same as themselves. A good example of this is in Scenario 1 where students visited locations around the world where the guest lecturer's native tongue wasn't always English; however, this was not a barrier to imparting knowledge. All guests spoke using text to ensure equality of experience as some students weren't able to access sound or use microphones.

The effect of culture, nationality, race and mother tongue with respect to socializing and participating in the virtual world is an interesting aspect for future research. The usage of avatars allows changing your actual body specifics and relations to cultural groups. People with disabilities or certain body attributes can choose to be anyone (or anything) they want and socialize without possible limitations. On the other hand, several experiments in Second Life were conducted with students that participated in a role play where they had to experience every day situation from another perspective: being handicapped in a wheel chair in a non-accessible building, member of a cultural group that is harassed or under influence of drugs. Students describe that the immersive experience in a 3D environment opened their eyes for other situations and that they start to understand the problems being involved with having limitations in the everyday life. University of Hamburg is currently developing a scenario simulator where students can experience controlled mobbing or sexual harassment situations. The idea is that a student is briefed for a scenario (eg a job interview) and either has to select an outfit from a wardrobe or an outfit is randomly assigned. Afterwards, the student teleports into the scene and confronted with a (recorded) voice that might or might not be offensive. The student has a selection of possible answers that can be used as a reaction. Afterwards, the student is teleported to an area where a multiple choice sheet has to be completed. The student has to decide if this was sexual harassment (or mobbing in a different scenario), if the clothing might have influenced the reply and if the avatar was using the right reaction on the offensive behaviour.

A study undertaken at Deakin University in 2007 looked at the culture and cultural differences in the online environment and considers what strategies were effective in teaching a culturally diverse cohort of online students (Goold et al., 2007). They concluded that online learning environments enabled greater numbers of students of diverse educational and cultural backgrounds as well as modes of study to come together within the one virtual classroom. The diversity within a virtual classroom is more likely to be greater than in a physical classroom. In an online environment, many of the clues that enable culturally sensitivity are missing. They conclude that students need better preparation for learning in an online environment, an understanding of diverse communication styles.

Economic

Virtual worlds also provide economic implications educational institutes and the involved students. There are costs implications on the real life campus, the educators and the students. For the students, the cost is limited to the technology required for the access. Generally, students are already equipped with computers capable to use Second Life and other worlds; therefore no further investment is required. On the other hand, the students need access to the Internet with high bandwidth and large amounts of free volumes. Not necessarily for the virtual worlds itself but for the voice and possible video usage during the lecture. In our case, the students were either in distance education and used to video and audio lecture, or it is common for the country to have the unlimited access to Internet resources.

The university might have to invest in the project. The universities would have to reconsider how their campuses are structured. Instead of creating lecture theatres and workshop areas, they may also have to create new computer labs, or alternatively, supply the students with computers for the duration of the studies. As we see it as an additional tool for studying, the need of computer and lecture halls might be the same, whereas the utilization decreases in advantage of more and smaller lectures. In addition, the institute needs to invest in the virtual worlds, which is the cost for the space as well as generating content. But this is comparable to other high quality material and therefore not increasing the cost but shifting the type of content. Other cost factors could be the hosting of virtual worlds in the future, which would require a server as well as administrator.

Meetings could be held in the virtual world where it would enable the best staff to be employed because they wouldn't have to physically be in location on campus. They could be located anywhere worldwide and have real discussions and presentations in the virtual world.

Education institutions could hold conferences in the virtual world and participants wouldn't have to endure the cost of travel, accommodation and time for the travel. They could also be more cost effective by attending a virtual world session and still be working at the same time.

As the virtual world is an environment that has been created to emulate real world physics, experiments could be held without the implications that occur in the real world, such as harming someone, using expensive equipment and using participants that in a real world would not be possible (such as demonstrating surgery without the need for a real patient). Dangerous chemicals could be used to demonstrate an experiment, without harming anyone. Spacecraft created to react with the environment as it does in the real world could be used without the costs of creating the spacecraft, the harm, or loss of life, if the mission was unsuccessful.

Social Factors

We generally argue that virtual worlds are one possibility to tear down barriers and work on a better environment for students, teachers, and every other user. Nevertheless, there is one barrier we like to have for individuals or as part of (social) experiments: no one knows who is controlling the avatar. An example of this was one guest lecturer was profoundly deaf and had difficulty speaking in real life, however, the students were totally unaware of this and he was treated as anyone else was, which may not have been the case in real life, particularly as it would have been difficult to understand him and he couldn't hear people very well. This session was undertaken using text only and was thoroughly enjoyed by the students. One comment from a student was "Virtual Worlds are here to stay; they are already being used in Universities so it is a matter of time before schools are employing the technology. They offer a plethora of opportunities for students with learning problems, disabilities and mainstream students to expand their learning and experience different ways of learning" (Gregory, 2008).

We are aware of the fact, that this is an ideal scenario, but unfortunately, virtual worlds have to handle the same problems as the real world. The social behaviour is unique as it provides other opportunities to, e.g., communicate, bond, or make new enemies. The avatars – and we assume that the personality of the avatar and user must not be necessarily the same – interact with others, group and share information about anything. Avatars will find their role in the group, while others leave or are excluded; see Minocha & Tingle (2008), Grove & Steventon (2008), Hollins & Robbins (2008), Gee (2008) for a deeper discussion on this issue as it will become an important needs to be part of future research. In our classes, social factors were not an issue besides the abovementioned cases as we used a closed environment where only students were invited to join and being asked to behave nicely to each other. Which worked perfectly in our cases as the group was small and friendly to each other. In cooperation with a German agency, we are currently experimenting with ideas that allow detection of misbehaviour in a defined setting. That is, for example, avatars disturb a lecture, try to destroy or modify the work of others or use inadequate language. The detection allows to initiate counter-measurements as communicate about the behaviour or to ban someone. Social behaviour is, similar to the real world, difficult to control in advance, but we take precautions to interfere as soon as possible by being present and keeping close relation to the participants such that any problems are reported and discussed.

FUTURE DIRECTIONS

The web has created new opportunities for the world's population to engage with each other. The explosion of the large scale social construction of knowledge via social computing software, social bookmarking, vast taxonomies and ontologies as in the Open Directory Project and Wikipedia, blogs, wikis and so on, has created engagement that is common in Web 2.0 technology environments. Latest projects are Twitter in Second Life or the integration of in-world information or status of avatars on common web-sites. Virtual worlds, whilst part of the explosion, are relatively unexplored in the education domain, perhaps because they stem from the role playing game phenomenon. When applied in the education field however, virtual environments such as Second Life do provide an emerging alternative for the creation of learning spaces that have the potential to offer students and teachers some exciting new possibilities for achieving educational objectives.

According to Fenn et al. (2008), public opinion regarding Virtual Worlds is currently in a stage that the Gartner Hype Cycle calls the *Trough of Disillusionment*. In contrast Hayes (2009) sees Virtual Worlds as mature for (higher) education and as being located in the upper part of the *Slope of Enlightenment,* and therewith near the *Plateau of Productivity*. Considering the change of acceptance in the research community and the start of numerous projects over the last months, we feel confident to predict that 3D spaces will become an integral part of education (ie in combination and seamless integration with other media and technology, and across a variety of learning paradigms). This expectation is supported by *the Internet community* where the search term *virtual worlds* is raising over the last years; see Figure 5.

Our future (research) influenced is based on the described experiences as well as the trend to bring the virtual and real world closer together. There was an extensive learning stage to identify the opportunities as well as possible scenarios for future integration. The lesson learned is used to define new and promising challenges for teaching and learning. We have several projects (besides the ones describes in the scenarios and the cited references) that explore the interconnectivity between virtual and real space focusing on tech-

Figure 5. Trend of the search volume of virtual worlds; Google Trends (2009)

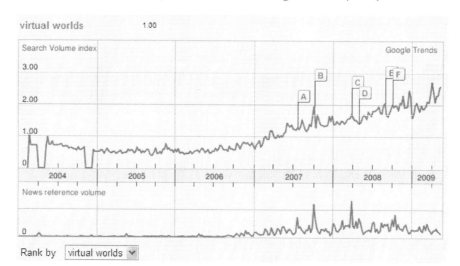

nology to intensify the immersive experience as well as lowering the access barrier even more; see also Dreher et al. (2009b), Dreher et al. (2009c) as well as Reiners et al. (2009) for some thoughts on how to bridge worlds. Note, that Dreher et al. (2009c) also describe how virtual worlds integrate at different learning stages, ie K-12 up to life-long-learning.

Nevertheless, we want to emphasize again, that we see virtual worlds as an integral part of future education, but not THE future, as education in the classroom and eLearning in a traditional LMS will co-exist and even be superior in terms of time being used. All *worlds* will come closer and melt to a new form of education as education always needs to adapt to the expectations and requirements of each individual learner. These learners are from a continuously evolving society with new technology, beliefs, socializing, etc. Educators need to be aware of the changes and have to react on them. Preparation by learning from existing examples will help to know what to do. No case is exactly like the next, so that self-experiments are the key element to be confident in the coming technology, which might not be Second Life but promising approaches like OpenSim, Croquet or Project Wonderland.

We outlined rather positive experiences that demonstrated the advantages of Second Life from our and our student's perspective. We described some drawbacks and risks that are connected to Second Life and being in a virtual world. We did not focus on this as learning in virtual worlds is most of the time very similar to distance learning (in the real world) so that the pros and cons are very comparable, especially considering social and group behaviour as well as pedagogical models; see eg Hollins & Robbins (2008), Carr et al. (2008), Ryan (2008), Minocha & Tingle (2008), Grove & Steventon (2008), Hollins & Robbins (2008), Gee (2008).

CONCLUSION

The virtual world of Second Life has been found to immerse students in the environment so that they have the feeling of actually being in a real life discussion with the educator and fellow students, undertaking tasks as required. This is an emerging technology that is being explored vastly by institutions worldwide and evidence is beginning to emerge to support the statements that this is an immersive, engaging and collaborative environment. Second Life lends itself to education and is an area where much more research should be conducted to identify its strengths, as well as any pitfalls it may have. This chapter has analysed the environment from two lecturer's perspectives and provided an insight, how an alternative way of presenting the learning material can be done if we are open to new media formats. We initiated the courses as an experiment to evaluate 1) the usability, 2) the acceptance of the students, 3) the learning effect 4) the behaviour of the students and 5) the integration of Virtual Worlds as part of courses in general. We found Virtual Worlds to be an excellent way to teach students the learning material that is required for their studies in a different format, Second Life, in a collaborative and engaging environment from different locations around the world, at the same time. The participation – involvement in the discussion and interest in the learning material – was above average, which was observed as well as shown in the later interviews with the students. Nevertheless, we see the technology at its beginning with a new generation that is used to be in a three dimensional environment. Virtual worlds might not replace the Internet but substitute content that requires a higher degree of visualization, interaction, dynamics, collaboration, etc. to have its full advantage. And with a growing number of use cases, institutions and companies start to implement new and innovative applications like 3D content management systems to build libraries, as it is common for the traditional literature.

REFERENCES

Addison, A., & O'Hare, L. (2008). How Can Massive Multi-user Virtual Environments and Virtual Role Play Enhance Traditional Teaching Practice? In *Researching Learning in Virtual Environments International Conference* (pp. 5-15). Milton Keynes, UK: The Open University.

Barnes, C., & Tynan, B. (2007). The adventures of Miranda in the brave new world: learning in a Web 2.0 millennium. *ALT-J . Research in Learning Technology, 15*(3), 189–200.

Belanger, F., & Jordan, D. H. (2000). *Evaluation and Implementation of Distance Learning: Technologies, Tools and Techniques*. Hershey, USA: Idea Group Publishing.

Bowers, K. (2008). Assessing the value of Virtual Worlds for post-secondary instructors: a survey of innovators, early adopters and the early majority in Second Life. *International Journal of Humanities and Social Sciences, 3*(1), 40–50.

Brown, B., & Bell, M. (2004). CSCW at play: 'there' as a collaborative virtual environment. In *Proceedings of the 2004 ACM conference on Computer supported cooperative work* (pp. 350-359). Chicago, USA: ACM.

Burmester, A., Burmester, F., & Reiners, T. (2008). Virtual environment for immersive learning of container logistics. In *Proceedings of ED-MEDIA 2008. World Conference on Educational Multimedia, Hypermedia & Telecommunications,* Vienna, Austria (pp. 5843–5852). Chesapeake, USA: AACE.

Calonge, C. (2007). A view from Second Life's trenches: are you a pioneer or a Settler? In R. Smith (Ed.), *NMC Summer Conference Proceedings* (pp. 111-119). Stanford, USA: The New Media Consortium.

Carr, D., Oliver, M., & Burn, A. (2008). Learning, Teaching and Ambiguity in Virtual Worlds. In *Researching Learning in Virtual Environments International Conference* (pp. 83-93). Milton Keynes, UK: The Open University.

Clark, A. (2003). *Minds, Technologies, and the Future of Human Intelligence*. Oxford, UK: Oxford University Press.

Collins, C. (2008, November 26). *AVWW 2008 Program: Australasian Virtual Worlds Workshop*. Swinburne University of Technology, Hawthorn Campus and Second Life. Retrieved March 1, 2009, from http://avww.org/?q=node/35

Constable, G. (2007). *Virtual Worlds: A short Introduction to SL*. YouTube. Retrieved March 1, 2009, from http://au.youtube.com/watch?v=CaLKFeJLnqI

Constance, J. (2007, April 5). *Second Life: Educational Precedents and Examples*. Second Life Feasibility Study. Retrieved March 1, 2009, from http://manfromporlock.wetpaint.com/page/Second+Life+Educational+Precedents+and+Examples

Darbyshire, P. (2005). *Instructional Technologies: Cognitive Aspects of Online Programs*. Hershey, USA: IRM Press.

Dreher, C., Reiners, T., Dreher, N., & Dreher, H. (2009a). *3D Virtual Worlds as Collaborative Communities Enriching Human Endeavours: Innovative Applications in e-Learning*. Accepted for publication at the DEST 2009 Conference.

Dreher, C., Reiners, T., Dreher, N., & Dreher, H. (2009b). *3D Virtual Worlds Enriching Innovation and Collaboration in Information Systems Research, Development, and Commercialisation*. Accepted for publication at the DEST 2009 Conference.

Dreher, H. Reiners, T., Dreher, N. & Dreher, C. (2009c). 3D Spaces in Software Engineering: From K-12 to Life Long Learning. Accepted for publication in *Proceedings of ED-MEDIA 2009. World Conference on Educational Multimedia, Hypermedia & Telecommunications, Vienna, Austria*. Chesapeake, USA: AACE.

Driver, E. (2008). *Forrester Principal Analyst Erica Driver on Virutal Worlds*. FIR Interview on Jan 16, 2008. Retrieved March 1, 2009, from http://www.nevillehobson.com/2008/ 01/17/ fir-interview-forrester-principal-analyst-erica-driver-on-virtual-worlds-jan-16-2008

Erlenkötter, A., Kühnlenz, C.-M., Miu, H.-R., Sommer, F., & Reiners, T. (2008). Enhancing the class curriculum with Virtual World use cases for production and logistics. In *Proceedings of E-Learn 2008. World Conference on E-Learning in Corporate, Government, Healthcare, & Higher Education*, Las Vegas (pp. 789–798). Chesapeake: USA: AACE.

Facebook. (2009). *Welcome to Facebook*. Retrieved May 25, 2009, from http://www.facebook.com

Fenn, J., et al. (2008). *Hype Cycle for Emerging Technologies*. http://www.gartner.com/DisplayDocument?doc_cd=159496 &ref=g_homelink

Gee, J. (2003). What video games have to teach us about learning and literacy? *ACM Computers in Entertainment, 1*(1), 1–4. doi:10.1145/950566.950567

Gee, J. P. (2008). *Social linguistics and literacies (3rd ed.)*. Oxon: Routledge.

Google Trends. (2009). *Google trends: Virtual Worlds*. Retrieved May 28, 2009, from http://www.google.com/trends?q=virtual+worlds&ctab=0&geo=all&date=all&sort=0

Goold, A., Craig, A., & Coldwell, J. (2007). Culture and cultural diversity in online teaching. *Australasian Journal of Educational Technology, 23*(4), 490–507.

Gregory, S. (2008). *Online Dialogue in Second Life Sessions*. Retrieved March 1, 2009, from http://www.virtualclassrooms.info

Gregory, S., & Smith, H. (2008a). How virtual classrooms are changing the face of education: using virtual classrooms in today's university environment. In *Proceedings of ISTE Conference Research in Teacher Education: International Perspectives*, Armidale, Australia.

Gregory, S., & Smith, H. *(2008b)*. Virtual Worlds: Can educators in higher education engage students in greater collaboration through the use of virtual worlds and do they engage the student in conversations (through text) that can lead to deeper thinking and responses compared to other social computing tools. *Technical Report, Armidale.*

Grove, P. W., & Steventon, G. J. (2008). Exploring community safety in a virtual community: Using Second Life to enhance structured creative learning. In *Researching Learning in Virtual Environments International Conference* (pp. 154-171). Milton Keynes, UK: The Open University. Retrieved April 22, 2009.

Hafner, K. (2008, April 30). At Sundance, a Second Life Sweatshop Is Art. *New York Times*. Retrieved March 1, 2009, from http://bits.blogs.nytimes.com/2008/01/25/at-sundance-a-second-life-sweatshop-is-art

Hayes, G. (2009). The Virtual Worlds Hype Cycle 2009: Business, education, marketing, social media, virtual worlds. Retrieved March 30, 2009, from http://www.muvedesign.com/the-virtual-worlds-hype-cycle-for-2009

Hollins, P., & Robbins, S. (2008). The Educational affordances of Multi User Virtual Environments (MUVE). In *Researching Learning in Virtual Environments International Conference* (pp. 172-180). The Open University, Milton Keynes, UK. Retrieved April 22, 2009.

Jennings, N., & Collins, C. (2008). Virtual or virtually: educational institutions in Second Life. *International Journal of Social Sciences*, *2*(3), 180–186.

Johnson, L. F. (2008). *Testimony of Laurence F. Johnson, Ph.D.: Committee on Energy and commerce; Subcommittee on the Telecommunications and the Internet: Online Virtual Worlds: Applications and Avatars in a User-Generated Medium.* US: US House of Representatives. Retrieved March 1, 2009, from http://energycommerce.house.gov/cmte_mtgs/110-ti-hrg.040108.Johnson-testimony.pdf.

Koch, G. (2007). *Teacher uses online Second Life for classes: Students take classes interact via cyberspace.* Retrieved March 1, 2009, from http://www.idsnews.com/news/story.aspx?id=41756&comview=1

Kovela, S. (2008). *3D Virtual Worlds and Education 2.0: The "Second Life" Perspective.* Retrieved March 1, 2009, from http://www.kingston.ac.uk/~ku07009/Uni2/Kovela.pdf

KZERO. (2008). *Research.* Retrieved March 1, 2009, from http://www.kzero.co.uk/blog/?page_id=2092

Lagorio, C. (2007, January 7). The Ultimate Distance Learning. *The New York Times: Education Life.* Retrieved March 1, 2009, from http://www.nytimes.com/2007/01/07/education/edlife/07innovation.html

Lamont, I. (2007, May 24). *Virtual Reality and Higher Education: Another Perspective.* Retrieved March 1, 2009, from http://terranova.blogs.com/terra_nova/2007/05/teaching_in_vr_.html

Linden Research. (2008a). *Economic Statistics.* Retrieved March 1, 2009, from http://secondlife.com/whatis/economy_stats.php

Linden Research. (2008b). *Second Life Official Site.* Retrieved March 1, 2009, from http://secondlife.com

LinkedIn. (2009). *LinkedIn: Relationships Matter.* Retrieved May 26, 2009, from http://www.linkedin.com

Marshall, S. (2008). Worlds in Collision: Copyright, Technology, and Education. *Innovate Journal of Online Education, 4*(5). http://www.innovateonline.info/ index.php? view=article&id=528.

MCT. (2008, July 22). Characters in Second Life polish their practical skills. *The Australian: Executive Tech*, 34.

Minocha, S., & Tingle, R. (2008). Socialisation and Collaborative Learning of distance learners in 3-D Virtual Worlds. In *Researching Learning in Virtual Environments International Conference* (pp. 216-227). Milton Keynes, UK: The Open University. Retrieved April 22, 2009.

Myers, J. P. Jr. (1989). The new generation of computer literacy. *ACM SIGCSE Bull, 21*(1), 177–181. doi:10.1145/65294.65307

N.N. (2008). *Second Life Business Communicators Wiki: Companies in Second Life*. Retrieved March 1, 2009, from http://slbusinesscommunicators. pbwiki.com/ Companies+in+Second+Life

NSW Department of Education and Training. (2004). *Framework of professional teaching standards*. Retrieved January 14, 2008, from https://www.det.nsw.edu.au/proflearn/areas/plp/standards.htm

Ondrejka, C. (2007). Education Unleashed: Participatory Culture, Education, and Innovation in Second Life. In *The Ecology of Games: Connecting Youth, Games, and Learning* (pp. 229-251).

Ostlund, B. (2008). Prerequisites for interactive learning in distance education: Perspectives from Swedish students. *Australasian Journal of Educational Technology, 24*(1), 42–56.

Prensky, M. (2001). *Digital Natives, Digital Immigrants*. Retrieved March 1, 2009, from http://www.marcprensky.com/writing/Prensky%20 -%20Digital%20Natives,%20 Digital%20Immigrants%20-%20Part1.pdf

Prensky, M. (2008). Digital Game-Based Learning. *ACM Computers in Entertainment, 1*(1), 21–24. doi:10.1145/950566.950596

Ramondt, D. (2008). Towards the adoption of Massively Multiplayer Educational Gaming. In *Researching Learning in Virtual Environments International Conference* (pp. 258-268). Milton Keynes, UK: The Open University. Retrieved April 22, 2009.

Reiners, T., Dreher, C., Büttner, S., Naumann, M., & Visser, L. (2009). Connecting Students by Integrating the 3D Virtual and Real Worlds: We need 3D Open Source Spaces to Keep Socialization, Communciation, and Collaboration alive. Accepted for publication in *Proceedings of E-Learn 2008. World Conference on E-Learning in Corporate, Government, Healthcare, & Higher Education,* Las Vegas (pp. 789–798). Chesapeake, USA: AACE.

Reiners, T., & Voß, S. (2008). Inter-world Business Perspectives: Integrating Virtual Worlds in the Real World Business (Process). In *Proceedings of IFSAM 2008,* Beijing, China.

Robbins, S. S. (2007). *Immersion and Engagement in a Virtual Classroom: Using Second Life for Higher Education*. Presentation on EDUCause Connect. Retrieved March 1, 2009, from http://connect.educause.edu/library/abstract/ImmersionandEngageme/39328

Ryan, M. (2008). 16 Ways to Use Virtual Worlds in your Classroom: Pedagogical Applications of Second Life. In *Researching Learning in Virtual Environments International Conference* (pp. 269-178). Milton Keynes, UK: The Open University. Retrieved April 22, 2009.

Salleh, A. (2008, July 10). *Switch on a chip to boost internet speed*. Retrieved March 1, 2009, from http://www.abc.net.au/news/stories/2008/07/10/2299688.htm

Second Life, F. A. Q. (2008). *Is Second Life a game?* Retrieved March 1, 2009, from http://secondlife.com/whatis/faq.php#02

Second Life Grid. (2008). *Getting Started: Second Life Grid.* Retrieved March 1, 2009, from http://secondlifegrid.net/gs/get-started

Second Life Wiki. (2008). *Main Page, Second Life Wiki.* Retrieved March 1, 2009, from http://wiki.secondlife.com

Second Life Wikia. (2008). *List of museums and galleries in Second Life.* Retrieved March 1, 2009, from http://secondlife.wikia.com/wiki/List_of_museums_and_galleries_in_Second_Life

SimTeach. (2008). *Institutions and Organizations in SL.* Retrieved March 1, 2009, from http://www.simteach.com/wiki/index.php?title=Institutions_and_Organizations_in_SL

Slater, R. (2004). *What is the future of Massively Multiplayer Online Gaming?* Dissertation. Retrieved from http://www.richard-slater.co.uk/university/dissertation

Stephenson, N. (1994). *Snow Crash.* London, UK: Penguin.

Tapley, R. (2007). *Designing Your Second Life.* Berkeley, USA: New Rider.

Toro-Troconis, M., Partridge, M., Mellstrom, U., Meeran, K., & Higham, J. (2008). Technical infrastructure and initial findings in the design and delivery of game-based learning for virtual patients in Second Life. In *Researching Learning in Virtual Environments International Conference* (pp. 334-350). Milton Keynes, UK: The Open University. Retrieved April 22, 2009.

Vieyra, G. (2006). *A Dialectical Interpretation of Factual Knowledge in Vygotskyan Terms vs Blooms Taxonomy as Interpreted by the Teaching Staff at 75th Street Elementary School (LAUSD).* Retrieved November 9, 2007, from http://66.102.1.104/scholar?hl=en&lr=&q=cache:o08N16jolVIJ:www.gestaltdialektik.com/content/Factual_Knowledge_in_Vygotskyan_Terms.pdf+blooms+taxonomy

White Paper, N. M. C. (2007, October 27). *Social Networking, the "Third Place," and the Evolution of Communication.* Retrieved March 1, 2009, from http://www.nmc.org/evolution-communication

Wikipedia. (2009). *Massively multiplayer online game.* Retrieved March 1, 2009, from http://en.wikipedia.org/wiki/Massively_multiplayer_online_game

Wriedt, S., Ebeling, M., & Reiners, T. (2008). How to Teach and Demonstrate Topics of Supply Chain Management in Virtual Worlds. In *Proceedings of ED-MEDIA 2008. World Conference on Educational Multimedia, Hypermedia & Telecommunications, Vienna, Austria* (pp. 5501–5508). Chesapeake, USA: AACE.

YouTube. (2009). *YouTube – Broadcast yourself.* Retrieved May 25, 2009, from http://www.youtube.com.

Zagami, J. (2008). Technology education through online virtual environments. In *Technology Education*, Gold Coast, Australia. Retrieved August 5, 2008.

Section 3
Learning Strategy and Challenges for Distance Learning

Chapter 16

Instructional Challenges in Higher Education Online Courses Delivered through a Learning Management System by Subject Matter Experts

George L. Joeckel III
Utah State University, USA

Tae Jeon
Utah State University, USA

Joel Gardner
Utah State University, USA

ABSTRACT

The authors are Instructional Designers developing online courses in higher education. These courses are facilitated by Subject Matter Experts and delivered through a Learning Management System. They propose that instructional alignment with pedagogic beliefs is the best instructional foundation for original course designs in this instructional context, and examine three factors unique to this context. They propose new instructional design models and a new instructional system of design to address the instructional challenges specific to their learning system context.

INTRODUCTION

As Instructional Designers (IDs) in higher education, one of our main responsibilities involves working with Subject Matter Experts (SMEs) to design online courses for delivery in a Learning

DOI: 10.4018/978-1-61520-672-8.ch016

Management System (LMS). We have identified three main factors specific to this instructional context. The first is the ongoing nature of the relationship between SMEs and IDs as they collaborate on the design and delivery of online courses. The second is the constraint that these never-delivered courses must be designed without the benefit of learner-generated data to inform the process. The

Figure 1. Taxonomy of Online Course designed by Instructional Designers

Course Type	Design Resources				Course Facilitator			
	ID	SME	SME/F	I	L-F	PA-F	I-F	SME/F
L-F	X	X			X			
PA-F	X	X				X		
I-F	X	X		X			X	
SME-F	X		X					X

L-F = Learner-facilitated   ID = Instructional Designer

PA-F = Pedagogical Agent-facilitated   SME = Subject Matter Expert

I-F = Instructor-facilitated   SME/F = Subject Matter Expert/Facilitator

SME-F = Subject Matter Expert-facilitated   I = Instructor

third is the foundational role which the course facilitator's pedagogical beliefs play throughout the course design process.

In this chapter we propose a taxonomy for an ID-designed Online Course and define the terms used in our discussion. We then discuss the three factors associated with our instructional context. We propose a model for achieving learner-driven course designs through a phased approach. We examine two elements which shape our learning system context: the pedagogical effects of LMS adoption and success factors related to Online Learning Environments (OLEs). We explore the role of context in ID. Finally, we present a framework for an Instructional System of Design (ISD) we are developing to produce original course designs for our learning system context.

TAXONOMY AND TERMS

In order to communicate more effectively about our instructional context, we have developed the term "SME-F (Subject Matter Expert-facilitated)

online courses" to refer to online courses taught by the same individual responsible for providing a course's content. We will refer to this person as the "SME/F" (Subject Matter Expert/Facilitator). We propose the following taxonomy in order to situate our terms within the larger context of online courses designed by IDs (see Figure 1).

We believe that there are critical distinctions between the instructional context for the type of course we have described and the instructional context for other types of online courses. For example, in an I-F online course the Instructor is facilitating a course with content provided by a SME, and she or he may or may not be an expert in the content. Also, the Instructor is not likely to have played a significant role in the course design process, so one would not expect to find course design choices aligned with his or her pedagogical strengths.

For the purposes of this chapter we will use the term "course design" to represent the entire process of Instructional Design as represented by the phases described in the ADDIE model: analysis, design, development, implementation and evaluation (see, for example, Dick & Carey, 1996). We will use the terms Learning Management System (LMS) and Course Management System (CMS) interchangeably. We will use the term "learning system context" as defined by Tessmer and Richey (1997): "those situational elements that affect both the acquisition and application of newly acquired knowledge, skills, or attitudes" (p. 87). We will use the term "pedagogical beliefs" to refer to "teacher's educational beliefs about teaching and learning" (Ertmer, 2005, p. 28).

THREE CONTEXTUAL FACTORS

We are part of a team of IDs providing ID (Instructional Design) services at a research-based university. Designing original online courses facilitated by SMEs is a major component of our responsibilities. In the course of our practice, we have identified three factors that we believe are unique to this instructional context.

Ongoing Relationship

Each ID on our team is assigned to work with specific university departments on an ongoing basis. Our IDs and SME/Fs work together throughout the entire pre- and post-semester cycle of course design. This arrangement creates an opportunity to make course design decisions driven by the pedagogical beliefs of the individual providing the course content and facilitating the delivery of the course.

Designing without Learner-Generated Data

By definition, never-delivered courses must be designed without the benefit of learner-generated data. According to Geber & Scott (2007), for designers operating "from the theoretical orientation of learning as interdependent with context and experience, it is not possible to know learners'

perspectives in advance of course development" (p. 464-465). The ID and SME/F are forced look to second-hand sources of information to construct assumptions about potential learners: data gathered from learners in similar traditional or online courses, research-based findings about online learners, learner characteristics implied by the LMS, etc. In their examination of ID practices using established instructional design methods, Sims and Stork (2007) state that IDs "...will often predict or assume certain characteristics of the learners" (¶3) and incorporate these assumptions into a course design.

For original course designs, we propose that IDs need to limit the assumptions made about the potential learners to one source: the SME/F. We posit that the SME/F's assumptions about how the course's future learners will achieve course objectives are inherently linked to their pedagogical beliefs and practices. We stipulate that documenting and incorporating these assumptions into a new course design will create an instructional foundation that maintains alignment with the SME/F's pedagogy, and consequently his or her pedagogical practices throughout the course.

SME/F Pedagogical Beliefs

Working with the same individual throughout the design and delivery process presents a unique opportunity for instructional continuity. Our experience has led us to conclude that the pedagogical beliefs held by the SME/F are the best instructional foundation for original designs of courses delivered online through a LMS. This conclusion is supported by Ertmer's (2005) examination of the research conducted on teacher beliefs: "... beliefs are far more influential than knowledge in determining how individuals organize and define tasks and problems" (p. 28). She also draws a direct connection between pedagogical beliefs and technology skills:

Given that these [technology] skills are unlikely to be used unless they fit with teachers' existing pedagogical beliefs, it is imperative that educators increase their understanding of and ability to address teacher beliefs, as part of their efforts to increase teachers' technology skills and uses (Ertmer, 2005, p. 37).

Zhao & Cziko (2001) also emphasize the importance of teacher beliefs when creating their Perceptual Control Theory (PCT) framework for understanding teacher adoption of technology. PCT defines three necessary conditions:

1. The teacher must believe that technology can more effectively meet a higher-level goal than what has been used.
2. The teacher must believe that using technology will not cause disturbances to other higher-level goals that he or she thinks are more important than the one being maintained.
3. The teacher must believe that he or she has or will have sufficient ability and resources to use technology. (Zhao & Cziko, 2001, p. 6)

Ertmer (2005) demonstrates how pedagogical beliefs have a global effect on a teacher's perceptions about new instructional tools and practices when she states "Even new information (about technology, alternative teaching methods, etc.), if attended to at all, will be filtered through these existing belief systems" (p. 30). Our instructional process recognizes and embraces this filter by systematically exploring, documenting, and integrating the SME/F's pedagogical beliefs into the course design. We share the hope that a greater understanding of the relationship between pedagogical beliefs and technology use:

...may enable us to facilitate a better alignment between research, practice, and beliefs and to provide more effective ways of supporting and

documenting teacher change. Ultimately, the goal is to facilitate uses of technology that lead to increased student learning (Ertmer, 2005, p. 27-28).

We propose that creating and maintaining instructional alignment with the core beliefs of the individual responsible for the course's content and for the facilitation of the course will lead to the most significant learner outcomes. We suggest that it is the responsibility of the ID to gather and interpret course data, and then present evidence of course outcomes which are aligned or misaligned with the SME/F's pedagogical beliefs. If the evidence induces a shift in the SME/F's pedagogical beliefs, the ID should recommend changes to the course design that will increase instructional alignment, and then implement the changes that are approved.

DATA-DRIVEN DESIGN EVOLUTION

An ongoing relationship between an ID and a SME/F may lead to an evolution of the course design. Ideally this evolution would be the result of evidence derived from course data that led to changes in the SME/F's pedagogical beliefs. We have created the term "data-driven design evolution" to describe this process. We propose a three-stage model in which the course design shifts from "SME/F-driven" towards "learner-driven" (see Figure 2).

In Stage I, there is an insufficient quality of course data to justify changes to the course design decisions/revisions based on learner feedback. This occurs in courses which have yet to be delivered, but it may also be the result of an insufficient quantity of course data. The ID creates a course design based on instructional alignment between the SME/F's pedagogical beliefs and assumptions about learners.

In Stage II, the quality of the course data is high enough to identify learner characteristics

Figure 2. Data-driven Design Evolution in SME-F Online Courses

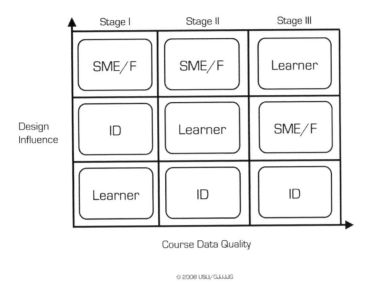

© 2008 USU/GJJJJG

that can replace the SME/F's assumptions. The ID provides the SME/F with evidence based on course data that demonstrates instructional alignment or misalignment. When the evidence produces a shift in the SME/F's pedagogical beliefs, the ID recommends changes to the course design that will increase instructional alignment, and implements the approved changes.

In Stage III, the increase in the quality of the course data has led to a fundamental shift in the SME/F's pedagogical beliefs. He or she has become willing to learner feedback drive design changes to the course. The ID assists the SME/F in interpreting the learner feedback from the latest cohort of learners by using the entire set of course data to control for anomalies. The ID recommends changes and implements the approved changes.

TWO CONTEXTUAL ELEMENTS

Researchers have explored the role of context in ID for more than a decade. In 1994 Edmunds, Branch & Mukherjee stated:

Concepts, theories and models have an ecology, a context within which they function. Importing a theory or model from a significantly different context, without attention to contextual differences, violates this ecology, and subsequently results in inefficient solutions to instructional problems (p. 66-67).

Tessmer & Richey (1997) described the context of a learning system as "those situational elements that affect both the acquisition and application of newly acquired knowledge, skills, or attitudes (p.87)." They identify the social, physical, and political elements which combine to create "a multilevel body of factors in which learning and performance are embedded (p. 87)." We have identified two contextual elements that interact with the previously-discussed instructional context to create our learning system context: the pedagogical effects of LMS adoption and the success factors associated with Online Learning Environments (OLEs).

Pedagogical Effects of LMS Adoption

The majority of the technological resources we use to deliver our courses are embedded in an LMS. In a comprehensive study of faculty and instructional staff in a multi-campus university system, Morgan (2003) found that more than a third of respondents stated "to solve a pedagogical problem or challenge" as their reason for CMS adoption (p. 3). Despite pedagogical problems or challenges being the number one reason stated for CMS adoption, Morgan (2003) found that "when probing below the surface, however, it seems that most of these needs have less to do with pedagogy, per se, and more to do with class management" (p. 2). Morgan (2003) reconciles this apparent contradiction:

Faculty using course management systems find that they achieve a number of pedagogical gains. This is something of a paradox given that faculty look to a CMS to provide them with organizational tools. But in the process of using these tools, many faculty members begin to rethink and restructure their courses and ultimately their teaching. The end result is a sort of "accidental pedagogy". Faculty teaching is improved through the use of a CMS, but this is a side effect of the use of the software rather than a direct result of its use (p. 4-5).

We have also seen shifts in pedagogical beliefs among the faculty and instructors we work with that they attribute to their use of a LMS. Because our process is designed to establish "baseline" pedagogical beliefs, we will be in a position to document the changes to these beliefs. By following a research-based model of success factors in online learning, we can recommend changes to the course design that utilize these pedagogical shifts to generate increased learner outcomes.

Success Factors in OLEs

In order to identify success factors in OLEs, Bekele (2008) reviewed 82 studies from educational technology journals. Based on his review, he developed a model that identifies seven success measures: learning outcomes, student satisfaction, higher learning, faculty satisfaction, sustainability, scalability, and rate of return. The model illustrates that "...success in the OLEs was a function of a complicated interplay of human, technologic, course, pedagogic, and leadership factors" (p. 237). We have adopted this model to guide our ongoing development of an ISD specific to our learning system context.

THE AERO ISD

The AERO ISD is being developed to create course designs for our learning system context. By focusing on a specific learning system context, we believe our process will be practical, detailed, dynamic and flexible. We also believe that by maintaining a strict vision of solving the instructional challenges presented in our environment (as opposed to taking on global instructional challenges), we are creating a process that will evolve to be not only systematic, but systemic, where "the outcomes of each component directly or indirectly impact every other component of the instructional design to some degree (Edmunds, Branch & Mukherjee, 1994, p. 56)." The AERO ISD utilizes two new context-specific ID models, incorporates the ADDIE design phases (see, for example, Dick & Carey, 1996), encompasses the instructional phases identified in Merrill's First Principles of Instruction (Merrill 2002, 2006), and is being guided by Bekele's model of success and success factors in Internet-supported learning environments (Bekele, 2008).

Assumptions

There are a number of assumptions that we have made as IDs in developing the AERO ISD. We assume that our process will be applied to courses for which: a) a needs analysis has been conducted, b) a need for the course has been established, and c) there is an institutional commitment to develop the course. We also assume that the SME/F has the necessary expertise in the subject area, and that they have, and/or can obtain, the necessary course content. We assume that IDs will be designing online courses to be delivered through a Learning Management System (LMS) or Course Management System (CMS).We assume that the extra effort expended in learning and utilizing our systematic process will be justified by increases in:

- Course usability for SME/Fs and learners
- Instructional alignment with the SME/F's pedagogical beliefs
- Data-driven design choices
- Learner outcomes

The OAR Model

The OAR model (Figure 3) is a visual tool which represents the components of SME-F online courses in higher education, and their relationship to each other. The OAR model was developed to meet four criteria: a) maintain a strict focus on our particular learning system context, b) create a simple graphic-based aid which facilitates communication among design stakeholders, c) remain inclusive by avoiding the use of jargon, and d) represent the basic order of operations in our ID process. The OAR model has proven effective in meeting these criteria by organizing the components of SME-F online courses in higher education into three domains: Resources, Objectives and Activities.

The OAR model defines resources as the physical, electronic and intellectual assets with which a course can be created. These resources are determined by an analysis of the learners, SME/F, ID, learning and performing environments, available instructional technology, and other relevant contextual factors associated with a course. IDs and SME/Fs use the results of this analysis to identify real-world problems and tasks to inform the design of objectives.

The objectives domain contains the learning and performance goals that are designed to guide the course. Objectives determine which resources will be delivered to influence learner behavior under specified conditions to meet defined criteria. Opportunities for learners to accomplish the objectives are created through activities that are as closely aligned with real-world problems and tasks as the available resources will allow.

Activities are the actual events that learners engage in to acquire and develop new knowledge and skills. At a minimum, these events involve an agent (most often the learner, but at times the facilitator) following an objective to engage with a resource. Activities are primarily delivered by a LMS and are facilitated and assessed by the SME/F.

Merrill's First Principles of Instruction

The AERO ISD is being designed to generate activity types which correlate strongly to a well-know instructional theory: Merrill's First Principles of Instruction (2002, 2006). In an effort to establish the most fundamental principles of instruction, Merrill reviewed and synthesized several instructional theories and research reports. Merrill writes that learning is promoted when:

- Instruction takes place in the context of real-world **problems** or **tasks** that are progressively difficult
- Learners **activate** relative cognitive structures by recalling or demonstrating prior knowledge or experience

Figure 3. The OAR model

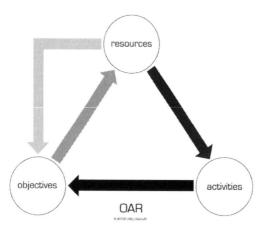

Figure 4. Merrill's First Principles of Instruction

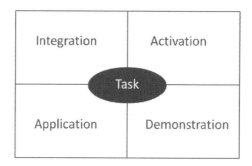

- Learners observe a **demonstration** of new knowledge
- Learners **apply** new knowledge, receiving feedback and coaching that is gradually withdrawn
- Learners **integrate** their new knowledge by reflecting on, discussing, defending, presenting new knowledge and creating personal ways to use it

Figure 4 illustrates these phases and their relationships to each other. The task/problem plays a central role by defining the learning context. The instruction begins with activation, moves clockwise to demonstration, followed by application, and ends with integration.

Figure 5 illustrates how Merrill's First Principles of Instruction relate to the three domains of the OAR model. The task/problem is a resource. Objectives determine how this and other resources will be delivered to create two types of activities: acquisition and application. Acquisition activities are the opportunities provided for learners to gain new knowledge and skills and encompass Merrill's activation and demonstration phases. Application activities are the opportunities provided for learners to use and develop the new knowledge and skills they have acquired, and correlate to Merrill's application and integration phases.

The OAR communication model is adapted to create an ISD-specific model by the addition of an evaluation component. The AERO model

Figure 5. Merrill's First Principles in the OAR domains

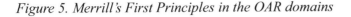
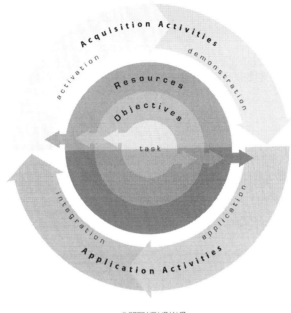

(Figure 6) represents the theoretical foundation of a new ISD for creating and revising SME-facilitated online courses developed by IDs in the higher education environment. The AERO ISD incorporates the ADDIE phases of instructional design and Merrill's First Principles of Instruction to create a systematic, research-based process targeted at this context.

An AERO ISD "cycle" represents the steps of the process when applied to one of three design levels: course, interunit or unit. The "course" design level refers to acquisition and application activities that may incorporate elements from all of the available objectives and resources, including introductory papers/discussions, assessments of prerequisite knowledge and skills, and comprehensive activities such as final exams, portfolios, capstone projects, etc. The "interunit" design level encompasses activities based on the objectives and resources from more than one unit such as midterm exams, projects, and learner presentations. The "unit" design level is the smallest grouping of

related objectives, resources and activities, and in our experience is labeled by SME/Fs with a term denoting a "chunk" of instruction (ie, "Module 1"), or with a temporal unit (ie, "Week 1").

An AERO ISD cycle (Figure 7) begins with an analysis of the resources available at the selected design level. The results of this analysis are used to design acquisition and application objectives. These objectives are used to select resources and develop the vehicles for delivery to learners. The cycle is implemented when the learner engages in activities which are facilitated by the SME/F. The results of the activities are evaluated and the results of the evaluation are used to make necessary revisions or additions to the relevant objectives, resources, and/or activities.

FUTURE TRENDS

In our practice as IDs, we have experienced positive outcomes and feedback from our use of

Figure 6. The AERO model

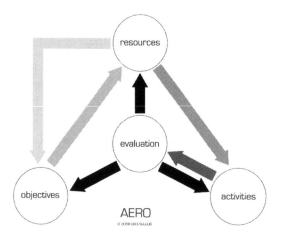

Figure 7. The AERO ISD cycle

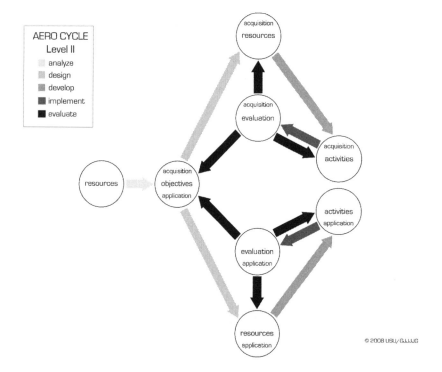

the OAR communication model. We are in the process of continuing to gather data from course stakeholders to design formal evaluations of this model. The results of these evaluations will allow us to determine the validity of its theoretical foundations and make research-based revisions.

The development of a systematic process based on the AERO ISD is in its preliminary stages, and continues to be challenged and revised based on the feedback we receive from our clients. We encourage other IDs operating in higher education to utilize any of its components that they might find helpful in developing a process for their own practices.

CONCLUSION

Three factors unique to new online higher education courses facilitated by Subject Matter Experts and designed by Instructional Designers create an instructional and learning systems contexts with unique challenges. We created the two context-specific ID models (OAR and AERO) and are continuing to develop the AERO ISD to address these challenges. Original designs in this context are most effective when aligned with the SME/F's pedagogical beliefs. As learner-generated data is gathered, our process documents shifts in the SME/F's pedagogical beliefs and encourages a data-driven evolution from SME/F-driven designs to learner-driven designs.

REFERENCES

Bekele, T. A. (2008). *Impact of technology supported learning environments in higher education: Issues in and for research*. Unpublished doctoral dissertation, University of Oslo, Norway.

Dick, W., & Carey, L. (1996). *The systematic design of instruction (4th ed.)*. New York: Harper Collins.

Edmonds, G. S., Branch, R. C., & Mukherjee, P. (1994). A Conceptual Framework for Comparing Instructional Design Models. *Educational Technology Research and Development, 42*(4), 55–72. doi:10.1007/BF02298055

Ertmer, P. A. (2005). Teacher Pedagogical Beliefs: The Final Frontier in Our Quest for Technology Integration? *Educational Technology Research and Development, 53*(4), 25–39. doi:10.1007/BF02504683

Gerber, S., & Scott, L. (2007). Designing a learning curriculum and technology's role in it. *Educational Technology Research and Development, 55*(5), 461–478. doi:10.1007/s11423-006-9005-6

Merrill, M. D. (2002). First principles of instruction. *Educational Technology Research and Development, 50*(3), 43–59. doi:10.1007/BF02505024

Merrill, M. D. (2006). First principles of instruction: a synthesis. *Trends and Issues in Instructional Design and Technology (2nd Ed.)*. Upper Saddle River, NJ: Prentice-Hall, Inc.

Morgan, G. (2003). *Faculty use of course management systems*. Boulder, CO: EDUCAUSE Center for Applied Research. Retrieved Dec. 23, 2008, from http://net.educause.edu/ir/library/pdf/ecar_so/ers/ERS0302/ekf0302.pdf

Sims, R., & Stork, E. (2007). Design for contextual learning: Web-based environments that engage diverse learners. In J. Richardson & A. Ellis (Eds.), *Proceedings of AusWeb07, Thirteenth Australasian World Wide Web Conference*. Lismore, Australia: Southern Cross University. Retrieved December 23, 2008, from http://ausweb.scu.edu.au/aw07/papers/refereed/sims/index.html

Tesser, M., & Richey, R. C. (1997). The role of context in learning and instructional design. *Educational Technology Research and Development, 45*(2), 85–115. doi:10.1007/BF02299526

Zhao, Y. & Cziko, G. A. (2001). *Teacher adoption of technology: A Perceptual Control Theory perspective*.

Chapter 17

Societal Issues, Legal Standards, & International Realities Universities Face in the Distance-Learning Market

Robert Hogan
University of the South Pacific, Fiji

ABSTRACT

In today's global economy, both students and workers need to be lifelong learners. While some universities have been slow to recognize these changing needs, others have quickly moved to serve this new academic market. The eLearning revolution empowers individuals to take courses and to earn degrees from local or foreign universities. In developing nations, a foreign degree may, in fact, be more attractive than a local degree if the student plans to migrate (Herbst, 2008). This chapter discusses societal, international, cultural, and technical issues that universities face in providing distance-learning programs to meet the needs of today and the demands of tomorrow. Universities that fail to adapt risk losing their students to competing local and foreign universities. Key issues discussed in this chapter are university barriers to change, changing needs of students, legal issues, cultural issues, and emerging international educational opportunities.

INTRODUCTION

In today's evolving global economy, information has a short shelf life. To stay competitive, not only scientists and engineers, but all sectors of the workforce must continuously upgrade their skills to stay competitive. Lifelong learning is no longer an option, but a career requirement. Some nontraditional learners who balance family needs

and career responsibilities are choosing to enroll in distance-learning programs that suit their busy life styles. Instead of spending nights and weekends on a college campus, today's learners can study at work, at home, and even when traveling. A few years ago, universities saw the eLearning classroom without walls as a way to meet the needs of students throughout their service regions. That view of eLearning has broadened. Today, universities are beginning to realize that their service regions cross state, province, and international borders. The

DOI: 10.4018/978-1-61520-672-8.ch017

advent of online learning, which is also referred to as eLearning in this chapter, dramatically increases student access to educational opportunities. In developing countries, eLearning can provide access to learning opportunities never before available. The eLearning revolution empowers learners to study online from grade school to graduate school, earning high school degrees, certificates, diplomas, undergraduate degrees, masters, and doctorates from educational institutions around the world

Students have become consumers who shop the Internet for their preferred academic programs and delivery methods. Institutions can no longer rely on the traditional post-secondary on-campus student; the demographic has changed. Some may discover too late that fraternities, football, the face-to-face lecture system and 16-week on-campus semesters are not meeting consumer needs. Just as workers must adapt to lifelong learning, so too universities need to recognize that online delivery is an important new market. According to the Asian Development Bank (2008), the interdependence of world markets, communication advances, and technology have created a new educational market for continued training for technical workers, managers, and administrators. Colleges and universities must adapt to the changing demands of the workplace.

In this evolving marketplace, working students understand that they can search the market for the educational products that best meet their needs. Throughout this chapter, the term *market* is frequently mentioned to emphasize the concept that universities must develop new products and new delivery methods to meet changing student demands if they are to retain their market share. Universities need to develop business plans to identify and develop new programs which meet market needs. In these financially uncertain times, academic institutions must generate more of their operating costs to replace declining government and donor funding. Therefore, institutions must deliver high quality educational programs that are also cost effective. Two challenges that universities face in developing distance-learning programs are their reluctance to adopt a customer-oriented approach (Magaud, 2007) and the resistance of faculty and administrators who believe that distance learning does not have the academic quality of face-to-face training (Wright, Dhanarajan, & Reju, 2009). The economic reality is that institutions of higher education must meet the needs of their customers or risk losing students to competitors Oblinger, 1999).

According to Adams (2008), private for-profit online universities have been quick to exploit this new academic market, recognizing that working customers and businesses are willing to pay higher tuition in return for shorter academic terms, greater access to courses, flexibility, and the opportunity to earn degrees more quickly. The University of Phoenix, the leader in online for-profit education, has an enrollment of 300,000 students and has generated significant profits (Tanzer, 2007). More recently, public universities like the University of Maryland have entered the international market by actively recruiting international students. In 2008, 10% of the university students were from foreign countries (Wolston, 2009).

This chapter discusses societal, legal, technical, international, and cultural issues facing universities considering online programs. Key issues this chapter discusses are existing barriers to academic change, the growing demand for eLearning, and new competition traditional universities face from higher-education competitors around the world. The chapter also describes barriers that limit the ability of organizations to make the changes needed to compete. The chapter proposes that universities must adjust to changing customer needs in order to remain competitive.

Figure 1. The growth of online learning in US higher education (Students taking at least one online course)

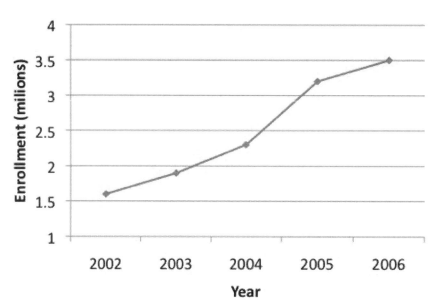

BACKGROUND

The Growth of Online Learning

As Figure 1 shows, the move to online learning has been dramatic. In 2006 nearly 3.5 million students took at least one online course and almost 20% of all higher education students took one online course (Allen & Seaman, 2006; Allen & Seaman, 2007). The authors report that while higher education enrollment increased in 2005 by 1.5%, online enrollment jumped by nearly 10%. The average online growth rate between 2002-2006 was 22% per year and shows no sign of in online learning shows no sign of leveling off.

Not all colleges and universities have experienced such dramatic increases in online enrollment. In the United States, community colleges have been the early leaders in developing online training (Bradburn & Zimbler, 2002), followed by public universities. The private universities have been much slower to adopt online instruction (Waits & Lewis, 2003; Allen & Seaman, 2003). According to Winter (2002), one reason online

programs grew most quickly in community colleges was that university students realized they could save money by taking some of their courses through community colleges and applying for cross credit. According to the College Board (2008), the average tuition in 2008 for community colleges was $2,402. The average cost at a public 4-year institution was $6,585, more than two and half times the community college rate. Also, most states have articulation agreements that award university credit for courses taken at in-state community colleges.

At U.S. public universities, online growth was slower as tenured faculty proved resistant to moving from the lecture mode of teaching (Shank, 2005). Although eLearning has been shown to promote critical thinking (Allen & Seaman, 2007), many faculty accustomed to face-to-face teaching still have concerns about the quality of online teaching (Gerlich, 2005; Myers, Bennet, Brown, & Henderson, 2004). Even today, some faculty and administrators view online learning as an inferior mode of delivery compared to traditional lecture classrooms (Adams, 2008). These faculty

Table 1. Selected Online University Enrollments In The United States

University	Web Site	Enrollment
Capella University	www.capella.edu	21,773
Franklin University	www.franklin.edu	7,559
Grand Canyon University	www.gcu.edu	13,415
Jones International University	www.jiu.edu	1,588
Kaplan University	www.kucampus.edu	32,734
Liberty University	www.liberty.edu	27,068
University of Phoenix	www.uopxonline.edu	224,880
Walden University	www.walden.edu	29,455
Western Governors University	www.wgu.edu	9,022
South University	www.southuniversity.edu	7,222
Western International Univ.	www.wintu.edu	8,909

Note. The enrollment data is compiled from a National Center for Educational Statistics report.

concerns are legitimate and as online programs grow, universities must actively evaluate the quality of their online courses (Badat, 2005; Hagel & Shaw, 2006), as well as faculty acceptance and attitudes. A study by Akdemir (2008) found that faculty attitude toward online learning influences the quality of online courses. Faculty who are concerned about the added time requirements of distance learning or are not convinced of the effectiveness of online pedagogy may limit their online involvement to depositing course materials, ignoring rich pedagogical opportunities.

Several studies (Bruner, 2007; Kemp, 2006) indicate that colleges and universities are increasingly offering both face-to-face and online delivery to meet student demand for flexibility and availability. Some higher educational institutions recognize that online learning is the next step in educational delivery (O'Malley & McGraw, 1999). In support of this notion, a study by Minotti and Giguere (2003) found that that Web learning can be as effective as face-to-face teaching, and that some students prefer online teaching to classroom learning. Students rated online courses much superior to face-to-face teaching for convenience and the opportunity for self pacing (Wuensch, 2008). These same students rated online teaching

inferior to classroom teaching in regard to student interaction with the instructor and other students, evaluation, and learning complex material.

The Growth of Online Universities

Twigg and Oblinger (1996) predicted that the campus-centered teaching model needed to shift to a consumer model that better supported the growing need for lifelong learning. For-profit universities quickly recognized and responded to this market change, offering online registration, shorter courses, and credit for life experiences. As Table 1 shows, by 2008 the University of Phoenix's enrollment was nearly a quarter million students at a time when many universities were experiencing declining enrollments.

One reason for the growth of online universities was their implementation of three business innovations. The first innovation was "design once – teach many times" (Epper & Garn, 2003). By using the materials in hundreds of courses, development costs are quickly recovered, which enables the university to create high quality online course materials that can equal or exceed that of traditional universities. The standardization of courses also demonstrates to employers and accrediting agencies that the same learning goals are covered in each course. The University of Phoenix expands this process by using the same curriculum in both its online and face-to-face courses, demonstrating that the training is consistent across all courses and delivery modes.

The second innovation was shortening course length from 16 weeks to 5-12 weeks. This approach increased revenue for the institution while enabling students to graduate in less time. A related innovation was offering a full menu of courses each term, helping students to progress more quickly. The third innovation was to employ a cadre of part-time faculty, rather than the traditional full-time cohort. Part-time instructors are paid fixed stipends that range between $1,500 and $2,000 to teach an undergraduate course. Employing part-time instructors eliminates retirement and health-benefit costs, greatly reducing operating costs. The use of part-time teachers also enables the institutions to maintain a supply of back-up instructors ready to teach whenever courses fill up. A traditional approach using the institution's full-time instructors could be cost prohibitive and limit the ability to scale-up its online program.

WHY UNIVERSITIES RESIST ONLINE LEARNING

Given the numerous models of successful programs, why have all universities not rushed into the field? Let's look at some of the hurdles they face.

Faculty Concerns

Faculty may not support eLearning for a variety of reasons. One major faculty concern is the added time needed to develop and teach Web-based courses (Allen & Seaman, 2006). In a survey by Pachnowski and Jurcyzk (2003), faculty reported that even with experience, online courses took more time to develop and to teach than face-to-face. Nearly 30%

of the faculty surveyed responded that they spent more time preparing online courses even in their third semester of teaching the course. Online courses take more time because the teachers engage with their students throughout the week. Some online universities require teachers to be online a minimum of four days per week, to respond to all student questions within 24 hours, and to return assignments within one week. Frey, Faul, and Yankelov (2003) reported that one of the major attractions of online teaching for students is interaction with the instructor. Unfortunately, teachers often find this interaction to be time consuming (Bradburn, 2002: Rockwell, Schauer, Fritz, & Marx, 1999; Wolcott & Betts, 1999). When instructors consider the additional time needed for eLearning, Parker (2003) reports that they may decide that their time is better spent doing research and publishing, which count toward promotion and tenure. Some institutions have addressed these concerns by implementing faculty motivators such as incentive pay, reduced course load, smaller class size, and credit toward career advancement. Another approach suggested by van Rosmalen, Sloep, Keste, Brouns, de Croock, Pannekeet and Koper (2008) is to use peer tutors to assist online teachers.

Another common faculty concern is technological support (Bower, 2001). While faculty may be subject specialists and excellent teachers, they may need assistance to learn how to upload files, enter grades, and solve student technical questions. In smaller universities and in developing countries, appropriate technical support can be an issue, especially in universities that lack adequate IT infrastructure and Internet connectivity to support online learning. While it is true that Internet access continues to improve, in many areas of Africa, Asia, and the South Pacific Internet access is still extremely limited (Gulati, 2008, Hogan, 2009). Slow Internet speed and limited student access to the Internet and computers can discourage teachers.

Faculty may resist new online learning simply because is very different from their previous experience (Wright et al., 2009). Older faculty often prefer face-to-face teaching (Gerlich, 2005; Myers, Bennet, Brown, & Henderson, 2004). Similarly, moving from the podium to the keyboard may be frightening for teachers who have limited computer experience. A key to convincing teachers to consider this new experience is training and support.

Online course quality remains a concern of faculty and administrators (Frey, Faul, & Yankelov, 2003). Some view it as a poor substitute for face-to-face teaching. Others argue that online degrees may be less acceptable to other universities and employers (Adams, 2008; Muilenburg & Berge, 2001). However, Allen and Seaman 2006 reported that the quality rating by administrators had risen from 57% in 2003 to 62% in 2006. The issue of plagiarism is the same for face-to-face and online classes. However, unsupervised eLearning examinations continue to be a vexing problem for faculty.

Societal Issues

According to Davis and Batkin (1994), organizations change only when confronted with external demands. However, for change to take place administrators must be open to change and they must create an organizational strategic plan to implement the innovation (Toffler, 1985). Unless an organization has leaders with both a vision and a plan, it will resist change. Even if an organization has the leadership and vision, political and other forces may make change impossible (Christensen, Horn, & Johnson, 2008). Implementing an online program is a major change that may be opposed by faculty, university boards, other universities, governing agencies, and donors. Some common concerns about online learning are shown in Table 2. Universities must convince faculty of the value and the necessity of online delivery. Universities must also reassure faculty that the development of new online programs will not threaten job security, academic quality, or professional growth. Another change inhibitor for traditional universities is often

Table 2. Barriers to Online Programs

Obstacle
• Perceived quality of online courses
• Lack of online teaching skills
• Cost and time needed to develop course materials
• Additional time needed to Teach online
• Industry acceptance of online courses and degrees
• Retention and pass rates
• University reputation

distrust of business models (Adams, 2005). Often, academic institutions view profit making as not their *business*. In contrast, for-profit universities, such as Walden University, Capella University, and the University of Phoenix eagerly develop new approaches designed to increase enrollment and profit by catering to the needs of students who want to earn their degrees online (Tanzer, 2007). These online universities differ from traditional institutions in that they use business plans to develop and expand their markets. For such universities, "profit" is a key consideration.

Another challenge for traditional undergraduate programs can be a reluctance to adopt smaller class sizes. Large classes have been a cost-effective approach that utilizes a single lecturer and a cohort of less expensive tutors. The problem such universities face is how to transition to smaller classes that incorporate active involvement between instructor and students to encourage critical thinking and team learning (Kanuka, 2002). Although large lecture classes are a mainstay, students are demanding smaller classes that promote active learning.

Legal Issues

At the onset of eLearning, critics questioned whether it would be accepted by accrediting organizations, the federal and state governments, and employers. Ten years later the six regional accrediting organizations recognized by the Council for Higher Education Accreditation (CHEA Directory of Regional Accreditation Organizations, 2009) have accredited the major eLearning universities. Moreover, the United State military now accepts online universities that have been accredited by these distance-learning organizations recognized by the military. Nevertheless, Adams (2008) found in a survey of businesses and industry that online degrees are still viewed as significantly less acceptable compared to face-to-face degrees. The reasons given were the absence of face-to-face learning and mentoring, and the reputation of the online university. According to Adams, this finding has implications for students since graduate schools and businesses may question the acceptability of online degrees.

One legal issue that inhibits the acceptance of online courses taken at other universities is a cumbersome system of cross crediting. Although public universities usually have articulation agreements with other state and private institutions within the region, the process is too localized because the bulk of the states are not included. When students apply to institutions of higher learning in other states, they must submit their transcripts for review. This absence of a nationwide articulation plan limits students' ability to take online courses from other universities because they cannot be certain that the course credits will be accepted. One option for entrepreneurial universities is to liberalize their cross-credit policies to attract students who want credit for completed courses.

A related issue faced by state colleges is whether they can or should solicit out-of-state students since they are funded by the state. They worry that government officials and taxpayers may question why their money is being used to support out-of-state or international students. However, some colleges, like California State University now serve a broader market by participating in a regional program offering lower tuition for students from 15 Western states (Glater, 2008). Joliet Junior College in Illinois has taken an even bolder step to attract out-of-state students). While the college still charges in-state, out-of-state, and out-of-country tuitions for on-campus

students, all students are charged in-district rates for online courses (Joliet Junior College Admissions, 2009.

Now that eLearning is going global, a new realm of legal issues appears. Audiovisual materials once shown only in campus classrooms are now transmitted electronically to students around the world. Therefore, universities delivering such online courses must ensure that they do not violate foreign copyright laws. Sharing certain types of information or streaming music may be legal in one country but not another. Copyright laws vary between countries (Switzer, 1994). Blogs raise a similar issue. In the United States, if what you say is true and not libelous you are within the law. However, the same statement may be illegal in a foreign country (Kazer, 2008). One advantage of course management software is that the material is restricted to your online students. However, in this era of cut and paste, that is no guarantee that information will stay put. Another fuzzy issue for online instructors is video exchange platforms such as YouTube, which have been sued for copyright infringement. These various copyright and libel examples will have to be addressed as online learning goes international.

A final legal issue is approval of online degree programs by other countries. One reality of online learning is that online programs do not require approval to deliver programs to students in other countries, unless the program includes face-to-face sessions in that country. Although foreign approval of online degrees is not required, it may be beneficial. If a program is not approved, government scholarship and loans may not be available. In such a case, that country's market will consist of students who have independent means to finance their education. Although these students may be the ones most likely to succeed in an online program, government approval can open access to a greater number of students.

Student Issues

Younger students tend to approach online learning with confidence. According to Picciano and Seaman (2007), approximately 700,000 K-12 U.S. students enrolled in online or blended courses in 2005. A blended (hybrid) courses as defined by Allen and Seaman (2006) has 30 to 80 percent of the course content delivered online. Many of today's students in developed countries have new skill sets that allow them to simultaneously watch TV, talk to friends, and text messages on their cell phones. Raised in a computer-technology environment, American students arrive at college equipped with the computer and typing skills for online learning. When these students enter college, their computer skills often rival or exceed those of their instructors.

Not all students are computer literate, however. Older working adults and students in developing countries frequently have weak or non-existent computer and Internet skills. For such students to be successful in online programs, they must be taught the necessary skills. For some students, this may even require teaching them to type. Once such students get computer access and are introduced to the Web and email, they have a new motivation to acquire the necessary online skills. In a recent survey by Hogan (2009), even students with poor typing and computer skills reported that they were able to navigate the course management system and that they considered online learning an essential part of their courses. Students said that they especially appreciated the increased interaction with the instructor and prompt feedback.

Not all students will be successful online learners. Online classes require more self-discipline than face-to-face classes (Allen & Seaman, 2007). Online courses require students to stick to schedules, to stay connected, and to meet deadlines. Therefore, universities should consider providing counseling and training in time-management for beginning online students. The attrition rate for distance learners is an issue. According to Angelo, Williams, and Natvig (2007), attrition rates for distance learners are 10% to 20% higher than for face-to-face learners.

A final student issue to be considered is plagiarism. The advent of the Internet search engines has opened a doorway to most human knowledge. Students can access libraries, museums, literature, art, music, research, and papers around the world. This access provides students in even the most remote parts of the world opportunities to access the latest information and discoveries. This easy access also can increase the risk of plagiarism. Therefore, students in online programs need to be given clear guidance as to what constitutes plagiarism. It is suggested that course syllabi or online student policies clearly detail the university policy on plagiarism.

Technological Issues

A key question is the type of online technology to select. A number of online universities have incorporated a two-way video capability into their course management software. Online instructors also can use Skype© or similar video and conferencing software. Some universities are using webcasting in blended courses to stream face-to-face lectures. The webcasting allows students to replay lectures from the web. Another popular option is to place audio portions of lectures on the web site so that students can download and play the lectures on their MP3 players.

All of these methods enrich the online learning experience. The one drawback is Internet speed and cost. Even in the United States, the cost of Internet access and a home computer may be more than some students can afford. In rural areas, the Internet connectivity may be slow. In developing countries, low Internet speed and high cost can be factors limiting the use of some newer technologies. In countries like Vanuatu, it may take five minutes to open a course web page and even simple tasks such as email can be time consuming and frustrating. Internet costs in such regions may be inflated by the presence of telecommunication monopolies. With no competition, there is little incentive to lower prices.

In India, where more than half of their 1.1 billion people earn approximately two dollars per day (World Bank, 2007), inhabitants cannot afford computers and must rely on Internet cafes for access. As a result access time to online courses will be limited. Similar conditions occur throughout the Third World. According to March 2008 statistics reported by the Association for Progressive Communication (APC, 2008) only 3.6% of global Internet users were from Africa. In regions where Internet access is not available or computers are too expensive, alternative delivery modes should be considered. In Africa, for example, governments are implementing mobile learning because more people have mobile phones than computers (Aderinoye, Ojokheta, & Olojede, 2007).

The lesson for online course providers is to limit the bandwidth requirements. Streaming video, teleconferencing, and software download requirements should be controlled. In poor regions, even if the student is able to download files, printing may be too expensive. These emerging technologies can further enhance online learning, giving students access to new resources and greater interaction with the instructor and classmates. Unfortunately, the full benefits of these new online tools will have to be introduced as the bandwidth allows.

Where Internet is not available, another option is to deliver educational training via correspondence courses, television, or radio. While these methods do not have the interactivity and student support offered by eLearning, they may be the most appropriate and cost-effective means of providing educational access to some populations. As Internet and computer costs decrease, eLearning may become viable. However, it is critical to provide the educational opportunities that will assist developing nations to upgrade their standard of living and the quality of their work force.

International Issues and Opportunities

By the year 2000, eLearning had spread throughout the United States. Now, less than a decade later online learning is poised to leap across oceans. Unlike face-to-face programs, students do not need passports and visas to attend online universities; international borders tumble with a click of the mouse. Universities in a number of countries are seizing the opportunity to attract foreign students. Unlike face-to-face teaching, students can remain in their home countries while earning their degrees. There is no need for visas or travel expense. Following the global economic meltdown in 2008, online learning takes on new relevance as countries tighten their immigration requirements and consumers become less able to travel. The question is which universities will be the innovators to tap this emerging international educational market.

In my role as an associate professor at the University of the South Pacific, one of only two regional universities in the world, I teach at campuses in our 12 member countries. I have observed that a few online universities have already come ashore on remote South Pacific islands. Students in Nauru, the Marshall Islands, and other developing countries can now earn their degrees online through Park University, San Diego State University, Brigham University, Divine Word University, Goroka College, the University of Papua New Guinea (UPNG), University of the Sunshine Coast, Charles Sturt University, and Revans University. The UPNG program is particularly attractive because it offers low tuition rates and delivers programs that meet the needs of local governments.

Just as American universities are experiencing competition from online universities, traditional universities in other foreign countries are beginning to lose enrollments to foreign online universities. A problem that will confront universities in developing countries is the attraction of online degrees from universities in the U.S., Canada, Great Britain, India, Australia, and New Zealand. Students who wish to migrate to Australia, New Zealand, Canada, and the United States are beginning to recognize that a degree from an accredited foreign university may provide greater employment opportunities in their destination country. As students begin to understand the benefits of accreditation, this will put further pressure on local universities that cannot offer accredited programs. One issue limiting the size of this international market is financial support. Like American taxpayers, foreign governments must consider whether to support students enrolled in foreign universities.

As universities in developing nations recognize this new competition from foreign online universities, some are moving to implement online programs to maintain their enrollments. However, this may not be the wisest choice. For such universities, it may be uneconomical to fund the needed infrastructure and to hire the staff needed to operate the online program. In such cases, the introduction of foreign online programs may actually be a benefit to the developing country. In the past, the best and the brightest students migrated to other countries to receive their undergraduate and graduate training. Often, these students did not return. Online training allows students to stay at home while earning their degree, making it more likely that they will remain in the country after graduation.

Cultural Barriers

At the beginning of this chapter, barriers to change for American universities were discussed. Christensen, Horn, and Johnson (2008) offer an excellent analysis of factors that limit the ability of academic institutions to change. For some foreign universities the local culture can make it even more difficult to adapt to changing market demands. In the South Pacific, for example, many educators view educational change as a cultural

threat imposed by Western imperialism. According to Taufe'ulungaki (2002: p.15) "The failure of education in the Pacific can be attributed to a large degree to the imposition of an alien system designed for western social and cultural contexts, which are underpinned by quite different values." Since educational reform is viewed as a cultural threat, local universities may be unable to unable to adapt to the online tsunami that is poised to sweep across the South Pacific.

Cultural characteristics, such as respect for authority, can also make it more difficult for foreign students to be successful in online courses. This attitude can cause students to be reluctant to participate in class discussions and activities, lest this be viewed as a sign of disrespect. Robbins (2004) noted this influence of culture on Web-based and multimedia learning in the South Pacific. Wang (2007) supports this finding, reporting that students raised in a culture of respect for elders and persons in authority are less inclined to participate in online activities.

A second cultural barrier for some foreign students is a reluctance to participate in mixed-gender and intercultural groups. Such students prefer to work in homogenous groups or to work alone. Therefore, online universities will need to assist such students to develop online team skills. A third barrier to online learning in some countries is language. Although English may be the language used in pre-college and university teaching, for many students, English is their second, third, or even fourth language. In Vanuatu, for example, there are three official languages – English, French, and Bislama. In addition, there are 113 indigenous languages that are still actively spoken. Therefore, online teachers must be alert that teaching materials are written at the appropriate level to accommodate such cultural diversity (Hussin, 2007; Rutherford and Kerr, 2008).

A fourth barrier to online learning can be a cultural predisposition to abhor deadlines. Some students, particularly older individuals, prefer correspondence courses that take longer to complete and offer more forgiving deadlines. In the South Pacific, this attitude is called *Fiji Time*, which refers to a very slow way of doing things. This *Fiji Time* effect, which is most prevalent among older students, is another issue online colleges will need to address, if such students are to be successful.

A fifth cultural barrier is concern whether online learning meets local needs. Matthewson and Thaman (1998) questioned whether eLearning, which they view as increasing student/teacher separation, might be in opposition to cultural needs. A study by Marsh and Hogan (2005) did not support this view. Instead, the authors found that students in Samoa and Vanuata eagerly worked in an international setting that culminated in a videoconference debate between the two student groups separated by thousands of miles from each other and the instructors. Although online providers must consider cultural issues, the new generation of learners is becoming members of the technology generation. Even in remote island settings, students watch MTV, own cell phones, and play computer games. While some countries may wish to resist cultural change, international borders cannot block technological change. The lure of technology is too strong, especially for the younger generation.

SOLUTIONS AND RECOMMENDATIONS

Online learning is costly to develop and to deliver, requiring an institution to invest in the technology, the network infrastructure, and the support staff. A successful online operation must also have administrative vision, a clear plan, adequate funding, and appropriate autonomy. Finally, the online unit must have the authority to evaluate the curriculum and the teaching to ensure the quality of the online courses. Although eLearning promises to expand access to higher education

in developing countries, Narayan (2007) and Sife, Lwoga, and Sanga (2007) point out that inadequate infrastructure and connectivity still persist. The point of this analysis is that universities will want to carefully consider whether it is in their best interest to offer entire degrees by eLearning. While eLearning can be one solution to increasing academic competition and changing market needs, it requires an administrative vision that supports innovation. If the management style is rule laden and top down, eLearning may not be viable. In such institutions, it may make more sense to partner with or buy eLearning courses from online universities.

Another reality facing universities is the new breed of online competitors that crosses state and national borders. If traditional universities are to compete, they need to adopt a business-like approach. Academics may scoff at turning academic institutions into businesses, but it is impossible to offer quality learning without money or resources. Universities will benefit from process that allows them to react quickly to meet the needs of their customers. Another necessary change is a more cooperative attitude toward business, other academic institutions, and governments. At one time it was comforting for academic institutions to be *ivory* towers, but in this time of economic change and growing competition, moats and drawbridges offer little protection.

Increasingly, universities realize that they must be more proactive in meeting their customers' need. One innovative example is the online program implemented by the University of the South Pacific (USP) to retrain teachers in the Cook Islands, which has experienced a student population shift that resulted in an over supply of primary teachers and a shortage of secondary teachers. In consultation with Cook Island educators and government officials, USP developed an online program to retrain primary teachers for secondary teaching. This innovative program is designed to allow teachers the flexibility to take

Table 3. Universities Offering Online Graduate Programs

University	University
American Intercontinental University	Park University
Argosy University	Penn State University
Athabasca University	Regis University
California State University	South University
Capella University	University of Colorado
Columbia Southern University	University of Florida
Duke University	University of Illinois
Florida State University	University of Liverpool
Franklin University	University of Massachusetts
Indiana University	University of Phoenix
Kaplan University	Walden University
Northeastern University	Western Governors University

the subject-area courses through a variety of South Pacific and New Zealand online universities. Teachers can work while upgrading their skills. One forward-thinking aspect of this initiative is the willingness to cross credit courses from foreign universities.

Another recommendation for universities is to increase their focus on the retraining needs of workers. This retraining may include both recertification courses and advanced degrees. One benefit for universities is that mid-career workers have the resources to pay the tuition. For example, the Duke University MBA program offers a blended approach to cater to career executives who want training, but are not willing to stop working for 18 months. This degree mixes online courses with short residential sessions in Asia, Latin America, Europe, and North America. The tuition for the degree is approximately $115,000, but executives are eager to enter a program that meets their needs, allowing them to continue working while earning their degree. A list of universities offering online graduate degrees is shown in Table 3. By 2005 nearly half of all face-to-face graduate programs were also offering online courses (Allen, 2005).

In developing nations, online learning is already proving its worth. As one student in Fiji wrote to the author, "I live near RakiRaki. Last year I had to drive three hours on a dirt road to bring my assignment to Suva. Now that you are using a course management system, I can submit my assignments from home. Thank you."

FUTURE TRENDS

Online learning will continue to become an essential part of educational programs at all levels. While this chapter focuses on the development of eLearning in higher education, online learning has already spread to primary and secondary schools. Picciano and Seaman (2007) estimated that in 2005 nearly 700,000 high school students were enrolled in an online course, which represents a tenfold increase in just six years. High schools already use online programs to assist at risk students and provide student mentoring. Online programs purchased from private providers allow high schools to offer advanced science and humanities courses that the schools could not afford to develop or to provide staff.

The implication of this spread of eLearning to pre-college learning is that entering university students will look for increased online learning options. As travel and shipping costs rise, online courses will become a cost-saving alternative. Online courses also have advantages in speed of development and course availability. ELearning can provide more courses, cost savings by using part-time teachers. . Table 4 lists other eLearning educational benefits for both students and educational institutions. The challenge for traditional universities can be to convince the faculty and administration to adapt to changing customer needs.

The demand for online training by government and industry will continue to grow. One example is the United States military. Although the services provide on-base training, online learning plays an important role in meeting the needs of personnel who often deploy to other assignments throughout the world. Online training solves this problem as shown in the following example. Recently, this author was teaching an online course that included a U.S. fighter pilot stationed in Europe. During the first week of the course, the pilot was stationed in England, during the second week in France, and in Germany for the third week. The pilot did very well in the course and reported that his travels had no negative effect on his course work. He simply logged on each night in the various countries.

The flexibility of eLearning is strength, but lack of acceptability is a liability. Therefore, universities must set up ongoing research to evaluate eLearning effectiveness and quality. One process that may assist in this regard is greater use of face-to-face examinations in online courses. For eLearning to be accepted, universities must demonstrate the value of their online product. Other research opportunities include measuring student satisfaction and success in online programs compared to face-to-face delivery. Finally, universities that deliver programs to markets with significant cultural differences will want to conduct research to ensure that the programs address the students' cultural needs.

Table 4. Rationale for Offering Online Course

Advantages of Online Courses
Increase student access to education
Enhance student/teacher interaction
Provide rapid feedback on assignments
Motivate student discussions
Promote critical thinking
Shorten time for degree completion
Increase enrollment and university reputation
Extend market beyond traditional service area
Provide training for industry
Promote student cultural interaction
Reduce strain on physical plant

CONCLUSION

Changing fiscal and economic realities present universities with three challenges: The first is reduced funding. The second is an unprecedented need to adapt to customer needs. The third is competition from national and international institutions of higher learning. In order to meet these challenges, universities will need to develop new strategies. As undergraduate students become less willing to spend five and six years to graduate (Epper & Garn, 2003), universities need to seek innovative alternatives. The *ivory tower* gatekeepers need to be replaced with customer greeters who smile as they say "Welcome."

The reality is that if universities do not offer eLearning opportunities, other institutions will step in to meet the market demand. It is a fact that education has become an international activity and that students realize that they are customers with choices.

The continued growth of eLearning offers a variety of research opportunities. In contrast to face-to-face classes and correspondence courses, online courses have a complete record of student-teacher interactions that can facilitate research. One topic of interest is undergraduate class size. It has been shown that student-centered online learning requires smaller class size, typically no more than 20 students. The smaller classes allow teachers to interact and to provide prompt feedback (Morgan, 2003).

At the close of this chapter, it is important to reiterate the need for adequate infrastructure since this is critical to develop a successful eLearning program. The university needs to start with a business plan and it needs to adopt a business approach with clear expectations. Is the goal to lose money, break even, or generate a profit? Who is the customer – existing students or a new market? Will online tuition be the same or different than for other delivery modes? How will tuition fees be set for local, regional, and foreign students? Other start-up decisions include funding, staffing, organizational structure, ITC backbone, and faculty training. Teachers must also be trained to use the technology (Mortera-Gutierrez, 2006) and to undergo a mental transformation from teacher-centered to student-centered learning (Ali, 2003). Often, teachers must be weaned from lecture to facilitation.

With the growth of eLearning, universities must think less locally and serve more globally. Universities that promote online learning will continue to develop new student markets. It was a dramatic environmental change that caused the demise of the dinosaur. The rise of eLearning is no less dramatic. The instructional approaches of today must evolve into electronic practices of tomorrow.

REFERENCES

Adams, J. (2008). Understanding the factors limiting the acceptability of online courses and degrees. *International Journal on E-Learning*, *7*(4), 573–587.

Aderinoye, R. A., Ojokheta, K. O., & Olojede, A. A. (2007). Integrating mobile learning into nomadic education programs in Nigeria: Issues and perspectives. *International Review of Research in Open and Distance Learning*, *8*(2), 1–17.

Akdemir, O. (2008). Teaching in online courses: experiences of instructional technology faculty members. *Turkish Online Journal of Distance Education*, *9*(2), 97–108.

Ali, A. (2003). Instructional design and online instruction: Practice and perception. *TechTrends*, *47*(5), 42–45. doi:10.1007/BF02763205

Allen, I. E., & Seaman, J. (2003). *Sizing the opportunity: The quality and extent of online education in the United States, 2002 and 2003*. Needham, MA: The Sloan Consortium. Retrieved September 1, 2008, from http://www.sloan-c.org/sizingtheOpportunity_survey02-03.pdf

Allen, I. E., & Seaman, J. (2005*). Growing by degrees: Online education in the United States*. Needham, MA: The Sloan Consortium. Retrieved September 1, 2008, from www.sloan-c.org/publications/survey/pdf/growing_by_degrees_southern.pdf

Allen, I. E., & Seaman, J. (2006). *Making the grade: Online education in the United States*. Needham, MA: The Sloan Consortium. Retrieved December 2, 2008, from http://www.sloanconsortium.org/publications/survey/pdf/making_the_grade.pdf

Allen, I. E., & Seaman, J. (2007). *Online nation: Five years growth in online learning*. Needham, MA: The Sloan Consortium. Retrieved October 9, 2008, from http://www.sloanconsortium.org/publications/survey/pdf/online nation.pdf

Asian Development Bank (ADB). (2008). *Education and skills: Strategies for accelerated development in Asia and the Pacific*. Manila. Retrieved March 15, 2009, from http://www.adb.org/Documents/Studies/Education-Skills-Strategies-Development/Education-Skills-Strategies-Development.pdf

Association for Progressive Communications (APC). (2008, October 13). *Why APC continues to obsess over Internet access.* Retrieved March 31, 2009 from http://www.apc.org/en/news/development/all/why-apc-continues-obsess-over-internet-access

Badat, S. (2005). South Africa: Distance higher education policies for access, social equity, quality, and social and economic responsiveness in a context of the diversity of provision. *Distance Education, 26*(2), 183–204. doi:10.1080/01587910500168843

Bower, B. L. (2001). Distance education: Facing the faculty challenge. *Online Journal of Distance Learning Administration, 4*(2), 1-9. Retrieved May 8, 2008, from http://www.westga.edu/~distance/ojdla/summer42/bower42.html

Bradburn, E. M., & Zimbler, L. (2002). *Distance education instruction by postsecondary staff: Fall 1998.* National Center for Educational Statistics, Statistical Analysis Report, February 2002, Postsecondary Education Descriptive Analysis Reports. 1-82. Retrieved December 24, 2008, from http://nces.ed.gov/pubs2002/2002155.pdf

Bruner, J. (2007). Factors motivating and inhibiting faculty in offering their courses via distance education. *Online Journal of Distance Learning Administration, 10*(2), 1–18.

CHEA Directory of Regional Accreditation Organizations. (2009). Retrieved on April 1, 2009 from http://www.chea.org/Directories/regional.asp

Christensen, C. M., Horn, M. B., & Johnson, C. W. (2008). *Disrupting class.* New York: McGraw-Hill.

College Board. (2008). *Trends in higher education series.* Retrieved on March 29, 2009 from http://www.collegeboard.com/trends

Davis, S. M., & Batkin, J. W. (1994). *The Monster Under the Bed: How Business is Mastering the Opportunity for Knowledge for Profit.* New York: Simon & Shuster.

Epper, R. M., & Garn, M. (2003). *Virtual college & university consortia: A national study.* (State Higher Education Executive Officers (SHEEO)). Retrieved August 15, 2008, from http://www.sheeo.org/publicat.htm

Frey, A., Faul, A., & Yankelov, P. (2003). Student perception of web-assisted teaching strategies. *Journal of Social Work Education, 39*(3), 443–449.

Gastfriend, H. (2008). *University System of Georgia Student Information Technology Survey.* Retrieved July 1, 2008, from www.alt.usg.edu/research/studies/USG_SIT_total%20aggregate.pdf

Gerlich, R. N. (2005). Faculty perceptions of distance learning. *Distance Education Report, 9*(17), 8. Retrieved July 25, 2008, from http://www.magnapubs.com/pub/magnapubs_der/9_17/news/597900-1.html

Glater, J. (2008, March 8). Colleges reduce out-of-state tuition to lure students. *New York Times.* Retrieved on March 15, 2009 from http://www.nytimes.com/2008/03/08/education/08states.html?_r=1

Gulati, S. (2008). Technology-enhanced learning in developing nations: A review. *International Review of Research in Open and Distance Learning, 9*(1), 1–16.

Hagel, P., & Shaw, R. N. (2006). Students' perceptions of study modes. *Distance Education, 27*(3), 283–302. doi:10.1080/01587910600940398

Hawksley, R., & Owen, J. (2002). *Going the distance: Are there common factors in high performance distance learning?* (Report No. 1225/02/02/2000). Learning and Skills Development Agency, London. ERIC Document Reproduction Service No. ED464231.

Herbst, M. (2008). The high barriers facing foreign workers. *Business Week Online.* Retrieved March 28, 2009, from Academic Search Premier database.

Hogan, R. (2009, June). *Attitudes of indigenous peoples toward distance learning in the South Pacific: An empirical study.* Paper presented at the ED-MEDIA 2009--World Conference on Educational Multimedia, Hypermedia & Telecommunications, Honolulu, HI.

Hussin, V. (2007). Supporting off-shore students: a preliminary study. *Innovations in Education and Teaching International, 44*(4), 363–376. doi:10.1080/14703290701602763

Joliet Junior College Admissions. (2009). Retrieved on April 1, 2009 from http://www.jjc.edu/admissions/pages/tuition.aspx?c=1

Kanuka, H. (2002). Guiding principles for facilitating higher levels of web-based distance teaching and learning in post-secondary settings. *Distance Education, 23*(2), 163–182. doi:10.1080/0158791022000009187

Kaser, D. (2007, November). Law of the blog. [from Academic Search Premier database.]. *Information Today, 24*(10), 14. Retrieved March 31, 2009.

Keller, C., & Cernerud, L. (2002). Students' perceptions of e-learning in university education. *Journal of Educational Media, 27*(1–2), 55–67. doi:10.1080/0305498032000045458

Kemp, J. E. (2006). Foundations for systemic change. *TechTrends, 50*(2), 20–21. doi:10.1007/s11528-006-7582-1

Maguad, B. (2007). Identifying the needs of customers in higher education. *Education, 127*(3), 332-343. Retrieved March 3, 2009, from Academic Research Database. Document ID 1268062551.

Marsh, C., & Hogan, R. (2005). Distance education the Pacific way. *The International Journal of Learning, 12,* 3–7.

Matthewson, C., & Thaman, K. (1998). Designing the Rebbelib: Staff development in a multicultural environment. In C. Latchem & F. Lockwood (Eds.), *Staff development in open and flexible learning,* (pp. 115-125). Florence, KY: Routledge.

Minotti, J., & Giguere, P. (2003). The realties of web-based training. *THE Journal, 30*(11), 41-44. Retrieved October 15, 2008, from Academic Research Library database (Document ID: 353845701).

Morgan, G. (2003). Faculty use of course management systems. *Educause Centre for Applied Research, 2,* 1–97.

Mortera-Gutiérrez, F. (2006). Faculty best practices using blended learning in e-learning and face-to-face instruction. *International Journal on E-Learning, 5*(3), 313–337.

Muilenburg, L., & Berge, Z. (2001). Barriers to distance education: A factor-analytic study. *American Journal of Distance Education, 15*(2), 7–22. doi:10.1080/08923640109527081

Myers, C., Bennet, D., Brown, G., & Henderson, T. (2004). Emerging online learning environments and student learning: An analysis of faculty perceptions. *Educational Technology and Society, 7*(1), 78–86.

Narayan, G. (2007). The digital divide: E-governance and m-governance in a hub and spoke model. *The Electronic Journal of Information Systems in Developing Countries, 31*(1), 1–14.

Ng, C. (2006). Academics telecommuting in open and distance education universities: Issues, challenges, and opportunities. *The International Review of Research in Open and Distance Learning 7*(2) 1-16. Retrieved November 1, 2007, from http://www.irrodl.org/index.php/irrodl/article/view/300/632

O'Malley, J., & McGraw, H. (1999). Student perceptions of distance learning, online learning, and the traditional classroom [Electronic version]. *Online Journal of Distance Learning Administration, 2*(4), 1-10. Retrieved on July 1, 2008, from http://www.westga.edu/~distance/omalley24.html

Oblinger, D. (1999). Global education: Thinking creatively. *Higher Education in Europe, 24*(2), 151–258. doi:10.1080/0379772990240212

Pachnowski, L., & Jurezyk, J. (2003). Perceptions of faculty on the effect of distance learning technology on faculty preparation time. *Online Journal of Distance Learning Administration, 6*(3), 1-10. Retrieved December 26, 2008, from http://www.westga.edu/~distance/ojdla/fall63/pachnowski64.html

Parker, A. (2003). Motivation and incentives for distance faculty. *Online Journal of Distance Learning Administration, 6*(3), 1-6. Retrieved November 7, 2008, from http://www.westga.edu/~distance/ojdla/fall63/parker63.htm

Picciano, A., & Seaman, J. (2007). *K-12 online learning: A survey of U.S. school district administrators*. Needham, MA: The Sloan Consortium. Retrieved December 27, 2008, from http://www.sloanconsortium.org/publications/survey/pdf/K-12_Online_Learning.pdf

Robbins, C. (2006). Providing cultural context with educational multimedia in the South Pacific. *Educational Technology & Society, 9*(1), 202–212.

Rockwell, K., Schauer, J., Fritz, S., & Marx, D. (1999). Incentives and obstacles influencing higher education faculty and administrators to teach via distance. *Online Journal of Distance Learning Administration, 2*(4), 1-8. Retrieved December 26, 2008, from http://www.westga.edu/~distance/ojdla/winter24/rockwell24.html

Rutherford, A., & Kerr, B. (2008). An inclusive approach to online learning environments: models and resources. *Turkish Online Journal of Distance Education, 9*(2), 64–85.

Shank, P. (2005). 5 common fears about teaching online — Fact vs. fiction. *Distance Education, 9*(24), 5-7. Retrieved February 8, 2008, from http://www.magnapubs.com/issues/ magnapubs_oc/5_10/news/598041-1.html.

Sife, A. S., Lwogoa, E. T., and Sanga, C. (2007). New technologies for teaching and learning: Challenges for higher learning institutions in developing countries. *International Journal of Education and Development using ICT. 3*(2), 57-67.

Switzer, J., & Switzer, R. (1994). Copyright question: Using audiovisual works in a satellite-delivered program. *T.H.E. Journal, 21*(10), 76–79.

Tanzer, A. (2007, February). Apollo goes back to school. *Kiplingers*, 19.

Taufe'ulungaki, A. (2002). Pacific education at the crossroads: Are there alternatives? In F. Pene, A. Taufe'ulungaki, & C. Benson (Eds.), *Tree of opportunity: Rethinking Pacific education* (pp. 5-21). Suva: USP.

Toffler, A. (1985). *The adaptive corporation*, New York. McGraw Hill.

Twigg, C., & Oblinger, D. (1997). *The virtual university*. Washington, DC: Educom. Retrieved on February 12, 2009, from http://net.educause.edu/ir/library/html/nli0003.html van Rosmalen, P., Sloep, P., Kester, L., Brouns, F., de Croock, M., Pannekeet, K., & Koper, R. (2008). A learner support model based on peer tutor selection. *Journal of Computer Assisted Learning, 24*(1) 74-86.

Waits, T., & Lewis, L. (2003). *Distance education at degree-granting postsecondary institutions: 2000–2001.* U.S. Department of Education, National Center for Education Statistics. Retrieved December 2, 2008, from http://nces.ed.gov/pubs2003/2003017.pdf

Wang, M. (2007). Designing online courses that effectively engage learners, from diverse cultural backgrounds. *British Journal of Educational Technology, 38*(2), 294–311. doi:10.1111/j.1467-8535.2006.00626.x

Wilson, C. (2001). Faculty attitudes about distance learning. *EDUCAUSE Quarterly, 24*(2), 70–71.

Winter, G. (2002, July 15). Junior colleges try niche as cheap path to top universities. *New York Times*, 1.

Wolcott, L., & Betts, K. S. (1999). What's in it for me? Incentives for faculty participation in distance education. *Journal of Distance Education, 14*(2), 34-39. Retrieved December 25, 2008, from http://cade.athabascau.ca/voll4.2/Wolcott_et_al.html

Wolston, V. (2009). *International education services.* Retrieved April 1, 2009, from http://www.international.umd.edu/ies

World Bank. (2007, August 29). *Inclusive Growth Consultations.* Retrieved March 5, 2009, from http://www.worldbank.org.in/WBSITE/EXTERNAL/COUNTRIES/SOUTHASIAEXT/INDIAEXT84,00.html

Wright, C., Dhanarajan, G., & Reju, S. (2009). Recurring issues encountered by distance educators in developing and emerging nations. *The International Review of Research in Open and Distance Learning, 10*(1), 11-25. Retrieved March 23, 2009, from http://www.irrodl.org/index.php/irrodl/article/view/608/1180

Wuensch, K., Aziz, S., Ozan, E., Kishore, M., & Tabrizi, M. (2008). Pedagogical characteristics of online and face-to-face classes. *International Journal on E-Learning, 7*(3), 523–532.

Chapter 18

Positioning the Learning Organization for a Successful Distance Education Strategy

Monique Fuchs
Wentworth Institute of Technology, USA

Stephanie Cheney
Wentworth Institute of Technology, USA

ABSTRACT

Compared to traditional educational offerings, Distance Education requires a significantly different business model involving factors such as learning culture, target audience, infrastructure, course and content development, support models, and others. The following perspective is put forth in an effort to illustrate particular concerns that may affect internal operations, perceptions, and attitudes as well as external reception and market positioning of distance education offerings. Recommendations and solutions will be discussed that center around organizational systemic anchoring and faculty development as a critical success factor. All of these pieces will help to provide a framework that could be utilized in building a successful, and more importantly, sustainable distance education strategy and associated process. Emerging developments in the realm of distance education will be presented and provide an outlook of how this educational field may change and evolve in the near future.

INTRODUCTION

Planning, developing, and launching a Distance Education program is a large undertaking that when done well, can launch your organization into a new realm of possibilities. Strategy is the heart of any successful distance education implementation and it should always be anchored and aligned with the overall mission of the university or college. A Dis-

tance Education strategy is a subset of the overall strategic direction the organization is venturing towards and should seamlessly support the guiding principles and goals of an organization.

The Distance Education strategy is an elaborate and systematic plan of action and must include a thoughtful vision that considers the institutional culture, organizational and faculty development. It involves everyone within the organization, requires stepping back from the daily routine and taking a

DOI: 10.4018/978-1-61520-672-8.ch018

higher-level view of the mission and goals and best ways to implement them.

It is easy to equate Distance Education with technology but failure to consider all of the other factors that make up a successful implementation strategy is dangerous. Determination of what Distance Education means to an individual organization is a key consideration. "True learning organizations aren't those with the most courses; they are characterized by the broader culture of open knowledge exchange" (Rosenberg, 2008, p. 25). Thinking about the culture of an organization allows the identification of potential roadblocks and addresses them proactively.

To position an organization for a successful Distance Education strategy, considering an assessment of environmental and internal factors as a means to better understand the Higher Education landscape in general and the individual institution in particular will help to formulate a sound framework. Conducting an environmental scan will reveal existing programs, the potential for new developments, and niche markets for Distance Education. The internal scan evaluates technology needs, course and content development, and campus support.

Recommendations for the strategy development process are derived from organizational development practice. Because faculty development is one of the critical aspects in establishing Distance Education programs, it is singled out and reflected upon separately. A closer look at organizational development should identify key stakeholders, support structures, and the evaluation process while striving to build a governance structure with strong internal and external collaborations. Faculty development should examine teaching strategies for online courses, implementation of learning technologies, and effective technology integration. Getting faculty ready to teach in an online environment provides a great opportunity to bring supporting departments, such as the library and counseling services, into

the conversation and encourage collaborations across the organization.

While each aspect, technology, content, assessment, and support structures could be considered separately, a strategic plan will link all these individual pieces of an organization together, orchestrating the process, providing guiding principles and a vision, helping people see the bigger picture and achieve step-by-step goals that are measurable within the strategy. A strategic plan is the roadmap – not set in stone, flexible enough for adjustments, but still a refined roadmap that supports sustainable decision-making and goal-oriented movement.

BACKGROUND

Considering Distance Education

The Distance Education market is very diverse ranging from individual course offerings to certificates, undergraduate and graduate degree programs for the adult and/or non-traditional learners. Non-profit organizations are the logical source for such offerings; however, there has been a significant growth in recent years within the for-profit sector. Online universities, providers of learning portals and learning management systems are on the rise. Publishers repackage their contents to develop learning applications that are sometimes sold separately as a standalone learning solution or frequently in combination with textbooks.

Although much movement is noticeable in the Distance Education sector, not all universities and colleges have branched out into the virtual learning market as Distance Education still struggles with acceptance problems and is critically monitored for a variety of reasons (Oblinger & Hawkins, 2005). "Given the tremendous knowledge base already existent in their communities, higher education institutions have a significant advantage in capturing this new market in learning – but only if they invest their resources wisely" (Massy & Zemsky, 1995, p. 11). Building and teaching online learning courses is only one side of the equation. It seems critical for an institution to identify a holistic internal distance education strategy and to achieve clarity of goals, expectations, benefits and challenges (Rosenberg, 2001). The intention of such strategy is to provide a framework and a roadmap for the organization in which to consider different stakeholders and to communicate the goals and concrete planned steps to realize Distance Education offerings.

Drivers for Higher Education to Integrate Distance Education

Organizations typically have a variety of goals and expectations when considering Distance Education. The two most critical ones are the economical and the educational values. From an economical aspect Distance Education could help scale educational offerings, attract new students, or serve current students while supporting recruitment and retention. Transferability of credits, cost-effectiveness, and collaborations with other institutions and industry offer attractive benefits in the age of globalization.

From an educational standpoint building learning communities, flexibility of learning, individualization, knowledge and experience exchange are only a few benefits of Distance Education.

The "Generation X" (Sacks, 1996) and "Digital Native" (Prensky, 2001) students have more technical experience and exposure to technology and are more comfortable in utilizing the internet, social learning networks, and online collaborations as learning tools. Higher flexibility of learning may attract professionals and non-traditional students, who have different work and family commitments but are highly motivated to go back to school and add a valuable industry perspective to the online classroom. In addition changing industries and global positioning of companies places employees

in different parts of the world for a short or longer period of time. Distance Education offerings can provide a stable yet flexible learning arrangement for this target audience.

Technology is a part of our everyday life at work, personally, and in the community and when it is thoughtfully integrated into the classroom, it helps students develop the skills necessary to contribute to a knowledge-based society, increase their employability, and build a career. Students don't think of it as technology, it is just how they live, how their work-environments function. When these "digital native" or non-traditional students come to class and are asked to turn off technology that they otherwise consider essential within their professional and personal sphere, we are encouraging a major disconnect between their daily lives and their educational experience.

Change Management: An Organizational Challenge

"To execute strategy is to execute change at all levels of an organization" (Norton, 2002, p.1). The culture together with the change readiness and willingness of the people within an organization should not be underestimated. Depending on the roll-out plan and the development work within one or multiple departments, it is vital to have the support and buy-in of critical stakeholders in order to elevate the Distance Education offerings to a successful launch. After all, many different business units and offices on campus are impacted and they are the ones who will need to champion the transition from traditional program offerings to Distance Education.

Change management is the combination of processes, activities, and approaches that manage the people of the organization through the transition from the old way of doing things to the new way, from the old way of training to e-Learning. Change management is about communication and exchange, dialogue and questions, leadership and support. The focus of change management is on attitudes and behaviors and the objective is to win the battle for the "hearts and minds" of the people – all of the people – within the organization (Dublin, 2008, p. 46).

It is fundamental to recognize the human aspect going through a major implementation such as the integration of Distance Education. Not all people will be equally excited, not everybody will immediately jump on board. Educating stakeholders, working to develop a business case, bringing people together and building bridges is necessary to gain momentum. In addition, getting all stakeholders such as faculty, students, alumni, and support staff involved in the process will result in greater commitment to the overall cause.

In general communication is critical to any change process. Human nature is to try to understand and find reasoning in processes or as Weick (1995) defined it: "Sensemaking is what it says it is, namely, making something sensible" (p.16). Sensemaking is an important factor within the framework of successful strategy development and the initiation of altered, new processes.

People hold on to status quo and are used to established processes. Removing these known entities can lead to anxiety. "Abandoning (of) the comfort zone that one survived or thrived on (…) has an emotional dimension to it" (Carr, 1997, p. 229). The key is to recognize individual anxieties and to reframe them as an engine for change supporting the definition and development of meaningful Distance Education strategy and realization processes.

DEVELOPING A DISTANCE EDUCATION STRATEGY

Issues and Considerations

Higher Education organizations considering Distance Education will need to take a close look at their goals and expectations. It is critical to understand why an organization is exploring Distance Education. It has to be for the right reasons based on the right drivers within the particular niche market that only this organization can serve best.

Launching Distance Education programs involves more than the development of online courses. Conducting a thorough environmental scan clarifies the understanding of how potential programs fit into the market and how the programs need to be positioned to attract prospective students. The identification of the target audience, competing programs and competing organizations, which might impact your target audience as well as the accreditation process are all factors that need to be evaluated.

An Internal Scan will weigh factors within your institution that could impact development of distance programs. These include the evaluation of current and required technology, subject matter experts and their content specialties, elements of a quality program, and the organization of a support team.

Environmental Scan

An environmental scan can help to determine all factors external yet relevant for the success of an organization in establishing Distance Education.

Market Position and Perception

Important questions focus on market positioning and perceptions. What is the standing of the organization within the Higher Education landscape? If it is a research institution it may be perceived as cutting edge and challenging status quo. If the college is more focused on hands-on education industry connections may be established and the focus for Distance Education could be on advancing careers of practitioners or positioning existing students better in the marketplace. Consider how this could translate into Distance Education and how this specific industry and target audience would perceive online learning.

Target Audience

If the potential target audience has no contact with computers in their daily lives, it would be more difficult to convince them to sign up for an online program than with prospective students who live and breathe technology. The location of the potential student body is another important factor, if the students are already on campus, e.g. in an undergraduate program, or if they are mainly expected to be professionals already working in the field. A blend of the two groups could be another alternative that needs to be carefully weighed in light of learning outcomes and student expectations. This determination is one of the main drivers of how an organization can position and market distance education offerings and how support structures need to be developed within the organization. Also relevant is a look at future learning developments and how the target audience may potentially adopt them going forward. To include such developments as part of the Distance Education strategy could be the key to staying competitive.

Competing Organizations

Equally necessary is an assessment of competing universities and colleges that are operating within the same industry field, with the same focus, hands-on or research, and who attract similar types of students. If those institutions offer Distance Education, engaging in conversations with them about their experiences may add valuable perspective. The kinds of programs they offer, the formats, success rate, and industry opinions could help the organization to formulate its own strategy that will set it apart from the competition.

In general, the possibility of collaborations should be explored. Industry relationships could be a stepping-stone for engaging in corporate university models as industry and university may serve the same objectives. Consortium models are also a valid option as they support the development of supplemental offerings, e.g. to satisfy the general education component with Math, Science, and English for degree offerings. Alternatively, Associations could be a great resource to formulate partnerships with. They can help promote offerings, have a rich pool of potential students, or function as exclusive provider of continuing education to their members.

Expectation of Accreditation Agencies

Another focus of the external scan should be accreditation agencies. The Council for Higher Education Accreditation (CHEA) is a private, nonprofit national organization that coordinates accreditation activity in the United States. According to their report, "Accreditation and Assuring Quality in Distance Learning" programs from 2002, both national and regional accreditation bodies have made changes to their process of certifying quality learning programs. While the standards vary depending on the accreditation organization, CHEA has identified seven areas of institutional activity that are reviewed in determining the quality of distance learning programs (Eaton, 2002):

- **Institutional Mission**: The programs should be consistent with the institution's area of expertise and mission.
- **Institutional Organizational Structure**: Programs must be approved and administered under institutional policies and procedures including appropriate evaluation.
- **Institutional Resources**: Programs must have a financial plan that provides equipment, faculty training, and other resources necessary to maintain the effectiveness of the program.

- **Curriculum and Instruction**: Content and learning experiences must be structured appropriately for Distance Education and align with institution-wide standards. The quality of the academic work must be the same as for on-campus programs.
- **Faculty Support**: Faculty members must be trained to teach at a distance and provided with appropriate support and resources.
- **Student Support**: Students must be provided with technical support and programs shall offer timely and meaningful interaction between faculty and students.
- **Student Learning Outcomes**: Institutions must document that they are meeting their educational mission and goals and that student outcomes are acceptable.

As Distance Education has become more prevalent in Higher Education, most accreditation bodies have adapted their process and provide guidelines to ensure that quality programs are becoming the norm. It is recommended to become familiar with these guidelines put forth by the various accreditation bodies while developing a Distance Education program to ensure a smooth accreditation process in the future.

Internal Scan

As important as the external scan is the fundamental understanding of the organization at its core. The evaluation of the existing infrastructure is essential homework to bridge the gap between status quo and desired state. The infrastructural needs are varied and range from hard to soft factors such as marketing, technology, academic support, faculty roles, content and course development cycle, delivery models to student preparedness.

Technology

Most of the time when considering Distance Education, discussions evolve around the integration of learning technology and technology support. This however, is only one part of the equation. "Organizations that focus exclusively on the deployment of an LMS (Learning or Course Management System), an LCMS (Learning Content Management System), or an online catalog of hundreds of courses, are accentuating means rather than ends—enablers rather than results" (Rosenberg, 2008, p.25). Although it is necessary to employ a solid technology infrastructure to guarantee a smooth learning experience for the students and a stable teaching environment for the instructors, it is more critical to determine the learning goals and objectives first. Learning technology has the potential to transform the student experience, providing opportunities for collaborative and team-based activities where students have the chance to apply what they've learned with the guidance of an instructor. What would a Distance Education course be worth with all technological bells and whistles, but the students did not reach the learning objectives, felt overwhelmed with activities driven by technology, and had no sufficient instructional support and interaction with other students? Technology should not drive pedagogy but rather vice versa.

Content Development and Quality

Curricula and content are in the academic domain and will emerge from within the respective school or department that seeks to branch out into Distance Education. It is necessary to determine if the planned online learning initiative should be from existing content or if new content needs to be developed. This makes a huge difference in terms of time and resources that need to be dedicated to this project.

Another critical factor is the decision on the educational quality of the program. What is considered quality education, and what are the specific quality standards that should be promoted within an organization's brand? This is one of the biggest disconnects among stakeholders in Higher

Education. Not knowing exactly what and how it should be delivered may detrimentally affect the way the development of Distance Education is positioned. Allow adequate time for planning and development of courses to ensure high-quality delivery. The use of quality standards such as the "Quality Matters" (Maryland Online, Inc., 2008) rubric ensures not only consistent content development across courses but also acts as an effective reference to inform the creation of organization-specific quality standards.

Subject Matter Expert and Support Team

In order to develop content it is important to identify who is going to be the subject matter expert (SME) and what role this person or a team of people is expected to play. Content could be generated through outside resources; For example, industry professionals could be the provider of content and support the development of the course material together with faculty or, one or multiple faculty members already employed by the university could be charged with developing course content for online delivery. Either way it is essential to define what the university's expectation level is towards content development and how involved the designated subject matter expert will be in building content within an online environment. The SME could be just that – somebody providing expertise and initiating a dialogue with content developers, who will take the material and translate it into instructional content online. In this case additional staff may be necessary to form a true support system around the SME.

Another scenario would be that the SME also functions as the builder of the content online, serving in a dual role. This scenario potentially poses different necessary support requirements to help the SME be as efficient as possible. To start, the person needs to be trained in instructional design and online course development, quality standards previously defined by the organization,

and receive technical insights on how to operate online tools available for course delivery such as course management systems, online communication and collaboration tools, online quizzes and assignments.

The decision on what role the SME will play and what scenario best fits into the organizational structure of the university may also be dependent on already existing expertise among faculty members with online tools as well as existing support functions such as instructional designers, course developers or centers for teaching and learning. A staged approach could also be utilized in the start-up phase of Distance Education, where cost-cautious decisions are made in order to get the process started and to test the market. Regardless of the chosen model, once Distance Education becomes an established entity at the university, support staff will be necessary to sustain operations, as the business model of Distance Education is quite distinct from traditional education.

Supporting Functions

Universities and Colleges typically have an established marketing function. However, it is necessary to examine, if specific marketing knowledge or different marketing strategies need to be employed in order to promote and position new Distance Education offerings successfully in the Higher Education market.

Other support functions include the Registrar's Office and Student Affairs. Online students may have different expectations than on-site students and could potentially require different service offerings. One of the main goals of residential colleges is to build a strong student community beyond the classroom environment. To replicate this within a cohort of online students who may be scattered nationally or even internationally can be challenging. The human aspect is a critical factor to create a social environment within an otherwise potentially anonymous medium. This will not only have great impact on student satisfaction but also on student retention and the identification with the university, which is considerably more difficult to accomplish online.

Depending on what kind of programs will be offered online the need for a revision of the career service offerings may also be necessary. If the school is primarily undergraduate, but is looking to move into advanced online degrees, students may expect different support in finding internships during studies or jobs after graduation. As the university is positioned as supplier of undergraduates this also requires a shift of industry perception to recognize that graduate students are now entering the market place with higher expectations in job opportunities, but also with more advanced skill sets.

Solutions and Recommendations

When it comes to defining a Distance Education strategy, broad based input and a holistic systemic approach is necessary. There are many structures in Higher Education that can hinder this process such as a lack of governance structure, leadership from bottom up as well as top down, academic and administrative divide, and academic groupings, e.g. faculty senate and union. It is critical to bridge any limitations that arise and arrive at a common vision. Two main factors are the cornerstone of a successful strategy development process and are identified as an important part of the framework: strategic organizational development and faculty development.

Strategic Organizational Development

Introducing or refining Distance Education within Higher Education is a major undertaking that deserves attention from an organization-wide systemic perspective. Existing business processes may be altered, job responsibilities modified and the potential impact it may have on the organization's reputation, industry acceptance, finances, faculty and student body need to be considered. Some measures can be taken to help position the organization for these changes and help identify the unknown.

Building a Governance Model for Transparency

Although governance may or may not exist within the organization or the level of credibility may be varied, it is good practice to introduce a structure related to Distance Education that assures campus wide input as well as promotes a decision-making body representing critical stakeholders. This could be in form of a Distance Education task force or committee with significant input to administration. However, governance is not only a structure, but also a process (Millett, 1974).

It is a process of encouraging, persuading, and even of directing others to make decisions and to perform in accordance with decisions. (Millett, 1974, p.1)

Within this process it is essential to enter a dialogue with different interest groups on campus, which should include but are not limited to:

- Academic leaders (provost, deans, department heads, chairs, etc)
- Faculty to consider content and curriculum development, expectations, attitudes, and existing and needed competencies to build and teach online courses
- Prospective students to highlight interest levels and possible delivery models
- Student affairs with all facets of student life and career development
- Business and finance to provide input on feasibility and cost-effectiveness
- Business or Higher Education leaders as external advisors to provide input on industry needs and expectations
- Learning Technology experts to help determine instructional design, tools, and vendors.

Including major stakeholders in this process ensures trust, transparency, and integrity to any decision that may be made representing a unified front to others on campus that may question the decision making process or the final decision. The task force or committee members function as source of information, communication, and feedback loop within the community and within the task force/committee. During the process each member will be educated about the different aspects, concerns, and ideas each member brings to the table, which in turn helps to formulate a more holistic understanding of the planned Distance Education undertaking. It also equips members to set and communicate realistic expectations to different involved parties on issues such as start-up conditions, process, roles and responsibilities.

Forming Collaborations

A governance model can help support the communication and transparency of decision making, but equally important is the forming of collaborations inside and outside the organization.

Many offices in universities and colleges serve a similar purpose and work towards common objectives. Although their overall missions may be different, the common goals would benefit from collaborative efforts. This becomes particularly crucial for the evaluation of existing resources necessary to start or refine the Distance Education endeavor. Student development for example may be anchored within Student Affairs, but is also served by teaching & learning centers, student leadership programs, library and counseling services. This is also true for faculty development. Learning technology units, training and development, library and counseling services may support different needs relevant to improve building and teaching online courses. Consolidating and streamlining efforts can be a powerful support model for faculty members and students as well as help to leverage existing knowledge within the organization.

Breaking down the barriers and entering each other's "area", however, is the biggest challenge. People are the change agents, but "real change in real organizations is intensely personal" (Nadler, 1998, p. 3) and it requires vision, persistence, and patience to bring people together to become part of a whole instead of performing as isolated parts with less impact on the organization as a whole.

Defining Support Structures

Examining existing support structures will assist in sensible decision-making about necessary services that are currently not in place within the organization. Trying to leverage existing skills and knowledge will help control cost and give individuals a chance to become active parts in the implementation process, educating others and disseminating their experience and background to build a foundation for knowledge growth.

Typical considerations when building or refining Distance Education stem from the requirements originally set forth. Different support structures will be necessary, if a university decides to utilize Distance Education for a couple of individual courses or if they plan on rolling out complete certificate or degree programs; If the content already exists and needs to be transitioned into the online environment or if the content needs to be developed from scratch. Depending on the extent of the program, the major considerations evolve around project management, market research, content/curriculum development, roles and responsibilities, faculty and student development, technology acquisition and support, vendor relationships, marketing, industry feedback, support requirements, and assessment.

Benchmarking and Evaluation

However beautiful the strategy, you should occasionally look at the results. – Winston Churchill

Once a framework for the Distance Education strategy is defined, benchmarking and evaluation will be a valuable mechanism to monitor progress and results as well as allowing for possible course corrections. The benchmarks help determine the current status quo before Distance Education is integrated and outline the desired state once Distance Education is realized. Throughout the development and implementation process forma-tive and summative evaluations can help determine if milestones have been reached and if necessary modify originally determined processes based on new data, experiences, and knowledge gained throughout the process.

While quantitative data support an objective data analysis, it is equally important to collect qualitative data from stakeholders involved. This will help inform the process, communication, at-titudes, perceptions, and emerging situations - in short it will allow for a reading between lines. In addition to intentionally collected data through a variety of formats such as surveys, interviews, polls, support statistics etc. unintentionally col-lected or "emergent" data will also influence the process. This is the kind of data that could not be foreseen, but delivers valuable insights about strategic direction and process and may cause unexpected modifications (Mintzberg & Waters, 1985).

Faculty Development

While organizational positioning for a Distance Education strategy is fundamental, faculty devel-opment plays a significant role in this process as faculty members are critical stakeholders in the governance process, building content, delivering online courses, and are the face of the university or college to the student body.

Contrary to students, faculty members are an entity that can be influenced by the university or college over a long period of time, causing the impact of faculty development to be sustain-able. Faculty members are the cornerstones of a successful Distance Education implementation and particular attention to faculty development is an essential success factor. This could be a two-pronged approach concerned with teaching strategies in online environments and community building on the one hand side and introduction to learning technology on the other.

Distance Education poses many challenges for faculty members who build and teach online courses. Not only may the medium and technol-ogy be unfamiliar, but also the teaching strategies that work in the face-to-face classroom may not be as effective in an online setting.

Prior to developing a comprehensive training plan it is important to administer a faculty needs assessment. The assessment should be structured to reveal the knowledge, skills, and attitude of faculty related to technology tools, teaching strate-gies, implementation, and integration with online course curricula. Personal interviews with faculty, though time consuming, allow for a clearer picture of how faculty members currently use technology and what they are interested in learning more about. Benchmarking of faculty feedback will show clear gaps of need resulting in more targeted development of either formal faculty development activities or informal collaborative efforts that foster the sharing and exchange of experiences with Distance Education.

When learning technologies are thoughtfully integrated into the classroom, they help students develop the skills necessary to contribute to a knowledge-based society. Effective technology integration is transparent, seamless, and supports course goals. "Successful technology-based learn-ing relies heavily on a context for use; classroom teachers play a significant role in facilitating student learning and aligning educational technol-ogy with content from complementary sources" (Marshall, 2002, p.ii). Before instructors can be expected to confidently and efficiently integrate technology and related teaching strategies across their curriculum, they must receive support and faculty development. Collaboration between faculty members, instructional designers, and other support staff such as library and counseling services to develop course content will result in high-quality curricula and a positive student experience. To ease the transition for faculty members to online learning it may be helpful to revise face-to-face curricula and develop blended/ hybrid course delivery models with face-to-face time as well as instruction online. This could benefit faculty members but potentially also students, who are not always savvy with online learning as it requires additional skill sets such as discipline, self-direction, motivation, and strong organizational skills.

FUTURE TRENDS

The concept of life-long learning is very powerful and certainly encourages a shift in perspective. Expansion of Distance Learning from an instruction-based model to an on-demand knowledge management application can directly influence performance (Rosenberg, 2001). For the establishment of an effective Distance Education strategy it is essential to examine some future trends that could influence the positioning of the institution, the learning behavior of the target audience, and the overall acceptance and success of Distance Education offerings.

Information & Instruction

External audiences such as prospective students and professionals as well as internal staff such as faculty members and students don't always need extensive training programs to improve their skills impacting performance; many times they just need access to knowledge and information. Supporting a "learning culture" rather than a "training culture" is a big shift for many organizations but if employees had to attend formal training for every teaching strategy, learning technology update or modification, they would be doing nothing but

going to class (Rosenberg, 2001). Often, providing access to documentation and other information sources facilitates the knowledge transfer in a more efficient, effective way leading to increased productivity.

It is easy to support a learning culture by employing even a few of the various electronic tools currently available. There are number of wikis in development and use of web-based tool-focused training is growing as well, both of which can be classified as on-demand Distance Education. Using wikis in an organization is one way to use information for knowledge management. This is different than using instruction, which can be done as online training and has defined learning outcomes, is sequenced for retention, and includes assessment (Rosenberg, 2001). Frequently access to both information and instruction are necessary for a comprehensive learning experience but it is important to recognize differences between the two. One advantage of information-based Distance Education is that it could continually be used after the instruction-based course is over, providing a platform for follow up, extended experience and knowledge exchange and a place to continue social networking among former classmates and peers.

Nokia, the Finnish mobile communications company, started using wikis (webpages that anyone with access can add to and edit) in 2004 to collaborate on solving product-design problems. Currently more than 20% of their 68,000 employees use wiki pages to develop project plans, edit documents, and brainstorm concepts. Where third party software was once used to facilitate collaboration, now "some of the most interesting stuff is emerging from within the company itself" says Stephen Johnson, senior manager for corporate strategy at Nokia (Carlin, 2007, p.1). Wikis can be used in a number of different ways to increase productivity; as a resource for software programs where the users add and edit for the benefit of others, instead of e-mail to increase collaboration and reduce the time spent e-mailing, and to improve participation, because everyone plays a part in the creation of a wiki, its easy to get involved and make a contribution. The number of companies that use wikis are exploding and include FedEx, General Dynamics, Oracle, Sony and the United States Coast Guard (Barton, 2008).

Identifying the importance of knowledge management and creating a balance between training and information are key elements that will become more important within Higher Education environments and industry. New offerings in the area of information and instruction or a combination of both could lead to transformational changes in the Distance Education market. A variety of Distance Education tools easily facilitate collaboration, improve participation, and increase productivity creating a variety of opportunities for Higher Education organizations to position themselves within existing and new target audiences.

Virtual Learning Environments

Virtual Learning Environments (VLE) are common on campuses across the United States and abroad. Sometimes referred to as Learning Management Systems, they are designed to support and enhance student learning. VLEs include many different communication and assessment tools that can augment face-to-face courses or be used to deliver blended and fully online classes. Commercial VLE products include Blackboard and Desire2Learn, a popular open source option is called Moodle. Increasingly, Virtual Learning Environments also include those where learning can happen virtually as in Second Life or Entropia. The intent of using any type of VLE is to create new opportunities for teaching and learning; from the student perspective, simply recreating a face-to-face course using technology tools is no longer an option.

There are many benefits of using a VLE for both students and faculty. Anecdotally, we know that using a VLE can decrease failure rates and increase performance (Ball, 2008). Considering

students are able to explore at their own pace, they are able to participate more actively in classroom activities. Most faculty use a VLE to post materials (syllabus, articles, handouts, etc) for students to use as part of the course but are not fully maximizing the potential of a VLE to manage interactions across real and virtual spaces. Using a VLE is an effective way to build community in a course; by design they facilitate a variety of interaction types, namely student to student, student to faculty, and student to content.

Interesting research is being done in the field of Adaptive Computer Assisted Instructions or Personalized VLEs (PVLEs). PVLEs are customized for diverse student communities and are able to identify learning needs and independently customize learning activities without an instructor to supplement instruction (Xu, 2005). PVLEs provide opportunities for online learning to enhance and extend higher-level thinking skills. The more customized a students' learning experience, the more effective and positive it is. When facilitating this individualized environment, it is important to "scaffold learner self-regulation and strategic process to help online learners manage the complexity of the learning situation" (Xu, 2005). As VLEs continue to evolve, faculty and students will have more exciting ways to connect with content and participate in relevant learning experiences.

M-Learning

Mobile devices are ubiquitous across campuses of higher education and mobile learning (M-Learning) has naturally grown as a way to put mobile devices to work in the many contexts where learning takes place. Using mobile devices allows learning to happen anywhere at anytime which supports an increasing population of students on the go. M-Learning fosters communication and collaborative work among students. It can also be used to deliver assessments and provide access to support and knowledge bases. Most mobile devices can easily deliver this type of content and can also capture and collect user created materials (Brown & Metcalf, 2008).

There have been many successful implementations of M-Learning from both business and Higher Education. Considering that the global Smartphone market grew 29% in the first quarter of 2008 over the first quarter of 2007, it would be fair to assume that mobile learning will become more prevalent in the near future (Brown & Metcalf, 2008). Merrill Lynch has piloted courses delivered on both the Blackberry and traditionally at Merrill Lynch University (MLU) and found that mobile users finished their training an average of 20 days earlier and with higher average scores than those using MLU. Duke University supplied iPods to faculty and freshmen in 2004 and has since furthered their partnership with Apple to distribute lectures, class materials, and campus news via iTunes University (iTunesU) (Brown & Metcalf, 2008).

It is easy to tap into the "coolness" factor as a way to motivate students to use a mobile device for learning. Because there are so many meaningful activities that take place outside the classroom, M-Learning is a great way to bridge formal and informal learning. This helps to place the "emphasis on *what* people learn" as opposed to *how* or *where* they learn (Sharples, 2007, p. 6). M-Learning seems like a natural fit when the goal is to support an individual throughout their journey as a learner with tools that let them capture, organize, create, share, and reflect. This could potentially become not only a way to recruit and retain students, but also expand into their professional spheres once they have graduated and allowing the university or college to stay connected with their alumni in meaningful ways.

Considering the student and faculty perspective of m-learning is worthwhile. Best practice of m-learning implementation from the student's point of view is when the experience enhances the authenticity of the learning. "Learning activities and resources can be developed to target use in particular places and at particular times" as in an activity on construction materials and methods that is completed on the job site (O'Connell and Smith, 2007). Other indicators of good m-learning from the student perspective include flexible access to materials which are easily loaded onto mobile device that they already own and are familiar with. Faculty who wish to develop strong m-learning opportunities should offer materials that are accessible in a variety of formats and support the full range of learning styles. Our lifestyles are increasingly mobile and the learning needs of students are more difficult than ever to address in the classroom. If nothing else, m-Learning "gives us a new channel to cover the space of learning needs" (Quinn, 2007).

CONCLUSION

Defining a successful Distance Education strategy that links all perspectives and aspects of the university together and provides a true roadmap for the development and implementation process is fundamentally important. To arrive at this point it is crucial to understand where the institution currently stands and to learn as much as possible about external and internal conditions while paying attention to the human aspect of change and transition.

Equally important, however, is to recognize the right moment to start the realization process. Sometimes it takes time to bring all critical stakeholders to one table, resolve individual concerns, and arrive at a common denominator. Waiting for the perfect strategy or the perfect conditions to implement Distance Education may result in a loss of opportunities and important learning moments.

Sometimes it is necessary to not "stop the train". If there are units within the organization that would like to try Distance Education with existing students or develop small-scale Distance Education offerings to new students, utilize those pockets of innovation as learning opportunities. Set clear expectations that these may be non-sustainable pilots depending on the actual success of the initiatives, but exploit them using extensive assessments, process definitions and refinements, and as a general testing ground for the larger scale project down the road. These kinds of projects may be flawed and not perfect, but they will inform future decision-making and deliver relevant feedback to task forces and committees as they try to determine the best overall strategy the university or college should take for Distance Education.

Research on future trends could also support and inform the decision making process. There maybe developments that could be easily realized within the organization without major change efforts while in addition allowing a heads up to the competition.

Regardless of the scope and objective of any Distance Education strategy, the bottom line is to find the best direction for the individual organization, getting the right people involved within the organization, and taking risks in a controlled environment.

REFERENCES

Ball, S. (2008). Effective Use of Virtual Learning Environments. *JISC InfoNet*. Retrieved March 10, 2009, from http://www.jiscinfonet.ac.uk/InfoKits/effective-use-of-VLEs

Barton, T. (2008). Customers. *Twiki*. Retrieved November 3, 2008, from http://www.twiki.net/customers.html

Brandon, B. (Ed.). (2007). *Handbook of e-Learning Strategy*. Santa Rosa, CA: The e-Learning Guild.

Brown, J., & Metcalf, D. (2008). *Mobile Learning Update*. Saratoga Springs, NY: The MASIE Center's Learning Consortium.

Carlin, D. (2007). Corporate Wikis Go Viral. *Business Week*. Retrieved November 3, 2008, from http://www.businessweek.com/technology/content/mar2007/tc20070312_476504.htm

Carr, A. (1997). The learning organization. New lessons/thinking for the management of change and management development? *Journal of Management Development*, *14*(4), 224–231. doi:10.1108/02621719710164517

Dublin, L. (2007). Marketing and Change Management for e-Learning: Strategies for Engaging Learning, Motivating Managers, and Energizing Organizations. In B. Brandon (Ed.), *Handbook of e-Learning Strategy* (pp. 45-49). Santa Rosa, CA: The e-Learning Guild.

Eaton, J. (2002). *Accreditation and Assuring Quality in Distance Learning*. Washington, DC: Council for Higher Education Accreditation, Institute for Research and Study of Accreditation and Quality Assurance.

Marshall, J. (2002). *Learning with Technology*. San Diego, CA: San Diego State University.

Maryland Online, Inc. (2008). Quality Matters Rubric Standards 2008-2010 edition with Assigned Point Values. *Quality Matters Institute*. Retrieved October 10, 2008 from http://qminstitute.org/home/Public%20Library/About%20QM/RubricStandards2008-2010.pdf

Massy, W. F., & Zemsky, R. (1995). Using Information Technology to Enhance Academic Productivity. *Educom National Learning Infrastructure Initiative (NLII)*. Retrieved November 14, 2008, from http://www.educause.edu/ir/library/html/nli0004.html

Millett, J. D. (1974). *Governance and Leadership in Higher Education*. Paper presented at the Presidential Seminar, Management Division of the Academy for Educational Development, Denver, CO and San Francisco, CA.

Mintzberg, H., & Waters, J. A. (1985). Of strategies, deliberate and emergent. *Strategic Management Journal, 6*, 257–272. doi:10.1002/smj.4250060306

Nadler, D. A. (1998). *Champions of Change: How CEOs and their companies are mastering the skill of radical change*. San Francisco, CA: Jossey-Bass.

Norton, D. P. (2002). Managing Strategy is Managing Change. *Balanced Scorecard Report, 4*(1).

O'Connell, M., & Smith, J. (2007). *A Guide to Working with M-Learning Standards*. Brisbane, Australia: Australian Flexible Learning Framework.

Oblinger, D., & Hawkins, B. (2005). The Myth about E-Learning: "We Don't Need to Worry about E-Learning Anymore. *EDUCAUSE Review, 40*(4), 14–15.

Prensky, M. (2001). Digital Natives. Digital Immigrants. *Horizon, 9*(5), 1–6. doi:10.1108/10748120110424816

Quinn, C. (2008) *Mobile Learning Devices: Performance to Go*. Santa Rosa, CA: The e-Learning Guild.

Rosenberg, M. (2001). *E-learning: Strategies for Delivering Knowledge in the Digital Age*. New York, NY: McGraw-Hill Professional

Rosenberg, M. (2008). Technology Euphoria: Taming the Irrational Expectations of High-Tech Learning. *Training +Development*, 24-27.

Sacks, P. (1996). *Generation X Goes to College. An Eye-Opening Account of Teaching in Postmodern America*. Chicago, IL: Open Court Publishing.

Sharples, M. (Ed.). (2007). *Big Issues in Mobile Learning*. Nottingham, UK: University of Nottingham, Learning Sciences Research Institute.

Weick, K. E. (1995). *Sensemaking in Organizations*. Thousand Oaks, CA: Sage.

Xu, D. (2005). *A Conceptual Model of Personalized Virtual Learning Environments*. St. Lucia, Australia: The University of Queensland.

Chapter 19
Structure and Change in E–learning:
An Ecological Perspective

Julia Penn Shaw
SUNY-Empire State College, USA

Fabio Chacon
Bowie State University, USA

ABSTRACT

This chapter provides a view of e-learning from the perspective of ecological systems with nested levels of structure, organizing principles, and emergent properties for use in accomplishing at least three goals: to evaluate emergent patterns in the development of e-learning; to assess current threats and enablers at any level; and to plan for successful growth within determinate niches. E-learning is structured into four levels: the International/National level; the Institutional level; the Class/Community level; and the Learning Object level. Within each level, and between them, there are organizing principles of integration and differentiation contributing to their stability or decay. Those that the authors have identified include: transactional distance in delivery of learning; industrialization of learning functions; functional equivalence of learning experiences; virtualization of knowledge; technological convergence of learning media; developmental growth of learning systems; and requisite variety in learning strategies. For administrators, practitioners, and faculty whose institutions have an identity within the ecology, the authors introduce the GEMS process to better control the Goals, Engagement, Management and Support of system elements between and across their levels of e-learning structures. Both the broad ecological view upon e-learning -and the specific tools of GEMS useful within it- are applied to existing structures in e-learning, such as open courseware and course management systems, and to e-learning innovations, such as mobile learning, meta-worlds, and virtual gaming.

INTRODUCTION

E-learning is not just the dissemination of instruction through electronic means; it has the potential to transform education, deeply changing it at all levels, bringing both benefits and challenges on an international scale. Changes have been so rapid in even the past few years that the concept of e-learning, representing all forms of electronic

DOI: 10.4018/978-1-61520-672-8.ch019

learning, has developed to get beyond the concept of 'online learning' with its implied metaphor of desktop access. E-learning, and the myriad forms of distributed learning that emerge from it, are transforming education with an impact not felt since the development of movable type, some 500 years ago. Just as printing made learning accessible to more than a select few, so does e-learning make learning accessible in an individually defined and virtualized time and space. Going beyond ecology as a metaphor (Garrison and Anderson, 2003; Henning, 2005), this chapter presents ecology as a viable tool for understanding the growth and usefulness of e-learning, providing guidelines for effective practice through the introduction of a practitioner's tool called GEMS (i.e., Goals, Engagement, Management and Support). The advantages of the ecological approach appear to be twofold: first, enhancing a broad understanding of e-learning across various environments and deeply within specific niches; and second, providing a useful tool to generate testable hypotheses.

BACKGROUND

E-learning is shorthand for electronic learning, and the universal distribution system for it is the World Wide Web. An analysis of two cases below elucidates the ecological relationships created by e-learning, complementing other well-know views of distance learning that capitalize on the systems perspective (Moore and Kearsley, 2005), technology (Spector et al, 2007) and virtual class (Laurillard, 1993).

The first case is MIT *OpenCourseWare* (MIT, 2009), initiated in 2001 and joined by many other outstanding higher education institutions. As of 2009, more than 1,800 courses are published on the MIT site, while hundreds more are published by associated institutions elsewhere. Faculty members create the content, a virtualized distribution system disseminates their intellectual products, and millions of users in several languages ben-

efit from this encapsulated knowledge for many purposes, some not foreseen when the system was established. Translations of the courses are disseminated in Chinese, Spanish, Portuguese, Thai and Persian, with most users from Asia. Several subsidiary institutions run fully online programs based on OCW. Because this is a non-profit initiative, there is very little exchange of money in the chain of transactions that go from the creators to the end users, further encouraging the distribution of the courseware. Faculty members as content producers and students as consumers are linked by many intermediate elements, including instructional technologists, virtualized distribution systems, connected institutions in North America and abroad, translators, and local curriculum organizers. Their joint efforts allow millions of users in several languages to use knowledge encapsulated in courses in multivariate ways. This loosely-coupled system is without a central command, with every associated organization having its own goals and clients. Whatever happens in one organization, however, has the potential of influencing others. Several factors influence the growth of this enormous array of organizations: the existence of the common environment of the web; the expectations generated by sharing first-rate knowledge; the myriad relationships created between creators and consumers; and the progressive diversification of programs based on OCW content.

The second case is the *University Of Phoenix (UOP)*, a well-known for-profit institution with more than 180,000 students in the United States and beyond. This university contracts hundreds of adjunct faculty, usually with "real world" experience in their fields. It uses a proprietary course management system (CMS) with tools enhanced for dialogue between instructors and students, and for carrying out teamwork among students in fully online or, less often, face-to-face sessions. UOP courses offer a variety of learning experiences such as electronic assignments, virtual organizations, teamwork, tutorials, peer feedback, and social simulations. The online library provides students and faculty access to a vast number of peer-reviewed journals and ebooks, the latter often products of agreements with publishers and specially tailored to curriculum requirements. Instructors and tutors submit to quality checks for performance such as the number and quality of interaction with students. A hierarchical organization exists with specialized functions in course development, marketing, student service, tutoring, evaluation and faculty training. UOP generally outsources content production, relying on close alliances with publishers that, in turn, have contracts with thousands of content creators. There are many steps for the process of sharing knowledge between creators and users, and in every step money transactions are involved. All process elements are tightly evaluated to provide corrective feedback.

Although opinions of experts differ (Bates, 2005; Garrison and Anderson, 2003), e-learning corresponds to the fourth generation of distance education, following 1) correspondence schooling, 2) instructional radio and television, and 3) modularized multimedia instruction. Of these, only e-learning has a distribution environment that is at the same time personal, local, national and international - the web. Earlier generations of distance education were also able in some instances to reach national or even international audiences, but never with the immediacy and capability of interaction offered by the web. Former distance learning paradigms (Bates, 2005) did not have the dynamic, interactive, emergent properties of the ecosystem of audiences, content providers, marketing agents, content intermediaries and learning facilitators. They were characterized as organizations formed mostly by the articulation of a course development system and a student support system; the first one in charge of the elaboration and dissemination of instructional content and the second of tutoring students and catering their needs (Rumble, 1986). The current

organizations are more diversified, interconnected and loosely coupled.

The e-learning paradigms of MIT and UOP move far beyond those of previous forms of distance education. When one compares the MIT and UOP e-learning models to brick and mortar institutions the differences are geometric. MIT and UOP reach very large national and international audiences far beyond those of their traditional counterparts. They offer a wide variety of educational interactions versus a few predominant models of classroom teaching. They embrace virtual spaces that become the "mode of living" for both students and faculty. They engineer a tight relationship between content producers publishers and user needs. They utilize an industrialized approach in most processes related to learning.

A number of ecological principles underpin the UOP mega-system, including central coordination that manages the major processes, such as course development, marketing and student support. UOP, using an industrialized approach, creates a replica of itself in each new region, acquiring local accreditation to obtain academic respectability. The university, following its lines of growth, adapts programs to local needs and clients. Its many links created with other organizations, such as publishers, tutor providers, training brokers, web marketing firms, financial aid providers, internet education resellers, client conglomerates (armed forces, governments, corporations), and media developers, enhance its chance for survival.

These two cases of MIT OCW and UOP, selected from many, highlight a number of distinctive traits that e-learning shares with other ecosystems, and help to demonstrate that an ecology model is an effective tool for understanding how programs arise, survive and grow or perish in a highly competitive environment. The first of these traits, which determines all others, is that almost all programs of this kind share the web as a common environment. This gives rise to forms of interaction and interdependence that were not present in previous forms of distance education. Among them are many interconnected "organisms" with specialized functions with respect to the whole; emergent "organisms" that permanently change the environment; "consumption chains" in which information produced by some people is consumed by others, and in turn repacked for further consumption with two or three intermediary links; and the mutual interdependence of these "organisms" for survival.

A model is successful when it contributes to increased understanding, and guides practice in a given realm of knowledge. The ecological approach of e-learning enables testing of relationships within and between levels of organization not afforded by other models. Viewing e-learning from an ecological perspective helps analysts answer crucial questions. What factors determine growth and survival of e-learning programs? What constitutes quality in e-learning? Which vehicles(s) are most effective for delivery within specific niches (online, pod cast, smart phones, etc.)? What are ways of increasing student and faculty satisfaction in courses? Which course elements promote engagement? How effective is an e-learning program against its proposed goals? The authors suggest that the systematic application of an ecological approach can help an emerging program to structure itself within a niche to assure early success and to maintain flexibility to both keep up with the "big players" and make use of innovations that develop within its virtual boundaries.

This Chapter Issue: E-Learning as an Ecosystem

John Seely Brown (2000) states: "An ecology is basically an open, complex adaptive system comprising elements that are dynamic and interdependent" and a learning ecology is "a collection of overlapping communities of interest (virtual), cross-pollinating with each other, constantly evolving, and largely self-organizing." Based on the previous observations, e-learning is an ecosystem formed by a diversity of educational programs that equally serve diverse audiences of students or users, all of them having a common environment of interaction constituted by electronic transmissions that transcend geographic, language and other cultural barriers. Major components of this ecosystem are the programs themselves, content authors, teachers and tutors, administrators, staff, students (actual and potential), course management systems, curricula, learning resources (including learning objects) and communication devices.

In natural ecosystems, the driving force is the exchange of energy among organisms at different levels through processes of nutrition, reproduction, waste and decay. In e-learning, exchange of knowledge drives interactions, which may or may not be accompanied by monetary transactions. The main reason for the interaction called learning may be to gain knowledge, but the definition of learning is still subject to controversy, although likely referencing transmission of sense information, understanding, skills, and values. The key processes and principles of interaction, growth, and success in this ecology are related to the electronic transmissions of knowledge. One knows that an e-learning program is working when people wanting knowledge engage in virtual interaction with other people wanting to share knowledge, and most users achieve their desired intent. "People wanting to have knowledge" and "people wanting to share knowledge" interact in moments of instruction where student and teacher roles can be interchanged or even exerted simultaneously.

When several organisms thrive or decay in the same geographic milieu and interact among themselves, they constitute an ecosystem that over time becomes more tightly interconnected and interdependent. In e-learning, when one program successfully adopts a certain technology, others follow suit in a few months. When one institution offers a certain "cutting edge" program in science, a few more will emerge with similar offerings in short span. Certain groups of potential students (i.e., armed forces, nurses, middle managers, law enforcement agents, and teachers) are the focus of so many online programs that they are over-served. When one adult student searches the web to pursue a career to improve her/his work eligibility, and leaves a few inquiry cards at some sites, thirty or more programs will send offerings through email. When one experienced professor is retired, she or he may apply as adjunct instructor simultaneously for three or four universities and be accepted by all of them.

Barriers that limit this pervasive flow of interactions, such as language, political borders, and geographic barriers, are beginning to be overcome by the presence of many international programs. Although language is still a major obstacle, some online programs now translate their instructional materials and hire local tutors to teach. Legal obstacles such as requirements of accreditation of some educational programs limiting the capability of graduates to work in certain regions or countries are being responded to by obtaining local accreditation for regional online programs.

Intense interest across e-learning systems is most evident within two areas. The first concerns devices used for communications. Desktop and laptop computers with many shared characteristics are the dominant tools as of 2010, while small devices capable of networked communication, such as hand-held computers and smart phones are growing fast as companions of, or replacements for, computers. Many devices are currently tested in educational environments and a whole movement of *mobile learning* is in expansion (Corbeil and Valdes-Corbeil, 2007). As a result, institutions are determining which the most successful models are and solving the multi-stage problems associated with the integration of small devices into existing hardware and software.

The second concerns consolidation of course or learning management systems (CMS or LMS), the main vehicles for disseminating and administer-

ing courses. Some twenty years ago, there were hundreds of them and many institutions created their own home-brewed solutions. Today, only a dozen platforms have a real world-wide presence, while many others remain in some niches threatened of becoming outmoded by the big players that have more money for research and development (Wexler *et al.*, 2008). There are a number of internet sites dedicated to surveillance of the CMS/LMS, such as *Edutools*, *Brandon Hall Research* and *Gartner*, distributing studies among current and potential users. Institutions actively seek a system that satisfies all criteria of administrative, pedagogical and technical prowess coupled with an acceptable cost/benefit ratio. Very soon, the surveillance of LMS will likely be integrated with that of mobile devices leading to learning systems with virtual presence.

TWO PERSPECTIVES ON THE ECOLOGY OF E-LEARNING: NESTED SYSTEMS AND IDENTITY THROUGH GEMS

The term, Ecology of E-learning was chosen by the authors because as people look ahead in the twenty-first century, e-learning systems and their constitutive elements become more and more interrelated. There is competition and collaboration as programs seeking to attract similar audiences are compelled to compete in terms of curriculum offerings, services, faculty, courseware, learning objects and communication devices. There is more than one way to usefully view e-learning as an ecology. The first perspective, the sociologist's 'etic' view, or view from the outside, sees e-learning as nested layers of organization. This perspective captures the ecology of the whole, similar to a physical map of a country that shows major formations such as mountains, rivers, lakes, seashores, and major population centers.

The second perspective, the 'emic', or view from the inside, is characterized as a look at e-learning from a point within the ecosystem out onto the larger whole. It is like studying the characteristics of a river by how it influences and is influenced by geographic landmarks around it. All of the knowledge of the larger system must be brought to bear to provide information relevant to that one point within the nested systems. It captures the motivations, actions, variations, 'developmental paths', goals of an element acting within the ecological system. This perspective is identified by the acronym 'GEMS' to capture four aspects of identity: Goals, Engagement, Management and Support.

E-Learning Ecological "Laws"

Despite their diversity of goals, these two perspectives share common "laws" in their operation. The term law is used here in a restricted sense as a statement that describes regularities found across many e-learning systems; no mathematical expression of them is implied. A brief examination of them is in order:

1. The law of transactional distance in delivery of learning determines how much a system can grow. Transactional distance (Moore, 1993) complements the concepts of teaching presence, social presence and cognitive presence proposed by Garrison and Anderson (2003). If a program is able to maintain short transactional distances, by means of adequate use of technology and course design, it can reach thousands of users. If transactional distance is too large, meaning lack of presence in the three categories, the program is bound to face the common phenomena of learner dropout and faculty alienation, two very common threats of the previous generations of distance education.

2. The law of industrialization (systematization of learning functions) is that the more able a system is to regularize its processes for course development, delivery and evaluation, the greater its potential for success as compared to other similar systems (Peters, 1983). Industrialization is common to all large e-learning systems and it can be observed in such features as establishment of a chain of production for instructional materials, division of labor (e.g., administrators, content authors, instructional designers, media specialist, etc.), standardization of desired products, mass production, continuous evaluation cycles, and marketing of products tailored to student needs.

3. The law of equivalence (functional equivalence of learning experiences) is the key for legitimacy of e-learning; an e-learning system is successful to the degree that it can provide all learners an equivalent experience without discrimination due to origin or time and space constraints of the learners (Simonson and Schlosser, 1995). This means that the experience provided by an e-learning program must be similar to that of a legally and socially accepted face-to-face program of the same kind. To do that, the e-learning program will provide interaction opportunities, instructional materials, individualized support, and assessment activities similar to these recognized programs.

4. The law of virtualization of knowledge. The process by which e-learning programs strive to achieve equivalence to features of face-to-face instruction is called virtualization (Michal, 2007), defined as creation of representations of environments and processes in virtual spaces while preserving the critical functionalities of their "real world" counterparts. Virtualization has advanced enormously in e-learning, from simple models of a lecture hall (Elluminate, Horizon Wimba, etc.) that allow synchronous communication via voice and screen board, to metaverses such as Second Life and Virtual Worlds, in which physical characteristics of imaginary worlds are constructed with a certain degree of realism, and users are represented as avatars with distinguishable personality traits.

5. The law of cyclical dissemination of knowledge. Ravet (2002) described a general process through which the interconnected knowledge and skills of a community or communities are transmitted from creators to users, with possibilities of interaction at several levels. Knowledge -as products of research or scholarly study, representation of reality, know-how about something, artistic creation, collection of facts and many other manifestations- is the core component of e-learning, as in any other form of education. However, e-learning knowledge is virtualized through digital processes, making it available almost instantly and in various forms. Thus, knowledge follows predictable cycles in an e-learning system. Usually, a central organization structures the curricula of programs and courses; based on these decisions, faculty and staff collect relevant materials in the form of books, e-books, journal articles, videos, interactive learning objects and others. Major sources for these materials are publishing companies and not-for-profit sources, such as the *Merlot.com* repository, the *Open Courseware Initiative* and *You-Tube*. Components are carefully organized in courses, with orientations for the learning and assessment activities of the students. Courses are accessible to learners through devices such as a desktop computer, digital player or a smart phone. Instructors or mentors act as mediators of this knowledge. The process of interaction and collaboration in online courses facilitates the construction and re-construction of knowledge by the learners, which in turn provide feedback to the organization about the quality of their experiences. By virtue of this dissemination cycle, one can find that many e-learning programs share common elements in their curricula and repositories of instructional materials.

6. The law of technological convergence of learning media is the capacity for digital systems to perform similar functions independent of the physical configuration of the systems (Jenkins, 2006). Separate technologies, such as video, radio, telephony and data processing have converged in a number of devices. Therefore, today it is possible to have similar experiences of multimedia communication in a large facility (auditorium with computer projection and cameras), medium-sized facility (desktop computer) and in a personal space (smart phone). All of these resources are capable of interacting with each other creating new pathways for synergy. Convergence appears not only with multimedia delivery through many levels of systems (cameras, phones, etc.), it also appears in the applications themselves as seen with the integration of digital imaging within films, for example. The more attractive and commercially-viable the attributes, the faster the integration. Today, we are surrounded by a multi-level convergent media world where all modes of communication and information are continually reforming to adapt to the enduring demands of technologies, "changing the way we create, consume, learn and interact with each other" (p. 18).

7. The law of developmental growth of learning systems. E-learning systems have an organic quality in the way they behave: goal-oriented, seeking equilibrium, absorbing resources to grow, and with central and local regulation. As such, Werner and Kaplan's model of gradual differentiation and integration of spheres of experience (Werner and Kaplan, 1963) applies to them. Experience or knowledge proceeds from simple, undifferentiated states to more complex, hierarchically-organized states. Similarly, e-learning systems usually evolve from a virtualized course or class approach to multi-departmental and multi-function systems, such as the in the UOP and MIT models. Units of these systems become specialized in functions such as marketing, course development, student support, and media management. Expansion, differentiation and integration are the rules of growth in these systems. Conversely, systems that do not succeed in applying these rules are imperiled. Differentiation occurs when one takes a new implementation of the E-world, such as the concept of virtual simulation, and applies it to a niche already established in the e-learning ecology such as an interest group (i.e., nurses), a region (i.e., Eastern Europe), an application (i.e., golf practice), or further exploration (i.e., research and social interactions in virtual communities). Such differentiation leads to the greater applicability of a particular technology across more diverse settings and applications, leading to integration. Growth may proliferate in many ways, including symbiotic relationships of small businesses with large (the bird on the back of the elephant), or parallel support of small emerging entities.

A correlate of the 'law of development' is the flexibility for the elements in the organic system to adapt readily. Being beautiful in the eyes of all of its beholders, transforming its name for different semiotic networks, using its structure for different functions, adapting to radical changes in scale, or expanding and contracting as needed over time are a few of the adaptations that help a system element maintain and grow, creating niches of differentiation within an increasingly more integrated system.

8. The law of requisite variety in learning strategies. The principle of cybernetics proposed by Ashby (1956) applies to e-learning. The principle can be expressed as "The larger the variety of actions available to a control system, the larger the variety of perturbations it is able to compensate." An e-learning system enables transactions for acquiring knowledge but each transaction at-a-distance has a potential to fail; for instance, if the student or the teacher do not meet their goal(s). In an empirical study, Chacon (2007) defined "incomplete learning", when the learner has an observable intent to learn but the outcomes show that the original intent was not achieved. This type of event can happen millions of times in a small e-learning program and even more often in much larger programs. Too many learning frustrations lead students to drop out from the programs. E-learning can compensate for this situation by providing a larger variety of instructional actions, a wider variety of learning events for different levels of learners, the variety of teaching and assessment strategies in each course, and the resourcefulness of instructors, tutors or counselors. The more these elements are in an e-

learning system, the higher its capability to turning educational transactions into successes.

A vigorous e-learning program usually accomplishes all these principles at a high level, while those that experience high dropout rates or are not able to sustain their offerings usually fail in one or more of them. It is possible to design research instruments that measure the quality of the programs, regarding each one of the principles, and provide feedback to administrators, faculty and students. It is by no means unusual that in a successful program some of these instruments are already in operation.

SOLUTIONS AND RECOMMENDATIONS: THE NS/GEMS MODEL

Those who are familiar with systems theory will immediately see the applicability of systems concepts to the ecology of e-learning. In fact, a systems view of distance education has been professed by many authors (Moore and Kearsley, 2005) since these types of programs became part of mainstream education. An ecological model simplifies the complexity of this international e-learning system. One immediate useful reduction of the complexity is to recognize that e-learning resides in nested systems (Saba, 1998), and another is to recognize that an organism within the ecology stabilizes four basic facets of its identity: goals, engagement, management, and support. The Ecology of E-learning schematic in Figure 1 expresses both the external ('etic') view of nested systems within the e-learning ecology (NS) and the internal ('emic') view of an identity within the nested systems which must develop goals and then engage, manage and support those goals within the ecology.

On the left are the Nested Systems, portrayed as a cone, from the most encompassing national and international levels, to their institutions and

Figure 1. The NS/GEMS Perspective of E-learning

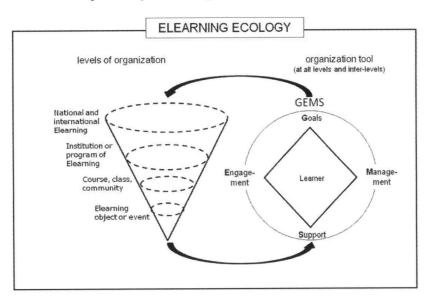

programs, to specific courses/communities/learning experiences offered by these institutions, to a particular e-learning event or object by itself. These levels are necessarily nested, because any larger level relies on lower levels for delivery of learning to consumers, and any lower level relies on higher levels for distribution of learning to consumers.

Next to the cone is the diamond symbolizing the facets of the conceptual tool, called "GEMS", which offers a succinct process for action of an organism within the ecological system towards Goals, Engagement, Management and Support of its identity. The nested systems (NS) view helps organize information about e-learning from multiple and varied sources. The GEMS helps an organism within the e-learning ecology to construct that information to meet their goals. GEMS represents the four points of the diamond structure of stability of an identity and is also a useful metaphor for the identity as a 'gem' within the ecological system. The NS/GEMS structure provides a grid for stabilizing a component's identity within the hierarchy of the nested systems. The GEMS concept helps an identity plan

and coordinate inter-level changes. This whole approach to the e-learning ecology is called NS/GEMS, to stress the components of nested systems and the stabilization tool GEMS.

Perspective 1: E-learning Nested Systems

The nested levels of e-learning will be briefly described in the following paragraphs.

Level 1: National and International E-Learning

At the international and national level, we find the "big players" of e-learning. These are digital technology companies, international publishers, very large universities with nationally and internationally operated programs, some professional organizations, and large practice and collaboration communities created through the Internet. Here we see ecological laws in full operation, as they inform how these various systems relate to each other. The emergence of a new provider of e-learning depends on how it creates a niche in an ecosystem that is becoming densely populated. World-wide, the absolute numbers of elearners are growing at fast pace, 15% to 25% per annum has been reported, but the proportion with respect to those in traditional programs grows more slowly, still in the single digits percentage range (van der Wende, 2002). The larger percentages reflect that there is a growing demand for education in the world both in the academic and corporate realms. How do some e-learning programs attract larger audiences than others? The ecological principles would indicate that this is done by maintaining short transactional distances, industrializing the content production and student support services, virtualizing knowledge, creating effective feedback across the knowledge dissemination cycles, maintaining legitimacy through equivalence with other forms of study, creating strategic alliances with other organizations and offering a large menu of opportunities and services to students. The authors hypothesize that these regularities will show in a large sample of e-learning programs with different rates of success.

Level 2: Institutional or Program E-learning

At the institutional or program level, we find the majority of e-learning programs currently delivered through the web. They share some basic features and differ in others. Among the shared features are structures for developing instructional content, for delivering instruction for learners, and for catering to their different needs. These are common with traditional distance learning programs, as identified by Rumble (1986). E-learning programs also need a robust system of digital networking, which can be internal or for hire. Harasim (2000) compared a number of online learning systems and found common elements in their structures, since they are all prepared to do the same job, as the law of equivalence suggests. It is their differences, however, that determine their possibility of success in a competitive environment.

The range of insourcing or outsourcing academic functions is an important factor. Primarily outsourced systems, which rely on many contracted personnel and services, can start and grow faster, but they are more prone to failure due to the difficulties of keeping the variety of perturbations under control. Insourced systems have a substantial number of people under full-time contracts, have a hierarchical organization and specialized divisions. Many e-learning systems emerging from traditional universities or colleges are of this type. They grow slowly and more firmly, finding it more difficult to change and adapt in the mercurial e-learning ecology. They can be very effective if, from the start, they have greater requisite variety, such as that of a college with a large number of courses corresponding to equally large faculty, many instructional resources and efficient counseling system. Outsourced systems rely mostly on short-term, part-time contracts of personnel and have a flatter structure. They grow faster and have more capability to adapt, but at the same time, find difficult to maintain quality control on all aspects of their operation. Very large e-learning systems, such as University of Phoenix, University of Maryland University College and Western Governors University show both a capability for adaptation of the permanent personnel, and efficient management of their numerous adjunct faculty bodies.

Delivery technology also differentiates programs; many still rely on technologies such as print and correspondence, while others are developing virtual worlds and new modes of collaboration. Mobile learning provides convergence towards which a whole campus experience is literally at hand. In the future, we can predict institutions to capitalize on the learner-centered devices, which extend the 'campus' to wherever the learner needs the information for 'just-in-time' use through networking. Numerous studies have failed to produce evidence that one mode of delivery is superior to others (Russell, 2001); the key factors of success reported in these comparative studies are rather related to instructional design and ability to form learning communities. Mobile learning, or learning through small devices, provides a convergence of media –telephone, wireless networks, geographic orientation systems, audio and video broadcasts and databases. A learning institution and beyond can be "at hand".

Is mobile learning the future generation of e-learning? If so, it is likely to be decided outside of the e-learning ecology, since no distance education systems, in all the generations that have existed so far, have created a technology of dissemination by themselves. They have absorbed technologies pre-existing in the social environment once they were sufficiently accepted and used for purposes different than learning. Radio and television were major entertainment media long before the first educational radio or television programs were aired. Computers were initially machines for data storage and calculation. They reached widespread dissemination in education only when they were capable of integrating other media, such as image, video and digital communications. Desktop and notebook computers are still superior to mobile devices for integrating other media, facilitated by larger screens, keyboards that are more functional, higher memory capacity and stable electrical supply. In the future, one can predict that small devices can lead e-learning when they become completely integrated to other devices that people have at home or at work, such as LCD screens, sound equipment and phone lines. The mode of input to these improved devices will be direct -via voice, writing tablets, on-screen or hand-contoured keyboards. Institutions will be able then to capitalize on these more learner-centered devices to extend the campus experience to wherever the learner is located. Currently many common course activities are very difficult if not impossible to do with small communication devices; think of conducting extensive library searches or typing an eight-page essay using the affordances of a smart-phone.

What about *metaverses*? These virtual worlds constructed in the internet attempt to reproduce visual and sound characteristics of the real world, while users are represented as avatars that have human-like or animal-like features. Several of them have achieved prominence in the educational arena, such as *Second Life*, *Active Worlds* and *Entropia Universe*. Initially, these special systems emerged from interactive games, in which avatars and simulated environments were used; even in the non-digital forms of games, such as the famed *Dungeons and Dragons*. They accomplish several principles of ecology: reduce transactional distance, increase equivalence and technological convergence and generate more engagement; in this, they are superior to static or interactive web pages. However, other principles are not served equally well. Virtual worlds promote synchrony of users while the largest e-learning systems are asynchronous, they charge users for membership according to amount of active resources while other sharing environments are cost-free, and they appeal to the more computer savvy and computer-resourceful users due to the complexity of the virtual worlds and the rules of use. Nevertheless, these new types of systems have introduced new pathways for differentiation and integration in the permanent quest for development of e-learning. Using the principle of convergence, one may predict that they will fuse with mainstream CMSs, probably through the appearance of free virtual worlds that interact with many of the existing resources for sharing. They likely will accept various modalities of asynchronous communication; for instance, participants in a discussion can record their avatar appearances and then any user can play them in the thematic order of the conversation versus the time in which they were recorded, much in the way that cinematographers make a film: short bits integrated later into sequences.

Level 3: Course, Class or Community

What we now perceive as the class, or course level, is a delivery unit for a unified sequence of learning events. This concept of 'course' may change, but this level of learning seems to be viable for long time. 'Courses' may increasingly be constructed by users, rather than deliverer (through searches on YouTube, for example), but there will continue to be a conceptual framework for unifying multiple learning events. The good organization of a course is part science and part art, and it needs to be seen from both from the deliverer's and the learner's perspective. Each actor has a different conception. Needs, learning styles, perceptual sets, intelligences, and atmosphere are key concepts in the learner's perspective; while from the teachers' (or creator's) perspective the most important are organization of knowledge, teaching presence, practice of competencies and tools, stability and flexibility of the course management system, and the applications supporting content creation. Some of the complexity of learner/provider interaction can be captured by use of the expert/novice paradigm adopted from information management (Shaw, 2005).

Henning (2005) suggests a schema that can be used to build such enhanced courses. She recommends organizing a course not around content, because different learners will need different content, but rather around goals that students are supposed to reach, to which they agree. Focus would be on the learning processes in which the students will engage in the course; some individual and some shared. These learning processes are guided by three major principles: Active Learning, Cognitive Apprenticeship and Distributed Cognition. The first one means that learners must enact what they are learning instead of just reviewing and repeating information; to this end, the instructor or developer will design or select activities for problem-solving, simulating processes, practicing skills and so forth. Dissonance in differing conceptual frameworks,

which leads to the construction of more resilient conceptual models by students, can be encouraged (Shaw, 2006). The second principle involves collaborative activities such as those in which students model behaviors to each other, discuss examples or cases presented by the teacher and peer-review products elaborated individually or in groups. The collaborative tradition in education is extensive with many models to consider such as those of (Garrison and Anderson, 2003, and Palloff and Pratt, 1999 and 20072007). The last principle relates to the content of the subject matter where students learn to create, use, and modify conceptual maps to organize knowledge; then share information through problem-solving or collaborative activities in which they view the concepts from multiple perspectives.

The learning community is a central concept for an e-learning class as already embedded in many best practices of the trade (Palloff and Pratt, 2007); however, it is not an absolute. "Community" is rather a property that ranges from the disaggregated e-learning class to the committed community; between these two extremes, probably one can find a familiar normal curve. A disaggregated class is characterized by few messages among members, most of them one-to-one and low level of emotional engagement. In the middle, where most e-learning classes are, there is a functional community, with frequent two-way communication, one-to-many messages, and emotional engagement expressed in styles such as praise, humor, recognition, and constructive critique. Functional communities usually dissolve once the class is finished. Committed communities are present in some programs that foster long-time relationships among groups of students, as they engage in communication out of the class environment, and have a high sense of collaboration. A few e-learning programs foster this type of community by means of face-to-face sessions characterized by ample social activities. The Open University of UK has been a pioneer in these formats with the Summer Schools.

Level 4: Learning Object or Event

Finally, at the resource/event level, we find learning objects, the granular components of 21st Century learning systems. They share the key characteristics of independence of platform, interoperability, sensory richness and engagement (Merrill, 2000; Wiley, 2000). Learning objects and, in general, any digital resource that can be used for learning, have acquired a new personality in the web. They can be reached from anywhere, used by anyone, and converted to any CMS; either by virtue of their original design or by availability on one of many digital conversion tools now in existence. Most importantly, these objects can be created by anyone through existing sharing services such as *You Tube*, *Google Video*, *iTunes*, *Wikipedia*, *Merlot.com*, *Slideshare* and many others. Learning objects and learning events portrayed in the web are closely related to the emergence of Web Science, as noted by (Shandbolt and Berners-Lee, 2008) and they follow ecology rules: "Concepts such as population dynamics, food chains, and consumers and producers all have counterparts on the Web. Perhaps methods and models devised for ecology can help us understand the Web's digital ecosystem..." p.81.

Frequency of use and semantic connectivity seem to govern use of content elements on the web. The first one is calculated by frequency algorithms that are embedded in the search engines; such that when one types certain keywords to locate resources in the internet the resulting list of web pages shows in order, from more to less frequent use by other inquirers, who typed similar words. Pick a few of these links, and you will have added new frequency data to the search engine. The presence of metadata, such as descriptive labels of web pages and their components, enhances this capability of search engines for finding the right resources of interest for a user. The second is related to the way web pages are interconnected by meaning relationships; certain pages have many links coming in, while others have just a few, which determine the semantic preeminence of the former. A useful learning object will have thousands of links coming in from anywhere in the world. It would be convenient to analyze how fast certain objects become preeminent due to their change of meaning for learners. Survival of the fittest applies to learning resources disseminated through the web; those suitable for learning are kept alive by virtue of many users benefiting from them, while others that are faulty or inadequate fall into oblivion.

Perspective 2: GEMS -Goals, Engagement, Management, and Support

The second perspective, GEMS, is from an "organism" within the e-learning ecology seeking a stable position from which to grow and thrive. It is based on the core concept of goal-oriented behavior, which is common to cognitive psychology and systems theory (Lord and Levy, 1994). Cognitive and man-created systems have goals, maintain engagement in their pursuit, manage internal and external forces to assure success, and provide relevant resources to support the desired intent. This principle applies both to self-directed systems such as a person or spontaneous social group, and to constructed entities such as an online class or an interactive learning object. Therefore, the agent who applies GEMS in e-learning, be it administrator, faculty, designer or technologist, has an understanding of the ecological mesh of relationships and takes advantage of this knowledge to be more effective in her/his purpose. Other action schemes may be also useful but this one is simple and straightforward. It encapsulates powerful concepts that can be generalized to the four levels of nested systems, as analyzed further below.

The GEMS model does not purport to present new information, but rather to help an 'organism' within the ecological system to organize ecological information for its own stability. The model forces goals to be prioritized with respect to each other and to the system as a whole. The GEMS arrangement is hierarchical with respect to the success of its goals. Creating a hierarchy of goals helps to keep the system functional during threat and keep all aspects of the system engaged during expansion. If the first goal is self-preservation, then subsequent goals -if they cannot be successfully be engaged- are not given resources for management and support. This is in keeping with the first goal of protecting the identity of the entity. The goals of a living entity are different from a mission statement or long-term direction. The GEMS concept simplifies goal-seeking behavior of an organism thereby conserving resources. For example, using the law of convergence, the closer the engagement, management, and support of the different goals, the more efficient the system is. Using the same advertising firm (engagement), legal firm (management), and computer support facilities (support) would help to keep the goals aligned, the communication lines easier to maintain, Clarifying the goals may make it clear, however, that as they are currently defined, this consolidation is not possible or advisable. Therefore, convergence needs to be measured against 'development', the increase in expansion and differentiation.

GEMS constitutes the link between analysis of nested systems and the needs of the institution or practitioner within the system. How can a practitioner benefit from the ecology of e-learning systems for planning for survival, planning for change, finding a niche or improving the quality of an existing program? Your reading of this book is an example of the use of GEMS perspective by an organic system – yourself. First, you read this book to seek knowledge that will help you interact more effectively in the complex e-learning system of which you are a part. You probably reviewed the table of contents to get an idea of the organization of the book. Your goal, related to your identity within an e-learning system, is to become more informed and effective in your role. If you find something interesting in this book (or in this chapter), you will engage with it. 'Engaging with it' means many things, but in all cases you will work to store (remember) what you have learned, reflect upon its applications, attempt to apply it, and review the success of that application. If the application is successful, you will manage that success – harness it for future use, and for uses beyond your immediate application of it. If your success at managing what you learn is of critical importance to your role in your system, you will find ways to support the structure you manage so you can effectively re-engage and continue to meet your goals. The strength of your identity with your e-learning system will affect your success in implementing your new GEMS.

GEMS as an Organizational Tool for E-Learning

GEMS reminds us that we are working within consecutive levels of 'organisms' called institutions which themselves have identities, some of which are out-of-reach and unknowable to us, some peripheral to our direct awareness, and some within our direct control. Living identities are concerned about their local stability, their resilience, their resistance to perturbations, their constancy across time, their persistence in the light of challenges, and their robustness. They are aware of their birth, their life course, and their potential demise. The GEMS process helps direct our focus to the moving, changing, and emerging identities around us that influence us. Any aspect at any level of the ecology of e-learning that has an identity will have the characteristics of a living entity, with goal-seeking behavior, desire to be sustained (and, more specifically self-sustaining), and composed of identifiable but interconnected organs and functions. Awareness of itself is an asset within an organism; so, an organizational chart, for example, enables an institution to strengthen communication among its parts, thereby strengthening its sustainability. A clear communication system - whether hierarchical or distributed - also enhances an institution's identity by making sure that messages -about student retention, for instance- get to units that respond appropriately to goals such as meeting yearly thresholds established by the institution or managing seasonal variations. GEMS is a somewhat different way to look at goal-oriented behavior, but its very simplicity is an asset in the achievement of the goals it describes.

Practitioners of e-learning can use GEMS as a framework to orient their actions to all levels of the ecology that influence their identity at a given time. Practitioners make decisions that have impact on one or more levels. Program managers work at the national and international level, and at the institutional level. Instructors and technology specialists usually work at the course or learning object level, although sometimes their decisions also affect the institutional level. Students typically work at the level of course or class, and occasionally at the learning object level when they suggest changes in the instructional materials that compose the course. The GEMS framework encourages people at different levels of the ecology to align their actions with each other, considering the implications of their actions to goals, engagement, management and support of levels above and below it in the nested system. The GEMS process provides direct communication links between functional aspects of different levels of an identity.

1. GEMS at the International/ National Level

Using NS/GEMS analysis at the international/ national level is probably the most difficult, because it is hard to view it from its own internal view - as an identity with goals, engagement, management and support. The *goals* at this level are similar to goals at any level, influenced by the ecological laws for e-learning outlined earlier. The sheer size of the entity, however, means that engagement, management and support must respond to complexity, diversity, flexibility and interactivity in a more critical way than at lower levels. These mega systems are at the top of the ecological food chain, consuming huge resources to deliver to myriad audiences. Although it may be difficult to consider the NS/GEMS of the huge e-learning mega systems, it is important that we do so because even small changes in their GEMS may have large consequences on the rest of the industry, including your niche. Your view on their GEMS may strongly influence your own GEMS. At the international/national level, goals for stability and sustainability must balance common denominators for services across multiple cultures and populations with unique opportunities for specific niches, which may expand and flourish in the future. They must also balance between short term and long-term e-learning opportunities and contracts, capital investments and media expenses, legal protection of prior innovations and investment in potential new creations. Recent financial crises show that a link in a management chain may lead to unexpected and significant consequences. Engagement must be responsive to new directions while keeping existing processes stable. Effective engagement assures that national and international cooperation and competition can be managed. Cooperation is frequently done at lower levels, and so is described in greater detail at the institution level. Management of innovation and cash cows may use different but compatible methods. Both established plans and emerging trends, such as variations in the student population, migration trends, and new challenges of the professions, must be addressed. Support is the most difficult level to both establish and to change; many international e-learning systems achieve it through critical alliances with other organizations under the principle of mutual benefit. A complex support chain is established and all aspects of it require permanent surveillance to survive.

2. GEMS at the Institution or Program Level

The goals at the institutional level are influenced by the identity of the larger systems of which it is a part, the identity it shares with parallel institutions, and the identity it projects to consumer audiences. A program mission seeks to address all of these perspectives at once. Managers of an e-learning system must always be able to answer the moving-target question: Who are our audiences and what do they expect from us? Some of these audiences are the encompassing international and national systems, and others are niches potentially encompassed by the particular program. Engagement elicits response from the broader learning community, which means actual and prospective students, instructors or faculty, staff, and alumni. The members of the e-learning program must feel that they can rely on the institution for any issue that they may have. Certain communication elements enhance this confidence, such as institutional themes, the "look and feel" of websites, advertising, student and faculty handbooks, and peer advising of the more experienced faculty to the newcomers. The institutions must furnish all aspects of their operation with these identity builders.

Each e-learning program is just one actor among many others that make possible the education of society; critical alliances are needed, for instance, to provision the knowledge and skills that constitute the core programs, to reach audiences that are very far from the program coordination center, and to assure that the programs match the changing needs of communities. There are several forms of cooperation possible in this realm. One of them is sharing curriculum resources, which may or may not involve cost; these are: books, e-books, learning objects, instructors, and infrastructure (particularly, information technology infrastructure or cyberinfrastructure). Another form of cooperation is for complementary func-

tions; each program does not have to do everything that is needed. Today, several organizations have specialized only on one aspect of the e-learning process, lending service to many programs. Specifically, there are organizations specialized in reaching and locating students, in publishing e-books, in developing tailored instructional materials, in evaluating quality of systems, in providing tutors that work around the clock, and in hosting course management systems. Based on these possibilities of cooperation, e-learning programs can focus their efforts in the essential: fulfilling learning needs of their audiences. Management at the institutional or program level must emphasize planning versus changes in the environment; for instance, be sensitive to variations in the student population, migration trends, new challenges of the professions, and look for topics of interest for larger communities and design curricula according to them. At this level, there are some considerations: first, integration, in the sense of building connectivity and feedback loops among all components of the system; and. second, management of the buy-in; be aware of the needs of faculty and students to respond to them with opportunity to guarantee that they would prefer e-learning to more traditional forms of education. Data gathering procedures such as surveys, focus groups, and help desk lines are used for this purpose.

On the Management and Support levels, some programs cooperate to form consortia from which all members benefit. An example of this is the SUNY Learning Network, formed by all public higher education institutions in New York. More than 60 universities, colleges and community colleges share a CMS, provide training to faculty and students, evaluate quality of programs, and exchange research outcomes, among other functions. In turn, this corporation feeds from resources of other institutions, such as the public libraries system of New York, *SmartThinking* (a private provider of developmental tutorials in mathematics, English, science, and other areas) and an outsourced company that maintains the corporate server pool and networks.

Support includes finding ways of reaching remote audiences, facilitate access of students to financial aid, and guarantee connectivity and appropriate devices for students. The most important concerns at this level are the smooth operation of the course management system or systems adopted by the program, and guaranteeing access to all program members, including potential students. Everybody must have equal opportunity of access to the technology chosen by the program for delivering the instructional content and communications. This requires paying special attention to minorities, disabled citizens and those living very far from the coordination center.

3. GEMS at the Course, Class or Community Level

The goals for stability of identity of the organization at this level must balance instructional objectives, the outcomes that are expected from student learning, with the capacity systematically to produce many courses, while keeping avenues open for creativity and innovation. Goals for a course must align with the institution of which the courses/communities are a part, so that classes can quickly respond to changes in institutional goals, such as the implementation of a corporate quality program. Engagement in both established systems for course production and innovation enable new methods to become a part of effective established processes, while maintaining high standards in both arenas for cognitive, social and teaching presence for students (Garrison and Anderson, 2003). Management refers here to keeping the course life-cycle efficient; every course must go through the stages of design, introduction, delivery, assessment, and quality evaluation; all this needs to be done on a tight timeline to avoid incomplete learning. Peer management increases the success of programs because learning is increased geo-

metrically as course creators and instructors interact. Teachers are assisted to convert every course incident in an opportunity for learning. Support is achieved through effective use of interactive tools present in the CMS, to which all instructors and tutors must acclimate. Assessment defines the critical path of a course, and it must be planned so that all assessment events are tightly connected to key objectives. The most important concerns at this level are the smooth operation of the course management system or systems adopted by the program, and guaranteeing access to all program members, including potential students. Everybody must have equal opportunity of access to the technology chosen by the program for delivering the instructional content and communications. This requires paying special attention to minorities, disabled citizens and those living very far with respect to the coordination center.

4. GEMS at the Learning Object or Event Level

When dealing with specific learning objects or events that integrate instruction in an online course, goals for stability of identity of the organization at this level relate largely to efficient reuse of learning events, and effective discovery of innovations for future use. The alignment of the institutional goals for capturing innovation with goals on this level will assure that instructors and developers create effective learning events that satisfy both learner needs and the institution's cost parameters. Engagement with educators, instructors, course developers and instructional designers encourages both opportunities for divergent creations and systematic paths for bringing those creations into the mainstream. Effective learning objects 'stage' interactions with a learner. A webpage that simply displays information is not the best means for engagement. The student needs to do something within the page; e.g.:, answer a question, input data for simulation, move objects in the screen, compare content of the webpage with something that the student can find in the textbook. Any prescription for increasing active and meaningful learning is valid here. Management relates to the selection, integration and creation of resources, nurtured both by the knowledge of how people learn and the craft of the experienced teacher. If any essential elements are missing in the equation, the internet provides multiple sources of advice and excellent models. Support uses metadata to improve efficiency for finding learning resources; both teachers and instructors must know rules for the efficient searches on the Web. Support also must exist for innovation and creativity. Both patents and grants support these processes, as do effective feedback cycles for student acceptance of established and new learning events.

Using GEMS to Connect Nested Levels of the Ecology Cone

As shown in the previous analyses, the goals, engagement, management and support of the stability of an institution can be aligned at each level of the nested ecological system. These GEMS can then be connected across levels. For example, an emerging goal at an international level can relate to goals at the institution, individual course, and individual learning events level. If an institution structures itself to make use of the concept of GEMS (if that becomes a goal of such an institution), then it engages the GEMS framework within the organization, organizing itself (managing itself) so that it can quickly and flexibly apply information learned at a higher level to nested inner levels of support.

An example of this might be that courses are designed as open systems where a new technology can first be tried as an aspect of a course as a test – and then, if monumentally successful, is used to develop the next course. One or more developers at the course level who are designated as *innovation-catchers* are immediately contacted if such new methods become available. And, conversely, *innovation-seekers* at different

levels are advised to be aware of the success of such innovations and immediately contact high levels of the institution so that they can become funded and considered as a part of the plans for the future. This already happens in some situations, but frequently rather haphazardly. Careful thought about institutional organization using a GEMS approach may increase success. For example, a strong and liberal patent policy (giving much ownership of the patent to the inventor) encourages innovation from below. And a relatively flat and flexible organization encourages communication from the top down.

Using a GEMS structure to compare the identity of the self-institution with the perceived GEMS of other institutions may expose areas of strength and weakness not otherwise visible, clarifying what other institutions are most willing to protect or let go, and exposing openings in their niches. A GEMS comparison can also show areas of possible agreement or merging, where desirable.

FUTURE TRENDS AND CONCLUSION

This NS/GEMS perspective of the Ecology of E-learning provides a framework to analyze one's position within the e-learning web, which could be implemented in a project management tool such as *MS Project*. Because e-learning systems are deployed within a globally-shared virtual space, users may ask: Where am I in that network? The question is not about a geographical location, but about location in the constellations of existing systems, determining associations with other systems, prevalence of pedagogical methods, availability of resources, and clienteles. If an online program director is working in India with one of the large online colleges from the USA, the typical environment of this director is more like an American college than an Indian university. This director can use NS/GEMS to assess whether the program should adapt the methods, resources and clienteles of Indian learning networks or remain encapsulated in a foreign environment. The NS/GEMS tool affords the director (or practitioner or institution) a finer level of granularity for gauging the position of one's 'self' within the web, while reducing complexity, and increasing orientations towards self-organization, self-optimization, and context-awareness. The NS/GEMS tool supports information generated by other mnemonic tools, such as the CATWOE tool (customers, actors, transformation processes, world-views, owners and environmental constraints (Checkland, 1990). Whereas CATWOE attends to the customer, GEMS attends to the producing system interested in survival.

On the other hand, NS/GEMS provides a language for communicating about relationships crossing levels of the nested system of e-learning. Each nested level creates semantic relationships unique to itself, even if the key words are also used on other levels. It is not the same, for instance, to speak of "environment" at the international level as at the class/course/community level because the concepts have different meanings in those different environments.

Use of the NS/GEMS tool at each nested level helps prevent an identity within the e-learning ecology from "mixing up levels" which causes miscommunication, misuse of resources, and problems with goals, engagement, management and resources. A separate NS/GEMS analysis at each level of the nested system helps to keep meaning contiguous with the unit of analysis (a principle for Contiguity of Meaning). For one example, 'assessment' has very different meanings when referring to a whole program than when referring to a learning outcome of a class; the NS/GEMS analysis at each level makes these distinctions salient. For a second example, a principle of design of learning resources, such as the concept of 'visualization of concepts' is assigned too narrow a spot if used only to talk about visual images on the course/class/community level. Visualization of concepts for the blind, for example, may require tactile and auditory channels for visualization. An NS/GEMS analysis will indicate that 'visualization' is a concept that crosses the institution, course/community and learning object levels.

The NS/GEMS reasoning method encourages the use of the ecological 'laws' as checkpoints for action within the web, assisting an identity (practitioner or institution) to detect current or potential problems in e-learning programs on any of the nested levels. Problems arise when these principles are not sufficiently attended to on each level. Common causes for an e-learning program to lose clientele, for example, may be due to transactional distances becoming too great (law of transactional distances), or may be due to students given unequal equality of service (law of equivalence). Certain e-learning programs remain for years as small initiatives, with just few courses and in a perennial attempt to reach audiences. Probably, they have not paid attention to the law of industrialization and the cycle of knowledge dissemination: Success in e-learning requires a certain degree of sophistication about "chains of production", as well as careful determination of roles within the institution for the organization and dissemination of knowledge through virtual environments.

The ecological view suggests the possibility of gauging the global dimensions of the e-learning environment, as the sum of all institutions and programs involved in it, altogether with associated services such as publishers of online instructional resources, online repositories, tutorial services and a few more. This is a permanently evolving meta-system but its expansion and mutations can be traced by using the suggested principles of nested systems. The e-learning world can be mapped through the internet. One can envision a new discipline of *E-learning Surveillance*, which uses network tracking methods, semantic webs and statistical analyses to provide a picture of the status of a determinate e-learning network or category of networks at a given time. It would be interesting to know, for instance, about the patterns of the flow of students to e-learning programs from different regions of the world. Do they prefer programs according to physical distance or based on prestige? Or do they prefer convenience? Who are the major providers of instructional resources for e-learning? What is the ratio of free versus proprietary providers in each level of instruction? What is the ratio of non-profit versus for-profit? The emerging discipline could answer these and many other interesting questions.

Finally, we can ask what the result of NS/GEMS is for people daily involved in e-learning as creators, workers or users. Researchers using NS/GEMS have a new framework for asking questions about e-learning at different levels of specificity - and with more precise granularity. The discipline of e-learning surveillance is a promising field for research grants and practical applications. Practitioners of e-learning, such as faculty, trainers and instructional designers can apply the full range of components of NS/GEMS to their work, as suggested in the many examples provided along this chapter. Administrators will find it a powerful tool for assessing the status of a program in critical dimensions for decision-making and for leading strategic action in order to improve results or eliminate shortcomings. The student, too, can make use of the NS/GEMS tool to guide actions: first, by clearly establishing goals of study and selecting the most appropriate program to meet them; second, by engaging in the program of their choice realizing that learning is proportional to their degree of engagement; third, by managing the critical resources available in the program such as time, tutoring, class collaboration, instructional materials, and assessment opportunities; and fourth, by creating a supportive environment for study at home, with instructors, in the workplace and through collaboration with peers. For any identity within the e-learning ecology, a thoughtful look at the NS/GEMS intersections can pay off.

REFERENCES

Bates, T. (2005). *Technology, e-learning and distance education (2nd Ed.)*. London: Routledge-Falmer Studies in Distance Education.

Bliznak, M. (2007). Virtualization technologies as an e-learning support in the academic environment. In *Annals of Proceedings of DAAAM International Vienna*.

Brown, J. S. (2000, March/April). Growing up digital: How the web changes work, education, and the ways people learn. *Change Magazine*, 11-20.

Chacon, F. (2006). Triangulating incomplete learning through student responses. In *Proceedings from EDMEDIA 2006*, Orlando, FL. Retrieved from http://www.editlib.org/j/EDMEDIA/v/2006/n/1

Checkland, P., & Scholes, J. (1990). *Soft systems methodology in action*. New York: Wiley.

Corbeil, J. R., & Valdes-Corbeil, M. E. (2007). Are you ready for mobile learning? *EDUCAUSE Quarterly, 30*, 2.

Garrison, D. R., & Anderson, T. (2003). *E-Learning in the 21st century: A framework for research and practice*. London: Routledge/Falmer.

Harasim, L. (2000). Shift happens: Online education as a new paradigm in learning, internet and higher education. *Elsevier Science 3,* 41-61.

Henning, E. (2005). Rural South-African teachers "move home" in an online ecology. In J. Weiss, J. Hunsinger, J. Nolan, & P. Trifonas (Eds.), *International Handbook of Virtual Learning Environments*. New York: Springer.

Jenkins, H. (2006). *Convergence culture: Where old and new media collide*. New York: New York University Press.

Laurillard, D. (1993). *Rethinking university teaching*. Milton Keynes, UK: Open University Press.

Lord, R. G., & Levy, P. E. (1994). Moving from cognition to action: A control theory perspective. *Applied Psychology*, *43*(3), 335–367. doi:10.1111/j.1464-0597.1994.tb00828.x

Merrill, M. D. (2000). Knowledge objects and mental models. In D. A. Wiley (Ed.), *The Instructional Use of Learning Objects: Online Version*. Retrieved June 7, 2008, from http://reusability. org/read/chapters/merrill.doc

MIT - Massachusetts Institute of Technology. (2009). *Evaluation*. Compilation of evaluation studies about *OpenCourseware*. Retrieved December 18, 2008, from http://ocw.uofk.edu/OcwWeb/ Global/AboutOCW/evaluation.htm

Moore, M. G. (1993). *Theory of transactional distance*. In D. Keegan (Ed.), *Theoretical principles of distance education* (p.22-38). New York: Routledge.

Moore, M. G., & Kearsley, G. (2005). *Distance education: A systems view (2nd Ed.)*. New York: Cengage Learning.

Palloff, R., & Pratt, K. (1999). *Building learning communities in cyberspace: effective strategies for the online classroom*. San Francisco: Jossey-Bass.

Palloff, R., & Pratt, K. (2007). *Building online learning communities: effective strategies for the virtual classroom*. San Francisco: Jossey-Bass.

Peters, O. (1983). Distance teaching and industrial production: a comparative interpretation in outline. In D. Sewart, D. Keegan & B. Holmberg (Eds.), *Distance education: International perspectives* (pp. 95-113). London: Croom-Helm.

Ravet, S. (2002). E-Learning and knowledge management. *Newsletter of PROMETHEUS Network*, *20*, 2–6.

Rumble, G. (1986). *The planning and management of distance education*. London: Croom Helm.

Russell, T. L. (2001). *The no significant difference phenomenon (5th Ed.)*. IDECC (The International Distance Education Certification Center).

Saba, F. (2007). A systems approach in theory building. In M. Moore (Ed.), *Handbook of distance education*. Mahwah, NJ: Lawrence Erlbaum.

Saba, F. (2007). A systems approach in theory building. In M. Moore (Eds.), *Handbook of distance education*. Mahwah, NJ: Lawrence Erlbaum.

Shadbolt, N., & Berners-Lee, T. (2008, October). Web science emerges. *Scientific American*, *229*(4), 81.

Shaw, J. P. (2005). Building meaning: Experts and novices in on-line learning. In *Proceedings from EdMedia International Conference*, Montreal, Canada. Retrieved from http://www.editlib.org/j/ EDMEDIA/v/2005/n/1

Shaw, J. P. (2006). The problem with Getting it right the first time. In *Proceedings from EdMedia International Conference*, Orlando, Florida. Retrieved from http://www.editlib.org/j/ EDMEDIA/v/2006/n/1

Simonson, M., & Schlosser, C. (1995). Theory and distance education: A new discussion. *American Journal of Distance Education*, *13*(1), 60–75. doi:10.1080/08923649909527014

Spector, J. M., Merrill, M. D., van Merrienboer, J., & Driscoll, M. P. (2007). *Handbook of Research on Educational Communications and Technology (3rd Ed.)*. London: Routledge.

Van der Wende, M. (2002). *The Role of US higher education in the global E-Learning market*. Research & occasional paper series: CSHE.1.02. Center for Studies in Higher Education. San Francisco: University of California, Berkeley.

Werner, H., & Kaplan, B. (1963). *Symbol formation: An organismic developmental approach to language and the expression of thought*. New York: John Wiley.

Wexler, S., Grey, N., Adams-Miller, D., Nguyen, F., & van Barneveld, A. (2008). *Learning management systems: The good, the bad, the ugly... and the truth*. Santa Rosa, CA: The e-learning Guild Publications.

Wiley, D. A. (Ed.). (n.d.). *The instructional use of learning objects: Online version*. Retrieved January 30, 2008, from http://www.reusability. org/read/

Compilation of References

Abilene Christian University. (2008). *Mobile learning and the connected campus.* Retrieved November 20, 2008, from http://www.acu.edu/technology/mobilelearning/index.html

Abrami, P. C. (2001). Understanding and promoting complex learning using technology. *Educational Research and Evaluation, 7*(2-3), 113–136. doi:10.1076/edre.7.2.113.3864

Adams, J. (2008). Understanding the factors limiting the acceptability of online courses and degrees. *International Journal on E-Learning, 7*(4), 573–587.

Addison, A., & O'Hare, L. (2008). How Can Massive Multi-user Virtual Environments and Virtual Role Play Enhance Traditional Teaching Practice? In *Researching Learning in Virtual Environments International Conference* (pp. 5-15). Milton Keynes, UK: The Open University.

Aderinoye, R. A., Ojokheta, K. O., & Olojede, A. A. (2007). Integrating mobile learning into nomadic education programs in Nigeria: Issues and perspectives. *International Review of Research in Open and Distance Learning, 8*(2), 1–17.

Akdemir, O. (2008). Teaching in online courses: experiences of instructional technology faculty members. *Turkish Online Journal of Distance Education, 9*(2), 97–108.

Alavi, M. (1994). Computer-mediated collaborative learning: an empirical evaluation. *MIS Quarterly, 18*(2), 159–174. doi:10.2307/249763

Alavi, M. (1994, June). Computer-mediated collaborative learning: An empirical evaluation. *MIS Quarterly, 18*(2), 159–174. doi:10.2307/249763

Alavi, M., Wheeler, B. C., & Valacich, J. S. (1995). Using IT to reengineer business education: An exploratory investigation of collaborative telelearning. *MIS Quarterly, 19*(3), 293–312. doi:10.2307/249597

Alexander, B. (2004). Going nomadic mobile learning in higher education. *Educause Review, 39*(5), 28-35. Retrieved October 8, 2008, from http://connect.educause.edu/Library/EDUCAUSE+Review/GoingNomadicMobileLearnin/40494

Alfonseca, E., Carro, R. M., Martin, E., Ortigosa, A., & Paredes, P. (2006). The impact of learning styles on student grouping for collaborative learning: a case study. *User Modeling and User-Adapted Interaction, 16*(2-3), 377–401. doi:10.1007/s11257-006-9012-7

Ali, A. (2003). Instructional design and online instruction: Practice and perception. *TechTrends, 47*(5), 42–45. doi:10.1007/BF02763205

Allen, E., & Seaman, J. (2003). *Sizing the opportunity: The quality and extent of online education in the United States, 2002 and 2003.* Retrieved February 2004, from http://www.sloan-c.org/resources/sizing_opportunity.pdf

Allen, E., & Seaman, J. (2007). *Online nation: Five years of growth in online learning.* The Sloan Consortium.

Allen, I. E., & Seaman, J. (2003). *Sizing the opportunity: The quality and extent of online education in the United States, 2002 and 2003.* Needham, MA: The Sloan Consortium. Retrieved September 1, 2008, from http://www.sloan-c.org/sizingtheOpportunity_survey02-03.pdf

Allen, I. E., & Seaman, J. (2005*). Growing by degrees: Online education in the United States.* Needham, MA: The Sloan Consortium. Retrieved September 1, 2008, from www.sloan-c.org/publications/survey/pdf/growing_by_degrees_southern.pdf

Allen, I. E., & Seaman, J. (2006). *Making the grade: Online education in the United States.* Needham, MA: The Sloan Consortium. Retrieved December 2, 2008, from http://

www.sloanconsortium.org/publications/survey/pdf/making_the_grade.pdf

Allen, I. E., & Seaman, J. (2007). *Online nation: Five years growth in online learning*. Needham, MA: The Sloan Consortium. Retrieved October 9, 2008, from http://www.sloanconsortium.org/publications/survey/pdf/online nation.pdf

Allen, I. E., & Seaman, J. (2008). *Staying the course: Online education in the United States, 2008*. Needham, MA: Sloan Consortium. Retrieved from http://www.sloanconsortium.org/publications/survey/pdf/staying_the_course.pdf

Allen, M. (2003). *Michael Allen's Guide to E-Learning: Building interactive, fun, and effective learning programs for any company*. New York: John Wiley & Sons.

Alliger, G., & Janak, E. (1989). Kirkpatrick's levels of training criteria: thirty years later. *Personnel Psychology, 42*(2), 331–342. doi:10.1111/j.1744-6570.1989.tb00661.x

Ally, M. (2004). Foundations Of Educational Theory For Online Learning. In T. Anderson & F. Elloumi (Eds.), *Theory and Practice of Online Learning* (pp. 3-31). Athabasca University. Retrieved December 31, 2008, from http://cde.athabascau.ca/online_book/

Anderson, B. (2005). Dimensions of learning and support in an online community. *Open Learning, 19*(2), 183–190. doi:10.1080/0268051042000224770

Anderson, T. (2006, February 25). Affinity groups in self-paced online learning. In *Virtual Canuck: Teaching and Learning in a Net-Centric World*. Retrieved November 12, 2008, from http://terrya.edublogs.org/2006/02/25/affinity-groups-in-self-paced-online-learning/

Anderson, T., & Elloumi, F. (Eds.). (2004). *Theory and Practice of Online Learning*. Athabasca University. Retrieved December 31, 2008, from http://cde.athabascau.ca/online_book/

Andreasen, M. S., Nielsen, H. V., Schrøder, S. O., & Stage, J. (2006). Usability in Open Source Software development: opinions and practice. *Information Technology and Control, 35*(3A), 303–312.

Apperley, M., Rogers, B., & Masoodian, M. (2002). LLC lecture capture and editing tool for online course delivery. In. *Proceedings of World Conference on E-Learning in Corporate, Government, Healthcare, and Higher Education, 2002*, 1866–1869.

Apple. (2008). *All the tools for mobile learning*. Retrieved October 18, 2008, from http://www.apple.com/education/teachers-professors/mobile-learning.html

Arbaugh, J. B. (2000a). Virtual classroom characteristics and student satisfaction in Internet-based MBA courses. *Journal of Management Education, 24*(1), 32–54. doi:10.1177/105256290002400104

Arbaugh, J. B. (2000b). How Classroom Environment and Student Engagement Affect Leaning in internet-based MBA Courses. *Business Communication Quarterly, 63*(4), 9–26. doi:10.1177/108056990006300402

Arcademic Skill Builders. (2009). *Ratio Stadium*. Retrieved March 7, 2009. from http://arcademicskillbuilders.com/games/ratio-stadium/ratio-stadium.html

Ardito, C., Costabile, M., De Marsico, M., Lanzilotti, R., Levialdi, S., Roselli, T., & Rossano, V. (2006). An approach to usability evaluation of e-learning applications. *Universal Access in the Information Society, 4*(3), 270–283. doi:10.1007/s10209-005-0008-6

Aronson, J., & Timms, M. (2003). *Net choices, net gains: Supplementing the high school curriculum with online courses* (WestEd Knowledge Brief). Retrieved December 21, 2008, from http://www.wested org/online_pubs/KN-03-02.pdf

Asian Development Bank (ADB). (2008). *Education and skills: Strategies for accelerated development in Asia and the Pacific*. Manila. Retrieved March 15, 2009, from http://www.adb.org/Documents/Studies/Education-Skills-Strategies-Development/Education-Skills-Strategies-Development.pdf

Association for Progressive Communications (APC). (2008, October 13). *Why APC continues to obsess over Internet access*. Retrieved March 31, 2009 from http://www.apc.org/en/news/development/all/why-apc-continues-obsess-over-internet-access

Athavaley, A. (2007, June 20). *A Job Interview You Don't Have to Show Up For: Microsoft, Verizon, Others Use Virtual Worlds to Recruit; Dressing Avatars for Success*. Microsoft, Verizon, Others Use Virtual Worlds to Recruit; Dressing Avatars for Success. Retrieved from http://online.

wsj.com/article/SB118229876637841321.html?mod=tff_main_tff_top

Bachfischer, A., Dyson, L., & Litchfield, A. (2008). Mobile Learning and Student Perspectives: An mReality Check! In *Proceedings of the Mobile Business.ICMB '08. Seventh International Conference* (pp. 287-295).

Badat, S. (2005). South Africa: Distance higher education policies for access, social equity, quality, and social and economic responsiveness in a context of the diversity of provision. *Distance Education, 26*(2), 183–204. doi:10.1080/01587910500168843

Baker, W., & Gloster, A. (1994). Moving towards the virtual university: A vision of technology in higher education. *Cause/Effect, 17*(2).

Ball, S. (2008). Effective Use of Virtual Learning Environments. *JISC InfoNet*. Retrieved March 10, 2009, from http://www.jiscinfonet.ac.uk/InfoKits/effective-use-of-VLEs

Barab, S. A., & Landa, A. (1997). Designing effective interdisciplinary anchors. *Educational Leadership, 54*(6), 52–55.

Barab, S. A., Squire, K. D., & Dueber, W. (2000). A Co-Evolutionary Model for Supporting the Emergence of Authenticity. *Educational Technology Research and Development, 48*(2), 37–62. doi:10.1007/BF02313400

Barnes, C., & Tynan, B. (2007). The adventures of Miranda in the brave new world: learning in a Web 2.0 millennium. *ALT-J. Research in Learning Technology, 15*(3), 189–200.

Barnes, L., Scutter, S., & Young, J. (2008). Using screen recording and compression software to support online learning. *Innovate, 1*(5).

Barton, T. (2008). Customers. *Twiki*. Retrieved November 3, 2008, from http://www.twiki.net/customers.html

Bates, A. (1991). Interactivity as a criterion for media selection in distance education. *Never Too Far, 16*, 5–9.

Bates, A. W., & Poole, G. (2003). *Effective teaching with technology in higher education: Foundations for success.* San Francisco: John Wiley & Sons, Inc.

Bates, T. (2005). *Technology, e-learning and distance education (2nd Ed.).* London: Routledge-Falmer Studies in Distance Education.

Beard, L. A., & Harper, C. (2002). Student perceptions of online versus on campus instruction. *Education, 122*, 658–663.

Beaudoin, M. F. (2002). Learning or lurking? Tracking the "invisible" online student. *The Internet and Higher Education, 5*(2), 147–155. doi:10.1016/S1096-7516(02)00086-6

Becker, H. J., & Ravitz, J. L. (2001). *Computer use by teachers: Are Cuban's predictions correct?* Paper presented at the annual meeting of the American Educational Research Association, Seattle, WA.

Bekele, T. A. (2008). *Impact of technology supported learning environments in higher education: Issues in and for research.* Unpublished doctoral dissertation, University of Oslo, Norway.

Belanger, F., & Jordan, D. H. (2000). *Evaluation and Implementation of Distance Learning: Technologies, Tools and Techniques.* Hershey, USA: Idea Group Publishing.

Bell, F., Zaitseva, E., & Zakrzewska, D. (2007). Evaluation: A link in the chain of sustainability. In N. Lambropoulos & P. Zaphiris (Eds.), *User-centered design of online learning communities* (pp. 186-214). Hershey, PA: Information Science Publishing.

Benbunan-Fich, R., Hiltz, R., & Harasim, L. (2005). The online interaction learning model: An integrated theoretical framework for learning networks. In S. R. Hiltz & R. Goldman (Eds.), *Learning together online: Research on asynchronous learning networks* (pp. 19-37). Mahwah, NJ: Lawrence Erlbaum.

Bender, T. (2003). *Discussion-based online teaching to enhance student learning: Theory, practice, and assessment* (1st ed.). Sterling, VA: Stylus Publishing, LLC.

Bielaczyk, K. (2006). Designing social infrastructure: critical issues in creating learning environments with technology. *Journal of the Learning Sciences, 15*(3), 301–329. doi:10.1207/s15327809jls1503_1

Blattberg, R., & Deighton, J. (1991). Interactive Marketing: Exploiting the Age of Addressability. *Sloan Management Review, 33*(1), 5–14.

Bligh, D. A. (2000). *What's the use of lectures?* San Francisco, CA: Jossey-Bass.

Bliznak, M. (2007). Virtualization technologies as an e-learning support in the academic environment. In *Annals of Proceedings of DAAAM International Vienna*.

Boettcher, J. (2007). Ten core principles for designing effective learning environments: Insights from brain research and pedagogical theory. *Innovate Journal of Online Education, 3*(3). Retrieved September 20, 2007, from http://innovateonline.info/index.php?view= article&id=54

Bonner, S. E. (1999). Choosing teaching methods based on learning objectives: An integrative framework. *Issues in Accounting Education, 14*(1), 11-39. Retrieved April 5, 2009, from ABI/INFORM Global database. (Document ID: 39568540).

Boss, S. (2007). *Twittering, Not Frittering: Professional Development in 140 Characters*. Retrieved October 22, 2008 from http://www.edutopia.org/twitter-professionaldevelopment-technologymicroblogging

Bower, B. L. (2001). Distance education: Facing the faculty challenge. *Online Journal of Distance Learning Administration, 4*(2), 1-9. Retrieved May 8, 2008, from http://www.westga.edu/~distance/ojdla/summer42/bower42.html

Bowers, K. (2008). Assessing the value of Virtual Worlds for post-secondary instructors: a survey of innovators, early adopters and the early majority in Second Life. *International Journal of Humanities and Social Sciences, 3*(1), 40–50.

Bozarth, J., Chapman, D. D., & LaMonica, L. (2004). Preparing for distance learning: Designing an online student orientation course. *Educational Technology & Society, 7*(1), 87–106.

Bradburn, E. M., & Zimbler, L. (2002). *Distance education instruction by postsecondary staff: Fall 1998*. National Center for Educational Statistics, Statistical Analysis Report, February 2002, Postsecondary Education Descriptive Analysis Reports. 1-82. Retrieved December 24, 2008, from http://nces.ed.gov/pubs2002/2002155.pdf

Brandon, B. (Ed.). (2007). *Handbook of e-Learning Strategy*. Santa Rosa, CA: The e-Learning Guild.

Bransford, J. D., Brown, A., & Cocking, R. (Eds.). (2000). *How people learn: Mind, brain, experience and school, Expanded Edition*. Washington, DC: National Academy Press.

Bransford, J. D., Sherwood, R. D., Hasselbring, T. S., Kinzer, C. K., & Williams, S. M. (1990). Anchored instruction: Why we need it and how technology can help. In D. Nix & R. Spiro (Eds.), *Cognition, education, and multimedia: Exploring ideas in high technology* (pp. 115-141). Hillsdale, NJ: Lawrence Erlbaum Associates.

Brookfield, S. (1995). Adult learning: An overview. In A. Tuinjman (Ed.), *International Encyclopedia of Education*. Oxford, UK: Pergamon Press. Retrieved November 23, 2008, from http://www.fsu.edu/~elps/ae/download/ade5385/Brookfield.pdf

Brower, H. H. (2003). On emulating classroom discussion in a distance-delivered OBHR Course: Creating an on-line learning community. *Academy of Management Learning & Education, 2*(1), 22–36.

Brown, B., & Bell, M. (2004). CSCW at play: 'there' as a collaborative virtual environment. In *Proceedings of the 2004 ACM conference on Computer supported cooperative work* (pp. 350-359). Chicago, USA: ACM.

Brown, E. (2001). *Mobile learning explorations at the Stanford Learning Lab. Speaking of Computers, 55*. Stanford, CA: Board of Trustees of the Leland Stanford Junior University. Retrieved October 8, 2008, from http://sll.stanford.edu/projects/tomprof/newtomprof/postings/289.html

Brown, J. S. (2000, March/April). Growing up digital: How the web changes work, education, and the ways people learn. *Change Magazine*, 11-20.

Brown, J. S., & Adler, R. P. (2008). Minds on fire: Open education, the long tail, and learning 2.0. *EDUCAUSE Review, 43*(1), 16–32.

Brown, J. S., Collins, A., & Duguid, P. (1989, Jan-Feb). Situated cognition and the culture of learning. *Educational Researcher, 18*(1), 32–42.

Brown, J., & Metcalf, D. (2008). *Mobile Learning Update*. Saratoga Springs, NY: The MASIE Center's Learning Consortium.

Brown, R. E. (2001). The process of community-building in distance learning courses. *Journal of Asynchronous Learning Networks, 5*(1). Retrieved from http://www.sloan-cwiki.org/wiki/index.php?title=The_Process_of_Communitybuilding_in_Distance_Learning_Classes%2c_JALN_5(2)

Brubacher, J. S., & Rudy, W. (1997). *Higher education in transition* (4th ed.). New Brunswick, NJ: Transaction.

Bruffee, K. A. (1993). *Collaborative learning: Higher education, interdependence, and the authority of knowledge.* Baltimore, MD: The Johns Hopkins University Press.

Bruner, J. (2007). Factors motivating and inhibiting faculty in offering their courses via distance education. *Online Journal of Distance Learning Administration, 10*(2), 1–18.

Bruning, R. H., Schraw, G. J., & Ronning, R. R. (1999). *Cognitive Psychology and Instruction.* Columbus, OH: Merrill.

Brush, T., Glazewski, K., Rutowski, K., Berg, K., Stromfors, C., & Van-Nest, M. H. (2003). Integrating Technology in a Field-Based Teacher Training Program: The PT3@ASU Project. *Educational Technology Research and Development, 51*(1), 57–72. doi:10.1007/BF02504518

Brusilovsky, P. (2001). Adaptive hypermedia. *User Modeling and User-Adapted Interaction, 11*(1-2), 87–110. doi:10.1023/A:1011143116306

Brusilovsky, P., & Peylo, C. (2003). Adaptive and intelligent web-based educational systems. *International Journal of Artificial Intelligence in Education, 13*, 156–169.

Bryant, T. (2008). *From Age of Empires to Zork: Using games in the classroom.* Retrieved March 22, 2009, from http://www.academiccommons.org/commons/essay/games-inclassroom

Bucy, M. C. (2003). *Online classes: The student experience* (No. AAT 3098412). Corvallis: Oregon State University (Proquest Digital Dissertations).

Burdet, B., Bontron, C., & Burgi, P. (2007). Lecture capture: What can be automated? *EDUCAUSE Quarterly, 30*(2), 40–48.

Burmester, A., Burmester, F., & Reiners, T. (2008). Virtual environment for immersive learning of container logistics. In *Proceedings of ED-MEDIA 2008. World Conference on Educational Multimedia, Hypermedia & Telecommunications,* Vienna, Austria (pp. 5843–5852). Chesapeake, USA: AACE.

Burns, M., Heath, M., & Dimock, V. (1998). *TAP into learning: Constructivism and technology: On the road to student-centered learning.* Austin, TX: Technology Assistance Program.

Butler, K. (2003). *How to Keep Online Students Motivated.* Australian Flexible Learning Community. Retrieved from http://community.flexiblelearning.net.au/TeachingTrainingLearners/content/article_3340.htm

California State University. Monterey Bay. (2005). *Mobile teaching and learning in action.* Retrieved October 18, 2008, from http://wetec.csumb.edu/site/x17155.xml

Callahan, P. (2003, March 28-30). *Proceedings of the University Council for Educational Administration 88th Annual Conference,* Chicago, IL. Retrieved November 24, 2008 from http://www.westga.edu/~distance/ojdla/fall63/howell63.html

Calonge, C. (2007). A view from Second Life's trenches: are you a pioneer or a Settler? In R. Smith (Ed.), *NMC Summer Conference Proceedings* (pp. 111-119). Stanford, USA: The New Media Consortium.

Campbell, G. (2005). There's something in the air: Podcasting in education. *EDUCAUSE Review, 40*(6), 32–47.

Cardoso, E., & Machado, A. (2000). Tools for Distributed Learning in the University. In *Proceedings of the Simposium Iberoamericano de Informática Educativa.*

Carlin, D. (2007). Corporate Wikis Go Viral. *Business Week.* Retrieved November 3, 2008, from http://www.businessweek.com/technology/content/mar2007/tc20070312_476504.htm

Carlson, S. (2004). The Next-Generation Classroom. *The Chronicle of Higher Education, 50*(25), A26.

Carney, A. L. (2003). *Factors in Instructional Design: Training versus Education.* Paper presented at the Instructional Technology Lab (ITL) Seminar, University of Illinois at Chicago.

Carr, A. (1997). The learning organization. New lessons/thinking for the management of change and management development? *Journal of Management Development, 14*(4), 224–231. doi:10.1108/02621719710164517

Carr, D., Oliver, M., & Burn, A. (2008). Learning, Teaching and Ambiguity in Virtual Worlds. In *Researching Learning in Virtual Environments International Conference* (pp. 83-93). Milton Keynes, UK: The Open University.

Carrell, L. J., & Menzel, K. E. (2001). Variations in learning, motivation, and perceived immediacy between live and distance education. *Communication Education, 50*(3), 230–241. doi:10.1080/03634520109379250

Carroll, T. G. (2000). If we didn't have the schools we have today, would we create the schools we have today? *Contemporary Issues in Technology and Teacher Education, 1*(1). Retrieved March 21, 2009, from http://www.citejournal.org/vol1/iss1/currentissues/general/article1.htm

Carter, M. (2008, May 15). Ikea to offer virtual furniture. *Guardian News and Media Limited.* Retrieved from http://www.guardian.co.uk/media/2008/may/15/marketingandpr.digitalmedia?gusrc=rss&feed=technologyfull

Caterpillar. (2008). *Caterpillar: Home.* Retrieved December 26, 2008, from http://www.cat.com/

Catton, M. (2006). Create Fearless Learners. *Learning and Leading with Technology, 34.* Retrieved September 18, 2008, from http://www.iste.org/Content/NavigationMenu/Publications/LL/LLIssues/Volume_34_2006_2007_/November_No_3_2/LandL_November_2006.htm

Cerbin, B. (2001, December 6). Teaching dogs to talk: Bill Cerbin on technology and student learning. *Teaching with Technology Today, 8*(3). Retrieved November 17, 2008, from http://www.uwsa.edu/ttt/articles/cerbin.htm

Cercone, K. (2008). Characteristics of adult learners with implications for online learning design. *AACE Journal, 16*(2), 137–159.

Cha, H. J., Kim, Y. S., Park, S. H., Yoon, T. B., Jung, Y. M., & Lee, J.-H. (2006). Learning styles diagnosis based on user interface behaviors for customization of learning interfaces in an intelligent tutoring system. In M. Ikeda, K. Ashley, & T.-W. Chan (Eds.), *Proceedings of the Intelligent Tutoring Systems, 8th International Conference* (LNCS 4053, pp. 513-524). Berlin, Germany: Springer-Verlag.

Chacon, F. (2006). Triangulating incomplete learning through student responses. In *Proceedings from EDMEDIA 2006,* Orlando, FL. Retrieved from http://www.editlib.org/j/EDMEDIA/v/2006/n/1

Chafe, A. (1998). *Computer technology and cooperative learning.* Retrieved September 25, 2007, from http://www.cdli.ca/~achafe/maj_index.html

challenges of participatory culture: Media education for the Twenty-first century [Electronic version]. Retrieved March 19, 2009, from http://www.macfound.org/atf/cf/%

7BB0386CE3-8B29-4162-8098-E466FB856794%7D/DML_ETHNOG_WHITEPAPER.PDF

Chamberlin, W. S. (2001). Face to face vs. cyberspace: Finding the middle ground. *Campus Technology.* Retrieved April 10, 2009, from http://campustechnology.com/Articles/2001/12/FacetoFace-vs-Cyberspace-Finding-the-Middle-Ground.aspx

Chandra, S. (2007). Lecture video capture for the masses. In *Proceedings of the 12th Annual SIGCSE Conference on Innovation and Technology in Computer Science Education,* Dundee, Scotland (pp. 276-280).

CHEA Directory of Regional Accreditation Organizations. (2009). Retrieved on April 1, 2009 from http://www.chea.org/Directories/regional.asp

Checkland, P., & Scholes, J. (1990). *Soft systems methodology in action.* New York: Wiley.

Chee, Y. S. (2002). Refocusing learning on pedagogy in a connected world. *Horizon, 10*(4), 7–13. doi:10.1108/10748120210452102

Chester, E. (2007). *From teacher to reacher: The common link between uncommon educators.* Retrieved December 12, 2008, from http://www.generationwhy.com/ images/stories/docs/ctr.pdf

Chickering, A. W., & Gamson, Z. F. (1987). Seven principles for good practice in undergraduate education. In *AAHE Bulletin,* March 3-7. Retrieved July 1, 2005 from http://honolulu.hawaii.edu/intranet/committees/FacDevCom/guidebk/teachtip/7princip.htm

Christensen, C. M., Horn, M. B., & Johnson, C. W. (2008). *Disrupting class.* New York: McGraw-Hill.

Christensen, R., Overall, T., & Knezek, G. (2006). Personal educational tools (PETS) for type II learning. *Computers in the Schools, 23,* 173-189. Retrieved October 15, 2008, from http://www.haworthpress.com/store/ArticleAbstract.asp?sid=P2GNR5WRN57M9HWPW66BWKBCMEC30E6&ID=71006

Christenson, C., & Horn, M. (2008). *Disrupting class: Student-centric education is the future.* Retrieved March 28, 2009, from http://www.edutopia.org/student-centric-education-technology

Clark, A. (2003). *Minds, Technologies, and the Future of Human Intelligence*. Oxford, UK: Oxford University Press.

Clouder, L., Dalley, J., Hargreaves, J., Parkes, S., Sellars, J., & Toms, J. (2006). Electronic re-constitution of groups: Group dynamics from face-to-face to an online setting. *Computer-Supported Collaborative Learning, 1*(1), 467–480. doi:10.1007/s11412-006-9002-0

Cognition and Technology Group at Vanderbilt. (1992). The Jasper series: An Exploration of Issues in Learning and Instructional Design. *Educational Technology Research and Development, 40*(1), 65–80. doi:10.1007/BF02296707

Cohen, D. (1990). A revolution in one classroom: The case of Mrs. Oublier. *Educational Evaluation and Policy Analysis, 12*(3), 327–345.

Cohen, S. L., & Pine, B. J., II. (2007). Mass Customizing the Training Industry. In *T+D* (pp. 50-54).

College Board. (2008). *Trends in higher education series.* Retrieved on March 29, 2009 from http://www.collegeboard.com/trends

Collins, C. (2008, November 26). *AVWW 2008 Program: Australasian Virtual Worlds Workshop.* Swinburne University of Technology, Hawthorn Campus and Second Life. Retrieved March 1, 2009, from http://avww.org/?q=node/35

Colorado Technical University. (2008). *Mobile learning at CTUMobile.com.* Retrieved October 28, 2008, from http://www.ctuonline.edu/ctumobile/ Corbeil, J. R., & Corbeil, M. E. (2007). Are you ready for mobile learning? *Educause Quarterly.* Retrieved October 8, 2008, from http://net.educause.edu/ir/library/pdf/eqm0726.pdf

Columbia University. (n.d.). *Virtual Worlds Research at Columbia University's Computer Graphics and User Interfaces Laboratory.* Retrieved from http://graphics.cs.columbia.edu/projects/virtual-worlds.html

Combs, L. (2004). The design, assessment, and implementation of a web-based course. *Association for the Advancement of Computing In Education, 12*(1), 27–37.

Comeaux, P. (2002). Introduction. In P. Comeaux (Ed.), *Communication and collaboration in the online classroom: Examples and applications* (pp. xxv-xxxiv). Boston, MA: Anker Publishing Company, Inc.

Comeaux, P., & McKenna-Byington, E. (2003). Computer-mediated communication in online and conventional classroom: some implications for instructional design and professional development programmes. *Innovations in Education and Teaching International, 40*(4), 348–355. doi:10.1080/1470329032000128387

Comer, J. P. (1999). *Waiting for a Miracle: Why Schools Can't Solve Our Problems and How We Can.* Canada: Penguin Group.

Community Intelligence Labs. (2001). *Communities of Practice Learning as a Social System by Eitenne Wenger.* Retrieved from http://www.co-i-l.com/coil/knowledge-garden/cop/lss.shtml

Conklin, M. S. (2006). *Difference between education and training.* Megan Squire Conklin blog. Retrieved from http://facstaff.elon.edu/mconklin/2006/10/difference-between-education-and.html

Conrad, R. M., & Donaldson, J. A. (2004). *Engaging the online learner: Activities and resources for creative instruction.* San Francisco: Jossey-Bass.

Constable, G. (2007). *Virtual Worlds: A short Introduction to SL.* YouTube. Retrieved March 1, 2009, from http://au.youtube.com/watch?v=CaLKFeJLnqI

Constance, J. (2007, April 5). *Second Life: Educational Precedents and Examples.* Second Life Feasibility Study. Retrieved March 1, 2009, from http://manfromporlock.wetpaint.com/page/Second+Life+Educational+Precedents+and+Examples

Conway, K. L. (2002). Foreword. In P. Comeaux (Ed.), *Communication and collaboration in the online classroom: Examples and applications* (pp. xvii-xix). Boston, MA: Anker Publishing Company, Inc.

Cook, T., & Sosin, K. (2006). Simulating a dynamic lecture online: Circular flow as an example. *The Journal of Economic Education, 37*(1), 121–121. doi:10.3200/JECE.37.1.121-121

Corbeil, J. R., & Valdes-Corbeil, M. E. (2007). Are you ready for mobile learning? *EDUCAUSE Quarterly, 30*, 2.

Cornell University. (2008). *eClips.* Retrieved December 19, 2008, from http://eclips.cornell.edu/homepage.do;jsessionid=7B78294693CBA0AE28AC3D60B6E47F8B

Crawford, M. A., & Yetton, P. W. (1985). Do Teaching Skills Matter? An Examination of the Relative Contributions of Teaching Skills and Student Ability in a Postgraduate Executive Development Program. In *Proceedings of the Academy of Management Proceedings* (pp. 124-128). Retrieved from Business Source Premier Database (AN 4978764)

CRE. (1998). *Restructuring the University - New Technologies for Teaching and Learning: Guidance to Universities on Strategy*. Geneva, Switzerland: Association of European Universities.

Cross, K. P. (1998, June). *Opening windows on learning* (The Cross Papers Number 2). Alliance for Community College Innovation. Mission Viejo, CA: League for Innovation in the Community College Educational Testing Service.

CTIA - The Wireless Association. (2008). *Teenagers a generation unplugged: A national survey by CTIA*. The Wireless Association and Harris Interactive. Retrieved October 8, 2008, from http://www.ctia.org/advocacy/research/index.cfm/AID/11483

Cuban, L. (1986). *Teachers and machines: The classroom use of technology since 1920*. New York: Teachers College Press.

Curtis, D. D., & Lawson, M. J. (2001). Exploring collaborative online learning. *Journal of Asynchronous Learning Networks*, *5*(1), 21–34.

Curtis, D. D., & Lawson, M. J. (2001, February). Exploring collaborative online learning. *Journal of Asynchronous Learning Networks*, *5*(1), 21–34.

Daniel, J. (1996). *Mega-Universities and Knowledge Media*. London: Kogan Page.

Darbyshire, P. (2005). *Instructional Technologies: Cognitive Aspects of Online Programs*. Hershey, USA: IRM Press.

Darrell, B. (1975)... *Peabody Journal of Education*, *53*(1), 45–48. doi:10.1080/01619567509538048

Davis, B. G. (1993) *Tools for Teaching*. San Francisco: Jossey-Bass Publishers.

Davis, S. M., & Batkin, J. W. (1994). *The Monster Under the Bed: How Business is Mastering the Opportunity for Knowledge for Profit*. New York: Simon & Shuster.

De Kreek, M., Krijgsman, A., Kromwijk, R., Van Kruining, M., Liemburg, M., & Wang, J. (2003). *Archeaological walk guided by a PDA*. Retrieved October 8, 2008, from http://www.geoinformatie.nl/courses/yes60504/posters2003/poster_gr3.pdf

De Marsico, M., & Levialdi, S. (2004). Evaluating web sites: exploiting user's expectations. *International Journal of Human-Computer Studies*, *60*(3), 381–416. doi:10.1016/j.ijhcs.2003.10.008

Dede, C. (2005). Planning for neo-millennial learning styles. *Educase Review, 28*(1). [Electronic Version]. Retrieved March 29, 2005, from http://www.educause.edu/ir/library/pdf/EQM0511.pdf

Deighton, J. (1996). The Future of Interactive Marketing. *Harvard Business Review*, *74*(6), 151–162.

DeLoughry, T. (1994). Pushing the envelope. *The Chronicle of Higher Education*, *8*(41), A36–A38.

Delwiche, A. (2006). Massively multiplayer online games (MMOs) in the new media classroom. *Educational Technology & Society*, *9*(3), 160–172.

Dennen, V. P. (2005). From message posting to learning dialogues: Factors affecting learner participation in asynchronous discussion. *Distance Education*, *26*(1), 127–148. doi:10.1080/01587910500081376

Dewey, J. (1978). How we think. In J. A. Boydston (Ed.), *How we think and selected essays, 1910-1911* (pp. 177-356). Carbondale, IL: Southern Illinois University Press.

Diaz, D. P. (2002, May/June). Online drop rates revisited. *The Technology Source*. Retrieved March 20, 2009, from http://technologysource.org/article/online_drop_rates_revisited

Dick, W., & Carey, L. (1996). *The systematic design of instruction (4th ed.)*. New York: Harper Collins.

Diekelmann, N., Schuster, R., & Nosek, C. (1998). *Creating new pedagogies at the millenium: The uncommon experience of University of Wisconsin-Madison teachers using distance education technologies*. Retrieved November 17, 2008, from http://www.uwsa.edu/ttt/ articles/

Dignan, L. (2006, December 1). *Second Life: Virtual world training wheels for corporate America*. ZDNet: CBS Interactive Inc. Retrieved from http://blogs.zdnet.com/BTL/?p=4039

Dillenbourg, P. (Ed.). (1999). *Collaborative learning: Cognitive and computational approaches.* New York: Pergamon.

Dodge, B. (2003). *The WebQuest Page* [Online]. Retrieved from http://webquest.sdsu.edu/

Doherty, K. M., & Orlofsky, C. (2001, May 10). The new divides. *Education Week on the Web* [Online serial]. Retrieved from http://www.edweek.org/sreports/tc01

Domine, V. (2006). 4 Steps to Standards Integration. *Learning and Leading with Technology, 34*. Retrieved September 18, 2008, from http://www.iste.org/Content/NavigationMenu/Publications/LL/LLIssues/Volume_34_2006_2007_/November_No_3_2/LandL_November_2006.htm

Downes, S. (2005). E-learning 2.0 [Electronic Version]. *eLearn Magazine.* Retrieved from http://elearnmag.org/subpage.cfm?section=articles&article=29-1

Draves, W. A. (2002). *Teaching online* (2nd Ed.). River Falls, WI: LERN.

Dreher, C., Reiners, T., Dreher, N., & Dreher, H. (2009a). *3D Virtual Worlds as Collaborative Communities Enriching Human Endeavours: Innovative Applications in e-Learning.* Accepted for publication at the DEST 2009 Conference.

Dreher, C., Reiners, T., Dreher, N., & Dreher, H. (2009b). *3D Virtual Worlds Enriching Innovation and Collaboration in Information Systems Research, Development, and Commercialisation.* Accepted for publication at the DEST 2009 Conference.

Dreher, H. Reiners, T., Dreher, N. & Dreher, C. (2009c). 3D Spaces in Software Engineering: From K-12 to Life Long Learning. Accepted for publication in *Proceedings of ED-MEDIA 2009.World Conference on Educational Multimedia, Hypermedia & Telecommunications, Vienna, Austria.* Chesapeake, USA: AACE.

Dreier, E. (2006). *Technology: A Catalyst for Teaching and Learning in the Classroom.* North Central Regional Educational Laboratory (NCREL) online publications. Retrieved September 18, 2008 http://www.ncrel.org/sdrs/areas/issues/methods/technlgy/te600.htm

Dringus, L. (1995). An iterative usability evaluation procedure for interactive online courses. *Journal of Interactive Instruction Development, 7*(4), 10–14.

Driscoll, M. (2002). *How people learn (and what technology might have to do with it).* Syracuse, NY. ERIC Document Reproduction Service No. ED470032

Driver, E. (2008). *Forrester Principal Analyst Erica Driver on Virutal Worlds.* FIR Interview on Jan 16, 2008. Retrieved March 1, 2009, from http://www.nevillehobson.com/2008/01/17/fir-interview-forrester-principal-analyst-erica-driver-on-virtual-worlds-jan-16-2008

Dublin, L. (2007). Marketing and Change Management for e-Learning: Strategies for Engaging Learning, Motivating Managers, and Energizing Organizations. In B. Brandon (Ed.), *Handbook of e-Learning Strategy* (pp. 45-49). Santa Rosa, CA: The e-Learning Guild.

Dufour, R. (2009). *The Power of Professional learning Communities: Bringing the Big Ideas to Life.* Paper presented at the Professional Learning Communities at Work, San Antonio, TX.

Dufour, R., Dufour, R., & Eaker, R. (2008). *Revisiting Professional Learning Communities at Work: New Insights for improving School.* Bloomington, IN: Solution Tree.

Dumont, R. A. (1996). Teaching and learning in cyberspace. *IEEE Transactions on Professional Communication, 39*(4), 192–204. doi:10.1109/47.544575

Dunn, S. (2000, March/April). The virtualizing of education. *The Futurist, 34*(2), 34–38.

Dyer, R., Reed, A., & Berry, R. (2006). Investigating the Relationship between High School Technology Education and Test Scores for Algebra 1 and Geometry. *Journal of Technology Education, 17*, 7-17. Retrieved June 15, 2008 from http://scholar.lib.vt.edu/ejournals/JTE/v17n2/pdf/index.html

Dziuban, C., Shea, P., & Arbaugh, J. B. (2005). Faculty roles and satisfaction in asynchronous learning networks. In S. R. Hiltz, & R. Goldman (Eds.), *Learning together online: Research on asynchronous learning networks* (pp. 169-190). Mahwah, NJ: Lawrence Erlbaum.

Eaker, R. (2009). *What it Means to be a Professional Learning Community.* Paper presented at the Professional Learning Communities at Work, San Antonio, TX.

Eaton, J. (2002). *Accreditation and Assuring Quality in Distance Learning.* Washington, DC: Council for Higher Education Accreditation, Institute for Research and Study of Accreditation and Quality Assurance.

Eberhard, S. (2005). *Can dual coding theory be used to develop reusable learning objects in a multilanguage distance education environment?* Retrieved March 19, 2009 from http://74.6.239.67/ search/cache?ei=UTF-8&p=cognit ive+artifact%2C+distance+learning&fr=moz2&u=www. unm.edu/~eberhard/Portfolio/Lit_review.doc&w=cognitiv e+artifact+artifacts+ distance+learning+learnings&d=XH 9S352uSiTJ&icp=1&.intl=us

Edmonds, G. S., Branch, R. C., & Mukherjee, P. (1994). A Conceptual Framework for Comparing Instructional Design Models. *Educational Technology Research and Development, 42*(4), 55–72. doi:10.1007/BF02298055

Egan, M., Sebastian, J., & Welch, M. (1991, March). Effective television teaching: Perceptions of those who count most... distance learners. In *Proceedings of the Rural Education Symposium,* Nashville, TN.

Eisenberg, A. (2007). What did the professor say? check your iPod. *New York Times.* Retrieved from http://www.nytimes.com/2007/12/09/business/09novel.html

Energames. (2005). *Big Kahuna Words* [Online computer game]. Retrieved March 28, 2009, from http://www.game-remakes.com/game.php?id=81

Enyedy, N., & Hoadley, C. M. (2006). From dialogue to monologue and back: Middle spaces in computer-mediated learning. *Computer-Supported Collaborative Learning, 1*(1), 413–439. doi:10.1007/s11412-006-9000-2

ePortfolio Portal. (2004). *What is an ePortfolio?* Retrieved March 29, 2009, from http://www.danwilton.com/eportfolios/whatitis.php#references

Epper, R. M., & Garn, M. (2003). *Virtual college & university consortia: A national study.* (State Higher Education Executive Officers (SHEEO)). Retrieved August 15, 2008, from http://www.sheeo.org/publicat.htm

Erekson, T., & Shumway, S. (2006). Integrating the Study of Technology into the Curriculum: a Consulting Teacher Model. *Journal of Technology Education, 18,* 27-37. Retrieved October 18, 2008 from http://scholar.lib.vt.edu/ejournals/JTE/v18n1/pdf/index.html

Erlenkötter, A., Kühnlenz, C.-M., Miu, H.-R., Sommer, F., & Reiners, T. (2008). Enhancing the class curriculum with Virtual World use cases for production and logistics. In *Proceedings of E-Learn 2008. World Conference on E-Learning in Corporate, Government, Healthcare, & Higher Education,* Las Vegas (pp. 789–798). Chesapeake: USA: AACE.

Erol, B., & Li, Y. (2005). An overview of technologies for e-meeting and e-lecture. In *Proceedings of the IEEE International Conference on Multimedia and Expo,* Amsterdam, The Netherlands (pp. 1000-1005).

Ertmer, P. (2003). Transforming Teacher Education: Visions and Strategies. *Educational Technology Research and Development, 51*(1), 124–128. doi:10.1007/BF02504522

Ertmer, P. A. (2005). Teacher Pedagogical Beliefs: The Final Frontier in Our Quest for Technology Integration? *Educational Technology Research and Development, 53*(4), 25–39. doi:10.1007/BF02504683

Ertmer, P., & Newby, T. (1993). Behaviorism, cognitivism, constructivism: Comparing critical features from an instructional design perspective. *Performance Improvement Quarterly, 6*(4), 50–71.

European Council of Education Ministers. (2000). *Bologna Declaration.* Retrieved from http://www.dges.mctes.pt/NR/rdonlyres/2EC14937-0320-4975-A269-B9170A722684/409/DeclaraçãodeBolonha1.pdf

Facebook. (2009). *Welcome to Facebook.* Retrieved May 25, 2009, from http://www.facebook.com

Federation of American Scientists. (2006). *National summit on educational games fact sheet.* Retrieved March 19, 2007, from http://www.fas.org/programs/ltp/policy_and_publications /summit/Fact%20Sheet.pdf

Feiner, S., MacIntyre, B., & Seligmann, D. (n.d.). *KARMA: Knowledge-based Augmented Reality for Maintenance Assistance.* Retrieved from http://graphics.cs.columbia.edu/projects/karma/karma.html

Felder, R. M. (1996). Matters of style. *ASEE PRISM, 6*(4), 18–23.

Felder, R. M., & Silverman, L. K. (1988). Learning and teaching styles in engineering education. *English Education, 78*(7), 674–681.

Felder, R. M., & Soloman, B. A. (2009). *Index of Learning Styles.* Retrieved March 20, 2009, from http://www.ncsu.edu/felder-public/ILSpage.html

Fenn, J., et al. (2008). *Hype Cycle for Emerging Technologies.*http://www.gartner.com/DisplayDocument?doc_cd=159496 &ref=g_homelink

Fern, E. (1983). *The use of focus groups: a review of some contradictory evidence implications, and suggestion for future research methods series.* Advances Consumer Research

Fingerhut, E. (2008). Raising educational attainment in Ohio. *Strategic Plan for Higher Education 2008-2017.* Retrieved November 21, 2008, from http://uso.edu/strategicplan/downloads/documents/strategicPlan/USOStrategicPlan.pdf

Fisher, M., & Baird, D. E. (2006). Making mlearning work: utilizing mobile technology for active exploration, collaboration, assessment and reflection in higher education. *Journal of Educational Technology Systems, 35*(1), 3–30. doi:10.2190/4T10-RX04-113N-8858

Ford Motor Company. (2008). *Ford Motor Company: Cars, Trucks, SUVs, Hybrids, Parts – Ford.* Retrieved from http://www.ford.com/

Forum, C. E. O. (1999). *Professional development: A link to better learning.* Washington, DC: CEO Forum.

Francescato, D., Mebane, M., Porcelli, R., Attanasio, C., & Pulino, M. (2007). Developing professional skills and social capital through computer supported collaborative learning in university contexts. *International Journal of Human-Computer Studies, 65*(2), 140–152. doi:10.1016/j.ijhcs.2006.09.002

Frey, A., Faul, A., & Yankelov, P. (2003). Student perception of web-assisted teaching strategies. *Journal of Social Work Education, 39*(3), 443–449.

Frey, B. A., & Alman, S. W. (2003). Applying adult learning theory to the online classroom. *New Horizons in Adult Education, 17*(1), 4–12.

Frost, S. (2000). Historical and Philosophical Foundations for Academic Advising. In V. N. Gordon & W. R. Habley (Eds.), *Academic Advising: A Comprehensive Handbook* (pp. 3-17). San Francisco: Jossey-Bass, Inc.

Frydenberg, J. (2007). Persistance in University Continuing Education Online Classes. *International Review of Research in Open and Distance Learning, 8*(3). Retrieved December 31, 2008, from http://www.nosignificantdifference.org/search.asp

Funderstanding. (2001). *Right Brain vs. Left Brain.* Retrieved from http://www.funderstanding.com/right_left_brain.cfm

Fung, Y. H. (2004). Collaborative online learning: interaction patterns and limiting factors. *Open Learning, 19*(2), 54–72. doi:10.1080/0268051042000224743

Gabriel, M. A., & MacDonald, C. J. (1996). Preservice teacher education students and computers: How does intervention affect attitude? *Journal of Technology and Teacher Education, 4*(2).

Gahala, Y. (2007). *Critical Issue: Promoting Technology Use in School.* North Central Regional Educational Laboratory (NCREL) online publications. Retrieved September 18, 2008 from http://www.ncrel.org

Gallagher, R. (2003, March). The next 20 years: How is online distance learning likely to evolve? In *Proceedings of the University Council for Educational Administration 88th Annual Conference*, Chicago, IL.

Garnham, C., & Kaleta, R. (2002, March). Introduction to hybrid courses. *Teaching with Technology Today, 8*(6). Retrieved November 17, 2008, from http://www.uwsa.edu/ttt/articles/garnham.htm

Garrison, D. R., & Anderson, T. (2003). *E-Learning in the 21st century: A framework for research and practice.* London: Routledge/Falmer.

Garrison, D. R., Anderson, T., & Archer, W. (2000). Critical thinking in text-based environment: Computer conferencing in higher education. *The Internet and Higher Education, 2*(2), 87–105. doi:10.1016/S1096-7516(00)00016-6

Gastfriend, H. (2008). *University System of Georgia Student Information Technology Survey.* Retrieved July 1, 2008, from www.alt.usg.edu/research/studies/USG_SIT_total%20aggregate.pdf

Gee, J. (2003). What video games have to teach us about learning and literacy? *ACM Computers in Entertainment, 1*(1), 1–4. doi:10.1145/950566.950567

Gee, J. P. (2008). *Social linguistics and literacies (3rd ed.).* Oxon: Routledge.

GeoSim Systems Ltd. (2008). *GeoSimPHILLY.* Retrieved from http://www.geosimphilly.com/index.aspx

Gerber, S., & Scott, L. (2007). Designing a learning curriculum and technology's role in it. *Educational Technology Research and Development, 55*(5), 461–478. doi:10.1007/s11423-006-9005-6

Gerlich, R. N. (2005). Faculty perceptions of distance learning. *Distance Education Report, 9*(17), 8. Retrieved July 25, 2008, from http://www.magnapubs.com/pub/magnapubs_der/9_17/news/597900-1.html

Glass, G. V. (2000). *Meta-analysis at 25*. Retrieved from http://glass.ed.asu.edu/gene/papers/meta25.html

Glass, G. V., McGraw, B., & Smith, M. L. (1981). *Meta-analysis in social research*. Beverly Hills, CA: Sage Publications.

Glater, J. (2008, March 8). Colleges reduce out-of-state tuition to lure students. *New York Times*. Retrieved on March 15, 2009 from http://www.nytimes.com/2008/03/08/education/08states.html?_r=1

Godwin-Jones, R. (2007). Emerging technologies e-texts, mobile browsing, and rich Internet applications. *Language Learning and Technology, 11*(3), 8. Retrieved October 18, 2008, from http://llt.msu.edu/vol11num3/pdf/emerging.pdf

Goggin, G. (2006). *Cell Phone Culture: Mobile Technology in Everyday Life*. New York: Routledge.

Gomes, M. J. (2005). E-learning: reflexões em torno do conceito, In Proceedings of the *Challenges 05: actas do Congresso Internacional sobre Tecnologias da Informação e Comunicação na Educação, 4,* Braga. Braga, Portugal: Centro de Competência da Universidade do Minho. Retrieved from: https://repositorium.sdum.uminho.pt/handle/1822/2896

Gomez, S. (2007). Scroll to 'E' for Education. *The Times Higher Education Supplement, 1780*, 13. Retrieved October 18, 2008, from http://www.timeshighereducation.co.uk/story.asp?storyCode=207730&sectioncode=26

Gonzalez-Rodriguez, M., Manrubia, J., Vidau, A., & Gonzalez-Gallego, M. (2009). Improving accessibility with user-tailored interfaces. *Applied Intelligence, 30*(1), 65–71. doi:10.1007/s10489-007-0098-3

Good, T. L., & Brophy, J. E. (1990). *Educational psychology: A realistic approach (4th ed.)*. White Plains, NY: Longman.

Google Trends. (2009). *Google trends: Virtual Worlds*. Retrieved May 28, 2009, from http://www.google.com/trends?q=virtual+worlds&ctab=0&geo=all&date=all&sort=0

Goold, A., Craig, A., & Coldwell, J. (2007). Culture and cultural diversity in online teaching. *Australasian Journal of Educational Technology, 23*(4), 490–507.

Grabe, M., & Christopherson, K. (2008). Optional student use of online lecture resources: Resource preferences, performance and lecture attendance. *Journal of Computer Assisted Learning, 24*(1), 1–10.

Graf, S. & Kinshuk. (2006). Considering learning styles in learning management systems: investigating the behavior of students in an online course. In P. Mylones, M. Wallace, & M. Angelides (Eds.), *Proceedings of the First IEEE International Workshop on Semantic Media Adaptation and Personalization, SMAP 06* (pp. 25-30). Los Alamitos, CA: IEEE Computer Society.

Graham, C. R. (2006). Blended learning systems: Definition, current trends, and future directions. In C. J. Bonk & C. R. Graham (Eds.), *The handbook of blended learning: Global perspectives, local designs* (pp. 3-21). San Francisco: Pfeiffer.

Grant, M. M., & Cheon, J. (2007). The Value of Using Synchronous Conferencing for Instruction and Students. *Journal of Interactive Online Learning, 6*(3), Retrieved December 31, 2008, from http://www.ncolr.org/jiol/issues/PDF/6.3.4.pdf

Greco, J. (1999). Going the distance for MBA candidates. *The Journal of Business Strategy, 20*(3), 30–34. doi:10.1108/eb040004

Green, H., & Hannon, C. (2007). *Their Space: Education for a digital generation* [Electronic version]. Retrieved March 24, 2009, from http://www.demos.co.uk/files /Their% 20 space%20%20web.pdf

Greeno and the Middle School Mathematics Through Applications Project Group. (1998). The situativity of knowing, learning and research. *The American Psychologist, 53*(1), 5–26. doi:10.1037/0003-066X.53.1.5

Gregory, J. R. (2008). *Automated classroom video streaming pilot at the University of Minnesota*. Paper presented at the EDUCAUSE 2008 Annual Conference, Orlando, FL. Retrieved from http://connect.educause.edu/Library/Abstract/AutomatedClassroomVideoSt/38874

Gregory, S. (2008). *Online Dialogue in Second Life Sessions*. Retrieved March 1, 2009, from http://www.virtual-classrooms.info

Gregory, S., & Smith, H. (2008a). How virtual classrooms are changing the face of education: using virtual classrooms in today's university environment. In *Proceedings of ISTE Conference Research in Teacher Education: International Perspectives*, Armidale, Australia.

Gregory, S., & Smith, H. *(2008b)*. Virtual Worlds: Can educators in higher education engage students in greater collaboration through the use of virtual worlds and do they engage the student in conversations (through text) that can lead to deeper thinking and responses compared to other social computing tools. *Technical Report, Armidale.*

Griesser, S. A. (2001). A Study of Problem Solving Abilities of Seventh Grade Students Who Receive Anchored Problem Solving Instruction. *Science, Mathematics and Environmnetal Education Clearinghouse.* (ERIC Document Reproduction Service No. ED456040)

Gronstedt, A. (2007, August 20). *Virtual Worlds Learning*. Sales and Marketing.com: Nielsen Business Media, Inc. Retrieved from http://www.salesand-marketing.com/msg/content_display/training/e3ic-b706624eaa6b047f367f6c5ec543baa

Gros, B. (2001). Instructional design for computer-supported collaborative learning in primary and secondary schools. *Computers in Human Behavior, 17*(4-5), 439–451. doi:10.1016/S0747-5632(01)00016-4

Grove, P. W., & Steventon, G. J. (2008). Exploring community safety in a virtual community: Using Second Life to enhance structured creative learning. In *Researching Learning in Virtual Environments International Conference* (pp. 154-171). Milton Keynes, UK: The Open University. Retrieved April 22, 2009.

Guidera, S. G. (2004). Perception of the effectiveness of online instruction in terms of the seven principles of effective undergraduate education. *Journal of Educational Technology, 32*(2/3).

Gulati, S. (2008). Technology-enhanced learning in developing nations: A review. *International Review of Research in Open and Distance Learning, 9*(1), 1–16.

Gunawardena, C., & Zittle, F. (1997). Social presence as a predictor of satisfaction within acomputer- mediated conferencing environment. *American Journal of Distance Education, 11*(3), 8–26. doi:10.1080/08923649709526970

Gustafson, K., & Branch, R. M. (1997). *Instructional design models.* Syracuse, NY: ERIC Clearinghouse on Information and Technology.

Hafner, K. (2008, April 30). At Sundance, a Second Life Sweatshop Is Art. *New York Times*. Retrieved March 1, 2009, from http://bits.blogs.nytimes.com/2008/01/25/at-sundance-a-second-life-sweatshop-is-art

Haga, H. (2004). Concept of video bookmark (videomark) and its application to the collaborative indexing of lecture video in video-based distance education. *International Journal on E-Learning, 3*(3), 32–37.

Hagel, P., & Shaw, R. N. (2006). Students' perceptions of study modes. *Distance Education, 27*(3), 283–302. doi:10.1080/01587910600940398

Hake, R. (2008, January). Can distance and classroom learning be increased? *International Journal for the Scholarship of Teaching and Learning, 2*(1). Retrieved November 7, 2008, from http://www.georgiasouthern.edu/ijsotl

Hall, D. (2006). Pluto is Gone, Is Mickey Next? *Learning and Leading with Technology, 34*. Retrieved June 7, 2008, from http://www.iste.org/Content/NavigationMenu/Publications/LL/LLIssues/Volume_34_2006_2007_/November_No_3_2/LandL_November_2006.htm

Han, X. (1999, November 15). Exploring an effective and efficient online course management model. *Teaching with Technology Today, 5*(2). Retrieved November 17, 2008, from http://www.uwsa.edu/ttt/articles/han.htm.

Hannafin, R. D. (1999). Can teacher attitudes about learning be changed? *Journal of Computing in Teacher Education, 15*(2), 7–13.

Hanny, R. J. (2001). *Teacher Made Tests and the Virginia SOL*. Retrieved January 5, 2003, from http://www.pen.k12.va.us/VDOE/Instruction/wmstds/solass.shtml

Hara, N., Bonk, C., & Angeli, C. (2000). Content analysis of online discussion in an applied educational psychology. *Instructional Science, 28*(2), 115–152. doi:10.1023/A:1003764722829

Harasim, L. (2000). Shift happens: Online education as a new paradigm in learning, internet and higher education. *Elsevier Science 3,* 41-61.

Harasim, L., Hiltz, S. R., Teles, L., & Turoff, M. (1995). *Learning networks: A field guide to teaching and learning online.* Cambridge, MA: The MIT Press.

Harley, D., Henke, J., & Maher, M. W. (2008). Rethinking space and time: The role of internet technology in a large lecture course. *Innovate, 1*(1). Retrieved from http://innovateonline.info/index.php?view=article&id=3&action=article

Harpp, D. N., Fenster, A. E., Schwarcz, J. A., Zorychta, E., Goodyer, N., & Hsiao, W. (2004). Lecture retrieval via the web: Better than being there? *Journal of Chemical Education, 81*(5), 688–705.

Harris Interactive. (2008). *National Study Reveals How Teens Are Shaping & Reshaping Their Wireless World.* Retrieved October, 8, 2008, from http://www.canvasseopinion.com/news/allnewsbydate.asp?NewsID=1334

Harvey, J., & Mogey, N. (1997). *Implementing Learning Technology.* Learning Technology Dissemination Initiative. Retrieved from http://www.icbl.hw.ac.uk/ltdi/implementing-it/motif.htm

Hawksley, R., & Owen, J. (2002). *Going the distance: Are there common factors in high performance distance learning?* (Report No. 1225/02/02/2000). Learning and Skills Development Agency, London. ERIC Document Reproduction Service No. ED464231.

Hayes, G. (2009). The Virtual Worlds Hype Cycle 2009: Business, education, marketing, social media, virtual worlds. Retrieved March 30, 2009, from http://www.muvedesign.com/the-virtual-worlds-hype-cycle-for-2009

Haythornthwaite, C. (2006, February). Facilitating collaboration in online learning. *Journal of Asynchronous Learning, 10*(1). Retrieved on December 31, 2008, from http://www.sloan-c.org/publications/jaln/index.asp

Heck, R., Wallick, M., & Gleicher, M. (2007). Virtual videography. *ACM Transactions on Multimedia Computing, Communications, and Applications, 3*(1), Article 4.

Hemmi, A., Bayne, S., & Landt, R. (2009). The appropriation and repurposing of social technologies in higher educa-tion. *Journal of Computer Assisted Learning, 25,* 19–30. doi:10.1111/j.1365-2729.2008.00306.x

Henning, E. (2005). Rural South-African teachers "move home" in an online ecology. In J. Weiss, J. Hunsinger, J. Nolan, & P. Trifonas (Eds.), *International Handbook of Virtual Learning Environments.* New York: Springer.

Herbst, M. (2008). The high barriers facing foreign work-ers. *Business Week Online.* Retrieved March 28, 2009, from Academic Search Premier database.

Herman, A. (2001). *How the Scots Invented the Modern World: The true story of how Western Europe's poorest nation created our world and everything in it* (1st ed.). New York, NY: Crown Publishers.

Herrington, J., & Oliver, R. (1999). Using situated learn-ing and multimedia to investigate higher-order thinking. *Journal of Educational Multimedia and Hypermedia, 8*(4), 401–421.

Hewson, L., & Hughes, C. (2005). Social processes and peda-gogy in online learning. *AACE Journal, 13*(2), 99–125.

Hillman, D. C. A., Willis, D. J., & Gunawardena, C. N. (1994). Learner interface interaction in distance education: An extension of contemporary models and strategies for practitioners. *American Journal of Distance Education, 8*(2), 30–42. doi:10.1080/08923649409526853

Hiltz, S. R. (1994). *The virtual classroom: Learning without limits via computer networks.* Norwood, NJ: Ablex Publish-ing Corporation.

Hiltz, S. R., & Goldman, R. (2005). Learning together online: Research on asynchronous learning networks. In S. R. Hiltz & R. Goldman (Eds.), *Learning together online: Research on asynchronous learning networks* (pp. 3-18). Mahwah, NJ: Lawrence Erlbaum Associates.

Hiltz, S. R., & Shea, P. (2005). The student in the online classroom. In S. R. Hiltz & R. Goldman (Eds.), *Learning together online: Research on asynchronous learning net-works* (pp. 145-168). Mahwah, NJ: Lawrence Erlbaum.

Hoegl, M., & Proserpio, L. (2004). Team member proximity and teamwork in innovative projects. *Research Policy, 33*(8), 1153–1165. doi:10.1016/j.respol.2004.06.005

Hogan, R. (2009, June). *Attitudes of indigenous peoples toward distance learning in the South Pacific: An empiri-*

cal study. Paper presented at the ED-MEDIA 2009--World Conference on Educational Multimedia, Hypermedia & Telecommunications, Honolulu, HI.

Hollins, P., & Robbins, S. (2008). The Educational affordances of Multi User Virtual Environments (MUVE). In *Researching Learning in Virtual Environments International Conference* (pp. 172-180). The Open University, Milton Keynes, UK. Retrieved April 22, 2009.

Hooper, S., & Rieber, L. (1995). *Teaching with technology*. Retrieved September 24, 2007, from http://www .nowhereroad.com/twt/

Hopper, C. (2008). *Left vs. Right Which Side Are You On?* Retrieved from http://frank.mtsu.edu/~studskl/hd/learn.html

Howe, N., & Strauss, W. (2000). *Millennials rising: The next great generation*. New York: Vintage Books.

Howell, S., Williams, P., & Lindsay, N. (2003). Thirty-two trends affecting distance education; an informed foundation for strategic planning. *Online Journal of Distance Learning Administration, 6*(3). Retrieved November 24, 2008, from http://www.westga.edu/~distance/ojdla/fall63/howell63.html

Hsiao, J. (n.d.). *CSCL theories*. Retrieved January 10, 2008, from http://www.edb.utexas.edu/csclstudent/Dhsiao/theories.html#vygot

Hunter, B. (2005). Learning, teaching, and building knowledge: A forty-year quest for online learning communities. In G. Kearsley (Ed.), *Online learning: Personal reflections on the transformation of education* (pp.163-193). Englewood Cliffs, NJ: Educational Technology Publications.

Hussin, V. (2007). Supporting off-shore students: a preliminary study. *Innovations in Education and Teaching International, 44*(4), 363–376. doi:10.1080/14703290701602763

Hutchins, E. (2000). *Distributed cognition*. Retrieved January 13, 2008, from http://eclectic.ss.uci.edu/~drwhite/Anthro179a/DistributedCognition.pdf

Hutchins, H. (2003). Instructional Immediacy and the Seven Principles: Strategies for Facilitating Online Courses. *Online Journal of Distance Learning Administration, 6*(3).

Hutchinson, D. (2007). Teaching Practices for Effective Cooperative Learning in an Online Learning Environ-

ment (OLE). [Retrieved from ABI/INFORM Global Database.]. *Journal of Information Systems Education, 18*(3), 357–367.

Indiana Higher Education Telecommunications System. (2003). *Guiding principles for faculty in distance learning*. Retrieved November 27, 2008, from http://www.ihets.org/archive/progserv_arc/education _arc/distance_arc/guiding_principles_ arc/index.html

International Organisation for Standardisation. (1998). *ISO 9241: Software ergonomics requirements for office work with visual display terminal (VDT)*. Geneva, Switzerland.

International Society for Technology in Education. (2008). *National Educational Technology Standards for Teachers*. Eugene, OR: International Society for Technology in Education. Retrieved March 29, 2009, from http://iste.org

Ireh, M., & Bell, D. (2002). *Implementing Faculty Professional Development: The Product-Based Model*. Paper presented at the Preparing Tomorrow's Teachers To Use Technology (PT3) Grantee Conference. Retrieved May 24, 2009, from http://www.eric.ed.gov/ERICWebPortal/custom/portlets/recordDetails/detailmini.jsp?_nfpb=true&_&ERICExtSearch_SearchValue_0=ED469001&ERICExtSearch_SearchType_0=no&accno=ED469001

ISCET. (2008). *Apresentação*. Retrieved from http://www.iscet.pt/index.php?vrl=10

Islam, K. (2004). Alternatives for Measuring Learning Success. *Chief Learning Officer, 3*(11), 32-37. Retrieved April 6, 2009, from Business Source Premier (AN 1505760)

Issue, C. Developing a School or District Technology Plan. (2007). *North Central Regional Educational Laboratory (NCREL) online publications*. Retrieved September 9, 2008 from http://www.ncrel.org/sdrs/areas/issues/methods/technlgy/te300.htm

Issue, C. Using Technology to Improve Student Achievement. (2007). *North Central Regional Educational Laboratory (NCREL) online publications*. Retrieved September 9, 2008 from http://www.ncrel.org/sdrs/areas/issues/methods/technlgy/te800.htm

Jackson, M.J., & Helms, M.M. (2008). Student Perceptions of Hybrid Courses: Measuring and Interpreting Quality. *Journal of Education for Business, 84*(1), 7-13. Retrieved from Business Source Premier (AN 34772191)

Jackson, R., Karp, J., Patrick, E., & Thrower, A. (2006). *Social constructivism vignette.* Retrieved March 20, 2009, from http://projects.coe.uga.edu/epltt/index.php?title=Social_Constructivism

Jenkins, H. (2006). *Convergence culture: Where old and new media collide.* New York: New York University Press.

Jenkins, H., Purushotma, R., Clinton, K., Weigel, M., & Robison, A.J. (2006). *Confronting the*

Jennings, N., & Collins, C. (2008). Virtual or virtually: educational institutions in Second Life. *International Journal of Social Sciences, 2*(3), 180–186.

Jiao, B. (2007). *Social constructivism: games, simulations, cases, and problem solving.* Retrieved March 21, 2009, from http://www.bjiao.com/tel7001/book/Games.htm

Johnson, D. W., & Johnson, R. T. (1975). *Learning together and alone: Cooperation, competition, and individualization.* Englewood Cliffs, NJ: Prentice Hall.

Johnson, D. W., Johnson, R. T., & Stanne, M. B. (2000). *Cooperative learning methods: A meta-analysis.* University of Minnesota, Minneapolis, MN: Cooperative Learning Center. Retrieved March 26, 2009, from http://www.cooperation.org/pages/cl-methods.html

Johnson, D. W., Johnson, R., & Smith, K. (1998). *Active Learning: Cooperation in the College Classroom.* Edina, MN: Interaction Book Co.

Johnson, L. F. (2008). *Testimony of Laurence F. Johnson, Ph.D.: Committee on Energy and commerce; Subcommittee on the Telecommunications and the Internet: Online Virtual Worlds: Applications and Avatars in a User-Generated Medium.* US: US House of Representatives. Retrieved March 1, 2009, from http://energycommerce.house.gov/cmte_mtgs/110-ti-hrg.040108.Johnson-testimony.pdf.

Johnstone, B. (2003). *Kitchen Magician: The surprising leader in the commercial VR sweepstakes is Matsushita?!* Wired Digital, Inc. Retrieved from http://www.wired.com/wired/archive/2.07/kitchen_pr.html

Joliet Junior College Admissions. (2009). Retrieved on April 1, 2009 from http://www.jjc.edu/admissions/pages/tuition.aspx?c=1

Jonassen, D. (1991). Objectivism vs. constructivism: Do we need a new philosophical paradigm? *Educational Technol-ogy Research and Development, 39*(3), 5–14. doi:10.1007/BF02296434

Jonassen, D. H., & Reeves, T. C. (1996). Learning with technology: Using computers as cognitive tools. In D. H. Jonassen (Ed.), *Handbook of research for educational communications and technology* (pp. 693-719). New York: Macmillan.

Jones, A. (2006). Should RFID Be Used to Monitor Students? *Learning and Leading with Technology, 34.* Retrieved September 18, 2008, from http://www.iste.org/Content/NavigationMenu/Publications/LL/LLIssues/Volume_34_2006_2007_/November_No_3_2/LandL_November_2006.htm

Jones, B. (2002). Students as Web Site Authors: Effects on Motivation and Achievement. *Journal of Educational Technology Systems, 31*(4), 441–461. doi:10.2190/UX5V-WVKL-3EJN-7L0C

Jones-Kavalier, B. R., & Flannigan, S. L. (2006). Connecting the Digital Dots: Literacy of the 21st Century. *Educause, 29*(2). Retrieved December 1, 2000, from http://connect.educause.edu/Library/EDUCAUSE+Quarterly/ConnectingtheDigitalDotsL/39969

Juni, P., Holenstein, F., Sterne, J., Bartlett, C., & Egger, M. (2001). Direction and impact of language bias in meta-analyses of controlled trials: Empirical study. *International Journal of Epidemiology, 31,* 115–123. doi:10.1093/ije/31.1.115

Kanter, R. (2004). *Confidence: How Winning Streaks and Losing Streaks Begin and End.* New York: Three Rivers Press

Kanuka, H. (2002). Guiding principles for facilitating higher levels of web-based distance teaching and learning in post-secondary settings. *Distance Education, 23*(2), 163–182. doi:10.1080/0158791022000009187

Kapp, K. (2006). *Design: Advantages of Interactivity.* Karl Kapp Blog. Retrieved from http://karlkapp.blogspot.com/2006/10/design-advantages-of-interactivity.html

Kaptelinin, V., & Cole, M. (1996). *Individual and collective activities in educational computer game playing.* Retrieved March 22, 2009, from http://lchc.ucsd.edu/People/MCole/Activities.html

Karger, D. R., & Quan, D. (2004, January). *Prerequisites for a personalizable user interfa*ce. Paper presented at the Workshop on Bahavior-Based User Interface Customization at the Intelligent User Interface 2004 Conference, Island of Madeira, Portugal.

Kaser, D. (2007, November). Law of the blog. [from Academic Search Premier database.]. *Information Today, 24*(10), 14. Retrieved March 31, 2009.

Katz, R. N. (2008). The Gathering Cloud: Is this the end of the Middle? The Tower and The Cloud: Higher Education in the Age of Cloud Computing. In R. N. Katz (Ed), *EDUCAUSE* (pp. 2-42). Retrieved from http://www.educause.edu/books/

Kay, A. C. (1972). *A Personal Computer for Children of All Ages.* Paper presented at the ACM Conference, Boston.

Kearsley, G. (n.d.). *Social development theory (L. Vygotsky).* Retrieved September 25, 2008, from http://www.gwu.edu/~tip/vygotsky.html

Keller, C., & Cernerud, L. (2002). Students' perceptions of e-learning in university education. *Journal of Educational Media, 27*(1–2), 55–67. doi:10.1080/0305498032000045458

Keller, J. M. (2006). *ARCS Design Process.* Retrieved from http://www.arcsmodel.com/Mot%20dsgn%20A%20prcss.htm

Kemp, J. E. (2006). Foundations for systemic change. *TechTrends, 50*(2), 20–21. doi:10.1007/s11528-006-7582-1

Kempfert, T. (2004, April). Quality online discussions in Women's Studies classes (or in any class). *Teaching with Technology Today, 10*(5). Retrieved November 17, 2008, from http://www.uwsa.edu/ttt/articles/forums.htm

Khan, B. (2005). Learning features in an open, flexible, and distributed environment. *AACE Journal, 13*(2), 137–153.

Kim, K. J., & Bonk, C. J. (2006). The Future of Online Teaching and Learning in Higher Education: The Survey Says... *Educause Quaterly, 29*(4), 22-30. Retrieved March 31, 2009, from http://net.educause.edu/ir/library/pdf/EQM0644.pdf

Kirkpatrick, D. L. (1959a). Techniques for evaluating training programs. *Journal of ASTD, 13*(11), 3–9.

Kirkpatrick, D. L. (1959b). Techniques for evaluating training programs: Part 2—Learning. *Journal of ASTD, 13*(12), 21–26.

Kirkpatrick, D. L. (1960a). Techniques for evaluating training programs: Part 3—Behavior. *Journal of ASTD, 14*(1), 13–18.

Kirkpatrick, D. L. (1960b). Techniques for evaluating training programs: Part 4—Results. *Journal of ASTD, 14*(2), 28–32.

Kirriemuir, J. (2006). *Literature review in games and learning.* Retrieved September 8, 2007, from http://www.futurelab.org.uk/resources/publications_reports_articles/literature_reviews/literature_Review378

Klein, J., & Fox, E. (2004). Performance Improvement Competencies for Instructional Technologists. *TechTrends: Linking Research & Practice to Improve Learning, 48*(2), 22–26.

Klopfer, E., Osterweil, S., & Salen, K. (2009). *Moving learning games forward: Obstacles, opportunities & openness.* Cambridge, MA: The Education Arcade, Massachusetts Institute of Technology.

Klopfer, E., Osterweil, S., Groff, J., & Haas, J. (2009). *Using the technology of today in the classroom today.* Cambridge, MA: The Education Arcade, Massachusetts Institute of Technology.

Knezek, D. (2006). Yes to Both. *Learning and Leading with Technology, 34.* Retrieved June 7, 2008, from http://www.iste.org/Content/NavigationMenu/Publications/LL/LLIssues/Volume_34_2006_2007_/November_No_3_2/LandL_November_2006.htm

Knowles, M. (1984). *Andragogy in Action.* San Francisco: Jossey-Bass.

Knowles, M. (1989). *The making of an adult educator: An autobiographical journey.* San Francisco: Jossey-Bass.

Koch, G. (2007). *Teacher uses online Second Life for classes: Students take classes interact via cyberspace.* Retrieved March 1, 2009, from http://www.idsnews.com/news/story.aspx?id=41756&comview=1

Kolb, L. (2006). From Toy to Toll. *Learning and Leading with Technology, 34.* Retrieved June 7, 2008, from http://www.iste.org/Content/NavigationMenu/Publications/LL/

LLIssues/Volume_34_2006_2007_/November_No_3_2/LandL_November_2006.htm

Koschmann, T., Hall, R., & Miyake, N. (Eds.). (2002). *CSCL 2: Carrying forward the conversation.* Mahwah, NJ: Lawrence Erlbaum Associates.

Kovela, S. (2008). *3D Virtual Worlds and Education 2.0: The "Second Life" Perspective.* Retrieved March 1, 2009, from http://www.kingston.ac.uk/~ku07009/Uni2/ Kovela.pdf

Kozol, J. (2006). *The Shame of a Nation: The Restoration of Apartheid Schooling in America.* CA: Three Rivers Press.

Kukulska-Hulme, A., & Shield, L. (2004). Usability and pedagogical design: are language learning websites special? In *Proceedings of the World Conference on Educational Multimedia, Hypermedia and Telecommunications 2004* (pp. 4235-4242). AACE Digital Library.

Kukulska-Hulme, A., & Traxler, J. (Eds.). (2005). *Mobile learning a handbook for educators and trainers.* London: Routledge.

Kurtus, R. (1999). *Difference Between Education and Training.* Retrieved from http://www.school-for-champions.com/training/difference.htm

Kzero. (2007a, November 25). *A buyers guide to Virtual Retailing. Part 3 – Dynamic Merchandising.* Retrieved from http://www.kzero.co.uk/blog/?p=1630

Kzero. (2007b, September 30). *Supersize Me. Design values in virtual worlds.* Retrieved from http://www.kzero.co.uk/blog/?p=1064

KZERO. (2008). *Research.* Retrieved March 1, 2009, from http://www.kzero.co.uk/blog/? page_id=2092

Kzero. (2008a, May 13). *Sunday Times covers BDO Second Life launch.* Retrieved from http://www.kzero.co.uk/blog/?p=2180

Kzero. (2008b, April 8). *The virtual Streets of Philadelphia and real-time geo-tagging.* Retrieved from http://www.kzero.co.uk/blog/?p=2066

Lage, M. J., Platt, G. J., & Treglia, M. (2000). Inverting the Classroom: A Gateway to Creating an Inclusive Learning Environment. *The Journal of Economic Education, 31*(1), 30–43. doi:10.2307/1183338

Lagorio, C. (2007, January 7). The Ultimate Distance Learning. *The New York Times: Education Life.* Retrieved March 1, 2009, from http://www.nytimes.com/2007/01/07/education/edlife/07innovation.html

Lamont, I. (2007, May 24). *Virtual Reality and Higher Education: Another Perspective.* Retrieved March 1, 2009, from http://terranova.blogs.com/terra_nova/2007/05/teaching_in_vr_.html

Laneways, M. (n.d.). *Would Your Business Benefit from a Second Life?* Retrieved from http://www.mmv.vic.gov.au/Assets/174/1/SecondLifeReport.pdf

Lankshear, C., & Knobel, M. (2006). *Blogging as participation: The active sociality of a new literacy.* Paper presented at the American Educational Research Association.

Laurillard, D. (1993). *Rethinking university teaching.* Milton Keynes, UK: Open University Press.

Laurillard, D. (2002). *Rethinking university teaching: A conversational framework for the effective use of learning technologies* (2nd ed.). New York: Routledge Falmer.

Laurillard, D. (2004). E-learning in Higher Education. In P. Ashwin (Ed.), *From Changing Higher Education.* London: RoutledgeFalmer. Retrieved from http://www3.griffith.edu.au/03/ltn/docs/E-Learning_in_Higher_Education.doc~

Lave, J., & Wenger, E. (1991). *Situated learning: Legitimate peripheral participation.* Cambridge, MA: Cambridge University Press.

Lavoie, M.-C. (2007). *Enabling contextual mlearning: Design recommendations for a context appropriate user interface enabling mobile-learning.* A Thesis in the Department of Education. Concordia University, Montreal, Quebec, Canada. Retrieved October, 8, 2008, from http://graduatestudies.concordia.ca/thesis/index.php?convocation_year=207&egree=M.A%20Educational%20Technology&f=list&supervisor=

Law, l. (2006). Fulldome Video: An Emerging Technology for Education. *Learning and Leading with Technology, 34.* Retrieved June 7, 2008, from http://www.iste.org/Content/NavigationMenu/Publications/LL/LLIssues/Volume_34_2006_2007_/November_No_3_2/LandL_November_2006.htm

Learning Company. (1995). *Math Munchers* [Computer Game]. Cambridge, MA: Learning Company.

Learning Theories Knowledgebase. (2008). *ADDIE Model at Learning-Theories.com.* Retrieved from http://www.learning-theories.com/addie-model.html

Lederer, A. L., Maupin, D. J., Sena, M. P., & Zhuang, Y. (2000). The technology acceptance model and the World Wide Web. *Decision Support Systems, 29*(3), 269–282. doi:10.1016/S0167-9236(00)00076-2

Lee, M. (2001). Profiling students adaptation styles in web-based learning. *Computers & Education, 36*(2), 121–132. doi:10.1016/S0360-1315(00)00046-4

Lee, M. J. W., McLoughlin, C., & Chan, A. (2008). Talk the talk: Learner-generated podcasts as catalysts for knowledge creation. *British Journal of Educational Technology, 39*(3), 501–521. doi:10.1111/j.1467-8535.2007.00746.x

Lehman, R. (2001, February 15). General principles and good practices for distance education. *Teaching with Technology Today, 7*(6). Retrieved December 13, 2008, from http://www.uwsa.edu/ttt/articles/lehman.htm

Leidner, D. B., & Jarvenpaa, S. L. (1995). The use of information technology to enhance management school education: A theoretical view. *MIS Quarterly, 19,* 265–291. doi:10.2307/249596

Liaw, Sh.-Sh., Chen, G.-D., & Huang, H.-M. (2008). Users' attitudes toward Web-based collaborative learning systems for knowledge management. *Computers & Education, 50*(3), 950–961. doi:10.1016/j.compedu.2006.09.007

Liegle, J. O., & Janicki, T. N. (2006). The effect of learning styles on the navigation needs of Web-based learners. *Computers in Human Behavior, 22*(5), 885–898. doi:10.1016/j.chb.2004.03.024

Lim, W. Y., Hedberg, J., Yeo, J., & Hung, D. (2005). *Fostering communities of practice of heads of IT departments using common projects.* Paper presented at the Association for Educational Communications and Technology Leadership and Technology International Convention, Orlando FL.

Linden Research, Inc. (2008). *Second Life Official Site.* Retrieved from http://secondlife.com/

Linden Research. (2008a). *Economic Statistics.* Retrieved March 1, 2009, from http://secondlife.com/whatis/economy_stats.php

LinkedIn. (2009). *LinkedIn: Relationships Matter.* Retrieved May 26, 2009, from http://www.linkedin.com

Lipponen, L., Hakkarainen, K., & Paavola, S. (2004). Practices and orientations of CSCL. In J. W. Strijbos, P. A. Kirschner & R. L. Martens (Eds.), *What we know about CSCL and Implementing it in higher education* (pp. 34-50). Dordrecht, Netherlands: Kluwer Academic Publishers.

Liu, C. (2007). Teaching in a wireless learning environment: A case study. *Educational Technology and Society, 10*(1), 107-123. Retrieved October 8, 2008, from http://www.ifets.info/journals/10_1/11.pdf

Liu, Q., Rui, Y., Gupta, A., & Cadiz, J. J. (2001). Automating camera management for lecture room environments. In *Proceedings of the SIGCHI Conference on Human Factors in Computing Systems,* Seattle, WA (pp. 442-449).

Liu, T., & Kender, J. R. (2004). Lecture videos for e-learning: Current research and challenges. In *Proceedings of IEEE Sixth International Symposium on Multimedia Software Engineering,* Miami, FL (pp. 574-578).

Liu, Y., & Shrum, L. J. (2002). What Is Interactivity and Is It Always Such a Good Thing? Implications of Definition, Person, and Situation for the Influence of Interactivity on Advertising Effectiveness. *Journal of Advertising, 31*(4). Retrieved December 31, 2008, from http://www.accessmylibrary.com/coms2/summary_0286-2773470_ITM

Locatis, C. (2001). *Instructional design theory and the development of multimedia programs.* Retrieved January 8, 2008, from http://lhncbc.nlm.nih.gov/lhc/docs/published/2001/pub2001048.pdf

Lord, R. G., & Levy, P. E. (1994). Moving from cognition to action: A control theory perspective. *Applied Psychology, 43*(3), 335–367. doi:10.1111/j.1464-0597.1994.tb00828.x

Lorenz, K. (2008). *Top 10 Soft Skills for Job Hunters.* Retrieved December 31, 2008, from http://jobs.aol.com/article/_a/top-10-soft-skills-for-job-hunters/20051107131509990011

Loucks-Horsley, S., Hewson, P. W., Love, N., & Stiles, K. E. (1998). *Designing professional development for teachers of science and mathematics.* Thousand Oaks, CA: Corwin Press.

Lowry, C. M. (1989). Supporting and facilitating self-directed learning. *ERIC Digest, 93.* Retrieved November 23, 2008, from http://www.ntlf.com/html/lib/bib/89dig.htm

Lu, J., Yu, C. S., & Liu, C. (2003). Learning style, learning patterns, and learning performance in a WebCT-based MIS course. *Information & Management, 40*(6), 497–507. doi:10.1016/S0378-7206(02)00064-2

Lundin, J., & Magnusson, M. (2003). Collaborative learning in mobile work. *Journal of Computer Assisted Learning, 19*(3), 273–283. doi:10.1046/j.0266-4909.2003.00029.x

Lynch, M. M. (November/December, 2001). Effective student preparation for online learning. *The Technology Source*. Retrieved March 31, 2009, from http://technologysource.org/article/effective_student_preparation_for_online_learning/

MacManus, T. (2002). Mobile what? The educational potential of mobile technologies. In *Proceedings of the World Conference on E-Learning in Corporations, Government, Health, and Higher Education* (pp. 1895-1898). Retrieved October 8, 2008, from http://www.editlib.org/INDEX.CFM?fuseaction=Reader.ViewAbstract&paper_id=9424

Maguad, B. (2007). Identifying the needs of customers in higher education. *Education, 127*(3), 332-343. Retrieved March 3, 2009, from Academic Research Database. Document ID 1268062551.

Malone, J. D. (2003). Shooting the past: An instructional case for knowledge management. *Journal of Information Systems, 17*(2), 7–14. doi:10.2308/jis.2003.17.2.41

Market Data Retrieval. (2002). *Technology in education, 2002*. Retrieved March 24, 2009, from http://www.school-data.com/publications3.html

Marsh, C., & Hogan, R. (2005). Distance education the Pacific way. *The International Journal of Learning, 12*, 3–7.

Marshall, J. (2002). *Learning with Technology.* San Diego, CA: San Diego State University.

Marshall, S. (2008). Worlds in Collision: Copyright, Technology, and Education. *Innovate Journal of Online Education, 4*(5). http://www.innovateonline.info/ index.php? view=article&id=528.

Martin, H. (2006). Remember the Mantra. *Learning and Leading with Technology, 34*. Retrieved June 7, 2008, from http://www.iste.org/Content/NavigationMenu/Publications/LL/LLIssues/Volume_34_2006_2007_/November_No_3_2/LandL_November_2006.htm

Maryland Online, Inc. (2008). Quality Matters Rubric Standards 2008-2010 edition with Assigned Point Values. *Quality Matters Institute.* Retrieved October 10, 2008 from http://qminstitute.org/home/Public%20Library/About%20QM/RubricStandards2008-2010.pdf

Massy, W. F., & Zemsky, R. (1995). Using Information Technology to Enhance Academic Productivity. *Educom National Learning Infrastructure Initiative (NLII)*. Retrieved November 14, 2008, from http://www.educause.edu/ir/library/html/nli0004.html

Matthewson, C., & Thaman, K. (1998). Designing the Rebbelib: Staff development in a multicultural environment. In C. Latchem & F. Lockwood (Eds.), *Staff development in open and flexible learning,* (pp. 115-125). Florence, KY: Routledge.

Mayer, M., & Leone, P. (2001). *Hypermedia and Students With E/BD: Developing untapped Talents and Fostering Success.* Retrieved May 24, 2009 From http://www.eric.ed.gov/ERICWebPortal/custom/portlets/recordDetails/detailmini.jsp?_nfpb=true&_&ERICExtSearch_SearchValue_0=ED458738&ERICExtSearch_SearchType_0=no&accno=ED458738

Mayer, R., & Moreno, R. (1997). *A cognitive theory of multimedia learning: Implications for design principles.* Retrieved January 7, 2008, from http://www.unm.edu/~moreno/PDFS/chi.pdf

McAlpine, I. (2000). Collaborative learning online. *Distance Education, 21*(1), 66–80. doi:10.1080/0158791000210105

McAnear, A. (2006). The Magic of Emerging Technology. *Learning and Leading with Technology, 34.* Retrieved June 7, 2008, from http://www.iste.org/Content/NavigationMenu/Publications/LL/LLIssues/Volume_34_2006_2007_/November_No_3_2/LandL_November_2006.htm

McCall, A. (2002). *Creating and Using Virtual Reality: A Guide for the Arts and Humanities.* Retrieved from http://vads.ahds.ac.uk/guides/vr_guide/vlib1.html

McClellan, S. (2008). Will Mobile Ads Take Off In '07, Or Be Put On Hold? *Adweek Magazine.* Retrieved June 27, 2008 from http://www.adweek.com/aw/magazine/article_display.jsp?vnu_content_id=1003526234

McConatha, D., Praul, M., & Lynch, M. (2008). Mobile learning in higher education: An empirical assessment of a new educational tool. *The Turkish Online Journal of Educational Technology, 7*(3), 1303-6521. Retrieved October 8, 2008, from http://www.scribd.com/doc/4494956/MOBILE-LEARNING-IN-HIGHER-EDUCATION-AN EMPIRICAL-ASSESSMENT-OF-A-NEW-EDUCATIONAL-TOOL

McCord, A. (2009). Detection and deterrence of plagiarism in online learning environments. In P. L. Rogers, G. A. Berg, J. V. Boettecher, C. Howard, L. Justice & K. D. Schenk (Eds.), *Encyclopedia of distance learning* (2nd ed.). Hershey, PA: IGI Global.

McElrath, E., & McDowell, K. (2008, March). Pedagogical Strategies for Building Community in Graduate Level Distance Education Courses. *MERLOT Journal of Online Learning and Teaching, 4*(1). Retrieved from http://jolt.merlot.org/vol14no1/mcelrath0308.htm

McInnis, C., & Hartley, R. (2008). *Managing study and work: The impact of full-time study and paid work on the undergraduate experience in Australian universities.* Retrieved December 13, 2008, from http://www.dest.gov.au/sectors/higher_education/publications_resources/profiles/managing_study_and_work.htm

McKavanagh, C., & Stevenson, J. (1992, November). *Measurement of Classroom Environment.* Paper presented at the 1992 joint conference of the Australian Association for research in education and the New Zealand Association for research in Education, Deakin University, Geelong.

McKeachie, W. J. (Ed.). (1999). *McKeachie's teaching tips: Strategies, research and theory for college and university teachers* (10th ed.). Boston, MA: Houghton Mifflin.

Mclean, M., Nikonchuk, A., Kaplo, P., & Wall, M. (2006). In sync with science teaching: Handheld computers support classroom and laboratory activities. *The Science Teacher, 73*(7), 26-29. Retrieved October 8, 2008, from http://eric.ed.gov:80/ERICWebPortal/custom/portlets/recordDetails.detailmini.jsp?_nfpb=true&_&RICExtSearch_SearchValue_0=EJ758661&ERICExtSearch_SearchType_0=no&accno=EJ758 661

Mclean, N. (2003). *The m-learning paradigm: an overview. A report for the Royal Academy of Engineering and the Vodafone group foundation.* Retrieved October 8, 2008, from http://64.233.169.132/search?q=cache:1HSfJMPzSgcJ:www.oucs.ox.ac.uk/ltg/reports/mlearningdoc+the+m-learning+paradigm+an+overview+by+neil+mclean&hl=en&ct=clnk&cd=1&gl=us

McManus, D. A. (2005). *Leaving the lectern: Cooperative learning and the critical first days of students working in groups.* Boston, MA: Anker Publishing Company, Inc.

MCT. (2008, July 22). Characters in Second Life polish their practical skills. *The Australian: Executive Tech*, 34.

Meinke, R. J. (1994). Appendix III: Introductory Sociology with EIES. In S. R. Hiltz (Ed.), *The virtual classroom: Learning without limits via computer networks* (pp. 334-348). Norwood, NJ: Ablex Publishing Corporation.

Mergel, B. (1998). *Instructional design and learning theory.* Retrieved December 14, 2008,

Merriam, S. B., & Caffarella, R. S. (1999). *Learning in adulthood* (2nd ed.). San Francisco: Jossey-Bass.

Merrill, M. D. (2000). Knowledge objects and mental models. In D. A. Wiley (Ed.), *The Instructional Use of Learning Objects: Online Version.* Retrieved June 7, 2008, from http://reusability.org/read/chapters/merrill.doc

Merrill, M. D. (2002). First principles of instruction. *Educational Technology Research and Development, 50*(3), 43–59. doi:10.1007/BF02505024

Merrill, M. D. (2006). First principles of instruction: a synthesis. *Trends and Issues in Instructional Design and Technology (2nd Ed.).* Upper Saddle River, NJ: Prentice-Hall, Inc.

Mielo, G. (2005). The medium is the moblog. [from http://direct.bl.uk/bld/]. *Etc.; a Review of General Semantics, 62*(1), 28–35. Retrieved October 8, 2008.

Miller, M. (2008). *Cloud computing:Web based applications that change the way you work and collaborate online.* Indianapolis, IN: Que Publishing

Miller, M., & Cruce, T. (2002). *A Twentieth Century timeline: Classroom use of instructional film, radio, and television.* Retrieved November 20, 2008, from http://www.arches.uga.edu/~mlmiller/timeline/1960s.htm

Miller, S. (1995). *Vygotsky and education: The sociocultural genesis of dialogic thinking in classroom contexts for open-forum literature discussions.* Retrieved January 11, 2008, from http://psych.hanover.edu/vygotsky/miller.html

Millett, J. D. (1974). *Governance and Leadership in Higher Education*. Paper presented at the Presidential Seminar, Management Division of the Academy for Educational Development, Denver, CO and San Francisco, CA.

Milter, R. G. (2002). Developing an MBA online degree program: Expanding knowledge and skills via technology-mediated learning communities. In P. Comeaux (Ed.), *Communication and collaboration in the online classroom: Examples and application* (pp. 3-22). Boston, MA: Anker Publishing Company, Inc.

Mingle, J. R. (1995). Vision and reality for Technology-based Delivery Systems in Postsecondary Education. In *Proceedings of the Governor's Conference of Higher Education*, St. Louis, MI.

Minocha, S., & Tingle, R. (2008). Socialisation and Collaborative Learning of distance learners in 3-D Virtual Worlds. In *Researching Learning in Virtual Environments International Conference* (pp. 216-227). Milton Keynes, UK: The Open University. Retrieved April 22, 2009.

Minotti, J., & Giguere, P. (2003). The realties of web-based training. *THE Journal, 30*(11), 41-44. Retrieved October 15, 2008, from Academic Research Library database (Document ID: 353845701).

Mintzberg, H., & Waters, J. A. (1985). Of strategies, deliberate and emergent. *Strategic Management Journal, 6*, 257–272. doi:10.1002/smj.4250060306

Mishra, P., & Koehler, M. J. (2006). Technological Pedagogical Content Knowledge: A new framework for teacher knowledge. *Teachers College Record, 108*(6), 1017–1054. doi:10.1111/j.1467-9620.2006.00684.x

MIT - Massachusetts Institute of Technology. (2009). *Evaluation*. Compilation of evaluation studies about *OpenCourseware*. Retrieved December 18, 2008, from http://ocw.uofk.edu/OcwWeb/Global/AboutOCW/evaluation.htm

Moffitt, M. (1996). *Importance of Teaching and Learning Implications When Making Decisions About Technology Acquisition*. North Central Regional Educational Laboratory (NCREL) online publications. Retrieved September 18, 2008 from http://www.ncrel.org

Moore, J.L., Lin, X., Schwartz, D.L., Petrosino, A., Hickey, D.T., Campbell, O., & Hmelo, C., & Cognition and Technology Group at Vanderbilt (CTGV). (1994). The relationship between situated cognition and anchored instruction: A response to Tripp. *Educational Technology, 34*(8), 28–32.

Moore, M. G. (1989). Three types of interaction. *American Journal of Distance Education, 3*(2), 1–6. doi:10.1080/08923648909526659

Moore, M. G. (1993). *Theory of transactional distance*. In D. Keegan (Ed.), *Theoretical principles of distance education* (p.22-38). New York: Routledge.

Moore, M. G., & Kearsley, G. (1996). *Distance Education: a Systems View*. Boston: Wadsworth Publishing Company.

Morgan, C. K., & Kinross, C. (2002). Facilitating Online Interactivity Among Remotely Located Land Management Students. *Electronic Journal of Instructional Science and Technology*. Retrieved from http://www.usq.edu.au/electpub/e-jist/docs/Vol5_No2/morganrevised.html

Morgan, G. (2003). *Faculty use of course management systems*. Boulder, CO: EDUCAUSE Center for Applied Research. Retrieved Dec. 23, 2008, from http://net.educause.edu/ir/library/pdf/ecar_so/ers/ERS0302/ekf0302.pdf

Morgan, G. (2003). Faculty use of course management systems. *Educause Centre for Applied Research, 2*, 1–97.

Mortera-Gutiérrez, F. (2006). Faculty best practices using blended learning in e-learning and face-to-face instruction. *International Journal on E-Learning, 5*(3), 313–337.

Moss, N. (2008). Incorporating a rich media presentation format into a lecture-based course structure. *Innovate, 1*(2). Retrieved from http://innovateonline.info/index.php?view=article&id=10&highlight=lecture

Mouza, C. (2002). Learning to teach with new technology: Implications for professional development. *Journal of Research on Technology in Education, 35*(2), 272–289.

Muilenburg, L., & Berge, Z. (2001). Barriers to distance education: A factor-analytic study. *American Journal of Distance Education, 15*(2), 7–22. doi:10.1080/08923640109527081

Murray, F. (2001). *The Use of PowerPoint to Increase Reading and Language Skills: A Research-Based Approach*. Retrieved May 24, 2009, from http://www.eric.ed.gov/ERICWebPortal/custom/portlets/recordDetails/detailmini.jsp?_nfpb=true&_&ERICExtSearch_SearchValue_0=ED458738&ERICExtSearch_SearchType_0=no&accno=ED458738

Myers, C., Bennet, D., Brown, G., & Henderson, T. (2004). Emerging online learning environments and student learning: An analysis of faculty perceptions. *Educational Technology and Society, 7*(1), 78–86.

Myers, J. P. Jr. (1989). The new generation of computer literacy. *ACM SIGCSE Bull, 21*(1), 177–181. doi:10.1145/65294.65307

N.N. (2008). *Second Life Business Communicators Wiki: Companies in Second Life.* Retrieved March 1, 2009, from http://slbusinesscommunicators.pbwiki.com/Companies+in+Second+Life

Nadler, D. A. (1998). *Champions of Change: How CEOs and their companies are mastering the skill of radical change.* San Francisco, CA: Jossey-Bass.

Nagel, D. (2008). *Lecture capture: No longer optional?* Retrieved October 23, 2008, from http://campustechnology.com/articles/67990/

Nam, C., & Smith-Jackson, T. (2007). Web-based learning environment: A theory-based design process for development and evaluation. *Journal of Information Technology Education, 6*, 23–43.

Narayan, G. (2007). The digital divide: E-governance and m-governance in a hub and spoke model. *The Electronic Journal of Information Systems in Developing Countries, 31*(1), 1–14.

National Aeronautics and Space Administration. (2008). *Beginner's Guide to Wind Tunnels.* Retrieved from http://www.grc.nasa.gov/WWW/K-12/windtunnel.html

National Aeronautics and Space Administration. (2008). *NASA MMO game.* Retrieved March 28, 2009, from http://ipp.gsfc.nasa.gov/mmo/index.html

National Aeronautics and Space Administration. (n.d.). *Hubble Space Telescope Servicing Mission 3A.* Retrieved from http://www.gsfc.nasa.gov/gsfc/service/gallery/fact_sheets/spacesci/hst3-01/reasons%20for%20hubble%20servicing.htm

National Council of Teachers of Mathematics. (2000). *Curriculum and evaluation standards for school mathematics.* Reston, VA: National Council of Teachers of Mathematics.

National Research Council (NRC). (2002). *How people learn.* Washington, DC: National Academy Press.

Ndahi, H. (2006). The Use of Innovative Methods to Deliver Technology Education Laboratory Courses via Distance Learning: A Strategy to Increase Enrollment. *Journal of Technology Education, 17*, 33-42. Retrieved September 18, 2008 from http://scholar.lib.vt.edu/ejournals/JTE/v17n2/pdf/index.html

New Media Consortium. (2007). Massively multiplayer educational gaming. In *The Horizon Report 2007 Edition* (pp. 25-27). Austin, TX: New Media Consortium.

New Media Consortium. (2008, January 22). *Virtual Worlds Case Study: Santa Clara Island.* Retrieved from http://secondliferesearch.blogspot.com/2008/01/virtual-worlds-case-study-santa-clara.html and http://virtualworlds.nmc.org/portfolio/santa-clara/

Ng, C. (2006). Academics telecommuting in open and distance education universities: Issues, challenges, and opportunities. *The International Review of Research in Open and Distance Learning 7*(2) 1-16. Retrieved November 1, 2007, from http://www.irrodl.org/index.php/irrodl/article/view/300/632

Ng, E., & Ma, A. (2002). An innovative model to foster Web-based collaborative learning. In *IS2002 Proceedings of the Informing Science+IT Education Conference* (pp. 1165-1171). Informing Science Institute.

Nielsen, J. (1993). *Usability engineering.* Boston, MA: Academic Press.

Nielsen, J. (1994). Heuristic evaluation. In J. Nielsen & R.L. Mack (Eds,), *Usability Inspection Methods* (pp. 25-64). New York: John Wiley.

Niess, M. L. (2005). Preparing teachers to teach science and mathematics with technology: Developing a technology pedagogical content knowledge. *Teaching and Teacher Education, 21*, 509–523. doi:10.1016/j.tate.2005.03.006

Nixon, M. A., & Leftwich, B. R. (2002). Collaborative instructional design for an internet-based graduate degree program. In P. Comeaux (Ed.), *Communication and collaboration in the online classroom: Examples and applications* (pp. 23-38). Boston, MA: Anker Publishing Company, Inc.

Nogier, J.-F. (2007). *What is usability?* Retrieved July 27, 2007, from www.usabilis.com/gb/whatis/usability.htm

Norstrom, B. (2006). Produce Employees. *Learning and Leading with Technology, 34.* Retrieved June 7, 2008, from http://www.iste.org/Content/NavigationMenu/Publications/LL/LLIssues/Volume_34_2006_2007_/November_No_3_2/LandL_November_2006.htm

Norton, D. P. (2002). Managing Strategy is Managing Change. *Balanced Scorecard Report,* 4(1).

NSW Department of Education and Training. (2004). *Framework of professional teaching standards.* Retrieved January 14, 2008, from https://www.det.nsw.edu.au/proflearn/areas/plp/standards.htm

Nyiri, K. (2002) Towards a Philosophy of M-Learning. In *Proceedings of the IEEE International Workshop on Wireless and Mobile Technologies in Education (WMTE, 2002),* Teleborg Campus.

O'Connell, M., & Smith, J. (2007). *A Guide to Working with M-Learning Standards.* Brisbane, Australia: Australian Flexible Learning Framework.

O'Malley, J., & McGraw, H. (1999). Student perceptions of distance learning, online learning, and the traditional classroom [Electronic version]. *Online Journal of Distance Learning Administration, 2*(4), 1-10. Retrieved on July 1, 2008, from http://www.westga.edu/~distance/omalley24.html

Oblinger, D. (1999). Global education: Thinking creatively. *Higher Education in Europe, 24*(2), 151–258. doi:10.1080/0379772990240212

Oblinger, D. G., & Hawkins, B. L. (2006). The Myth about Online Course Development. *EDUCAUSE Review, 41*(1), 14–15.

Oblinger, D., & Hawkins, B. (2005). The Myth about E-Learning: "We Don't Need to Worry about E-Learning Anymore. *EDUCAUSE Review, 40*(4), 14–15.

Ohio Board of Regents. (2004). *Adult Educational Attainment by Age Group 1990 and 2000 Census Results. Prepared for the Governor's Commission on Higher Education and the Economy.* Retrieved November 22, 2008, from http://regents.ohio.gov/perfrpt/special_reports/Degree_Attainment_by_Age_Group_90_2000_Census.pdf

Ohio Board of Regents. (2004). *The Performance Report for Ohio's Colleges and Universities, 2003.* Retrieved March 19, 2009, from http://regents.ohio.gov/perfrpt/2003/

Olaniran, B. A. (2006). Applying synchronous computer-mediated communication into course design: Some considerations and practical guides. *Campus-Wide Information Systems, 23*(3). doi:10.1108/10650740610674210

Ondrejka, C. (2007). Education Unleashed: Participatory Culture, Education, and Innovation in Second Life. In *The Ecology of Games: Connecting Youth, Games, and Learning* (pp. 229-251).

Orrill, C. H. (2001). Building Technology-Based, Learner-Centered Classrooms: The Evolution of a Professional Development Framework. *Educational Technology Research and Development, 49*(1), 15–34. doi:10.1007/BF02504504

Ostlund, B. (2008). Prerequisites for interactive learning in distance education: Perspectives from Swedish students. *Australasian Journal of Educational Technology, 24*(1), 42–56.

Paavola, S., Lipponen, L., & Hakkarainen, K. (2004). Models of innovative knowledge communities and three metaphors of learning. *Review of Educational Research, 74*(4), 557–576. doi:10.3102/00346543074004557

Pachnowski, L., & Jurezyk, J. (2003). Perceptions of faculty on the effect of distance learning technology on faculty preparation time. *Online Journal of Distance Learning Administration, 6*(3), 1-10. Retrieved December 26, 2008, from http://www.westga.edu/~distance/ojdla/fall63/pachnowski64.html

Palloff, R. M., & Pratt, K. (2001). *Lessons from the cyberspace classroom: The realities of online teaching.* San Francisco: Jossey-Bass Publishers.

Palloff, R., & Pratt, K. (1999). *Building learning communities in cyberspace: effective strategies for the online classroom.* San Francisco: Jossey-Bass.

Palloff, R., & Pratt, K. (2007). *Building online learning communities: effective strategies for the virtual classroom.* San Francisco: Jossey-Bass.

Papert, S. (1998). *Does easy do it? Children, games and learning.* Retrieved September 25, 2007, from http://www.papert.org/articles/Doeseasydoit.html

ParallelGraphics. (2008). *Virtual Reality in the Mining Industry.* Retrieved from http://www.parallelgraphics.com/products/sdk/success/dsk/

Parker, A. (2003). Motivation and incentives for distance faculty. *Online Journal of Distance Learning Administration, 6*(3), 1-6. Retrieved November 7, 2008, from http://www.westga.edu/~distance/ojdla/fall63/parker63.htm

Parlangeli, O., Marchigianni, E., & Bagnara, S. (1999). Multimedia system in distance education: effects on usability. *Interacting with Computers, 12*(1), 37–49. doi:10.1016/S0953-5438(98)00054-X

Pask, A. G. S. (1976). *Conversation Theory: Applications in Education and Epistemology.* Amsterdam: Elsevier.

Pattillo, R. E. (2007). Decreasing transactional distance in a Web-based course. *New Educator, 32*(3), 109–112.

Paulus, T. M. (2005). Collaborative and cooperative approaches to online group work: The impact of task type. *Distance Education, 26*(1), 111–125. doi:10.1080/01587910500081343

Pea, R., & Maldonado, H. (2006). WILD for learning: Interacting through new computing devices, anytime, anywhere. In K. Sawyer (Ed.), *Cambridge Handbook of the Learning Sciences* (pp. 427-442). New York: Cambridge University Press.

Peneul, W. R. (2006). Implementation and effects of one to one computing initiatives: A research initiative. *Journal of Research on Technology in Education, 28*(3), 329–343.

Peters, K. (2007). M-learning: Positioning educators for a mobile, connected future. *International Review of Research in Open and Distance Learning, 8*(2), 3831–1492.

Peters, O. (1983). Distance teaching and industrial production: a comparative interpretation in outline. In D. Sewart, D. Keegan & B. Holmberg (Eds.), *Distance education: International perspectives* (pp. 95-113). London: Croom-Helm.

Philips, D. C. (1995). The good, the bad, the ugly: The many faces of constructivism. *Educational Researcher, 24*(7), 5–12.

Phung, D., Valetto, G., Kaiser, G. E., Liu, T., & Kender, J. R. (2007). Adaptive synchronization of semantically compressed instructional videos for collaborative distance learning. *International Journal of Distance Education Technologies, 5*(2), 56–73.

Picciano, A. (2002). Beyond student perceptions: Issues of interaction, presence, and performance in an online course. *Journal of Asynchronous Learning, 6*(1).

Picciano, A., & Seaman, J. (2007). *K-12 online learning: A survey of U.S. school district administrators.* Needham, MA: The Sloan Consortium. Retrieved December 27, 2008, from http://www.sloanconsortium.org/publications/survey/pdf/K-12_Online_Learning.pdf

Plotrowski, C., & Vodanovich, S. J. (2000). Are the reported barriers to Internet-based instruction warranted? A synthesis of recent research. *Education, 121*, 48–53.

Polhemus, L., Shih, L., Richardson, J., & Swan, K. (2000). *Building an affective learning community: Social presence and learning engagement.* Paper presented at the World Conference on the WWW and the Internet (WebNet), San Antonio, TX.

Polly, D. (2006). *Examining the influence of learner-centered professional development on elementary mathematics teachers' instructional practices, espoused practices, and evidence of student learning.* Unpublished doctoral dissertation, University of Georgia, Athens, GA.

Polly, D. (2008). Modeling the influence of calculator use and teacher effects on first grade students' mathematics achievement. *Journal of Technology in Mathematics and Science Teaching, 27*(3), 245–263.

Polly, D., & Mims, C. (2009). Designing professional development to support teachers' TPACK and integration of Web 2.0 technologies. In T.T. Kidd & I. Chen (Eds.). *Wired for Learning: Web 2.0 Guide for Educators*, 301-316.

Powers, S., & Rossman, M. (1985). Student satisfaction with graduate education: Dimensionality and assessment in a college education. *Psychology: A Quarterly Journal of Human Behavior, 22*(2), 46-49. Retrieved April 10, 2009. from Education Resource Information Center, EJ327602.

Preece, J. (2000). *Online communities: Designing usability, supporting sociability.* New York: John Wiley & Sons.

Preece, J., Rogers, Y., & Sharp, H. (2002). *Interaction design: Beyond human-computer interaction.* New York: John Wiley & Sons.

Prensky, M. (2001). *Digital Natives. Digital Immigrants.* Retrieved December 2, 2008, from http://www.marcprensky.com/writing/Prensky%20-%20Digital%20Natives,%20Digital%20Immigrants%20-%20Part1.pdf

Prensky, M. (2008). Digital Game-Based Learning. *ACM Computers in Entertainment, 1*(1), 21–24. doi:10.1145/950566.950596

President's Committee of Advisors on Science and Technology. (1997, March). *Report on the use of technology to strengthen K-12 education in the United States.* Retrieved from http://www.whitehouse.gov/ WH/EOP/OSTP/NSTC/PCAST/k-12ed.html

Primary Research Group. (2007). *The Survey of Distance Learning Programs in Higher Education, 2007-08 Edition.* Retrieved from http://tinyurl.com/23zep8

Proserpio, L., & Gioia, D. A. (2007). Teaching the Virtual Generation. *Academy of Management Learning & Education, 6*(1), 69–80.

Quinn, C. (2000). M-learning: Mobile wireless in-your-pocket learning. *LineZine,* 1-5. Retrieved November 6, 2008, from http://www.linezine.com/2.1/features/cqmmwiyp.htm

Quinn, C. (2008) *Mobile Learning Devices: Performance to Go.* Santa Rosa, CA: The e-Learning Guild.

Quinn, C., Alem, L., & Eklund, J. (1999). A pragmatic evaluation methodology for an assessment of learning effectiveness in instructional systems. In S. Brewster, A. Cawsey, & G. Cockton (Eds.), *Human-Computer Interaction INTERACT99 vol. II* (pp. 55-56). UK: British Computer Society.

Ramondt, D. (2008). Towards the adoption of Massively Multiplayer Educational Gaming. In *Researching Learning in Virtual Environments International Conference* (pp. 258-268). Milton Keynes, UK: The Open University. Retrieved April 22, 2009.

Rauch, L. (2002). *Critical Issue: Using Technology to Support Limited-English-Proficient (LEP) Students' Learning Experiences.* North Central Regional Educational Laboratory (NCREL) online publications. Retrieved September 18, 2008, from http://www.ncrel.org/sdrs/areas/issues/methods/technlgy/te900.htm

Ravet, S. (2002). E-Learning and knowledge management. *Newsletter of PROMETHEUS Network, 20,* 2–6.

Rawitsch, D., Heinemann, B., & Dillenberger, P. (1974). *The Oregon Trail* [Computer Game]. Lauderdale, MN: Minnesota Educational Computing Consortium.

Reid, K. (1995). *Purchasing Technology Without Making Plans for Student Learning and Curriculum Application.* North Central Regional Educational Laboratory (NCREL) online publications. Retrieved September 18, 2008, from http://www.ncrel.org

Reiners, T., & Voß, S. (2008). Inter-world Business Perspectives: Integrating Virtual Worlds in the Real World Business (Process). In *Proceedings of IFSAM 2008,* Beijing, China.

Reiners, T., Dreher, C., Büttner, S., Naumann, M., & Visser, L. (2009). Connecting Students by Integrating the 3D Virtual and Real Worlds: We need 3D Open Source Spaces to Keep Socialization, Communciation, and Collaboration alive. Accepted for publication in *Proceedings of E-Learn 2008. World Conference on E-Learning in Corporate, Government, Healthcare, & Higher Education,* Las Vegas (pp. 789–798). Chesapeake, USA: AACE.

Ressler, S. (1994). *Virtual Reality for Manufacturing – Case Studies.* Open Virtual Reality Testbed: National Institute of Standards and Technology. Retrieved from http://ovrt.nist.gov/projects/mfg/mfgVRcases.html

Reynard, R. (2008). *Mobile learning in higher education: multiple connections in learning spaces. Campus Technology.* Retrieved February 26, 2008, from http://campustechnology.com/articles/2008/04/mobile-learning-in-higher-education.aspx

Rice, J. (2006). *New media resistance: barriers to implementation of computer video games in the classroom.* Retrieved September 18, 2007, from http://www.eduquery.com/papers/Rice/games/New_Media_Resistance.pdf

Richardson, J., & Swan, K. (2003). Examining social presence in online courses in relation to students' perceived learning and satisfaction [Electronic version]. *Journal of Asynchronous Learning Networks, 7*(1), 68–88.

Rismark, M., Solvberg, M. A., Stromme, A., & Hokstad, L. M. (2007). Using mobile phones to prepare for university lectures: Student's experiences. Norwegian University of

Science and Technology. *The Turkish Online Journal of Educational Technology, 6*(4), Article 9. Retrieved October 4, 2008 from http://www.eric.ed.gov/ERICDocs/data/ericdocs2sql/content_storage_01/ 0000019b/80/3c/19/e9.pdf

Robbins, C. (2006). Providing cultural context with educational multimedia in the South Pacific. *Educational Technology & Society, 9*(1), 202–212.

Robbins, S. S. (2007). *Immersion and Engagement in a Virtual Classroom: Using Second Life for Higher Education.* Presentation on EDUCause Connect. Retrieved March 1, 2009, from http://connect.educause.edu/library/abstract/ImmersionandEngageme/39328

Roberts, T. S. (Ed.). (2004). *Online collaborative learning: Theory and practice.* Hershey, PA: Information Science Publishing.

Robinson, C. C., & Hullinger, H. (2008). New Benchmarks in Higher Education: Student Engagement in Online Learning. *Journal of Education for Business, 84*(2). doi:10.3200/JOEB.84.2.101-109

Roblyer, M., & Davis, L. (2008). Predicting success for virtual school students: Putting research-based models into practice. *Online Journal for Distance Learning Administration, 11*(4). Retrieved December 15, 2008, from http://www.westga.edu/~distance/ojdla/ winter114/ roblyer114.pdf

Rockwell, K., Schauer, J., Fritz, S., & Marx, D. (1999). Incentives and obstacles influencing higher education faculty and administrators to teach via distance. *Online Journal of Distance Learning Administration, 2*(4), 1-8. Retrieved December 26, 2008, from http://www.westga.edu/~distance/ojdla/winter24/rockwell24.html

Rodriguez, M. C., Ooms, A., & Montañez, M. (2008). Students' Perceptions of Online-learning Quality given Comfort, Motivation, Satisfaction, and Experience. *Journal of Interactive Online Learning, 7*(2), 105–125.

Roschelle, J. (2003). Unlocking the learning value of wireless mobile devices. *Journal of Computer Assisted Learning, 19*, 260–272. doi:10.1046/j.0266-4909.2003.00028.x

Roschelle, J., & Teasley, S. D. (1995). The construction of shared knowledge in collaborative problem solving. In O. M. C. E (Ed.), *Computer-supported Collaborative eLearning* (pp. 69–97). New York, NY: Springer-Verlag.

Roschelle, J., Hoadley, C., Pea, R., Gordin, D., & Means, B. (2000, Fall/Winter). Changing how and what children learn in school with collaborative cognitive technologies. *Children and Computer Technology issue of The Future of Children, 10*(2), 76-101. Los Altos, CA: The David and Lucile Packard Foundation.

Rosenberg, M. (2001). *E-learning: Strategies for Delivering Knowledge in the Digital Age.* New York, NY: McGraw-Hill Professional

Rosenberg, M. (2008). Technology Euphoria: Taming the Irrational Expectations of High-Tech Learning. *Training +Development*, 24-27.

Rovai, A. P. (2001). Building classroom community at a distance: A case study. *Educational Technology Research and Development, 49*(4), 33–48. doi:10.1007/BF02504946

Rovai, A. P. (2003). The relationships of communicator style, personality-based learning style, and classroom community among online graduate students. *The Internet and Higher Education, 6*(4), 347–363. doi:10.1016/j.iheduc.2003.07.004

Rui, Y., Gupta, A., Grudin, J., & He, L. (2004). Automating lecture capture and broadcast: Technology and videography. *Multimedia Systems, 10*(1), 3–15. doi:10.1007/s00530-004-0132-9

Rumble, G. (1986). *The planning and management of distance education.* London: Croom Helm.

Rumble, G. (2001). Reinventing distance education, 1971-2001. *International Journal of Lifelong Education, 20*(1/2), 31–43.

Russell, T. L. (2001). *The no significant difference phenomenon (5th Ed.).* IDECC (The International Distance Education Certification Center).

Rutherford, A., & Kerr, B. (2008). An inclusive approach to online learning environments: models and resources. *Turkish Online Journal of Distance Education, 9*(2), 64–85.

Ryan, L. (2007). *Advantages and Disadvantages of mobile learning.* Retrieved October, 8, 2008, from the E-articles database.

Ryan, M. (2008). 16 Ways to Use Virtual Worlds in your Classroom: Pedagogical Applications of Second Life. In *Researching Learning in Virtual Environments International*

Conference (pp. 269-178). Milton Keynes, UK: The Open University. Retrieved April 22, 2009.

Rybarczyk, B. J. (2007). Tools of Engagement: Using Case Studies In Synchronous Distance-Learning Environments. *Journal of College Science Teaching, 37*(1), 31–33.

Saba, F. (2007). A systems approach in theory building. In M. Moore (Eds.), *Handbook of distance education*. Mahwah, NJ: Lawrence Erlbaum.

Sacks, P. (1996). *Generation X Goes to College. An Eye-Opening Account of Teaching in Postmodern America.* Chicago, IL: Open Court Publishing.

Saettler, P. (2004). *The Evolution of American Educational Technology.* Englewood, CO: Libraries Unlimited.

Salaway, G., & Caruso, J. B. (2008). *The ECAR study of undergraduate students and information technology, 2008.* Retrieved November 1, 2008, from http://connect.educause.edu/Library/ECAR/TheECARStudyofUndergradua/47485

Salleh, A. (2008, July 10). *Switch on a chip to boost internet speed.* Retrieved March 1, 2009, from http://www.abc.net.au/news/stories/2008/07/10/2299688.htm

Sapieha, S. (2007). *Essay on adult education for use by RM advisory.* Prepared for ARMA Calgary Chapter Board. Retrieved from http://www.arma.calgary.ab.ca/pdfs/Education%20Report2007/Appendix%2024.pdf

Sargent, M. (2003). Spanish for Beginners. *Technology and Learning, 7*(6), 8–9.

SCANS (Secretary's Commission on Achieving Necessary Skills). (1991). *What work requires of schools: A SCANS report for America 2000: Executive Summary.* Washington, DC: U.S. Dept. of Labor.

Scardamalia, M. (2002). Collective cognitive responsibility for the advancement of knowledge. In B. Smith (Ed.), *Liberal education in a knowledge society* (pp. 67-98). Chicago: Open Court.

Scardamalia, M., & Bereiter, C. (1996) Adaptation and understanding: A case for new cultures of schooling. In S. Vosniadou, E. De Corte, R. Glaser, & H. Mandl (Eds.), *International perspectives on the psychological foundations of technology-based learning environments* (pp. 149-163). Mahwah, NJ: Erlbaum.

Scardamalia, M., & Bereiter, C. (2006). Knowledge building: Theory, pedagogy, and technology. In K. Sawyer (Ed.), *Cambridge handbook of the learning sciences* (pp. 97-118). New York: Cambridge University Press.

Schank, R. (2004). *Making minds less well educated than our own.* Mahwah, NJ: Erlbaum.

Schlager, M. S., Fusco, J., & Schank, P. (2002). Evolution of an online education community of practice. In K. A. Renninger & W. Shumar (Eds.), *Building virtual communities: Learning and change in cyberspace* (pp. 129-158). Cambridge, MA: Cambridge University Press.

Schrader, P., Zheng, D., & Young, M. (2006). Teachers' perceptions of videogames: MMOGs and the future of teacher education. *Innovate Journal of Online Education, 2*(3). Retrieved September 18, 2008, from http://innovateonline.info/index.php?view= article&id=125&action=article

Schrage, M. (1990). *Shared minds.* New York: Random House.

Schwier, R. A. (1995). Issues in emerging interactive technologies. In G. J. Anglin (Ed.), *Instructional Technology: Past, present, and future* (2nd ed., pp. 119-127). Englewood, CO: Libraries Unlimited.

Second Life Grid. (2008). *Getting Started: Second Life Grid.* Retrieved March 1, 2009, from http://secondlifegrid.net/gs/get-started

Second Life Wiki. (2008). *Main Page, Second Life Wiki.* Retrieved March 1, 2009, from http://wiki.secondlife.com

Second Life Wikia. (2008). *List of museums and galleries in Second Life.* Retrieved March 1, 2009, from http://secondlife.wikia.com/wiki/List_of_museums_and_galleries_in_Second_Life

Second Life, F. A. Q. (2008). *Is Second Life a game?* Retrieved March 1, 2009, from http://secondlife.com/whatis/faq.php#02

Selim, H. M. (2003). An empirical investigation of student acceptance of course websites. *Computers & Education, 40*(4), 343–360. doi:10.1016/S0360-1315(02)00142-2

Senge, P. M. (1990). *The fifth discipline: The art & practice of the learning organization.* New York: Currency Doubleday.

Sensiper, S. (2000). Making the case online: Harvard business school multimedia. *Information Communication and Society, 3*(4), 616–621. doi:10.1080/13691180010002134

Seppala, P., & Alamaki, H. (2003). Mobile Learning in Teacher Training. *Journal of Computer Assisted Learning, 19*, 330-335. Retrieved October 8, 2008, from http://www3.interscience.wiley.com/journal/118838489/abstract?CRETRY=1&SRETRY=0

Sfard, A. (1998). On the two metaphors for learning and the danger of choosing one. *Educational Researcher, 27*(2), 4–13.

Shachar, M. (2008). Meta-analysis: The preferred method of choice for the assessment of distance learning quality factors. *International Review of Research in Open and Distance Learning, 9*(3), 1–15.

Shadbolt, N., & Berners-Lee, T. (2008, October). Web science emerges. *Scientific American, 229*(4), 81.

Shank, P. (2005). 5 common fears about teaching online — Fact vs. fiction. *Distance Education, 9*(24), 5-7. Retrieved February 8, 2008, from http://www.magnapubs.com/issues/magnapubs_oc/5_10/news/598041-1.html.

Shanker, M., & Hu, M. Y. (2006). A Framework for Distance Education Effectiveness: An Illustration Using a Business Statistics Course. *International Journal of Web-Based Learning and Teaching Technologies, 1*(2), 1–17.

Sharples, M. (2000). The Design of Personal Mobile Technologies for Lifelong Learning. [from http://www.elsevier.com/locate/compedu]. *Computers & Education, 34*, 177–193. Retrieved October 8, 2008. doi:10.1016/S0360-1315(99)00044-5

Sharples, M. (Ed.). (2007). *Big Issues in Mobile Learning.* Nottingham, UK: University of Nottingham, Learning Sciences Research Institute.

Sharples, M., Taylor, J., & Vavoula, G. (2005). Towards a Theory of Mobile Learning. In H. van der Merwe & T. Brown (Eds.), *Proceedings of the Mobile Technology: The Future of Learning in Your Hands, mLearn 2005* (pp. 1-9).

Sharples, M., Taylor, J., & Vavoula, G. (2007). A theory of learning for the mobile age. In R. Andrews & C. Haythorn-thwaite (Eds.), *The Sage Handbook of E-learning Research* (pp. 221-247). London: Sage.

Shaw, J. P. (2005). Building meaning: Experts and novices in on-line learning. In *Proceedings from EdMedia International Conference*, Montreal, Canada. Retrieved from http://www.editlib.org/j/EDMEDIA/v/2005/n/1

Shaw, J. P. (2006). The problem with Getting it right the first time. In *Proceedings from EdMedia International Conference,* Orlando, Florida. Retrieved from http://www.editlib.org/j/EDMEDIA/v/2006/n/1

Shaw, T. (2003). Finding Time to Teach Tech Skills in Context. *Multimedia Schools, 10*(1), 41–42.

Shepherd, C. (2001). *M is for Maybe Tactix: Training and communication technology in context.* Retrieved September 16, 2008, from http://www.fastrak-consulting.co.uk/tactix/features/mlearning.htm

Sherry, L. (1996). Issues in Distance Learning. [from http://www.cudenver.edu/ ~lsherry/ pubs/issues.html]. *International Journal of Educational Telecommunications, 1*(4), 337–365. Retrieved November 25, 2008.

Shih, T. K., Wang, Y., Liao, Y., & Chuang, J. (2003). Video presentation recording and on-line broadcasting. *Journal of Interconnection Networks, 4*(2), 199–209. doi:10.1142/S0219265903000829

Shih, Y. E., & Mills, D. (2007). Setting the new standard with mobile computing in online learning. *International Review of Research in Open and Distance Learning, 8*(2), 1492–3831.

Shneiderman, B. (1997). *Designing the user interface.* Reading MA: Addison-Wesley.

Short, J., Williams, E., & Christie, B. (1976). *The social psychology of telecommunications.* London: John Wiley and Sons.

Shyu, H. C. (2000). Using video-based anchored instruction to enhance learning: Taiwan's experience. *British Journal of Educational Technology, 312*(1), 57–69. doi:10.1111/1467-8535.00135

Siemens, G. (2004, December 12). *Connectivism: A Learning Theory for the Digital Age.* Retrieved from http://www.elearnspace.org/Articles/connectivism.htm

Sife, A. S., Lwogoa, E. T., and Sanga, C. (2007). New technologies for teaching and learning: Challenges for higher learning institutions in developing countries. *In-*

ternational Journal of Education and Development using ICT. 3(2), 57-67.

Sikora, A., & Carrol, D. (2002). *A profile of participation in distance education: 1999-2000.* National Center for Education Statistics. Retrieved December 31, 2008 from http://nces.ed.gov/pubs2003/ 2003154.pdf

Simonson, M., & Schlosser, C. (1995). Theory and distance education: A new discussion. *American Journal of Distance Education, 13*(1), 60–75. doi:10.1080/08923649909527014

Sims, R., & Stork, E. (2007). Design for contextual learning: Web-based environments that engage diverse learners. In J. Richardson & A. Ellis (Eds.), *Proceedings of AusWeb07, Thirteenth Australasian World Wide Web Conference.* Lismore, Australia: Southern Cross University. Retrieved December 23, 2008, from http://ausweb.scu.edu.au/aw07/papers/refereed/sims/index.html

SimTeach. (2008). *Institutions and Organizations in SL.* Retrieved March 1, 2009, from http://www.simteach.com/wiki/index.php?title=Institutions_and_Organizations_in_SL

Slater, R. (2004). *What is the future of Massively Multiplayer Online Gaming?* Dissertation. Retrieved from http://www.richard-slater.co.uk/university/dissertation

Slavin, R. (1991). *Student Team Learning: A Practical Guide to Cooperative Learning (3rd Ed.).* Washington, DC: National Education Association.

Smith, P. L., & Ragan, T. J. (2005). *Instructional Design* (3rd ed.). Hoboken, NJ: Wiley.

Smith, P. L., & Ragan, T. J. (2005). *Instructional Design Third Edition.* San Francisco: Jossey-Bass Education.

So, H. J. (2009). When groups decide to use asynchronous online discussions: Collaborative learning and social presence under a voluntary participation structure. *Journal of Computer Assisted Learning, 25*(2), 143–160. doi:10.1111/j.1365-2729.2008.00293.x

So, H. J., & Kim, B. (2009). Teaching and learning with mobile technologies: Educational applications. In M. Pagani (Ed.), *The Encyclopedia of multimedia technology and networking* (2nd ed., pp. 1366-1372). Hershey, PA: Information Science Reference.

Soegaard, M. (2006). *Cognitive artifacts.* Retrieved March 19, 2009, from http://www.interactiondesign.org/encyclopedia/ cognitive_artifacts.html

Soloway, E., Jackson, S. L., Klein, C., Quintana, C., Reed, J., & Spitulnik, J. (1996). Learning theory in practice: case studies in learner-centred design. In [New York: ACM Press.]. *Proceedings of Computer Human Interaction CHI, 96,* 189–196.

Soloway, E., Norris, C., Blumenfeld, P., Fishman, B., Krajick, J., & Marx, R. (2001). Devices are ready at-hand. *ACM Communications.* Retrieved October 10, 2008, from http://www.handheld.hice- dev.org/readyATHand.htm

Sonak, B., et al. (2002). *The Effort of a Web-Based Academic Record and Feedback System of Student Achievement at the Junior High School Level.* Paper presented at the Annual Meeting of the American Educational Research Association, New Orleans. Retrieved May 24, 2009, from http://www.eric.ed.gov/ERICWebPortal/custom/portlets/recordDetails/detailmini.jsp?_nfpb=true&_&ERICExtSearch_SearchValue_0=ED465768&ERICExtSearch_SearchType_0=no&accno=ED465768

Sonic Foundry. (2008). *University of Wisconsin study finds strong undergraduate student preference for classes with lecture capture.* Retrieved October 23, 2008, from http://www.sonicfoundry.com/company/pressroom/press-release/University-of-Wisconsin-Study-Finds-Strong-Undergraduate-Students-Preference-for-Classes-with-Lecture-Capture.aspx

Soong, M. H., Chan, H. Ch., Chua, B. Ch., & Loh, K. F. (2001). Critical success factors for on-line course resources. *Computers & Education, 36*(2), 101–120. doi:10.1016/S0360-1315(00)00044-0

Spector, J. M., Merrill, M. D., van Merrienboer, J., & Driscoll, M. P. (2007). *Handbook of Research on Educational Communications and Technology (3rd Ed.).* London: Routledge.

Spitzer, I. (2003). Students Dial Up Cell Phone Service. *North Gate News Online.* Retrieved June 27, 2008 from http://journalism.berkeley.edu/ngno/stories/001538.html

Spodick, E. (1995). The evolution of distance learning. Retrieved November 24, 2008, from http://sqzm14 .ust.hk/distance/evolution-distance-learning.htm

Squire, K., & Klopfer, E. (2007). Augmented reality simulations on handheld computers. *Journal of the Learning Sciences, 16*(3), 371–413.

Squires, D., & Preece, J. (1996). Usability and learning: Evaluating the potential of educational software. *Computers & Education, 27*(1), 15–22. doi:10.1016/0360-1315(96)00010-3

Squires, D., & Preece, J. (1999). Predicting quality in educational software: evaluating for learning, usability, and the synergy between them. *Interacting with Computers, 11*(5), 463–466. doi:10.1016/S0953-5438(98)00062-9

Stacey, E. (2002). Quality online participation: establishing social presence. In T. Evans (Ed.), *Research in Distance Education 5* (pp. 138-253). Geelong, Australia: Deakin University Press.

Stash, N., Cristea, A., & De Bra, P. (2004). Authoring of learning styles in adaptive hypermedia: Problems and solutions. In *Proceedings of the Thirteenth International World Wide Web Conference* (pp 114-123). New York: ACM Press.

State of Victoria. Australia. (2008). *Virtual Worlds.* Retrieved from http://www.mmv.vic.gov.au/VirtualWorlds

Stein, M. K., Grover, B. W., & Henningsen, M. (1996). Building student capacity for mathematical thinking and reasoning: An analysis of mathematical tasks used in reform classrooms. *American Educational Research Journal, 33*, 455–488.

Stenerson, J. (1998). Systems analysis and design for a successful distance education program implementation. *Online Journal of Distance Learning Administration, 1*(2). Retrieved October 15, 2008, from http://www.westga.edu/%7Edistance/ojdla/summer12/stener12.html

Stephenson, N. (1994). *Snow Crash.* London, UK: Penguin.

Steuer, J. (1992). Defining Virtual Reality: Dimensions Determining Telepresence. *The Journal of Communication, 42*(4), 73–93. doi:10.1111/j.1460-2466.1992.tb00812.x

Storey, V. A., & Tebes, M. L. (2008, Summer). Instructor's privacy in distance (online) teaching: Where do you draw the line? *Online Journal of Distance Learning Administration, 11*(2). Retrieved December 31, 2008, from http://www.westga.edu/%7Edistance/ojdla/summer112/storey112.html

Sundberg, P. (2003). *Learning and Human Development with Educational Technologies.* EdPsy 317 course offered at University of Illinois, Urbana-Champaign. Retrieved from http://www.ed.uiuc.edu/courses/edpsy317/sp03/learning-maps/sundberg-learning-theories.gif

Swan, K. (2005). A constructivist model for thinking about learning online. In J. Bourne & J. C. Moore (Eds.), *Elements of quality online education: Engaging communities.* Needham, MA: Sloan-C. Retrieved March 31, 2009, from http://www.kent.edu/rcet/Publications/upload/constructivist%20theory.pdf

Swigonski, M. (1994). Appendix III: Peer writing groups in the virtual classroom. In S. R. Hiltz (Ed.), *The virtual classroom: Learning without limits via computer networks* (pp. 363-368). Norwood, NJ: Ablex Publishing Corporation.

Switzer, J., & Switzer, R. (1994). Copyright question: Using audiovisual works in a satellite-delivered program. *T.H.E. Journal, 21*(10), 76–79.

Tabula Digita. (2009). *DimensionM.* Retrieved March 17, 2009, from http://dimensionm.com

Tanzer, A. (2007, February). Apollo goes back to school. *Kiplingers*, 19.

Tapley, R. (2007). *Designing Your Second Life.* Berkeley, USA: New Rider.

Taufe'ulungaki, A. (2002). Pacific education at the crossroads: Are there alternatives? In F. Pene, A. Taufe'ulungaki, & C. Benson (Eds.), *Tree of opportunity: Rethinking Pacific education* (pp. 5-21). Suva: USP.

Teo, H.-H., Chan, H.-C., Wei, K.-K., & Zhang, Z. (2003). Evaluating information accessibility and community adaptivity features for sustaining virtual learning communities. *International Journal of Human-Computer Studies, 59*(5), 671–697. doi:10.1016/S1071-5819(03)00087-9

Tesser, M., & Richey, R. C. (1997). The role of context in learning and instructional design. *Educational Technology Research and Development, 45*(2), 85–115. doi:10.1007/BF02299526

The Boeing Company. (2008). *The Boeing Company.* Retrieved from http://www.boeing.com/

The New Media Consortium, & EDUCAUSE Learning Initiative. (2008). *The 2008 Horizon Report.* Stanford, CA: The New Media Consortium. from http://www.educause.edu/

Thinking Machine. (2008). *Using mobile phones to learn.* Retrieved October 8, 2008, from http://thinkingmachine. pbwiki.com/Think%20Mobile%20Phones%20for%20 Learning

Thompkins, W. (2007). *Brain-Based Learning Theory: An Online Course Design Model.* Dissertation, Liberty University.

Thornton, P., & Houser, C. (2002). M-learning in transit. In P. Lewis (Ed.), *The changing face of CALL* (pp. 229-243). Lisse, The Netherlands: Swets and Zeitlinger. Retrieved October, 8, 2008, from http://studypatch.net/mobile/#General

Threlkeld, R., & Brzoska, K. (1994). Research in distance education. In B. Willis (Ed.), *Distance Education: Strategies and Tools.* Englewood Cliffs, NJ: Educational Technology Publications, Inc.

Toffler, A. (1985). *The adaptive corporation,* New York. McGraw Hill.

Toro-Troconis, M., Partridge, M., Mellstrom, U., Meeran, K., & Higham, J. (2008). Technical infrastructure and initial findings in the design and delivery of game-based learning for virtual patients in Second Life. In *Researching Learning in Virtual Environments International Conference* (pp. 334-350). Milton Keynes, UK: The Open University. Retrieved April 22, 2009.

Traxler, J. (2007). Defining, Discussing, and Evaluating Mobile Learning: The moving finger writes and having writ…. *International Review of Research and Distance Learning, 8*(2).

TRCLARK LCC. (2008). *In Search of Learning Agility: Assessing Progress from 1957 to 2008.* The eLearning Guild. Retrieved from http://www.elearningguild.com/content. cfm?selection=doc.1054

Trifonova, A. (2003). *Mobile learning: A review of the literature* (Technical Report DIT-03-009). Retrieved October 8, 2008, from http://eprints.biblio.unitn.it/archive/00000359/

Trifonova, A., & Ronchetti, M. (2003). *Where is mobile learning going?* Retrieved October 28th, 2008, from http:// www.trifonova.net/docs/Where%20is%20Mobile%20 Learning%20Going%20(E- Learn2003).pdf

Trinder, J. (2005). Mobile Technologies and Systems. In A. Kukulska-Hulme & J. Traxler (Eds.), *Mobile Learning a handbook for educators and trainers* (pp. 7-24). London: Routledge.

Twigg, C., & Oblinger, D. (1997). *The virtual university.* Washington, DC: Educom. Retrieved on February 12, 2009, from http://net.educause.edu/ir/library/html/nli0003.html

van Rosmalen, P., Sloep, P., Kester, L., Brouns, F., de Croock, M., Pannekeet, K., & Koper, R. (2008). A learner support model based on peer tutor selection. *Journal of Computer Assisted Learning, 24*(1) 74-86.

U.S. Government. Budget. (2008, June 27). *FY 2008 Budget Summary: Elementary and Secondary Education.* Retrieved June 27, 2008 from http://www.ed.gov/about/overview/ budget/budget08/summary/edlite-section2a.html

U.S. Government. Education. (2008). *Authentic Uses of Technology.* Retrieved June 6, 2008 from http://www.ed.gov/ pubs/EdReformStudies/EdTech/overview.html

U.S. Government. Education. (2008). *Executive Summary of the No Child Left Behind Act of 2001.* Retrieved June 11, 2008 from http://www.ed.gov/print/nclb/overview/intro/ execsumm.html

UNESCO. (1998). World Declaration on Higher Education for the Twenty-first Century: Vision and Action. In *Proceedings of the World Conference on Higher Education,* Paris. Retrieved from http://www.unesco.org/education/educprog/ wche/declaration_eng.htm

UNESCO. (2001). *Teaching Education Through Distance Learning.* Retrieved June 16, 2009 from http://unesdoc. unesco.org/images/0012/001242/124208e.pdf

University of Maryland Baltimore County. (2008). *UMBC Blackboard - adaptive release.* Retrieved December 19, 2008, from http://www.umbc.edu/oit/newmedia/blackboard/help/audio/audio_directions.html

Uribe, D., Klein, J. D., & Sullivan, H. (2003). The effect of computer-mediated collaborative learning on solving ill-defined problems. *Educational Technology Research and Development, 51*(1), 5–19. doi:10.1007/BF02504514

Valda, V. A. (1998). What is technical and vocational education and training? *Quarterly Newsletter of the Technical and Vocational Education and Training (TVET) Council, 1*(1). Retrieved from http://www.tvetcouncil.com.bb/Resource_Centre/TECVOC_Jan_Mar_1998.doc

Valdez, G. (2007). *Technology: A Catalyst for Teaching and Learning in the Classroom*. North Central Regional Educational Laboratory (NCREL) online publications. Retrieved June 6, 2008 from http://www.ncrel.org/sdrs/areas/issues/methods/technlgy/te600.htm

van 't Hooft, M. (2008). Mobile, wireless, connected information clouds and learning [Electronic Version]. *Emerging technologies for learning, 3*. Retrieved from http://partners.becta.org.uk/upload-dir/downloads/page_documents/research/emerging_technologies08_chapter2.pdf van Aalst, J., & Chan, C. K. K. (2001). *Beyond "sitting next to each other": A design experiment on knowledge building in teacher education*. Paper presented at the first European conference on computer-supported collaborative learning. Maastricht, The Netherlands: University of Maastricht.

Van Auken, S. V., & Chrysler, E. (2005). The Relative Value of Skills, Knowledge, and Teaching Methods in Explaining Master of Business Administration (MBA) Program Return on Investment. *Journal of Education for Business, 81*(1), 41–45. doi:10.3200/JOEB.81.1.41-46

Van der Wende, M. (2002). *The Role of US higher education in the global E-Learning market*. Research & occasional paper series: CSHE.1.02. Center for Studies in Higher Education. San Francisco: University of California, Berkeley.

Vaz de Carvalho, C. (2001). *Uma Proposta de Ambiente de Ensino Distribuído*. Unpublished doctoral dissertation, University of Minho, Portugal.

Vaz de Carvalho, C., & Cardoso, E. (2003). O E-Learning e o Ensino Superior em Portugal. In *Proceedings of the Revista do SNESUP – Sindicato Nacional do Ensino Superior*. Retrieved from http://www.snesup.pt/htmls/EEZykEyEVurTZBpYlM.shtml

Vaz de Carvalho, C., & Machado, A. (2001a). A Virtual Environment for Distributed Learning in Higher Education, In *Proceedings of the 20th ICDE World Conference on Open Learning and Distance Education*, Dusseldorf.

Velduis-Diermanse, A. E. (2002). *Csclearing? Participation, learning activities and knowledge construction in computer-supported collaborative learning in higher education*. Unpublished doctoral dissertation, Wageningen University.

Vieyra, G. (2006). *A Dialectical Interpretation of Factual Knowledge in Vygotskyan Terms vs Blooms Taxonomy as Interpreted by the Teaching Staff at 75th Street Elementary School (LAUSD)*. Retrieved November 9, 2007, from http://66.102.1.104/scholar?hl=en&lr=&q=cache:o08N16jolVIJ:www.gestaltdialektik.com/content/Factual_Knowledge_in_Vygotskyan_Terms.pdf+blooms+taxonomy

Virtual Worlds News. (2007a, August 26). *Blogging the SLCC: Case Studies – Selling Real Life Products*. Retrieved from http://www.virtualworldsnews.com/2007/08/blogging-the--8.html

Virtual Worlds News. (2007b, November 12). *Virtual MTV a Hit for Pepsi*. Retrieved from http://www.virtualworldsnews.com/2007/11/virtual-mtv-a-h.html

Virtual Worlds News. (2008a, May 5). *Case Study: vMTV's Virtual Hills Makes Pepsi Cooler than MTV's On-Air "The Hills."* Retrieved from http://www.virtualworldsnews.com/2008/05/case-study-vmtv.html

Virtual Worlds News. (2008b, May 12). *IRS Rules Electric Sheep's Second Life Greeters as Part-Time Employees*. Retrieved from http://www.virtualworldsnews.com/2008/05/irs-rules-elect.html

Virtual Worlds, N. M. C. (n.d.). *Virtual Worlds Case Study: Second Health*. Retrieved from http://virtualworlds.nmc.org/portfolio/second-health/

Vygotsky, L. (1962). *Thought and Language*. Cambridge, MA: MIT Press.

Vygotsky, L. (1987). *Thinking and speech*. In R.W. Rieber & A.S. Carton (Eds.), *The collected works of L.S. Vygotsky. Volume 1: Problems of general psychology* (pp. 37-285). New York: Plenum.

Vygotsky, L. S. (1935). *Mental development of children during education*. Moscow-Leningrad, Russia: Uchpedzig.

Vygotsky, L. S. (1962). *Thought and Language*. Cambridge, MA: MIT Press.

Vygotsky, L. S. (1978). Internalization of higher psychological functions. In M. Cole, V, John-Steiner, S. Scribner, & E. Souberman (Eds.), *Mind in society: The Development of higher psychological processes* (pp. 53-57). Cambridge, MA: Harvard University Press.

Vygotsky, L. S. (1978). *Mind in Society*. Cambridge, MA: Harvard University Press.

Vygotsky, L. S. (1981). The genesis of higher mental functions. In J. V. Wertsch (Ed.), *The concept of activity in Soviet Psychology*. Armonk, NY: Sharpe.

Wahl, L., & Duffield, J. (2006). Multi-modal Vocabulary Building. *Learning and Leading with Technology, 34*. Retrieved June 7, 2008, from http://www.iste.org/Content/NavigationMenu/Publications/LL/LLIssues/Volume_34_2006_2007_/November_No_3_2/LandL_November_2006.htm

Waits, T., & Lewis, L. (2003). *Distance education at degree-granting postsecondary institutions: 2000–2001*. U.S. Department of Education, National Center for Education Statistics. Retrieved December 2, 2008, from http://nces.ed.gov/pubs2003/2003017.pdf

Wang, M. (2007). Designing online courses that effectively engage learners, from diverse cultural backgrounds. *British Journal of Educational Technology, 38*(2), 294–311. doi:10.1111/j.1467-8535.2006.00626.x

Wang, W., Tzeng, Y., & Chen, Y. (2000). A comparative study of applying Internet on cooperative traditional learning. In *Proceedings of The 8th International Conference on Computers in Education/International Conference on Computer-Assisted Instruction 2000* (pp. 207-214). AACE-APC/National Tsing Hua University, Taiwan.

Waterhouse, S. (2005). *The Power of eLearning*. Upper Saddle River, NJ: Pearson Education, Inc.

Watson, G. (2006). Technology Professional Development: Long Term Effects on Teacher Self Efficacy. *Journal of Technology and Teacher Education, 14*(1), 151–165.

Weber, K., & Custer, R. (2005). Gender-based Preferences towards Technology Education Content, Activities, and Instructional Methods. *Journal of Technology Education, 16*, 55-71. Retrieved September 18, 2008 from: http://scholar.lib.vt.edu/ejournals/JTE/v16n2/pdf/index.html

Webster, J., & Hackley, P. (1997). Teaching effectiveness in technology-mediated distance learning. *Academy of Management Journal, 40*, 1282–1309. doi:10.2307/257034

Wedman, J., & Tessmer, M. (1991). Adapting instructional design to project circumstance: The layers of necessity model. *Educational Technology, 31*(7), 48–52.

Weick, K. E. (1995). *Sensemaking in Organizations*. Thousand Oaks, CA: Sage.

Weisenmayer, R., Kupczynski, L., & Ice, P. (2008, Winter). The role of technical support and pedagogical guidance provided to faculty in online programs: Considerations for higher education administrators. *Online Journal of Distance Learning Administration, 11*(4). Retrieved December 31, 2008, from http://www.westga.edu/~distance/ojdla/winter114/wiesenmayer114.html

Wenger, E. (1998). *Communities of Practice – Learning, Meaning, & Identity*. New York: Cambridge University Press.

Werner, H., & Kaplan, B. (1963). *Symbol formation: An organismic developmental approach to language and the expression of thought*. New York: John Wiley.

Wertsch, J. V. (1985). *Cultural, Communication, and Cognition: Vygotskian Perspectives*. Cambridge, UK: Cambridge University Press.

Wexler, S., Grey, N., Adams-Miller, D., Nguyen, F., & van Barneveld, A. (2008). *Learning management systems: The good, the bad, the ugly... and the truth*. Santa Rosa, CA: The e-learning Guild Publications.

White Paper, N. M. C. (2007, October 27). *Social Networking, the "Third Place," and the Evolution of Communication*. Retrieved March 1, 2009, from http://www.nmc.org/evolution-communication

Whitney, J. (2007). *The Use of Technology in Literacy Instruction: Implications for Teaching Students From Lower Socioeconomic Backgrounds*. Retrieved May 24, 2009, from http://www.eric.ed.gov/ERICWebPortal/custom/portlets/recordDetails/detailmini.jsp?_nfpb=true&_&ERICExtSearch_SearchValue_0=ED498986&ERICExtSearch_SearchType_0=no&accno=ED498986

Wiedenbeck, S., & Davis, S. (1997). The influence of interaction style and experience on user perceptions of software packages. *International Journal of Human-Computer Studies, 46*(5), 563–588. doi:10.1006/ijhc.1996.0106

Wikipedia. (2008). *Mashup (web application hybrid)*. Retrieved from http://en.wikipedia.org/wiki/Mashup_(web_application_hybrid)

Wikipedia. (2009). *Massively multiplayer online game*. Retrieved March 1, 2009, from http://en.wikipedia.org/wiki/Massively_multiplayer_online_game

Wilder, L. (2001). *Integrating technology on program Development for Children/Youth with E/BD.* Retrieved May 24, 2009, from http://www.eric.ed.gov/ERICWebPortal/custom/portlets/recordDetails/detailmini.jsp?_nfpb=true&_&ERICExtSearch_SearchValue_0=ED458738&ERICExtSearch_SearchType_0=no&accno=ED458738

Wiley, D. A. (Ed.). (n.d.). *The instructional use of learning objects: Online version.* Retrieved January 30, 2008, from http://www.reusability.org/read/

Wilkes, C., & Burnham, B. (1991). Adult learner motivations and electronics distance education. *American Journal of Distance Education, 5*(1), 43–50. doi:10.1080/08923649109526731

Williams, K. (1995). *The Incredible Machine* [Computer game]. Bellevue, WA: Sierra On-Line.

Willis, B. (1995). What's different about distant teaching? In *Strategies for Teaching at a Distance, Distance Education at a Distance, Guide 2.* Retrieved November 9, 2008, from http://www.uiweb.uidaho.edu/eo/guide2.pdf

Willis, B. (2004). Common research questions. In *Distance Education at a Glance, Guide 9: Distance Education: Research.* Retrieved December 9, 2008, from http://www.uiweb.uidaho.edu/eo/dist9.html

Wilson, C. (2001). Faculty attitudes about distance learning. *EDUCAUSE Quarterly, 24*(2), 70–71.

Winter, G. (2002, July 15). Junior colleges try niche as cheap path to top universities. *New York Times,* 1.

Wolcott, L., & Betts, K. S. (1999). What's in it for me? Incentives for faculty participation in distance education. *Journal of Distance Education, 14*(2), 34-39. Retrieved December 25, 2008, from http://cade.athabascau.ca/vol14.2/Wolcott_et_al.html

Wolston, V. (2009). *International education services.* Retrieved April 1, 2009, from http://www.international.umd.edu/ies

World Bank. (2007, August 29). *Inclusive Growth Consultations.* Retrieved March 5, 2009, from http://www.worldbank.org.in/WBSITE/EXTERNAL/COUNTRIES/SOUTHASIAEXT/INDIAEXT84,00.html

Wriedt, S., Ebeling, M., & Reiners, T. (2008). How to Teach and Demonstrate Topics of Supply ChainManagement in VirtualWorlds. In *Proceedings of ED-MEDIA 2008. World Conference on Educational Multimedia, Hypermedia & Telecommunications, Vienna, Austria* (pp. 5501–5508). Chesapeake, USA: AACE.

Wright, C., Dhanarajan, G., & Reju, S. (2009). Recurring issues encountered by distance educators in developing and emerging nations. *The International Review of Research in Open and Distance Learning, 10*(1), 11-25. Retrieved March 23, 2009, from http://www.irrodl.org/index.php/irrodl/article/view/608/1180

Wuensch, K., Aziz, S., Ozan, E., Kishore, M., & Tabrizi, M. (2008). Pedagogical characteristics of online and face-to-face classes. *International Journal on E-Learning, 7*(3), 523–532.

Xu, D. (2005). *A Conceptual Model of Personalized Virtual Learning Environments.* St. Lucia, Australia: The University of Queensland.

Yang, Y., & Cornelious, L. F. (2005). Preparing Instructors for Quality Online Instruction. *Online Journal of Distance Learning Administration, 8*(1).

Young, J. R. (2008a). MIT creates version of its web site for smartphones (and plans to share code). *Chronicle of Higher Education.* Retrieved from http://chronicle.com/wiredcampus/article/3486/mit-creates-version-of-its-web-site-for-smartphones-and-plans-to-share-code

Young, J. R. (2008b). Study finds hybrid courses just as effective as traditional ones. *Chronicle of Higher Education.* Retrieved from http://chronicle.com/wiredcampus/article/3321/study-finds-hybrid-courses-just-as-effective-as-traditional-model

Young, J. R. (2009). The lectures are recorded, so why go to class? *Chronicle of Higher Education.* Retrieved from http://chronicle.com.ezproxy.ltu.edu:8080/free/v54/i36/36a00103.htm

Young, M. F. (1993). Instructional Design for Situated Learning. *Educational Technology Research and Development, 41*(1), 43–58. doi:10.1007/BF02297091

YouTube. (2009). *YouTube – Broadcast yourself.* Retrieved May 25, 2009, from http://www.youtube.com.

Zagami, J. (2008). Technology education through online virtual environments. In *Technology Education*, Gold Coast, Australia. Retrieved August 5, 2008.

Zappe, S., et al. (2002). *The Effort of a Web-Based Academic Record and Feedback System of Student Achievement at the Junior High School Level*. Paper presented at the Annual Meeting of the American Educational Research Association, New Orleans. Retrieved May 24, 2009, from http://eric.ed.gov/ERICDocs/data/ericdocs2sql/content_storage_01/0000019b/80/1a/6b/19.pdf

Zhang, J. W., Scardamalia, M., Reeve, R., & Messina, R. (2009). Designs for collective cognitive responsibility in knowledge-building communities. *Journal of the Learning Sciences, 18*(1), 7–44. doi:10.1080/10508400802581676

Zhao, Y. & Cziko, G. A. (2001). *Teacher adoption of technology: A Perceptual Control Theory perspective.*

Zhu, E. (2006). Interaction and cognitive engagement: An analysis of four asynchronous online discussions. *Instructional Science, 34*, 451–480. doi:10.1007/s11251-006-0004-0

About the Contributors

Holim Song is an assistant professor of Instructional Technology in the College of Education at Texas Southern University. Song's primary research focus is in faculty's technology use in the classroom, instructional design methods integrating instructional technology, and instructional strategies for web-based instruction. He recently published, "Handbook of Research on Instructional Systems and Technology" (1st edition, New York: Hershey, 2008). Song has also written many articles published in journals such as *International Journal of Information and Communication Technology Education, and International Journal of Web-Based Learning and Teaching Technologies.*

* * *

Born in 1965, **Hyacinth Eze Anomneze** is the last of eight children; he grew up in Lagos Nigeria, and spent time in other countries of West Africa and Central Africa. Mr. Anomneze received his B.A. from Loyola University, New Orleans, U.S.A. 1993; M.A. from University of New Orleans, New Orleans, U.S.A. 1995; currently working on his Doctorial degree in Educational Administration and Supervision at Texas Southern University, Houston, U.S.A. Mr. Anomneze previously taught at St. Martin's Episcopal School in the New Orleans area and at Xavier University Preparatory School, New Orleans, and he currently teaches English Language Arts at Aldine High School, Houston, U.S.A. Mr. Anomneze is married to Stephanie and they have two children: Adanna and Dylan.

Kate Carey joined the Ohio Board of Regents in November, 2008 to create a program sharing network and develop the state's first distance learning plan. Previously Carey was the Executive Director of the Ohio Learning Network (OLN), a Regents initiative (www.oln.org). Carey held communications positions at the campus and state level and teaching positions at The Ohio State University (1994-96) and Jackson State University (1991). Prior to founding OLN, she was director of external relations at the Ohio Supercomputer Center (1996-99). Dr. Carey holds an associate of applied science in natural resources from Muskingum Area Technical College (now Zane State), and bachelor's and master's degrees in journalism from The Ohio State University. Her doctorate in educational policy and leadership is from Ohio State. Carey is a recipient of the Outstanding Alumni Award from the Ohio Association of Community Colleges.

Carlos Vaz de Carvalho has a "Licenciatura" degree in Electrical Engineering and an MSc degree in Industrial Informatics by the Faculty of Engineering of the Porto University. He has a PhD degree in Information Systems and Technologies. Currently he leads the GILT R&D group (Graphics, Interaction and Learning Technologies) and was e-Learning Director (2001-2005) of ISEP, Head of the Distance Learning Unit of the Porto Polytechnic (1997-2000) and Dean of the Computer Eng. Dep (2003-2005). He has published more than 75 references on the subject, including several books.

Fabio J. Chacon was born in Venezuela and is aresident in the USA. He is a researcher and practitioner of elearning. Dr. Chacon worked in the creation and development of elearning systems both in academic and corporate worlds. He is author of training materials and several online courses, and contributed to international publications. He teaches undergraduate and graduate courses, mostly online. His main research interests and publications are in cognitive learning, distance education and assessment. Currently works at Bowie State University, Maryland.

Stephanie Cheney is an Instructional Designer at Wentworth Institute of Technology in Boston, MA, USA. As part of the Training & Development team, she works with faculty to help them effectively integrate technology into curriculum to meet course goals. The unique 1-1 laptop initiative at Wentworth provides students and faculty with powerful tools to transform the educational experience. Stephanie worked in K12 education for a number of years, partnering with teachers across New England to develop and implement technology-rich curricula. She has delivered engaging presentations at state, regional, and national conferences including Association of Supervision and Curriculum National Conference and the National Educational Computing Conference. Stephanie was named an Apple Distinguished Educator in 2005 for her innovative work with iPods in the language learning process.

Caroline M. Crawford, Ed.D., is an Associate Professor of Instructional Technology at the University of Houston - Clear Lake, in Houston, Texas, USA. She earned her doctorate from the University of Houston in Houston, Texas, USA, where she focused her doctoral studies upon the areas of Instructional Technology and Curriculum Theory. At this point in Dr. Crawford's professional career, her main areas of interest focus upon communities of learning and the appropriate and successful integration of technologies into the learning environment, no matter whether a face-to-face, hybrid, learning course management system-based or virtual world learning environment.

Virginia Dickenson, A.B.D. Ed.D., is an educational, training, and technology consultant. She has worked extensively in the corporate arena with major oil and chemical companies for over 19 years as a consultant, and with institutions of higher learning as a consultant and professor for 9 years. Her areas of specialization are Adult Learning, Organizational Development, Educational Research, and Instructional Systems Design. She is President of eLumenata, Inc. In April 2006, Virginia created the avatar Xenon Darrow. She now owns four sims – one of which is dedicated to educational development in Second Life and two sims focus upon the delivery of her Instructional Systems Design course, Designing Dynamic Learning Events (DDLE). Virginia is currently the global provider for ISD training for the Shell MATPC refineries. Virginia invites her corporate clients to explore her sims to investigate the virtual universe. The sims are eLumenata, DDLE 1 & DDLE 2, and ICS Connect.

William Drummond has taught at colleges and universities in Korea, notably Yonsei University and Hankuk University of Foreign Studies, served as the Associate Director of the Fulbright office in Korea, and held positions with U.S. Military Education including U.S. Forces Korea, 8th U.S. Army,

Defense Activity for Non Traditional Education Support, and HQ U.S. Army. In Michigan he has served as Associate Dean, Distance Learning and Learning Support at Delta College, Multimedia/eLearning Specialist for the Veraldi Instructional Technology Resource Center, Lead Producer for LTU Online, and eLearning Architect and Online Program Producer for eLearning Services at Lawrence Technological University.

Jennifer Ehrhardt is an assistant professor of Communication at Pensacola Junior College (PJC), USA. She has been teaching online communication courses since 2002, including Public Speaking, Basic Speaking/Listening Skills, Survey of Mass Communication, and Interpersonal Communication. In teaching, she is particularly interested in developing cross-disciplinary and cross-generational online learning communities. Jennifer was awarded PJC's Teaching Excellence Award in 2008. Her research interests include educational outcome differences between face-to-face and online students and knowledge construction through student-student interaction in online discussion forums. She has presented papers and workshops on online learning communities and professional development at regional, national and international conferences. Jennifer holds a B.A. degree in Public Relations/Advertising and a M.A. in Communication from the University of West Florida (UWF), USA, and is currently a graduate student in the IT-Supported Distance Education program of netuniversity.se, Sweden, and a doctoral student in Distance Education at UWF.

Monique Fuchs has nearly 15 years experience in international settings ranging from higher education to various industries. She has managed significant organizational development and change initiatives such as initiating and establishing educational innovations as new lines of business and building competence centers for performance improvement on all levels. Fostering overall organizational positioning and growth while paying close attention to the human condition has been at the core of her work. During her career she has taught a variety of courses in adult education and has presented at international conferences in North America and Europe. Topics ranged from change management, strategic planning, organizational and professional development to curriculum building, instructional design, and learning technology/e-learning integration. Currently she is an Associate Vice President at Wentworth Institute of Technology in Boston, MA, USA overseeing Learning Technologies, Training & Development, Web and User Services.

Joel Gardner is an Instructional Designer in the Department of Information Technology at Utah State University (USU) and has several years of experience teaching, training, and designing instruction. He is also a Ph.D. student in the Department of Instructional Technology and Learning Sciences at USU. His research interests include the effective implementation of First Principles of Instruction and the Systematic Design of Instruction.

Sue Gregory is a long term adult educator and currently a Lecturer in Information Communication Technology in the School of Education at the University of New England, Armidale, Australia. She teaches pre service and post graduate education students how to incorporate technology into their teaching. Sue uses Web 2.0 tools extensively and the focus of her PhD is on the use of virtual worlds to enhance (Adult) learning. Sue, through her avatar Jass Easterman, has been using Second Life by applying her virtual world knowledge to expose her students, both distance and internal, to the learning opportunities in virtual worlds since 2007. She has been involved with many university projects on creating learning spaces in virtual worlds.

Robert Hogan is associate professor in the School of Education at the University of the South Pacific. His areas of research and teaching are science education and online learning. Ideally suited for eLearning, USP is one of two regional universities in the world. With a service area of 33 million km^2 and five time zones, USP has campuses in 12 member countries. Bob's research focuses on developing eLearning within developing countries subject to cultural differences and work technological limitations. Previously, Bob received a FIPSE grant to develop online partnerships among eight colleges in France, Germany, Spain, the United States, and England. He received his M.S. from New York University and his doctorate from the University of Central Florida. Bob has also worked as a systems engineer and as a science editor for Harcourt Brace. He has taught online for 10 years.

Hyo-Jeong So is an assistant professor in the Learning Sciences & Technologies Academic Group and the Learning Sciences Lab at the National Institute of Education, Nanyang Technological University (NTU). She obtained a Ph.D. in Instructional Systems Technology at Indiana University, Bloomington. Her current research focuses on teachers' epistemological beliefs about learning and technology, video technology for teacher learning, and students' knowledge building through collaborative knowledge building in technology-mediated learning environments. Dr. So has published and presented in the fields of distance education, teacher education, learning sciences, and computer-supported collaborative learning (CSCL).

Tae Keun Jeon is an Instructional Designer at the FACT Center with 10 years of multimedia design and development experience. He earned B.S. degree in ART with Computer 3-D and 2-D graphic design emphasis and a M.S. degree in Instructional Technology department at Utah State University with emphases in simulation, multimedia learning, augmentative learning-environment, and cognitive information processing. He is currently progressing Ph.D. degree in Instructional Technology department at Utah State University. He likes reading, programming, and writing. He also has professional career in teaching speed skating and skiing. He is always waiting for winter season.

George Joeckel is an Instructional Designer at Utah State University's Faculty Assistance Center for Technology (FACT). He earned his M.S. in Instructional Psychology and Technology from Brigham Young University with an emphasis in evaluation. He enjoys attending and presenting at conferences. His interests include reading, cooking and gardening.

Jennifer Lee is the Assistant Director of Academic Services for the College of Education at the University of North Texas. She is working on her PhD in Learning Technologies through the College of Information, Library Science, and Technologies. Her research interests are new media and technologies, distributed learning, and the scholarship of teaching and learning.

Pamela Lowry is currently Associate Professor, Department of Math and Computer Science and Co-Director, Master of Educational Technology Program at Lawrence Technological University. She held the position Director of Veraldi Instructional Technology Resource Center from June 2001 – January 2009. Pam holds a Ph.D. in Instructional Technology from Wayne State University and has been teaching full-time at the university level since 1980. Full-time positions were held at Lawrence Technological University and Oakland University. Prior to 1980 she taught part time at Schoolcraft College, Oakland Community College, and Eastern Michigan University. From 1971-1976 she taught full time at Brighton High School. She also holds a M.A. and B.S. degree in Mathematics from Eastern Michigan University along with a secondary teaching certificate.

José Magano holds a "licenciatura" in Electrical Engineering and Computer Science and a Master in Business Administration, both from University of Porto. He lectures Project Management at the Department of Economics, Management and Industrial Engineering at University of Aveiro, and he's the Marketing coordinator at the Institute of Management Sciences and Tourism (ISCET). At ISCET he has been the coordinator of e-Learning activities, and he's been engaged in several research initiatives related to e-Learning platforms and courses, namely aimed at supporting advanced studies and companies' training. Other research interests include innovation management and entrepreneurship. Since 2000 he's been working as a consultant at INESC Porto – Institute for Systems and Computer Engineering of Porto, where he's been involved with the formulation of new business projects, aimed at creating market value out of research and development university efforts. He has, himself, become an entrepreneur, having created several service and technology based start-up companies.

Kamna Malik's teaching and research focus lies in enabling better use of information technology for improved business value. Her current research areas are Software Quality, Strategic Information Systems and Online Education. She has authored / edited several books and published research articles in refereed journals and conferences. Her experience spans practice, teaching, research and academic administration. She has handled key roles in IT management and software projects across different stages of life-cycle and worked very closely with end-users. She has headed various academic offices such as research, MBA Programme, IT Infrastructure and has held positions of conference chair, session chair and member of program committee in multiple refereed conferences. She also conducts management development programmes for middle- and senior-level management in the area of Strategic Information Systems, Software Quality and Testing, Knowledge management and contemporary technologies.

Alan McCord teaches doctoral and master's level courses in Lawrence Technological University's College of Management and leads the University's eLearning and online program efforts. He previously served in senior IT roles at the University of Michigan (UM) and Eastern Michigan University. McCord holds a bachelor's degree from UM as well as master's and doctorate degrees in instructional technology from Wayne State University. He is active in the Higher Learning Commission, the Sloan Consortium, and EDUCAUSE. He is an editorial board member for the Innovate journal or online education. He has authored many professional papers and book chapters on IT infrastructure, IT outsourcing, virtual work technologies, plagiarism in online learning environments, and the use of technology to support organization development. He has consulted for businesses and higher education institutions and has served on nonprofit boards and advisory groups for regional technology initiatives.

Matthew E. Mooney is a Lecturer of Instructional Technology in the Department of Secondary Education and Foundations of Education of the School of Education at Indiana University South Bend. He earned his Ph.D. in Curriculum and Instruction with an emphasis in Educational Technology from Purdue University. He has worked as a university administrator, private consultant, web developer, and application analyst.

Anjum Najmi is a Teaching Fellow in the Learning Technologies Department at the University of North Texas. She is working on her PhD. in Educational Computing through the College of Information, Library Science and Technologies. Her research interests are emerging technologies, games and simulations, and distance learning.

Joanna Ochelska-Mierzejewska received the PhD, Eng. degree in computer science from Polish Academy of Sciences in 2006 and M.Sc., Eng. degree from the Institute of Computer Science from Technical University of Lodz, Poland, in 2001 where she currently works as an assistant professor. Her research interests are in soft computing, machine learning, fuzzy data, data mining, distance learning. She is authored or coauthored more than 15 papers in these areas.

Gail Peters joined the Ohio Learning Network in September, 2000 to provide distance learning support to Ohio's colleges and universities and manage one of six regional distance learning outreach programs. She has provided coordination and leadership for the E 4 ME Program since 2006. Previously, Peters led customer technical education programs across The Ohio State University (OSU) campus, including the University Technology Services, for 20 years. Peters also taught part-time for the Office of Continuing Education (1987-1999) at OSU and for Columbus State Community College - Business and Industry (1990-1993). Peters holds a bachelor's degree in interpersonal/organizational communication and a master's degree in adult education from The Ohio State University. Peters has three certifications: in instructional design/development, in training management, and as a master trainer. She is an award recipient of the International Who's Who of Professional and Business Women.

Drew Polly is an Assistant Professor in Mathematics Education and Instructional Technology at the University of North Carolina at Charlotte. His research agenda focuses on examining how to best prepare teachers to implement learner-centered instruction in mathematics and across the curriculum with educational technologies.

Torsten Reiners is a postdoctoral researcher at the University of Hamburg, Germany, and University Associate with the Curtin University of Technology in Perth, Australia. His research and teaching experiences are in the areas of clustering and mining large data sets, online-algorithms and the incorporation of bio-analogous meta-heuristics in simulations models (applied to container terminals), fleet logistics, information systems as well as several topics in eLearning and software development. Within his PhD-thesis "Simulation and OR with SmartFrame" he demonstrated concepts for didactical models. Besides scientific publications, he is currently doing research in semantic networks to improve cross-border communication and (e)learning as well as machine translation. Another interest is about (virtual) worlds and their interconnectivity and exchange without barriers. This research includes the development of highly adaptive systems, automatic processing of documents and their analysis as well as evaluation, the usage for educational purposes in a multicultural setting, the usage of innovative platforms like virtual worlds integrating emerging technologies like mobile devices. Torsten Reiners is co-founder of the Second Life Island University of Hamburg and Students@work, an initiative to promote education in Web 3D as well as the value of students' work.

Julia Penn Shaw has integrated a systems view of elearning through prior practice in software development and process management at IBM; through education in a doctorate in developmental learning from the Harvard Graduate School of Education and an MS in system science/computer science; and through current application of an online learning program at the SUNY-Empire State College Center for Distance Learning requiring curriculum and course development and coordination of academic delivery. Her research, teaching and publication interests focus on elearning, the construction of meaning, and adolescent and adult learning.

Marion S. Smith earned her doctorate in business from the University of Houston. She obtained her MBA and undergraduate degree in mathematics from Rensselaer Polytechnic Institute. Dr. Smith is an Associate Professor of Management Science at Texas Southern University. Her areas of research interests are in evaluation and distance learning. Dr. Smith has taught the following graduate courses: Management Information Systems, C++ Programming, Java Programming, C# Programming, Database Management Systems, System Analysis and Design, Business Statistics, Special Topics in Quantitative Methods. Additionally, Dr. Smith has taught the following undergraduate courses in courses: Business Statistics I and II, Production Management, Introduction to Business Government and Society Information Technology, C# Programming, College Algebra, Trigonometry, Finite Mathematics and Introduction to Business Statistics and Symbolic Logic.

Bruce Spitzer is Assistant Professor of Instructional Technology and Head of the Department of Secondary Education and Foundations of Education of the School of Education at Indiana University South Bend. He earned his Ed.D. in Curriculum and Instruction with an emphasis in Educational Technology from Oklahoma State University. His career history includes stints as a high school drama coach, English teacher, and journalism advisor; a community college English instructor; and a corporate vice president.

Belinda Tynan is the Academic Director of the Faculty of The Professions at the University of New England. She develops and aligns academic activities in the Faculty to achieve outcomes, in relation to learning and teaching, specified in the university's Strategic Plan and the Teaching and Learning Plan. Belinda contributes to the development of academic strategy and policy at Faculty and University level, including fostering strategic change and development in coursework programs, teaching and learning and student affairs. She has worked internationally and received a range of internal and competitive funds. Her research background is in the area of academic development, distance education, new technologies and models of research collaboration. She has more than 30 refereed research publications. She is also the treasurer of the Open and Distance Learning Association of Australia and has extensive project management experience and is currently involved in supporting a range of projects.

Wei-Ying Lim is a lecturer at the National Institute of Education, Singapore. She has research interests in socio cultural notions of learning, teacher learning and identities and communities of practice. She is currently pursuing a Ph.D. in the area of teacher identities, using concepts from discourse/conversation analysis and ethnomethodology.

Robert Wright is a doctoral candidate in Educational Computing at the University of North Texas. He received his MA in Instructional Technology and his BA in Information & Communication Studies from California State University, Chico. His career in technology and training has included work as an Instructional Television Producer/Director, Community College Instructor, Media Director, Textbook

Production Manager, and Quality Development Manager. His research and academic interests include memory and cognition, technology adoption and implementation, distributive learning, mobile technologies, and the use of technology in medical education. He currently serves as Director of Biomedical Communications at the University of North Texas Health Science Center at Fort Worth.

Jennifer Yeo is a lecturer in the Natural Sciences and Science Education Academic Group at National Institute of Education, Singapore. She has recently obtained a Ph.D. in Learning Sciences. Her current research focuses on students' meaning making process in collaborative inquiry-based learning environments such as Problem-based Learning and Knowledge Building. Her interest in this area extends to the use of computer-supported collaborative learning systems in supporting science meaning making.

Danuta Zakrzewska is Assistant Professor at the Institute of Computer Science, Technical University of Lodz. She received her Ph.D. in Mathematics in 1987. Her current research interests focus on intelligent e-learning systems especially considering personalization and applications of such techniques as data warehousing and data mining. She has been also involved in organizing international students' collaborative activities, with emphasis on peer review and discussions. She has published more than 40 articles in conferences, journals, and books.

Index